FIELDWORKING

Reading and Writing Research

FieldWorking

Reading and Writing Research

Second Edition

Bonnie Stone Sunstein

University of Iowa

Elizabeth Chiseri-Strater

University of North Carolina—Greensboro

Bedford/St. Martin's
Boston ◆ New York

For Bedford/St. Martin's

Developmental Editor: Diana M. Puglisi
Production Editor: Bernard Onken
Senior Production Supervisor: Dennis J. Conroy
Marketing Manager: Brian Wheel
Art Director: Lucy Krikorian
Text Design: DeNee Reiton Skipper
Copy Editor: Rosemary Winfield
Cover Design: Robin Hoffmann
Cover Art: Hundertwasser, Garden of the Happy Dead, 1953, © 2001, J. Harel, Vienna, Austria
Authors Photo: Courtesy of Jane McVeigh Schultz
Composition: Stratford Publishing Services
Printing and Binding: R. R. Donnelley & Sons Company

President: Charles H. Christensen
Editorial Director: Joan E. Feinberg
Editor in Chief: Nancy Perry
Director of Marketing: Karen R. Melton
Director of Editing, Design, and Production: Marcia Cohen
Managing Editor: Erica T. Appel

Library of Congress Control Number: 00–111167

Manufactured in the United States of America.

7   6   5   4   3   2
f   e   d   c   b   a

For information, write: Bedford/St. Martin's, 75 Arlington Street, Boston, MA 02116
(617-399-4000)

ISBN: 0–312–25825–9

Acknowledgments

Acknowledgments and copyrights can be found at the back of the book on pages 493–495, which constitute an extension of the copyright page.

Implicit in this book is our philosophy of teaching: that teaching is a way of learning. We dedicate this book to all the students who have been our teachers.

To the Instructor

You are about to "step in" to a whole different way of teaching with the second edition of *FieldWorking: Reading and Writing Research*. When you decide that your students will conduct fieldstudies, you'll join a subculture of instructors across the country who have already worked closely with the first edition of this text. Several instructors, from a variety of academic disciplines and teaching cultures, have contributed exercises and samples of their own fieldwriting, along with writing done by their students, to this new edition. So although this approach may be a new step in your teaching, you'll have much support from colleagues who have successfully used *FieldWorking*.

Adopting a new book takes a certain kind of courage and confidence—in both your students and yourself. It's risky to depart from what you already know to try out new ideas. As you are considering this fieldworking approach, you may have some questions about whether or not this type of research can really be part of your course. Our answer is, yes, it definitely can, as long as you are committed to having your students *act on* ideas of diversity and multiculturalism rather than just *read about* those ideas. *FieldWorking* exposes students to cultures different from their own by asking them to "step out," observe, then write.

Why do fieldwork? Fieldwork invites students to be more engaged and involved in the research process. To a much greater extent than their counterparts whose research activities are confined to the library and the Internet, students who work in fieldsites and archives learn to observe, listen, interpret, and analyze the behaviors and language of "others" around them. Because doing fieldwork allows students actual contact with people and cultures different from their own, they will often be more invested in the topics they investigate. Doing fieldwork also encourages a greater understanding of self as each student reads, writes, researches, and reflects on relationships with "others" in the culture. But the most compelling reason for any instructor to use this investigative approach is that through the process of fieldworking, a student will become a better reader, writer, and researcher.

What's Fieldworking?

Each chapter in FieldWorking introduces specific research concepts and then offers short writing activities ("Boxes") that give students an opportunity to practice. In addition, our readings offer examples of fieldworking, by both professional and student writers, that will inspire and enrich students' work. We firmly believe that to become good writers students must also be accomplished readers. In all cases, we've written about the readings in our text, explaining why we've chosen them and what relevance they have to the topic we're introducing. In short, each reading is purposely set in the chapter where we think it will serve as a sample or an expansion of the topic at hand. We hope the range of readings will challenge and encourage students to develop the complex skills and strategies needed to make them better readers, writers, and researchers.

As students learn and practice fieldworking, they begin to build, interpret, and analyze a cumulative record of their research process. We've designed this book to accommodate either a single large fieldwork project or a collection of shorter field projects on different topics, from various research sites. But in both cases, the writing that students do can become part of a research portfolio.

How's the Second Edition Like the First Edition?

- **Wide-ranging examples.** We have drawn the readings for *FieldWorking* from an array of related disciplines—anthropology, folklore, sociology, journalism, natural science, and education—in the genres of fiction, nonfiction, and journalism, both historical and contemporary. The book reflects a range of voices, including those of Horace Miner, Gloria Naylor, Jamaica Kincaid, Maxine Hong Kingston, Jan Harald Brunvand, and Oliver Sacks. Our field-reading sections at end of each chapter offer related readings for students.

- **Ethnographic exercises.** We've designed each of the thirty-two "Boxes" around a specific research skill, such as observing, taking notes, interviewing, using archives, and responding to text. Students may either write about a different short topic for each box or use the exercise to explore their larger fieldwork projects.

- **Opportunities to develop a research portfolio.** Appearing toward the end of each chapter, these sections show students how to reflect, interpret, and share both the processes and the products of their field research as they gradually create a portfolio to represent their research.

- **FieldWriting in every chapter.** Our "FieldWriting" sections discuss writing strategies related to each chapter's focus. Here we handle issues of grammar, convention, style, and craft, reminding students that fieldwork is always about writing.

- **FieldWords in every chapter.** Terms specific to fieldwork, like "artifact," "informant," and even "culture," may seem confusing to anyone who has not used them in the context of research and writing. To support teachers and students, we have included in each chapter a short glossary of specific terms introduced within that chapter. We've tailored these definitions so they relate to the fieldworker's vocabulary.

WHAT'S NEW IN THE SECOND EDITION?

Since the 1997 publication of the first edition, we've been collecting comments from students and instructors who have used *FieldWorking* both in formal class settings and in independent field projects. We've been lucky enough to hear from many people, and we've tried to incorporate their suggestions and meet their needs while also developing new ideas of our own. Among the new features in the Second Edition of *FieldWorking* are the following:

- **Two chapters devoted entirely to writing.** Many instructors wanted more coverage of the writing process at the beginning of the book, which prompted us to add a new Chapter 2, Writing Self, Writing Cultures: Understanding FieldWriting. This chapter will help students understand how the rhetorical concepts of purpose, audience, and voice are integral to their research; moreover, it will show them how to begin writing fieldnotes. In addition, we expanded the book's concluding chapter on writing. Chapter 8, FieldWriting: From Down Draft to Up Draft, will help students extract the most pertinent information from their accumulated data, shape this material into a draft, and then move from draft to polished final essay.

- **A new chapter on archives.** Chapter 4 helps student researchers recognize the value of the letters, journals, and artifacts people have stored in their homes, local buildings, museums, and historical societies. A set of journals, box of photos, pile of mementos, or sheaf of letters can unlock a large slice of cultural history. During the years since we wrote our first edition, the World Wide Web has become an important tool for daily research and communication, and in this edition we recognize the Web as both a complex critical source of information and as a giant archive itself.

- **An increased number and variety of readings.** Of the thirty-six readings in *FieldWorking*, almost half are new to this edition. New readings include selections by such well-known writers as William Least Heat-Moon, Garrison Keillor, and Shirley Brice Heath.

- **New student readings.** In this edition, we present five complete and accessible student research essays to help students set realistic goals for their own projects. We treat the student essays with the same level of analysis and explication as the professional writing.

- **Writing activities in every chapter.** Instructors and students who used the first edition responded so positively to the "Boxes"—ethnographic exercises designed around a specific skill—that we've expanded them in this edition.

First, we've included several "guest boxes," activities our colleagues across North America have developed in their classes. Second, every chapter in *FieldWorking* now includes several boxes. And third, each box now contains three easily identifiable components: "purpose" (a rationale for and explanation of the exercise), "action" (the exercise itself), and "response" (a sample of student work).

■ **An exploration of the relationship between poetry and fieldworking.** A new idea we've experimented with in this edition of *FieldWorking* is the "FieldPoem" section at the end of each chapter, which attempts to answer the question "Can a poem be 'ethnographic'?" This is a question we and our students ask as we consider the genres a fieldworker can choose for presenting a study. We've ended each chapter with a relevant poem, eight in all, and invited additional poets to share their responses ("Commentary"). Most of these contributors are graduate students with some fieldwork experience who are (or were) enrolled in the MFA in Poetry programs at one of our home institutions, the University of Iowa and the University of North Carolina–Greensboro.

HOW CAN I USE FIELDWORKING?

We've designed this book to provide enough material for a semester-long course, and our accompanying Instructor's Manual offers many different ways to put together a course, along with sample syllabi. You can easily organize or assign *FieldWorking*'s contents in different or abbreviated ways. It's not necessary, for example, to read the book from beginning to end, although we intended this order to offer a full introduction to reading, writing, and research.

How you use *FieldWorking* will depend on your overall course purpose or theme and the other texts you want to include. It can serve alone in an undergraduate composition/research course. Or you can use it in an ethnographic reading/writing course in which students also read several full-length ethnographies, such as *Mules and Men, Translated Woman, Ways with Words*, or a collection of ethnographic essays such as *Women Writing Culture* or *An Anthropologist on Mars*. We've compiled lists of our current favorite options for further reading in the "FieldReading" bibliographies.

You might have students start out with the three introductory chapters, which introduce them to the key theories about studying cultures as well as writing and reading strategies, and then move around in the book, depending on the specific focus of your course. For example, Chapter 6, Researching Language: The Cultural Translator, includes many short readings and exercises focused on language and culture that could serve as a unit of language study within any course.

Service learning and university-community project collaborations provide wonderful opportunities for the kind of student fieldwork this book facilitates.

In Chapter 4, for example, you'll see an essay by one student, an immigrant to the United States and former refugee, whose university service learning project took her to a homeless shelter.

There is a detailed Instructor's Manual to accompany this edition of our text that offers you ways to integrate the features of *FieldWorking* into your syllabi, assignments, and courses. To obtain a copy of the Instructor's Manual, contact your local Bedford/St. Martin's sales representative or e-mail <sales_support@ bfwpub.com>.

We believe strong teaching requires the courage to learn alongside your students. It also requires the hope that students will reflect on their own lives through the processes of reading and writing about others. In *FieldWorking*, we invite you and your students to engage in that reflective process together.

ACKNOWLEDGMENTS

Effective writing, as we have tried to convey in this book, requires collaboration. It requires a subculture of selected readers—writers' own trusted "insiders"— before it can successfully move to an outside audience. For this book, we shared each reframed idea and each revision with our own subculture of trusted colleagues, whom we wish to acknowledge and thank.

The initial supporters of our text tried out drafts of both editions "in progress" and helped us refine our ideas: Janet Bean, Meg Buzzi, Julie Cheville, Lee Torda, and Sarah Townsend—all initially students of ours who are now professionals working with their own students and teaching with *FieldWorking*. Seth Kahn of Syracuse University introduced us to a network of colleagues and students around the country who do fieldwork with our book. Our thanks to him and to all our new colleagues whose work we've seen in three successive sessions at the annual Conference on College Composition and Communication.

We would like to thank our long-lived writing group of academic sisters, the "Daughters of Discourse," Danling Fu, Cindy Gannett, Sherrie Gradin, Donna Qualley, Hephzibah Roskelly, and Pat Sullivan, whose voices mix with our own and always blur the boundary between "self and other." And during the writing of the Second Edition, we had special support from Minshall Strater, Arthur Hunsicker, Jan Stone, and Judy Rosenwald (who reads more nonfiction than anyone we know).

Our confidence in the value of *FieldWorking* for so many different classes is the result of so many students having used it successfully in a variety of academic settings. We thank these students for their responses—and for their fieldwork. Ethnographic essays by Karen Downing, Cindie Marshall, Rick Zollo, Ivana Nikolic, Pappi Tomas, and Sam Samuels appear in this book. We also thank the many students whose shorter works appear in this new edition. In particular, we acknowledge Paul Russ for his contribution from his MFA thesis in Film Studies and Yolanda Majors for her research on hair, a project that has spanned three universities.

Teaching assistants at both of our institutions contributed their own students' work to this text: from the University of North Carolina–Greensboro, Janet Bean, Lee Torda, and Katie Ryan; and from the University of Iowa, Julie Cheville. We also appreciate Katie Ryan (now at the University of West Virginia–Morgantown) for contributing the box "Fieldworking Book Clubs," and Julie Cheville (now at Rutgers University) for contributing "From Ethos to Ethics." Our thanks go, too, to David Seitz at Wayne State University for the box "Listening to the Voices in Your Draft." We'd like to specially thank Lee Torda for writing the Instructor's Manual for the Second Edition.

And, of course, we thank the students and teachers from the courses we have taught with this text: in Iowa, in Greensboro, at the Martha's Vineyard Summer Institute of Northeastern University, the Smithsonian Institution, and several summer cultural studies institutes: The Fife Conference at Utah State University, the Louisiana Voices Institute at the University of Louisiana in Lafayette, "Celebrate New Hampshire" and the New England Community Heritage Project at the University of New Hampshire.

We greatly appreciate the thoughtful comments we received from the reviewers of the Second Edition: Janet Bean, University of Akron; Meg Carroll, Rhode Island College; Seth Kahn, Syracuse University; Carrie S. Leverenz, Florida State University; and David Seitz, Wayne State University.

Our own universities were generous with fellowships to help us complete our project. We thank as well the Obermann Center for Advanced Studies at the University of Iowa, the Woodrow Wilson Foundation in Princeton, New Jersey, and the National Network on Folk Arts in Education in Washington, D.C. Our colleagues' and students' enthusiasm, careful work, and faith in us allows us to share our confidence about the value of *FieldWorking* with our readers. As we prepared both editions, Sandie Hughes and Beth McCabe were always available for collegial support, clearheaded response, and technical preparation.

Between one important taxi ride a decade ago and a published book, now in its second edition, Nancy Perry's vision, judgment, expertise, business acumen, and personal support have helped us both envision this project and carry it through—always the way we wanted to do it. No meeting, meal, phone call, or e-mail was ever too much. We thank, too, our development editor at Bedford/St. Martin's, Diana Puglisi, who wrote with us, learned with us, and treated this book as her own. We also thank production editors Colby Stong and Bernard Onken, who respected our collaborative writing efforts and helped us to bring this project to fruition.

Finally, we thank our children: Tosca Chiseri, Alisha Strater, Amy Sunstein, and Stephen Sunstein. In four different ways they have grown and shared with us over the writing of both editions of this text. As we wrote this book, they taught us, as our students do, more than we ever thought we could learn.

BONNIE STONE SUNSTEIN
ELIZABETH CHISERI-STRATER

To the Student

There's both joy and satisfaction in understanding people and situations different from our own. *FieldWorking* will give you special license and formal ways to hang out, observe carefully, and speculate about talk and behavior. This book will show you how to see and interpret the lives and surroundings of others—through their eyes as well as your own. And this book will also help you see yourself and your own cultural attitudes more clearly because any study of "an other" is also a study of "a self."

FieldWorking assumes that you will want to *do* fieldwork, not *just read* about it. In the doing of fieldwork, we want you to consider your process as both art and craft: art in the writing and craft in the research. Fieldwork as an artistic craft implies cultural methods and expectations in the same way that woodcarving, quilting, and music making showcase the cultures they represent. Understanding and presenting other cultures requires the engaged reading, writing, listening, speaking, and researching activities we hope to share with you in this book.

UNDERSTANDING THIS BOOK

Perhaps, like many students, you need to learn how to do research and writing that will help you throughout your academic career, but aren't yet sure what direction you want to take. Or perhaps you plan to focus on cultural studies, anthropology, or education. There is no single way to read our book, and your instructor will surely have ideas about using it. Wherever you begin and whatever your ultimate goals may be, *FieldWorking* will help you to work with ideas, readings, and assignments that we know are effective with all new fieldworkers and in courses about fieldwork.

We also invite you to make the book work for your own purposes. We know one student, for example, who took *FieldWorking* to Mount Everest and used it by himself to study the culture of the sherpas and the climbers at the base camp. Other students have used it as guides for extended fieldwork in India and Ecuador. We'd like to encourage you to read the entire book, but the way you choose to proceed within it will depend entirely upon your own research plans.

Chapter 1, Stepping In and Stepping Out, introduces the idea that field researchers simultaneously act as both participants in a culture and observers. Then, in Chapter 2, we focus on writing strategies for the early stages of field-work—thinking of a topic, taking fieldnotes for the first time, and considering voice and audience. We deal directly with the writing process again in Chapter 8, the last chapter of the book. At the end of a field research project, when you're staring at piles of your own writing, other people's words, and materials you've collected, you'll need to think about shaping your study so that someone else will want to read it. So our final chapter suggests more writing strategies—ones you can use as you compose your final drafts.

The middle chapters don't ignore writing, but we've devoted each one to a different category of collecting data in the fieldworking process. Chapter 3, Reading Self, Reading Cultures, handles the fundamental idea that when you set out to study a culture, you "read it" as if it were a text. Chapter 4, Researching Archives, is devoted to archives, the "stuff" of a culture, from family letters to the World Wide Web. If your project involves mostly archival research, you might want to consult this chapter before the others. Chapter 5, Researching Place, focuses mainly on how to write about a cultural setting, the sense of place that a researcher finds—both as you experience it yourself and as you understand its meaning to the people who live and work there. Chapter 6 is Researching Language, and if you're interested in looking closely at the language behaviors of a person or group, you may want to work first with this chapter. Chapter 7, Researching People, may be the chapter you'll want to start with if your research centers on interviews or oral histories. Chapter 8, From Down Draft to Up Draft, draws together the threads about writing that we've woven throughout our book (for instance, establishing a voice, considering point of view, using published and unpublished written sources, creating an annotated bibliography, moving from details to verbal portraiture, and writing analytic section headings) so that you'll have some more support from us as you "write up" your study.

UNDERSTANDING FIELDWORKING'S SPECIAL FEATURES

With the help of our students, colleagues, and their students, we've designed some special features that help *FieldWorking* work in multiple ways. We're hoping you notice, soon after you start reading, that although *FieldWorking* looks a little bit like a traditional textbook, it doesn't necessarily act like one. There are no end-of-chapter questions, for example, or summaries of the ideas we've presented. We trust that you will ask your own questions and summarize what you need. Instead, we want to help you with your fieldwork in a variety of ways, each represented in one of the book's special features. Here is a brief description of each:

- **Boxes:** Each chapter has several "boxes," or fieldwork exercises, that provide you with opportunities to try out your research skills before working them into a major research project. You may want to do these activities with a range of people and places, or you may already know your primary research site and want to explore it with each exercise. Whichever way you choose to use the boxes, we and our students have found them good ways to practice research habits or change the direction of a project. We hope they'll save you from obstacles or problems you may not have thought about.

- **Readings:** We hope you'll enjoy reading our students' and colleagues' actual writing from their fieldwork—as well as the previously published professional pieces, fiction and nonfiction, that we've chosen. We offer these readings to give you confidence as you do your own research and write about it. These readings connect with our text to illustrate the ideas we're describing to you, and we hope our own responses to them will help you as you read.

- **The Research Portfolio:** Keeping an ongoing research portfolio, we believe, offers a place for a fieldworker to gather her work together, review it, and represent the process of her research to herself, her fellow researchers, and her instructor. It also is a means by which the researcher can determine what she wants to accomplish next. Your instructor may give you specific requirements for creating, maintaining, and submitting a research portfolio. We've handled a different idea about portfolio keeping in each chapter, with the hope that you'll work—and rework—your portfolio as you work your way through this book.

- **FieldWriting:** Because writing is such a critical part of the research process, in each chapter we've taken the opportunity to introduce a very specific issue of grammar, style, or convention that is related to the chapter's topic. We've chosen these ideas according to the concerns our own students have had as they've gone about the many processes of writing. Some of the fieldwriting suggestions will be reminders to you; others will offer old ideas with the new perspective of writing about fieldstudies; others will be new and useful to almost any writing you do.

- **FieldWords:** All subcultures have specialized language, and the world of a field researcher is no exception. In this section of each chapter, we introduce you to the special words that we think are important for researchers to know—words that we have printed in **boldface** as we mention them in each chapter. You may think of the fieldwords as a glossary, a handbook, or a nomenclature. We prefer to think of them as simply some of the tools all fieldworkers need, share, and use to make their work easier and more precise.

- **FieldReading:** When a particular idea moves you, we hope you'll consider doing more reading about it. Each chapter includes a short list of our own favorite readings, ones we often recommend to our own students. These lists are not complete, but we hope they will offer you a place to start if you want to learn more about what we've presented in each chapter. Of course, we'd love to include lists of websites, museums, archives, and recordings, but we did not want to write a book of lists. (Please note that the "FieldReading" toward the end of each chapter is different from the "Works Cited," the bibliographic list at the back of *FieldWorking*, which offers information about works we've quoted and that have influenced our own text.)

- **FieldPoems:**   Sometimes artwork itself conveys an ethnographic portrait or reveals something significant about the culture from which it comes. At the conclusion of each chapter we offer you a "fieldpoem," one that we feel illustrates a slice of the ethnographic process; in short, the fieldworker's art. For each poem, we've asked a student poet to share a personal response. We hope you'll enjoy both the poems and your fellow students' thoughts. In addition to fieldpoems, we and our students have experimented with various other literary genres and many arts: music, sculpture, photography, drawing, and printmaking, as well as documentary film, video, and Web production.

ABOUT US

The single voice that addresses you in this book is really a double voice. We wrote this book together—every single word of it—many drafts' worth—on a laptop Macintosh Powerbook. As we write this second edition, we have shared this project for over a decade. Because we've used drafts of our book in our own courses, from first-year classes to graduate classes, we acknowledge the huge role that our students' voices and contributions have played in helping us shape and reshape both the first edition and this one.

As you read through *FieldWorking*, take what is useful to you. Ignore what you can't use. Skip around—or read it from beginning to end. But please remember this: The field research you do should be meaningful and valuable to you and the others you study. We hope most that you will find your own voice in your fieldwriting. Work on a project you care about, and you'll make others care about it too.

One final note. Throughout this book, we've adopted the personal pronoun "she" over "he/she," s/he, he/she, they, or the more traditionally used "he." We do not mean this to be radical or off-putting, but merely to provide a corrective to the long history of textbooks that employ the pronoun "he." We mean our use of "she" to encompass and embrace every "she" and "he" who reads this book.

BONNIE STONE SUNSTEIN
ELIZABETH CHISERI-STRATER

CONTENTS

4   Researching Archives: Locating Culture   159

5   Researching Place: The Spatial Gaze   217

6   Researching Language: The Cultural Translator   293

7 Researching People: The Collaborative Listener 345

8   FieldWriting: From Down Draft to Up Draft   417

Stepping In and Stepping Out: Understanding Cultures

Long before I ever heard of anthropology, I was being conditioned for the role of stepping in and out of society. It was part of my growing up process to question the traditional values and norms of the family and to experiment with behavior patterns and ideologies. This is not an uncommon process of finding oneself.... Why should a contented and satisfied person think of standing outside his or any other society and studying it?

— HORTENSE POWDERMAKER

Ordinary living involves all the skills of fieldworking—looking, listening, collecting, questioning, and interpreting—even though we are not always conscious of these skills. Many of us enjoy people-watching from the corners of our eyes, checking out how others talk, dress, behave, and interact. We question the significance of someone's wearing pig earrings or displaying a dragon tattoo on the left shoulder. We wonder how a certain couple sitting in a restaurant booth can communicate when they don't look each other in the eye or wonder who made the rules for children we see playing stickball in the middle of a busy street. Fieldworkers question such behaviors in a systematic way.

What is a "field"? And how does a person "work" in it? The word *field* carries a wide range of meanings. It can mean open cleared land, such as a field of corn, and it can also mean the ground devoted to playing sports, such as a soccer field. In military operations, the word suggests a battleground, whereas at the university, a field relates to an area of professional study, such as the field of rhetoric and composition or the field of Latin American studies. In photography and in art, a field can mean a visible surface on which an image is displayed, like a field of color or a field of view. In science, it relates to a region of space under the influence of some agent, such as an electrical field or a magnetic field. Business people, naturalists, and anthropologists all talk about "being in the field" as part of their jobs. Working "in the field" for an anthropologist means talking, listening, recording, observing, participating, and sometimes even living in a particular place. The field is the site for doing research, and **fieldworking** is the process of doing it.

Close looking and listening skills mark trained fieldworkers who study groups of people in contexts—others' and their own. The job of this book is to help you become more conscious as you observe, participate in, read, and write about your own world and the worlds of others. Although we don't claim to turn

1

you into a professional ethnographer, we borrow **ethnographic** strategies to help you become a fieldworker, and we focus on showing you effective ways to write about your process. We'll guide you as you conduct and write up your own field-work and as you read about the fieldwork of others. *FieldWorking* will make you consider your everyday experiences in new ways and help you interpret other people's behaviors, language, and thoughts. But most of all, the fieldwork itself will help you understand why you react and respond in the ways you do. Some-times, without much consciousness, we watch others. This book will encourage you not only to watch others but also to watch yourself as you watch them—consciously.

You've probably spent many hours noticing behavior patterns and question-ing routines among the people you've lived with and learned from. In the quota-tion that introduces this chapter, anthropologist Hortense Powdermaker suggests that as we grow up, we "step out" a bit; we "adopt the **outsider** stance" as we watch the people inside our own group. We also "step in" to unfamiliar groups and examine them closely, which is the fieldworker's "**insider** stance." As insiders, we wonder if there might be a better technique for mincing garlic or cooling pies that is less laborious than our family's method. Or we wonder if it is always necessary to dry dishes with a towel since, after all, they *do* dry by them-selves. As outsiders moving to a new school, we might question the ritual cheers aimed against the rival or different rules for submitting papers. When we visit another country, we need to learn new rules for introductions and farewells in order to behave appropriately. Fieldworkers study the customs of groups of people in the spaces they inhabit.

Inquiry into the behavior patterns of others prepares us for doing fieldwork. Powdermaker also asks why any "satisfied and contented person" would want to research everyday ways of behaving, talking, and interacting. One answer is that fieldworking sharpens our abilities to look closely at surroundings. People, places, languages, and behaviors can be familiar because we've lived with them, but when we move or travel and find ourselves strangers, the very same things can be unfamiliar or uncomfortable. Another answer is that knowing our assumptions and recognizing our stereotypes helps develop tolerance and respect for customs and groups different from ours. For example, head coverings—turbans, veils, yarmulkes, ceremonial headdresses, and even baseball caps worn backward—may seem strange to us until we understand their history and sig-nificance. Studying and writing about diverse people and **cultures** does not nec-essarily make us accept difference, but it can make us aware of our assumptions and sometimes even of our prejudices.

DEFINING CULTURE: FIELDWORK AND ETHNOGRAPHY

Culture is a slippery term. To some people, it implies "high culture"—classical music, etiquette, museum art, "Great Books," or extensive knowledge of Western history. For those people, culture is gained through exposure and socioeconomic status. But fieldworkers who have studied cultures around the world and in their own backyards know that individuals acquire culture from others in their group. Every group has a culture, so there is no useful distinction between "high" and "low" cultures. Anthropologists have tried to define what culture is for as long as they've been thinking about it, and they have developed contrasting definitions.

We define *culture* as an invisible web of behaviors, patterns, rules, and rituals of a group of people who have contact with one another and share common languages. Our definition draws from the work of many anthropologists:

- "Culture is local and manmade and hugely variable. It tends also to be integrated. A culture, like an individual, is a more or less consistent pattern of thought and action" (Benedict 46).
- "A society's culture consists of whatever it is one has to know or believe in order to operate in a manner acceptable to its members…. [I]t does not consist of things, people, behavior, or emotions. It is rather an organization of those things" (Goodenough 167).
- "Cultures are, after all, collective, untidy assemblages, authenticated by belief and agreement" (Myerhoff 10).
- "Man is an animal suspended in webs of significance which he himself has created. I take culture to be those webs" (Geertz 14).

Cultural theorist Raymond Williams writes that *culture* is one of the most difficult words to define, and these anthropologists' definitions illustrate this. While Ruth Benedict and Ward Goodenough emphasize patterns in their definitions, Barbara Myerhoff highlights messiness. Clifford Geertz uses the metaphor of a web to describe how a culture hangs together invisibly. And still another anthropologist, James Peacock, draws a metaphor from photography. Using the lens of a camera, he describes its "harsh light" and "soft focus" to show how ethnographers try to capture the background and the foreground of a group. As you can see, definitions of culture can be both metaphorical ("webs" and "lenses") and structured (patterns of belief and behavior as well as untidy deviations from those patterns).

In your fieldworking experiences, you will be constantly asking yourself, "Where is the culture?" of the group you are investigating. The goal of fieldworking is to find it. You will find evidence in the language of the group you study, in its cultural **artifacts**, or in its rituals and behaviors. Fieldworkers investigate the cultural landscape, the larger picture of how a culture functions: its rituals, its rules, its traditions, and its behaviors. And they poke around the edges at the stories people tell, the items people collect and value, and the materials people use to go about their daily living. By learning from people in a culture what it is like to be part of their world, fieldworkers discover a culture's way of being, knowing, and understanding.

Fieldworkers who live, observe, and describe the daily life, behaviors, and language of a group of people for long periods of time are called *ethnographers*.

This book draws on the work of classic and contemporary anthropologists and folklorists: Hortense Powdermaker, Henry Glassie, Barbara Myerhoff, Zora Neale Hurston, Paul Stoller, and Renato Rosaldo, among others. Ethnography, the written product of their work, is a researched study that synthesizes information about the life of a people or group. Researchers in many disciplines rely on ethnographic methods: anthropologists, folklorists, linguists, sociologists, oral historians, and those who study popular culture. Ethnographic researchers conduct fieldwork in an attempt to understand the cultures they study. And as they study the culture of others, they learn patterns that connect with their own lives and traditions.

Powdermaker, who did her fieldwork during the 1930s and 1940s, wrote about the Melanesians she studied as both "strangers" and "friends." Her book, in fact, is called *Stranger and Friend*. Powdermaker, a product of her time, also refers to the Melanesians as "stone-aged" and "natives," revealing an unconscious Westernized attitude toward people different from herself. Without realizing it, Powdermaker judged the Melanesian culture to be less sophisticated or developed than her own. This attitude—domination of one culture by the values of another—is called **colonization**, and fieldworkers of all backgrounds must guard against it.

Like Powdermaker, fieldworkers historically studied foreign or exotic cultures, but no longer do they restrict their research to non-Western cultures. Contemporary fieldworkers also investigate local cultures and subcultures. Jennifer Toth, for example, wrote a book called *The Mole People: Life in the Tunnels beneath New York City*, describing her time with homeless people who shelter themselves in subways, sewer systems, and work stations under city streets. Rather than depicting these people as somehow less than herself, Toth likens them to people who have more conventional homes. Because all fieldworkers risk projecting their own **assumptions** onto the groups they study, they must be ready and willing to unpack their own cultural baggage and embark on a collaborative journey with those they study.

STEPPING IN: REVEALING OUR SUBCULTURES

As coauthors of this book, we have ourselves come to our interest in ethnography from membership in a dizzying array of **subcultures**. As collaborators, we share the culture of academia. We are graduates of the same Ph.D. program in which we learned to conduct ethnographic fieldwork. As middle-aged professors, we've both taught in public urban, suburban, and rural schools, directed college writing centers and programs, and taught many college English and education courses. And as mothers of young adults, both of us have spent years navigating the child-centered cultures of nursery school carpools, pediatric waiting rooms, and soccer and Special Olympics teams.

Yet our subcultures vary. Although she doesn't think about it much, Bonnie grew up with one Yiddish-speaking Jewish grandmother and another grandmother who denied her Jewish heritage. Elizabeth is a midwestern WASP whose grandfather was a farmer and whose father became a businessman who spoke Spanish and traveled to Cuba before Fidel Castro came to power. We both grew up as American baby boomers, with conformity and optimism in the post–World War II '50s, which by the '60s turned to protest of the Vietnam War. Bonnie played the guitar, wrote folk songs for a friend's coffeehouse, and joined the civil rights march on Selma. Elizabeth belonged to the Anti-Complicity War Movement, hung out in Greenwich Village wearing black clothes, and grew organic vegetables on a cooperative farm. But we were not only followers of these "countersubcultures"; we also belonged to more mainstream American ones. Bonnie, who was vice president of her high school student council, skipped school occasionally to take the train downtown to sneak into a broadcast of *American Bandstand* but also wrote features for her college newspaper and joined a sorority. Elizabeth was a member of the National Honor Society, drag raced a souped-up red and cream-colored Chevy, and was sent off to finishing school, where she wore white gloves, stockings, and little hats.

In each of these subcultures, we communicated through special languages with insiders. We knew the ways of behaving and interacting, and we shared belief systems with the others in each group. Yet we held membership in many subcultures at the same time, and we could move among them. As members over the years, we were unaware of those groups as actual cultures, but looking back as fieldworkers, we now understand that we, like you, have always been in a position to research the people around us. And we probably did do some informal inquiry but not the disciplined fieldwork of the ethnographer that this book describes.

As researchers, we've both studied the literacies of American subcultures. Because we are interested in language, both written and oral, we research everyday places where people read, write, speak, and listen. Elizabeth has studied college students' conversation patterns, collaborative journal writing, middle school writing workshops, and kindergarteners' book talk. Bonnie has studied talk in a high school teachers' lounge, interactions in a college writing center, a recording session for a Hollywood movie, the writing and reading of handicapped teenagers, and a school superintendent's writing **portfolio**.

Neither of us has "stepped out" of our North American culture to find our research sites, but the more research we do, the more interest we have in researching familiar places. We are a bit like tourists who need only to travel a little way from home to find something very different and very fascinating to research. Less than an hour away from Elizabeth's home, for example, is a small town called Seagrove that has over 100 working potters. They form a community that shares similar technical language, crafting skills, and aesthetic values. Each spring the potters of Seagrove stage a ritual opening of the kilns to the public. Pots are thrown and glazes are applied as potters share their insider knowledge with outsiders. This group of artisans, whose craft goes back eight or nine generations, represents a subculture unknown to Elizabeth and many others who live just outside Seagrove. We don't always need to go very far from home to find groups of people whose ways of behaving and communicating are different and interesting, yet unfamiliar to us.

As you begin to think about conducting field research projects, review your own subcultures; you may find that they offer intriguing possibilities for research.

BOX 1

Looking at Subcultures

Purpose

We consider any self-identified group of people who share language, stories, rituals, behaviors, and values a subculture. Some subcultures define themselves by geography (southerners, Texans, New Yorkers). Others define themselves by ethnicity or language (Mexicano, Irish, Belgian, Filipino, Ghanaian). And others define their interests by shared rituals and behaviors (fraternities, Girl Scouts, Masons, Daughters of the American Revolution, computer hackers). Whether it's your bowling league, your neighborhood pickup basketball team or group of bicycle freestylers, your church, your community government, or your school's ecology club, you simultaneously belong to many different subcultures. With this box, we'd like you to recall your subculture affiliations and share them with others in your class.

Action

List some of the subcultures to which you belong. For each subculture you mention, jot down a few key details that distinguish the group—behaviors, insider phrases, rules, rituals, and the specific locations where these behaviors usually occur. You might want to divide your list into a few categories or columns, such as

Group	Rituals	Insider Phrases	Behaviors

Write a paragraph or short essay describing one of these subcultures, either seriously or satirically.

Response

Some of our students belonged to these subcultures: computer interest groups, online discussion groups, listservs, deer hunters, gospel singers, specialty book clubs, volleyball teams, science fiction conventioneers, auctiongoers, fly fishermen, billiard players, bull riders, lap swimmers, bluegrass musicians, stock car racers.

Chinatsu Sazawa is a native of Japan, where as a teenager she experienced karaoke quite differently from the way Americans do. Here is what she writes about the subculture of Japanese karaoke participants:

The Karaoke Box is a small soundproof room with a karaoke machine, a table, and sofas. Customers can reserve it for $5 to $20 an hour and sing as much as they like. This habit is to weekend Karaoke Box warriors as a sports gym is to exercise lovers. We enjoy karaoke and perform extensively to release our stress by singing, shouting, and dancing. The most important thing for weekend Karaoke Box warriors is to be efficient at the Box. Paying by the hour, we do our best to sing as many songs as possible. As we enter the Karaoke box, we go directly to a remote control and the book listing the available songs. While we take off our jackets and put our bags down, we check "the code" of our opening song and punch in the number on the remote. During the one minute while the machine searches for the song, we prepare to sing, taking off the sanitary plastic covering on the microphone and connecting it to the machine. We adjust the key of the song by pressing the Key Changer button.

It is an understood rule among us that we take turns and sing only one song each turn. It's also a courtesy to avoid singing too many long songs (songs that would last over five minutes, such as "Hotel California"). While others are singing, instead of listening we constantly flip the pages of the book of available songs and select the songs we will sing in our following turns. It's important to punch in the code numbers before the other people's songs end so that the next song starts immediately without down time. We even press the Stop Performance button just as the song begins its ending.

We talk very little in the Box except to ask questions like "Whose song is that?" or say "That was good!" Seven or eight minutes before our time expires, we receive a phone call from the front desk. That's the cue to punch in the number of our closing songs. We often select closing songs that everyone in the room can sing together. While the last person is singing, the rest of the people clean up the room—pile the books of available songs, place the mikes on the table, throw garbage in the bin—and get ready to leave. When we pass the front desk, we look for discount coupons for our next visit.

INVESTIGATING PERSPECTIVES: INSIDER AND OUTSIDER

Fieldworkers realize that ordinary events in one culture might seem extraordinary in another. When people say "that's really weird" or "aren't they strange," a fieldworker hears these comments as signals for investigation. When you first ate dinner at someone's home other than yours, you may have felt like an outsider. You "stepped out" of your own home and "stepped in" to a set of routines and rituals different from your own. You may have noticed who set the table, passed the food, served, ate first, talked, signaled that the meal was over, cleared off the table, and washed the dishes. Or as an insider among your own relatives, you always observed their quirky behaviors: you learned not to disturb the bronze baby shoes in Aunt Sonia's TV room or never to descend into Uncle Fred's cellar. To avoid a head cold, your mother may use crystals and a spiritual chant, but your best friend's mother may depend on warm milk and honey, minted tea, echinacea, or vitamin C.

Although we would not classify modern families as subcultures, they do have some of the features of a subculture and prepare us to observe outside our own home territory. When you visit another place, you may notice that people move and talk more slowly or quickly, more quietly or noisily, or that they use space differently than you're used to. A fieldworker "steps out" to adopt an outsider's perspective when investigating unfamiliar (or even familiar) patterns, attempting to penetrate or unveil the many layers of behaviors and beliefs that make people think as they think and act as they act.

Anthropologist Renato Rosaldo offers a good example of "stepping out," using the outsider's detached perspective to look at a familiar routine, the family ritual of making breakfast:

> Every morning, the reigning patriarch, as if in from the hunt, shouts from the kitchen, "How many people would like a poached egg?" Women and children take turns saying yes or no.
>
> In the meantime, the women talk among themselves and designate one among them the toastmaker. As the eggs near readiness, the reigning patriarch calls out to the designated toastmaker, "The eggs are about ready. Is there enough toast?"
>
> "Yes" comes the deferential reply. "The last two pieces are about to pop up." The reigning patriarch then proudly enters, bearing a plate of poached eggs before him. Throughout the course of the meal, the women and children, including the designated toastmaker, perform the obligatory ritual praise song, saying, "These sure are great eggs, Dad" (47).

In this passage, Rosaldo has made a familiar routine seem unfamiliar: father makes poached eggs, women make toast, all eat. By analyzing his family's well-known breakfast-making process, Rosaldo exposes the power and gender relationships involved in this ordinary event. He describes the father as the "reigning patriarch" and the women as subsidiary toast makers and praise singers. With his detached language and his careful detailing of their routine, he depicts this North American middle-class family as if it were part of a different tribe or culture. He uses his interpretive skills as an ethnographer to create a **parody**—in jest and fun—to allow his family to see them as an outsider might describe them.

But fieldworkers do not depend entirely on the detachment or objectivity that comes from stepping out of a culture. They rely on basic human involvement—their gut reactions or subjective responses to cultural practices—as well. In another example from Rosaldo's fieldwork, he shows how his own personal life experience shaped his ability to understand headhunters. As a ritual of revenge and grief over a deceased relative, the Ilongots of the Philippines sever human heads. When Rosaldo and his anthropologist wife, Michelle, lived and studied among the Ilongot people for several years, they were unable to understand the complex emotions surrounding headhunting. But after Michelle died in an accident during fieldwork, Rosaldo began to understand the headhunters' practice of killing for retribution. It was his own experience—rage and grief over his wife's death—that allowed him insight into the cultural practice of the people he was studying. Rosaldo writes:

> [N]othing in my own experience equipped me even to imagine the anger possible in bereavement until after Michelle Rosaldo's death in 1981. Only then was I in a position to grasp the force of what the Ilongots had repeatedly told me about grief, rage, and headhunting (19).

Rosaldo's reaction to Michelle's dying, his subjective feelings, connected him with the Ilongots' practice of killing as an act of revenge. Even though their value systems were different, Rosaldo and the Ilongots shared the basic human response to a loved one's death.

So it is not always **objectivity** or detachment that allows us to study culture, our own or that of others. **Subjectivity**—our inner feelings and belief systems—allows us to uncover some features of culture that are not always apparent. As a fieldworker, you will conduct an internal dialogue between your subjective and objective selves, listening to both, questioning both. You combine the viewpoints of an outsider "stepping in" and an insider "stepping out" of the culture you study. And studying culture is as much about the everyday practices of cooking and eating, such as poaching eggs, as it is about the unfamiliar tribal practices of killing as a part of grieving, of achieving revenge by severing a human head. Detachment and involvement, subjectivity and objectivity, insider and outsider stances are equally coupled in fieldworking.

STEPPING OUT: MAKING THE FAMILIAR STRANGE AND THE STRANGE FAMILIAR

Rosaldo's parody of the family breakfast and his understanding of the Ilongots' headhunting practices display the coupled skills of detachment and involvement a fieldworker needs. To understand the Ilongots' perspective on headhunting—a crucial part of what anthropologists would call their **worldview**—Rosaldo had to suffer the intensity of rage and grief that the bereaved Ilongots did. Though not intentionally, he achieved this empathy by making what seemed to him a strange event (cutting off people's heads for revenge) totally familiar as a researcher.

What is often more difficult to achieve than making the unknown become familiar is making the familiar seem strange. Rosaldo was able to accomplish the outsider view of his family's breakfast-making practices mainly through satire, a technique that distances the reader from the event or practice under consideration. In the following reading written in 1956, "Body Ritual among the Nacirema," anthropologist Horace Miner also depends on satire to depict an ordinary set of daily practices as strange and unfamiliar. As you read this essay, try to figure out what everyday rituals Miner is satirizing.

Body Ritual among the Nacirema
Horace Miner

The anthropologist has become so familiar with the diversity of ways in which different peoples behave in similar situations that he is not apt to be surprised by even the most exotic customs. In fact, if all of the logically possible combinations of behavior have not been found somewhere in the world, he is apt to suspect that they must be present in some yet undescribed tribe. This point has, in fact, been expressed with respect to clan organization by Murdock (1949:71). In this light, the magical beliefs and practices of the Nacirema present such unusual aspects that it seems desirable to describe them as an example of the extremes to which human behavior can go.

Professor Linton first brought the ritual of the Nacirema to the attention of anthropologists twenty years ago (1936:326), but the culture of this people is still very poorly understood. They are a North American group living in the territory between the Canadian Cree, the Yaqui and Tarahumare of Mexico, and the Carib and Arawak of the Antilles. Little is known of their origin, although tradition states that they came from the east. According to Nacirema mythology, their nation was originated by a culture hero, Notgnihsaw, who is otherwise known for two great feats of strength—the throwing of a piece of wampum across the river Pa-To-Mac and the chopping down of a cherry tree in which the Spirit of Truth resided.

Nacirema culture is characterized by a highly developed market economy which has evolved in a rich natural habitat. While much of the people's time is devoted to economic pursuits, a large part of the fruits of these labors and a considerable portion of the day are spent in ritual activity. The focus of this activity is the human body, the appearance and health of which loom as a dominant concern in the ethos of the people. While such a concern is certainly not unusual, its ceremonial aspect and associated philosophy are unique.

The fundamental belief underlying the whole system appears to be that the human body is ugly and that its natural tendency is to debility and disease. Incarcerated in such a body, man's only hope is to avert these characteristics through the use of the powerful influences of ritual and ceremony. Every household has one or more shrines devoted to this purpose. The more powerful individuals in the society have several shrines in their houses and, in fact, the opulence of a house is often referred to in terms of the number of such ritual centers it possesses. Most houses are of wattle and daub construction, but the shrine rooms of the more wealthy are walled with stone. Poorer families imitate the rich by applying pottery plaques to their shrine walls.

While each family has at least one such shrine, the rituals associated with it are not family ceremonies but are private and secret. The rites are normally only discussed with children, and then only during the period when they are being initiated into these mysteries. I was able, however, to establish sufficient rapport with the natives to examine these shrines and to have the rituals described to me.

The focal point of the shrine is a box or chest which is built into the wall. In this chest are kept the many charms and magical potions without which no native believes he could live. These preparations are secured from a variety of specialized practitioners. The most powerful of these are the medicine men, whose assistance must be rewarded with substantial gifts. However, the medicine men do not provide the curative potions for their clients, but decide what the ingredients should be and then write them down in an ancient and secret language. This writing is understood only by the medicine men and by the herbalists who, for another gift, provide the required charm.

The charm is not disposed of after it has served its purpose, but is placed in the charm-box of the household shrine. As these magical materials are specific for certain ills, and the real or imagined maladies of the people are many, the charm-box is usually full to overflowing. The magical packets are so numerous that people forget what their purposes were and fear to use them again. While the natives are very vague on this point, we can only assume that the idea in retaining all the old magical materials is that their presence in the charm-box, before which the body rituals are conducted, will in some way protect the worshipper.

Beneath the charm-box is a small font. Each day every member of the family, in succession, enters the shrine room, bows his head before the charm-box, mingles different sorts of holy water in the font, and proceeds with a brief rite of ablution. The holy waters are secured from the Water Temple of the community, where the priests conduct elaborate ceremonies to make the liquid ritually pure.

In the hierarchy of magical practitioners, and below the medicine men in prestige, are specialists whose designation is best translated "holy-mouth-men." The Nacirema have an almost pathological horror of and fascination with the mouth, the condition of which is believed to have a supernatural influence on all social relationships. Were it not for the rituals of the mouth, they believe that their teeth would fall out, their gums bleed, their jaws shrink, their friends desert them, and their lovers reject them. They also believe that a strong relationship exists between oral and moral characteristics. For example, there is a ritual ablution of the mouth for children which is supposed to improve their moral fiber.

The daily body ritual performed by everyone includes a mouth-rite. Despite the fact that these people are so punctilious about care of the mouth, this rite involves a practice which strikes the uninitiated stranger as revolting. It was reported to me that the ritual consists of inserting a small bundle of hog hairs into the mouth, along with certain magical powders, and then moving the bundle in a highly formalized series of gestures.

In addition to the private mouth-rite, the people seek out a holy-mouth-man once or twice a year. These practitioners have an impressive set of paraphernalia, consisting of a variety of augers, awls, probes, and prods. The use of these objects in the exorcism of the evils of the mouth involves almost unbelievable ritual torture of the client. The holy-mouth-man opens the client's mouth and, using the above mentioned tools, enlarges any holes which decay may have created in the teeth. Magical materials are put into these holes. If there are no naturally occurring holes in the teeth, large sections of one or more teeth are gouged out so that the supernatural substance can be applied. In the client's view, the purpose of these ministrations is to arrest decay and to draw friends. The extremely sacred and traditional character of the rite is evident in the fact that the natives return to the holy-mouth-men year after year, despite the fact that their teeth continue to decay.

It is to be hoped that, when a thorough study of the Nacirema is made, there will be careful inquiry into the personality structure of these people. One has but to watch the gleam in the eye of a holy-mouth-man, as he jabs an awl into an exposed nerve, to suspect that a certain amount of sadism is involved. If this can be established, a very interesting pattern emerges, for most of the population shows definite masochistic tendencies. It was to these that Professor Linton referred in discussing a distinctive part of the daily body ritual which is performed only by men. This part of the rite involves scraping and lacerating the surface of the face with a sharp instrument. Special women's rites are performed only four times during each lunar month, but what they lack in frequency is made up in barbarity. As part of this ceremony, women bake their heads in small ovens for about an hour. The theoretically interesting point is that what seems to be a preponderantly masochistic people have developed sadistic specialists.

The medicine men have an imposing temple, or *latipso*, in every community of any size. The more elaborate ceremonies required to treat very sick patients can only be performed at this temple. These ceremonies involve not only the thaumaturge but a permanent group of vestal maidens who move sedately about the temple chambers in distinctive costume and headdress.

The *latipso* ceremonies are so harsh that it is phenomenal that a fair proportion of the really sick natives who enter the temple ever recover. Small children whose indoctrination is still incomplete have been known to resist attempts to take them to the temple because "that is where you go to die." Despite this fact, sick adults are not only willing but eager to undergo the protracted ritual purification, if they can afford to do so. No matter how ill the supplicant or how grave the emergency, the guardians of many temples will not admit a client if he cannot give a rich gift to the custodian. Even after one has gained admission and survived the ceremonies, the guardians will not permit the neophyte to leave until he makes still another gift.

The supplicant entering the temple is first stripped of all his or her clothes. In everyday life the Nacirema avoids exposure of his body and its natural functions. Bathing and excretory acts are performed only in the secrecy of the household shrine, where they are ritualized as part of the body-rites. Psychological shock results from the fact that body secrecy is suddenly lost upon entry into the *latipso*. A man, whose own wife has never seen him in an excretory act, suddenly finds himself naked and assisted by a vestal maiden while he performs his natural functions into a sacred vessel. This sort of ceremonial treatment is necessitated by the fact that the excreta are used by a diviner to ascertain the course and nature of the client's sickness. Female clients, on the other hand, find their naked bodies are subjected to the scrutiny, manipulation and prodding of the medicine men.

Few supplicants in the temple are well enough to do anything but lie on their hard beds. The daily ceremonies, like the rites of the holy-mouth-men, involve discomfort and torture. With ritual precision, the vestals awaken their miserable charges each dawn and roll them about on their beds of pain while performing ablutions, in the formal movements of which the maidens are highly trained. At other times they insert magic wands in the supplicant's mouth or force him to eat substances which are supposed to be healing. From time to time the medicine men come to their clients and jab magically treated needles into their flesh. The fact that these temple ceremonies may not cure, and may even kill the neophyte, in no way decreases the people's faith in the medicine men.

There remains one other kind of practitioner, known as a "listener." This witch-doctor has the power to exorcise the devils that lodge in the heads of people who have been bewitched. The Nacirema believe that parents bewitch their own children. Mothers are particularly suspected of putting a curse on children while teaching them the secret body rituals. The counter-magic of the witch-doctor is unusual in its lack of ritual. The patient simply tells the "listener" all his troubles and fears, beginning with the earliest difficulties he can remember. The memory displayed by the Nacirema in these exorcism sessions is truly remarkable. It is not uncommon for the patient to bemoan the rejection he felt upon being weaned as a babe, and a few individuals even see their troubles going back to the traumatic effects of their own birth.

In conclusion, mention must be made of certain practices which have their base in native esthetics but which depend upon the pervasive aversion to the natural body and its functions. There are ritual fasts to make fat people thin and ceremonial feasts to make thin people fat. Still other rites are used to make women's breasts larger if they are small, and smaller if they are large. General dissatisfaction with breast shape is symbolized in the fact that the ideal form is virtually outside the range of human variation. A few women afflicted with almost inhuman hypermammary development are so idolized that they make a handsome living by simply going from village to village and permitting the natives to stare at them for a fee.

Reference has already been made to the fact that excretory functions are ritualized, routinized, and relegated to secrecy. Natural reproductive functions are similarly distorted. Intercourse is taboo as a topic and scheduled as an act. Efforts are made to avoid pregnancy by the use of magical materials or by limiting intercourse to certain phases of the moon. Conception is actually very infrequent. When pregnant, women dress so as to hide their condition. Parturition takes place in secret, without friends or relatives to assist, and the majority of women do not nurse their infants.

Our review of the ritual life of the Nacirema has certainly shown them to be a magic-ridden people. It is hard to understand how they have managed to exist so long under the burdens which they have imposed upon themselves. But even such exotic customs as these take on real meaning when they are viewed with the insight provided by Malinowski when he wrote (1948:70):

Looking from far and above, from our high places of safety in the developed civilization, it is easy to see all the crudity and irrelevance of magic. But without its power and guidance early man could not have mastered his practical difficulties as he has done, nor could man have advanced to the higher stages of civilization.

Works Cited

Linton, Ralph. 1936. *The Study of Man*. New York, D. Appleton-Century Co.

Malinowski, Bronislaw. 1948. *Magic, Science, and Religion*. Glencoe, The Free Press.

Murdock, George P. 1949. *Social Structure*. New York, The Macmillan Co.

As you read this parody of American (*Nacirema* spelled backward) personal hygiene, you probably noticed how Miner's descriptions of everyday bathroom objects and grooming practices seemed like something you never before engaged in. He describes the medicine chest as a "shrine" that holds magic potions and "charms." The toothbrush is "a small bundle of hog hairs" for the application of "magical powders."

We laugh at Miner's parody because we see ourselves and our American obsession with cleanliness. This reading makes fun of our own cultural attitudes about bathing and cleansing habits, our American belief in dentists, doctors, and therapists, and our reliance on hospitals and diets. Miner defamiliarizes our everyday behaviors so that we can see ourselves as outsiders might describe us: a highly ritualized people who believe in magical customs and potions.

Making the Ordinary Extraordinary

B O X 2

Purpose

As the preceding excerpts from Renato Rosaldo (p. 8) and Horace Miner (p. 10) show, shifting oneself from insider to outsider and trying to describe language and behavior from those perspectives are not only the essence of parody but also activities of enormous value when we try to "make the familiar strange and the strange familiar" as fieldworkers must do. This box offers you an opportunity to recognize the value of seeing ourselves as outsiders might describe us.

Action

Take something that's familiar to you—an ordinary routine or ritual in your everyday life that would seem extraordinary to someone else in another culture or subculture—and reexamine it as if you were seeing it for the first time. Try something simple—like the way you fix your hair, listen to music, change a tire, take in the mail, or get ready for a sporting event. List the specific behaviors of your routine, and identify what might seem strange or extraordinary to others. Prepare your list to share with others, or write a short paragraph that describes the process.

Response

Our student Angela Harger wrote this response:

> I pay thousands of dollars a year—dollars I resent giving up but give up anyway. For all this money, I get the privilege of awakening early, long before my body wants to. I groggily get ready and then drive east for half an hour, through rain, snow, or blinding sun. I shell out another extraordinary amount of dollars each day for the privilege of leaving

my vehicle. I then subject myself to the weather's elements, trudging off to far-flung buildings so I can sit for hours at a time, always feeling restless. I listen to older people talk and talk, and I write it all down so I can remember it later when I submit myself to stressful testing for days at a time so that these older people can determine whether I've learned anything. For these sessions, I spend exorbitant amounts of time and more dollars for books I will have to force myself to read. But I can't give up this ritual: I have been doing it and perfecting it for more than thirteen years, and I am nowhere close to being finished.

POSING QUESTIONS: ETHNOGRAPHIC AND JOURNALISTIC

An ethnographer and a journalist may both gather information about the same event but write up their accounts very differently. Miner's satire on American body rituals is a parody of the kind of traditional research that anthropologists have often published about foreign or exotic cultures. Nonfiction exposés, reports of personal experiences, and historical and documentary writings may read like fieldwork projects, but the difference lies in the research processes that led up to them. A standard daily newspaper reporter, for example, conducts research in an attempt to be objective: to give the who, what, where, when, and why of an event for a readership that expects facts without too much interpretation. As a fieldworker, your purpose is to collect and consider multiple sources of information, not facts alone, to convey the perspective of the people in the culture you study.

The fieldworker asks big, open questions such as "What's going on here?" and "Where is the culture?" as he or she observes, listens, records, interprets, and analyzes. The journalist often writes from the outsider perspective, quoting from insiders. The fieldworker must combine an outsider's point of view with an insider's perspective. Anthropologists use the term *emic* to mean the insider perspective and *etic* to refer to that of the outsider.

The following piece, "Church Opens Doors to Vietnamese," from the front page of a small city's newspaper, provides an example of reportage. But if we examine the article with an ethnographer's eye, we'll ask different questions that help us examine information that a newswriter usually doesn't consider. To read for the complexity that this article implies, we need to uncover many layers of cultural meanings.

Church Opens Doors to Vietnamese

St. Louis de Gonzague Holds First Mass in Vietnamese and Welcomes the Community to Its Parish

Byron Brown, Telegraph Staff

NASHUA—The one o'clock Mass at St. Louis de Gonzague Church was a little different Sunday. The choir and congregation sang "Meet Me in St. Louis" to greet its new minister, the Rev. Louis Nhien.

Nhien greeted his new parishioners by conducting Mass in Vietnamese.

Nhien's sermon was the first of what will be a weekly Vietnamese Mass at the church on West Hollis Street.

Before the 90-minute Mass, Nhien led about 200 Vietnamese worshipers into the church as hundreds of St. Louis' current parishioners stood and applauded. Nhien took a seat behind the altar alongside Pastor Roland Cote and Bishop Leo O'Neil of the Manchester diocese.

Older Vietnamese women wearing flowing silk blouses and pants, and younger Vietnamese families toting small children all filed into the pews in the center of the church.

There, they listened as O'Neil praised, with the help of an interpreter, the union of the Vietnamese community and the Roman Catholic Church.

"No matter what language we speak, no matter what country we come from, baptism has made us all brothers," he said. "We are one church as we profess one faith."

O'Neil spoke of St. Louis' history as a French-speaking church and how that had prepared its older parishioners for the new Vietnamese Mass.

"The French people of Nashua decided to build their own church where they could feel at home and speak their own language," he said. "The people of St. Louis want to welcome you here today, so you can feel at home."

Nhien then led the entire church in prayer and song.

Nhien, 38, was ordained last year and came to New Hampshire three weeks ago from Carthage, Mo. The New Hampshire Catholic Charities, led by Monsignor John Quinn, specifically brought him to the state to conduct Mass for the Vietnamese refugee community, which is centered in Greater Nashua and Manchester.

Older parishioners welcomed the Vietnamese worshipers and said their arrival makes St. Louis a stronger and more diversified church.

Veronica Barr, an Englishwoman who now lives in Nashua, said, "I'm excited. I think enthusiasm is an extension of us all being Catholic."

Ethnography and journalism differ not only with respect to the writing process but also with respect to the depth of research, the time allotted to it, and, most significantly, the perspective that the researcher adopts. Many ethnographers write journalistically, and many journalists write ethnographically. In the example above, journalist Byron Brown's responsibility was to report on the special church service—that event as it happened at that church on that day—against a deadline and for a specific audience of newspaper readers. This journalist's goal was to gather the church's news, and his responsibility was to get it out quickly. But as a fieldworker, your responsibility would be to conduct extensive research, to discover knowledge that might take months or even years to complete. The fieldworker's commitment is an emic one—to capture the perspective of the insiders in the culture.

The newspaper account is the story of a Vietnamese priest from Carthage, Missouri, who has been invited to conduct a weekly Catholic Mass for Vietnamese refugees. The Mass takes place in a New Hampshire church whose pastor and parishioners are primarily French Canadian and whose bishop is Irish. The article states that the choir sings a song from an American musical, "Meet Me in St. Louis," playing off the name of the church (St. Louis de Gonzague), its newest minister (Louis Nhien), and the state from which he has recently come (Missouri).

The article describes young Vietnamese women as "wearing flowing silk blouses and pants" and an Englishwoman as saying "I'm excited. I think enthusiasm is an extension of us all being Catholic." In the newspaper account, the bishop announces, "The people of St. Louis want to welcome you here today, so you can feel at home." The accompanying photograph shows an American flag, a bilingual banner that says "Welcome/Bienvenue," and a large stained-glass crucifix. Under these artifacts stand the three Catholic clergymen, posed before the congregation in their religious vestments. The caption reminds readers that the clergy recited the welcoming Mass in three languages: English, French, and Vietnamese.

As a fieldworker, you would ask focused questions about this cultural moment. You would emphasize issues that differ from the journalist's focus on the who, what, where, when, and why. You would ask questions like these: Who belongs to the Vietnamese refugee community? How do they see themselves here at this church? What languages do *they* speak? Do they define themselves as Catholic? Vietnamese? French? Americans? Immigrants? Settlers? Why are they associated with this French Canadian church? What is the history of French speakers in New Hampshire? What is the history of the French influence in Vietnam? Whether you choose the perspective of the Vietnamese priest, a non-Catholic Vietnamese refugee, the Irish bishop, or the mayor of Nashua, you will offer the insiders' perspective along with your own as you translate your cultural **data** into ethnographic text for your readers.

When Bishop O'Neil states in the article that he wants the Vietnamese worshipers to feel "at home," what does he mean by "at home"? Home to the people already in the church? to the Vietnamese refugee community of parishioners? to the other clergy? to the greater Nashua community? The older Vietnamese women are reported to be wearing silk blouses and pants, but what were the younger women wearing? The men? The non-Vietnamese parishioners? Who was included in the "hundreds" who stood and applauded? Why did they applaud? Why was Veronica Barr specifically described as "an Englishwoman"? And how do we read her perspective that "enthusiasm is an extension of us all being Catholic"? What, for example, would one of the Vietnamese parishioners say about the multicultural service?

As a fieldworker, investigating all these questions and trying to understand this cultural moment, you would collect more information (data) and do more fieldwork. You might, for example, gather artifacts (material objects that belong to and represent a culture)—the printed service, prayerbooks and hymnals, documents or pamphlets describing the church and its programs—in any or all of the three languages. You might do some research at the library on the French occupation of Vietnam and on the history of the Catholic Church in the United States, Canada, France, and Vietnam. Or you might go to the Nashua Historical Society to learn about the French Canadian settlers in Nashua. But you would not be able to write your account until you had begun to decipher where the culture is.

One way you could begin would be to locate key **informants** to interview— a few people to help guide you and explain their culture. Such guides represent the "others," those who are different from the researcher. To describe their guides, fieldworkers use the terms *informants, consultants, subjects, natives, the other,* or *insiders.* Which term we use is our own decision, but since such descriptions reveal our attitudes toward the people we study, it is a crucial decision to make. Throughout this book, we use anthropology's term *informant* to refer to insiders in a culture. We realize that some readers may associate this term informant with police work (a "snitch," for instance). But we like this term because it emphasizes the knowledge—the *information*—that insiders have. For similar reasons, some fieldworkers like the term *consultant.*

So you would choose key informants in Nashua to interview, using a translator if necessary, holding conversations in homes and in other community settings as well as in the church. Your informants might offer different perspectives on the extent to which the church has welcomed the Vietnamese into its community. You might, for example, interview the three clergy, the Englishwoman Veronica Barr, one of the Vietnamese women, or even Byron Brown, the newswriter who wrote the account of the Sunday afternoon Mass. Other informants could include the church's choir director or Monsignor John Quinn, who brought Reverend Nhien to New Hampshire. You would tape your interviews and then transcribe them.

Throughout the process, you would keep careful fieldnotes describing the details in the places you go and the people you observe as they go about living in those places. You would also record your own subjective responses and feelings and how they affect your data: things that bother you, ideas you don't understand, events or comments that interest you. Looking over all this data, you would begin to formulate hypotheses about what is important in the culture of the St. Louis de Gonzague Church, Nashua's Vietnamese community, the larger refugee community, or the French Canadian Catholic community. As you thought about your data, you would then make choices about which part of it you would use to represent the people in the culture.

Engaging the Ethnographic Perspective

Purpose

Knowing the difference between the insider ("emic") perspective and the outsider ("etic") perspective is an important skill for a fieldworker, as it is for a journalist. But for a fieldworker, being sure to represent many perspectives—those of the researcher as well as those of the various people important to the "moment" in a given cultural event—is deeply important to the principles of ethnographic research.

Action

Find a news article in your local paper that shows a cultural moment and might challenge a fieldworker to do more research. A cultural moment need not be a major political or social event such as the dissembling of the Berlin Wall or a march on Washington. Local headlines often mark insider culture in smaller places: the opening of an ethnic restaurant, a local hero's action, a community conflict, a group or institution that's made a major shift. Share the article and your answers to the following questions with your colleagues:

- What cultural information does the article include?
- What kinds of questions might the fieldworker ask to further uncover the culture the article describes?
- How would the fieldworker's questions differ from those of a journalist?
- What information would the fieldworker want to gather to answer the question "What's going on here?"
- What other sources of information might the fieldworker use to penetrate the insider perspective?
- Where would she need to go to find those sources?

Response

Here are some sample headlines of newspaper articles our students chose: "Amish Community Copes with Rare Murder," "Korean University Professor Develops Education Program in Finland," "Art Teacher Saves Drowning Child in Treacherous River Dam," "Small Business Grant Slashed in Favor of Community Fireworks Display," "Kiwanis Club Donates Funds toward Little Juanita's New Kidney." Note that the headlines are specific, full of cultural details. Our students' analyses were twice as long as the news articles they chose. They asked more questions than they were able to answer as they peeled back layers of information to find out "Where is (or are) the culture(s)?" An example, consisting of a news story accompanied by a student's analysis, follows:

Black Astronaut Carries Navajo Flag

CAPE CANAVERAL, FLA. (AP)—Before Bernard Harris Jr. was allowed to take a Navajo flag aboard *Discovery,* tribal medicine men had to bless it with corn pollen and make sure the space shuttle's path fit with their beliefs: It had to orbit clockwise.

When the Navajo decided that from their viewpoint, *Discovery*'s orbit met the requirement, all signals were go for Harris to carry the first Navajo item to fly in space. NASA allows astronauts to carry up a few small belongings.

"I'm flying this flag for them because being there I could see their plight as the original Americans," said Harris, a 38-year-old black physician who lived on a Navajo reservation from ages 7 to 15. His mother taught at boarding schools run by the U.S. Bureau of Indian Affairs.

Harris, who today will become the first black to spacewalk, approached the Navajo in December about taking some tribal item with him on the mission.

Navajo Nation President Albert Hale decided on a flag after consulting with medicine men to make sure no spiritual traditions would be violated. The flag was blessed last month by Navajo medicine man Ross Nez.

Through a ceremony, Nez "was told by the Creator and the Holy People that it would strengthen the Navajo Nation for this flag to go around Mother Earth," Navajo spokeswoman Valerie Taliman said Wednesday.

Bernard Harris Jr., an astronaut
aboard the space shuttle *Discovery*.

"The flag is a symbol of our nation and reminds us of how we must live in balance with our Mother Earth to survive," Hale said.

Nez blessed the flag by sprinkling it with corn pollen, which has an importance for the Navajo roughly similar to holy water in the Catholic church.

Hale sent the blessed flag to NASA. A few days later, he said, a NASA official called: "We have the flag, but we have a question. What is this yellow stuff on it?"

Hale assured NASA the powder was sacred pollen used in prayers.

The Navajo flag depicts the four mountains that delineate traditional Navajo territory.

Using the Ethnographic Perspective

Steve Gates

"Black Astronaut Carries Navajo Flag," Cedar Rapids Gazette, *February 10, 1995*

The article discusses Bernard Harris Jr.'s choice to carry a Navajo flag on board the NASA shuttle plane, *Discovery.* Harris is an African American who spent eight years of his youth on a Navajo reservation. The article reveals general details about the circumstances and the way in which the decision was approved by Navajo tribal leaders.

Regarding the cultural issues, there are several things the article doesn't include. Why does Harris consider the Navajo the "first Americans," as he is quoted as saying? What daily interaction did Harris have with the Navajo during his youth, and what specific influence did they have on him? Why did he leave when he was 15? Did he maintain contact with the Navajo after he left the reservation? How much does he know about his African American heritage compared to the Navajo culture? Did he also take an artifact from his African American heritage? Why or why not? If so, what was it, and is there any connection to the Navajo flag?

Other questions worth pursuing might be knowing how Navajo officials and tribal leaders felt about Harris's choice for an artifact. Perhaps one could interview childhood friends of Harris's from the reservation to hear their reflections and opinions. Do they have the same opinion of him now that they did then? Why or why not? Did Harris actively participate in the Navajo culture and rituals as a young person? To what extent does his choice to carry their flag represent a sincere and genuine belief in their culture?

I would think tribal elders and the medicine man referred to in the article would be good sources for more insight into the cultural implications and details of this event. Another curiosity is the writer's choice to compare the use of corn pollen in Navajo rituals to the use of holy water in the Catholic Church. This could be an example of a "mixed" metaphor since the frame of reference of the writer is Christianity, and although there are some obvious general similarities (i.e., creation stories and the hereafter), there are many contradictions between the two, especially if one starts to pursue the concept of land ownership and its relationship to Christianity.

Obviously, an ethnographer could find numerous trails and sources to pursue.

FIELDWORKING WITH THIS BOOK

In the preceding section, as our imaginary fieldworker, you used one cultural moment at a church service to begin your field research. Researching involves making sense of cultural events. As one of the main goals of your research will be to share what you learn with others, you'll need to organize your research process as you work toward your final written project.

To help you organize, we've arranged this book around four learning strategies: reading, writing, fieldworking, and reflecting. Using these strategies will help you build two projects of your own: a research portfolio and either a fieldwork essay or a series of shorter fieldworking pieces. To help you, we've gathered readings from a variety of genres, academic disciplines, and voices to show how to do fieldwork and how to write about it. Since writing is so integral to fieldworking, we've included a number of boxes with writing activities that will help you develop the fieldworking skills you'll need. You may do the short exercises on topics that interest you and collect them in your portfolio. Or you may decide to build these pieces toward one fieldwork essay, as Rick Zollo does in his study of a truck stop, which is reproduced later in this chapter. In either instance, the writing you do becomes part of your research portfolio. The aim of a fieldworking portfolio is to develop personal insights and reflections on the research process as you go along, not just at the end of your project. We recommend that you share your work in progress several times during your research process. You may want to choose a portfolio partner among your colleagues to read your work regularly or form a research group to do the same.

With this book, you'll read published texts, but you'll also learn to "read" objects as cultural artifacts: baskets, buildings, quilts, clothing. And you'll learn to "read" places, events, and people: truck stops, restaurants and bars, mall stores, and town meetings. In the process of "reading" places and people, events and artifacts, you will dig into layers of meaning that lie inside language in words, expressions, stories, jokes, proverbs, and legends.

This book will initiate you into the gritty part of fieldwork. You will learn to keep researcher's notes, tape-record interviews with informants, collect material culture, gather multiple types of information (research data), develop questions and hunches, analyze patterns, and offer interpretations. A pencil and a notebook are your bare necessities, although you might consider other technologies (a camera, a laptop computer, a tape recorder). Far more important than the skills you develop or the equipment you use for controlling your data, however, is the understanding that *you are the main tool for your research.* As a researcher, you'll need to develop a kind of bidirectional lens as you research, allowing you to look out at others and back at yourself.

For example, as our imaginary fieldworker on page 18, if you were French Canadian and Catholic yourself, you might not recognize the interesting collision of Asian, French, Canadian, and Catholic cultures in a French Canadian Catholic church in Nashua. Or you might have a biased view of history because your own father was killed in the Vietnam War. Or you might not notice the significance of the song "Meet Me in St. Louis" and its connection to the name of the church, St. Louis de Gonzague. Through the process of writing and reflecting on your fieldwork, you'll become aware of the cultural lenses through which you look and how they affect what you understand, what you don't yet understand, and what you may never understand.

In this book, we'll review some of the basic writing strategies that fieldworkers use. Short writing exercises will help you hone your skills of description, specificity, mapping, organization, and analysis. You'll learn about constructing a researcher's voice in your ethnographic study and developing yourself as a narrator who guides your reader through your research. Particulars of audience, purpose, and focus will help you shape your data for your reader. You will also study and try out some of the aesthetic features of ethnographic writing: metaphors, sensory images, dialogue patterns, thematic structures.

Writing is both the process and the product of doing fieldwork. It is both the means for your thinking and the end result of your fieldwork project. All the writing you do—from brainstorming about possible research sites and topics through keeping fieldnotes, writing reflective memos to yourself, designing interview questions, and taking notes from other research sources to drafting your final fieldworking project—will become part of your research portfolio.

AN ETHNOGRAPHIC STUDY: "FRIDAY NIGHT AT IOWA 80"

We present here a fieldworking project completed by one of our students to give you a sample of the kind of research and writing we hope you'll ultimately do. We want to show you how a fieldworker "steps in" to a culture to investigate it, at the same time "stepping out" as he maintains the outsider's perspective while he observes. Rick Zollo wrote this study about a truck stop in Iowa as his major paper for a course centered on researching and writing about fieldwork. Though your study will probably be shorter than Rick's, it will share many features of his approach, particularly the emphasis on the self as part of the research process.

Rick is an older student with a background in journalism who is new to ethnographic research and has long been interested in truck drivers—so much so that he attended trucking school the summer after finishing his study. You'll notice immediately that Rick's study of the truck stop is written as a narrative and reads like a nonfiction article from a magazine, a genre often called literary journalism or creative nonfiction. As a reader new to ethnographic writing, you may not immediately distinguish the features of this study that make it ethnographic research and not journalism or reportage. You'll need to slip underneath Rick's smooth narrative line to see what goes into the fieldworking process. Look for places where Rick interweaves his own feelings, beliefs, and reflections. While reading, ask ethnographic questions like the ones we asked as we read the newspaper article "Church Opens Doors to Vietnamese": What were Rick's sources of data? How does he confirm or disconfirm his ideas? What interpretations does he offer? What is the culture he describes? What makes it a culture? Does his writing convince you? Can you see the places and people he describes? Do you understand what it would be like to be an insider in this culture?

You'll need to keep in mind some background knowledge as you read Rick's interesting journey into the culture of truckers that he has captured by describing one truck stop, Iowa 80, on a Friday night. First, it's clear that although Rick writes about a single Friday evening, he's spent many Fridays and other days gathering data and working his way into this fieldsite. He writes with the authority of having been there, and he makes us feel that we've been there too. It's also obvious that Rick has permission from the owner of the truck stop, Delia Moon, to hang out and interview truckers and staff members. Finally, it's also apparent from his study that Rick has read other articles and books about the trucking culture. He has knowledge about what he expects to see there. In some ways, this background information could put blinders on Rick as he sets out to confirm or disconfirm the ideas of other writers who claim that truckers form a community with shared interests, values, and language. Because, like Rick, you will be researching a place you are already interested in and want to know more about, you'll need to admit your possible biases about your topic and look at how other researchers have written about it.

As you read Rick's study, make a list of questions about his research process so that you'll be prepared to discuss the piece from that point of view. We realize that Rick's research may be the first ethnographic study you've read, so we'd like you to recognize its form and content. For example, Rick provides headings to guide you through his study and help you organize the questions you may have. His form takes the shape of a journalistic essay and his content focuses on the trucker subculture, but most important, Rick describes his fieldworking process within the essay.

Friday Night at Iowa 80
The Truck Stop as Community and Culture
Rick Zollo

> Truck stops are the center of trucking culture. "Trucker Villages"…offer the driver an equivalent to the cowboys' town at trail's end or the friendly port to sailors.
>
> —James Thomas, *The Long Haul*

A Modern Trucking Village

Friday nights are a special time all across America, for big and small towns alike, and it's no different at a "trucker town." Iowa 80 is advertised as "the largest Amoco truck stop in the world" and is located off Interstate 80 at exit 284, outside the small town of Walcott, about 10 miles from downtown Davenport and 40 miles from my Iowa City home.

I arrived at suppertime one fall Friday evening, with the intention of enjoying a meal in the full-service restaurant. But before I could even consider eating, I had to walk the grounds. In my experience, the best way to observe a community is with a walkabout, observing climate and current social interactions.

A huge hole occupied what had most recently been the south-side front parking lot. The hole was filled with a bright blue fuel tank roughly 40 by 60 feet in size and topped by five large green plastic sprials. The operation was a result of another government mandate, concerning leaky fuel storage containers. Delia Moon, company vice president, told me this operation would cost Iowa 80 $180,000 ($40,000 to take out the old tanks and $140,000 for replacements), another example of "government interference." According to Delia, the tanks dug up so far were in good condition.

The truck stop is laid out in the form of a huge rectangle, taking up over 50 acres on the north side of the interstate exit. The first building facing incoming traffic is the main headquarters, which includes a restaurant at the front, video and game room next, a sunken shopping mall, and a stairway leading to second-floor corporate offices, hair salon, laundry room, movie theater (seats 40) and TV room, dental offices, exercise room, and private shower stalls. The last renovations were completed in 1984, about the time I first began noticing the village, but Delia stated that a large building project was planned for 1994.

The evening had yet to begin, and the yard was only a quarter full, without that convoy pattern of trucks coming and going in single file, an orderly parade that in several hours would take on Fellini-like dimensions. I sauntered through the yard (in my usual loping stride), notebook in hand, making eye contact with truckers when they passed, not trying to act like one of them so much as feeling comfortable in their company.

(Photo: Susan Zollo)

Will Jennings, a former trucker and personal friend, talked about the insularity of the trucker community in Frederick Will's *Big Rig Souls*. "You go in truck stops and they have their own section.... Most of them [truckers] could tell from the minute you walk in the door you're not a driver. They hold most people who aren't drivers...with a good deal of disdain" (27).

I had already been spotted by employees of Iowa 80 as "not a driver," and in my many youthful years of hitchhiking around the country, I had been made to feel the outsider whenever I'd stumble into one of these trucking lairs. I had trouble understanding this resentment of outsiders, especially when I was on the road in need of a ride. But familiarity with the culture was bringing what scholar Sherman Paul calls "the sympathetic imagination," and I now felt I was beginning to understand.

On this late afternoon, the lot was rather calm, even though rigs waited in line to diesel up at the Jiffy fuel station, all four bays at the Truckomat truck wash were filled, and service was being rendered at the mechanics' and tire shop. The three buildings stood in a row on the north side of the lot, each about a third the size of the main complex and separated by several truck lanes for traffic.

The truckyard occupied the southern half of the property, with the interstate in its full glory to the south of that. Every time I stood in the middle of

(Photo: Susan Zollo)

this immense yard, with truck traffic in full promenade, I'd experience a thrill. But for now, with walkabout complete, I doubled back to the restaurant. I was hungry.

Truck Stop Restaurant

By 6 p.m., Iowa 80's restaurant was full to capacity. Customers appeared to be divided equally between truckers and four-wheelers. After a short wait, I was led to a small table in the back section, where at an adjacent booth, a young waitress was serving supper to a grizzled veteran. I detected a mild flirtation passing between them.

The night's special was catfish, which I ordered. I ate heartily, fish fried light and crispy, a scoop of potatoes adorned with gravy, cole slaw, and a fresh warm roll. Every book on truckers I've read describes truck stop food as rich, plentiful, and greasy.

Ditto!

(Photo: Susan Zollo)

I sat opposite the veteran and watched him. He ate with gusto, enjoyed a smoke (truck stop restaurants are not smoke-free), and wrote in his logbook. Should I approach him? Why not?

"Excuse me, I'm doing research on truckers and truck stops. Can I talk to you?"

He looked up from his logbook and smiled. "Yeah, sure. I've got time."

I grabbed my gear and joined him. His name was Gordy,* and he drove out of Oklahoma City for Jim Brewer, a company that hauls racks of automobiles to dealerships. Gordy spoke with easy affability, and underneath his three-day growth of beard, I detected once boyish good looks reminiscent of the actor Lee Majors.

Gordy drove all over the country, hauling General Motors vehicles. He stopped at this truck stop often, but only because of the food. He made it a point to let me know that he generally didn't frequent truck stops.

"Your truck have a sleeper?"

"No. Wouldn't drive a truck that had one."

That was a surprise, since I thought that just about all long haulers used sleepers.

Gordy was a veteran, with 22 years of service on the road. "How does driving compare now with twenty years ago?"

"Worse. Things are worse now." So are the truck stops, he said, which are bigger, with more features, but run by national chains with no feeling for the trucker.

He blamed deregulation for today's problems. Before deregulation, freight rates were controlled, and a trucker knew what he could make from each delivery. Then came deregulation, and "all these fly-by-night companies" flooded

---

*The names of all truckers and employees, except those in management, have been changed.

(Photo: Susan Zollo)

the market. The power of the Teamsters was also curtailed, and Gordy, a union man, found his position threatened. "I'm real bitter about it."

He once owned his own truck, was out on the road for long periods of time, and made good money. Today, he drove only four-day runs, for a company that was the highest bidder for his services. He slept in motels and had his choice of destinations.

As for the cursed paperwork that so many truckers complain about: "Hardly got any. Just this logbook. And they're fixin' to do away with that. By '96, they figure it'll all be on computer."

No issue galvanizes a trucker more than the logbook. Any time I wanted to test a trucker's spleen, I'd only have to mention the issue.

"I've been told that most truckers cheat on their logbooks," I said. "If they computerize it, you won't be able to cheat."

Gordy gave me a sly Lee Majors grin. "Oh, there'll be ways."

The Arcade

Fortified by a meal and a successful encounter, I ventured into the arcade area separating restaurant from shopping mall. The area was packed. During my hour with catfish and Gordy, many truckers had pulled off the road, and a handful of them were engaged in pinball games, laser-gun videos, a simulated NBA game, and in front of one large glass case with a miniature pickup shovel, a man and a woman were trying to win a pastel-colored stuffed animal. I stopped to watch. After several tries the man succeeded, and the couple rejoiced. I waited for their enthusiasm to wane and then introduced myself.

The driver's name was Morris, and he wasn't sure he wanted to talk to me. Like Gordy, he was middle-aged and grizzled, but where Gordy's three-day growth covered handsome features, Morris was a buzzard, with a hawk nose, a pointy chin, and a leather motorcycle cap pulled low over his forehead.

I assured him that my questions were for research purposes only, but he looked at me suspiciously, as if I were an authority sent to check on him.

Had he ever been at this truck stop before?

"First time, but I'm coming back. It's got everything."

How long had he been on this particular run? (Gordy was careful to emphasize that he made only four-day hauls.)

"Been home three and a half hours in the past four months."

Did he drive his own truck?

He was a lease operator (leasing his own rig to a company that moves furniture), presently hauling a load from Lafayette, Louisiana, to Cedar Rapids, Iowa.

How long did it take him to drive from Lafayette? (Knowing geography, I tried to calculate the time.) The question of time raised Morris's suspicions again, and instead of answering, he fixed me with a hard gaze. Sensing I had crossed some invisible boundary, I thanked him for his time. Obviously, my question related to logbook procedures, and I made a mental note to avoid that type of inquiry.

Also, I noticed that Morris and the woman for whom he had so gallantly won a prize were not together. Seeking a couple who actually drove in tandem, I walked into the mall area, past the cowboy boot display and chrome section ("the world's largest selection of truck chrome"), and spotted a couple with a baby moseying down the food aisles.

"Excuse me. I'm doing a research paper on truckers and truck stops. Are you a trucker?" I asked, directing my question to the presumed dad in the group.

"No, I'm not," he said emphatically.

Iowa 80 Employees

Truckers, four-wheelers (about 20 percent of the business at Iowa 80), and employees make up the truck stop community. The employees keep the community functioning, like municipal employees without whom towns and cities could not operate.

Two such employees stood at the end of one of the food aisles, stocking shelves. Sally and Maureen knew about me, thanks to a letter that General Manager Noel Neu had sent out a month ago, asking Iowa 80 workers to cooperate with my study. Sally was the shift manager of the merchandise area, and Maureen was one of her staff. I directed most of my questions to Sally.

How long had she been working at Iowa 80?

Eight years. Maureen had been with the company for only a year.

Which was the busiest shift?

"I think it's four to midnight, but if you ask someone on the day shift, they'd probably say their shift."

What did she most like about working four to midnight?

"The people. We get all kinds here. Down-to-earth people…crazy people." And she told me about a woman who several weeks ago came into the store ranting and raving, apparently in the throes of paranoid delusions. Authorities were called, and it was determined that "she was on some kind of bad trip— cocaine or something."

Sally mentioned that the police were out in the yard at this moment, making a drug bust. "How'd they know somebody was selling drugs?" I asked.

"A trucker reported it at the fuel center. Heard someone over the CB. We called the cops."

Apparently truckers police themselves. Sally also said that drivers will even turn in shoplifters. "They know if we get too much shoplifting, prices will go up."

I asked Sally about those prices, which I considered reasonable. She replied that they were cheap enough for most truckers, but there were always those who wanted to haggle.

"You're allowed to barter over costs?" I asked.

"Oh, yeah. Not as much as the day manager."

Sally came from a small town north of Walcott, and Maureen was from one of the Quad Cities.* Iowa 80 employed over 225 workers and was one of the largest employers outside of the Quad Cities municipal area.

"One of the things that most impresses me is how friendly the workers are here," I said.

"We try to be the trucker's second home," said Sally.

Talking to Truckers

Business continued to pick up. As with previous Friday night visits, I found much conversation in the aisles, as if the truckers could afford to be expansive, find community with colleagues, socialize at the end of a workweek. Many of these drivers, though, still had loads to deliver; others were settling in for the weekend, waiting for a Monday morning pickup.

I had hoped to talk to women and minorities. The popular image of the trucker is that of a Caucasian blue-collar male, and for the most part, that group represents the majority of the industry. But more women are entering the field, and from my observations, black men make up 10 to 20 percent of the population. Two black truckers stood behind displays of music tapes, engaged in spirited conversation. I didn't want to interrupt them. Near the cash register, I spotted another black trucker, a beefy 40-something fellow with flannel jacket and flat driving cap. He was reluctant and wary, but he agreed to answer questions.

Ronald was a long hauler from Detroit, making his third stop at Iowa 80. He had been driving for five years, after serving a 12-year hitch in the armed services. He drove all over the country, going out for three to five weeks at a

---

*Bettendorf and Davenport, Iowa, and Moline and Rock Island, Illinois.

time. He didn't mind sleeping in his rig. For every week on the road, he got a day off. He was presently hauling a load from Omaha to New Jersey, with plenty of time to get there. (I consciously steered my questions away from time lines.)

He wore a forced smile, which served as a shield, and any question that might seem personal made the smile stiffen. He didn't give off the scent of danger I detected from Morris, but he definitely eyed me more as an adversary than as a friendly interlocutor.

Our session was interrupted by a midsized white fellow, probably in his midthirties, sporting an orange pony tail, two diamond studs in his left ear-lobe, and several menacing facial scars.

"What you up to, man? Who you workin' for?" His voice had a manic edge that reminded me of Gary Busey in one of those action adventures they watched in the movie theater upstairs.

"I'm a researcher from the University of Iowa." I described my project.

"Oh, yeah?" he said, as if he didn't believe me. Then he turned his high-voltage attention on Ronald. They started talking about the rigs they drove.

Cal spoke so fast it was hard to keep up with him. He was telling Ronald that he had bought his own truck and would soon go independent, a status he encouraged Ronald to seek. Ronald's smile by this time had tightened like a band of steel. He was cornered by white guys, one with a notebook, the other a speed rapper with a pony tail. Ronald was clearly on guard.

Cal was from a nearby town, and he mentioned a motorcycle-driving buddy who was writing a book with help from someone in the Iowa Writer's Workshop. I dropped a few names Cal recognized, and he suddenly decided I was OK. When he couldn't convince Ronald to use his method to buy a truck, he ducked away to collar someone else. Ronald kept smiling and muttering, "Man, I don't want my own truck."

Before I could finish questioning Ronald, a well-built 30-something trucker with finely brushed hair and trimmed moustache jumped before me, arms folded, ready to unload his truck.

The atmosphere was getting uncomfortable. Who did these people think I was? I recalled a previous visit, when I was down at the truck wash. A woman named Connie, a road veteran who bragged of living on the highway for years as a hitchhiker, told me, "We though you were a spotter."

Not knowing what that meant but reckoning that it couldn't be in my favor, I assured her I was only a writer. "What's a spotter?" I asked.

"They go around checking on company drivers, to see that they're not screwing up, taking riders, that kind of stuff."

My new friend's name was Dan, and he was at the truck stop because a trailer he was supposed to pick up at a nearby meat products plant was late being loaded. "Never come down here normally. Know why?" I sure didn't. "No counter in the restaurant. They took out the counter. And the food's greasy."

Dan presented me with a challenge. "Want to know what makes me mad? Want to know what pisses me off?"

A Trucker's Lament

Dan started in on his own speed rap. His eyes weren't glazed like Cal's but instead fixed on me, as if I were an authority he wanted to confront, an ear that would be judged by its sympathy or lack thereof.

I wanted Dan to know I was sympathetic. I'm all ears, good buddy.

As Dan began ticking off his grievances, I asked him the same questions I had asked the others. He didn't stop at Iowa 80 often. His schedule enlisted him on 3,000-mile hauls (however long they took—it varied, he said). He drove for a company, was nonunion (didn't like the Teamsters but wanted to organize truckers into a national force), and had been driving for 12 years.

With that said, most of our conversation dealt with Dan's copious grievances, a litany other truckers voiced to various degrees.

Grievance number one: "I'm pissed about multiple speed limits. Iowa, the speed limit's the same, sixty-five for cars and trucks. In Illinois, it's sixty-five for cars but only fifty-five for trucks. Know why it's set up like that? Supposed to be for safety, have the trucks go slower, but it creates two flows of traffic, and that's a hazard. No, the real reason is revenue. Easier to give us a ticket."

Dan was angry, and I had trouble writing down all his words in a standing position. I suggested we go upstairs, where we found a spot by the shoeshine area just outside the movie theater, giving me a better position to get everything down. The Illinois complaint was not new; other truckers had sounded off about that state's split speed limit, as well as their war against radar detectors. The opinion in the trucker community was that the authorities in Illinois were against them.

Once we were seated in comfortable chairs, Dan went off on another tangent. "They take three million basically honest people and force us to break the law to make a living."

I assumed he was talking about the infamous logbook. I just so happened to have one with me. Dan grabbed it. "Know what we call this? A comic book. It's a joke!"

He proceeded to show me why. The logbook was symbol and substance of what was wrong with the industry, a monitoring device that was set up so it couldn't be followed except by lying. Once lawbreaking becomes institutionalized, other more serious laws become easier to break until the small man is truly the outlaw of romantic legend. And the trucker, in Dan's mind, at least, was a small man caught in the snares (Clifford Geertz's "webs of suspension") constructed by government and big business, a conspiracy of sorts designed to keep the proverbial small man down.

Dan opened the logbook and ran through a typical workweek. The trucker had two formats: 60 hours in seven days or 70 hours in eight. Time frames are broken into four categories: off duty, sleeper berth, driving, and on duty. The last slot was what most agitated Dan. As he simulated a California run, he showed that loading and unloading is held against the trucker, since it is considered on-duty time. (Note that the trucker does have the option of leaving the site where his trailer is located, which is what Dan was doing when he met me, but that involves risk, especially in terms of truck hijacking and other forms of larceny.) "Sometimes we gotta wait eight hours before they load or unload our truck. That time is held against us, against our sixty- or seventy-hour week. We get paid by the mile. I don't make a cent unless my truck is moving."

Dan was convinced that big business and government were in a conspiracy. "Suppose I've got to deliver a load from Monfort [Illinois] to San Francisco. That's two thousand miles. Then they want me to turn around and bring a load back. How can I do it if I honestly report my hours?" He tapped the logbook nervously.

"You have to cheat," I said.

"Cheat or starve. Because if I follow the laws, I get no work. Company won't say anything. They'll just stop giving me orders."

"And if you get caught cheating, does the company back you?"

Dan's eyes lit up, and he gave me a manic half grin, half grimace, as if to say, "Now you're catching on."

"We get caught cheating, breaking the speed limit, you name it, the trucker pays all fines. Our fault, so we gotta pay."

Gripe number three: who is supposed to load and unload the truck? Dan waited for me to record this complaint. The company sells his services, which are to deliver meat products to supermarket warehouses. He's not paid to load and unload the truck. But the supermarket chains will not provide the service.

"I have a choice," he said. "Unload the truck myself, which I'm not supposed to do. Or hire a lumper."

Mere mention of the term *lumper* sent Dan into another paroxysm of indignation. Lumpers are scab laborers who hang around warehouses and get paid under the table ("out of my money!"). Dan was convinced that most of them were on welfare and made as much as $300 a day that they don't declare.

"I pay taxes on my wages. Lumpers get government welfare plus this other money." Another symbol and symptom of what was wrong with America. And who was to blame? The Department of Transportation.

"All the DOT does is drive up and down the highway busting truckers. They never go to the grocers and make sure we're not forced to unload our trucks." And the reason for the conspiracy? Simple. The supermarkets "get all this free labor."

The combination fuel tax and low-sulfur diesel oil requirement was another gripe. (A government-mandated low-sulfur fuel plus an additional 4 cents fuel tax had been imposed as of October 1.)

"Truckers are supposed to pay to clean up the air, but not airlines or bus companies or farmers. They all get exemptions. Farmers are exempt because of off-road use. Yet how many tractors we got running in this state?"

I asked if he thought conditions would improve. One trucker told me the split speed limits in Illinois were supposed to be abolished.

"Rumors. To keep truckers in line. They know if we organize a work stoppage, this nation'll stop running."

Dan believed in truckers organizing but felt that the trucker's independent nature prevented this from happening. He dismissed the Teamsters. "We need an organization run by and for truckers. Teamsters are not the answer, and this organization, the American Truckers Association, has sold us out, backing every law that's ever hurt us."

On and on. Dan's monologue was complicated by his nervously darting eyes, which kept sizing me up for sympathy. He talked about disparities in fines ($70 for a logbook violation in Nebraska; the same violation in California can cost you $1,500), unfriendly state police and DOT officials ("California, Ohio, and Virginia are the worst"), and big business and government collusion to keep the small man down.

"This country depends on truckers for survival. Trains and airplanes can't deliver like the truckers. Yet if this country is so dependent on us, why are we treated like scum?"

I could not adequately answer Dan's complaints, nor could I ascertain their complete veracity, except to say that similar complaints had been made by other informants. Yet even in the midst of these difficult working conditions, there was the sense that a living wage was being made. One particular trucker, who was vehement about the split speed limits and logbook absurdities (he drove from Omaha to Chicago and back twice a week), bragged that he made $600 to $1,000 a week.

Even Dan admitted to making more money driving a truck than he could ever earn in the small Iowa town where he lived when he wasn't on the road. His complaints were less about pay than about being forced to break the law to earn his living and about the lack of sympathy shown by greater society to this blue-collar occupation so responsible for America's land of plenty.

My sympathies were aroused. I've always felt sympathy for blue-collar concerns. My European forebears had fled to America for better jobs, freedom from persecution, rights to pursue an individual lifestyle. And I was nothing if not an advocate of individuality.

Dan and I traded addresses—he promised to send me a flyer for his own fledgling organization— and I thanked him for his time.

Town Meeting around the Cash Register

I wandered back downstairs and moved about the merchandise aisles, tired from my talk with Dan. Who did I meet in one of the back aisles but Cal, in the company of a tall, slender woman with a well-used look. He still had that manic glint in his eye. "Man, you're all right. You really are a writer. I thought you were government, but you're not."

My wandering brought me to the cash register, a good place to meet truckers. Drivers were either coming or going and were most receptive to exchange. I found a middle-aged driver paying for a purchase, and we passed pleasantries. No heavy conversations or even probing questions—Dan had exhausted me of that.

The woman working the register and the driver were comparing horror stories about truck-stop robberies. I had noticed the woman before. She was one of the friendly employees who liked to talk to drivers. Many of the workers at Iowa 80 had this friendly conversational manner about them, and it always contributed to the atmosphere in the building.

The trucker knew a driver who had been robbed recently at a truck stop in Atlanta, where he was now heading. The woman told of another robbery at a truck stop outside Tampa. Both robberies occurred in the parking lot, and in both cases, the drivers were getting out of their rigs when someone stepped out of the shadows and robbed them at gunpoint.

The trucker left, and I lingered to talk to the woman. Her name was Bea. Her husband had been a trucker until last week, when he was involved in an accident outside Atlanta, caused by a drunk driver three cars ahead of his rig. Nobody was hurt, but there was $8,000 in damage. "Five years without an accident, and they fire him. I sent the guy who fired him a thank-you letter. We got two teenagers at home."

How was her husband taking his dismissal?

"He's broken up about it, but I'm glad."

What's he doing now?

"He's farming with relatives."

I pulled out my notebook and introduced myself. Bea knew about me, again thanks to Noel Neu's letter. She was convinced I had picked a great subject for research. She had been working for Iowa 80 part time, then left for a full-time job in Davenport. "But I came back because I missed it. Took a pay cut, but it's worth it to work here."

I mentioned my interview with Delia Moon and how many Iowa 80 employees seem to love the work atmosphere.

"Isn't Delia wonderful? I love this family." Bea told me a story about Bill Moon, founder of Iowa 80 and an empire builder in the truck stop industry. Years ago, Bea's son had a paper route in downtown Walcott. One morning, her son was stymied by a blizzard. Bill Moon saw the boy struggling to cover his route. The businessman got his car and helped her son finish the job. "That's the kind of guy he was."

Bill Moon died of cancer over a year ago. "You should have seen this place," said Bea. "Everyone was so sad."

Truck Yard at Night

Back outside, three hours after my arrival, I moved through the huge truck yard, filling my lungs with air and trying to catch a second wind. Trucks pulled in and out of the lot in promenade. Diesel fumes filled the air, and the lot was noisy with the sounds of transmissions shifting.

The yard was teeming. Large spotlights mounted on 50-foot poles outlined the scene. Puddles in the middle of the parking lot reflected blue and pink neon from the Jiffy Shop fuel center. A computerized sign facing the interstate spilled a cascade of shifting letters, advertising the night's menu, chrome supplies, free showers with tank of fuel, guaranteed scales to weigh freight.

I loped across the yard, tired but feeling fine, realizing that the more I learned about the trucking community, the more I would never know. I was a four-wheeler, a writer temporarily tangled in all these "webs of significance," an outsider whose sympathies could never connect all the many lives spent in forced but voluntary isolation. Long haulers were sentenced to a solitary voyage, and the truck stop was the oasis where they found temporary community.

Old-Timer at the Fuel Center

Inside the Jiffy Shop: quiet. Iowa 80's fuel center is built like your average convenience store, with fuel and sundries sold at a discount, except that here the fuel is diesel instead of gasoline and the sundries are marketed for truckers' needs.

A young black trucker was buying a sandwich at a back counter. Several of his white comrades were paying for their fuel up front. In one of the two-person booths that line the windows along the west wall sat an older gray-haired gentleman, resplendent in a green polo shirt and reading a trucker magazine.

I sat across from the old-timer in an adjoining booth and, after a few minutes of sizing up the situation, made my introduction. "May I ask you a few questions?"

He looked up from his magazine and admitted to being a trucker but added, "I don't like to get involved."

Fair enough. Still, we talked. Gradually he warmed up, and eventually I opened my notebook and began recording his remarks.

He had been driving trucks for some time but wouldn't say how long. He was at the truck stop getting an oil change for his tractor. He was primarily a short hauler, though he had done long hauls in his time.

I placed his age in the midsixties. Books I had read on over-the-road trucking mention how the long haul prematurely ages the driver. I could understand that this old-timer would change to shorter routes. As he warmed up to me, he revealed more information. He was articulate and had the face of a learned man. Perhaps he had retired from another profession. (More and more truckers were coming from other professions; many were veterans from the armed services.)

He asked me questions as well. His early pose of disinterest belied an avid curiosity. I soon had the impression that he would rather interview me.

He lived in the Quad Cities and had been a trucker all his life, starting at age 17 when he drove for construction outfits in the Fort Dodge area. He let slip that he was 60, an owner-operator of his own rig. Allusions to problems from years gone by hinted at previous financial difficulties.

Dan's populist appeal was still ringing in my ear, so I mentioned the rigors placed on truckers by big business and government. But the old-timer was not buying. True, big business and government put obstacles in the way, but there was a good living out there for anyone willing to put in the time. He told me a story similar to the fable of the tortoise and the hare. He always obeyed speed limits. He was in no hurry. Younger drivers would pass him, impatient with his caution. But the old-timer always got the job done on time. He clearly identified with the tortoise.

I found myself taking a shine to this man. There was something strong-willed and flinty about him, even in his refusal to give me his name. We talked about trucks, and he became a font of information. He pointed to his rig in the yard, a Ford. He would have preferred a Freightliner but couldn't get financing. He made disparaging remarks about Kenworths, called the Rolls-Royces of the profession, and about another highly rated competitor—"Why, I wouldn't even drive a Peterbuilt. Cab's too narrow."

He was presently leasing his truck and services to a company that hauls general merchandise to stores like Pamida, Kmart, and Sam's Warehouse. Earlier in the day, he had hauled 45,000 pounds of popcorn, but at present he had a trailer full of supplies for a Sam's Warehouse in Cedar Rapids. As for his earlier mention of being a short-hauler, well, that wasn't quite the truth. He tried to limit his runs to the Midwest—within the radius of Kansas City, Omaha, Fargo, and Youngstown—but sometimes he ventured as far as Atlanta or Dallas.

What about the complaint, first voiced by Gordy, that times were worse now than 20 years ago?

Yes in some instances, no in others. True, the logbook was a joke, especially concerning off-duty time. ("Why, when I hauled steel out of Gary, sometimes they made you wait 12 hours to get your load. That's all your driving time.") Yet the trucks these days were better, and the money was still good. ("I can drive from Kansas City to Des Moines without hardly changing gears. Couldn't do that 20 years ago." And, "I'm not saying I'm not making money. Making more money now than I was three years ago.")

He had to get back to his work, make his Cedar Rapids drop by 11. Otherwise he'd continue the conversation. I could tell he enjoyed our talk, and I had the urge to ask him if I could go out on the road with him. I was sure several weeks of riding with this old-timer would have given me an education.

But we parted as comrades, although when I asked again for his name, he declined to give it.

"I'll just refer to you as 'an esteemed older gentleman in a green shirt,'" I said. He enjoyed that description immensely and left me with a loud, ringing laugh.

Conclusion

My night at Iowa 80 was coming to a close. I had only to walk back through the truck lot and get into my little Japanese-made sedan. I was a four-wheeler, but that didn't stop me from making eye contact with the truckers in the yard, waving a hearty hello before I made my Hi-ho Silver.

What was I to make of this experience? I was exercising what Clifford Geertz calls "an intellectual poaching license" (*Local Knowledge* 12), engaging in what John Van Maanen terms "the peculiar practice of representing the social reality of others through the analysis of [my] own experience in the world of these others" (ix).

But had I truly experienced the community and culture? Had I penetrated the veils of unfamiliarity to become a reliable scribe of trucker life?

I had no doubts on that Friday night, as I returned to my car and drove home. I felt flush. My informants, reluctant at first, had been forthcoming. Employees were friendly, and the truckers, although initially suspicious of my motives, spoke from both head and heart.

My experiences with the culture reflected what I had read by James Thomas and Michael Agar. I sensed a community that felt both proud and put upon, holding to perceived freedoms yet reined in by new regulations and restrictions. Some company drivers, like Gordy and Ronald, felt insulated from variables over which they had no control (fluctuating fuel prices), but others, like Dan, were angry about issues both on the road (DOT and highway patrolmen) and off (time and money constraints involving the unloading of deliveries). The owner-operator, my green-shirted older gentleman, did not feel like an endangered species, and the fact that Cal, however reliable his testimony might have been, was becoming an owner-operator attested to some of the virtues of that status.

The metaphor of the road cowboy certainly has significance. I surveyed the boot and shoe shop and found three varieties of cowboy boots (but not a loafer or a sneaker in sight), ranging from the economical $40 model with non-leather uppers to $150 snakeskin cowboy boots. Not far from the boot section were belts and buckles with a decidedly Western cast and enough cowboy hats to populate a Garth Brooks concert.

But connections to cowboys run deeper than clothes. Thomas writes that the "outstanding characteristics of both the trucker and the cowboy are independence, mobility, power, courage, and masculinity" (7). With all due apologies to the many women now trucking, that definition seems to apply. But it might be more mental than physical since, as my old-timer professed, driving a truck these days is not the physically rigorous activity it once was, and Dan's complaints about loading and unloading aside, truckers are not supposed to touch the product they deliver.

The cowboy element of the culture might seem like romantic accouterment rather than realistic assessment. Yet as Agar has pointed out, even romantic notions of the cowboy were more nonsense than truth, since that species in actuality "wore utilitarian clothes, engaged in long days of hard work, and ate boring and nutritionally deficient food" (*Independents Declared* 10), a description that sounds like trucker life.

I also found some agreement with Agar's assessment of present versus past times. The old-timer had a healthy attitude: "Some things are better, some things are worse." But for the most part, the veteran truckers I talked with see the past as "a better time…because regulations were simpler, enforcement was more lax, and fines were lower. Although the technology of trucks and roads has improved, the culturally spun webs of regulation have thickened into a maze" (44).

As for trucker grievances, one thing I found for certain, which Frederick Will documents in *Big Rig Souls*, is that "the trucker is condemned to rapid turn-arounds after each load, to physical discomfort, to little or boring leisure, to being forever harried" (29).

I believe I found a community at Iowa 80. Delia Moon described the company's goal as turning the truck stop into a "destination." The dictionary defines *destination* as "the place to which a person or thing travels or is sent." Iowa 80, for all its scope and size, is still a truck stop. But a good many of my trucker informants were regulars, and the ones who were there for the first time were impressed by what they found.

Thomas states that "providing personal services for drivers is not where a truck stop gains most of its profits. The extras…are to lure truckers in from the road to the fuel pumps and service area" (17). Delia Moon supported this view. "We're working primarily to satisfy the…trucker. That's why you see the movie lounge and so much parking and chrome and everything" (interview, Oct. 7, 1993).

Yet in the process of giving truckers these amenities, as varied as a part-time dentist or a portable chapel for those needing to be born again, Iowa 80 is creating a context, setting up a multiplicity of complex structures that are both conceptual and real. A Friday night at this village is truly an adventure and, for those willing to engage experience as a form of education, an introduction into a dynamic community and culture.

Works Consulted

Agar, Michael. *The Professional Stranger: An Informal Introduction to Ethnography*. New York: Academic, 1980.

Agar, Michael. *Independents Declared*. Washington, DC: Smithsonian Inst., 1986.

Geertz, Clifford. *The Interpretation of Cultures*. New York: Basic, 1973.

Geertz, Clifford. *Local Knowledge*. New York: Basic, 1983.

Horwitz, Richard. *The Strip: An American Place*. Lincoln: U Nebraska, 1985.

Kramer, Jane. *Trucker: Portrait of the Last American Cowboy*. New York: McGraw, 1975.

Paul, Sherman. University of Iowa, English Dept., personal communication.

Thomas, James. *The Long Haul: Truckers, Truck Stops and Trucking*. Memphis: Memphis State U, 1979.

Van Maanen, John. *Tales of the Field*. Chicago: U Chicago P, 1988.

Will, Frederick. *Big Rig Souls: Truckers in the American Heartland*. West Bloomfield: Altwerger, 1992.

Wyckoff, D. Daryl. *Truck Drivers in America*. Lexington: Lexington, 1979.

Rick Zollo's research study has many features of a full-blown ethnography, which is a book-length study that often takes years to complete. Over the course of one semester, or even a year, neither Rick nor you could expect to write a complete ethnography of a subculture. Rick's study, however, includes most of the parts of a fuller piece of research: library and archival research, cultural artifacts, fieldnotes, photographs, interviews and transcripts, reflective memos, and multiple drafts of his writing. (We will explore these aspects of research in later sections of this book.) In his portfolio, Rick mentions having read Michael Agar's *Independents Declared,* an ethnography about truckers. In his reading at libraries and in private collections, he read Walt Whitman's poem "Song of the Open Road," Jack Kerouac's novel *On the Road,* and Woody Guthrie's road songs. He studied trucker magazines, truck school brochures from a community college, trucker trade journals, truck stop menus, and government regulations about the trucking industry. He also attended a two-day "truckers' jamboree," where he took more notes.

In "Friday Night at Iowa 80," Rick begins with descriptions of both the inside and the outside of the truck stop, to establish a full sweep of the landscape. He starts by guiding his reader on a walk around the outside of the truck stop, moving from the huge unfilled hole that marks the uprooted fuel containers to the parking lot that holds 500 trucks. Once inside the mall-like complex, Rick shows us around the restaurant, where we watch him eat a meal of catfish and lumpy potatoes. We next accompany him into the arcade of pinball machines and laser-gun videos and then into the aisles of the convenience store, where employees are stocking shelves.

In addition to the sense of authority he gains through his thick and rich physical descriptions of Iowa 80, Rick also collects an interesting range of interviews from both truckers and employees at the truck stop. Rick is able to get his informants to talk by hanging out and chatting with them. Sometimes informants don't talk to him because they're suspicious of him and think he is a "spotter" or some kind of spy from the Department of Transportation. Sometimes they don't trust him because he is a student-researcher. Other times that prompts a stream of valuable information. But because he persists and gathers a range of informants—male and female, black and white, trucker and nontrucker—weaving his interviews into the overall narrative, he advances his study toward an analysis of the information he's collected.

The data he relies on come mainly from informant interviews, but within these he sorts through a range of responses to his questions: insider terms, insider knowledge, and insider stories. Some informants supply terminology about the jobs, such as the words *lumper* and *spotter*. Others offer insider knowledge about how truckers do their jobs, answering questions about mileage, speed limits, logbooks, and truck preferences. From still others, he gathers occupational stories by inviting informants both to brag and to complain about their jobs.

After Rick has spent considerable time collecting this data about trucker beliefs and gripes, he introduces an unnamed informant who disconfirms and complicates much of what other drivers have said. Unlike the others, this lifetime driver felt trucking was a solid job and a good way to make a living and had little to complain about. Fieldworkers always try to disconfirm and complicate the theories that they are trying out. Rather than tossing out this interview data as something that doesn't fit, Rick includes it. An ethnography is compelling only when the author persuades us of his credibility. Rick does this by allowing the voices of his informants to speak. The fieldworker's obligation is both to inform and to persuade.

Rick's data analysis leads toward his initial hunch that the truck stop is a kind of community and a subculture for many of the truckers who spend time there. One of the Iowa 80 employees claims that the place is like the truckers' second home—a home away from home—which provides the central metaphor for Rick's paper. By the end of the study, Rick is able to link his own findings with other research that draws on the image of the trucker as cowboy.

What makes Rick's study ethnographic, then, is the wide range and depth of description and interview data, the amount of time he spent gathering it, and his commitment to show the insider's perspective on the trucking culture. As a writer, Rick creates a "slice-of-time" device. He uses one Friday night at Iowa 80 to represent all the days and nights he's collected data there. In actuality, though, he spent weeks and months there. As a researcher, Rick writes himself into the study to show what he's in a position to see and understand, but he also points out what eludes him, who won't talk to him, and who walks away. All along, Rick reads and uses outside sources from other writers to test his own hunches about what trucking life and trucking culture are like. As a writer, Rick makes choices about how he will present his data from a wide range of writing strategies that are open to all contemporary ethnographers. But as a researcher, Rick conforms to the process of gathering, analyzing, interpreting, and validating his data, which is what *doing* fieldwork is all about.

The Research Portfolio: Definitions and Purpose

During the course of his study, Rick kept a research portfolio, which housed both the process and the product of his fieldwork. We recommend developing working files for tracking your learning and documenting your work throughout the research process, and we will discuss further aspects of portfolio keeping in each of the subsequent chapters in this book.

You might keep your files organized on your computer with backup disks or written out and stored in file folders or boxes. Once you have plentiful, accurate, organized working files, you can create a portfolio from them—not merely for final course evaluation or assessment but for your own self-reflection and evaluation. The working files will help you select documents to present in your portfolio so that you can lay out an array of your research in progress.

As you assemble and revise your portfolio, you'll develop a behind-the-scenes account of the story of your research, which you'll want to share with others. Naturally, the research portfolio will include your final ethnographic essay, but your selections will also show the thinking process that led to this project. You'll want to represent selections from the reading, writing, and materials you've relied on along the way: writing exercises, fieldnotes, interview questions, charts, methods of analysis, and whatever helped you think your way through the final written report. You may include maps, transcripts, sketches or photographs, summaries of related reading materials (poems, songs, newsletters, advertisements), and any items unique to your study of a particular subculture. At the end of each chapter, we will offer ways to review the working files of your research to make selections for your research portfolio. In Chapter 5, we present the research portfolio completed by one of our students, Karen Downing, along with the full text of her field study.

To keep track of your project, you'll move back and forth among four key activities: collecting, selecting, reflecting, and projecting. Each time you work on the portfolio, and each time you share it with others, you'll be engaged in these processes.

Collecting   At first, you might find it strange to **collect** wrinkled scraps of paper, lists on napkins, or snippets of conversation you've overheard, but by gathering them in your portfolio, you'll see how they might fit into your larger project. In fact, the portfolio may look more like a scrapbook to you at first. But over time, you will see that it is a focused, not random, collection of artifacts and writing that lend shape to your fieldwork. Unlike a scrapbook, where the pieces are fastened down, in this portfolio you can move, remove, and replace your data to see potential patterns and structures. As you work with it, you'll move data around, determine other sources of evidence, and confirm or discard insights or hunches that you're making about your data. *The portfolio allows flexibility.*

Selecting   Another advantage of a research portfolio is that you can **select** from parts of it for your final ethnographic writing. While your initial fieldnotes may capture something different from the final report, you'll always be able to use some parts of your fieldnotes. If you've studied firefighters, for example, you may have collected pages and pages of fieldnotes describing the fire station even when your final project focuses on the firefighters' language. In your final project, you'll still need to describe the firehouse before describing the words used there because your reader will need to understand the whole context of your field site before looking at specific parts of the culture. The skills of collecting and selecting, as you move between them, are important to your research portfolio.

Reflecting and Projecting   At critical points during the fieldwork process, you will need to take time to **reflect** on the data in your portfolio—to look at your fieldnotes and informant interviews and begin to analyze and synthesize the data that are most important to your work. Every item that you include in the portfolio will require reflective writing on your part, from short fieldnote entries to longer memos to yourself. When you review your data alongside your thinking, you'll find options for further focus and analysis. Reflection is complex. As you look over what you've read, thought, said, written, and collected, you will begin to find meanings and patterns across your data that may surprise you and instruct you about where your work is headed. This reflective reviewing will enable you to **project**—to see your progress and form your goals: where you've been, where you are, and where you'll want to head next.

One of the most important parts of the portfolio process is to share your portfolio with others who are also conducting fieldwork. You may share it as hard copy or online through e-mail, or you may even want to create or join an electronic discussion group or listserv with colleagues whose interests match yours. Keeping a research portfolio makes little sense if it's relegated to the status of end-of-course activity. The major evaluation or assessment ought to be your own. We suggest that you choose a portfolio partner or a small group at the outset of your research and set aside regular times to meet and share your portfolios. At these meetings, you may ask your partner(s) to respond to your descriptions, offer ways of filling gaps in your data, suggest further resources for your research, point out themes or patterns in your data, or help verify your hunches. The process of talking about your data, your hunches, and your research plans and hearing those of others as you look through their portfolios in process will generate new ideas and strategies for your own fieldwork.

FieldWriting: Establishing a Voice

Research writing, like all good writing, has voice. And this voice should be yours—not that of a faceless third person, as in "it was determined" or "this researcher found." It's preferable, we believe, to use *I* in **fieldwriting**. *I* allows you to write with your own **authority** and with the authenticity of your own fieldwork, and it will ensure your credibility. Contemporary fieldwork, as a research methodology shared by anthropology, sociology, folklore, cultural studies, and linguistics, doesn't claim to be a totally objective social science, as either process or product, fieldworking or fieldwriting.

There's always been a vigorous conversation among scholars about writing up fieldwork—from notes to publication. (We'll discuss this in more depth in Chapter 8.) Even several generations ago, during Hortense Powdermaker's time, fieldworkers debated how to incorporate their personal responses—feelings and emotions, sensory and aesthetic details—in their writing about others. In her classic book *Stranger and Friend,* from which we have borrowed the idea of "stepping in and stepping out," Powdermaker writes about the similarity between fieldwriters and fiction writers:

> The novelist and the playwright, as well as the anthropologist, write out of their immersion and participation in a particular situation from which they have been able to detach themselves. But they write of the particular.... [T]he particular illuminates the human condition (296).

This conversation continues. Some scholars argue that social science field reports should be "scientific" and detached. They fear that blurring the boundaries between ethnography and journalism, fiction and nonfiction, the personal and the impersonal will weaken the credibility of their findings. But others, including ourselves, think that a distanced, objective stance would be dishonest. To ignore yourself as part of the data distorts your findings: you are the researcher who selects the particular details, records informants' particular voices, chooses what to leave in and what to take out, and decides how to write about the "particular" as it "illuminates the human condition" you studied. Your reader needs to know you as the person who has been there. To create a writing voice, you must invite yourself onto the page. To invite yourself onto the page means to ignore conventions that you've already learned—the formula for an essay, the passive voice, overuse of the third person, or the taboo against the personal pronoun *I*. Rather, the content and the language of your project should suggest its form as you shape it. The form should be an extension of the content. There is no fixed form for an ethnographic essay.

When we began to write this book together, one of our first challenges was to establish a common voice. There we sat, Macintosh Powerbooks side by side on an old dining room table, a small fan blowing cool air at us. Works by our favorite anthropologists and folklorists—all of them fieldworkers who write well—lay in stacks, organized in our homemade library in the corner. Our students' and colleagues' writing hung in folders in a blue plastic file box. Our books, our own field experiences, and the research of our students and colleagues lent silent support to our project. And yet, even with all the data and support, we faced the problem that all writers face: how to create a voice to bring life to our pages for our readers. We were two separate writers, friends and colleagues who respected each other and shared similar training and philosophies about writing, teaching, and doing fieldwork. We knew the information we wanted to convey in this book. Our data were already collected and in order. But how to write the book?

We tried writing separately, thinking that that would be more efficient. But we kept looking at each other's screens, unable to ignore each other's texts. "Wait a minute," Elizabeth would admonish. "That's not what you mean!" Bonnie would peer over, shocked at what she read: "Don't you know about passive voice? You've robbed that sentence of all its action." Elizabeth teased Bonnie for her "baby sentences," which Bonnie claimed were for emphasis. Like this. Bonnie ribbed Elizabeth for getting so involved in her thoughts that her voice vacated the page entirely, disappearing into the words on the page. Soon we began to work on one computer, writing, rereading, and revising every line together.

We'd like to show you how we wrote the opening paragraph in this chapter. Elizabeth drafted long, complex sentences, junked up with scholarly phrases and extra jargon: "The anthropological fieldworker—one who has been trained to look through the eyes of the 'other'—positions herself three ways (textually, fixed, and subjectively), both in the field and on the page, to observe, listen, question, and interpret the behaviors and language patterns of those she is studying." Bonnie reacted, "Phew, Elizabeth! This sentence says everything we want to say in the first chapter—and even some stuff for the second. Actually, this sentence is the whole book. We may need to simplify this a bit." Bonnie would then begin to simplify by writing long strings of endless examples: "We question why someone would wear pig earrings, pierce her tongue, drive a certain kind of car, clench his fists, pick her fingernails, wear a rose or a snake or a dragon tattoo on a shoulder, a forearm, or an ankle." Elizabeth would read it and say, "This stuff is terrible. There are way too many examples, Bonnie. By the end of the example, the reader will forget what we're talking about."

After weeks of writing side by side, 12 hours a day, we forged a collaborative writing voice that represents us both. Whether you choose to write with someone else or whether you write alone with your resources as colleagues, you'll need to think about and establish a voice for your fieldwriting. What we learned most, of great value to us as we developed our voice, was to write ourselves into our text, to be there on the page with the reader.

Similarly, writing research means first "being there"—in the field, as Rick Zollo was at the truck stop, and then on the page, as he is in his ethnographic study in this chapter. If you've never stopped at Iowa 80, Rick's research will take you there—cruising the parking lot, eating fried catfish and potatoes, hearing the truckers' gripes and recording their lingo, reading their logbooks, and noticing their musical tastes. Rick shows that fieldworkers who care about their topics want their readers to learn as much as they did. He knew that his major challenge was to make the culture come alive for other people. So he researched his field site and its background, established relationships with insiders, and thought hard about the data piled high on his desk and stuffed into boxes on his living room floor. As a researcher, he temporarily becomes a trucker, and through his writing, you, as his reader, become one too. Here are some of the ways he makes this happen:

1. *He begins by writing himself into his fieldnotes.* In this passage from his October journal, Rick contrasts his own mood as a researcher with the surroundings at the truck stop:

> When I hear that Mrs. Moon will be returning from a funeral, I feel uneasy, like perhaps I am partly responsible for this state of affairs, a harbinger of bad times…. That leaves me sauntering across the back lot heading for the Jiffy Stop and trying to shake off my uneasiness. The sun is high in the sky, giving no indication of the coming cold front…. Dark clouds slash in diagonals across the northwest and southeast skies, and I give silent thanks for this bit of good weather…. I am determined to get off my dime and get to work on this project. If it's going to amount to anything, I have to talk to *people.*

2. *He writes his interviews as dialogues, capturing both his own voice and that of his informants in his transcripts.* In his interview with Delia Moon, the founder's daughter and company vice president, Rick records some company history. But he also records his own questions as part of the interview:

Delia Moon has an office in back, parallel to the movie theater. She's brown-haired, fair-complected, in her late twenties, thin with nervously attentive features. Her office is crowded with a large desk and trucking industry mementos.... After a few introductory moments dealing with research objectives, we begin:

RZ: This truck stop was founded by your father?

DM: He worked for Standard Oil, in the engineering department, and when the interstate system was built, Amoco targeted places for stops, and my father would go in and buy the land and set up a dealer. He was responsible for setting up places all over the Midwest.

RZ: So he was a visionary? He had a vision of what truck stops in the future should be? Did he see it coming to this, places like Iowa 80 and Little America?

DM: I'd say it happened over time. Traffic here kept building. He was very...he really liked people, truckers. He'd sit in the restaurant and talk to them. The customers can always tell you how you can be better.

3. *He rejects his early drafts because his voice depends too much on other authorities.* In this short excerpt from the beginning of a first draft of "Friday Night at Iowa 80," Rick cites two outside sources and even quotes the roadside sign he recorded in his fieldnotes. He struggles to balance his own voice with the recognized authorities from his reading. You might want to compare this early draft with the first few paragraphs of his final essay (see p. 26).

"Truckstops are the center of the trucking culture," writes James Thomas in *The Long Haul,* and the new trucker villages "offer the driver an equivalent to the cowboys' town at trail's end or the friendly port to sailors" (111). One trucking village that exemplifies this roadside oasis is Iowa 80, "the largest Amoco truckstop in the world" (roadside advertisement), located off Interstate 80 in Walcott, Iowa, some dozen miles from Davenport and 40 miles from my Iowa City home.

I spent selected days and evenings at this site during the fall of 1993, with hopes of discovering "those webs of significance" that make up the context of this very particular culture (Geertz, *Interpretation of Cultures* 5). I am interested in trucker life for a variety of reasons and have wanted to write about Iowa 80 since first noting its sprawling growth almost a decade ago. My time there was well spent, "sorting out the structures of signification" that I had to "first grasp and then render" (9–10).

4. *He experiments with another genre.* In a fiction-writing class he took while conducting his research, Rick began a novella about trucking that he describes as "pulp fiction." For this story, he invents a character, trucker Dick Deacon, and uses the setting he's learned about in his research. Sometimes field-

workers discover that writing in another form—fiction, poetry, dramatic dia-logue—helps them enter the worldview of their informants. When he later returned to the final draft of his ethnographic essay, Rick felt more confident that he could transform his real-world data into an interesting text for his read-ers. Though an ethnographic essay is certainly not fiction, it relies on many of the techniques that writers use to craft other genres.

Truck Drivin' Man

Rick Zollo

Chapter 1

"Ten four, this is the Deacon on the Beacon."

The sun was peeking over a small ridge of oak trees when Dick Deacon guided his '92 Peterbuilt conventional down Illinois I-88 and prepared to downshift for the turn-off onto I-80. He was heading for home, a free weekend in his home state of Iowa. He was tired and dragged out from twenty-one straight days of hauling, but he had to remind himself to look out for Smokies and watched ruefully as a comrade in an International cab-over hauling reefer blew by him.

"Watch out, good buddy. This is Illinois," muttered Deacon, as he spot-ted a speed sign that said it all. "Sixty-five for automobiles, fifty-five for commercial trucks"—one of those states with split limits. Illinois was not a favorite place of truckers. But Deacon took it all in stride. He was an over-the-roader, having taken to this way of life as soon as he could get his C.D.L. He drove tandem for five years with his Dad, then his Dad took sick. He missed his old man and was looking forward to their meeting later that evening.

5. *He combines some of these techniques in his ethnographic study.* Playing with technique, revising, and redrafting helped Rick establish his fieldworker's voice for "Friday Night at Iowa 80." In the final draft, his authority comes from com-bining his personal feelings and observations with those of his informants and of the texts he read.

The challenge in fieldwriting, as Rick learned, is to create a writer's voice that will engage a reader, based on the data gathered in the field. Often the most com-pelling techniques for writing up research are ones that fiction writers use. "As I undid necklaces of words and restrung them," writes anthropologist Ruth Behar, "as I dressed up hours of rambling talk in elegant sentences and paragraphs of prose, as I snipped at the flow of talk, stopping it sometimes for dramatic empha-sis long before it had really stopped, I no longer knew where I stood on the bor-der between fiction and nonfiction" (16). This borderland, where a fieldwriter experiments with voice, is an exciting place. It challenges us both as writers and as researchers. It is a borderland in which, as writers, we can step in and step out.

FIELDWORDS

We end each chapter with a list of key terms we've used and their definitions. Here is our first set of fieldwords.

Artifact Any material object that belongs to and represents a culture.

Assumptions Untested attitudes or theories you hold (based on your own experiences) about unfamiliar people, places, or ideas.

Authority An expert within a field, usually someone who has done reliable research and clearly presented data.

Colonization The takeover of less powerful people by more powerful people who demand conformity to their group's ideas and values, as in a territory ruled or annexed by another country.

Culture The invisible web of behaviors, patterns, rules, and rituals of a group of people who have contact with one another and share common languages.

Data All the information, both written and material artifacts, that a researcher uses as the basis of evidence.

Ethnocentric Projecting one's own cultural values onto others.

Ethnography The study of people in other cultures and the resultant written text from that study. (Note that a fieldworker can adapt ethnographic methods for research and writing without producing a full-length ethnography.)

Fieldwriting A study based on data gathered during field research, as well as the process of drafting such a study.

Fieldwork The process of living and studying among other people in their own context, with their permission and cooperation. Fieldworking involves gathering, interpreting, and validating data via notetaking, interviewing, collecting material artifacts, and other methods.

Genre Classification of an artistic form (as in painting, music, film). Creative nonfiction, for example, is a genre of nonfiction. Reportage is a genre of news story.

Informant A person who shares information about the meanings of his or her culture with a researcher; sometimes also referred to as a consultant, a subject, or "the other."

Insider/Outsider The dialectical stance of detachment (outsider) or involvement (insider) that a researcher adopts toward the informants in the culture studied.

Objectivity In social science research, an unbiased perspective.

Parody A work that imitates the style or voice of an author or other artist for comic effect.

Portfolio A collection of material artifacts that displays and explains a learning process, complete with a reflective analysis. Using it, the portfolio keeper can evaluate progress and accomplishments. When the portfolio is used as an instrument to look at others, as in a research portfolio, it becomes both reflective and *reflexive*. When you build your portfolio, you depend on four key recurring processes:

Collecting Gather data continually and organize it in your portfolio as you go along.

Selecting Lay your data out in front of you, eliminate some of it, describe some of it, analyze the choices that you make, and weigh how the choices fit your current plans.

Reflecting Each time you work on your portfolio, write a one- or two-page reflection about the major items you include. In this reflective writing, address either yourself or your portfolio partner to explain and interpret your data. Discuss your choices and organizational patterns.

Projecting Your reflective writing will point to gaps in your data, emerging patterns, and questions you might follow in further data collection and analysis. It will help you state a few goals for your project.

Reflection The act of considering thoughtfully, looking back to gain insight.

Reflexivity The process of self-scrutiny that results from studying others. To be reflexive demands both an "other" and some self-conscious awareness. Without the aid of an "other," the process is only self-reflective. To be reflective does not demand an "other."

Subculture A group of people who share common language, rituals, and behaviors.

Subjectivity One's own personal inner feelings and attitudes toward a given subject or topic, as opposed to objective, verifiable, concrete, factual evidence.

Worldview The perspective or point of view of any particular culture.

FIELDREADING

Behar, Ruth. *Translated Woman: Crossing the Border with Esperanza's Story.* Boston. Beacon, 1993.

Benedict, Ruth. *Patterns of Culture.* New York: New American Library, 1953.

Fiske, John. *Understanding Popular Culture.* Boston: Unwin, 1989.

Goodenough, Ward. *Culture, Language, and Society.* Menlo Park: Benjamin, 1981.

Graves, Donald H., and Bonnie S. Sunstein. *Portfolio Portraits.* Portsmouth: Heinemann, 1992.

Hebdidge, Dick. *Subculture: The Meaning of Style.* New York: Methuen, 1984.

Moffatt, Michael. *Coming of Age in New Jersey: College and American Culture.* New Brunswick: Rutgers UP, 1989.

Peacock, James. *The Anthropological Lens: Harsh Light, Soft Focus.* Cambridge: Cambridge UP, 1986.

Powdermaker, Hortense. *Stranger and Friend: The Way of an Anthropologist.* New York: Norton, 1966.

Rosaldo, Renato. *Culture and Truth: The Remaking of Social Analysis.* Boston: Beacon, 1989.

Toth, Jennifer. *The Mole People: Life in the Tunnels of New York City.* Chicago: Chicago Review P, 1993.

FIELDPOEM

Self and Other
Sal Biondello

groping for a footing with oneself
   assessing the images of others
attempting to find oneself
   by explaining the other,

deflating them
   with our pins of inquiry
we collect them like butterflies
   pinned to a page,

often we ignore the breathing
   behind the images,
the sentence behind
   our seen patterns,

can we explain their shimmering
   by pinning them to a page,
can we forestall our loneliness
   with our explanations,

we can only reach out,
   allowing another's vibrations to
affect our own shimmering,
   glimpsing for a moment the same
you from another perspective,

not a synchrony,
   or a harmony,
but rather a momentary
   change in oneself,

to experience the same life
   in a new way,
to compare that experience
   with the unchanged you,

thereby glimpsing for a moment
   another world
another possible you.

Commentary
Sarah Townsend

Have you ever seen an old insect collection? My mother or father at some point inherited an old relative's cigar boxes full of pinned beetles and dragonflies and bees. I remember being fascinated and appalled by the prospect of those strangely still wings. What I love about Sal Biondello's poem as a comment on doing fieldwork is its ability to walk that tightrope between science and art that is ethnographic study. Biondello is playing with the image of the insect collector that T. S. Eliot used so wonderfully in "The Love Song of J. Alfred Prufrock"—a poem I treasure teaching to my students as an introduction to internal and external realities and conceptions of "self." Biondello riffs on Eliot here, bringing to our attention again that nineteenth-century entomologist pinning the objects of his study still wriggling to the page—a microscopic metaphor for torture suggesting the violence we can do to another through careless inspection. The work of the fieldworker instead must be full of gentle care, "allowing another's vibrations to / affect our own shimmering." We must rigorously imagine our own selves in the place of that "object" of study, never objectify her with our gaze or fix her with the pin of our preconceptions. Biondello reminds us delicately to have a care for the "breathing," "shimmering" other—and her light will illuminate our own mysterious selves.

Sarah Townsend received her MFA in poetry from the Iowa Writers' Workshop and is currently studying toward her Ph.D. in language, literacy, and culture with an emphasis on the media of literary production.

Writing Self, Writing Cultures: Understanding FieldWriting

2

The fieldworker must choose, shape, prune, discard this and collect finer detail on that, much as a novelist works who finds some minor character is threatening to swallow the major theme, or that the hero is fast talking himself out of his depth. But unlike the novelist…the fieldworker is wholly and helplessly dependent on what happens…. One must be continually prepared for anything, everything—and perhaps most devastating—for nothing.

—MARGARET MEAD

This book is about conducting fieldwork, but it's also very much about fieldwriting. The writing process of a fieldworker, as anthropologist Margaret Mead describes in the quotation above, is somewhat like that of a novelist. The fieldworker must "choose, shape, prune, discard…and collect" data, transforming words and images into text. Mead, whose fieldwork reached both scholarly and popular audiences, knew how to write for both. She instinctively understood what compositionists call rhetoric—the art and craft of persuasion. Her research on Samoan family life in the 1920s informed not only her professional colleagues but the readers of *Redbook, Parent,* the *Nation,* and other magazines—and later the viewers of television talk shows. She learned how to translate her distant field experiences to her home culture in the United States in an inviting and accessible way. This is what you'll want to do, too, as you re-create the conversations and experiences of your fieldwork into writing for an audience.

Mead reminds us that fieldworkers invent neither informants nor descriptions of their cultural spaces. Rather, as she wrote in 1977, we, as fieldworkers, are "helplessly dependent" on what actually takes place in the field—as we see it and as our informants see it. Yet representing or writing about reality depends on how fieldworkers use language—their own and that of their informants—to describe "what's going on." Today, perhaps more than ever before, fieldworkers pay close attention to how language interactions shape and influence their work.

In conversations with our informants we make a contract to try to understand them and represent their ideas in writing as they presented those ideas to us. And as in any negotiation, the ability to understand and interpret the point of view and situation of an "other" depends on both participants. It depends on how deeply our informants allow us to enter their worldviews and on how well we participate and listen. The special ethics of writing about fieldwork demand that we respect and represent our informants' voices. At the same time, we must respect and represent ourselves as narrators, as fieldworkers telling a story about an "other." Your fieldwork ultimately involves *what* you write as well as *how* you write it.

At the outset of your fieldwork, you may question the importance of writing. Why not just hang out, observe, and listen to others? Why take notes at all? Why can't a good fieldworker just be a participant-observer—a person who can scope out a place, schmooze with other people, and make witty or astute observations about whatever new group she happens to meet? Why not just develop your observational powers by sitting around, watching people and places?

The difference between doing fieldwork and just "hanging out" is the *writing*. Without writing, the sharp, incisive details about people, places, and cultures are lost to us. The overheard conversation, the aftereffect of an image, or the undertone of an encounter with an informant dissipates unless it is written down. Fieldworkers turn hanging out into a scholarly art form. They begin by choosing from a variety of exploratory writing strategies and developing a dependable system for taking **fieldnotes**.

Since the days when Margaret Mead did her fieldwork, researchers' thinking has shifted about the writing of fieldnotes. No longer are fieldnotes considered a mirror, or direct reflection, of the research experience; rather, a researcher's fieldnotes are recognized as a **construction** of that field experience. The fieldnotes you gather and record will not be like anyone else's. They will represent your perspective—gathered, recorded, mapped, and written according to your own conscious and unconscious choices about what you see and hear at your fieldsite.

In this chapter we discuss how writing about the self links with writing about the culture you are investigating. We feel that it's critical for you to understand your personal curiosity or fascination with the subculture you plan to study. To help you start gathering data and taking fieldnotes, we share some of the ways our students began their field projects. We offer you some exploratory writing techniques as well as some examples from both students and professional writers who have used these techniques to write themselves into their topics about subcultures. Some common informal composing options—such as freewriting, mapping, listing, outlining, and journaling—can help you to jump-start field projects, just as they assist writers in jump-starting any writing. You may find that some of your initial exploratory writing will find its way into your actual fieldnotes or even into your final project, but you may also choose to ignore it as you move toward writing about the culture you have selected. We hope that by reviewing these exploratory writing techniques along with student and professional examples, you'll find a way into your fieldwork topic as you begin to craft your initial fieldnotes.

Choosing a subculture, an event, or a site you want to learn more about is critical to the success of your project, although we also believe that almost any event, subculture, or site can be fascinating and instructive as long as you keep an open mind. Throughout this book, we will caution you not to choose places or events that are particularly sensational. The culture of a children's playground can be as complex and engaging to write about as the subculture of witch covens or gang warfare. Since we wrote the first edition of this book, students who've used it have researched hundreds of subcultures, fieldsites, and cultural events all over the United States and the world. Our colleagues and their students have shared fieldprojects with us, some of which you'll read in this new edition.

In the first chapter, we saw how Rick Zollo's fieldnotes helped him construct his stance for looking at the culture of the truck stop. His study shows his fascination with and investment in the subculture of truckers—and from studies our other students have done, we understand this investment. We're proud of the following partial listing of the many interesting studies we have read and hope it will help you think about what you might want to study for your own project:

Subcultures

drag racers, Boy Scouts, people who live in RVs

cloggers, country music dancers, female impersonators

role-players, Pokemon players, Bingo players

chat room "talkers," Internet "cyber-lebrities"

soccer parents, street hockey players, skateboarders

a group of quilters who have met once a week for fifty years

the World War II Women's Airforce Service Pilots (WASPs)

Events

a rodeo, a harvest festival, a rave, a gathering at a meditation center

a one-time controversial TV show, an Academy Award–winning movie

a distance learning college course

a convention of Nancy Drew novel readers

services in a Catholic church, the summer restaging of the Mormon walk westward

base-camp preparations for a climb of Mt. Everest

design, rehearsals, and performance of a ballet

military reenactments

Places

a telemarketing company, a law office, a sorority house

a tailor shop, a health club, a beauty parlor, a barber shop, a fish bait shop a comic book store, an old family hotel, a fast-food kitchen

a teacher's room in a high school, an alternative high school housed in a trailer

the kitchen of a woman with Parkinson's disease

an adult book and video store, a tattoo parlor

a traveling circus, a playground, a movie music recording studio

a city cemetery, a dog kennel, an art studio, a homeless shelter

One of the best ways to brainstorm ideas for fieldwork projects is to write informally about possibilities. We'd like you to explore some additional ways to write before writing—drafting informally before writing more formally, sometimes called exploratory writing or *prewriting*. The strategies we offer here are options for all writers: freewriting and mapping, keeping a personal notebook, and drafting notes in a research journal. Such exploratory writing helps you think on the page and generates more ideas as you enter the field. We'll address not only the skills that are part of keeping fieldnotes, but the uses of language for different purposes and audiences involved when a fieldworker writes.

CONSIDERING SELF

Freewriting

Freewriting belongs to a category of informal writing designed to release your mind from worrying about an audience of readers. A kind of uninhibited doodling with words, freewriting is helpful when you have trouble getting started. Peter Elbow, a scholar of composition, writes extensively and powerfully about the potential of freewriting as a way of "priming the pump." In his book, *Writing without Teachers*, he opens with a chapter about freewriting, excerpts of which we include here.

Freewriting
Peter Elbow

Freewriting is the easiest way to get words on paper and the best all-around practice in writing that I know. To do a freewriting exercise, simply force yourself to write without stopping for ten minutes. Sometimes you will produce good writing, but that's not the goal. Sometimes you will produce garbage, but that's not the goal either. You may stay on one topic, you may flip repeatedly from one to another: it doesn't matter. Sometimes you will produce a good record of your stream of consciousness, but often you can't keep up. Speed is not the goal, though sometimes the process revs you up. If you can't think of anything to write, write about how that feels or repeat over and over "I have nothing to write" or "Nonsense" or "No." If you get stuck in the middle of a sentence or thought, just repeat the last word or phrase till something comes along. The only point is to keep writing.

Or rather, that's the first point. For there are lots of goals of freewriting, but they are best served if, while you are doing it, you accept this single, simple, mechanical goal of simply not stopping. When you produce an exciting piece of writing, it doesn't mean you did it better than the time before when you wrote one sentence over and over for ten minutes. Both times you freewrote perfectly. The goal of freewriting is in the process, not the product. [...]

The Benefits of Freewriting

Freewriting makes writing easier by helping you with the root psychological or existential difficulty in writing: finding words in your head and putting them down on a blank piece of paper. So much writing time and energy is spent *not* writing: wondering, worrying, crossing out, having second, third, and fourth thoughts. And it's easy to get stopped even in the middle of a piece. (This is why Hemingway made a rule for himself never to end one sheet and start a new one except in the middle of a sentence.) Frequent freewriting exercises help you learn simply to *get on with it* and not be held back by worries about whether these words are good words or the right words.

Thus, freewriting is the best way to learn—in practice, not just in theory—to separate the producing process from the revising process. Freewriting exercises are push-ups in withholding judgment as you produce so that afterwards you can judge better.

Freewriting for ten minutes is a good way to warm up when you sit down to write something. You won't waste so much time getting started when you turn to your real writing task and you won't have to struggle so hard to find words. Writing almost always goes better when you are already started: now you'll be able to start off already started.

Freewriting helps you learn to write when you don't feel like writing. It is practice in setting deadlines for yourself, taking charge of yourself, and learning gradually how to get that special energy that sometimes comes when you work fast under pressure.

Freewriting teaches you to write without thinking about writing. We can usually speak without thinking about speech—without thinking about how to form words in the mouth and pronounce them and the rules of syntax we unconsciously obey—and as a result we can give undivided attention to what we say. Not so writing. Or at least most people are considerably distracted from their meaning by considerations of spelling, grammar, rules, errors. Most people experience an awkward and sometimes paralyzing *translating* process in writing: "Let's see, how shall I say this." Freewriting helps you learn to *just say* it. Regular freewriting helps make the writing process *transparent*.

Freewriting is a useful outlet. We have lots in our heads that makes it hard to think straight and write clearly: we are mad at someone, sad about something, depressed about everything. Perhaps even inconveniently happy. "How can I think about this report when I'm so in love?" Freewriting is a quick outlet for these feelings so they don't get so much in your way when you are trying to write about something else. Sometimes your mind is marvelously clear after ten minutes of telling someone on paper everything you need to tell him. (In fact, if your feelings often keep you from functioning well in other areas of your life frequent freewriting can help: not only by providing a good arena for those feelings, but also by helping you understand them better and see them in perspective by seeing them on paper.)

Freewriting helps you to think of topics to write about. Just keep writing, follow threads where they lead and you will get to ideas, experiences, feelings, or people that are just asking to be written about.

Finally, and perhaps most important, freewriting improves your writing. It doesn't always produce powerful writing itself, but it leads to powerful writing. The process by which it does so is a mysterious underground one. When people talk about the Zen of this or that I think they are referring to the peculiar increase in power and insight that comes from focusing your energy while at the same time putting aside your conscious controlling self. Freewriting gives practice in this special mode of focusing-but-not-trying; it helps you stand out of the way and let words be chosen by the sequence of the words themselves or the thought, not by the conscious self. In this way freewriting gradually puts a deeper resonance or voice into your writing.

But freewriting also brings a surface coherence to your writing and it does so immediately. You cannot write *really* incoherently if you write quickly. You may violate the rules of correctness, you may make mistakes in reasoning, you may write foolishness, you may change directions before you have said anything significant. That is, you may produce something like "Me and her we went down and saw the folks but wait that reminds me of the thing I was thinking about yester oh dam what am I really trying to say." But you won't produce syntactic chaos: language that is so jumbled that when you read it over you are frightened there is something the matter with you.

However, you wouldn't be frightened if you looked more closely at how you actually produced that verbal soup. If you had movies of yourself you would see yourself starting four or five times and throwing each start away and thereby getting more and more jumbled in your mind; finally starting; stopping part way through the sentence to wonder if you are on the wrong track and thereby losing your syntactic thread. You would see yourself start writing again on a slightly different piece of syntax from the one you started with, then notice something really wrong and fix it and lose the thread again; so when you finally conclude your sentence, you are actually writing the conclusion of a different sentence from the ones you have been writing. Thus, the resulting sentence—whether incorrect or just impossibly awkward—is really fragments of three different syntactic impulses or sentences-in-the-head tied together with baling wire. When you write quickly, however, as in freewriting, your syntactic units hang together. Even if you change your mind in mid-sentence, as above, you produce a clear break. You don't try to plaster over two or three syntactic units as one, as you so often do in painstaking writing. Freewriting produces syntactic coherence and verbal energy which gradually transfer to your more careful writing.

In this excerpt, Elbow reminds us that informal writing helps to produce more writing; it gives us "all around practice" in writing. The goal for informal writing is to loosen up the process, not to create a perfect product. In fact, as Elbow mentions, "so much time is spent not writing" that such informal writing can just help us "get on with it"—help us get actual words on the page. We and our colleagues have favorite expressions, like "lower your standards," "outrun your censor," "just get down some language," or "generate a brain dump." Freewriting, brainstorming, and mapping are all similar to conversation in that they have no predetermined plan. Words call up other words and consequently words call up ideas.

Freewriting can be useful at any stage of the fieldwork process, but it is particularly helpful at the beginning of a research project when you are trying out ideas and thinking about yourself in different research sites and subcultures. One of our students, Nora Markum, did some freewriting when she was considering a study of skateboarders. Here are three excerpts from her in-class freewrites, written at different times, in which she explores her history with skateboarding, anticipates problems she might have studying this subculture, and expresses her continuing fascination with skateboarders:

Nora's freewriting #1: This past hot summer I had a crush on Mo. Among other things, Mo was tall, lanky, and dirty. One night at Mo's house, a bunch of boys decided to go skating. I looked down at my bare belly poking out from in between the edge of my shorts and the edge of my tank top and felt old frustrations surface within me. I felt past resentments from feeling left out and bored while my boyfriend Jamie gawkily learned how to "Ollie." "I'm going home," I said. The boys wanted me to come, and I told them that I hated watching skaters. Mo said I didn't have to watch, I could skate. Within 10 minutes we were at a downtown parking deck. The night was warm, and I felt excited and scared. I didn't even know how to stand on a skateboard. That night I learned that and then some…it was fun, and I felt a sense of togetherness with the boys.…

Nora's freewriting #2: Before this summer I considered myself an outsider to the skating community, and with this position came certain beliefs and opinions about skaters. In ninth grade my girlfriend Erin had some skater friends. In between classes we would all clump together, and I would comment on the insider lingo by saying to Erin, "Shhh, skater talk." I definitely felt left out. Despite my feelings of being left out, I have always felt attracted to talented skaters and the laid-back attitude and style of dress skaters have.…

Nora's freewriting #3: Since this is predominantly a male sport/recreation, the fact that I am a girl might pose a challenge. I have a couple of friends I know who skate, and I want to interview different ages and races. This Saturday, there's going to be a skate demo with a bunch of really talented skaters. I think this would be a good opportunity to interview. I'm worried that they (skaters) might look at me and not accept me in this situation. A fieldsite that I was thinking about is Funky's (a local skate shop) and The Slip Side (a place where kids pay to skate indoors).…

Nora's freewriting enabled her to brainstorm possible ideas about a field project on the skateboard subculture: her insider-outsider position and potential places she might conduct interviews. She was also able to recall previous memories and feelings about skateboarding from her point of view as a former ninth-grader. While she might not use all of this writing in her final project, freewriting has energized her thinking and released many ways for her to consider skateboarders as a subculture.

Mapping

Nora also used another strategy for unlocking her memories and organizing her ideas. Like many students, she benefited from "mapping," a visual way of inventorying what you know and making plans for a project (see Figure 2.1). To begin

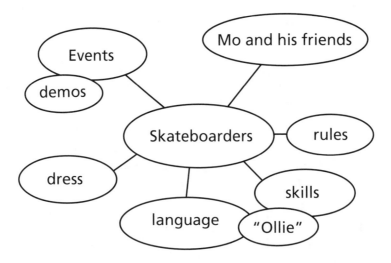

Figure 2.1

mapping, place a keyword in the center of the page, and draw a circle around it. Use the word to free-associate. Words call up words; place these related items in circles around the key phrase. Mapping can be as extensive and complex as you want. Some word-processing programs accommodate this type of visual planning, so you might want to try mapping with your computer.

Exploratory Writing

Purpose

One way of thinking about the pros and cons of possible subcultures or field-sites to study is through informal exploratory writing: brainstorming, list-making, mapping, clustering, and outlining. Turn off your internal censor, and free your mind. These strategies help you hold conversations with yourself on paper about your interests, your memories, and your curiosities.

Action

Choose one exploratory writing strategy to think about a site or subculture you may want to investigate, and consider some of these questions:

1. What do you already know about this subculture? What insiders do you know?
2. What kinds of connections do you have with the site or subculture now?
3. How easy or difficult would it be to enter this subculture as either insider or outsider?
4. In what ways are you either an insider or an outsider already?
5. What do you hope to find out?

Response

When Terra Savage was considering a study of a tattoo parlor, she freewrote to discover her background knowledge and feeling about tattoos:

> Grunge. Class. No Stress. Responsibility. Lacking education. Over-achiever. Artistic. Artistic? Family. Tattoo artisan. Me. At first glance, there seems to be no relationship between my life and this tattoo parlor. But take another look; the more I stare I am not so different.
>
> Men with tattoos ride Harley Davidsons and are running from middle age. Putter putter rev rev. When my stepdad turned fifty, he wanted a Harley I guess to feel masculine and in control; all I could envision was him getting a tattoo. One with "I ❤ MY MAMA"

written across his chest. Have you seen it before? Tattoos on teenage kids are a way for them to rebel. My mom would threaten me with my life....

My sister wanted her nose pierced; she chose Harry's Tattoo in order to get the job done. She had to have all the correct documents to prove she was my mom's daughter, an infinite amount of paperwork. Employees must be meticulous with their work....

A girl I graduated high school with worked nights @ the gas station so she could have enough $$$ saved up to apprentice a tattoo artist. She was a good girl who made decent grades in high school. I tend to be very narrowminded when it comes to a traditional education (a typical thought for me, the only reason they're working in the tattoo business, is b/c they can't do anything else).... However, all that aside, as I have matured, I realize that a person who would like to work in a tattoo parlor is just as valid as someone who has 2 bachelors degrees, 3 masters degrees and a Ph.D.

A tattoo artist has a special talent for drawing, but instead of using an easel and paper they choose to use skin. The flesh. Maybe this is one of the most organic forms of art work. I have touched a weak spot—Art. At one time I considered myself an artist, a dancer and choreographer, to be more precise. Have I stumbled on common ground by sheer coincidence? I understand the need to be around your field; I understand the need to be enthused.

CONSIDERING AUDIENCES

In a fieldworking project titled "Much Ta-Too about Nothing," Terra Savage, the student whose freewriting is excerpted in Box 4, eventually decided to include direct quotes from her early freewriting so that her readers would understand her position as a person who was ambivalent about tattooing until she recognized its artistic nature. At the outset of her study, it was important that Terra ignored her audience and wrote in an uncensored way to discover both what she did know and didn't know about the subculture of tattoo parlors. When Terra looked through her research portfolio, she saw that her **thesis**— tattooing is an art—lay in her early freewriting. To shape her nascent ideas for an eventual reader, however, she needed to gather thick piles of information, observations, and data about other people's perspectives. She shifted her writing from "self" to "other," from informal to formal, from writer to reader. It was the information she gathered, the actual data, that helped her complete her study. Throughout her fieldwork project, Terra engaged in a highly *rhetorical* process.

All writing is rhetorical. You may have heard someone respond to a politician or a magazine advertisement by saying, "Oh, that's just rhetoric." **Rhetoric** is commonly defined as the art of persuasion, but it involves far more than the verbal devices that are often connected with propaganda. It is the shaping of discourses (or simply the uses of language) for different purposes and audiences. Rhetoric has many positive uses, and writers or speakers who are aware of their rhetorical situation are far more prepared to shape oral or written texts than writers who know little of the power and options in word choice and delivery. Even a young child who writes a letter to the tooth fairy or who argues to eat pizza for breakfast is employing persuasive rhetorical devices.

The Greek philosopher Aristotle described the rhetorical event, which can be either oral or written, as having three important elements: ethos (the self), logos (the information), and pathos (sensitivity to an audience). This triadic idea crosses historical periods and academic disciplines. You may have learned, for example, in computer or basic communications courses that the paradigm of sender, message, and receiver describes how people convey ideas to one another. Folklorists and anthropologists see a similar pattern when they study verbal art (like joking, rapping, and storytelling): a three-way interaction among a performer, a performance, and an audience. In contemporary composition, we refer to these three elements as voice, purpose, and audience. As you conduct your fieldwork and then share it with others, you become a rhetorician, making decisions about how to use your own voice (ethos), as well as the voices of your informants and the information from your fieldnotes (logos), and, too, a sense of your audience (pathos).

Writing for an audience can be scary, especially when you're in the initial stages of a project. Terra's exploratory freewriting helped her discover what she knew when she wasn't yet ready to think about an audience of readers. In fact, she hadn't yet done field research. We could say that Terra's freewrite helped her develop her voice, which many of these exploratory writing strategies are designed to do. As she gathers more data from more sources, reflects on her ideas, and decides what to use in her drafts, Terra will become more confident about all her material. Most important, she will begin to think about ways to shape her writing away from her writer "self" and toward a reader, an audience of an "other." You can't shape your text for someone else until you can explain it yourself. Freewriting is just one of many ways to discover how interested you are or how much you already know about a subculture.

There are more formal ways of writing about your interest and history in a fieldwork topic. Luke E. Lassiter, a professor of anthropology, has been interested in Native American studies all his life. In the following excerpt from his book *The Power of Kiowa Song,* he describes his passion for "Indianness," which began when he was a Boy Scout and developed into his professional scholarship. Like Nora's and Terra's freewriting, this excerpt explores the interest of an outsider in the insiders he plans to study. In Lassiter's case, this selection tracks his deepening awareness of Native American cultures. With each participation in Indian events, he grows more conscious of his need to understand the people of these cultures on their own terms, not his preconceived ones. Notice that, despite the presentation of complex information and scholarly references, Lassiter engages his audience by using a personal, friendly, crafted voice, much like we often seen in freewriting.

Before you read this selection, you may want to review in your own mind your cultural assumptions or the stereotypes you have about Native Americans.

Boy Scouts, Hobbyists, and Indians
The Power of Kiowa Song
Luke E. Lassiter

Any American, when asked, can tell you about Indians. Without much thought, most of us envision feathers, turquoise jewelry, reservations, alcohol, or tipis. Such images are among an overabundance of conventional knowledge. Yet this knowledge is rarely derived from a deep understanding of Native American experience. It emerges instead from a long legacy of imagined encounters with Indians, images that we pass from generation to generation.

Several studies have shown that American children have crystallized their ideas of "Indians" by age six or seven (see, e.g., Hirschfelder 1982). When asked, children often position Indians in a historical, natural, and wild setting; they portray them as close to nature, sparsely clothed, decorated with war paint, and carrying weapons (usually a rifle or bow and arrow). These stereotypes may evolve into more sophisticated ones as they learn about Indians in school and in youth organizations such as the Boy or Girl Scouts. But the dominant images seem to change little from those most Americans acquire as children. They pervade American thought in the media, in literature, and even in academia (Clifton 1989, 6–8).

My own most memorable rendezvous with this world of imagery began at age eleven in the Boy Scouts of America (BSA). Scouts beheld "the Indian" as exotic, as mysterious, and most predominantly, as a figure of antiquity. The first requirement listed in the Indian lore merit badge pamphlet began: "Give the history of one Indian tribe, group, or nation…." The seven chapters on seven culture areas, the final chapter on Indian dancing and games, and the table in the back entitled "Indian Life at a Glance" authoritatively delivered us knowledge of an authentic past. Our duty as Scouts was to preserve this past. Consider this passage excerpted from the latest edition of the Indian lore merit badge pamphlet:

> Fortunately, people all over America have the chance to see Indian dancers perform. Unfortunately, in many cases, what they see are feathered dancers haphazardly hopping up and down. They see uncontrolled frenzy

and dancers wearing Sioux war bonnets with Chippewa bustles. In Scouting, in our Indian lore groups, *we have a chance to preserve the proper past* [my emphasis]. (Boy Scouts of America [1959] 1992, 74)

At eleven or twelve, I wasn't really sure what "the proper past" meant, but it certainly didn't contradict anything that I had learned before. To be sure, all the additional reading I did about Indians ministered to an image of antiquity far beyond my merit badge training.

When I was thirteen or fourteen, my immersion into an enactment of "Indianness" came with my induction into the Boy Scouts' Order of the Arrow (OA), a fraternal order of experienced boy and adult scouters for whom a variety of Indian representations epitomize principles and rituals that are actually more in line with Freemasonry than with Indianness. Although the point of the OA was not Indianness, for me and several other boy and adult scouters, our fascination with Indians extended far beyond our Indian-style induction ceremonies. We sought to enact Indianness on much deeper levels. Our fascination was not unusual; we met and networked with Arrowmen from all over the country at OA-sponsored national, regional, and local conventions and seminars on Indians. There we cultivated our impersonation of the "proper past." One text from a Boy Scout conference on Indians I attended as a boy reads:

Research is the key to the outstanding outfit. Action photographs are best for finding good combinations—posed photographs tend to reflect the contents of the studio. Museum pieces are best for designs and colors, provided they are properly labeled. When looking at a photo, note how the item is worn, and look at the same item on half a dozen dancers—for instance, how long is a breechclout? *You are trying to duplicate a culture that no longer exists—therefore, don't be original* [my emphasis]. (Anonymous n.d.)

With our handbooks in hand, Arrowmen worked hard to summon these Indian ghosts from a vanishing American landscape. In OA ceremonies, shows, and powwows, we reproduced costuming and dance as near as possible to "the original"—often situated in the nineteenth century. As one might expect, most of us impersonated Plains Indians. In Order of the Arrow Indian dance troupes, for example, we tended to replicate our vision of an early-twentieth-century version of the Plains Grass Dance. Scouters called it old style or old time, a dance form combining late-nineteenth-century Plains Indian dress (particularly of the Lakota Sioux) with early-twentieth-century clothing such as top hats and wool vests. My cohorts and I never considered the fact that Native Plains communities had long since abandoned and replaced such dance styles. And although we knew of living, breathing Indians (who often taught at the conventions and seminars), the "real" authority rested in the pictures.

As the Boy Scout motto, "Be Prepared," suggests, my childhood training equipped me for enthusiastic participation with a larger international movement as I grew older—the so-called Indian hobbyists, who, simply put, are non-Indians having "a wide range of interests in American Indian subjects, but mainly arts and crafts, Indian dancing, and singing" (Powers 1988, 557). While I was staffing a Boy Scout summer camp at age sixteen, some Native American scouts insisted I attend a "real" powwow with "real" Indians; they said that my Boy Scout training had fallen short. The following August I seized the opportunity to attend a powwow not sponsored by the BSA.

A secluded site in the Smoky Mountains served as the mystical backdrop for my perceived journey into the past. Half-hidden bundles and streamers fastened to tree limbs guided motorists to an undisclosed location and heightened my expectations. (In retrospect, the brightly painted powwow signs bearing American flags and colored banners typical of contemporary Oklahoma powwows would have disappointed me.)

At this, my first "real" powwow, Boy Scouts, hobbyists, and Indians combined an absorbing array of elements from scouting, hobbyism, and "pan-Indianism." Indians provided the songs for the event; the few Indian dancers wore modern War Dance outfits (e.g., those used for fancy war dance and shawl dance); hobbyists dressed either in elaborate and costly traditional outfits (e.g., the Lakota Sioux version of the Grass Dance outfit) or in straight dance clothing (the Oklahoma version of the Plains War Dance outfit); and Boy Scouts wore their usual "old style" garb (cf. Powers 1988).

My participation in the BSA-Indian tradition had been marginal, but when I attended this powwow, I caught what hobbyist participants called the bug—an irresistible urge to do "Indian things." I decided that the convictions I learned as a Boy Scout had led me astray; I now had achieved a new and "genuine" understanding of Indians. Over the course of a couple of years, I began tanning my own leather, grew my hair long so I could braid it (which I did), made Indian clothes, and even set up a sixteen-foot-high canvas tipi in my parents' backyard to get out of our "square" house (a move that did not last very long). That I had never set foot in an Indian community and knew relatively few Indian people was of no consequence.

Lassiter writes in an informal voice, somewhat like Nora and Terra do, to review for himself his history of ideas about Native Americans, mainly derived from his membership in the Boy Scouts. He arrives at an ironic juncture when he realizes that despite all the powwows he has attended and despite his extensive reading, he has had virtually no contact with Native Americans. Lassiter's book is an in-depth study of the songs of a particular group, the Kiowa. It took Lassiter many years of study to enter the Kiowa culture and be accepted there as a fieldworker. The most important writing he did was to own up to how and why he became interested in Native American culture and what he needed to know to study it.

CONSIDERING VOICE

Many writers find that a personal daybook, journal, or log is useful as a seedbed of ideas. Keeping a notebook, systematically or even sporadically, allows writers to capture observations and emotions that otherwise might dissipate. In Chapter 1, we reproduce the finished version of Rick Zollo's study "Friday Night at Iowa 80." During his fieldwork, Rick kept his notes in the form of a narrative research journal. He used a spiral notebook on site and then later expanded his notes into a longer document using his computer's word-processing program. In these **expanded fieldnotes**, Rick not only recorded but also reflected on what he had seen. Here is one page from the file, dated Friday, October 1, 11 a.m. We've used italics to highlight his reflective comments on what he's observing and hearing:

My next stop is the truck wash, where lines of trucks wait at each bay. Business is booming on this sunny day, and I want to see how it's done.

Inside, a trucker waits at the counter to talk to a sales rep. The price of a truck wash is $43.95 for tractor and trailer, $26.95 or $24.95 for cab only, depending on the type of cab. The trucker is an old gent, gray hair covered by a black cowboy hat decked with pins and medallions, his rangy arms marked with faded tattoos. He talks over his shoulder to a woman drinking coffee and smoking a cigarette

"Government pays real good…it's just that you might have to wait 6 months to be paid." He then goes on to recount a story about a trucker he knows from Texas who's assembled millions in back pay that the government continues to owe in arrears. "He's retired now. Gets a check from the government every month."

The woman seems suitably impressed in her reply, but her tone betrays a bored casualness that hints at possible disbelief.

My notebook is open, and I'm writing down information as fast as I can observe it. I'm still nosing around. I'm listening to these guys B.S.ing loudly. They want people to listen to them. I don't want to be strictly with just the colorful characters. I have a weakness for characters. I have to give voice to quiet people. They are the people who do all the work. The loud and noisy people are trying to sell you their con.

Past the office area, into the first bay, watching two workers in rubber boots steam spray both sides of an Atlas Van Line…. A third worker stands on a moving platform and scrubs down the top of a cab with a brush broom. Overhead, a steamer runs along a track and sprays the truck from above…. A young worker in bay 2 notices me and saunters over to talk.

"On a real good day we have four people to a bay, and we can wash 20 trucks a shift in each bay." Times 4 bays, times 3 shifts tells me that on an ideal day, this truck-o-mat can clean 240 trucks.

I'm back outside looking at rigs and writing in my notebook when a woman trucker yells out, "Don't write my license plate down in that notebook!"

"I'm not writing down your license plate," I say defensively. "I'm doing research for the University of Iowa on this truck stop."

She looks at me like I'm crazy. She looks like she's interested in me but she doesn't believe I'm doing a term paper. Truckers have a real "them–us" mentality. To them I'm a real nerd. I'm driving a "Jap 4-wheeler" and walking around with a notebook in my hand. I feel very existential, tentative, have to be circumspect. That sense of the "other." Polite. Respectful. It's hard to make an introduction at a truck stop.

These italicized sections serve the same purpose as freewriting by permitting the researcher to explore himself—his feelings, attitudes, and perceptions—as he records data from the culture. Although few of Rick's notes from his truck-washing scene appear in his final paper, his journal reflections helped him to construct theories about truckers. As he began to see truckers as cowboys and outlaws, Rick sought to confirm (and disconfirm) this theory with his continued observations and interviews at Iowa 80. With each field visit, Rick's fieldnotes became sharper and more complete, whether or not the specific facts became part of his final project. He learned and wrote about who would be a good informant and who wouldn't, and he came to feel more like an insider as he stepped further and further into the truck stop culture. And so, parts of what was in Rick's notebook reappeared in his final essay, which theorizes about the truck stop, as well as in his research portfolio, which tells the whole story of his research process.

Rick's notes were unique to him and his research project. Many types of writers—including journalists, poets, novelists, technical writers, and scriptwriters—record their thoughts and collect their self-reflections in notebooks and refer to them as they draft their work. Scholars study writers' notebooks because they often reveal the personal source of a writer's ideas. When we return to our recorded notebook scratchings, we also return to those unrecorded circumstances that surrounded the written notes. Like a snapshot or a home video, our jottings trigger a flood of information and remembrance about people and places. Writer Joan Didion reminds us that any types of personal notes will always be unique to the keeper. "Your notebook will never help me, nor mine you." In the following well-known essay, Didion meditates on the value of her own personal notebook. It is a way, she writes, of "keeping in touch" with the self. "*How it felt to me:* that is getting closer to the truth about a notebook."

As you read this essay, notice how Didion talks about collecting details that she describes as the "bits of the mind's string too short to use": cracked crab, sauerkraut, a woman in a dirty crepe-de-Chine wrapper, an orchid-filled sitting room, a New York blizzard. When Didion returns to these bits in her notebook, her memory will pull up a version of her original experience.

On Keeping a Notebook
Joan Didion

"'That woman Estelle,'" the note reads, "'is partly the reason why George Sharp and I are separated today.' *Dirty crepe-de-Chine wrapper, hotel bar, Wilmington RR, 9:45 a.m. August Monday morning.*"

Since the note is in my notebook, it presumably has some meaning to me. I study it for a long while. At first I have only the most general notion of what I was doing on an August Monday morning in the bar of the hotel across from the Pennsylvania Railroad station in Wilmington, Delaware (waiting for a train? missing one? 1960? 1961? and Wilmington?), but I do remember being there. The woman in the dirty crepe-de-Chine wrapper had come down from her room for a beer, and the bartender had heard before the reason why George Sharp and she were separated today. "Sure," he said, and went on mopping the floor. "You told me." At the other end of the bar is a girl. She is talking, pointedly, not to the man beside her but to a cat lying in the triangle of sunlight cast through the open door. She is wearing a plaid silk dress from Peck & Peck, and the hem is coming down.

Here is what it is: the girl has been on the Eastern Shore, and now she is going back to the city, leaving the man beside her, and all she can see ahead are the viscous summer sidewalks and the 3 a.m. long-distance calls that will make her lie awake and then sleep drugged through all the steaming mornings left in August (1960? 1961?). Because she must go directly from the train to lunch in New York, she wishes that she had a safety pin for the hem of the plaid silk dress, and she also wishes that she could forget about the hem and the lunch and stay in the cool bar that smells of disinfectant and malt and make friends with the woman in the crepe-de-Chine wrapper. She is afflicted by a little self-pity, and she wants to compare Estelles. That is what that was all about.

Why did I write it down? In order to remember, of course, but exactly what was it I wanted to remember? How much of it actually happened? Did any of it? Why do I keep a notebook at all? It is easy to deceive oneself on all those scores. The impulse to write things down is a peculiarly compulsive one, inexplicable to those who do not share it, useful only accidentally, only secondarily, in the way that any compulsion tries to justify itself. I suppose that it begins or does not begin in the cradle. Although I have felt compelled to write things down since I was five years old, I doubt that my daughter ever will, for she is a singularly blessed and accepting child, delighted with life exactly as life presents itself to her, unafraid to go to sleep and unafraid to wake up. Keepers of private notebooks are a different breed altogether, lonely and resistant rearrangers of things, anxious malcontents, children afflicted apparently at birth with some presentiment of loss.

My first notebook was a Big Five tablet, given to me by my mother with the sensible suggestion that I stop whining and learn to amuse myself by writing down my thoughts. She returned the tablet to me a few years ago; the first entry is an account of a woman who believed herself to be freezing to death in the Arctic night, only to find, when day broke, that she had stumbled onto the Sahara Desert, where she would die of the heat before lunch. I have no idea what turn of a five-year-old's mind could have prompted so insistently "ironic" and exotic a story, but it does reveal a certain predilection for the extreme which has dogged me into adult life; perhaps if I were analytically inclined I would find it a truer story than any I might have told about Donald Johnson's birthday party or the day my cousin Brenda put Kitty Litter in the aquarium.

So the point of my keeping a notebook has never been, nor is it now, to have an accurate factual record of what I have been doing or thinking. That would be a different impulse entirely, an instinct for reality which I sometimes envy but do not possess. At no point have I ever been able successfully to keep a diary; my approach to daily life ranges from the grossly negligent to the merely absent, and on those few occasions when I have tried dutifully to record a day's events, boredom has so overcome me that the results are mysterious at best. What is this business about "shopping, typing piece, dinner with E, depressed"? Shopping for what? Typing what piece? Who is E? Was this "E" depressed, or was I depressed? Who cares?

In fact I have abandoned altogether that kind of pointless entry; instead I tell what some would call lies. "That's simply not true," the members of my family frequently tell me when they come up against my memory of a shared event. "The party was *not* for you, the spider was *not* a black widow, *it wasn't that way at all.*" Very likely they are right, for not only have I always had trouble distinguishing between what happened and what merely might have happened, but I remain unconvinced that the distinction, for my purposes, matters. The cracked crab that I recall having for lunch the day my father came home from Detroit in 1945 must certainly be embroidery; worked into the day's pattern to lend verisimilitude; I was ten years old and would not now remember the cracked crab. The day's events did not turn on cracked crab. And yet it is precisely that fictitious crab that makes me see the afternoon all over again, a home movie run all too often, the father bearing gifts, the child weeping, an exercise in family love and guilt. Or that is what it was to me. Similarly, perhaps it never did snow that August in Vermont; perhaps there never were flurries in the night wind, and maybe no one else felt the ground hardening and summer already dead even as we pretended to bask in it, but that was how it felt to me, and it might as well have snowed, could have snowed, did snow.

How it felt to me: that is getting closer to the truth about a notebook. I sometimes delude myself about why I keep a notebook, imagine that some thrifty virtue derives from preserving everything observed. See enough and write it down, I tell myself, and then some morning when the world seems drained of wonder, some day when I am only going through the motions of doing what I am supposed to do, which is write—on that bankrupt morning I will simply open my notebook and there it will all be, a forgotten account with accumulated interest, paid passage back to the world out there: dialogue overheard in hotels and elevators and at the hat-check counter in Pavillon (one middle-aged man shows his hat check to another and says, "That's my old football number"); impressions of Bettina Aptheker and Benjamin Sonnenberg and Teddy ("Mr. Acapulo") Stauffer; careful *aperçus* about tennis bums and failed fashion models and Greek shipping heiresses, one of whom taught me a significant lesson (a lesson I could have learned from F. Scott Fitzgerald, but perhaps we all must meet the very rich for ourselves) by asking, when I arrived to interview her in her orchid-filled sitting room on the second day of a paralyzing New York blizzard, whether it was snowing outside.

I imagine, in other words, that the notebook is about other people. But of course it is not. I have no real business with what one stranger said to another at the hat-check counter in Pavillon; in fact I suspect that the line "That's my old football number" touched not my own imagination at all, but merely some memory of something once read, probably "The Eighty-Yard Run." Nor is my concern with a woman in a dirty crepe-de-Chine wrapper in a Wilmington bar. My stake is always, of course, in the unmentioned girl in the plaid silk dress. *Remember what it was to be me*: that is always the point.

It is a difficult point to admit. We are brought up in the ethic that others, any others, all others, are by definition more interesting than ourselves; taught to be diffident, just this side of self-effacing. ("You're the least important person in the room and don't forget it," Jessica Mitford's governess would hiss in her ear on the advent of any social occasion; I copied that into my notebook because it is only recently that I have been able to enter a room without hearing some such phrase in my inner ear.) Only the very young and the very old may recount their dreams at breakfast, dwell upon self, interrupt with memories of beach picnics and favorite Liberty lawn dresses and the rainbow trout in a creek near Colorado Springs. The rest of us are expected, rightly, to affect absorption in other people's favorite dresses, other people's trout.

And so we do. But our notebooks give us away, for however dutifully we record what we see around us, the common denominator of all we see is always, transparently, shamelessly, the implacable "I." We are not talking here about the kind of notebook that is patently for public consumption, a structural conceit for binding together a series of graceful *pensées*; we are talking about something private, about bits of the mind's string too short to use, an indiscriminate and erratic assemblage with meaning only for its maker.

And sometimes even the maker has difficulty with the meaning. There does not seem to be, for example, any point in my knowing for the rest of my life that, during 1964, 720 tons of soot fell on every square mile of New York City, yet there it is in my notebook, labeled "FACT." Nor do I really need to remember that Ambrose Bierce liked to spell Leland Stanford's name "£eland $tanford" or that "smart women almost always wear black in Cuba," a fashion hint without much potential for practical application. And does not the relevance of these notes seem marginal at best?:

> In the basement museum of the Inyo County Courthouse in Independence, California, sign pinned to a mandarin coat: "This MANDARIN COAT was often worn by Mrs. Minnie S. Brooks when giving lectures on her TEAPOT COLLECTION."

> Redhead getting out of car in front of Beverly Wilshire Hotel, chinchilla stole, Vuitton bags with tags reading:

> MRS LOU FOX
> HOTEL SAHARA
> VEGAS

Well, perhaps not entirely marginal. As a matter of fact, Mrs. Minnie S. Brooks and her MANDARIN COAT pull me back into my own childhood, for although I never knew Mrs. Brooks and did not visit Inyo County until I was thirty, I grew up in just such a world, in houses cluttered with Indian relics and bits of gold ore and ambergris and the souvenirs my Aunt Mercy Farnsworth brought back from the Orient. It is a long way from that world to Mrs. Lou Fox's world, where we all live now, and is it not just as well to remember that? Might not Mrs. Minnie S. Brooks help me to remember what I am? Might not Mrs. Lou Fox help me to remember what I am not?

But sometimes the point is harder to discern. What exactly did I have in mind when I noted down that it cost the father of someone I know $650 a month to light the place on the Hudson in which he lived before the Crash? What use was I planning to make of this line by Jimmy Hoffa: "I may have my faults, but being wrong ain't one of them"? And although I think it interesting to know where the girls who travel with the Syndicate have their hair done when they find themselves on the West Coast, will I ever make suitable use of it? Might I not be better off just passing it on to John O'Hara? What is a recipe for sauerkraut doing in my notebook? What kind of magpie keeps this notebook? "He *was born the night the Titanic went down.*" That seems a nice enough line, and I even recall who said it, but is it not really a better line in life than it could ever be in fiction?

But of course that is exactly it: not that I should ever use the line, but that I should remember the woman who said it and the afternoon I heard it. We were on her terrace by the sea, and we were finishing the wine left from lunch, trying to get what sun there was, a California winter sun. The woman whose husband was born the night the *Titanic* went down wanted to rent her house, wanted to go back to her children in Paris. I remember wishing that I could afford the house, which cost $1,000 a month. "Someday you will," she said lazily. "Someday it all comes." There in the sun on her terrace it seemed easy to believe in someday, but later I had a low-grade afternoon hangover and ran over a black snake on the way to the supermarket and was flooded with inexplicable fear when I heard the checkout clerk explaining to the man ahead of me why she was finally divorcing her husband. "He left me no choice," she said over and over as she punched the register. "He has a little seven-month-old baby by her, he left me no choice." I would like to believe that my dread then was for the human condition, but of course it was for me, because I wanted a baby and did not then have one and because I wanted to own the house that cost $1,000 a month to rent and because I had a hangover.

It all comes back. Perhaps it is difficult to see the value in having one's self back in that kind of mood, but I do see it; I think we are well advised to keep on nodding terms with the people we used to be, whether we find them attractive company or not. Otherwise they turn up unannounced and surprise us, come hammering on the mind's door at 4 a.m. of a bad night and demand to know who deserted them, who betrayed them, who is going to make amends. We forget all too soon the things we thought we could never forget. We forget the loves and the betrayals alike, forget what we whispered and what we screamed, forget who we were. I have already lost touch with a couple of people I used to be; one of them, a seventeen-year-old, presents little threat, although it would be of some interest to me to know again what it feels like to sit on a river levee drinking vodka-and-orange-juice and listening to Les Paul and Mary Ford and their echoes sing "How High the Moon" on the car radio. (You see I still have the scenes, but I no longer perceive myself among those present, no longer could even improvise the dialogue.) The other one, a twenty-three-year-old, bothers me more. She was always a good deal of trouble, and I suspect she will reappear when I least want to see her, skirts too long, shy to the point of aggravation, always the injured party, full of recriminations and little hurts and stories I do not want to hear again, at once saddening me and angering me with her vulnerability and ignorance, an apparition all the more insistent for being so long banished.

It is a good idea, then, to keep in touch, and I suppose that keeping in touch is what notebooks are all about. And we are all on our own when it comes to keeping those lines open to ourselves: your notebook will never help me, nor mine you: "*So what's new in the whiskey business?*" What could that possibly mean to you? To me it means a blonde in a Pucci bathing suit sitting with a couple of fat men by the pool at the Beverly Hills Hotel. Another man approaches, and they all regard one another in silence for a while. "So what's new in the whiskey business?" one of the fat men finally says by way of welcome, and the blonde stands up, arches one foot and dips it in the pool, looking all the while at the cabaña where Baby Pignatari is talking on the telephone. That is all there is to that, except that several years later I saw the blonde coming out of Saks Fifth Avenue in New York with her California complexion and a voluminous mink coat. In the harsh wind that day she looked old and irrevocably tired to me, and even the skins in the mink coat were not worked the way they were doing them that year, not the way she would have wanted them done, and there is the point of the story. For a while after that I did not like to look in the mirror, and my eyes would skim the newspapers and pick out only the deaths, the cancer victims, the premature coronaries, the suicides, and I stopped riding the Lexington Avenue IRT because I noticed for the first time that all the strangers I had seen for years—the man with the seeing-eye dog, the spinster who read the classified pages every day, the fat girl who always got off with me at Grand Central—looked older than they once had.

It all comes back. Even that recipe for sauerkraut: even that brings it back. I was on Fire Island when I first made that sauerkraut, and it was raining, and we drank a lot of bourbon and ate the sauerkraut and went to bed at ten, and I listened to the rain and the Atlantic and felt safe. I made the sauerkraut again last night and it did not make me feel any safer, but that is, as they say, another story.

In this essay, we heard Didion's playful voice as it inventories her mind's collection of thoughts. Hers is a writer's notebook. As a novelist and essayist, Didion uses the notebook as a playground to toy with ideas she'll later draft into more formal writing. At the beginning of her essay, Didion offers us a few short clips about a hotel bar across from a railroad station in Wilmington, Delaware, during an unspecific year in the early 1960s. For her, these notes signal an imagined scenario that she creates for us in this essay. She might have used the same notes to write a piece of fiction. However, a fieldworker researching out of those notes would need to talk to the woman in the crepe-de-Chine wrapper, the bartender, and the woman in the plaid silk dress at the other end of the bar to confirm what they said about what was going on there. A fieldworker's notebook probably won't become an essay or a novel, but it will draw on the same writerly skills of close observation and description. Since fieldnotes eventually shape a research study, a fieldworker has a responsibility to inventory not only what's in the mind but also what's actually at the fieldsite and what informants say.

For writer or fieldworker, keeping a notebook can serve two purposes: it documents a moment and contemplates that moment as well. This double process or recording and being conscious of oneself recording allows for many levels of awareness. As experienced anthropologists and journal writers Barbara Myerhoff and Deena Metzger have noted, this journaling process is "a means for acquiring, not merely recording, knowledge." We think that all exploratory writing, whether it's in a notebook from a fieldsite or a five-minute freewrite in a quiet classroom, carries the potential to generate further writing and more informed thinking.

Exploratory Notetaking

Purpose

When several people take notes at the same fieldsite, each person's set of notes, as Joan Didion suggests, is unique. In a field research project, especially at the beginning, it can be instructive to share notes among researchers. We often take our new students to a public event for this purpose of taking and sharing notes. We ask students to record as many details, concrete and personal, as they can about what they experience while they're at the site. This activity will encourage you to develop different notetaking formats and share them in class afterward.

Action

With a group or in pairs, attend a public event at your school or in a local community—a lecture, symposium, reading, recital, planning board meeting, or business presentation. It's difficult to do this exploratory exercise at a large event with many presenters or performers, so try to stay away from concerts, plays, or sports events. Plan to spend at least an hour taking many pages of notes. Many beginning fieldworkers find that they leave out important details of context—the time frame, the composition of the audience and its response, the conditions of the room, the conversation that surrounds them, and some details of the event itself. After taking notes, compare them with others', and think about and develop an efficient notetaking system that works for you.

Response

After Bonnie and her students attended an hour-long poetry reading on campus, they reconvened in class and shared their exploratory notes. There were many kinds of notes: some had recorded the ambiance of the auditorium; others focused on the age, gender, and dress of audience members; still others looked at the gestures and behaviors of the poet himself. Some recorded smells, temperature, lighting, and the sound equipment they saw. Most people included their personal responses to being at a poetry reading in a large auditorium at night when they might have been watching television, hanging out with friends, or studying. The class shared both informational and personal responses to this event. Below are some snippets from their exploratory notes:

Informational Notes
"students quiet, cross-legged, leaning, hands clasped, arms crossed, still, chewing gum,

Personal Notes
"I don't associate poetry readings with packed auditoriums unless, you know, Jewel is reading"

"baseball caps front and back, French braids, corn rows, pierced eyebrows"

"a young man in a black tee shirt with his back toward me and the words 'no speed limit' on his shirt"

"a man with black glasses and a goatee, carrying a bike helmet and a backpack, enters the auditorium and stands"

"a lot of people are chewing gum"

"there is a lot of motion in this listening audience—coughs and sneezes"

"mustard and white striped ceiling, ceiling tiles like it's a hanging ceiling, square lights and vents, holes around the light fixtures"

"what's the maximum seating by fire code?"

"poet licks his lips as he looks from poetry book to poetry book, telling us he's not organized."

"8:18: poet says 'eh, let's see, it's hot in here, I might take off my jacket.'"

"There are eleven blonds in the front row."

"the air smells of a mix of musk oil, Liz Claiborne, sweet to spicy oriental scents, dust and mold"

"audience laughs bigtime when poet uses the word 'shit'"

"Two people are wearing red scarves. I wonder if red scarves have something to do with the poet or poetry reading."

"How do the different generations, genders, and styles of poets present themselves during such public negotiations of identity?"

"How did the popular habit of crossing one's legs begin? Which cultures do this, and what do they have in common? What are the associations with different styles of sitting?"

"My foot is falling asleep. The velcro of my sandal is sticking to the carpet"

"What a peculiar custom, to position one person before, indeed in the midst of, a crowd, have him speak, to no reply."

"That was too long to stand on an empty stomach. I'm hungry, tired, and bitter. How different would my notes have been? What business do I have 'spying' on people attending the reading?"

"The poet is reading about clocks. How many people have never owned a clock that ticks? What does that say about progress in our society?"

"What is audience etiquette? What function do the long pauses serve?"

"I wonder why more women than men have notebooks."

CONSIDERING FIELDNOTES

When you first enter your fieldsite, sensory impressions surround you. You feel as if you'll never get them all down. One of our students tried to describe a band's outdoor concert in a New England harbor town and was initially over-whelmed by how much there was to notice. Should she listen to the sounds of the band she came to hear? Try to eavesdrop on people's conversations about the band as they sat on their blankets? Describe the foghorn in the background? The drawbridge siren? or should she focus on the outdoor smells? The flowers in the formal gardens surrounding the park? Hot dogs? Popcorn? Gyros? Cal-zones? Or the fish harbor air? Her "gaze" expanded as she took more notes. The more she looked, the more she saw. She noted everything in order to capture the feeling of being at the harbor concert, even though she knew her research focus was the band itself, which had been playing together for 20 years.

To become a good fieldworker, you must observe closely and participate intimately, returning to your fieldsite and informants again and again—and still again. As you take fieldnotes, you become better at appreciating what you initially took for granted. You start to gather a thick collection of notes, which will serve as a body of data. Later, you'll turn these notes into descriptions of your fieldsite and your informants. You will take far more fieldnotes than you will ever use in your final description. Professional writers publish perhaps a fifth of the writing they do, and movie directors use only about a tenth of the footage they shoot. A few focused hours with a notebook, a pencil, and receptive senses will help you practice capturing good descriptive details. But for your final project, you'll need to plan many visits at different times to gather details, data, and materials before your writing begins.

No matter how you decide to collect your fieldnotes, it is important to find a system that works for you and the project you've chosen. As you create a note-taking system for your particular study, you organize your data to see what's important. There is no one single accepted format for taking fieldnotes. Each fieldstudy demands a different design for notetaking; each fieldworker needs to adapt notetaking strategies a different way. Because the essence of field research is not to duplicate what someone else saw and thought but to describe and inter-pret data in its particulars, it's not surprising that each study and each researcher's notes are unique.

Your fieldnote system needs to be more organized than the freewrite or the exploratory writing and notetaking we've considered so far. Our experience as researchers has shown us that any fieldnote format that you borrow or design needs to be organized enough so that you can retrieve specific pieces of data eas-ily, even months later. To retrieve the note about red scarves from the poetry mentioned in Box 5, for instance, you'd need to have recorded the time, date, and place at the very least. Or if you wanted to work with the question about crossed legs as body language, you'd need to be able to find it in your pile of research data.

Fieldnotes actually provide a rhetorical construct: they help a fieldworker begin the movement from self to audience. While your personal observations, opinions, and questions can help form your writerly voice (ethos), the informational notes add to your collection of data (logos), and this combination starts to provide you with the authority to write about your fieldwork for different audiences (pathos). As you shuttle back and forth between your personal reflective observations and your increasing piles of data from fieldnotes and other sources, you'll begin to form theories, see connections, follow hunches, and confirm understandings of the culture you're investigating.

Professional fieldworkers take their notes in a variety of ways, using codes and systems they've developed themselves. Here, we show two different samples of anthropologists' fieldnotes to give you further ideas about formats. The first example comes from Roger Sanjek's 1988 study in Queens, New York, which he composed using a word-processing program. He uses his informants' names— Milagros, Carmela, Phil, Jenny, and Mareya. The second study is from Margery Wolf's 1966 notes taken in a village in Taiwan. She assigns numbers and letters —such as 48 (F 30) and 48I (F 12)— to her informants. Although their coding systems are different and their informants are from different times and places, both excerpts are thick with descriptive detail.

Roger Sanjek's Fieldnotes

7 May 1988—*Carmela George's Cleanup Day**

Milagros and I arrived at 10 am, as Carmela told me, but 97th Street, the deadend, was already cleaned out, and the large garbage pickup truck, with rotating blades that crushed everything, was in the middle of 97th Place. I found Carmela, and met Phil Pirozzi of Sanitation, who had three men working on the cleanup, plus the sweeper that arrived a little later. The men and boys on 97th Place helping to load their garbage into the truck included several Guyanese Indians in their 20s, whom Carmela said have been here 2–3 years ['They're good.']; several families of Hispanics, and Korean and Chinese. They were loading TV sets, shopping carts, wood, old furniture, tree branches and pruning, and bags and boxes of garbage. Most houses had large piles of stuff in front, waiting for the truck. The little boys hanging on and helping were Hispanic, except for one Chinese. They spoke a mixture of Spanish and English together, when painting the LIRR walls.

Carmela had put flyers at every house on Wednesday, and Police 'No Parking Saturday' signs [D] were up on the telephone poles. A few cars were parked at the curb, but most of the curbside on the three blocks was empty so the sweeper could clean the gutters.

The sweeper this year was smaller than the one in 1986, and there was no spraying of the streets, only sweeping the gutters. As before, people

---

*A page from Roger Sanjek's 1988 Elmhurst-Corona, Queens, New York, fieldnotes, printed from a computer word-processing program. (Size: 8.5 by 11 inches.)

swept their curbs, and in some cases driveways, into the gutter. Carmela was a whirlwind. She asked her elderly Italian neighbor Jenny, who did not come out, if she could sweep the sand pile near Jenny's house in their common driveway. Jenny said don't bother, but Carmela did it anyway. She was running all around with plastic garbage bags, getting kids to help paint off the graffiti on the LIRR panels she had painted in the past, and commandeering women to clean out the grassy area near the LIRR bridge at 45th Ave and National Street. She got a Colombian woman from 97th Place, and gave her a rake and plastic bag. She then rang the door bell across from the grassy area, behind the bodega, and an Indian-looking Hispanic woman came down, and later did the work with the Colombian woman.

Mareya Banks was out, in smock, helping organize and supervising the kids doing the LIRR wall painting. Milagros helped with this, and set up an interview appointment with Mareya. She also met a Bolivian woman, talking with Mareya, and sweeping her sidewalk on 45th Avenue.

Carmela also had potato chips and Pepsi for the kids, which the Colombian woman gave out to them, and OTB T-shirts.

Phil said this was the only such clean up in CB4. A man in Elmhurst does something like this, but just for his one block. The Dept. likes this, and hopes the spirit will be contagious. We like anything that gets the community involved. He said it began here because the new people didn't understand how to keep the area a nice place to live. Carmela went to them, and now they are involved.

Margery Wolf's Fieldnotes

March 5, 1960*
Present: 153 (F 54), 154 (F 31), 254 (F 53), 189 (F 50), 230 (F 17)

Yesterday 48 (F 30) was taken by her husband to a mental hospital in Tapu. 48I (F 12) told Wu Chieh that the woman ran out into the field, and her husband had to come to pick her up and take her to the hospital. The women were talking about this today and said that she was sent to a big mental hospital, and that her husband went there to see her but was not allowed to see her because she was tied up. The doctor said there was nothing else he could do with her. Someone told Wu Chieh that something like this had happened to 48 once before, but she was not hospitalized then. The women say that her illness this time came about as the result of her worrying about losing NTS90. She couldn't find the money and asked 49 (her seven-year-old son) about it, and he told her that his father took it to gamble. Her husband said that this was not true. They said that she may have known that she was going to get sick, because the day before she took her baby (3 months) over to her sister's house and asked her to take care of the baby.

---

*A page from Margery Wolf's fieldnotes taken in Taiwan. Wu Chieh is her informant/assistant, and Wolf assigns numbers to other informants.

They said that 47 (her 32-year-old husband) was very dumb. If he knows that his wife has this kind of illness, he should not let her worry. He should have said that he had taken the money even if he didn't. Instead, when she started to get sick, he stood there and told everyone, "She is going to go crazy, she is going to go crazy." The women said that this is the reason 47 is called "Dumb Tien-lai." 154: "When 492's (F28) children and 48's children got into a fight and 48 went to talk with 492 about it, 492 scolded 48. She said: 'If children fight and kill each other it serves them right. If your children get killed, then you come and take your children home and bury them. You don't need to come and talk to me about it.' But once when 48's child hit 492's child, 492 went out and said something to 48, and she just said this back to her and then she had nothing to say." (All of the women agreed that 492 had said this to 48.)

Wu Chieh heard that 47 is going to go ask T'ai Tzu Yeh [a god] to help his wife get well. The women also said that when 48 fell into the field, she lay there saying: "Just because of children's things other people bully me, other people bully me just because of children's things. I won't forget this. I won't forget this." The women said that when a person is like this, you shouldn't let them worry and should encourage them to sleep a lot.

Entire books and scholarly articles are devoted to writing and analyzing fieldnotes and explaining researchers' attitudes about their fieldnotes. Anthropologist Jean Jackson, who interviewed field researchers, discovered that many have nightmares about losing their fieldnotes to fires or thieves: "Anxiety about loss of fieldnotes has come up so many times and so dramatically—Images of burning appear quite often.... The many legends, apocryphal or not, about lost fieldnotes probably fits into this category of horrific and yet delicious, forbidden fantasy." Since fieldnotes become the backbone of any fieldstudy, it's no wonder that professional fieldworkers attribute such power and fear to this kind of writing.

Fieldnotes can range from scraps taken furtively on small bits of paper when a researcher wants to be unobtrusive to complex computer programs designed specifically for organizing large amounts of data. The first time you enter your chosen fieldsite, your biggest challenge is figuring out *what* to record. Like freewriting and exploratory notes, fieldnotes include sensory impressions, nascent thoughts, and snippets of conversation. Our own students often feel so overwhelmed by the sheer amount of possible data to record that at first they write very little. As beginning researchers, we both had the same problem.

Elizabeth remembers her first visit to a classroom as a fieldworker. Although she'd spent many years in many classrooms as a teacher, she felt helpless. Should she write down everything or nothing? What was important? Was it the words on the teacher's handouts, the configuration of the furniture, the banging of a jackhammer outside, the heat of the late afternoon, the stickers on the students' notebooks, the patterns of conversation, the flyers pinned to the walls, the flickering of the fluorescent lights? Forty-five minutes later, she had scribbled very little in her research notebook: "Why did the teacher waste so much time explaining her handout when the students could have read it? I wish that wiggly kid would quit talking under his breath when I can't hear what he has to say. I wonder how long it's been since this room has been painted." She wanted to change her topic and find another fieldsite. But she didn't.

The next day, Elizabeth entered the classroom, turned to a fresh page in her notebook, and began to make lists. First, she wrote down important identifying information: the time, the date, the name of the building, the number on the classroom door. She sketched a small map showing where everyone was sitting, noting windows, doors, and placement of furniture. She developed a code for noting genders, assigning M's and F's, and gave a number to each student. She then made lots of lists—kinds of shoes, colors and sayings on T-shirts, types of bookbags and backpacks. Then she counted things—how many windows were open and how many were closed, who wore nose rings and who wore engagement rings, how many students brought their textbooks to class and how many didn't. She noted specific **underlife** behaviors—who was taking notes and who was asleep, who was whispering and who was putting on makeup. She concentrated on writing down as much dialogue as possible—both the topics and the patterns of what the teacher and students were saying—who spoke and for how long. Although she was not sure what was important or what information would make it into her final study, she trained herself to record more systematically, and over time her fieldnotes became more and more focused. By the end of a month she knew her study would be about gender and conversation in a college writing classroom.

Sharing Your Initial Fieldnotes

BOX 6

Purpose

It's a good idea to spend some time at your possible fieldsite making yourself feel at ease there, before you start taking fieldnotes. Once you do begin writing, it's also a good idea to get feedback from one or more colleagues who can help you identify strengths and weaknesses in your initial notes.

Action

Take a set of fieldnotes at a site you are considering or at which you have decided on becoming a **participant-observer**. Note important information like time, location, date, weather, and your vantage point. You may also draw a sketch or a map of the space, indicating shapes, objects, focal points, and movement patterns. Listen and look at the people there, and record as much information about them as possible. Create a consistent shorthand or code that you understand in order to develop a notetaking scheme that you will be able to follow throughout your project. Practice ways to differentiate between verifiable information (12 spotted cows) and your own subjective responses to or reflections on the data ("Yuck. It stinks. It reminds me of my great-uncle's outhouse"). Once you have 10 pages of notes or so, review them, and try to write a short summary of the fieldsite using your best details, so that a research partner will understand them. While you may develop a personal code (as Margery Wolf's or Roger Sanjeck's fieldnotes show), at this point, your notes should be clear enough to share with someone else. This is your first step toward shaping your work for an audience.

Bring your fieldnotes and your summary to a research partner for sharing. Here are some questions you and your partner should consider as you read and respond to one another's fieldnotes:

1. Are the notes readable? Are the pages numbered and dated?
2. What background material does someone need to understand the history and location of this place?
3. Does the researcher include information about her subjective feelings as she observes?
4. What other details should she include so that another person could see, hear, and become immersed in the daily routines of this place?
5. What details are most interesting? What would you like the researcher to write more about?
6. What other data do you need to confirm some of the researcher's initial observations about this place?

Response

In one of our classes, Simone Henkel read Tara Tisue's fieldnotes on the morale captains at an annual university event, the dance marathon. The dance marathon is a charity fund-raiser, held in a large auditorium. Students volunteer to dance for hours; the more hours they dance, the more money they raise. The morale captains, whom Tara observes, are the leaders who keep students' spirits up. After reading Tara's study, Simone responded to the above questions as follows:

1. The notes are neatly printed and numbered and dated. The location of the site is also noted.
2. The background material regarding the history of the dance marathon included where it started, how long it's been happening here at our university. Tara might include the details of what happens at various other sites, since every university will shape this event a bit differently depending on the time of year and the students who choose to participate.

3. I am not sure what feelings Tara brings to her site. This is interesting that she excludes her feelings since Tara has been involved prior to this year. Tara might include how she thought the first year she was a morale captain herself.

4. Tara offers a good picture of what the people are doing, the feeling of being there (smells, sounds, sights, etc.). I can picture the auditorium because I know what it looks like. I think a more detailed description would be helpful, specifically, an expanded description of the auditorium.

5. The most interesting description was of all the water bottles, the soaked red T-shirts, the pony tails flying, the scuffing sounds on the floor, and the specific songs they played over the speakers.

6. I think I'd like to hear more about how the morale captains meet regularly, how long before the event itself, and who trained them. It would also be interesting to know what other students think about the dance marathon through a series of interviews. What about students who won't go? I'd also like to know what they think about the event!

CONSIDERING DETAILS

Most of us need to train ourselves to become better observers of our surroundings by exercising our vision along with expanding other senses. In her book *A Natural History of the Senses,* Diane Ackerman writes that "seventy percent of the body's sense receptors cluster in the eyes, and it is mainly through seeing the world that we appraise and understand it" (230). Of course, seeing can also be deceptive; we can become overreliant on what we think we see, screening the world through predetermined filters.

Anthropologist Paul Stoller suggests that personal experiences affect what people see and how they think. We experienced this ourselves when we rented a house in Maine together to write this book, and searched for the mailbox that the owner said was attached to the garage. Elizabeth returned empty-handed from her first mail run and reported to Bonnie that the only nearby box read "169." When we complained to the owner, she laughed and said, "Oh, that really means 199. The nine turned upside-down into a six, and we never fixed it." "How very Maine," we both thought, as we reprimanded ourselves for not reading these numbers with the same "gaze" that the postal carrier, the owner, and perhaps all Downeasterners do. Ethnographic fieldworkers teach themselves to see in new ways. They test what they think they see against their preconceptions and assumptions.

As art historian John Berger writes, "We only see what we look at. To look is an act of choice" (8). In your first trip to the field, details might seem so familiar that you do not lift your pencil to record a single thing. You don't record sounds or smells or textures; you passively wait. You're frustrated. You decide to change field sites. You have not yet learned to look. Seeing—establishing a gaze—requires receptivity, patience, and a willingness to penetrate the outer layer of things.

Our student Karen Downing studied a glamour photography business called Photo Phantasies (which you'll read more about in Chapter 5). Karen took seven pages of fieldnotes on what she saw when she gained entry to Photo Phantasies for the first time. Figure 2.2 shows two excerpts from her notes (two visits on the same day). Notice that her fieldnotes come from descriptions of the site and interviews with staff and customers.

Like Karen, you should develop a personal, systematic way of taking field-notes. Your system should allow enough room to record details at the site, but it should also allow space to expand your initial impressions away from the site. Some people like to use spiral notebooks, some use three-ring binder paper, some use papers to be filed in folders, and some use laptop computers, keeping a separate file for each visit. Fieldnotes are your evidence for confirming theories you make about the observations you record. They are the permanent record of your fieldworking process, and they become part of your research portfolio. Without accurate fieldnotes, you have no project. Although each fieldworker develops his or her own system, any set of fieldnotes needs to include all of the following details:

- Date, time, and place of observation ("Friday, April 6, 11:45 in the store")
- Specific facts, numbers, details ("last appointment at 7 p.m.," "3 customers present," "sign: 'professional makeup artist'")
- Sensory impressions: sights, sounds, textures, smells, tastes ("caramel corn smells, footsteps on tile, children crying, pop music playing fairly loud, gray carpet with muted pink, white walls, black modern furniture, notebook of thank-you notes")
- Personal responses to the act of recording fieldnotes and how others watch you as you watch them ("Giant pictures of Phantasy Phaces. They look pretty darn good. Are these pics taken in this store?")
- Specific words, phrases, summaries of conversations, and insider language ("Girl inquires about modeling special. Asks, 'Do you do it now?' Response: 'Not really, but you really have a nice forehead. You could be a runway model.'")
- Questions about people or behaviors at the site for future investigation ("dressing rooms are small—they don't want you there for long")
- Continuous page-numbering system for future reference ("4/4 studio visit, page 5")

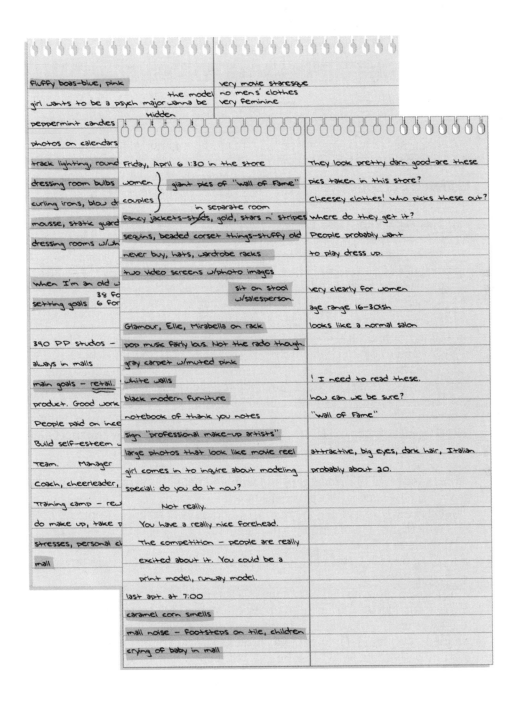

Figure 2.2. Karen's fieldnotes

We develop observational skills through practice and careful notetaking. In the following short essay, "Look at Your Fish," Samuel Scudder, a student in the nineteenth century who aspired to study entomology (insects), first learns to observe from his professor Louis Agassiz (1808–73) whose lessons in natural science are legendary.

Look at Your Fish
Samuel H. Scudder

Samuel H. Scudder (1837–1911), a naturalist who specialized in the study of insects, wrote this amusing account for a Boston literary journal in 1873. He tells of enrolling at Harvard's Lawrence Scientific School and of his first lesson under the inspired teacher and popularizer of science, Louis Agassiz (1807–1873), then professor of natural history. After hours of detailed but unpatterned observation, Scudder let his problem incubate during an evening away from the laboratory.

It was more than fifteen years ago that I entered the laboratory of Professor Agassiz, and told him I had enrolled my name in the Scientific School as a student of natural history. He asked me a few questions about my object in coming, my antecedents generally, the mode in which I afterwards proposed to use the knowledge I might acquire, and, finally, whether I wished to study any special branch. To the latter I replied that, while I wished to be well grounded in all departments of zoology, I purposed to devote myself especially to insects.

"When do you wish to begin?" he asked.

"Now," I replied.

This seemed to please him, and with an energetic "Very well!" he reached from a shelf a huge jar of specimens in yellow alcohol. "Take this fish," he said, "and look at it; we call it a haemulon; by and by I will ask what you have seen."

With that he left me, but in a moment returned with explicit instructions as to the care of the object entrusted to me.

"No man is fit to be a naturalist," said he, "who does not know how to take care of specimens."

I was to keep the fish before me in a tin tray, and occasionally moisten the surface with alcohol from the jar, always taking care to replace the stopper tightly. Those were not the days of ground-glass stoppers and elegantly shaped exhibition jars; all the old students will recall the huge neckless glass bottles with their leaky, wax-besmeared corks, half eaten by insects, and begrimed with cellar dust. Entomology was a cleaner science than ichthyology, but the example of the Professor, who had unhesitatingly plunged to the bottom of the jar to produce the fish, was infectious; and though this alcohol had a "very ancient and fishlike smell," I really dared not show any aversion within these sacred precincts, and treated the alcohol as though it were pure water.

Still I was conscious of a passing feeling of disappointment, for gazing at a fish did not commend itself to an ardent entomologist. My friends at home, too, were annoyed when they discovered that no amount of eau-de-Cologne would drown the perfume which haunted me like a shadow.

In ten minutes I had seen all that could be seen in that fish, and started in search of the Professor—who had, however, left the Museum; and when I returned, after lingering over some of the odd animals stored in the upper apartment, my specimen was dry all over. I dashed the fluid over the fish as if to resuscitate the beast from a fainting fit, and looked with anxiety for a return of the normal sloppy appearance. This little excitement over, nothing was to be done but to return to a steadfast gaze at my mute companion. Half an hour passed—an hour—another hour; the fish began to look loathsome. I turned it over and around; looked it in the face—ghastly; from behind, beneath, above, sideways at a three-quarters' view—just as ghastly. I was in despair; at an early hour I concluded that lunch was necessary; so, with infinite relief, the fish was carefully replaced in the jar, and for an hour I was free.

On my return, I learned that Professor Agassiz had been at the Museum, but had gone, and would not return for several hours. My fellow-students were too busy to be disturbed by continued conversation. Slowly I drew forth that hideous fish, and with a feeling of desperation again looked at it. I might not use a magnifying-glass; instruments of all kinds were interdicted. My two hands, my two eyes, and the fish: it seemed a most limited field. I pushed my finger down its throat to feel how sharp the teeth were. I began to count the scales in the different rows, until I was convinced that that was nonsense. At last a happy thought struck me—I would draw the fish; and now with surprise I began to discover new features in the creature. Just then the Professor returned.

"That is right," said he; "a pencil is one of the best of eyes. I am glad to notice, too, that you keep your specimen wet, and your bottle corked."

With these encouraging words, he added:

"Well, what is it like?"

He listened attentively to my brief rehearsal of the structure of parts whose names were still unknown to me: the fringed gill-arches and movable opercu-lum; the pores of the head, fleshy lips and lidless eyes; the lateral line, the spinous fins and forked tail; the compressed and arched body. When I finished, he waited as if expecting more, and then, with an air of disappointment:

"You have not looked very carefully; why," he continued more earnestly, "you haven't even seen one of the most conspicuous features of the animal, which is as plainly before your eyes as the fish itself; look again, look again!" and he left me to my misery.

I was piqued; I was mortified. Still more of that wretched fish! But now I set myself to my task with a will, and discovered one new thing after another, until I saw how just the Professor's criticism had been. The afternoon passed quickly; and when, towards its close, the Professor inquired:

"Do you see it yet?"

"No," I replied, "I am certain I do not, but I see how little I saw before."

"That is next best," said he, earnestly. "But I won't hear you now; put away your fish and go home; perhaps you will be ready with a better answer in the morning. I will examine you before you look at the fish."

This was disconcerting. Not only must I think of my fish all night, studying, without the object before me, what this unknown but most visible feature might be; but also, without reviewing my discoveries, I must give an exact account of them the next day. I had a bad memory; so I walked home by the Charles River in a distracted state, with my two perplexities.

The cordial greeting from the Professor the next morning was reassuring; here was a man who seemed to be quite as anxious as I that I should see for myself what he saw.

"Do you perhaps mean," I asked, "that the fish has symmetrical sides with paired organs?"

His thoroughly pleased "Of course! Of course!" repaid the wakeful hours of the previous night. After he had discoursed most happily and enthusiastically —as he always did—upon the importance of this point, I ventured to ask what I should do next.

"Oh, look at your fish!" he said, and left me again to my own devices. In a little more than an hour he returned, and heard my new catalogue.

"That is good, that is good!" he repeated; "but that is not all; go on"; and so for three long days he placed that fish before my eyes, forbidding me to look at anything else, or to use any artificial aid. "Look, look, look," was his repeated injunction.

This was the best entomological lesson I ever had—a lesson whose influence has extended to the details of every subsequent study; a legacy the Professor had left to me, as he has left it to many others, of inestimable value, which we could not buy, with which we cannot part.

A year afterward, some of us were amusing ourselves with chalking outlandish beasts on the Museum blackboard. We drew prancing starfishes; frogs in mortal combat; hydra-headed worms; stately crawfishes, standing on their tails, bearing aloft umbrellas; and grotesque fishes with gaping mouths and staring eyes. The Professor came in shortly after, and was as amused as any at our experiments. He looked at the fishes.

"Haemulons, every one of them," he said; "Mr. _____ drew them."

True; and to this day, if I attempt a fish, I can draw nothing but haemulons.

The fourth day, a second fish of the same group was placed beside the first, and I was bidden to point out the resemblances and differences between the two; another and another followed, until the entire family lay before me, and a whole legion of jars covered the table and surrounding shelves; the odor had become a pleasant perfume; and even now, the sight of an old, six-inch, worm-eaten cork brings fragrant memories.

The whole group of haemulons was thus brought in review; and, whether engaged upon the dissection of the internal organs, the preparation and examination of the bony framework, or the description of the various parts, Agassiz's training in the method of observing facts and their orderly arrangement was ever accompanied by the urgent exhortation not to be content with them.

"Facts are stupid things," he would say, "until brought into connection with some general law."

At the end of eight months, it was almost with reluctance that I left these friends and turned to insects; but what I had gained by this outside experience has been of greater value than years of later investigation in my favorite groups.

Scudder's observational training comes from Agassiz, a natural scientist, but it is equally important for the social scientist. Both researchers learn to gaze beyond the obvious—to look and then to look again. Scudder used many of the same skills that ethnographic researchers rely on—drawing pictures, asking focused questions, and "sleeping on the data."

The fieldworker can model Scudder's experience by looking at something unfamiliar, too. With time, knowledge, and familiarity, the fieldworker's boredom will turn to interest. With constant practice and attention, almost any fieldsite and the people in it become fascinating. Scudder faced one of the most humbling experiences a fieldworker can have—to discover how little he actually saw the first time. After looking long and hard, Scudder also realized that the mere recording of data—"facts are stupid things"—is not important unless you connect it with some larger idea. Before you undertake fieldwork in your chosen site, as Karen did, it is good practice to observe an everyday object or event to consider its significance.

Here's what we've imagined that Scudder might have written in his few hours with the fish:

Record	Respond
9–9:10 (first 10 minutes):	
jar—yellow alcohol	does yellow alcohol indicate old?
called a "haemulon"	is that its classification? phylum? kingdom? species?
"keep fish moistened?"	why keep it wet if it's dead?
	will it crumble? dry out? is it old?
9:30–12:00 (next 2 ½ hours):	
dries after 10 minutes	how much alcohol can a fish absorb?
all views the same (5 views:	why does it look ghastly from all positions,
under, over, side, ¾, behind)	perspectives?
throat-teeth sharp	must eat hard things—shells, fish skin?
scales in rows	possible symmetry?
(sketch)	fish looks like a fish, but more complicated than at first

We wrote these notes above to demonstrate another way of keeping field-notes, one that we and our students have found most useful. We borrow this notetaking idea from composition theorist Ann Berthoff, who developed this form as a way to encourage her students to both look, reflect, and write about natural objects. In her book *The Making of Meaning* (1981), she shows how writers can audit their own thoughts as they create them, searching for patterns and bringing order to what may have seemed random observations:

> Critical awareness is consciousness of *consciousness* (a name for the active mind). Minding the mind, being conscious of consciousness, is not the same sort of thing as thinking about your elbows when you are about to pitch a baseball: nor is it *self-consciousness*. Consciousness, in meaning-making activity, always involves us in interpreting our interpretations. (11)

Like all exploratory writing, the **double-entry notes** are designed to make your mind spy on itself and generate further thinking and text. To write double-entry fieldnotes, divide the page vertically, using the left-hand side for direct observations—concrete, verifiable details. The right-hand side is the place to capture your personal reactions, opinions, feelings, and questions about the data on the left side. It's a good idea to number each observation (the left side) and response (the right side) to keep track of your data collection. Like Samuel Scudder, these closely honed notes allow you to "look at your fish." Our students have adapted this phrase as a research mantra. In reading one another's field-notes, exchanging early descriptions of fieldsites, we often hear them suggesting to one another, "LOOK AT YOUR FISH!"

Figure 2.3. Fish Scales (Anthony Guyther)

Double-Entry Notes

Purpose

To practice the art of double-entry notetaking, it's useful at first to focus on something that's not at your fieldsite (where the actions and sensory details can be overwhelming and you know there's a whole project at stake). Instead, try this exercise. Select an ordinary object or event in nature to observe every day for a week. Our students have taken notes on such different things as snow forming and melting on a windshield, coffee grounds accumulating in a trash can, a finch's nesting activities, a cut on a finger as it develops into a scar, and dirt forming in an unattended bathtub.

Action

Record your notes over the course of a week in double-entry format, using the left-hand side of the page to list specific details of the changes you observe and the right-hand side of the page to reflect on the meaning of these changes. Your subject must be one that alters in some way within a week's time. At the end of the week, look over the notes carefully, see what's changed and what hasn't, and write a short reflection on what you learned by keeping these field-notes. Discuss what surprised you most and what you would do differently if you were to continue with this observation. How might you connect what you have seen with an overall hunch or hypothesis?

Response

Our student Grant Stanojev observed the bathtub he shares with his two room-mates and kept a double-entry notebook over the course of six days. These are his recorded notes and reflective responses:

OBSERVATION OF A BATHTUB IN NEED OF A SHOWER

Grant Stanojev

Record	Respond
2/12 White tub around edges with brown crust along the doors. Rings under each shampoo bottle. New bar of Dial soap. The drain drains slowly.	Most of this observation is pretty typical of the apartment. Three guys shower in here once a day and it shows.
2/13 The visible soap has stray hairs plastered to it. One bottle of	Not too much going on. The guys had a basketball game last night so

conditioner is placed upside down. Unused washcloth hangs stiffly on bar.

the tub got an extra workout. Kind of gross that none of us use the washcloth.

2/14   Soap is starting to have a slimy film surrounding it. The bottom of the tub is slippery and a little on the beige side. The crust around the edges is particularly dark today. Drain is backing up and is about halfway up the foot as shower proceeds.

The theme of today seems to be film (tub, soap, me). Starting to realize just how big of slobs we really are.

2/15   Bar of soap has dwindled considerably. Water actually covers the feet today and rests around the ankles. Cannot even see through the water.

This is getting disgusting. Went to a concert last night so the soap had to scrub off the layer of smoke and the "legal" stamp on each of our right hands.

2/16   Water is around the ankles again. Dishcloth is wet. There is a nasty clump of black hair wadded on top of the drain. More gone from the soap.

Another night out for the guys so same results. A little repulsed by the hair that has accumulated. More repulsed that no one has removed it yet.

2/17   Crust around the edges of everything is a nice golden bronze. Filth lines the bottom of the tub.

Roommates are getting restless at the sight of the bathroom. It even became the subject of conversation. Still no one does anything. I think the end is near though. Everyone is sick of the crust on the tub.

What really struck me was the lack of motivation in our apartment. It was important enough for the guys to play basketball for our health but not to bathe in a sanitary environment. Standing in my own filth is something I would never do if I still lived with my parents. I knew that we were pigs, but I never really documented the decay of our bathing facilities. Bacteria is probably everywhere in our bathroom, and to tell you the truth I am not sure exactly why that is bad. I know it is not sanitary though and it is disgusting to wash yourself in it. I told my roommates that I brought it up in class and Dave cleaned the tub the next day.

CONSIDERING ANALYSIS

Most fieldworkers write their notes while they're in the field, but some find themselves in situations where they can take only minimal notes on site. They must return to their desk to flesh out and expand the scanty notes they took while they were in the field. Bonnie and Elizabeth have both worked in teacher-preparation programs in which students are often required to observe classrooms. In such sites, observers see so much activity and evoke so many emotions and memories that they find it impossible at the time to write it all down. When we do fieldwork in schools, we follow the advice we give our students. Before you go back to your busy life with all its distractions, take some time to sit quietly and write in your notebook. Expand your fieldnotes by reading them, by adding details of conversations, sensory impressions, and contextual information, by noting your observations and reflections, and by jotting down possible questions and hunches. Analysis begins with reviewing your notes.

Just as fieldworkers develop many systems for notetaking, they invent, develop, and devise systems for organizing, coding, and retrieving data. Colored folders, highlighters, stick-on (or "sticky") notes, hanging folder boxes, and three-ring binders can be a researcher's best friends. Computers, too, have organizing features that can help you label and find pieces of your fieldnotes when you need them. Accumulating a solid set of fieldnotes is only one step in the process of creating a fieldwork project. You probably know that taking notes in a lecture class does you little good if you try to review them all for the first time the night before a test. Just as periodic review of your lecture notes helps you understand complicated material, your fieldnotes will speak to you if you read them regularly. In reviewing your fieldnotes, you will begin to find recurring themes, images, metaphors that will form patterns. These patterns will help you form your beginning interpretations. Some fieldworkers write weekly memos culled from their fieldnotes, pulling together pieces of data around an emerging idea.

We have developed a helpful kind of analysis memo that involves three key questions to ask and write about regularly as you review your data. These questions will guide the work we discuss throughout this entire book. While we haven't yet introduced you to some of these concepts in detail, we feel that these questions are worth considering even at the beginning of your fieldwork project:

1. **What surprised me? (tracking assumptions)**   This question helps you keep track of your assumptions throughout the fieldwork process. When you ask yourself this question regularly, you'll articulate your preconceived notions about this project and also record how they change.

2. **What intrigued me? (tracking positions)**   Asking this question makes you aware of your personal stances in relationship to your research topic. As we've already suggested, you as the fieldworker are the instrument (recorder and presenter) of the research process. So what interests and attracts you about your project will always influence what you record and how you write about it.

This question helps you understand the complex idea of positioning, which we discuss in Chapter 3.

3. **What disturbed me? (tracking tensions)** This question exposes yourself to yourself. It requires honesty about your blind spots, stereotypes, prejudices, and the things you find upsetting, no matter how small. Focusing on what bothers you about a field project is not always comfortable, but it often leads to important insights.

In time, these three questions should become a kind of mantra for your field study.

Fieldnotes enhance your ability to step in and step out of the culture you've chosen. From your earliest freewriting as you think about a topic, through the notes you take as you enter your fieldsite, to the reflections you write for yourself as you look back and question what you wrote, fieldnotes offer you the details, language, perspectives, and perceptions that will eventually become your final written product. We hope you'll take fieldnotes with care and patience and treat them as you would any other kind of source material. Although you may not realize it, your fieldnotes create an original source, a primary source that no one else has recorded in the same way you have, at the site you've chosen, and with the people you've studied.

BOX 8

Questioning Your Fieldnotes

Purpose

During the course of your research, your assumptions, positions, and tensions will probably change a lot, and looking over your notes will help you see how you learn about your site and your informants as your research progresses. Continually asking the three key questions introduced on p. 95 will help you check in on your research and become aware of your own changing attitudes, stances, and even blind spots as you gather new data. You will actually see your knowledge deepen in your researcher's journal.

Action

Look over the notes you've taken in your researcher's journal so far. Try for the first time to ask these three key questions:

- **What surprised me?**
- **What intrigued me?**
- **What disturbed me?**

Response

Holly Richardson is a high school teacher in Alaska who grew up in western New York and worked with us in Massachusetts. To prepare to teach her Alaskan students how to do fieldwork, she practiced by doing a field study of her own. Holly decided to study a bingo game at an American Legion hall:

> Ever since I was a young girl, I have accompanied my mother and a slew of her friends to bingo games at various Veterans of Foreign War posts, Indian reservations, Catholic churches, and volunteer fire stations in Western New York. In my adult life, I have attended bingo games in central Alaska—sometimes just for fun and sometimes to raffle off items or do 50/50 drawings for my student government group. I've always been intrigued by the superstitions and rituals that surface at these games. Although I am not particularly superstitious, I find myself rubbing my neighbor's winnings or coding a particular game by marking an edge with the dabber, hoping that the game will bring me luck. There are mostly women at the games, and usually there is a mix of ages, although the majority are probably over 50. The men seem to accompany the women, not vice versa. Until now, I never actually took notes on what people around me were doing at these games.
>
> *What surprised me?* I went outside before the game started and during the 10-minute break to smoke a cigarette and talk to some of my fellow addicts. As usual, the chitchat was of gas prices, cigarette prices, and our terrible habits. But there was an underlying feeling of camaraderie in this group that didn't seem directly related to bingo, but maybe it was. I realized I was being accepted into their bingo circle merely because we were smoking together. This surprised me; I just haven't thought about it before.
>
> *What intrigued me?* As I began to think about the 10 years I have spent on front porches or in smoking sections, I realized that these strangers whom I meet have shared their life stories with me. I remember and am intrigued by the hundreds of people whose wisdom about life, strengths, and failures have been in my life. I wanted the smoking area to become my central area of focus.
>
> *What disturbed me?* I went to the bingo game to observe the players, not to focus on the smokers! I was disturbed by my feeling when I was with them. They took me into their lives and shared with me. This has been happening for 10 years, and I am only now realizing it. I wonder if the kindness and closeness I feel with my fellow smokers is part of the addiction I can't seem to kick. I understand why AA meetings can be so important to people. But I'm here to study bingo!

As she reread her fieldnotes and wrote in her journal, Holly realized that she needed to either write more about the bingo games—or focus on the cluster of interesting and talkative people with whom she'd developed a relationship during their smoking breaks. You can see that these three questions helped Holly understand that she had many different ways of researching this site and finding a focus for her study.

THE RESEARCH PORTFOLIO: REFLECTING ON YOUR FIELDNOTES

In Chapter 1, we called the research portfolio a "behind-the-scenes account of the story of your research" and mentioned four key activities of portfolio keeping: collecting materials, selecting according to your emerging focus, reflecting on the overall data and themes, and projecting as you look forward toward further progress and continue to form your plans. Collecting and selecting are activities that come with the abundance of data you gather and sort. Projecting, as we use it here, is a sophisticated kind of goal setting that naturally emerges as you work with your fieldsite and recognize what more you need to learn. Having gotten to college, you've already had practice with similar forms of these activities.

Reflecting, as we see it, is a skill with which most people need particular practice and strategies. To reflect is to think about your own thinking, to monitor the evidence of your mind's work. Although it may seem a bit counterintuitive and self-indulgent to spend time looking over, judging, assessing, and evaluating the growing products of your own learning, of course it's quite the opposite. And all you need to start the process of thinking about your thinking is a pack of stick-on notes (such as Post-its) or index cards.

Gathering pages and pages of fieldnotes won't help you unless you take the time to reread them and reflect about what they mean—to you, to your site, and to your informants. What data relate to your positions as a researcher? What information confirms your initial hunches? What artifacts speak about your site and your informants? Which of your informants' words explain larger ideas about the subculture you're studying? Try writing one- or two-line summaries on stick-on notes or index cards explaining what's important about certain pieces of data and then affix them to your fieldnotes. While you're doing this, you'll begin to understand more about your project and your position in relationship to it. Then you'll get better at choosing material for your research portfolio that's a representation of your work. For an example of a whole research portfolio complete with little note summaries, see Karen Downing's portfolio in the special portfolio section in Chapter 5.

As you collect fieldnotes, pictures, and artifacts, data will accumulate quickly. Stick-on notes are particularly useful tools because their small size forces you to summarize succinctly and they're easy to replace as your insights change over the course of your project. Once you have your fieldnotes captioned with a stick-on note, you can lay out the array of data to see what kinds of larger themes emerge.

Writing teachers refer to this type of thinking about thinking as **metacognition**. Metacognitive work, such as periodically taking notes on your notes, helps you with analysis, the complex thinking you'll need to do about what all this data might mean—to you, to your informants, and in relationship to other similar research. By monitoring your thinking as your data and research material accumulate and testing your ideas with captions or summaries on stick-on notes, you will begin the process of analysis.

Holly Richardson's initial fieldnotes (discussed in Box 8 on page 97), were about superstitions, rituals, and gender at bingo games:

> I've always been intrigued by the superstitions and rituals that surface at these games. Although I am not particularly superstitious, I find myself rubbing my neighbor's winnings or coding a particular game by marking an edge with the dabber, hoping that the game will bring me luck. There are mostly women at the games, and usually there is a mix of ages, although the majority are probably over 50. The men seem to accompany the women, not vice versa. Until now, I never actually took notes on what people around me were doing at these games.

It wasn't until Holly reread her notes that she realized she could track all three of these important aspects of bingo games in her study: superstitions, rituals, and gender. The process of rereading enabled her to write the following analysis on a stick-on note: "The bingo dabber is only one of the rituals I need to keep track of. I know that there are many others." Another note says, "Gender: I counted so many more women than men. My experience tells me this is representative." And another says, "Superstitions: bingo is a game of chance, and people have their lucky charms." Holly's analysis will guide her further fieldnotes because she has alerted her mind to some significant themes she might pursue as she continues this project.

FIELDWRITING: POINT OF VIEW

You may have encountered the term *point of view* in a literature course in which discussions focus on the angle of vision from which a story is told. Telling a story from inside a character's head, as you know, is significantly different from telling a story through an omniscient third-person narrator. As our colleague Jim Marshall says, "Where you stand is what you see." But as a fieldworker, your job is to stand in several places and see through multiple sets of eyes.

Ethnographic writing needs to include many different points of view, and that means you'll need to find ways to signal to your reader when you're shifting from one to another. You need to include your own first-person point of view (often, as in Nora's writing in this chapter, you'll want to represent both your present perspective and your former point of view). You also need to include the points of view of your informants as you've gathered them through interviews, as well as a third-person outsider point of view to report on background information and to present events as readers might see them.

Using double-entry notes as we've described them in this chapter will force your reflective observations (the notes on the right side of the page) to connect to or correspond with details and facts (the notes on the left side of the page). It's useful from the outset to take some of your exploratory writing or initial fieldnotes, turn them into short descriptions of people or places, and experiment —for example, try shifting points of view from first-person insider to third-person outsider. Changing point of view can help you locate missing or underdeveloped information about your fieldsite and the informants and, in turn, suggest another round of research you'd want to do.

Here is how Terra Savage moved from the exploratory writing she did about her conflicting feelings as she entered the tattoo parlor (Box 4) to more of a description of the tattoo parlor subculture as she listens to Chance, the tattooist, talk about the artistry of his work. We'll include a few key phrases from her first freewrite:

> Grunge. Class. No Stress. Responsibility. Lacking education. Overachiever. Artistic. Artistic? Family. Tattoo artisan. Me. At first glance, there seems to be no relationship between my life and this tattoo parlor. But take another look, the more I stare I am not so different.
>
> Men with tattoos ride Harley Davidsons and are running from middle age.... Tattoos on teenage kids are a way for them to rebel. My mom would threaten me with my life.

Over several drafts, Terra moves from her early exploratory first-person freewriting to this point of view in her final field study in which she describes Chance and quotes from what he has to say. She is doing the delicate job of giving us both her perspective and Chance's, by using a third-person narrative point of view:

> Chance is a tattoo artist at Infinite Arts Tattoo who enjoys what he does. He has a medium build and black hair that he wears in a ponytail. He has quite a few tattoos. The one big one that was visible on his arm is of a dragon. Chance explains, "Getting started in the tattoo business"—he seems to drift back to what may have been a lifetime ago—"spent a long time in kitchens and doing construction work, also doing a lot of drawing, trying to get my name out there. Going to lots of tattoo shops. Pretty much working for minimum wage and trying to find someone to teach me how to tattoo."
>
> Chance gives a picture of a poor starving artisan trying to make his way. Chance goes on, "You can't go to the university and say here's five thousand dollars, give me a trade. You have to find someone who is willing to teach you."

Chance describes how he takes on the role of the customer. He says, "By me being an artist, I still try to let the others have enough artistic freedom without my interfering. There becomes a thin line between a piece of painting that you hang on the wall and a piece of painting that you put on your skin."

Gradually Terra comes back to herself in this fieldstudy, and includes some of the earlier feelings she wrote about in her exploratory writing:

Can a connoisseur of tattoos tell the difference between one artist and the next by examining your skin? As I began thinking more through the eyes of the tattoo artist, I realized that there were similarities between me and them. I saw them as artists and understood.

Try taking some of your exploratory writing about the subculture you are studying and some of your early fieldnotes to play with point of view. Ask yourself where you can best include your own perspective and where you need to change your angle of vision and include third-person description as well as the actual words of your informants. Be aware of the multiple points of view that ethnography attempts as it constructs different stances and positions for the reader. When a field researcher is conscious of manipulating or working with different points of view, she is using her knowledge of rhetoric to achieve desired effects. In ethnographic writing, the more perspectives you include within a study and the more detailed your data, the stronger and more convincing your final essay becomes.

FieldWords

Construction In writing, the building of text by borrowing from a variety of language sources, including your own words as well as those of others. Ethnographic writing in particular is constructed from many text sources: fieldnotes, descriptions of artifacts, glossaries of vocabulary, informants' words, archival sources, and reflective commentary.

Double-entry notes Fieldnotes that are divided into a fieldworker's observations of a fieldsite and informants and the fieldworker's personal reflections about the site and informants. The purpose of this division is to make the fieldworker more aware of the difference between verifiable, tangible facts and his or her thoughts and feelings about those facts.

Expanded fieldnotes Additional comments and reflections made by the researcher once he or she has left the research site.

Fieldnotes Observations written by a researcher at a research site, during an interview, and throughout the data collection process.

Freewriting The spontaneous writing done to release or free the mind from concerns about grammar, punctuation, or other sentence-level distractions. Freewriting is done without stopping and without editing.

Metacognition Knowledge about one's own knowing, sometimes accomplished by trying to assess and evaluate the learning process.

Participant-observer A researcher who has become involved in the daily life of a culture in addition to observing it.

Rhetoric The shaping of discourses (or simply the uses of language) for different purposes and audiences. Often defined as "the art of persuasion," this term has a long Western tradition that began with the classical Greek teachings of Plato, Aristotle, and the Sophists. The three key elements of rhetoric—speaker or writer (ethos), content (logos), and audience (pathos)—shape all written and oral messages.

Thesis The controlling idea of an essay. A thesis does not have to appear anywhere in the text but must be firmly embedded in the writer's mind and should be clear to the reader. The term is also used to refer to an extended original study about a subject (such as a master's thesis).

Underlife Classroom activity that generally goes unrecognized by teachers, such as passing notes, whispering, sleeping, and so on.

FIELDREADING

Bishop, Wendy. *Ethnographic Writing Research: Writing It Down, Writing It Up, and Reading It.* Portsmouth: Boynton, 1999.

Didion, Joan. "On Keeping a Notebook." *Slouching toward Bethlehem.* New York: Farrar, 1968.

Elbow, Peter. *Writing without Teachers.* New York: Oxford, 1973.

Emerson, Robert M., Rachel I. Fretz, and Linda L. Shaw. *Writing Ethnographic Fieldnotes.* Chicago: U of Chicago P, 1995.

Goodall, H. L. *Writing the New Ethnography.* Walnut Creek: Altamira, 2000.

Jackson, Bruce. *Fieldwork.* Chicago: U of Illinois P, 1987.

Lassiter, Luke E. *The Power of Kiowa Song.* Tucson: U of Arizona P, 1988.

Sanjek, Roger. *Fieldnotes: The Makings of Anthropology.* Ithaca: Cornell U P, 1990.

Stoller, Paul. *The Taste of Ethnographic Things: The Senses in Anthropology.* Philadelphia: U of Pennsylvania P, 1989.

Wolf, Margery. *A Thrice-Told Tale: Feminism, Postmodernism, and Ethnographic Responsibility.* Stanford: Stanford UP, 1992.

Woolcott, Harry. *The Art of Fieldwork.* Walnut Creek: Altamira, 1995.

FieldPoem

Education by Stone
Translated by James Wright

An education by stone: through lessons,
to learn from the stone: to go to it often,
to catch its level, impersonal voice
(by its choice of words it begins its classes).
The lesson in morals, the stone's cold resistance
to flow, to flowing, to being hammered:
the lesson in poetics, its concrete flesh:
in economics, how to grow dense compactly:
lessons from the stone (from without to within,
dumb primer), for the routine speller of spells.

Another education by stone: in the backlands
(from within to without and pre-didactic place).
In the backlands stone does not know how to lecture,
and, even if it did would teach nothing:
you don't learn the stone, there: there, the stone,
born stone, penetrates the soul.

A Educação Pela Pedra
João Cabral de Melo Neto

Uma educação pela pedra: por lições;
para aprender da pedra, freqüentá-la;
captar sua voz inenfática, impessoal
(pela de dicção ela começa as aulas).
A lição de moral, sua resistência fria
ao que flui e a fluir, a ser maleada;
a de poética, sua carnadura concreta;
a de economia, seu adensar-se compacta:
lições da pedra (de fora para dentro,
cartilha muda), para quem soletrá-la.

Outra educação pela pedra: no Sertão
(de dentro para fora, e pré-didática).
No Sertão a pedra não sabe lecionar,
e se lecionasse, não ensinaria nada;
lá não se aprende a pedra: lá a pedra,
uma pedra de nascença, entranha a alma.

Commentary

Hillary Gardner

I'm not a relativist, I tell my writing students. I don't believe that everything depends, even less so when I consider poetry. I believe the art of poetry shows us time and again that what is human is not particular to biography or geography, that the voice of the human thought becomes one in a unique place. Translation makes this all the more evident to me since, when something in a poem speaks to us, we tend to respond to it without regard for the age in which it was created or the gender or nationality of its creator. For me, this is Cabral de Melo Neto's stone that "penetrates the soul."

I love how when we look at a poem in translation, the translator's name usually appears in small font as an aside from the text, like a soldier's name, lucky even to exist. We never know how much of the translator is in fact author without considering the poem in both its versions; nevertheless, we accept the poet-translator's humble crumb of a confession of having been there, which seemingly demands no thanks.

As time goes by, one's resistance learns to flow, a lot does become relative, we learn to revise words and opinion to the lessons of reality in flux. Then some things do depend, and depend on us revisiting them, which is why I like reading and writing poems. When I do, words take on both weight and flight, a physical reality comes forth, we experience the "impersonal voice" of human thought made personal to us. We inhabit Cabral de Melo Neto's predidactic place, a kind of sense of understanding without ever having fully known. Then everything feels in place.

Hillary Gardner holds an MFA from the University of Iowa Writers' Workshop. A published poet and translator, she has over 10 years of teaching experience in ESL and creative writing. She has also taught Spanish and tutored adult literacy classes. She is currently a reading specialist at The Grow Network in New York City, where she is developing teaching tools for language arts teachers.

Reading Self, Reading Cultures: Understanding Texts

The reader performs the poem or the novel, as the violinist performs the sonata. But the instrument on which the reader plays, and from which he evokes the work, is—himself.
—LOUISE ROSENBLATT

We all read differently. Literary theorist Louise Rosenblatt suggests that a reader's main instrument for making meaning is the self. And meaning is an intertwining of our past reading experiences, current tastes, attitudes about genres and forms, and history of teachers, mentors, friends, and relatives. No one reads exactly as you do. No one but you listened to your grandfather's stories on the front stoop. No one but you heard your second-grade teacher read *Charlotte's Web* on the day you lost your first front tooth. No one but you searched the guide words in the phone book for the name of your boyfriend's family (and no one but you called him). No one but you has stayed up on a hot summer night finishing *To Kill a Mockingbird.* No one reads exactly as you do because no one has exactly the same experiences.

Your own choice of a good author is both personal and situational. For a plane trip, you may take Danielle Steele or John Grisham. Or you may be so frightened by flying that you read *Field and Stream* magazine or an economics text to keep your mind occupied. You may plow through the manual for your new Macintosh while your best friend ignores it and expects you to answer his constant questions. Yet this same person is willing to spend hours scrolling through America Online's restaurant guide to cities he has never visited. We read differently because we have different needs as readers.

We also read differently at different times in our lives. When you reread *Charlotte's Web* as an adult, you may not be as devastated for Wilbur, but instead you might notice that Charlotte the spider is a spiritualist and a philosopher. When Bonnie read *Little Women* to her daughter, she was surprised to find that she felt connected with the character of the mother "Marmee," although as a 10 year-old reading *Little Women*, she hadn't noticed the mother at all. We bring our current lives into the reading we do.

As a reader, you have formed tastes and predispositions from your many past experiences. What are your attitudes toward reading? Are you a reluctant reader? Do you like to whip through a book quickly, or do you luxuriate in how an author uses words? Do you read novels differently than textbooks? Poetry differently than magazines and newspaper? Online magazines and websites differently than print versions? What expectations do you carry for a bestseller? What behaviors do you engage in while you read? Do you like to mark your own comments in the margins of a book? Do you respond to your reading in a journal? Do you like to talk with a friend about what you read?

Meaning itself is a process of negotiation among the reader, the text, and the writer. This negotiation takes place both on and off the page. *On the screen* of your computer, for example, the text explains how to insert footers and page numbers. You take the technical writer's directions, negotiate them with your personal skills as a reader and a computer user, and carry that meaning directly to your keyboard to make footers and numbers on your page. You may find yourself rereading pages of a mystery novel for clues to the murder as you are reaching the conclusion of the book. But negotiation *off the page* is a less visible process. When you read a poem or hear a song, for example, the words on the page may have little meaning without your off-the-page experience. Sometimes it is through talk with others that you discover new meanings. At other times, knowing about the writer's background helps you negotiate meaning. Your understanding of a poem or song may come entirely through an emotional response. One metaphor may explode an entire image in your head. If no other person reads exactly like you do, it follows that no text has the same meaning for another reader. Meaning is a subjective experience.

Fieldworkers research cultures in the same way as readers approach novels. As you read the following excerpt from the opening of Gloria Naylor's *Mama Day*, we'd like you to "read yourself" into this text. This bestseller about the fictional sea island of Willow Springs invites you into an entire culture—one that you may approach by "stepping out" or one that you may already know by having "stepped in." You may know something about the novel's setting, the Georgia–South Carolina sea islands. You might think about Hilton Head, an island full of resort hotels, condominiums, and golf courses purchased (colonized) by land developers from the people born and raised there. Or you may have vacationed there with your family or worked at one of the hotels. You may think about the special Gullah dialect spoken there, which fascinates historians and linguists. You may have read or seen the movie based on Pat Conroy's book *The Water Is Wide*, another novel set in the sea islands. In other words, how do you situate yourself as a reader?

You probably approach any text with expectations based on your membership in different subcultures, including your readership preferences, which represent subcultures in themselves. For example, all of Linda Barnes's mystery readers belong to a subculture, as do all followers of James Morrow's science fiction novels, whether they know one another or not. Gloria Naylor is an African American female novelist. What other writers does Naylor remind you of? William Faulkner, who created the fictional world of one county in the American South? Anne Tyler, who constructs characters enmeshed in complicated family situations? Ray Bradbury, whose fictional future worlds are filled with odd but familiar places and people? Does Gloria Naylor make you think of other

African American women writers, such as Alice Walker or Toni Morrison? If you're male, how will you approach a novel about a black matriarch? Do you think your ethnicity and gender affect the way you read, or are they irrelevant?

We chose this excerpt from a novel because it depicts a fieldworker researching his culture. Reema's boy, though fictional, represents the novice fieldworker—a position you'll take when you enter your fieldsite. He puzzles over an unfamiliar term he hears, "18 & 23," and tries to make sense of it. Notice both what he does as he researches this culture—in which he once lived—and what he forgets to do. As you read, use your subjective experiences to negotiate meaning—your personal background and your history as a reader. Add your response to that of the text. Take notes, pose questions, and write about your process of reading.

Mama Day

Gloria Naylor

Willow Springs. Everybody knows but nobody talks about the legend of Sapphira Wade. A true conjure woman: satin black, biscuit cream, red as Georgia clay: depending upon which of us takes a mind to her. She could walk through a

lightning storm without being touched; grab a bolt of lightning in the palm of her hand; use the heat of lightning to start the kindling going under her medicine pot: depending upon which of us takes a mind to her. She turned the moon into salve, the stars into a swaddling cloth, and healed the wounds of every creature walking up on two or down on four. It ain't about right or wrong, truth or lies; it's about a slave woman who brought a whole new meaning to both them words, soon as you cross over here from beyond the bridge. And somehow, some way, it happened in 1823: she smothered Bascombe Wade in his very bed and lived to tell the story for a thousand days. 1823: married Bascombe Wade, bore him seven sons in just a thousand days, to put a dagger through his kidney and escape the hangman's noose, laughing in a burst of flames. 1823: persuaded Bascombe Wade in a thousand days to deed all his slaves every inch of land in Willow Springs, poisoned him for his trouble, to go on and bear seven sons—by person or persons unknown. Mixing it all together and keeping everything that done shifted down through the holes of time, you end up with the death of Bascombe Wade (there's his tombstone right out of Chevy's Pass), the deeds to our land (all marked back to the very year), and seven sons (ain't Miss Abigail and Mama Day the granddaughters of that seventh boy?). The wild card in all this is the thousand days, and we guess if we put our heads together we'd come up with something—which ain't possible since Sapphira Wade don't live in the part of our memory we can use to form words.

But ain't a soul in Willow Springs don't know that little dark girls, hair all braided up with colored twine, got their "18 & 23's coming down" when they lean too long over them back yard fences, laughing at the antics of little dark boys who got the nerve to be "breathing 18 & 23" with mother's milk still on their tongues. And if she leans there just a mite too long or grins a bit too wide, it's gonna bring a holler straight through the dusty screen door. "Get your bowlegged self 'way from my fence, Johnny Blue. Won't be no 'early 18 & 23's' coming here for me to rock. I'm still raising her." Yes, the *name* Sapphira Wade is never breathed out of a single mouth in Willow Springs. But who don't know that old twisted-lip manager at the Sheraton Hotel beyond the bridge, offering Winky Browne only twelve dollars for his whole boatload of crawdaddies— "tried to 18 & 23 him," if he tried to do a thing? We all sitting here, a hop, skip, and one Christmas left before the year 2000, and ain't nobody told him niggers can read now? Like the menus in his restaurant don't say a handful of crawdaddies sprinkled over a little bowl of crushed ice is almost twelve dollars? Call it shrimp cocktail, or whatever he want—we can count, too. And the price of everything that swims, crawls, or lays at the bottom of The Sound went up in 1985, during the season we had that "18 & 23 summer" and the bridge blew down. Folks didn't take their lives in their hands out there in that treacherous water just to be doing it—ain't that much 18 & 23 in the world.

But that old hotel manager don't make no never mind. He's the least of what we done had to deal with here in Willow Springs. Malaria. Union soldiers. Sandy soil. Two big depressions. Hurricanes. Not to mention these new real estate developers who think we gonna sell our shore land just because we ain't fool enough to live there. Started coming over here in the early '90s, talking "vacation paradise," talking "pic-ture-ess." Like Winky said, we'd have to pick their ass out the bottom of the marsh first hurricane blow through here again. See, they just thinking about building where they ain't got no state taxes— never been and never will be, 'cause Willow Springs ain't in no state. Georgia and South Carolina done tried, though—been trying since right after the Civil War to prove that Willow Springs belong to one or the other of them. Look on any of them old maps they hurried and drew up soon as the Union soldiers pulled out and you can see that the only thing connects us to the mainland is a bridge—and even that gotta be rebuilt after every big storm. (They was talking about steel and concrete way back, but since Georgia and South Carolina couldn't claim the taxes, nobody wanted to shell out for the work. So we rebuild it ourselves when need be, and build it how we need it—strong enough to last till the next big wind. Only need a steel and concrete bridge once every seventy years or so. Wood and pitch is a tenth of the cost and serves us a good sixty-nine years—matter of simple arithmetic.) But anyways, all forty-nine square miles curves like a bow, stretching toward Georgia on the south end and South Carolina on the north, and right smack in the middle where each foot of our bridge sits is the dividing line between them two states.

So who it belong to? It belongs to us—clean and simple. And it belonged to our daddies, and our daddies before them, and them too—what at one time all belonged to Bascombe Wade. And when they tried to trace him and how he got it, found out he wasn't even American. Was Norway-born or something, and the land had been sitting in his family over there in Europe since it got explored and claimed by the Vikings—imagine that. So thanks to the conjuring of Sapphira Wade we got it from Norway or theres about, and if taxes owed, it's owed to them. But ain't no Vikings or anybody else from over in Europe come to us with the foolishness that them folks out of Columbia and Atlanta come with— we was being un-American. And the way we saw it, America ain't entered the question at all when it come to our land: Sapphira was African-born, Bascombe Wade was from Norway, and it was the 18 & 23'ing that went down between them two put deeds in our hands. And we wasn't even Americans when we got it —was slaves. And the laws about slaves not owning nothing in Georgia and South Carolina don't apply, 'cause the land wasn't then—and isn't now—in either of them places. When there was lots of cotton here, and we baled it up and sold it beyond the bridge, we paid our taxes to the U.S. of A. And we keeps account of all the fishing that's done and sold beyond the bridge, all the little truck farming. And later when we had to go over there to work or our children went, we paid taxes out of them earnings. We pays taxes on the telephone lines and electrical wires run over The Sound. Ain't nobody here about breaking the law. But Georgia and South Carolina ain't seeing the shine off a penny for our land, our homes, our roads, or our bridge. Well, they fought each other up to the Supreme Court about the whole matter, and it came to a draw. We guess they got so tired out from that, they decided to leave us be—until them developers started swarming over here like sand flies at a Sunday picnic.

Sure, we coulda used the money and weren't using the land. But like Mama Day told 'em (we knew to send 'em straight over there to her and Miss Abigail), they didn't come huffing and sweating all this way in them dark gaberdine suits if they didn't think our land could make them a bundle of money, and the way we saw it, there was enough land—shoreline, that is—to make us all pretty comfortable. And calculating on the basis of all them fancy plans they had in mind, a million an acre wasn't asking too much. Flap, flap, flap—Lord, didn't them jaws and silk ties move in the wind. The land wouldn't be worth that if they couldn't *build* on it. Yes, suh, she told 'em, and they couldn't build on it unless we *sold* it. So we get ours now, and they get theirs later. You shoulda seen them coattails flapping back across The Sound with all their lies about "community uplift" and "better jobs." 'Cause it weren't about no them now and us later—was them now and us never. Hadn't we seen it happen back in the '80s on St. Helena, Daufuskie, and St. John's? And before that in the '60s on Hilton Head? Got them folks' land, built fences around it first thing, and then brought in all the builders and high-paid managers from mainside—ain't nobody on them islands benefited. And the only dark faces you see now in them "vacation paradises" is the ones cleaning the toilets and cutting the grass. On their own land, mind you, their own land. Weren't gonna happen in Willow Springs. 'Cause if Mama Day say no, everybody say no. There's 18 & 23, and there's 18 & 23—and nobody was gonna trifle with Mama Day's, 'cause she know how to use it—her being a direct descendant of Sapphira Wade, piled on the fact of springing from the seventh son of a seventh son—uh, uh. Mama Day say no, everybody say no. No point in making a pile of money to be guaranteed the new moon will see you scratching at fleas you don't have, or rolling in the marsh like a mud turtle. And if some was waiting for her to die, they had a long wait. She says she ain't gonna. And when you think about it, to show up in one century, make it all the way through the next, and have a toe inching into the one approaching *is* about as close to eternity anybody can come.

Well, them developers upped the price and changed the plans, changed the plans and upped the price, till it got to be a game with us. Winky bought a motorboat with what they offered him back in 1987, turned it in for a cabin cruiser two years later, and says he expects to be able to afford a yacht with the news that's waiting in the mail this year. Parris went from a new shingle roof to a split-level ranch and is making his way toward adding a swimming pool and greenhouse. But when all the laughing's done, it's the principle that remains. And we done learned that anything coming from beyond the bridge gotta be viewed real, real careful. Look what happened when Reema's boy—the one with the pear-shaped head—came hauling himself back from one of those fancy colleges mainside, dragging his notebooks and tape recorder and a funny way of curling up his lip and clicking his teeth, all excited and determined to put Willow Springs on the map.

We was polite enough—Reema always was a little addle-brained—so you couldn't blame the boy for not remembering that part of Willow Springs's problems was that it got put on some maps right after the War Between the States.

And then when he went around asking us about 18 & 23, there weren't nothing to do but take pity on him as he rattled on about "ethnography," "unique speech patterns," "cultural preservation," and whatever else he seemed to be getting so much pleasure out of while talking into his little gray machine. He was all over the place—What 18 & 23 mean? What 18 & 23 mean? And we all told him the God-honest truth: it was just our way of saying something. Winky was awful, though, he even spit tobacco juice for him. Sat on his porch all day, chewing up the boy's Red Devil premium and spitting so the machine could pick it up. There was enough fun in that to take us through the fall and winter when he had hauled himself back over The Sound to wherever he was getting what was supposed to be passing for an education. And he sent everybody he'd talked to copies of the book he wrote, bound all nice with our name and his signed on the first page. We couldn't hold Reema down, she was so proud. It's a good thing she didn't read it. None of us made it much through the introduction, but that said it all: you see, he had come to the conclusion after "extensive field work" (ain't never picked a boll of cotton or head of lettuce in his life—Reema spoiled him silly), but he done still made it to the conclusion that 18 & 23 wasn't 18 & 23 at all—was really 81 & 32, which just so happened to be the lines of longitude and latitude marking off where Willow Springs sits on the map. And we were just so damned dumb that we turned the whole thing around.

Not that he called it being dumb, mind you, called it "asserting our cultural identity," "inverting hostile social and political parameters." 'Cause, see, being we was brought here as slaves, we had no choice but to look at everything upside-down. And then being that we was isolated off here on this island, everybody else in the country went on learning good English and calling things what they really was—in the dictionary and all that—while we kept on calling things ass-backwards. And he thought that was just so wonderful and marvelous, etcetera, etcetera…Well, after that crate of books came here, if anybody had any doubts about what them developers was up to, if there was just a tinge of seriousness behind them jokes about the motorboats and swimming pools that could be gotten from selling a piece of land, them books squashed it. The people who ran the type of schools that could turn our children into raving lunatics—and then put his picture on the back of the book so we couldn't even deny it was him—didn't mean us a speck of good.

If the boy wanted to know what 18 & 23 meant, why didn't he just ask? When he was running around sticking that machine in everybody's face, we was sitting right here—every one of us—and him being one of Reema's, we woulda obliged him. He coulda asked Cloris about the curve in her spine that came from the planting season when their mule broke its leg, and she took up the reins and kept pulling the plow with her own back. Winky woulda told him about the hot tar that took out the corner of his right eye the summer we had only seven days to rebuild the bridge so the few crops we had left after the storm could be gotten over before rot sat in. Anybody woulda carried him through the fields we had to stop farming back in the '80s to take outside jobs—washing cars, carrying groceries, cleaning house—anything—'cause it was leave the land or lose it during the Silent Depression. Had more folks sleeping in city streets and banks fore-closing on farms than in the Great Depression before that.

Naw, he didn't really want to know what 18 & 23 meant, or he woulda asked. He woulda asked right off where Miss Abigail Day was staying, so we coulda sent him down the main road to that little yellow house where she used to live. And she woulda given him a tall glass of ice water or some cinnamon tea as he heard about Peace dying young, then Hope and Peace again. But there was the child of Grace—the grandchild, a girl who went mainside, like him, and did real well. Was living outside of Charleston now with her husband and two boys. So she visits a lot more often than she did when she was up in New York. And she probably woulda pulled out that old photo album, so he coulda seen some pictures of her grandchild, Cocoa, and then Cocoa's mama, Grace. And Miss Abigail flips right through to the beautiful one of Grace rest-ing in her satin-lined coffin. And as she walks him back out to the front porch and points him across the road to a silver trailer where her sister, Miranda, lives, she tells him to grab up and chew a few sprigs of mint growing at the foot of the steps—it'll help kill his thirst in the hot sun. And if he'd known enough to do just that, thirsty or not, he'd know when he got to that silver trailer to stand back a distance calling Mama, Mama Day, to wait for her to come out and beckon him near.

He'da told her he been sent by Miss Abigail and so, more likely than not, she lets him in. And he hears again about the child of Grace, her grand-niece, who went mainside, like him, and did real well. Was living outside of Charleston now with her husband and two boys. So he visits a lot more often than she did when she was up in New York. Cocoa is like her very own, Mama Day tells him, since she never had no children.

And with him carrying that whiff of mint on his breath, she surely woulda walked him out to the side yard, facing that patch of dogwood, to say she has to end the visit a little short 'cause she has some gardening to do in the other place. And if he'd had the sense to offer to follow her just a bit of the way—then and only then—he hears about that summer fourteen years ago when Cocoa came visiting from New York with her first husband. Yes, she tells him, there was a first husband—a stone city boy. How his name was George. But how Cocoa left, and he stayed. How it was the year of the last big storm that blew her pecan trees down and even caved in the roof of the other place. And she woulda stopped him from walking just by a patch of oak: she reaches up, takes a bit of moss for him to put in them closed leather shoes—they're prob-ably sweating his feet something terrible, she tells him. And he's to sit on the ground, right there, to untie his shoes and stick in the moss. And then he'd see through the low bush that old graveyard just down the slope. And when he looks back up, she woulda disappeared through the trees; but he's to keep pushing the moss in them shoes and go on down to that graveyard where he'll find buried Grace, Hope, Peace, and Peace again. Then a little ways off a group-ing of seven old graves, and a little ways off seven older again. All circled by them live oaks and hanging moss, over a rise from the tip of The Sound.

Everything he needed to know coulda been heard from that yellow house to that silver trailer to that graveyard. Be too late for him to go that route now, since Miss Abigail's been dead for over nine years. Still, there's an easier way. He could just watch Cocoa any one of these times she comes in from Charleston. She goes straight to Miss Abigail's to air out the rooms and unpack her bags, then she's across the road to call out at Mama Day, who's gonna come to the door of the trailer and wave as Cocoa heads on through the patch of dogwoods to that oak grove. She stops and puts a bit of moss in her open-toe sandals, then goes on past those graves to a spot just down the rise toward The Sound, a little bit south of that circle of oaks. And if he was patient and stayed off a little ways, he'd realize she was there to meet up with her first husband so they could talk about that summer fourteen years ago when she left, but he stayed. And as her and George are there together for a good two hours or so—neither one saying a word—Reema's boy coulda heard from them everything there was to tell about 18 & 23.

But on second thought, someone who didn't know how to ask wouldn't know how to listen. And he coulda listened to them the way you been listening to us right now. Think about it: ain't nobody really talking to you. We're sitting here in Willow Springs, and you're God-knows-where. It's August 1999—ain't but a slim chance it's the same season where you are. Uh, huh, listen. Really listen this time: the only voice is your own. But you done just heard about the legend of Sapphira Wade, though nobody here breathes her name. You done heard it the way we know it, sitting on our porches and shelling June peas, quieting the midnight cough of a baby, taking apart the engine of a car—you done heard it without a single living soul really saying a word. Pity, though, Reema's boy couldn't listen, like you, to Cocoa and George down by them oaks—or he would left here with quite a story.

Responding to Text

Purpose

We hope you found yourself reading the excerpt from *Mama Day* more than once. We did. When each of us first read it, we realized we needed to read it again. Bonnie's interest in the character of the bumbling young researcher, Reema's boy, focused her reading so that she excluded other characters. Elizabeth found herself looking at Naylor's map, imagining how close it might be to where she lives in North Carolina. As Elizabeth read the code word "18 & 23," she found herself trying to substitute other words each time she encountered it. But as we reread the text together for the purpose of writing this book, we talked about it and found ourselves discovering much more. We began to read the text in two ways: one as a parody of fieldworking and the other as a rich fictional account of a cultural group with its own codes, behaviors, stories, and rituals.

Action

We'd like you to describe your own process of reading and rereading *Mama Day* in a page or two. If you're keeping a journal or a process log, you might want to use these questions to guide your response:

- What personal assumptions did you bring to this text? About this region's geography? This group of sea islanders? Rural families and their belief systems and values?

- What other books have you read or movies have you seen that this excerpt reminds you of? In what ways?

- How do your previous reading experiences affect the way you appreciate Naylor's writing? How would you describe Naylor's style?

- What was hard for you to understand in this text? Which words, phrases, or paragraphs made you stop and reread? How did you solve this problem?

- What stood out for you? Where in the text did you find yourself entertained? Immersed? Confused?

- What information was helpful as you read the first time? In your second reading, what did you discover that you missed the first time?

- Which of the characters interested you most, and why? Cocoa? Mama Day? Reema's boy? Sapphira Wade? The narrator?

- What details of the setting involved your imagination? When you share your response with your colleagues, notice how they might have read differently.

Response

Our student Cheri Kreclic's response to this exercise looked like this:

> Reading *Mama Day,* I was reminded of the movie *Daughters of the Dust,* which is the story of the Gullahs on a very similar island during the early part of the twentieth century. This movie greatly influenced my visualization of the events in *Mama Day* and helped me understand the historical events and the writer's perspective. I am also acquainted with what happened to the Gullah people's redevelopment of their property in Hilton Head because of a series of programs on the subject on National Public Radio a few years ago. The dialect is also familiar since during a course called "The Black Experience," we listened to the language of the Gullahs.
>
> I was most intrigued with the character of Sapphira Wade. The narrator gives a very clear characterization of her, but I wanted to know more—how did she persuade Bascombe Wade to deed this land to the slaves, and how did she escape the hangman's noose? I had no trouble reading this excerpt and quickly fell into the rhythm of the words.

And Cheri's colleague, Brenda Yarish, found herself less confused on each rereading:

> The first time I read *Mama Day,* I was so confused by the language that I completely missed the story. As I read it the second time, the language cleared up, and the third time, I finally grasped the story. The one thing in the language that threw me was "18 & 23." It later became clearer when I started inserting other words to make the sentence have meaning for me. In the first paragraph where the narrator tells of Sapphira Wade's life, he says she "escaped the hangman's noose, laughing in a burst of flames." "Laughing in a burst of flames" still eludes me. I'm also still confused how Sapphira could have smothered a man, then married him, given him seven sons, then put a dagger through his kidney, then poisoned him, then bore him seven sons. Wow! She must have been quite a woman to have killed the same man so many times. The character that interested me the most was the narrator. He or she (not sure what gender) knew everything about the culture yet remains unidentified. My second favorite was Reema's boy. I related to him in his search for "culture" after having to write ethnographically. When you read ethnography, it seems so simple until you try it.

READING CULTURES AS TEXT AND TEXT AS CULTURE

The kinds of questions that we list in Box 9 can be asked of any text you read. Reading any complex text can also involve reading a culture. In the excerpt from *Mama Day,* we see culture's ordinary life in dailiness that fieldworkers always try to penetrate—catching crawdaddies, chewing tobacco, truck farming. But we also see this culture's uniqueness through Naylor's specific characters and setting.

Our own collaborative reading of Naylor's text helped us see the layers of culture she created. She begins with an omniscient insider narrator who takes us into Willow Springs, a place with its own folklore and folkways. Willow Springs is not easily accessible to outsiders; it requires crossing a bridge between the mainland and the island. Crossing this bridge, as we read it, symbolizes the differences between mainland and island cultures, and many islanders are required to move back and forth between these two very different worlds, to be bicultural.

With the character of Reema's pear-headed nameless boy, Naylor offers us a parody of a field researcher. He is an insider, born on the island, and he returns from his fancy college, "dragging his notebooks and tape recorder and a funny way of curling up his lip and clicking his teeth, all excited and determined to put Willow Springs on the map." He conducts "extensive field work," which includes recording the sound of Winky Brown spitting tobacco and intensive interviews about "18 & 23." Reema's boy writes up his field study and gives it to his informants, who never even finish reading the introduction and dismiss the conclusions he makes about "18 & 23."

Reema's boy's college education had so shaped him that he was unable, even as an insider, to do what fieldworkers need to do: listen, observe, and participate in the life of the people he studied. Even the residents of Willow Springs knew more about how to do his fieldwork than he did: "If the boy wanted to know what 18 & 23 meant, why didn't he just ask?" The narrator concludes that a researcher who doesn't know how to form questions would never be in a position to understand answers. "But on second thought," the narrator reminds us, "someone who didn't know how to ask wouldn't know how to listen."

You'll need to think about how your background can affect what you see in another culture just as it does when you read a written text. What you see is affected by who you are. Your education, geography, family history, personal experiences, race, gender, or nationality can influence the way you do research. Learning to read a culture like a text is similar to learning to read a text like a culture.

BOX 10

From Ethos to Ethics

Julie Cheville, Rutgers University, New Jersey

Purpose

"Ethos" in speakers' or writers' texts, implies their ethics and emerges in writing or speech as their credibility: When my students and I read *Mama Day,* many of us sympathize with Reema's boy. The tactical errors of a college student turned fieldworker hit close to home. And they raise imposing questions. How do we enter a cultural space and earn the trust of insiders? And how, as outsiders just stepping in, do we recognize the essence of identities and relationships?

I like to read this selection from *Mama Day* to students so we can concentrate less on processing language than on listening to the rich images of character and culture. I ask groups of students to notice particular "informants" so that when we finish the story, we can interpret the lives Naylor writes about without obsessing first on the question of "18 & 23." Rather than attend to the single and most obvious question, as Reema's boy does, we focus on informants' habits of mind, language, and body—all features of cultural life that answer the question implicitly.

While notetaking and audiotaping are essential field techniques, they can become liabilities and get a fieldworker into trouble. For Reema's boy, these tools are a means to his particular end—the "truth" about "18 & 23." But in the same way that Sapphira Wade "ain't about truth or lies," the culture that memorializes her resists a single interpretation. When Reema's boy contrives his own interpretation, the residents resist him. For the descendants of Sapphira Wade, "18 & 23" represents the totality of the unsaid.

From the experiences of Reema's boy, we understand that entering the field is not about exerting oneself on others but about emerging into delicate relationships with those who guide us where they choose. In this way, our credibility, or "ethos," arises from our receptiveness to what and to whom we're introduced.

So how do fieldworkers position themselves without overriding informants' identities, relationships, and histories? This is where this excerpt from *Mama Day* invites a discussion of ethics. As you'll learn in this book, fieldworkers by profession rely on written ethical principles to monitor their interactions. These principles ensure that research involving human subjects protects the welfare of all involved. In this activity, you will research many of the professional codes that govern fieldworkers in a variety of disciplines.

Action

In small groups, analyze the online ethics statements of some of the professional organizations that monitor fieldwork. Here are a few of them:

American Anthropological Association: www.ameranthassn.org/stmts/ethstmnt.htm

American Folklore Society: www.afsnet.org/ethics.htm

American Psychological Association: www.apa.org/ethics/homepage.html

American Sociological Association: www.asanet.org/members/ecostand2.html

The Society of Professional Journalists: spj.org/ethics/code.htm

Each group can study a single statement for principles that might have helped Reema's boy to make more sensitive choices. As a class, talk about the strengths of each association's code. From this discussion, you may either come to consensus about the code that seems most relevant to your work or create a code of your own. During fieldwork, as you encounter particular dilemmas, you will be able to use the guidelines to identify options and obligations.

Response

Here is the preamble the students in one of my classes wrote:

Preamble

We have created this code of ethics to guide our behavior as we enter fieldwork. Because our subcultures are not the same, we will face different ethical questions. This code of ethics will help us to remember our responsibilities to informants and to their perspectives and histories. As researchers, we understand the importance of the following:

1. Before fieldwork begins, we should explain the process and purposes of our project to members of the subculture. This should be done in such a way that allows informants an opportunity to ask questions. We should avoid using technical language that informants might not understand, and we should listen and respond to each question they ask.

2. Before fieldwork begins, we should understand that the purpose of our research is not to put a subculture "on the map." We must focus on accurate portraits of those we observe and interview. Final products should be shared with informants before they are due. This should be done either orally or in writing, in whatever form our informants choose.

3. During fieldwork, we should protect the anonymity of informants at all times. Whenever possible, we should offer our services and support as a way of compensating for the help our informants provide us.

4. We should develop interview questions that reflect not just what we don't understand but, most important, what informants say and do. As much as possible, we should take part in rituals of the subculture so that our questions arise from the actual behaviors and objects that are important to members. We should never let notetaking or taperecording become the most important ritual.

5. We should make conclusions about a subculture based on beliefs that are shared across several informants. We should realize that the emphasis in field research is not on discovering the truth but on discovering how informants perceive their subculture.

POSITIONING: READING AND WRITING ABOUT YOURSELF

As we conduct our fieldwork, we must be conscious of ourselves as the key instruments of the research process. When you begin to research a site, you will need to "read" yourself in the same way that you have deciphered texts, and you will want to write that perspective into your study. Had Reema's boy thought or written about his insider status, education and field training, family history, and geography, he might have asked different questions and gotten different answers. Instead of leaving out personal, subjective information, fieldworkers should write it in. The subjective perspective—as opposed to the objective one—admits the researcher's presence as she goes about her fieldwork.

Horace Miner's study of the Nacirema (reprinted in Chapter 1) satirizes the so-called objective traditions of natural science that once dominated the field of anthropology by describing everyday routines such as brushing our teeth as stylized ceremonies or rituals. Today, most contemporary scientists, in both the natural and the social sciences, realize that objectivity is not possible—that the observer is part of the person or culture observed.

In fieldwork, **positioning** includes all the subjective responses that affect how the researcher sees data. Readers of ethnography sometimes wonder how this kind of research could be considered social "science" if the researcher is not offering "objective" data. In fact, fieldworkers achieve a type of objectivity through **intersubjectivity**, the method of connecting as many different perspectives on the same data as possible. These multiple sources encourage the fieldworker to interpret patterns and interrelationships among various accounts alongside the researcher's own account and to leave other interpretations open as well.

Being the researcher so influences your fieldwork that it would be deceptive *not* to include relevant background information about yourself in your study. From our own experiences as fieldworkers, we believe that as a researcher you position or situate yourself in relationship to your study in at least three ways: fixed, subjective, and textual.

Fixed Positions

Fixed positions are the personal facts that might influence how you see your data—your age, gender, class, nationality, race—factors that do not change during the course of the study but are often taken for granted and unexamined in the research process. Does it matter that you are middle-aged and studying adolescents? Or that you grew up on a kibbutz in Israel? Does being a middle-class African American affect the way you interpret the lives of homeless African Americans? How does your gender affect your perspective?

In Elizabeth's research on college students' literacies, for example, her position as a woman was a key to understanding differences in the ways that men and women talk in college classrooms. Her gender helped her see why women were often silent in certain classrooms while male students dominated the talk. Being female enhanced her project and enabled her to see and record behaviors that might have been inaccessible to her had she been male. One of her male informants asked her, "What is this women's way of knowing?" implying that he just didn't understand how gender affected someone's knowledge and understanding. Rather than overlook the fixed positions of age, gender, nationality, class, or race, researchers need to reflect on these influences and include their reflections in their fieldnotes.

Our word *fixed* is problematic; nothing is truly "fixed." Sometimes fixed factors are subjected to change during the research process, and then that, too, demands the researcher's attention. If, for example, a male researcher looking at the play behaviors of preschool children becomes the father of a girl during his study, he may find himself looking at his fieldsite data not only through his own eyes but also through those of his infant daughter. If what originally seemed a fixed influence in the researcher's position becomes more fluid, then that process of changed perspectives would become part of the researcher's data.

Subjective Positions

Subjective positions such as life history and personal experiences may also affect your research. As we described in Chapter 1, fieldworker Renato Rosaldo found that his wife's death altered his perspective toward studying another culture. As he began to understand his grief and rage, he relied on his subjective feelings to understand the Ilongots. Living through a flood, an earthquake, or a hurricane may change your stance toward the world around you. But it does not take disaster, death, divorce, or illness to alter our perspective. Someone who grew up in a large extended or blended family will see the eating, sleeping, and conversation patterns of groups differently than someone from a small nuclear family. What seems to be a crowded room in a small household is not a crowded room in a home with extended family. Many people who grew up in large families confess that they learned to eat quickly at family meals because they wanted to get their fair share before the food disappeared. During their thirty-year marriage, Bonnie's husband, an electronics engineer with a history of "do-it-yourself" repairs, insisted on fixing their own appliances. For four years they lived with two jury-rigged interconnected TV sets—one for the picture and one for sound. Bonnie saw them both as broken, and her husband saw them both as usable. The children just watched the two sets.

Textual Positions

Textual positions—the language choices you make to represent what you see—affect the writing of both fieldnotes and the final ethnographic report. The way that you position yourself in the field with respect to the people you study—how close or how far away you focus your research lens—determines the kind of data you'll gather, the voice you'll create in your finished text, and to some extent your credibility as a researcher.

BOX 11

Positioning Yourself

Purpose

This activity will help you uncover the assumptions, preconceptions, personal experiences, and feelings that influence you as a fieldworker by writing about them throughout your research process. In this way, you will become conscious of your positioning as a researcher.

Action

Consider a site or subculture you might choose to research: a tattoo parlor, the lobby of a nursing home, a community theater, a convenience store, a finger-nail salon, a group of pheasant hunters, workers on break, an airport check-in desk. What are your reasons for choosing this subculture? Which of your own "fixed positions" may affect what you see? What "subjective positions" do you carry into your site? Write a short commentary describing how your positions might affect what you'll see at your fieldsite. (Writing short commentaries regularly will help you understand how fixed, subjective, and textual positions affect your continuing research process.)

Response

Rick Zollo, who wrote the ethnographic study presented in Chapter 1, "Friday Night at Iowa 80," wrote short commentaries while he conducted his study, and they helped him to think about and prepare for the textual position he would take in his final study—a position in which he keeps himself very visible as the researcher guiding his reader throughout the text. In the following excerpt from his commentary, called "My Gig at the Truckstop," Rick discusses how his previous experiences and his own preconceptions about truck drivers initially affected his position as a researcher at Iowa 80. He is honest as he discovers his own subjective position—the baggage he carries into the research site from his past experiences:

> For many years I enjoyed hitchhiking as a way to travel. Cheap and purposeful, it allowed me to wander when occasion arose, in a manner suiting my personality and economic means. These days it is no longer safe to hitchhike, and I lament this loss of engaged travelling, for every journey was an adventure and every ride was an existential meeting with new souls.
>
> During my so-called "hippie" days (I preferred to call myself a "freak"), I found a great unfriendliness toward me and people like me from the truckdriving community. Truckers would rarely pick up a long-haired hitchhiker, and whenever they did, it was usually because it was late at night and the truck was without a C.B. radio or perhaps because the driver had a weirder personality than what hippie personalities were thought to be.
>
> Visits to truckstops were always accompanied by a chill emanating from those so-called cowboys of the highway. I can remember vividly spending the greater part of one night—three hours in an Indiana interstate truckstop—begging truckers for a ride, their derision burning fires of indignation into my soul.
>
> …Thus I had misgivings as I prepared to follow this truckstop gig along the line of a standard story: rising action, climax, falling action,

and denouement. The trucking industry has undergone many changes since my last hitchhiking adventures. The redneck versus hippie tension has dissipated, as many of those truckers now wear ponytails and have pierced ears, the two classes of outlaws merging and mingling in the various contact zones of this great boiling pot of America.

UNDERSTANDING POSITIONING: CHECKING IN ON YOURSELF

Throughout the process of conducting your field study, you'll need to continue to ask how who you are affects how you understand yourself and your fieldwork. In Chapter 2, we offered you three questions to help you monitor your assumptions, stances, and blind spots: "What surprised me?" "What intrigued me?" and "What disturbed me?" These questions help provide ways of "checking in" on yourself as well as ways of interrogating the different features of your positions as you bring them to your study. This kind of monitoring will eventually help you see how your fixed and subjective positions contribute to the textual voice you'll develop as you write about your topic. Even more important, checking in will heighten your awareness of the extent to which the instrument of your data gathering is not statistical information or a computer program or an experiment but *you*—with all of your assumptions, preconceptions, past experiences, and complex feelings.

Sometimes it's easier to understand the idea of positioning when you look at someone else's set of issues rather than your own. For example, the narrator of *Mama Day* (see page 107) can see other people's flaws; she says "Reema was always a little addle-brained" and is convinced that Reema's son's college education has made him unable to understand the simplest truths about his home town—but she does not seem to understand her own part in constructing the history of Willow Springs.

A humorous essay by Laura Bohannan about her fieldwork experience in West Africa, "Shakespeare in the Bush," illustrates the importance of checking in on yourself—on your assumptions, expectations, and feelings—throughout your research experiences. Bohannan is an anthropologist by profession who also writes fiction. In fact, Bohannan has written a wonderful novel about being a fieldworker, *Return to Laughter*, under the pseudonym Elenore Smith Bowen. In "Shakespeare in the Bush," Bohannan draws on the craftsmanship of fiction to make fun of herself as a fieldworker. After recounting a brief conversation that suggested a cultural conflict between English and American readers of Shakespeare's play *Hamlet*, Bohannan goes on to expose how she tried to import the "universal" message of *Hamlet* to the Tiv tribe she was studying.

At one point in the essay, Bohannan decides to skip summarizing the famous "To be or not to be" speech because she feels her listeners would misinterpret it; she then proceeds to try to explain Hamlet's father's "ghost" to her audience. She finds herself interrupted at every turn in the telling of what she had previously thought to be a "universal" and "transcultural" story:

> I decided to skip the soliloquy. Even if Claudius was here thought quite right to marry his brother's widow, there remained the poison motif, and I knew they would disapprove of fratricide. More hopefully I resumed, "That night Hamlet kept watch with the three who had seen his dead father. The dead chief again appeared, and although the others were afraid, Hamlet followed his dead father off to one side. When they were alone, Hamlet's dead father spoke."
>
> "Omens can't talk!" The old man was emphatic.
>
> "Hamlet's dead father wasn't an omen. Seeing him might have been an omen, but he was not." My audience looked as confused as I sounded. "It *was* Hamlet's dead father. It was a thing we call a 'ghost.' I had to use the English word, for unlike many of the neighboring tribes, these people didn't believe in the survival after death of any individuating part of the personality.
>
> "What is a 'ghost?' An omen?"
>
> "No, a 'ghost' is someone who is dead but who walks around and can talk, and people can hear him and see him but not touch him."
>
> They objected. "One can touch zombis."
>
> "No, no! It was not a dead body the witches had animated to sacrifice and eat. No one else made Hamlet's dead father walk. He did it himself."
>
> "Dead men can't walk," protested my audience as one man.
>
> I was quite willing to compromise. "A 'ghost' is a dead man's shadow."
>
> But again they objected. "Dead men cast no shadows."
>
> "They do in my country," I snapped.

In order to appreciate the full scope of Bohannan's mistaken assumptions, you will need to read her complete essay online. When you access <fieldworking. com>, you will find a downloadable version of the essay in "the library"; you can also link to "Shakespeare in the Bush" via <bedfordstmartins.com/ fieldworking> or by searching for the essay's title with a search engine. As you read, you'll want to notice the ways the author monitors herself as she relates the story of Hamlet to the audience of informants she is trying to win over through her storytelling.

The mental checking Bohannan does in this reading is what we are suggesting you do as well, seeing yourself as outsiders like the Tiv might see you. Just as Renato Rosaldo uses satire to convey the rituals of breakfast, and Horace Miner makes fun of Americans' bathroom habits, Bohannan also employs satire in this essay to convey to her readers how she is the cultural outsider.

Of course, it's important that Bohannan's fixed position is that she is American and female. As you read "Shakespeare in the Bush," check to see if there are other fixed factors that are important to how the people she studies perceive her.

Bohannan's essay also raises the many ethical issues she faced in the field. Should she drink beer in the morning with her informants? Should she try to change parts of *Hamlet* to make the story more culturally relevant to her audience? Should she defend the way her own culture thinks of family relationships when clearly her audience thinks differently? Although Bohannan constructs herself textually as a bewildered fieldworker in "Shakespeare in the Bush," she also makes it clear that the ethical issues she faced are serious ones, worthy of lengthier consideration than she was able to give them in this essay.

NEGOTIATING THE ETHICS OF ENTRY

When you enter a fieldsite and make yourself known, you must follow many courtesies to make yourself and the people you're observing feel comfortable. All places in which you are a participant-observer involve an official process for "negotiating entry." As a beginning researcher, don't enter a site where you feel at risk in the subculture. For the kinds of projects this book suggests, you will not have adequate time to gain entry or insider status in an intimidating group. One of our students, for example, wanted to research a group of campus skinheads. They permitted Jake to hang out on the edges of their subculture, even allowing him to read their "code of honor," which included these statements:

- Be discreet about new recruits; check them out thoroughly.
- For prospects, we must have at least a ninety-day contact period in which we can attest to your character. A probationary period and productivity report will be given.
- Outsiders need no knowledge of what goes on or is said in our meetings.
- No racial exceptions whatsoever! All members must be 100% white!

Early on, Jake began to realize that his research position was unworkable, that he was stuck. While the skinheads had let him into their subculture as a potential recruit, he could never fully enter their subculture or worldview. Their code of honor, which excluded minority groups, stood against his personal ethics. In an early portfolio reflection, Jake wrote, "I never hung out with them in public. I never went to an organizational meeting. I realized I was an outsider to this subculture."

Jake's negotiation experience was so dramatic that he was unable to gain full access, and so he was unable to collect the data he wanted. No matter how interested in and enthusiastic we are about a possible fieldsite, we must be conscious of our own comfort levels and even potential dangers in investigating certain groups or places.

Harvey, another of our students, experienced difficulty negotiating entry into a fieldsite owing mainly to his own assumption that it would be easy for him to do so. He is a Native American, a Sioux, who wanted to research a gambling casino on another tribe's reservation. Because of his heritage, he assumed that he would be welcomed. But he wasn't. He had enormous difficulty finding people who were willing to talk to him, and he never really knew whether it was because of his Sioux background or because he was perceived as a student. Eventually, he had a conversation with the woman who ran the gift shop at the casino, and she introduced him to others. As his informant, she helped him gain an insider status in a place where he had assumed he already had it.

Any fieldsite you enter requires that you be conscious of your own personal assumptions and how they reflect your ethics, but you must also be respectful of the people whose lives you are watching. It is common courtesy for researchers to acknowledge time spent with informants with gestures as small as writing thank-you notes or as large as exchanging time (tutoring or babysitting, for example) or obtaining grant-funded stipends to pay them. As you work your way through the process of "negotiating entry," be sure to follow these guidelines:

- Explain your project clearly to the people you will study, and obtain the requisite permission from those in charge.
- Let your informants understand what part of the study you'll share with them.
- Think about what you can give back to the fieldsite in exchange for your time there.

Some sites may require official documentation, as in the case of two of our students who collaborated on a study of a day-care center. The center required them to have an interview, submit a proposal describing their project, and sign a document attesting that they had reviewed all of the center's rules and procedures. Entry might be simple, laborious, or even impossible. For this reason, don't wait too long to make yourself visible to the insiders you study. One student we worked with spent over a month in the field observing a Disney store. When she attempted to get official permission to write about this store, however, she was denied entry and could not continue her project.

Once you finalize your site, you might want to check with your instructor to find out your university's policy with respect to research on human subjects. For long-term projects, the university's **human subjects review board** usually requires that you file a proposal and submit permission forms from your informants. They are called "**informed consent** forms," and on page 127 we present a sample of one of our own forms as a model. Universities usually have less formal procedures for the kind of short-term fieldwork that you might do for a one-semester course, and often have no requirements for filing permissions. Fieldworkers, no matter what size their projects, are ethically responsible for accurately showing the voices of their informants on the page. We feel strongly that you should receive permission from all the informants whose work you audiotape or video-tape as well as from any official person at your fieldsite, such as the manager in the following example.

Karen Downing, a high school teacher, chose to research Photo Phantasies, a beauty photography studio at a suburban shopping mall. Her full-length study appears in Chapter 5, but in one section of her final project, reproduced here, she discusses the difficulties she encountered with the managers of the studio while she attempted to negotiate entry. Karen opens this section of her paper by nar-rating a telephone call she made to Photo Phantasies:

"Hello, this is Photo Phantasies. My name is Mindy. Today's a great day." I am not calling Photo Phantasies to inquire about specials. I am not calling because I want to know if they have any free time today for a last-minute appointment. I am not calling to see if a $220 package of photographs has arrived. I am calling to speak to Ginny James, the manager. When I make this request and tell Mindy who I am, she says, "Oh. Hang on a sec," in a voice without intonation. Her hand covers the receiver, muffling sounds.

When I talk with Ginny, I will not say that I have an aversion to her store and the whole Photo Phantasies concept. I will tell her I am fascinated by the photographs my high school students, always female, bring to school to show off. I will present myself as curious.

"This is Ginny James. It's a great day! What can I do for you?" Her voice rises at the end of the question.

I tell Ginny my name and ask her if she has received the letter I sent four days ago requesting to visit her store.

"Letter? What letter are you referring to?"

I am caught off guard by her response and feel slightly uneasy. I take a deep breath before explaining my "research project."

Silence. And more silence. Finally, this from Ginny: "I'll need this in writing. Call me back after 11:30. That's when the mail comes. If there's no letter, you'll need to provide adequate documentation. You'll have to deliver it in person." Despite the mall noise in the background, I sense immediately that Ginny is guarded with me. Her changed tone results in sentences with periods, no longer exclamation points. I wait until 12:30 and try again.

"Hello, this is Photo Phantasies. My name is Stacey! It's a great day, and we're searching for models! How may I help you?"

When I finally talk with Ginny during this second phone call, she leaves out the conversational niceties. Yes, my letter had arrived in the mail after all. "I'll have to clear this request with headquarters, which I can do tomor-row. I'm leaving for a Photo Phantasies meeting in Chicago. What kind of class is this for? Business? Sociology? I'll call you Wednesday night and leave a message about whether or not it's OK."

Wednesday night, no reply.

Friday morning, no reply.

Mary Smith
Dormitory Hall
State University
City, State
Telephone number

I give my permission to Mary Smith to use my written and spoken words in her research project written for "Composition/English 102" at State University. I understand that I may read and approve the final draft of the material she uses about me in her project.

Signature: _____ Date: _____

Address: _____

_____

Telephone number: _____

I prefer to use this pseudonym: _____

Informed consent form.

My third call to Photo Phantasies is on Friday afternoon. "Hello, this is Photo Phantasies. My name is Ginny! Ask me about our model search! How may I help you?"

"Ginny, this is Karen Downing. You may help me by telling me that headquarters granted me permission to spend some time in your store." I try to be personable and charming.

"Karen Downing?"

"Yes, the one that sent the letter about doing research for..."

"Oh. Right. Well. Yes. You can come to the store, but I don't want an extra body around when customers are here. You could come to an in-store training session from 5:30 to 6:30 on Sunday night. And I have some material about Photo Phantasies that you could read."

"Huh. Well...huh. Ummm...when could I come out to pick up the material?"

"Saturdays are nuts. Sunday's the meeting day. Monday's my paper day...and I'm still catching up from Chicago..." She trails off into a sigh.

"How about today. This afternoon?"

"Fine." Click. When she hangs up, I realize that in three phone calls, I have never heard the official Photo Phantasies telephone goodbye.

I leave the house to go to the mall at 11:30, even though I know that, technically, it's not yet afternoon. But I have work to do in the afternoon and would rather not face more traffic and a busier mall. Before I leave, I think about what I am wearing. My standard look—black turtleneck and brown jeans, minimal gold jewelry, lipstick, powder, blush and eyeliner, curly and full hair tucked behind my right ear. I decide not to do anything differently to my appearance for this particular errand, but I am aware that I am thinking about how I look a lot more than I normally would. I hear the words of my mother, words I have grown up with: "You need more blush! And remember the lipstick! Without it, you don't look alive!" Today, I follow her advice, advice I usually ignore, and add just a bit more makeup to be sure it's noticeable.

Not only was Karen concerned about her attitude about Photo Phantasies; she was also concerned with how she presented herself. She thought about makeup more than usual because she wanted to fit into the culture she was seeking to enter. Her fieldnotes began long before she actually walked into the studio. She recorded her phone conversations, her impressions of how she was being interpreted by those she sought to interview, and her previous knowledge of Photo Phantasies' products. Karen was careful to monitor her feelings and her assumptions as she moved into her fieldsite. She wrote, "I have an aversion to her store and the whole Photo Phantasies concept." She recorded feeling "caught off guard" and "slightly uneasy." She noted sarcastically that in three phone calls she never heard "the official Photo Phantasies telephone goodbye." She worries about makeup and thinks about her outfit, her jewelry, and her mother's advice. As an outsider stepping into a world in which she feels uncomfortable but to which she is nevertheless drawn, she is careful to be, in her own words, "personable and charming." But at the same time, she is honest about her own assumptions and attitudes toward Photo Phantasies and records these fieldnotes reflectively. After negotiating with her subjective feelings and with her potential informants, she was ready to enter the studio.

READING AN OBJECT: THE CULTURAL ARTIFACT

As you enter the field, you should train yourself to notice material objects—**artifacts**—that represent the culture of that site. Karen's writing about the three phone calls (see pp. 126–28) revolves around one particular artifact, the letter she has sent to Ginny, the manager who finds reasons not to talk with her. She also uses artifacts—the black turtleneck, brown jeans, minimal jewelry—to explain what she calls her "standard look" and contrast it with the glamorized look that belongs, she thinks, to Photo Phantasies.

In his journal, Rick Zollo (whose fieldwork we present in Chapter 1) wrote about an "old gent's black cowboy hat decked with pins and medallions." This artifact eventually connected with Rick's metaphor of the trucker as a cowboy. During his research, he became sensitized to truckers' musical tastes, cravings for home-cooked food, and their ways of passing time at the truck stop. To represent those features of the trucking culture, he collected trucking magazines, tapes and CDs of particular songs, menus from the diner, and pictures of the pinball machines. As he wrote about the truck stop later, he was able to include detailed descriptions of the artifacts he had collected. In his final project, the trucker's logbook became the primary cultural artifact that revealed values about the subculture. The logbook itself encouraged truckers to unveil their attitudes and politics about their jobs and the trucking industry as a whole. Researchers gather artifacts for what they reveal about subcultures. And researchers use artifacts to learn about insiders' perspectives on their subcultures.

Objects, then, are readable texts. As you read an object, your position as researcher affects your reading just as it affects the way you read a fieldsite. You can investigate the surface details of an object, research its history, or learn about people's rules and rituals for using and making the object. Researchers—folklorists and anthropologists—use the term **material culture** to refer to those objects, personal artifacts loaded with meaning and history that people mark as special: tools, musical instruments, foods, toys, jewelry, ceremonial objects, and clothes.

Everyone wears jeans. But not all jeans convey the same cultural meanings. Some mean utility, some fashion, some status. Jeans that have been painted, beaded, patched, stone-washed, bleached, ripped, or tie-dyed by their owner (not purchased that way in a store) can be read as objects that mark the wearer's place in popular culture. But we cannot know the meaning of an object through observation alone because our eyes can deceive us and there are meanings that lie beyond the surface of an object. Japanese collectors, for instance, pay thousands of dollars for old pairs of American denim jeans. To search for the meanings of any cultural artifact, we need to look at the people who create, collect, and use it. The best way to learn about the meaning and value of an artifact is to ask questions about the object and listen carefully.

As you look at the photographs of the basket on page 130, think about the kinds of questions you might want to ask the owner or the basketmaker. How is it made? How old is it? What is it used for?

On the surface, it is a woven basket with a lid. But the basket holds a coiled history, a collection of stories that belongs to its makers, its sellers, and its owners. The basket itself is an artifact produced by several interconnected cultures. It is made by African American women on the coast of South Carolina, near the city of Charleston, not far from Gloria Naylor's fictional Willow Springs. The

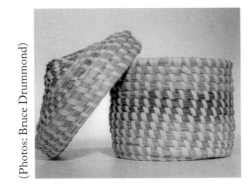

(Photos: Bruce Drummond)

South Carolina Low Country coil basket.

basketmakers use natural materials (coastal sweetgrass, palmetto fronds, and pine needles) found on the southeastern coast of the United States, much like the plants their ancestors knew on the western coast of Africa. These baskets come out of a strong craft tradition of using available materials to make everyday objects. It is a tradition that daughters learn from mothers, who learned it from their mothers, who learned it from their mothers. The basketmaking technique represents a long chain of informal instruction over many generations of craftswomen. And each generation—in fact, each basketmaker herself—adds her own technique and her own circumstances to what she has learned. During their years of American slavery, for example, African American women modified kitchen implements, such as spoons, to create the tools they needed to continue making baskets according to their traditional designs.

But knowing the history of this craft and even holding the basket in your hand does not speak about the object the way the maker does. When Bonnie interviewed a basketmaker in the Charleston marketplace, a middle-aged woman named Wilma, she learned more than the observable and historical details we described here. Bonnie was already positioned by knowing the history of this craft from reading about the tradition and having heard her mentor, folklorist Burt Feintuch, lecture on exactly this topic. So when she visited Charleston, she was eager to find a basketmaker who would talk about her craft. Bonnie wanted to buy one of Wilma's baskets, one with a beautifully tight-fitting top. As they examined it together, Wilma explained the challenge of pulling the fresh sweetgrass, weaving in palmetto fronds, and keeping the pine needles fresh enough to bend. After the basket is finished, Wilma said, it is important to coil it all carefully and work it with an awl-like tool made from a spoon. Bonnie complimented her on the top.

"Oh, I didn't make this," Wilma answered as she stroked the top that fit so well. "My cousin is the only person in the family who can make a tight top. My tops just float around. She's good at making tops. I'm good at selling them." This conversation contained important firsthand information about the stories that lie inside cultural objects. The information from Wilma—about her cousin, the awl-like tool made from a spoon, and the separate roles she and her cousin took—explained that the craft of basketmaking, like much folk art, is a collective endeavor that involves not only a long history of instruction but also a family of craftspeople who establish rules, determine roles, and invent new methods to carry on an old tradition. Bonnie's subjective positioning from her knowledge of folklore and her history as a basket collector affected the way she "read" Wilma's basket. And Wilma's story of her family's craft unpacked another layer of meaning and cultural knowledge.

When researchers read an artifact, they try to unpack the stories that lie inside it and to understand the interplay between tradition and creativity. Objects carry traditions of form, function, and symbol: how they are made, how they are used, and what they mean to people. But while they carry on a cultural tradition such as making pottery, cooking foods, or working with wood, objects can also show how individuals digress from tradition. Each craftsperson remakes the object in a unique way according to what materials are available, what needs it must serve, and what the craftsperson's artistic sensibility brings to it. Wilma, her cousin, and her great-grandmother each had an opportunity to put their own creative mark on the basket-weaving tradition. They were reproducing an ancestral tradition in their culture, a stable core of purpose and technique. But at the same time, each had an opportunity to remake it as her own.

Reading an Artifact

BOX 12

Purpose

The everyday objects people use inside a culture are often so utilitarian and taken for granted that the members of the culture don't recognize them as being important or symbolic of their history. An outsider is more likely to notice them and wonder where the objects come from, what they're used for, who makes them, and why they're made the way they are. All of these facts become clues to the traditions, rituals, values, rules, and behavior of a cultural group.

Action

Try your fieldworker's gaze on an everyday object: a musical instrument, a tool, a piece of furniture, or an article of clothing. If you are already involved in your fieldwork, you'll probably want to choose something you've collected from your site for this exercise. Observe it. Take fieldnotes while you study it. As Professor Agassiz would have said, "Look at your fish!" (For more on being a trained observer, see Chapter 2.)

With the help of your notes, try to describe the external details of the object. Sketch it, map it, or photograph it. If you can, read about its history in the library or online, and interview either the owner or the creator. Then make an interpretation: What does it say about the person who uses it? The person who made it? How are you positioned to see the object? What did you already know? Why did you choose the object? Finally, what does the object teach about the culture from which it comes?

Response

Our colleague and student Jeanne Janson wrote about the cotton quilt made by a Lakota woman on the reservation where Jeanne taught. Her positioning among Native Americans allowed her to read this quilt in ways that an outsider might not see. The quilt maker was the grandmother of one of Jeanne's high school students who was grateful for the extra help that Jeanne had offered her grandson. This excerpt from Jeanne's written account of this quilt as an artifact shows how she reads its history and culture, its tradition and creativity:

> Even though this quilt was made on Standing Rock Indian Reservation in South Dakota, I suppose it does have much in common with the

(Photo: Jeanne Janson)

Lakota Sioux star quilt.

European and North American tradition of quilting. The materials and techniques used—the appliquéd scraps and the double layers of cloth with batting between—were no doubt borrowed from the European quilt tradition. But the designs the Lakota Sioux women use go back in their own culture for at least a thousand years, long before the arrival of Columbus.

Originally the designs appeared in porcupine quillwork, which used either normal porcupine quills laid out and sewn into hide or flattened porcupine quills, which were dyed colors and were wound around cords to form intricate designs when the cords were sewn beside each other on the hide. When Queen Victoria made beads popular in England and they spread to North America, Native Americans took to beadwork instead of quillwork because the beads were already dyed and they were much more durable than the delicate porcupine quills. But the designs used for the beadwork remained the same as they had been for the porcupine quillwork.

I think the Lakota's exposure to cotton quilts came a bit later—I'd guess the 1890s, when they were forced to stay on the reservation and use government-issue wool blankets on beds in houses instead of buffalo robes on hides in teepees. The Bureau of Indian Affairs schools taught girls how to sew the "white man's way," so that was probably where they learned how to make quilts. But the designs they use today on the quilt covers are the same star designs used in the traditional quillwork and beadwork.

READING EVERYDAY USE:
THE USES OF CULTURAL ARTIFACTS

Like Gloria Naylor's novel *Mama Day*, Alice Walker's short story "Everyday Use" explores the theme of the college-educated insider returning to her own culture. In *Mama Day*, Reema's boy sought to decipher cultural codes of the citizens of Willow Springs. In "Everyday Use," Dee, the daughter of the narrator, places value on her family's artifacts without recognizing their cultural meanings or functions. Here are some questions to think about while you read the story:

■ What are the different values the characters place on the cultural artifacts in the story? The butter churn and its dasher? The table benches? The food? The quilts?

■ How are different characters positioned to value the cultural artifacts? What subjective history affects their positioning? How do the fixed positions of age, race, and gender affect the way they see these artifacts?

- Where are the indications of the interaction between tradition and creativity? Dee's old and new names, for example? The quilts?
- How does the narrator position herself in relationship to each of her daughters? What scenes show this?
- In what kind of culture do Maggie and her mother live? What everyday details stand out for you as they would for a fieldworker? The mother's outdoor work? The role of the church in the community? The use of snuff?

Everyday Use
Alice Walker

for your grandmama

I will wait for her in the yard that Maggie and I made so clean and wavy yesterday afternoon. A yard like this is more comfortable than most people know. It is not just a yard. It is like an extended living room. When the hard clay is swept clean as a floor and the fine sand around the edges lined with tiny, irregular grooves, anyone can come and sit and look up into the elm tree and wait for the breezes that never come inside the house.

Maggie will be nervous until after her sister goes: she will stand hopelessly in corners, homely and ashamed of the burn scars down her arms and legs, eying her sister with a mixture of envy and awe. She thinks her sister has held life always in the palm of one hand, that "no" is a word the world never learned to say to her.

You've no doubt seen those TV shows where the child who has "made it" is confronted, as a surprise, by her own mother and father, tottering in weakly from backstage. (A pleasant surprise, of course: What would they do if parent and child came on the show only to curse out and insult each other?) On TV mother and child embrace and smile into each other's faces. Sometimes the mother and father weep, the child wraps them in her arms and leans across the table to tell how she would not have made it without their help. I have seen these programs.

Sometimes I dream a dream in which Dee and I are suddenly brought together on a TV program of this sort. Out of a dark and soft-seated limousine I am ushered into a bright room filled with many people. There I meet a smiling, gray, sporty man like Johnny Carson who shakes my hand and tells me what a fine girl I have. Then we are on the stage and Dee is embracing me with tears in her eyes. She pins on my dress a large orchid, even though she has told me once that she thinks orchids are tacky flowers.

In real life I am a large, big-boned woman with rough, man-working hands. In the winter I wear flannel nightgowns to bed and overalls during the day. I can kill and clean a hog as mercilessly as a man. My fat keeps me hot in zero weather. I can work outside all day, breaking ice to get water for washing; I can eat pork liver cooked over the open fire minutes after it comes steaming from the hog. One winter I knocked a bull calf straight in the brain between the eyes with a sledge hammer and had the meat hung up to chill before nightfall. But of course all this does not show on television. I am the way my daughter would want me to be: a hundred pounds lighter, my skin like an uncooked barley pancake. My hair glistens in the hot bright lights. Johnny Carson has much to do to keep up with my quick and witty tongue.

But that is a mistake. I know even before I wake up. Who ever knew a Johnson with a quick tongue? Who can even imagine me looking a strange white man in the eye? It seems to me I have talked to them always with one foot raised in flight, with my head turned in whichever way is farthest from them. Dee, though. She would always look anyone in the eye. Hesitation was no part of her nature.

"How do I look, Mama?" Maggie says, showing just enough of her thin body enveloped in pink skirt and red blouse for me to know she's there, almost hidden by the door.

"Come out into the yard," I say.

Have you ever seen a lame animal, perhaps a dog run over by some careless person rich enough to own a car, sidle up to someone who is ignorant enough to be kind to him? That is the way my Maggie walks. She has been like this, chin on chest, eyes on ground, feet in shuffle, ever since the fire that burned the other house to the ground.

Dee is lighter than Maggie, with nicer hair and a fuller figure. She's a woman now, though sometimes I forget. How long ago was it that the other house burned? Ten, twelve years? Sometimes I can still hear the flames and feel Maggie's arms sticking to me, her hair smoking and her dress falling off her in little black papery flakes. Her eyes seemed stretched open, blazed open by the flames reflected in them. And Dee. I see her standing off under the sweet gum tree she used to dig gum out of; a look of concentration on her face as she watched the last dingy gray board of the house fall in toward the red-hot brick chimney. Why don't you do a dance around the ashes? I'd wanted to ask her. She had hated the house that much.

I used to think she hated Maggie, too. But that was before we raised the money, the church and me, to send her to Augusta to school. She used to read to us without pity; forcing words, lies, other folks' habits, whole lives upon us two, sitting trapped and ignorant underneath her voice. She washed us in a river of make-believe, burned us with a lot of knowledge we didn't necessarily need to know. Pressed us to her with the serious way she read, to shove us away at just the moment, like dimwits, we seemed about to understand.

Dee wanted nice things. A yellow organdy dress to wear to her graduation from high school; black pumps to match a green suit she'd made from an old suit somebody gave me. She was determined to stare down any disaster in her efforts. Her eyelids would not flicker for minutes at a time. Often I fought off the temptation to shake her. At sixteen she had a style of her own: and knew what style was.

I never had an education myself. After second grade the school was closed down. Don't ask me why: in 1927 colored asked fewer questions than they do now. Sometimes Maggie reads to me. She stumbles along good-naturedly but can't see well. She knows she is not bright. Like good looks and money, quickness passed her by. She will marry John Thomas (who has mossy teeth in an earnest face) and then I'll be free to sit here and I guess just sing church songs to myself. Although I never was a good singer. Never could carry a tune. I was always better at a man's job. I used to love to milk till I was hooked in the side in '49. Cows are soothing and slow and don't bother you, unless you try to milk them the wrong way.

I have deliberately turned my back on the house. It is three rooms, just like the one that burned, except the roof is tin; they don't make shingle roofs any more. There are no real windows, just some holes cut in the sides, like portholes in a ship, but not round and not square, with rawhide holding the shutters up on the outside. This house is in a pasture, too, like the other one. No doubt when Dee sees it she will want to tear it down. She wrote me once that no matter where we "choose" to live, she will manage to come see us. But she will never bring her friends. Maggie and I thought about this and Maggie asked me, "Mama, when did Dee ever *have* any friends?"

She had a few. Furtive boys in pink shirts hanging about on washday after school. Nervous girls who never laughed. Impressed with her they worshiped the well-turned phrase, the cute shape, the scalding humor that erupted like bubbles in lye. She read to them.

When she was courting Jimmy T she didn't have much time to pay to us, but turned all her faultfinding power on him. He *flew* to marry a cheap city girl from a family of ignorant flashy people. She hardly had time to recompose herself.

When she comes I will meet—but there they are!

Maggie attempts to make a dash for the house, in her shuffling way, but I stay her with my hand. "Come back here," I say. And she stops and tries to dig a well in the sand with her toe.

It is hard to see them clearly through the strong sun. But even the first glimpse of leg out of the car tells me it is Dee. Her feet were always neat-looking, as if God himself had shaped them with a certain style. From the other side of the car comes a short, stocky man. Hair is all over his head a foot long and hanging from his chin like a kinky mule tail. I hear Maggie suck in her breath. "Uhnnnh," is what it sounds like. Like when you see the wriggling end of a snake just in front of your foot on the road. "Uhnnnh."

Dee next. A dress down to the ground, in this hot weather. A dress so loud it hurts my eyes. There are yellows and oranges enough to throw back the light of the sun. I feel my whole face warming from the heat waves it throws out. Earrings gold, too, and hanging down to her shoulders. Bracelets dangling and making noises when she moves her arm up to shake the folds of the dress out of her armpits. The dress is loose and flows, and as she walks closer, I like it. I hear Maggie go "Uhnnnh" again. It is her sister's hair. It stands straight up like the wool on a sheep. It is black as night and around the edges are two long pigtails that rope about like small lizards disappearing behind her ears.

"Wa-su-zo-Tean-o!" she says, coming on in that gliding way the dress makes her move. The short stocky fellow with the hair to his navel is all grinning and he follows up with "Asalamalakim, my mother and sister!" He moves to hug Maggie but she falls back, right up against the back of my chair. I feel her trembling there and when I look up I see the perspiration falling off her chin.

"Don't get up," says Dee. Since I am stout it takes something of a push. You can see me trying to move a second or two before I make it. She turns, showing white heels through her sandals, and goes back to the car. Out she peeks next with a Polaroid. She stoops down quickly and lines up picture after picture of me sitting there in front of the house with Maggie cowering behind me. She never takes a shot without making sure the house is included. When a cow comes nibbling around the edge of the yard she snaps it and me and Maggie and the house. Then she puts the Polaroid in the back seat of the car, and comes up and kisses me on the forehead.

Meanwhile Asalamalakim is going through motions with Maggie's hand. Maggie's hand is as limp as a fish, and probably as cold, despite the sweat, and she keeps trying to pull it back. It looks like Asalamalakim wants to shake hands but wants to do it fancy. Or maybe he don't know how people shake hands. Anyhow, he soon gives up on Maggie.

"Well," I say. "Dee."

"No, Mama," she says. "Not 'Dee,' Wangero Leewanika Kemanjo!"

"What happened to 'Dee'?" I wanted to know.

"She's dead," Wangero said. "I couldn't bear it any longer, being named after the people who oppress me."

"You know as well as me you was named after your aunt Dicie," I said. Dicie is my sister. She named Dee. We called her "Big Dee" after Dee was born.

"But who was *she* named after?" asked Wangero.

"I guess after Grandma Dee," I said.

"And who was she named after?" asked Wangero.

"Her mother," I said, and saw Wangero was getting tired. "That's about as far back as I can trace it," I said. Though, in fact, I probably could have carried it back beyond the Civil War through the branches.

"Well," said Asalamalakim, "there you are."

"Uhnnnh," I heard Maggie say.

"There I was not," I said, "before 'Dicie' cropped up in our family, so why should I try to trace it that far back?"

He just stood there grinning, looking down on me like somebody inspecting a Model A car. Every once in a while he and Wangero sent eye signals over my head.

"How do you pronounce this name?" I asked.

"You don't have to call me by it if you don't want to," said Wangero.

"Why shouldn't I?" I asked. "If that's what you want us to call you, we'll call you."

"I know it might sound awkward at first," said Wangero.

"I'll get used to it," I said. "Ream it out again."

Well, soon we got the name out of the way. Asalamalakim had a name twice as long and three times as hard. After I tripped over it two or three times he told me to just call him Hakim-a-barber. I wanted to ask him was he a barber, but I didn't really think he was, so I didn't ask.

"You must belong to those beef-cattle peoples down the road," I said. They said "Asalamalakim" when they met you, too, but they didn't shake hands. Always too busy: feeding the cattle, fixing the fences, putting up salt-lick shelters, throwing down hay. When the white folks poisoned some of the herd the men stayed up all night with rifles in their hands. I walked a mile and a half just to see the sight.

Hakim-a-barber said, "I accept some of their doctrines, but farming and raising cattle is not my style." (They didn't tell me, and I didn't ask, whether Wangero (Dee) had really gone and married him.)

We sat down to eat and right away he said he didn't eat collards and pork was unclean. Wangero, though, went on through the chitlins and corn bread, the greens and everything else. She talked a blue streak over the sweet potatoes. Everything delighted her. Even the fact that we still used the benches her daddy made for the table when we couldn't afford to buy chairs.

"Oh, Mama!" she cried. Then turned to Hakim-a-barber. "I never knew how lovely these benches are. You can feel the rump prints," she said, running her hands underneath her and along the bench. Then she gave a sigh and her hand closed over Grandma Dee's butter dish. "That's it!" she said. "I knew there was something I wanted to ask you if I could have." She jumped up from the table and went over in the corner where the churn stood, the milk in it clabber by now. She looked at the churn and looked at it.

"This churn top is what I need," she said. "Didn't Uncle Buddy whittle it out of a tree you all used to have?"

"Yes," I said.

"Uh huh," she said happily. "And I want the dasher, too."

"Uncle Buddy whittle that, too?" asked the barber.

Dee (Wangero) looked up at me.

"Aunt Dee's first husband whittled the dash," said Maggie so low you almost couldn't hear her. "His name was Henry, but they called him Stash."

"Maggie's brain is like an elephant's," Wangero said, laughing. "I can use the churn top as a centerpiece for the alcove table," she said, sliding a plate over the churn, "and I'll think of something artistic to do with the dasher."

When she finished wrapping the dasher the handle stuck out. I took it for a moment in my hands. You didn't even have to look close to see where hands pushing the dasher up and down to make butter had left a kind of sink in the wood. In fact, there were a lot of small sinks; you could see where thumbs and fingers had sunk into the wood. It was beautiful light yellow wood, from a tree that grew in the yard where Big Dee and Stash had lived.

After dinner Dee (Wangero) went to the trunk at the foot of my bed and started rifling through it. Maggie hung back in the kitchen over the dishpan. Out came Wangero with two quilts. They had been pieced by Grandma Dee and then Big Dee and we had hung them on the quilt frames on the front porch and quilted them. One was in the Lone Star pattern. The other was Walk Around the Mountain. In both of them were scraps of dresses Grandma Dee had worn fifty and more years ago. Bits and pieces of Grandpa Jarrell's Paisley shirts. And one teeny faded blue piece, about the size of a penny matchbox, that was from Great Grandpa Ezra's uniform that he wore in the Civil War.

"Mama," Wangero said sweet as a bird. "Can I have these old quilts?"

I heard something fall in the kitchen, and a minute later the kitchen door slammed.

"Why don't you take one or two of the others?" I asked. "These old things was just done by me and Big Dee from some tops your grandma pieced before she died."

"No," said Wangero. "I don't want those. They are stitched around the borders by machine."

"That'll make them last better," I said.

"That's not the point," said Wangero. "These are all pieces of dresses Grandma used to wear. She did all this stitching by hand. Imagine!" She held the quilts securely in her arms, stroking them.

"Some of the pieces, like those lavender ones, come from old clothes her mother handed down to her," I said, moving up to touch the quilts. Dee (Wangero) moved back just enough so that I couldn't reach the quilts. They already belonged to her.

"Imagine!" she breathed again, clutching them closely to her bosom.

"The truth is," I said, "I promised to give them quilts to Maggie, for when she marries John Thomas."

She gasped like a bee had stung her.

"Maggie can't appreciate these quilts!" she said. "She'd probably be backward enough to put them to everyday use."

"I reckon she would," I said. "God knows I been saving 'em for long enough with nobody using 'em. I hope she will!" I didn't want to bring up how I had offered Dee (Wangero) a quilt when she went away to college. Then she had told me they were old-fashioned, out of style.

"But they're *priceless*!" she was saying now, furiously; for she has a temper. "Maggie would put them on the bed and in five years they'd be in rags. Less than that!"

"She can always make some more," I said. "Maggie knows how to quilt."

Dee (Wangero) looked at me with hatred. "You just will not understand. The point is these quilts, *these* quilts!"

"Well," I said, stumped. "What would you do with them?"

"Hang them," she said. As if that was the only thing you *could* do with quilts.

Maggie by now was standing in the door. I could almost hear the sound her feet made as they scraped over each other.

"She can have them, Mama," she said, like somebody used to never winning anything, or having anything reserved for her. "I can 'member Grandma Dee without the quilts."

I looked at her hard. She had filled her bottom lip with checkerberry snuff and it gave her face a kind of dopey, hangdog look. It was Grandma Dee and Big Dee who taught her how to quilt herself. She stood there with her scarred hands hidden in the folds of her skirt. She looked at her sister with something like fear but she wasn't mad at her. This was Maggie's portion. This was the way she knew God to work.

When I looked at her like that something hit me in the top of my head and ran down to the soles of my feet. Just like when I'm in church and the spirit of God touches me and I get happy and shout. I did something I never had done before: hugged Maggie to me, then dragged her on into the room, snatched the quilts out of Miss Wangero's hands and dumped them into Maggie's lap. Maggie just sat there on my bed with her mouth open.

"Take one or two of the others," I said to Dee.

But she turned without a word and went out to Hakim-a-barber.

"You just don't understand," she said, as Maggie and I came out to the car.

"What don't I understand?" I wanted to know.

"Your heritage," she said. And then she turned to Maggie, kissed her, and said, "You ought to try to make something of yourself, too, Maggie. It's really a new day for us. But from the way you and Mama still live you'd never know it."

She put on some sunglasses that hid everything above the tip of her nose and her chin.

Maggie smiled; maybe at the sunglasses. But a real smile, not scared. After we watched the car dust settle I asked Maggie to bring me a dip of snuff. And then the two of us sat there just enjoying, until it was time to go in the house and go to bed.

In Walker's story, you may have noticed that Dee seeks to remove the cultural artifacts from the cultural site as she leaves her culture behind. Whereas Reema's boy saw himself as a fieldworker in training, Dee considers herself a sophisticated collector of valuable folk art. Neither was successful at listening or looking at the language, the rituals, or the artifacts of their home culture. Dee's desire to collect the quilt, perhaps even hang it, takes it out of its everyday context, distances it, and makes it more an object of art than of the living culture. In "Everyday Use," Dee's sister Maggie lives quietly inside the everyday community that her sister tries to interrupt. Notice that the voice of this narrator, Dee's mother, is similar to the narrator in *Mama Day*, both full members of their communities, who already value and appreciate their culture.

These stories provide us with a contrast between "stepping in" and "stepping out." Dee and Reema's boy serve as both insiders and outsiders. Their misinterpretations of artifacts and rituals mark them as outsiders. Their histories and kinships mark them as insiders. Yet they have each left their home cultures and returned, no longer able to read the culture or its artifacts in the same way as the people who continue to live there.

Both of these readings are reflective pieces of fiction intended to invite you into another distinct culture: its rituals, rules, behaviors, codes, and artifacts. Both Naylor and Walker illustrate culture as everyday lived experience that is not easily understood by outsiders. They show culture as more than kinship or geography, more than language and ways of behaving, but as a combination of all of these. And your own history as a close reader of texts has, we hope, taught you to enter fictional culture—to live within it and understand it from a character's point of view. Fictional worlds are both satisfying and neat for the reader. By starting and ending with fiction, we've drawn on your strengths as a reader, the same kinds of strengths you will need while you are reading and researching in the field.

READING ETHNOGRAPHY AND MEDIA CULTURES

One way to understand how to write fieldwork is to read it. In our book we offer you many samples of students' and teacher's fieldstudies as well as excerpts from published fieldworkers to illustrate the very different ways that fieldworkers write about their data. These are essays, ethnographic in nature and method, done over a semester or a year, but of course not full ethnographies. Most studies that can claim themselves as "ethnographies" are done over long periods of time. We and many of our teaching colleagues believe that sometimes, to get a fuller range of ideas, styles, and formats for writing, it's also helpful to read a full-length ethnographic account of a much longer piece of research. We realize, however, that it can be difficult to read more than one study during a semester in which you're conducting your own fieldwork. One way of exposing yourself to many approaches to doing fieldwork is to form book clubs within a class and have each small group read an ethnographic study or an ethnographic novel. After each group meets and talks about the book it has selected and read, the groups then report back to the rest of the class about not only the study itself, but what they've learned about doing and writing up fieldwork. In Box 13, our colleague Katie Ryan shares her process for forming book clubs in a first-year writing course devoted to fieldwork.

BOX 13

Fieldworking Book Clubs

by Kathleen Ryan, University of West Virginia, Morgantown, West Virginia

Purpose

The point of fieldwork is to tell the story of your "reading" of a culture, and the point of a fieldworking book club is to figure out the story of the book you are reading. This project shows you how doing fieldwork, like reading, is about acts of interpretation. In other words, the abilities you use for fieldworking translate into the abilities you use for reading, and, of course, the opposite is also true.

In a fieldworking book club, you will read an ethnography, an oral history, or an ethnographic fiction work with four or five of your classmates. The point of this book club is to collectively figure out what your book can teach you about being a fieldworker and what being a fieldworker can teach you about your book. The five phases of the project include choosing a book, writing in a reading journal, meeting regularly in class for book club discussions, presenting your book to the class with your book club at the end of the semester or year, and finally, individually reflecting on the entire project.

Action

1. Choose a Book.

When my students did fieldworking book clubs, each club chose one of these three books: *The Mole People,* an ethnography by Jennifer Toth about the homeless communities who live beneath the streets in New York City; *Mules and Men,* a historical study by Zora Neale Hurston of African American stories from Florida and hoodoo practices in Louisiana; and *The Handmaid's Tale,* novelist Margaret Atwood's futuristic fiction written from the viewpoint of Offred, a vital participant and outsider in a post–nuclear war society. I call this book ethnographic fiction because Offred writes from the perspective of a participant-observer in her culture and the text asks readers to read as fieldworkers. My students grouped themselves according to the book they chose.

2. Keep a Reading Journal.

Once you have a book and a club, you are ready to begin writing and talking together. You'll write regularly in a reading journal as you read. Bring at least a two-page journal entry and your book to each book club meeting. The reading journal serves as a place that documents your process of reading, a starting point for your club discussions, and a place for you to write about the text on your own. Here are some sample questions to ask of your reading:

- What's the book about? How do I know?
- How does the field researcher/narrator position himself or herself?
- What choices do you imagine the author made in writing the book?

- How do authorial choices in detail and style affect your reading?
- How does reading with a club affect your reading?
- How does the organization of the book help you think about the arrangement of your own research?
- What do you bring to your book as a fieldworker? What do you bring to your book as a reader?

Here is an excerpt from my student Matt Furbish's reading journal on *The Mole People:* "If Toth had not positioned herself in the story, she could not have shown exactly how much underground life changes a person. At the beginning of the book, she's just a sweet, innocent graduate student from Columbia. At the end, however, she comes to find a part of herself she never knew existed: her animal side."

3. Have Regular Book Club Meetings.

In my class, fieldworking book clubs meet once every two weeks. Students bring their book and most recent journal entry to each meeting. As a book club, their assignment is to explore reading and fieldworking by talking about this book. Each group is responsible for determining a reading schedule and an agenda of discussions aimed at fulfilling the assignments and the general goals of the fieldworking book club. Since they know they will be writing evaluations of the books and offering them to the others, their readings and discussions need to move in that direction. Here are some tips to help book club meetings run smoothly:

- Exchange e-mail addresses and phone numbers to reach other members.
- Give clear book club assignments for each meeting.
- Do long-range planning by creating a reading schedule and preparing for the group review and presentation.
- Be sure someone takes notes during class discussions.
- Plan discussions around recurring questions, interests, and ideas that come up in journals.
- Plan ahead for assignments.

4. Write a Group Paper, and Give a Presentation.

Each fieldworking book club writes a collaborative review of the book according to its qualities as ethnography, oral history, or ethnographic fiction, answering the question "How did this work contribute to your understanding of fieldworking and reading?" This review also becomes the content material for a creative and informative 20-minute class presentation.

5. Write an Individual Reflection

Each club member also writes a one- or two-page summary reflection on the entire book club project. Students reread their journals, reread their group notes, and answer these questions:

- What did you notice about the way you made sense out of the book as you read?
- How did reading and talking about the book with others shape or change your thinking? Your reading?
- What did you learn about the process of fieldworking?
- What did you learn about your own project?
- How does this book relate to your life in this class as a fieldworker and your life beyond this class as a writer and reader of books and culture?

Response

One of my former students, Kelli Frazier, describes how her book club read *Mules and Men* by applying their growing knowledge of oral histories to their reading:

> As I look back over the semester, I see that our group really made a lot of progress. I must admit that during the first few weeks of class, I was discouraged about the way our group discussions were going. We seemed unable to get past the fact that we were not enjoying the book and spent all of our time reiterating just how much we disliked it. Finally, I think everyone realized that we were not getting anywhere with the attitudes we had and the way we were handling the assignment. From that point on, we were able to start to look at the book from a different perspective, and we gained a new appreciation for it and the author's purpose in writing it. I was really proud of us because we made a huge change as we began to focus on it as an oral history. Once we began to evaluate it on that basis, we really discovered a lot of things to discuss: Hurston's method of transcribing in the 1930s by candlelight at night, the old male storytellers who were part of her own past as they sat on the porch in the evening, etc. By that point our book group conversations were becoming really interesting as each of us brought different ideas to the group but no longer in a negative way.

READING ELECTRONIC COMMUNITIES

Most of the time we think of a fieldsite as being a physical place you can enter, a place that is "out in the world," a place where you can talk with people face to face. But with the advances of electronic technologies, the idea of place is widening to include chatrooms, mailing lists, Web-based message boards, and other sites of interaction. Although the Web may seem disembodied to some, others find a virtual conversation more comfortable than an actual one. Participating in electronic communities can bring you a wealth of information relevant to your fieldworking study—from "insider" sources of data to "stepping in" yourself, learning how a community operates from the inside and, in a sense, doing virtual fieldwork as you "read" the culture electronically.

Not all cultures exist in the electronic world as completely as others, but it is worthwhile to check whether something related to your fieldsite exists on the Internet. Its presence will depend on how comfortable the culture's members are with emerging technologies—whether they build webpages, exchange e-mail, or participate in hypertext discussions. You may turn up nothing, or you may discover a host of insiders conversing as if they were meeting face to face.

It's important to "read" the electronic media with the same ideas we've been discussing about conventional print texts. Linking and interactive participation are new skills our electronic culture requires of us as readers. Because of this, you may want to do a survey of a few mailing lists, chatrooms, and Web-based discussion forums. Take a brief look at websites you know about, or search for sites by using a few keywords. As you search, you'll notice whether your fieldsite's subculture engages in electronic conversations. If so, you can develop your skills in "reading" that community. If not, choose any other electronic community that interests you.

Now your real participation begins. To sign up as a member of a chatroom or a Web-based discussion forum, you'll probably need to create an account with a user name and password to gain access. For listservs or mailing lists, you'll have to subscribe with your e-mail address. After you're registered as a member of your electronic community, listen in or "lurk" for a while before posting your own comments. Once you begin actively participating, don't forget your common-sense "Netiquette," which calls for respect, courtesy, and playing by the basic rules that govern all communities.

After you have participated in some exchanges, do some analysis offline, thinking about the data as well as the interactions you've witnessed and taken part in. Make notes on all the topics that suggest data you might explore further and potentially **triangulate** for your study. Think about how the members of the community you've joined interact with one another. How do they address one another, for instance? What names have they given themselves in the virtual world? What tone does each conversation take? How do informants seem to conceive of themselves as a community or culture? Pull particular pieces from your data for closer scrutiny to see whether they suggest general trends to pursue in either your data collection or essay writing. And don't forget that the people you meet online are potentially valuable resources to you for your study. Keep those contacts you make. In the course of group discussions, you can plan to e-mail individuals later.

In her ethnographic study of a college student chatroom, Bridgewater State College student Sarah-Rose Hollis focused on the culture particular to this online social niche: its behaviors, prejudices, likes, and dislikes. Most of Sarah-Rose's informants were engaging in chat as a leisure activity rather than as a way of exchanging any particular information. In the course of interviewing people she met online, she discovered her informants' views about the medium of online chat. In this statement, she framed herself as the researcher, noting her own goals and thoughts and procedures:

> In the beginning of my research, I discovered that my screen name did not make me as inconspicuous as I wanted. Because my name implies my sex, I constantly received PMs (private messages) from guys—never from girls. With the constant PMs I found it impossible to observe the chatroom conversation and therefore had to create a new and less identifying screen name, "getting_research." I chose not to disclose any personal information with my observation name and was far more successful in remaining an invisible observer.
>
> Although many don't admit they held biases beforehand, Peter confesses that he "thought only freaks and perverts chatted." One informant, whose name was alluded to only as "for me to know and you to find out" viewed chatting as a "stupid concept" but now chats every day. Gil, 23, is a daily chatter who was able to put the whole idea into perspective: "I think that people are still highly skeptical about the whole chatting arena, it is so vast and impersonal. No one knows who anyone truly is, and there is no way of knowing who you are really talking to, but some find that anonymity a comfort. It helps some people vent while protecting their dignity from the 'known' world." Despite their biases, plenty of new people begin chatting each day. Sue, 21, was skeptical: "I felt it could be very dangerous, if one was not careful"; but now she is dating someone she met online. Her caution, however, has not diminished. "I still think it is dangerous.... It is sort of unorthodox, but I was lucky. I wouldn't recommend someone going and meeting someone from the chatrooms."
>
> In the University Years chatroom, I found that chatters have the chance not only to meet people they wouldn't otherwise get to meet but also to be people they wouldn't otherwise get to be. Anybody has the opportunity to pretend they are someone else and enter any type of room they wish. Gil says the reason he was attracted to chatting the first time was because he "found it interesting that you could be anybody, from anywhere, that you wanted to be." The anonymity of the Internet makes this possible, and everyone can make it a reality.
>
> Due to the free-for-all basis, a huge variety of tensions are constantly created. Many heated conversations erupt that stem from battles of the sexes, sports, pornography, location, and many other topics. Ethics are not an essential tool of chatting, as there are no consequences. The worst thing that can happen in the room is that you are ignored or badmouthed. (You cannot be "booted" from a Yahoo!-sponsored room for profanity.)... Gil does not believe in chatroom censorship, as "the beauty of chatting is that it is no-holds-barred.... Regulation would take away a lot of what people

come to chatrooms for—the craziness and freedom of speech that makes chatting such an eye-opening and enlightening experience."… As a college student myself, I know that the topics discussed in the room are ones that college students will discuss anyway—online or off.

By investigating the social behaviors of her chatroom fieldsite, Sarah-Rose's study reveals certain aspects of the medium and her own college-age culture that ultimately lead her to conclude that this chatroom is "the pickup bar of the twenty-first century." Through informants online she is able to gather data from a wide range of people: "I've met many people from all around the world and of many different ages and races in the room," which gives her essay a breadth of perspective not readily accessible to her through other means.

In Chapter 4, we continue to look at how our subcultures are expanding with technology but also, as Sarah-Rose observed, how our virtual world offers ways to organize and archive the very human materials we've shared for generations.

THE RESEARCH PORTFOLIO: OPTIONS FOR REFLECTION

The portfolio is the site of your research reflections. It gives focus to a researcher's abstract thoughts and feelings. All your data—the writing you do, the artifacts you collect, and the readings you complete—are options for putting into your portfolio. The portfolio contains the artifacts, both the written and cultural material, of your work in progress. It records your fieldnotes: anxieties about looking at others and perhaps their anxieties about being researched. The portfolio captures both your fieldwork and your deskwork. And your written commentary about your ongoing research process reflects your positioning as a researcher. The key word in developing a research portfolio is *reflection*.

We hope you'll work with a portfolio partner or a small group to share your project in progress. This is a way to clarify your own ideas and get new ideas from other researchers who are working in sites and on projects different from yours. We've attended several professional ethnography conferences that held a Festival of Data session where researchers shared their work in progress. Sharing your portfolios can serve the same purpose. Our own students have found such data-sharing sessions useful and valuable.

Reflections on Artifacts

Rick Zollo, for example, wrote several short reflections about his positioning as he researched Iowa 80. In them, he was able to explore how his own personal history linked with his research and affected his work in the fieldsite. His portfolio included artifacts from the truck stop as well as his related reading and writing: a menu, a few brochures about trucking regulations, photocopies of articles he'd read about truckers, a trucker magazine, photographs he had taken at the truck stop, five writing exercises describing his fieldsite, and a **transcript** of an interview with one of his informants. Each time he reviewed his portfolio, he wrote a short commentary about where he found himself in the research process. In one reflection about his position, he writes:

> This truck stop story has been gestating for years. I first conceived a project about truck drivers and their hangout several years ago. The Iowa 80 truck stop became my place for planned inquiry, since it was along a major highway near my home, was practically in the center of our nation and its interstate highway system, and had grown into a strange (to my eyes, at least) little community that seemed to have its own life.

Researching another culture can be both messy and confusing, but if you reflect on the process, you'll find yourself sorting out the mess and clarifying much of the confusion. We believe that the process of reflecting is just as important as the final end product of an ethnographic study. For this reason, we want you to take time to think and write about what you've actually learned from each exercise you do at different stages of your research process. Get together with your portfolio partner, and share your work. Have your partner ask questions about your project, and include those questions and responses in your portfolio as well: How does your own personal history affect what you've chosen? What does each artifact represent about a growing theme in your research? How do the artifacts connect to one another? In Rick's portfolio, he might have looked at the relationship between the menu, the trucking magazine, and his photographs, for example. With each reflective commentary, Rick had a chance to see the scope and depth of his project, and the reflection moved him toward the next phase of his research process.

Reflections on Reading

For your portfolio, you'll want to review each of the short readings you did and reflect on them: Gloria Naylor's introduction to her novel *Mama Day*, Laura Bohannan's essay "Shakespeare in the Bush," and Alice Walker's short story "Everyday Use." Which of your responses do you prefer, and why? Which ones gave you more insight into researching another culture? Review the pieces you wrote on Naylor, Bohannan, and Walker, and choose one (or more) as an example of "reading culture" to place in your portfolio. You might also want to add other related readings you have done.

Reflections on Writing

If you've worked on the boxes in this chapter, you may have already

- Written about your positionality (the assumptions you carry into your fieldsite),

- Written about an everyday object or event using the double-entry format,
- Kept notes for a book club,
- Considered the process of negotiating entry and worked with ethics statements,
- Selected and "read" a cultural artifact.

Review the writing exercises you have completed, and look for common themes or concerns they represent. What is important about them to you as a writer, a researcher, and a beginning fieldworker? How have you have positioned yourself within your written responses? What have you left out, and why? If you've started to work in a fieldsite or in a subculture that you want to continue with, compare your exercises to the actual fieldnotes you have started to take. Notice similarities and differences.

The portfolio itself is like a researcher's trips to the field. It shows the journey to the places you've observed and the people you've interviewed. It documents the resources you use throughout your field trips along with the books and guides you've relied on to get there. When you see the evidence of your trip laid out in a portfolio, you can reflect on what you've done and plan for the work that lies ahead.

FieldWriting: Published and Unpublished Written Sources

Fieldwriting depends far more on oral source material than on written sources. Your informants, along with your fieldnotes, will contribute the most important data to your fieldprojects. When fieldworkers write up their research, they treat informants' words in the same way that library researchers cite textual references. (See Chapter 6 for information on taping, transcribing, and presenting oral language on the page.)

But you'll still need to refer to written texts from both published and unpublished library and archival sources, as well as documents you've collected at your fieldsite, to support your fieldwork's oral sources. As all research writers know, the basic role of documentation is to attribute ideas that are not your own to their original source. For example, when we use the phrase "stepping in and stepping out" in this book, we put quotation marks around it to indicate that it is not our original idea. We do this because we want to attribute this term to Hortense Powdermaker, whose quote from *Stranger and Friend* opens our book and whose idea has given us a new way to explain the insider-outsider researcher stance.

One exception to information that requires documentation is common knowledge. Common knowledge refers to information that everyone might be expected to know, such as the presidents or the population of the United States. A fieldwriter might consult an almanac, a map, a time chart, or an encyclopedia to verify such common knowledge, but she would not need to include that source in a final paper. Sometimes it's difficult to determine, however, what common knowledge particular readers will have. In this chapter, for example, we have assumed that our readers know that Gullah is an English dialect. However, they may not know that it is a creole form of English spoken in the South Carolina and Georgia low country of the United States; we write that information into our text to show this. We mention where Gullah is spoken and a novel and movie about people who speak Gullah. Writers who are unsure of their own readers' common knowledge should include contextual information, which itself often comes from published written sources.

Because this book is about fieldworking and the conventions associated with writing about it, we've limited our discussion of textual documentation to the issues directly related to writing about fieldwork. When you use documentation (published or unpublished) to support your fieldwork, you should refer to a more complete handbook or research manual. We like the Modern Language Association's *MLA Handbook for Writers of Research Papers,* fifth edition, because it illustrates how to cite movies, electronic publications, diskettes, tapes, and online databases, as well as personal interviews, letters, journals, e-mail, and more conventional text sources. Because we work in English departments, we follow the MLA documentation conventions; in other subject areas, your instructors may guide you toward other, equally thorough research manuals, such as the *Publication Manual of the American Psychological Association,* used in psychology and education; the *Chicago Manual of Style,* which many book publishers use; or one of the many other manuals of style specific to other disciplines, such as law, mathematics, science, medicine, linguistics, or engineering.

The current convention for documenting any source—informant or text, published or unpublished—is to give as much information about the source as possible within your actual written text. This is called *intertextual citation,* and it is a simpler convention than the older ones, which required footnotes, endnotes, and abbreviations of Latin phrases (*op. cit.* and *ibid.,* for example). Intertextual (or "in-text") citation might include the author or informant's name and the book or document title, depending on how you introduce the material into your writing. Your first citation must always refer to the original source. For published sources, this would be the page number (for example, "Naylor 7" or "*Mama Day* 7"). For unpublished written sources, how you cite depends on the type of material you have collected. When you cite a written source intertextually, you must provide information that allows a reader to find the complete citation in your "Works Cited" section—or "References," "Bibliography," or "FieldReading"—at the end. Intertextual documentation provides helpful context without interrupting the flow of your text and cluttering it with information that readers can find elsewhere. On the following pages, we present examples from this book of the many ways intertextual citation can be used.

Incorporating Published Sources

We used intertextual citation in Chapter 2 when we quoted from writers Diane Ackerman and John Berger (see pages 85 and 86). When you want to cite only a sentence or two (no more than four lines), you try to weave someone else's words into your own text. You want to quote the source and let your reader understand why you've called on it to support your own ideas. Include enough information about the citation for your reader to locate the source at the end of your work.

Here is an example of a direct quotation from art historian John Berger. In Chapter 2, we used Berger's quote to amplify what we wanted to say about Samuel Scudder's essay, "Look at Your Fish." It is a straightforward example of intertextual citation that identifies only the author and page number:

As art historian John Berger writes, "We only see what we look at. To look is an act of choice" (8).

This source would require the following bibliographic entry:

Berger, John. *Ways of Seeing.* New York: Penguin, 1972.

On page 230 of her book *A Natural History of the Senses,* Diane Ackerman writes: "Seventy percent of the body's sense receptors cluster in the eyes, and it is mainly through seeing the world that we appraise and understand it." We wanted to use her words but incorporate them into a sentence of our own. Here's how we did that:

In her book *A Natural History of the Senses,* Diane Ackerman writes that "seventy percent of the body's sense receptors cluster in the eyes, and it is mainly through seeing the world that we appraise and understand it" (230).

Had we wanted to use only part of her sentence, we would have used ellipsis points within brackets to indicate the part that has been omitted:

In her book *A Natural History of the Senses,* Diane Ackerman writes that "seventy percent of the body's sense receptors cluster in the eyes[…]" (230).

Note that capitalization of the first word of the quote matches the grammar of our own sentence, not necessarily that of the original.

A quote of more than four lines of published text is called a *block quotation.* Instead of using quotation marks, a block quotation is set off by skipping a line and indenting both margins. Introduce a block quote by giving as much information about the source as possible. For example, to introduce Scudder, we wrote about his essay on studying entomology in the nineteenth century with his Harvard professor, Louis Agassiz. Here's a block quotation taken from Scudder's essay:

It was more than fifteen years ago that I entered the laboratory of Professor Agassiz, and told him I had enrolled my name in the Scientific

School as a student of natural history. He asked me a few questions about my object in coming, my antecedents generally, the mode in which I afterwards proposed to use the knowledge I might acquire, and, finally, whether I wished to study any special branch. To the latter I replied that, while I wished to be well grounded in all departments of zoology, I purposed to devote myself especially to insects. (1)

When a writer summarizes another person's words, there is no need to include quotation marks or page numbers as long as the reader can locate that information in your final list of references. If you've listed three books by Louise Rosenblatt, for instance, you would need to distinguish which book you were summarizing. We open this chapter with a quote from Louise Rosenblatt's book *Literature as Exploration* and follow it up immediately with our summary of her theory of reading. We write:

We all read differently. Literary theorist Louise Rosenblatt suggests that a reader's main instrument for making meaning is herself.

In another part of this chapter, when we summarized parts of Gloria Naylor's novel *Mama Day* and also included directly quoted material, we indicated the page from which we took the quote. The combination of quoting directly and summarizing is yet another way of documenting written source material, just as it is when we cite our informants:

With the character of Reema's pear-headed nameless boy, Naylor offers us a parody of a field researcher. He is an insider, born on the island, and he returns from his fancy college, "dragging his notebooks and tape recorder and a funny way of curling up his lip and clicking his teeth, all excited and determined to put Willow Springs on the map." (115)

Incorporating Unpublished Sources

Many times in your fieldwork, you'll want to quote from your informants' unpublished written texts or from documents you collect at your fieldsite. This might include, for example, journals, letters, diaries, photocopies meant for insiders, or notes written by informants that provide evidence you want to cite. Rick Zollo, for example, received a letter from one of his informants at Iowa 80 that illustrated the truckers' complaints about growing government regulations. Rick included this letter only in his research journal, but here's one way he might have quoted from it in his final essay:

Dean Self, a truck driver who wanted his fellow truckers to organize, wrote this letter:

Drivers:
Enough is enough, we're finally fed up. We have shown unity through protest convoys and even a shutdown.

No matter how much we protest, we will gain nothing due to the fact that we have no representation. We must have a national organization founded, funded, and operated by us drivers. With no outside interests. Then and only then will we be represented.

Another example of an unpublished written source in this chapter is the "code of honor" from the skinheads our student Jake began to study. (We present this material in a block quotation on page 124 because it is over four lines.) Since it has no verifiable source, like Rick's letter from Dean Self, the full bibliographic reference for this code will indicate that it is unpublished. Here is the skinheads' "code of honor" that Jake photocopied:

- Be discreet about new recruits; check them out thoroughly.
- For prospects, we must have at least a ninety-day contact period in which we can attest to your character. A probationary period and productivity report will be given.
- Outsiders need no knowledge of what goes on or is said in our meetings.
- No racial exceptions whatsoever! All members must be 100% white!

Both of these unpublished sources would be cited in the Works Cited. In the first instance, Rick Zollo knew the author of the letter and so would place the entry among his references in alphabetical order like this:

Self, Dean. Letter to the writer. October 1994.

By contrast, Jake had limited information about the original source of the skinheads' honor code. Although he too would place this citation among his references in alphabetical order, it would look like this:

"Code of Honor." Unpublished document. 1993.

You'll find that fieldwriters draw from a wide range of unpublished materials that include flyers, brochures, menus, business statements, letters, signs, captions in family albums, photocopied or mimeographed pages meant for a group of insiders, and other kinds of personal and unpublished writing.

As a fieldwriter, your major responsibility in using your sources, both published and unpublished, is to amplify and support what you have to say by incorporating the written source material smoothly into your text. You also need to make it possible for another researcher to be able to locate whatever written resources you have cited, both by including information about the reference within your text and by making it available in your list of cited source materials.

FIELDWORDS

Artifact   Any material object that belongs to and represents a culture.

Human subjects review board   An administrative department at a university that processes researchers' applications for conducting studies with people as their subjects. This board protects human subjects from inappropriate or unethical projects and protects researchers by helping them anticipate problems they may encounter in working with people.

Informed consent   The agreement between a researcher and a human subject (informant, consultant, collaborator) that gives the researcher permission to use the informant's observations, interviews, comments, and artifacts. Sometimes a researcher must also obtain such an agreement to enter a fieldsite and conduct a study there.

Intersubjectivity   The process of collecting and connecting many different perspectives on one piece of data. In photography, this would translate into taking many pictures of the same object from different angles.

Material culture   The artifacts that represent meaning, history, and values for a group. These artifacts can be tools, printed or written materials, musical instruments, foods, toys, jewelry, ceremonial objects, and clothes.

Positioning   The researcher's stance toward the place and people he or she studies, as well as the representation of that stance in a final written text. This chapter describes three aspects of this stance: fixed, subjective, and textual.

Transcript   The written, word-for-word record of an interview or other oral event.

Triangulation   The process of verifying data using multiple sources of information. Triangulation does not mean simply obtaining three pieces of evidence or three perspectives. Researchers use the term to discuss ways that data is validated, cross-checked, or disconfirmed.

FIELDREADING

Ackerman, Diane. *A Natural History of the Senses.* New York: Vintage, 1991.
Atwood, Margaret. *The Handmaid's Tale.* New York: Anchor, 1998.
Baldwin, James. *Nobody Knows My Name: More Notes of a Native Son.* New York: Dial, 1961.

Berger, John. *Ways of Seeing*. New York: Penguin, 1972.

Bowen, Elenore Smith. *Return to Laughter*. New York: Anchor, 1964.

Cary, Lorene. *Black Ice*. New York: Knopf, 1991.

Fitzgerald, Frances. *Cities on a Hill: A Journey through Contemporary American Cultures*. New York: Simon, 1986.

Hurston, Zora Neale. *Mules and Men*. 1939. New York: Harper, 1989.

Lurie, Alison. *Imaginary Friends*. New York: Avon, 1991.

————. *The Language of Clothes*. New York: Random, 1986.

Naylor, Gloria. *Mama Day*. New York: Vintage, 1988.

Rosenblatt, Louise. *Literature as Exploration*. 5th ed. New York: Modern Language Association, 1995.

Sims, Norman, and Mark Kramer, eds. *Literary Journalism*. New York: Ballantine, 1995.

Stoller, Paul. *The Taste of Ethnographic Things: The Senses in Anthropology*. Philadelphia: U Pennsylvania P, 1989.

Toth, Jennifer. *The Mole People: Life in the Tunnels of New York City*. Chicago: Chicago Review, 1993.

Wolf, Margery. *A Thrice-Told Tale: Feminism, Postmodernism, and Ethnographic Responsibility*. Stanford: Stanford UP, 1992.

FieldPoem

The Voice You Hear When You Read Silently

Thomas Lux

is not silent, it is a speaking-
out-loud voice in your head: it is *spoken*,
a voice is *saying* it
as you read. It's the writer's words,
of course, in a literary sense
his or her "voice" but the sound
of that voice is the sound of *your* voice.
Not the sound your friends know
or the sound of a tape played back
but your voice
caught in the dark cathedral
of your skull, your voice heard
by an internal ear informed by internal abstracts
and what you know by feeling,

having felt. It is your voice
saying, for example, the word "barn"
that the writer wrote
but the "barn" you say
is a barn you know or knew. The voice
in your head, speaking as you read,
never says anything neutrally—some people
hated the barn they knew,
some people love the barn they know
so you hear the word loaded
and a sensory constellation
is lit: horse-gnawed stalls,
hayloft, black heat tape wrapping
a water pipe, a slippery
spilled *chirr* of oats from a split sack,
the bony, filthy haunches of cows...
And "barn" is only a noun—no verb
or subject has entered into the sentence yet!
The voice you hear when you read to yourself
is the clearest voice: you speak it
speaking to you.

Commentary
Todd McKinney

One reason this poem is so memorable is that we all know this voice Lux
writes about, this voice that speaks to us when we read. So reading this
poem is a lot of fun because we hear that voice as we read. But what's really
exciting is how this poem teaches us about this voice: that it is unique to
each individual, that it is something that occupies the "dark cathedral of our
skull" in the same way a bird occupies a birdcage, that it is a perspective
shaped by experience, and that it is not neutral precisely because of
experience (which then validates everyone's voice and existence and, more
important, our right to speak about that existence). All of this should make
us want to hear that voice, to understand it, to live in it.

When we think of this poem in terms of this chapter, all of a sudden
this voice becomes something much larger. It becomes a personal space
within a landscape. It becomes a voice that speaks not only when we read a

*Todd McKinney received his MFA from the University of North Carolina at
Greensboro, where he now teaches. He has recently published work in* The
Greensboro Review *and* Puerto del Sol.

page from a book but also when we "read" what is in our gaze: people, landscape, culture. The voice is still there in our heads, informing our present experience with our past. And if we listen closely enough to this voice in our heads, it will be our understanding of all that makes up the landscape of this world.

CHAPTER 4

Researching Archives: Locating Culture

Culture is elusive. It passes secretly, often silently, telepathically.… it ripens, untended, often unconsciously in dreams, suddenly unexpectedly to reveal itself in an expression or a turn of phrase…or, at another level, in our musical and pictorial preferences, in the narratives we construct about ourselves and others or to which we turn for understanding. It may arise by accident, from a half-remembered memory, from fingers or hands idling with instruments and tools.

—ROBERT CANTWELL

As folklorist Robert Cantwell suggests above, culture is elusive—hard to capture and even harder to retain. One way people capture culture is by assembling **archives**—collections of documents and artifacts. An archive can be a shoe box full of mementos from your volleyball career, a storage trunk of letters from an uncle who fought in Vietnam, a collection of pens used by a local mayor to sign laws, an elderly neighbor's egg cup collection that attracts visitors from throughout the region, a room in your town hall showing maps and photographs tracing the town's historical development on top of a floodplain, a display of embroidery that tells the story of the Hmong's entrapment in refugee camps, or a large city's aerospace museum. Simply, an archive contains important "stuff" so that family, ethnic, local, or national cultures and subcultures don't—to paraphrase Cantwell's words—pass secretly, silently, or untended.

One of the largest archives in the United States, the Smithsonian Institution in Washington, D.C., describes itself as "the nation's attic." In this attic, as in any archive, you will find stored a dazzling and surprising variety of artifacts, records, correspondence, historical documents, and audiovisual media. The Smithsonian has 10 separate archives, which hold an estimated 50,000 cubic feet of paper documents, 7 million still photographs, and thousands of motion picture films, videos, and audio recordings. Smithsonian's National Museum of American History, only one of its many constituent "attics," includes over 150 million items and acquires more all the time. A few of our favorite examples of its holdings are the ruby slippers Judy Garland wore in *The Wizard of Oz,* the Woolworth's lunch counter stools from one early civil rights sit-in, the first typewriter, from 1870, which weighs 165 pounds, and a 1918 Oldsmobile

Model 37. One specialized collection includes a urologist's surgical case from the 1830s, a ritual circumcisionist's kit, a piano maker's tool chest, a shoe-shine kit from the 1950s, and even a computer technician's tool case from the 1990s.

Our computer culture allows us access to many archival sources through the Internet. In fact, some exhibits are available only as "virtual tours," like the Hard Rock Cafe website's Memorabilia Gallery, which displays artifacts from its franchised cafes across the world. Online, you can view rock star Jim Morrison's leather pants, Eric Clapton's favorite bar stool, the wool herringbone suit Rex Harrison wore when he played Professor Henry Higgins in the 1964 movie musical *My Fair Lady*. (The site can be accessed at <http://www.hardrockcafe.com/Memorabilia/Gallery>.)

All cultures and subcultures hold on to collections of representative artifacts to hand down to group members. To an outsider, those collections may appear to be mere clutter; to an insider they are the most precious identity markers and artifacts of a subculture's history. These are the concrete objects of tradition—symbols of the rituals, behaviors, language, and beliefs that teach a culture about itself as it shifts and changes with time. Even when a cultural group is oppressed or exiled from its place of origin, human ingenuity prevails, finding ways to preserve old traditions and apply them in new settings.

Hmong embroidery, for example, is intricate and beautiful, but not merely decorative. Rather, it stitches the story of the Hmongs' life for 2,000 years in their homeland and later in refugee camps as they prepared for relocation in cultures very different from theirs. "Flower cloth stitching" (*paj ntaub*), is an old art form of appliqué and embroidery in geometric patterns, often depicting animals and other forms of nature. In the 1970s, after the Vietnam War, the Hmong were pushed into refugee camps in Thailand. Since they had no written language, they developed the concept of the "storycloth" (*pa ndau*) in an effort to retain their history and pass it on. Not only was the storycloth an artistic document of the Hmongs' recent history, it also allowed them to become small entrepreneurs in their new locations in the Western world. They used the ancestral traditions of embroidery to record the stories of their past, share their current situation, and anticipate their future lives (see page 161).

In this chapter, we explore a wide range of archival materials—the stuff of collections—from private family diaries, journals, letters, and scrapbooks to the bigger institutional archives like museum holdings and the very public archive, the Internet. We intend for you to use the ideas in this chapter in two different ways: as a way of choosing a fieldwork topic and as support for the fieldwork you are already doing.

We feel that all archival work, including traditional library research, strengthens fieldwork through triangulation. Researchers use the term triangulation to discuss ways they validate, check, confirm, or disconfirm data. And, of course, accumulating and analyzing multiple data sources can make fieldstudies more persuasive.

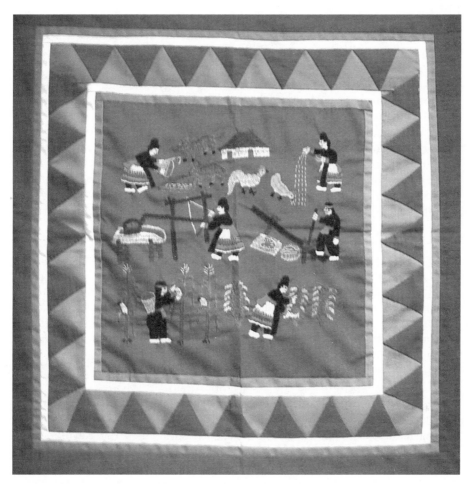

Hmong storycloth.

FAMILY ARCHIVES

Digging through any archive can be just as overwhelming as entering a fieldsite for the first time. Even if it's a small private archive like your grandmother's attic, you have no idea at first how to sort through and make use of it in any systematic way. The way to organize someone else's clutter does not announce itself to you; that process is the job of the fieldworker.

Tradition-bearing archives are part of almost every family's legacy. There is great joy and pleasure in knowing that you have an artifact or an archive of stuff from someone in your own family. And yet trunks full of family heirlooms often go unexplored and unexamined in attics and cellars until someone in the family is interested enough to look. Boxes of old photographs, bundles of letters, diaries, journals, daybooks, family Bibles with genealogies and notes, jumbles of mementos, and business ledgers can all open up a family's connection with the cultures that define it.

Every family in the United States that is able to trace its roots has some version of an "arrival narrative," although sometimes it is the story of displacement or oppression. Our student Meg Buzzi grew up in a large Italian American family in Pittsburgh, Pennsylvania, where she is called "the main cousin" by the 17 younger ones. Meg's recorded family story begins in Naples, Italy, where, as the oral tale goes, her great-great-grandfather was a switch operator for the railroad and lost both his legs in an accident. This event somehow prompted her great-grandfather "Peep" to immigrate to the United States, where he hopped a train to Cleveland and labored on an auto assembly line there. At night he took a real estate correspondence course, and two years later he landed in Pittsburgh with a real estate license and no money. Somehow, he found a financial backer, founded a real estate company, and found himself a wife. Over the years, they prospered and had four children, the oldest of whom was Meg's grandfather, Raymond Barone, born in 1922. Raymond eventually took over Peep's business and expanded its success. He was in the right place at the right time; Pittsburgh was experiencing its urban renaissance, and real estate was a key to that renewal. So Raymond, known to his family as "Rad-Rad," completed the family's Horatio Alger story by funding the college educations of his eight children and 18 grandchildren.

But Raymond left another legacy far more valuable to his family. Feeling both proud and abandoned when his children left home for college, he began writing family letters as a way of keeping them together. For Raymond, the extended family was his most important community and his way of maintaining the traditions he wanted to pass on. His handwritten letters on yellow legal paper cover a nearly 30-year period. Each letter, about nine to 12 pages long, begins with the salutation "Dear Kiddies," and is addressed to the collective audience of children and grandchildren. Each person's name is underlined when Raymond mentions noteworthy information about them. Because these letters were an entertaining, literary accounting of family activities, they were often read aloud at family parties and holidays. In fact, on the day that the relatives were notified of Raymond's sudden death, they gathered at his home, and his children read aloud from many of the letters. Later, Meg's mother and aunts lovingly typed the letters and placed them in two large binders of 500 pages each.

Meg saw these letters as a family archive and chose to use them as a basis of a field study incorporating family research, interviews, history, and her own reflective commentary. Her study is full of her grandfather's humor (which she inherited): "Our family uses humor because it is entertaining," she writes, "and because it teaches lessons and communicates arguments without as much hostility." She expands on the importance of family humor as it's represented in the letters: "It is our drug of choice, our solace, our subversion, and our sneak attack.

This satire we employ relies on the assumption that there will always be a force above us. Always a power with whom to negotiate. Always someone to ridicule."

She loved poring through hundreds of her grandfather's letters recalling events she had been part of and many which she had not. It excited her to see that the letters were so full of history, politics, and family details that she felt she could spend a lifetime, rather than just a semester, on her study. In the back of her mind, Meg knew that she was searching for a theme or a focus within this mass of paper. When she began telephone and in-person interviews with her relatives—Aunt Monica, her mother, brother, and cousins—she noticed that they each recalled hilarious events that featured Rad-Rad's outrageous humor. She looked back through her own personal journals to connect dates with facts in the letters and found that she too had recorded funny family stories. Then she e-mailed her brother Nathan and her cousins Ben and Bryan, asking them to add their own memories and confirm the details of the letters. As a researcher, Meg knew enough not to take personal letters on their face value alone. Any stories written down privately need more confirmation from a broader, more public range of evidence. To get a feel for the times her grandfather wrote about, she familiarized herself with a 30-year period in politics and popular culture by looking at newspapers, magazines, and books. So in addition to the collection of Raymond's personal letters, Meg triangulated these other data sources and in the process discovered the theme of family humor.

In this excerpt called "The Fridge," from her larger study called "Dear Kiddies," Meg incorporates and analyzes three letters. But notice that she draws on the following data sources—letters about the vegetable drawer, a family photograph that she now owns, and refrigerator notes written to her grandmother.

The Fridge

When our freezer section is opened something invariably falls to the floor… of late things don't just fall straight down; they kind of leap out about 3–4 feet. Actually, the most interesting thing about our "fridge" is the various textures which can be achieved in its various sections. From your crisper sections comes your "no-noise" carrots…it works for celery and radishes too. One week in the CRISPER takes all the noise out. On the other hand, the bottom shelf will put snap, crackle, and pop in cooked spaghetti, put the snap back into cooked green beans and even make stewed prunes crunchy… I believe that "fridges" should be seen and not heard. (1/26/79)

Meg writes:

There is a story about a photograph my grandfather took. It is a picture of rotting vegetables: carrots, onions, tomatoes, and peppers in varying degrees of decay, all carefully arranged on my grandmother's heirloom serving platter. Entitled "Still Life?" this 40" × 28" masterpiece hung in his dining room as a constant reminder to my grandmother that her produce-preservation

Still Life?

skills were less than acceptable. Currently it graces my dining room wall in a black and gold Baroque-style frame with cream-colored matting. Previous to that, it was I who dared to remove it from the basement bowels it had been condemned to by my grandmother. His aim to satirize her treatment of the vegetable drawer had never been well received.

In addition to the art projects he endeavored to torture her with, Rad-Rad also played a passive-aggressive note game with her on the front of their monster appliance. "We must get stronger magnets soon. Our messages are now three deep and they tend to slide down the door as it's used (2/28/79)." When the magnets gave up, he bought a blackboard and hung it on the front of the basement door.

Meg could not have accomplished her study of her grandfather's humor without the collection of letters that her mother and aunts kept. The boxes you discover in your own family archives can come in all shapes and sizes. Meg's family consciously built an archive of letters by typing and binding them, but many families have more informal archives of stuff they don't quite know what to do with—a relative's diary, a scrapbook of pictures and newspaper clippings, a box or drawer full of random-looking odd items.

It is both puzzling and thrilling to find family letters, journals, and artifacts that explain—or complicate—hunches you've always had about traits you've inherited, stories you've overheard, histories your family has witnessed. Finding personal archives can lead you into further research to confirm and expand the data. Writer Edward Ball used his extended family's personal archives to move into conducting his institutional research. Through deeds, documents, and ledgers in the South Carolina Historical Society, Ball continued constructing the story of his family. In his book *Slaves in the Family*, Ball rhapsodizes on the emotions he experiences as he works with old documents:

> Old papers are beautiful things. Coarse, mottled parchment containing business records sometimes has the look of white skin. The pages are veiny, with age spots, the black ink coursing down them like hair. In some places, the ink is as dark as the day it was unbottled, and the paper as blotchy as an English cheek. I read through the Ball papers, beginning with the story of the first Elias Ball, who died in 1751, at 75; his will filled four pages with script. The paper was pierced here and there by holes, signatures of book-worms. A rip had been mended on the second page, and there in the splotch of a dried glue stain, a thumb print appeared.
>
> The deeds were the most beguiling. They came with maps, or "plats," that showed the layout of a plantation and the location of its buildings. One plat had a red border, faded like a child's watercolor, while some pages had brown splatter marks, perhaps from ancient splashes of tea. Other papers had curled up from dryness or changes in chemistry. In the old days, each deed was folded into an envelope shape, tied shut with a strip of parchment, and sealed with red wax. The wax was crusty, with black streaks where the burning candle had dripped carbon into the seal.
>
> I read the papers slowly, lingering on the chatty letters, smiling at the quirks of the garrulous Balls, savoring their loopy signatures. Then I found the slave lists.
>
> There were bundles of them, in thick sheaves, each sheaf containing a stack. When a rice planter handed out shoes, he wrote down the names of who got them. To pay taxes, he made an inventory of his human property. If he bought fabrics so people could make clothes, he noted how many yards were given to each person. When a woman gave birth, the date and the name of the child appeared. And when Mr. Ball died, his executor appraised everyone before title passed to the heir. I began to count the names on some of the bigger lists, up to a few hundred, then lost track.
>
> …Shut in the vaults of the historical society's pink stucco building, I read as much as I could absorb. One family at a time, the stories surfaced, and in glimpses and parts, I began to piece together what happened.

Ball did research on his own family based on documents that were housed in institutions open to the public. In his book he hunts down the history of his family, which includes both the plantation owners in South Carolina and the intermarriages with their slaves. In the following excerpt from this nonfiction bestseller, Ball traces his genealogy to a "mixed-blood" namesake born in 1740. Notice how, as archivist, he adopts the stance of a detective toward the records he examines to make this discovery. As you read this short selection from *Slaves in the Family*, try making a mental or a written list of all the types of documents you think Ball needed to consider in his genealogical detective work.

Slaves in the Family
Edward Ball

In the early 1730s, a young black woman named Dolly came to work in the Comingtee big house. Elias's second wife had three children at the time, and Dolly probably helped with the young ones, cleaned house, and cooked. A little homage to Dolly appears in the published Ball memoir. "Perhaps the name that stands out above the others is 'Dolly,'" wrote one of the Ball women at the beginning of the twentieth century. "We know little about her, but enough to show that she was well thought of in the family. Perhaps she had 'minded' the children, and been a faithful nurse in illness. The ministrations of such humble friends of the family—they were surely no less—have soothed many a bed of suffering; and in death their hands have tenderly performed the last offices."

It seems strange that the name of a slave would evoke sentimental memories in the family of her owners some 150 years after her death. Just as strange is the aside "We know little about her," which seems to contradict the familiarity of the memory.

Dolly was born in 1712, though I cannot say where and I can only fix the year of her birth from a note about her death that states her age. Dolly was evidently more than a good housekeeper. In his will, dictated in 1750, Elias devoted considerable thought to Dolly, whom he called his "Molattoe Wench." As used then, the word "mulatto" described children of black mothers and white fathers. (In Elias's day, the children of one Native and one black parent were called "mustees" by whites.) Since the colonial legislature had already passed a law forbidding sex between white women and enslaved blacks, the white mother of a daughter of color would have been subject to prosecution. Therefore, in all likelihood, Dolly's father was white, her mother black.

It is undeniable that white men on the plantations forced and persuaded black women to have sex with them, and evidence of white-black sex appears in official records from the earliest days. In one case, from 1692, a woman named Jane LaSalle filed a petition with the Grand Council, the highest authority in Charleston. The petition involved her husband, who had left her for a black woman, probably one of the white couple's slaves. The abandoned wife appealed for help, and the Grand Council ordered the husband to return to his spouse, or else pay her a sum of money. The public nature of the case and matter-of-fact way in which it was disposed give reason to believe that interracial sex was a common part of Elias's world.

Because the earliest Ball plantation records date from 1720, and Dolly was born in 1712, it is difficult to say who her parents were. I don't believe her father was Elias Ball. I suspect, from much circumstantial evidence, he bought her as a child and later grew fond of her. During her youth Dolly seems to have gotten unusual attention. At age sixteen, according to plantation accounts, Dolly fell ill and Elias quickly summoned a doctor to the plantation to treat her. The following year, he again called a doctor for Dolly and paid a high fee for the cure. It almost never occurred, on the remote plantations, that a slave was singled out for individual medical care. Physicians were scarce, and doctors had to be enticed with large sums of money to make trips to the country, since they could easily find patients in Charleston. But thanks to Elias, Dolly received house calls, the only black person on Comingtee to warrant such attention.

The pattern of care continued throughout Dolly's young life. On one occasion Elias had special shoes made for her. Beginning in the colonial days, plantation owners hired shoemakers to sew one kind of footwear for themselves and their families and another kind, called Negro shoes, for slaves. Once, Elias hired a shoemaker from the nearby settlement of Goose Creek to sew shoes for his son, and, in the same order, to make similar high-priced footwear for Dolly. There is no evidence that other slaves ever received such treatment.

Dolly was about twenty when she went to work in the Ball house. After a year or two there, she began to have children. Her son Cupid was born April 1735. Because the slave owners often left out the name of the father in records of slave births, I cannot say who Cupid's father was. In all likelihood he was another slave on Comingtee, because Cupid went on to become a field hand, lived his entire life on Ball plantations, and died sometime after 1784.

In the 1730s, Elias and Mary were also having children. Mary gave birth to her last, a son, in 1734; he died as an infant. There is no record of Mary's death, but soon after the birth of her final child, Mary herself passed away and Elias buried her sometime around 1735, ending a marriage of fifteen years. Upon Mary's death, Elias was left with three daughters to look after—Mary, Eleanor, and Sarah—ages two to thirteen. In 1736, he turned sixty. When Elias married Mary Delamare, he had made clear his preference for younger women. Now Dolly, twenty-four, was on hand.

Mary's death seems to have made possible a liaison between Elias and Dolly. On September 16, 1740, Dolly gave birth to her second child, who was given the name Edward. Among the slaves on Comingtee, none carried English forenames. What's more, when Edward grew up, records show that the Ball family paid him respect. Edward was given his freedom and lived among the Balls, who handled his business affairs. When he died, at eighty, his will and other papers went into the Ball family collection. According to probate records, Edward was a mulatto, described in his estate papers as "a free yellow man." If Edward had been able to take the name of the man whom I believe was his father, he would have been called Edward Ball.

A few years later, while still working in the big house, Dolly had another child who received an English name, Catherine. Like her brother Edward, Catherine would also later gain freedom, evidently granted to her by the Balls. The two siblings, Catherine and Edward, were the only people owned by Elias who would ever be freed from slavery.

Around the time Dolly began to have her mulatto children, sex between whites and blacks was a topic of sharp discussion in the local newspaper. The frequency of the editorials suggests that Elias and Dolly's relationship had plenty of precedent. In July 1736, one writer for the *South Carolina Gazette* pleaded with "Certain young Men" of Charleston to hide their relationships with colored women. He called on them to "frequent less with their black Lovers the open Lots and the . . . House on the Green between old Church street and King street." If they did not keep their heads down, he added, other whites might step in "to coole their Courage and to expose them." The writer ended his cranky editorial with an appeal to white men to stay away from women slaves, if only in solidarity with other whites. White women, he maintained, were "full as capable for Service either night or day as any Africain Ladies whatsoever."

When he sat down to write his will, Elias kept young Dolly high in his mind. After declaring that his property would pass to his white children, he added this unusual clause: "I give & Bequeath the Molattoe Wench called Dolly to such of my children as she shall within three months next after my Decease make her Election for her master or mistress." Elias wanted Dolly to be able to decide her fate after he was gone: she was to choose which among Elias's white children would give her a home. It was an incomplete gesture—Dolly could select only her next master or mistress, not freedom—but in this way Elias acknowledged her humanity. The telltale clue is the phrase "within three months next after my Decease." Dolly would have a period of mourning to collect herself before deciding her next step, a graceful interval of grief.

If Dolly and Elias kept up a relationship for several years, was it rape? Or could they have cared for each other? Mockery and danger would have faced the couple on both sides. Not only would Elias have felt ostracized by some whites, but Dolly may have angered some of the other slaves at Comingtee by sleeping with the master. As for the sex itself, could Elias and Dolly both have felt desire? Or did Dolly trade sex (willingly or not) for more lenient treatment? Despite the pitiful circumstances of their attachment, could these two have, somehow, loved each other?

I imagine several of these things may simultaneously have been true.

As a researcher, writer Edward Ball used a range of institutional archives and special collections as he studied his family history to find evidence of inter-marriage between his white rice-plantation owner relatives and their slaves. To make sense of how the mulatto slave Edward (Ball), son of Dolly, may have been his distant relative, he had to read family histories, plantation records, wills, and business records, as well as newspapers of the times. His primary sources were the oral histories he recorded from his relatives. You will learn more about recording oral history in Chapter 7. To confirm (and sometimes disconfirm) parts of the oral histories, Ball relied on an interesting array of public archives—the Afro-American Historical and Genealogical Society in New York, family papers that he found in several states' historical society archives and university libraries, United States census records, warrants and deeds, mortgage records, town papers, genealogies and maps, birth records, statutes, contracts, probate records, estate inventories, wills, medical and death records, and even gravestones. He consulted books on Indian history, American slavery, economic life and rice farming in the southern United States, life in seventeenth- and eighteenth-century Africa, and more specific resources as he needed them in his research.

Not all archival research projects are this complex. Edward Ball wondered about his roots throughout his lifetime and even moved to Charleston, South Carolina, to conduct the research for his book.* Some fieldworkers—anthropologists, journalists, historians, and other writers—spend decades of their professional lives conducting in-depth studies. Your study won't demand as much time of you but will require you to examine and consider a wide range of different sources.

INSTITUTIONAL ARCHIVES

Edward Ball's book shows us how we can use institutional archives to do research on our own families. Institutional archives are far more organized than family archives and therefore easier to access. Many fieldworkers overlook the rich resources of local and institutional archives that reside in their own town halls, in schools and colleges, and in large and small corporations.

Many of us are unaware of the archival resources we have in our hometowns or nearby cities. Bonnie comes from the Philadelphia area, the home of some of our nation's most important museums (the Philadelphia Museum of Art, the Rodin Museum, the Franklin Institute, the Wyeth museum) as well as buildings that hold collections of historical artifacts (the Betsy Ross House, the United States Mint, and the Independence Hall plaza with the Liberty Bell, to name a few). Elizabeth grew up in a small Ohio town and while she was a child visited the Pioneer Historical Society, of which both her parents were members. Although Bonnie had early contact with rich metropolitan resources through

---

*Like Ball, many African Americans encounter challenges in doing genealogical research since few records of slave families exist. New archival sources are helping African Americans trace their roots. For example, a CD-ROM contains the records of the Freedman's Bank, an institution that was created for freed slaves after the Civil War and that required depositors to list all members of their families, even relatives who had been sold to others. This database will be helpful in doing research on African American families and is available from <www.ldscatalog.com>.

her art-teacher mother, Elizabeth didn't realize that her hometown was important, historically or artistically, as a ceramic center until she moved to New York City and found that many people collected Roseville and Zanesville pottery. (Her hometown now has a modest pottery museum.)

We like to tell the story of a high school student we know in a small town in New Hampshire who, when assigned a fieldwork project, complained to his teacher, "There's nothing in this town—nothing to do, nothing to research, no one to talk to. All I'm interested in is basketball."

"Okay," his teacher replied, "Why don't you try to find out about the history of basketball in this town?"

He grumbled all the way to the town archives in the small Historical Society building where he began his research. There he discovered pictures and newspaper clippings about a family basketball team formed at the turn of the last century in New England, just a few decades after basketball was invented in the Midwest. This was a family with five children, just enough for a team, and one of the player-siblings happened to be a girl. They were the town's first team and won a claim to fame because of the sister, who helped win many a contest. Our young researcher was intrigued, much to his surprise, and he traced the local family until he found a living relative, one of the original team members. He interviewed this elderly man and wrote a compelling study of the town's family team, which eventually became part of the school district's collective fieldproject called "The Four Towns Museum." So even with a skeptical attitude, this young student was able to use archival research to inspire his rediscovery of a local family's sports fame long ago. Sometimes a fieldworker can overlook a small-town archive or even a small institutional archive.

Another of our students, Bill Polking, made use of an institutional archive in his study of a Catholic boarding school for Native American tribes of the Southwest United States. Bill had been a teacher and dorm counselor before the school closed its doors in 1998. His project posed a special challenge because the fieldsite as he once knew it no longer existed. It also posed an ethical challenge to him because of the way Native Americans had previously been studied and represented by other fieldworkers. He writes, "Ethnography, rightfully, has a bad name in Native America, and I didn't want to see myself as another bone collector, another collector of artifacts." And yet Bill had access to personal and historical archives as well as Internet connections with his former colleagues and students. Bill began the study with his own archives, a few boxes full of mementos from his years at this school, since, as he writes, "I am my own best and worst informant." He supplemented the study with e-mail interviews of former students and colleagues, as well as a return visit to the site of the school. In his reflection about doing this study, he catalogs the data sources, many of them archives, from which he drew:

Obviously, my own observations are a continual source throughout the essay. But I have also "borrowed" from license plates, signs, school newspapers, city newspapers, day students, girls' dorm students, boys' dorm students, Sisters, girls' dorm staff, boys' dorm staff, the language of my informants, the official publications of the Sisters and the school, histories of Indian education, and Peshkin's book on Santa Fe Indian School.

Eventually, a visual artifact helped Bill understand and determine his focus. A framed rectangular sign had hung above the door of the boys' dorm announcing "Nothing But the Best for the Boys Because the Boys are the Best." This motto ultimately became the title and the controlling thesis of his fieldwork essay. Before he settled on this saying as a focus, Bill had been aware of all the directions his study might take and worried about how to use the archives he had at his disposal. How would he use his personal journal? What was important about the order of nuns who ran the school? What was the value of the other fieldstudies he'd read? How would he bring the voices from personal e-mails into this study? Although he was aware of his many options, he needed to find one way to represent his complicated understanding of the school's culture. Using the motto as his thesis helped to guide his awareness of the ethics of his position, the needs and opinions of the former students and colleagues who were his informants, and his wish for his readers to understand the tangled cultural amalgamation of this Catholic coed boarding school for Native Americans. Based on a flood of e-mails from friends, Bill noticed that dorm life seemed to be an important theme in people's memories:

A small school, down to just over two hundred students by the time it closed, St. Catherine prided itself on its sense of community: "Some seek St. Kate's to escape the hardships at home. We welcome them. Some come here to escape other hardships of life. We welcome them. Some come here because they belong nowhere else. We welcome them, too" (Belin Tsinnajinnie, boys' dorm student).

"Everyone was like a family here," said day student Nicole Hernandez, and from my beginnings in 1992, as a volunteer freshly graduated and looking for a year apart from the life he had seen and the life he foresaw, to the end in 1998, when one year had drawn into six and I had become assistant director of the dorm, St. Catherine and the boys' dorm in particular were my family, my home. Home in the literal sense, as I lived in the dorm, in a small room next to the ninth graders and (unfortunately) the bathroom. And home also in the sense poet Michael Blumenthal describes, "…Anywhere/ that makes the relentless heart/ relent, friends, can be your home."

Others saw the boys' dorm in similar fashion: "Although it was infused with respect for the cultural/tribal traditions from which its students came, the boys' dorm seemed to form an identity, a 'culture,' quite apart from those traditions, and in this way it was able to unite students from diverse backgrounds" (Jenn Guerin, girls' dorm director).

"I believe the main objective of the boys' dorm, aside from introducing a person to a very diverse community and making sure they did well academically, was to create an environment where a sense of brotherhood evolved and a comfortable form of reliance on one another was developed" (Oscencio Tom, boys' dorm student).

"The thing that has stood out in my memory…is the respect the boys seemed to show for each other. The fact that we didn't have one fist fight all year is remarkable…. Even the tougher kids treated each other with dignity or indifference" (Tom McGrory, boys' dorm staff).

"Nothing but the best for the boys because the boys are the best" (sign made by Jerry Payne, boys' dorm director).

"The boys are spoiled" (numerous girls' dorm students).

Whether you choose to supplement your study with archival research or to suggest a topic for your study from personal, historical, or online sources, archives offer shape, texture, depth, and color to help bring a study to life. Even though institutional archives are organized more formally than family archives, the challenge of the research is still the same—finding a focus. Eventually a visual artifact—a framed rectangular sign—helped Bill figure out his focus.

BOX 14   A Box about Boxes

Purpose

Sometimes dusty boxes, even boxes in our homes or belonging to people we know, are important sites for archival study. Bill Polking's fieldstudy of St. Catherine's School began with a box of mementos—artifacts, newspaper clippings, notes, and photographs from his years as dorm counselor and English teacher at the school. Meg Buzzi's study of family stories began with two binders full of her grandfather's letters. Looking with the eyes of a researcher can shift the way we sort through a collection of "stuff," whether that stuff comes from a family member, someone we know like a teacher or a student, or some anonymous figure whose stuff promises the beginning of a fascinating fieldstudy.

Action

Locate a box of archival stuff—a grouping of artifacts or documents that someone has collected for some purpose, even if the purpose is simply "to keep because it's important." This box could belong to you, a member of your family, or someone else. List the contents of the box. Try organizing or mapping the contents in different patterns: chronological, by size, by type or shape, by order from beginning to end or from inside to outside—see if there are one or more overall logical shapes to the data, determine how the organizing patterns would show different themes about the contents of the box.

Response

David Jakstas, one of our students, comes from a family that owns a hotel on a lake in a small town in Illinois, not too far from Chicago. The hotel is an old, stately one, known to city weekenders as "the big white building on the lake." It was built in 1884 with 100 rooms, a 240-foot porch, a ballroom, a tower, and a bar. Only the bar exists today for business, though the family is planning to restore both the bar and the hotel. David's uncle, who plans the restoration, manages a successful marina next to the hotel. David claims that the hotel itself is an archive, full of information, documents, and artifacts from basement to tower. Already equipped with the family stories he's heard all his life and knowing he could listen to other family versions of them, David's early fieldwork consisted of uncovering archival material from the old hotel, much of which was in the bar. "One particular slot machine," he writes, "sits in a showcase of the bar, but was found in one of the storage rooms in the hotel. The sign below the machine reads, 'a switch underneath the machine quickly makes this machine dispense candy instead of money, in case of a police raid.' " Also in the showcase is a hat with this caption: "This hat was worn by Al Capone. It was left by him in the back seat of a cab after leaving the hotel."

David's research led him to wonder how much of a role the hotel had played in the lives of Chicago gangsters, who would "pull off a big heist in the city" and head for the lake-area hotels. His family's stories involve bullet holes in the walls, ghosts in the rafters, boating accidents, and floods. David studied a scrapbook of news articles about the hotel that had been clipped by various family members throughout the hotel's lifetime. He found an original lease, evidence that the hotel had once been a clubhouse for a Board of Trade, several old maps, menus, and souvenir programs from celebrations, as well as the news articles with pictures, details, and stories spanning a hundred years of history. David writes: "I did not start with this topic; I literally walked into it one day. My problem was that I had never looked at the place as a place for research…. My dad and I went through boxes of things about the hotel in our basement before I talked to anyone at the bar. Although my mom thought we'd trashed the basement, I found plenty of information and a lot of history. I had the main material for my project."

Museum Archives

Even experienced fieldworkers sometimes ignore possible archival resources. We suffered from a kind of unawareness when we visited Ball State University in Muncie, Indiana, to give a talk about doing fieldwork. Little did we know that we would find a fascinating museum that would unlock the whole culture of this interesting midwestern town. We knew we were going to be writing this chapter on archives and knew that transplanted college students often feel disconnected from the culture of their surroundings. So we wanted to see what sources might be available for a student to discover at the beginning of a fieldstudy.

From our Ball State colleagues, we learned that Muncie had a history of being studied as a typical American city. Muncie has been the subject of three separate sociological studies—*Middletown* (1929), *Middletown in Transition* (1935), and *Middletown III* (1977). A student at Ball State, for instance, who wanted to investigate the connections between the university and the town might begin with these books or with the town's history. In the town's history, this fieldworker would discover that for over a hundred years, between 1888 and 1998, Muncie was the world headquarters of the Ball Corporation, makers of glass jars for preserving foods.

The Muncie story goes like this. The region had an abundance of natural gas, so much that it attracted the glass and steel manufacturing industries because they needed the enormous amounts of heat and energy the gas produced. The five Ball brothers moved their manufacturing plant from Buffalo, New York, to Muncie, made their fortune, and left their mark on the town. At the crest of a hill overlooking the muddy White River, the Ball brothers' impressive homes and gardens once stood watch over the town. Two of these homes are now the sites of a cultural museum and a conference center. Our fieldworker might start with a visit to Muncie's Minnetrista Cultural Center, which displays rooms full of old-fashioned glass Ball jars, both utilitarian and unusual. Our favorite was a huge Ball jar of preserved pears from a nineteenth-century world's fair, claimed to still be edible.

We became fascinated with the kinds of archives and talented people who would teach us about how the culture of a town is reflected in its history. Folklorist Beth Campbell, curator and exhibits developer at Minnetrista Cultural Center, guided us through the exhibits and shared with us the kind of archival research projects she develops for the museum. We learned from Beth that her background research resulted in two kinds of scripts for recent museum exhibits. Both became part of the museum's archives. The first had been written for a recent exhibition on the restoration of the center's gardens. The other was a transcript from an oral history project, interviews of senior citizens who had once worked in the Ball brothers' glass jar factory. To our delight, Beth shared the exhibition script and the interview transcript with us, and we realized how valuable such rich sources could be for a fieldwork project.

Although you'll never read a full exhibition script on the walls of a museum, the script is the curator's organizational blueprint. When you tour an exhibit, you'll see little snippets of text placed for the visitor near the materials, objects, pictures, or displays. But these short texts don't begin that way. A curator must first develop a longer script to focus and sharpen the huge amount of information about the exhibit. Here are three small sections from the full 25-page script that describes the unearthing and reconstruction of Elisabeth Ball's dollhouse:

3D. Rediscovering the Grounds

...the project team used a three-step "triangulated" analysis. During the first step, team members superimposed a fifty-foot grid over each section of the grounds, made a list of each species and its location within the grid, and noted structural remains. They then conducted archival research in order to map buildings and grounds.... During the fieldwork, the team made many discoveries, including old gardens and evidence of an arbor and a dollhouse....

3E. Rehabilitating the Grounds

In 1990, the gardens looked wild and overgrown. Having made the decision to rehabilitate the gardens...thickets of invasive plants were removed so that dormant plants might find new life.... A sunken rock garden similar to Elisabeth's "sunk" was designed, using her notes and plant invoices as a guide...bellflowers, buttercups, daylilies, lamb's ear, and creeping phlox....

3F. Recreating Vistas

...after researchers learned of Elisabeth's garden dollhouse, they tracked down the people who had purchased it at a charity auction.

Beth was interested in the factory's owners, their gardens, and their dollhouses. But she also wanted to gather data about the lives of everyone in the town, from the original gardens' owners to the factory workers. And so Beth offered us another document, an interview with Almeda Mullin, who had been a "stamper" (of the Ball logo on the glass gar) and "spare girl" at the Ball factory. Mullin, born in 1907, began working in the factory at age 13 and worked there for 40 years—the same years that the Ball women worked their gardens.

In the following excerpt, Almeda Mullin gives us a sense of her working conditions:

BC: What was [your boss] like to work for?

AM: *(laughs)* He was just as cocky as you'd let him be. I hated that bloody glass house with a purple passion. So one night, after I got off work at the glass house, I came out, my hands were swollen, my fingers were cut, and I was a-crying. I must have been 17, 18. I said "Sam, I can't work in that glass house." "Oh," he said, "shut up you big old baby and go on home...."

BC: What was it about the glass house that people hated so much?

AM: They pushed those jars on a conveyor, and you had to stick your hands into them...it just pinched pieces and cut, your hands would just bleed and be so sore....

Beth's interview with Almeda will become part of an exhibition about the everyday lives of workers at the Ball factory. As museum curator, Beth was interested in collecting data about the lives of everyone in the town, from the original gardening of the Ball wives to the everyday routines of the factory workers. As a fieldworker, Beth collected materials to document the class differences in Muncie, Indiana, during the 1920s. She also consulted other sources, such as diaries, journals, letters, and newspapers written at the time, and interviewed town residents about their memories of the Ball family. But that's only one researcher's choice. There are many ways to use archival resources to develop a project. This material could be used as a backdrop for a field study of class differences in the culture of contemporary Muncie or for a historical study of the glass industry or a study of the history of landscaping.

You can find scripts and transcripts in many different places. We were happy to learn that Garrison Keillor had devoted a radio segment to the Ball jar connections when he visited Muncie in 1997. When Keillor visits a city to broadcast a show, he depends on local researchers to feed him background information about the culture of the place. Our colleague, Professor Joe Trimmer of Ball State University, did the research for Keillor's Muncie visit, including the following information:

> The Ball Brothers' Glass Manufacturing Company set up shop in 1886. Its glass containers and Ball jars enabled the business to dominate the local economy.... Most of what's distinctive in Muncie is the direct result of the generosity of the Ball family.... Everything in town is named Ball—there's Ball Corporation, Ball Foundation, Ball Gym, Ball Memorial Hospital, Ball Field, Ball Building, Ball Avenue, and, of course, the town's currently largest employer, Ball State University.

A seasoned storyteller, Keillor typically uses humor to engage his audience. In his 1997 Muncie broadcast, he shaped his commentary for his many radio fans across the United States as well as the local live audience of Muncie's college students, their parents, and townspeople. He also drew on the Minnetrista Cultural Center's museum archives, Joe Trimmer's research notes, and other sources to tell the story of the Ball jar culture. We found the citation for Keillor's show online through National Public Radio's Performance Archives, ordered the tape, and transcribed it with Keillor's permission as follows:

Ball Jars
Monologue from March 15, 1997, Muncie, Indiana
Garrison Keillor

Well, it's been a quiet week in Lake Wobegon, my hometown, out here on the prairie. It's been a week of interesting weather. It started to thaw earlier in the week, and some of the snow melted even in the woods, and we actually saw mud for a while. And then it all switched around Wednesday night and Thursday. And the mud froze, and we got about a foot of snow, and everything is covered with white again, sort of like you change the sheets on your bed. And it's very pretty.

But some people are getting tired of winter, of course, but some people are sort of longing for spring and wishing it were here. But, you know, there are people in northern California, folks, who have had spring all of their adult lives. And has this done them any good? I mean, I'm just asking. Take a look. Make up your minds for yourself.

Winter is good for you. And if winter lasts a little bit longer than you wish it did, perhaps it is because there is more good to be gotten out of winter. Winter focuses the mind in all sorts of ways. When you're in a warm climate, your mind wanders. You think about your career. You think about whether or not you were happy as a child or things of that sort. These people on daytime TV shows who are talking about their childhoods and how they didn't get the positive reinforcement from their parents that they really needed and that's why they shot them: these people are not from the North. These are not northern people. We know that.

Winter is good for you in so many different ways. Winter cures people of self-pity. You learn as a child: if it's cold, don't talk about it because the others are just as cold as you are. Winter is not a personal experience. You learn this by the time you are seven or eight years old.

Now, when I was a boy, the way you combated the winter blues was very simple. You went down the basement. You went to those shelves that were behind the wash tubs, and you reached up there, and there were all of your mother's canned vegetables and jams and peaches. And there was corn, and there was applesauce and apple butter. And you reached down to the end, and you got a jar of stewed tomatoes. You took that up and took off the lid, and you put some of it in a pan. You heated it up, and you put butter on it. And in those stewed tomatoes that you yourself had picked and had helped your mother can last August: you found in those tomatoes the courage or sunshine or whatever it was you needed to buck yourself up and get on with winter and not complain about it. And, of course, those were Ball fruit jars. Those were Ball canning jars. They were always Ball jars with Kerr lids in our family.

So it always made me want to come to Muncie, Indiana—sort of the home of the mother church. Then I come here and found out that the Ball Corporation has gotten out of the fruit jar business. Which is all well and good, until I start to think that there may be children who are growing up not knowing of the existence of Ball fruit jars—not knowing about canning. The children are missing out on this. There was a time in my lifetime when everyone all across the Midwest saved their Ball jars and filled them up in the month of August. They were sealed, and they were put away. And you ate this over the next fall and winter and spring—produce from your own garden.

I'm just going to wait a moment and let that sink in. Nowadays, of course, your parents can go to the produce section of an upscale grocery in town, and they buy everything fresh: December, January, February, March. Buy a little carton of raspberries from Mexico, some little blueberries from New Zealand, buy a pack of salad hand-picked, hand-selected from twelve different varieties of baby lettuce, hand-raised in the coastal foothills of northern California by liberal arts graduates.

But children, the money that your parents are expending on these foods—buying them out of season fresh in the produce section—is money that could have gone towards your college tuition. This is money that could have been spent to send you to a good school. But because your parents don't can their own food, you may have to go to some college that is a sort of little cluster of cinder block buildings that's around a parking lot. There will be 500 other students in calculus class. And you will have to put yourself through school working nights at the 7-11 so that college for you will be four years of just trying to stay awake. And at the end of it all, you'll get a degree that when job interviewers take a look at the name of your college they will think "dumb." All because your parents didn't have the industry, the gumption, the wit, to grow their own tomatoes—grow their own tomatoes and put them in jars, Ball canning jars from Muncie, Indiana.

And it's not that your parents don't love you. They do love you. Your parents love you through thick and thin. They loved you in days when you were not that attractive at all. They loved you back when you used to scream whenever they would leave the room. Back when they would lay you down on the floor and change your poopy diaper, and it was disgusting. It was foul. They would carry this evil-smelling thing over to the garbage, and then you would stand up, and you would walk leaving a little brown trail behind you.

Your parents still loved you back in those days when you used to grab up things in your hands and stick everything in your mouth. They'd turn their back for two minutes, and you'd be standing by a potted plant, and you'd have dirt in both of your fists and dirt trailing down out of the corners of your mouth. And they would get as much of it out with their fingers as they possibly could. And they would take you into the bathroom, and they would hold you under one arm under the sink. They would try to make you throw up by sticking a finger up your throat. And you would not throw up. You would gag, but nothing would come out. So they would pour a little Listerine in you and just hope for the best. And they'd lay you in bed, and then you threw up. Then you threw up: you threw up quarts, quarts of stuff.

No, your parents loved you through some pretty dark days, indeed. But your parents have a sense of economics that's like drunken cowboys on a Saturday night. And that is why you may not be able to go to a good college. And that is why when you are ready for it, there will be no Social Security, there will be no Medicare whatsoever, and America will be basically just a series of malls connected by interstates. People will live in sort of walled compounds. It will be like the Middle Ages. And that's all because people didn't put vegetables in the canning jars. They didn't take care of business at home.

It was the basis of a whole social order—home canning—and Muncie, Indiana, was the mother church. Right here, this is where it all came from. It all had to do with order because in the month of August in all of this humidity and rain, the garden had lost any semblance of order whatsoever. It was teeming with vegetation. The rows of vegetables had disappeared; it was just all vines all over. In the spring it was neat. It was like a patchwork quilt. But now the quilt was off, and these plants were openly making out with each other—all writhing around. The most obscene zucchini growing, and plants lolling all over and extending their lewd long tendrils towards each other—groping and grasping and lots of heavy breathing out there. So canning was to impose a kind of Lutheran order on this—gathering up everything that was usable. Prepare it, and put it into jars that would be labeled and put in rows on shelves where you can find them, and thus put the world as it ought to be. I think of it as Lutheran culture, home canning.

Everybody in the Midwest is Lutheran. Even Catholics are. Everybody is basically Lutheran. Even atheists are Lutheran. It is a Lutheran God they do not believe in. The Lutherans have always had this chasm—the schism between the happy Lutherans and the dark Lutherans. And the dark Lutherans believed that man is inherently corrupt and degraded. They believe in separation from the things of the world and absolute adherence to truth. The happy Lutherans believe in sprinkling a child with a little water and put the child through confirmation, and then after that you come on Sundays and bring a hot dish for afterwards. The dark Lutherans were the ones, of course, who were the canners. They believed in canning. They believed in frugality. In a flush time you save some of your riches, and you hold it for a time when there will be snow on the ground and you won't have corn—whereas the happy Lutherans believed in feasting and eating up all of the sweet corn and not thinking too much about January and February.

There was also the danger of canning, which appealed to the dark side of Lutherans. The danger of botulism, ever present. The process of disinfection had to be followed precisely otherwise you might come up with botulism. Yes, *Clostridium botulinum*, which is Latin for "you bought yourself a small closet with handles on the side." Botulism, one of the deadliest germs there is. One ounce can kill 100 million people. So that one jar of asparagus gone bad would have the lethal potency of a thermonuclear weapon. You thought about that when you canned. Yes you did. You thought about that. One minute you're a woman who serves on the altar guild on the Lutheran church, and the next minute you're Henry Kissinger, thinking about weapons of mass destruction.

There was a time, children—there was a time back before things changed in the Lutheran church. There was a time before when people did not openly discuss the virginity of their olive oil in front of other people. This was not a topic of conversation. This was not important. We had Crisco, we had Wesson oil, we didn't need anything else. "Extra virgin olive oil": What does that mean? What does that mean—"extra virgin"? That's sort of like saying "slightly pregnant."

Which brings me to another use of the fruit jar. The fruit jar was the container of choice for a segment of the adult beverage market. Back when your parents were in college, people gave parties, and a punch was served—an alcoholic punch known as "purple death." The host provided grape Kool-Aid, and then the guests were supposed to bring something alcoholic. They would usually take something from their parents' liquor cabinet, and seeing as they were Lutherans, they didn't have any good stuff. They took things that parents would not miss. They took things like Creme de Banana, Licorice Schnapps, an off-brand of bourbon (Old Buzzard Breath Bourbon). And they combined all of these into the grape Kool-Aid, and you drank this stuff out of Ball fruit jars. And you gave yourself a hangover that would remain vivid for years to come. You woke up the next morning, and suddenly you understood where surrealism came from. You now had a taste of what mental illness might be like. And you'd resolve never ever to do anything like this ever again. They were good days, the fruit jar days, and I miss them. It was a part of the world that I grew up in. It was the symbol of the goodness of life. It was also the symbol of frugality: that one should take care against the morrow.

The canner had to have a good ear. After she had disinfected the jar and she had cooked the food and packed it in the jars and put the lids on, the canner had to tap the lid with a knife to see if it would ring. If it rang that meant the seal was good and your family wouldn't all drop dead of botulism. But it shouldn't have that hollow sound that would indicate that the seal was not good, and that this could breed botulism.

It's a wondrous thing—canned food in a jar. It was the way in which parents saved money to put their children into good colleges. It was a way in which young people were able to experience absolute degradation when they were young so they wouldn't have to keep searching for it the rest of their lives. They knew what it was. And it was a way of detecting hollowness, which is always good. There's so much in life that's hollow, and you don't want to waste your time on any of it.

To find radio and television transcripts, you can use the educational resources of National Public Radio, the Public Broadcasting System, and most other mass media resources. As you probably know, at the end of most radio and TV news broadcasts, magazine shows, talk shows, and other informative presentations, there is information about the website or phone number to access for a tape or a transcript.

Sorting through Public Archives

Purpose

It's interesting to think about the collections that we might label as public archives. For the kind of fieldwork we describe in this book, our definition is broad: a public archive is a place where collections of public and private records, as well as other historical documents and artifacts, are stored. It can be a town hall, for example, or a special museum, a library's special collection, or a collection held by a business, a school, a club, or a church. A public archive might be as small as a scrapbook or as large as a building.

The archive's organizational patterns will probably be less than efficient; patterns could range from files in chronological order with codes to organize items by type to jumbles of papers in large boxes. Looking for his slave and slave owner legacy, Edward Ball reflected as he pored through wills, deeds, ledgers, and town records: "Shut in the vaults of the historical society's pink stucco building, I read as much as I could absorb. One family at a time, the stories surfaced, and in glimpses and parts, I began to piece together what happened." Working your way through a public archive can be frustrating and sometimes daunting; it takes time and patience, and there are no quick answers ready for you. But as we mention at the beginning of this chapter, you will find that the data begin to come alive as you find what you need.

Action

To see how archival material coincides with other sources of data, check out a few public archives related to your topic of interest, or your site, or your informants. These archival materials can be any documents or artifacts that are part of an organized (or a disorganized) collection. List the sources you've looked at, and see what connections or correspondences turn up or what gaps you can perceive. Freewrite about the archives themselves and how they relate to your topic, your site, and your informants. Try to triangulate this information with other material you might find about your topic while cruising the giant technological archive we have quite literally at our fingertips these days, the World Wide Web. (We'll discuss doing research on the Web starting on page 183.) As you might notice, the job of collecting and selecting—and making sense out of archival data sources—is one of reflective critical analysis, much like the strategies used in creating a research portfolio.

Response

Brenda Boleyn prepares students to become elementary public school teachers. She writes about an archival search she did on the conflicts young men face when they choose to become elementary teachers. Notice the range of archival material she considers. Brenda writes:

I located several items that I felt could be viewed as archival when trying to understand from the male perspective the culture tied to becoming an elementary teacher:

1. *An article* from the *USA Today* archive entitled "Elementary School Students Need More Male Teachers." It is relevant to my study for a couple of different reasons. It gives percentages of males who are currently in elementary education and compares today's statistics with those in 1981 and 1961. What's important to me is that the trend is downward. The article speculates about why males are choosing the field of teaching less often.

2. *A website address* for readers to access to further discuss the topic of males and their roles in elementary education. I went to this website to get a glimpse of the public conversation surrounding this topic, and it proved very interesting. Everything from classroom discipline to pay/respect issues to bashing feminists surfaced in this discussion. Most seemed to agree that there is a shortage, but no one seemed surprised.

3. *A brochure,* among our college's collection of brochures, about education as a career. For those students who *do* decide to consider early childhood or elementary education majors, the common path is to meet with an advisor and discuss coursework, requirements, field experience options, etc. I serve as advisor for 30 students, and one is male. Most of this is factual information, but I found the image of "teacher" in the brochure photos was definitely female. That's why this brochure is important.

4. *Two lists:* A list for teachers at a local elementary school where I place preservice teachers for their practicum experiences. It shows that out of 15 teachers in kindergarten through third grade, only one is male. Also, a list of students from the fall semester—all female. This document speaks to the demographics of students in our program and also to the available teacher models and classrooms we have to mentor our preservice teachers.

5. *Textbooks:* One of the first courses our students take is literacy methods. Usually after this course students have a pretty good idea if they want to remain in teaching. I looked at a stack of texts (in a sense, an archive in a book closet), books I'm considering using in my course, and made photocopies of every literacy text that featured teachers and students working together on the cover. Although the representations of teachers on (and in) these texts show ethnic diversity (in both students and teachers), the gender of the teacher is always the same—female. Scary!

6. *Artifacts:* I examined and photographed some of the items various education professors had in or displayed in their offices. Although I found more gender-neutral items around the department, I looked long and hard for images of males working with young children. I was not successful in my search. The items highlighted for me the dominant image of female

"teacher" and caused me to wonder about the impact that may have on prospective male teachers. Can they see themselves in the images that are portrayed? Or do they position themselves in opposition to these images, encouraging them to seek out more traditionally masculine roles in middle schools and high schools, science rooms and gymnasiums?

ELECTRONIC ARCHIVES: THE WORLD WIDE WEB

Brenda Boleyn couldn't have done the **Web (World Wide Web)** research discussed in Box 15 without using her **browser** to see what was out there. Not very long ago, doing research using a website on your personal computer at your own desk would have sounded like an idea for a science fiction novel. But now it is difficult to imagine doing any research without using the Web as one of our tools. The term **website** refers to one or more "pages" that your computer can find at a certain "address" known as a **URL** (Uniform Resource Locator). Think of each site as a "place" holding collected, linked information. To "visit" the Web is an apt metaphor for this process. We like to think of the Web as a giant, very decentralized, very public archive. Because of that, using the Web for research and using it well are two different things. Having so much information available immediately means that we're not sure how to value what we see. As with any kind of research, it takes skill and knowledge to surf and sift through large amounts of data, make choices about what is credible, decide how it might be useful, and link your sources together with one another and with your project as a whole.

Like the kind of research you do at your actual fieldsite, conducting research with a website requires patience, attention to detail, selectivity, and analysis. We will be careful in this section to refer to *fieldsite* or *website* and not to confuse you with the shorter term *site*. Web "surfing" can make people think that doing research online will be quick and easy, but in fact it takes time, care, and rigor. Just as you might sit and sit and watch and watch your fieldsite, piecing together information as you find it, you ought to spend much time simply sitting and sitting and reading and reading information on the Web until you know what focus you need, what data seem appropriate, and how the information will fit with the other parts of your research. You may uncover a wealth of information quickly but will need time to assess it. Is what you've found useful to your project? Does it answer any questions you or your informants have raised? Does it supplement incomplete facts and details about people, places, histories, ideas, and artifacts you've already heard about? Are the sources up-to-date? What evidence do you have that they're believable? These are all questions requiring your patience, attention to detail, and ability to be selective.

And then there are questions of analysis—how the details fit into your broader ideas. You will need to decide what fieldsites and websites are telling you. How can the websites enhance your ideas about your fieldsite and about your informants and their culture? How does each website relate to the others—and to your fieldsite? Is the information similar? If it's not, how is it different? Would one website have a different purpose for displaying itself than another? And is its information consistent with its purpose? How is that consistent with what you know or think already about your fieldsite?

What you find on the Web works in three ways. First, it is a source of basic information to supplement all that you've gathered at your fieldsite, much like library books or journal articles that offer facts, histories, and descriptions about the culture or subculture you're studying. Second, it can offer you potential contact information—telephone numbers or **e-mail** addresses of possible informants. As Bill Polking discovered from his online chats with former students and colleagues from the Indian school no longer in existence and Meg Buzzi found in her correspondence with relatives, e-mails from distant but involved people can be an enormously rich source of data. But probably the most important way the Web works is that the online information itself becomes an artifact that a culture or subculture has produced. We think, in fact, that these new electronic resources blur the traditional boundaries between primary and secondary sources.

When we wrote about Hmong storycloths, for example, in one short paragraph at the beginning of this chapter, we used the Web to confirm what we'd learned from two Hmong embroiderers, a local folklorist who collects storycloths, a few presentations we've attended, and Hmong students we've known. But we wanted to be sure we had the history right, so we used the word *Hmong* as a keyword in a search on the Web. Instantly, we found a wealth of written material, both published and unpublished, about the Hmong people, traditions, and histories. We found virtual museum exhibits displaying detailed pictures of Hmong crafts, foods, and music traditions, websites in which Hmong in various parts of the world can talk with one another in chatrooms, and newsletters with activities and invitations to participate. In a few hours, we had confirmed what we'd learned from informants about storycloths and felt more confident about writing the paragraph you read at the beginning of this chapter. But we also had found the connected websites themselves to be artifacts of the Hmong culture itself, offering us much new knowledge of the culture in the words and choices of the informants who manage the websites. This way, we were able to access the Hmong's perspective on their own transplanted American culture.

This all seems familiar, suspiciously, in fact, like the library work you have always done in order to write a report. Online research is research, of course.

Electronic Resources and Options

We like Yahoo!—not only as a **directory** with a major presence online but also an acronym for "You always have other options." Yahoo! continues to be the Old Faithful of indexing sites, easy to navigate and simple to understand. The acronym is worth noting because it explains exactly what electronic resources offer us—other options, multiple choices for finding out interesting information. The Web is the most obvious of electronic archives, but it's really only one of many, including these:

- Websites,
- Institutional electronic archives and databases,
- **Newsgroups,**
- **Listservs** (electronic mailing lists),
- E-mail collections, correspondences, and conversations,
- **Bulletin boards** and **chatrooms** (Web discussion forums), and
- Other electronic communities (**MUDs**, MOOs, MUSHs).

The Internet began decades ago as a product of the cold war and the U.S. military-industrial complex. In the 1960s, a group of governmental computer scientists belonging to the Advanced Research Projects Agency (ARPA) collaborated to create a resource for keeping critical electronic documents safe from the threat of nuclear destruction. The result of their efforts—a "distributed platform network" called *ARPAnet*—allowed computers that were geographically separated to share their content so that if a bomb wiped out the computers in one region, the computers in another region could continue to store important information. Eventually, the Internet as we know it evolved from this data-sharing concept. And so what we call the **Internet** comprises the whole mass of distributed electronic resources: the Web, e-mail, and probably other sources we can't yet predict.

The piece of the Internet that receives the most attention is, without doubt, the Web, partly because it is so user-friendly. The Web holds a large portion of the material available online and provides any field researcher with a rich resource. The Internet as a whole, in fact, is an electronic version of the kinds of archives field researchers have used for years to supplement their fieldwork. Fieldworkers, for example, have traditionally consulted archives of handwritten letters, and we now can consult enormous piles of e-mail correspondence, already transcribed (with permission, of course, from the informants).

We must take certain cautions when we use electronic media. Because anyone who has the means to transfer files (such as an **ftp** or **file transfer protocol**) from a local machine to a **server** can do so, publication is more available to the average person than ever before. Home computers and dialup accounts allow millions to publish words, sounds, and images for the world to read. On the one hand, this is a great opportunity for all of us to have our public say. But on the other hand, it creates difficulties for the electronic researcher. Online documents don't necessarily pass through the kind of prior-to-publication editorial or peer review that writing intended for publication in periodicals and books commonly undergoes. And so it becomes a challenge to determine the reliability of material we encounter on the Web. How do we know that the websites we find are reliable? How do we determine the authority of the information we gather online? Fieldworkers know how to answer these questions: as with any other data we collect in the field, we can rely on triangulation to substantiate our research.

Thus, the same rule applies to electronic data that applies to any field data: when we find something that confirms or contradicts our research, we must also collect complementary data from additional sources before we can be sure that our conclusions and theories are valid and believable. That the Web offers us an almost limitless supply of information presents another challenge for the online researcher—simply navigating the sheer volume of information out there. Web directories (such as Yahoo!) and other **search engines** are useful, but they don't replace the human thinking and real time necessary to sift through data to determine the story you want to tell. It's important to collect data you want to rely on, whether it's offline or online. But beyond that, as Professor Louis Agassiz taught Samuel Scudder a century ago, we simply must stare at our fish for a good long while before we come to understand all that it has to teach us.

Web Search Resources

Web Directories or Subject Guides   Web directories constitute painstakingly human-engineered listings of websites sorted by category. Yahoo! is the granddaddy of Web searching. It's been around the longest, is the friendliest with visitors, and although reliable can be a little slow. Here are some examples of Web directories that are available as we write this book:

- Yahoo!   http://www.yahoo.com
- NBCi   http://www.nbci.com
- LookSmart   http://www.looksmart.com
- Google Web Directory   http://directory.google.com

Search Engines   A search engine uses a program called a *spider* to crawl through all of the documents on the Web at a given time. Because this number of documents is huge and continually increasing, updating the search engine's database is a slow process. A search engine's effectiveness depends on the efficiency and size of its database as well as on the frequency with which its records are updated. Some well-known examples of search engines:

- AltaVista   http://www.altavista.com
- Excite   http://www.excite.com
- Google   http://www.google.com
- HotBot   http://hotbot.lycos.com
- Go.com   http://www.go.com

- Lycos   http://www.lycos.com
- Magellan   http://www.magellan.excite.com

Search Engine Compiler Sites   Some sites further automate the searching process to maximize the breadth of a search by querying several engines at once. Some examples of these "meta search" engines:

- Dogpile   http://www.dogpile.com
- Metacrawler   http://www.metacrawler.com/index_power.html

Other Helpful Sites

- Web Searching Tips   http://searchenginewatch.com/facts/index.html
  Tips on using search engines effectively.
- Introduction to Search Engines   http://www.kcpl.lib.mo.us/search/srchengines.htm
  Overview and reviews of Web search tools compiled by a reference librarian at the Kansas City Public Library. A handy chart compares features of six major search engines.
- Accessibility and Distribution of Information on the Web   http://www.wwwmetrics.com
  Overview of searching the Web. Research found that search engines are lacking in comprehensiveness and timeliness and do not index sites equally.
- Comparing Search Engines   http://web.hamline.edu/administration/libraries/search/comparisons.html
  A collection of articles on search engines.

To demonstrate the process of using **electronic archives**, we asked our colleague Sarah Townsend how she'd search the Web as part of a research project. Sarah has had experience as a Web developer as well as a student. "Choose any topic," we urged. "And show us what you'd do." Join Sarah here as she begins forming ideas for a 10- to 20-page fieldstudy on comic books.

A Comic-Book Search
Sarah Townsend

Doing Research on the Web—and a False Start

In doing my online research on comic books, I hardly know where to begin—so many search engines, so much information. So I begin with what was the beginning of my own Web browsing—the trusty Yahoo!, which I know is useful for structuring a top-down approach to organizing online research. To get myself rolling, I do a simple search for the text string *comic books* on Yahoo!'s homepage and see what turns up. In this case, several subcategories emerge, and I need to figure out which ones are relevant to my study. I decide to ignore all of the regional subcategories (for instance, *Regional>Countries>Singapore> Entertainment>Comics and Animation*) for the time being, although this may be a sign that regions have their own comic-book styles. But that's not what I'm interested in. At this stage I decide I'll start by looking in the most general of the listed categories: *Entertainment>Comics and Animation>Comic Books*.

Following this **link,** I see a listing of further subcategories as well as a list of website links. A quick glance down this page tells me right off the bat that I'd better narrow my search. I'm lost already. While it's good that I've chosen a topic broad enough to work with, I'm realizing that the world of comic books is far more extensive than I could possibly treat in any 10- to 20-page essay. What I need to think about right now is what interests me and why it would make it a good subject for a fieldstudy. I realize that I've maybe jumped online too soon— that this is, in a sense, a false start. Without a clearer idea of where I want to go, I'm going to get lost in the limitless forest of information out there. Like Hansel and Gretel as they followed a trail of breadcrumbs to help them find their way, I need to find a way to find my way. Time to step back from the computer, go back to the beginning, and think about where I want to go with my online research.

Asking the "What Intrigues Me?" Question

When I was considering potential topics, why did I decide on comic books in the first place? My Web browser isn't going to help me answer this, so I turn it off and take up paper and pen. I sit down to think on my own, jotting notes and ideas, doing some freewriting, circling in closer to the heart of what most interests me about my topic.

I think about my first associations with comic books when I was little— how as a girl my older brother gave me a vintage *Spiderman* book encased in plastic and how I kept it safe in my sock drawer for years. My brother particularly loved Spiderman and the Hulk; there was a kind of tragic glamour to both of them, a dark side maybe shared by all superheroes—the inevitable doom of being separated from the rest of humanity. There was something that appealed to my brother in that and to me on his behalf.

And then there was the time, several years later, when I saw my first copy of *Love and Rockets* on the coffee table at a friend's house. This was a comic book like I'd never imagined before. Instead of superheroes, it was populated by regular neighborhood people, dealing with real-life dramatic scenarios—similar, in some ways, to serial soap operas, but with an edge. This darkly drawn book featured strong women characters—a far cry from the whitewashed images of girls gracing the pages of *Seventeen* magazine. At a time in my life when I was beginning to deal with my own maturity, these more complicated and realistic images of young women were a profound relief.

But I still need to think about how this topic can become a fieldwork project. Where, indeed, is the culture of comic-book lovers? That, I believe, is where I need to focus my online research. And what do I already know? I'm pretty sure there is a substantial comic-book culture. I've also known some wannabe comic-book artists in passing—young people my age who prefer bikes and skateboards to cars, who sport the clothes of the urban geek. And who, I wonder, reads comic books regularly? I've noticed comic-book stores tucked away in every urban center I've ever visited. Although this may not be a very visible community, it's definitely there. I need to talk to the proprietor of the local comic-book store, but before I do that active fieldwork, I want to educate myself a little bit and come up with a list of questions to help direct the conversation. And so I come back to electronic resources: along with printed matter, they are a good way for me to begin my self-education.

Continuing My Comic-Book Research Online

I've decided that what most interests me about comic books is the community that gathers around their production and use. Who reads them? Who writes them? And who sells them? I can now return to my online research with more confidence that I have specific questions I want answered. And while I am surfing the Web for relevant material, I can be looking into other electronic resources as well.

Having glimpsed the kinds of resources Yahoo! turns up, I decide to start out with another big search engine. Google simply searches and lists matches rather than giving an overview index of the topic. Once again I type in *comic books*, and Google returns several promising links. The snippet of text indexed by this search engine can tell me a lot at a glance. As Figure 1 shows, I can see how the first site describes itself ("A Research Guide"), and I can learn from the site's URL whether it's an institutional site (like <www.nypl.org>, the New York Public Library's *org* address) or somebody's personal page (like <www.geocities.com/SoHo/55371/>, a personal site hosted by a free service, Geocities). I also can read a little snippet of text from the actual site, which suggests the tone or the intention of the writing ("Comic books are, at least, as old as…").

The first link I pursue (labeled 1) attracts me with its description, which seems relevant to my goal, and turns out to be a section of the New York Public Library's official site. The site details ways to go about researching comic books using materials in the library. While this information doesn't seem particularly helpful to me for conducting online research, I make a note of it as a potentially helpful model to follow when I get to the point of doing research in a library. Then I take a quick look around the site for any other bits that might prove useful. Well, here's something: "Comics and comic books are one of the most pervasive and influential media forms of 20th-century popular culture." Wow. This is a pretty big validation of my topic's cultural significance, posted by the esteemed New York Public Library. I file it away for potential use as a quote for my own writing. If I do quote from this website, I'll be sure to use

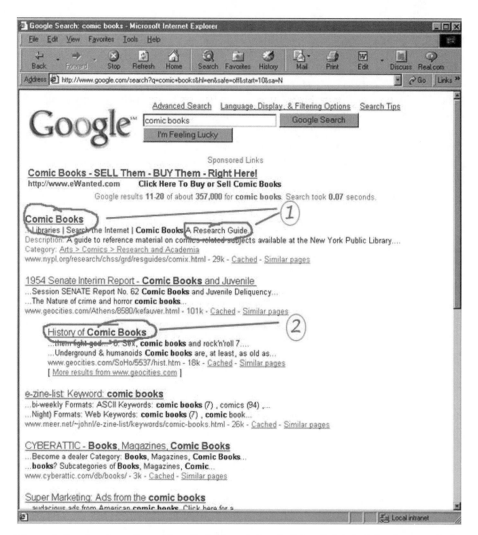

Figure 1. Result of search on Google for "comic books." Sarah labeled the first two links I followed.

citation standards from the MLA or the *Chicago Manual of Style*, noting the URL and the entity I took the information from—just like I would with any other published source.

And now this site gives me an idea for an angle for my piece of research. In a section entitled "The Comic Book Controversy," it briefly introduces the debate about the "moral influence of comic books" in the 1940s and 1950s. I consider my own introductory thoughts about the culture of comic books and their readers—how I notice the shops in places I visit but how they don't seem to have much of a presence; how I've noticed, through my own observations of comic books, that they can have a sophisticated, precise, and sometimes countermainstream social agenda despite the seeming childishness of their artwork. And I find that I've begun to identify a point of interest in comic books stemming from 50 years ago or more—how they serve or cut through the mainstream—and how their readership accepts or rejects standards set by authorities. It is possible that comic-book culture, in some ways, continues to exist and define itself as a counterculture. I think about some of the comic-book readers I've known and how they've intersected with other countersubcultures (skateboarders, computer geeks). I'll need to think about this some more and see what evidence I can turn up to support or contradict it.

The next link I follow (labeled 2) in my Google search takes me to a "history of comic books" compiled by someone who seems to be a student in Brazil. My hunch is based on details I notice in the text of the site rather than on any direct statement. There is, for instance, a Brazilian flag graphic on the homepage linking to a Portuguese version of the site, and I notice that the author's name, Rafael de Viveiros Lima, suggests South American roots. As I cruise around the site, I decide that it's pretty well researched and responsibly constructed. Not only does the author strive to portray an array of comic-book types in his list of his "preferred comics," but he's careful to attribute in a bibliography page the artwork and information he uses. This impresses me. It's not something I've seen often on sites, and it serves a couple of different purposes. Besides respectfully acknowledging Rafael's research sources, it also gives me a list of books and authors I might find reason to consult for my own research.

Apart from his being a responsible researcher, what appeals to me most is Rafael's portrayal of himself as a lifelong reader of comic books. Reading his webpage is equivalent to talking with an aficionado of the comic-book culture at length but with the discussion carefully organized and summarized with illustrations. I get a kind of Web-based portrait of his history of reading comic books and a log of what he's found most appealing and influential in them. Rafael conveys his overview of the history of comic books engagingly and with the air of an authority:

> The '50s staged the greatest witchhunt of comics ever, and a lot of prejudice from those days still remains. Psychiatrist Frederic Wertham wrote a book, *The Seduction of the Innocent*, where he accused comic books of causing youth corruption and juvenile delinquency. Among many other weird subjects, he accused comics of inciting youth to violence (what had already happened with rock 'n' roll). A Comics Code was then created destined to limit and rule on what could appear (and what could not) in the pages.

Rafael's site, in fact, seems almost like formal research rather than a collection of light commentary. Even better, he's got a section entitled "Alternative Comics," which seems promising to my current working thesis that comic-book culture is alternative or countercultural:

> [In alternative comics] the scope is widened. Superhero parody, trash, futurism, ecological concern, social commentary, action, history, fantastic realism—anything can be shown in a comic page. The space for unusual issues was already opened, and the new authors used their creativity to capture the readers' attention. Even in the superhero genre, changes conquer space with new views on old characters and concepts.

His comments are so interesting that I decide to write Rafael an e-mail, and thus my search takes me into another electronic space. In less than 24 hours, I participate in an online conversation:

> ST: Hi Rafael. I came across your comic-book site recently and wanted to tell you how much I liked it…it certainly is well-presented and informative for your audience. How did you assemble the site? Who's your audience? How would you advise a student to find out more? Thank you. :-)…I'm working on a piece about comic books as a subject for an online search—because I'm intrigued by them and don't know much…. Thanks again!
>
> RL: Hi Sarah…Thanks for your comments. Hope you enjoyed the site. I would say that the site is the result of an assemblage of 15 years or so of information about comic books, when my taste about comics changed much. Scott McCloud is the main scholar nowadays, and both his books are the most up-to-date sources. I'd recommend them to students, amateurs, researchers with the same enthusiasm…. I hope that your work will help to bring back to the comics the respectability and cultural relevance they've always deserved…. You are welcome.

Both Rafael and his website are important sources for me, as well as a great motivation to keep going. From here my Web-based research will continue through who knows how many more layers of branching links. Each step I take will inform my next step, just as after I read through the New York Public Library's site, I became more aware that history determines comic books' moral influences and brought that particular perspective with me when viewing Rafael's commentary about "alternative comics." For an illustration of how a Web search works, see Figure 2.

My path through further layers of websites will grow complex, and I need to be careful to note the steps I take along the way if I'm going to responsibly account for my online research. I know from past experience how easy it is to click from one webpage to another, reading related information, following the trail farther into the forest until I finally find myself far from home with little

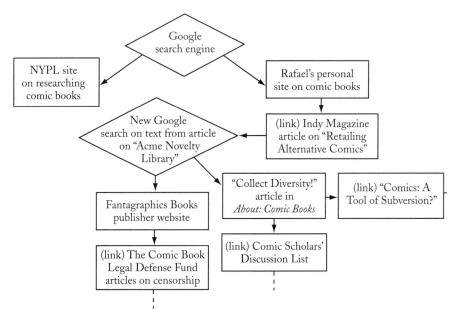

Figure 2. The Way a Web Search Works.
Note that some Web search paths lead only to unhelpful or incidentally helpful information, while others lead to more and more branching sites of related information. When I link to the New York Public Library's site, it turns up one page of somewhat interesting data but doesn't lead me anywhere else. Rafael's site, on the other hand, leads me to a whole constellation of related Web sites, with which I feel my Web search has finally really begun.

idea of what the path looked like that took me there. This is both the wonder and the problem with doing Web-based research. Like a good book, the Web is a medium that's easy to lose myself in. As with other fieldwork, however, I know that making careful notes about where I've been, what I've seen, and how it's all influenced my thinking is essential: these notes will be my trail and will be valuable as I digest, sort, and plan with my data. Of course, there is also the "live" fieldwork part of this project—the local comic-book store owner and the comic-book readers I'll interview, both the young and the middle-aged people who were at one time "counterculture" comic readers. With a bit more research online, I'll know enough to feel confident when I'm in actual places talking to actual people.

Branching Out from the Web

Although webpages are at this point the most accessible medium for finding information by computer, I know that it's important not to forget about other sorts of electronic archives and fields of information. Figure 2 illustrates what is perhaps the second most common—the listserv, or e-mail discussion group. When I come across a webpage for the "Comics Scholars' Discussion List," I know I've struck gold: Here is a community of people asking some of the same sorts of overview questions I'm asking in my study. In addition to the discussion list for which the site is named, this site also includes links to information about several other comparable electronic discussion communities based on comic-book research. From here, I can sign up as a member or "subscribe" to one of these lists and, through e-mail, listen to and ask questions of other comic-book scholars.

Related to the listserv, there are also several other versions of electronic communities I might join while I'm working on this project, communities built around particular areas of interest. Electronic bulletin board systems (BBSs), while not as prevalent as they were in the years before the Web, are also a means of joining an electronic discussion. Chat, or synchronous messaging, is another electronic venue for the exchange of ideas between individuals, and chatrooms are set up through corresponding websites for likeminded people to "get together" and talk. Some websites also set up a version of a guest book or Web-based bulletin-board system that lets visitors post questions and answers that are then written to the page and sorted by "thread" or item of discussion. By browsing through the chronological conversation, you can find data relevant to your study and also other people interested in your topic.

Some Final Words on My Comic-Book Project

To be honest I'm just getting started on the electronic part of my research into comic-book culture, and I haven't yet entered a fieldsite. Figure 2 gives an idea of the kind of paths I'll continue to follow in my Web search, "surfing" for online information. Before I'm done, I will visit many more sites and glean much more information than what I've outlined here. But this is a start. And I hope it helps you envision how you might start your own study online. Throughout the course of online research we'll both need to keep a few things in mind:

1. *Evaluate.*   A website or other electronic resource is only as good as the information it provides. Be a smart researcher who carefully gauges the value and verifiability of that information. Triangulate it using information from other kinds of data sources.

2. *Document.*   Be responsible and carefully document, cite, and attribute the text, graphics, and data you use from electronic sources the way you would any other published material, both out of respect for the author as well as for your readers' benefit.

3. *Research.*   There is more to electronic media than the World Wide Web! Look around the electronic world. See who's talking where—in listservs or e-mail discussion groups, chatrooms, and other online forums. And always remember to be a courteous member of the communities you join.

4. *Mark Your Trail (or, track your breadcrumbs).*   Don't forget to make notes about the divergent paths your Web search takes you on. You never know when you're going to want to go back later and check something that you barely noticed or thought was unimportant when you first saw it.

Finding Your Way in the Online Forest

B
O
X 16

Purpose

Learning to navigate around the Web is one of the first things most of us do online, but doing a focused study with the help of electronic tools requires that you use a more systematic approach to Web browsing, as well as a more discerning eye about what you turn up. Because the Web is nonlinear, as Sarah Townsend points out in the reading on pages 187–95, searches can take you in several directions in a single sitting; therefore, keeping notes serves as a scattering of virtual bread crumbs, marking your path and allowing you to go back later and revisit information you might want.

Action

Starting with a major search engine, try inputting a word or phrase related to your fieldwork subject, and track the links you follow. Keep a notepad beside your keyboard for jotting down notes and brief thoughts on each stop along your way. Limit your time to, say, half an hour or so, to cruise around different sites, and then close down your Web browser. Afterward, map out the path your search took, noting surprises, unpursued possibilities, and general trends you noticed.

As you look over the steps you took, consider the following questions: How many different trails did you use simultaneously in this short period of browsing? How were some of the sites you turned up more helpful than others? What details suggested a given site's authority or value from your researcher's perspective? What telltale signs made you dismiss other sites as unreliable or irrelevant? Where was the most helpful information?

Response

As she did her Web-based research on comic books, Sarah realized it would be easy to become lost in multiple and simultaneous layers of sites. As a means of retracing her steps, she made brief notes in a notebook (see page 196).

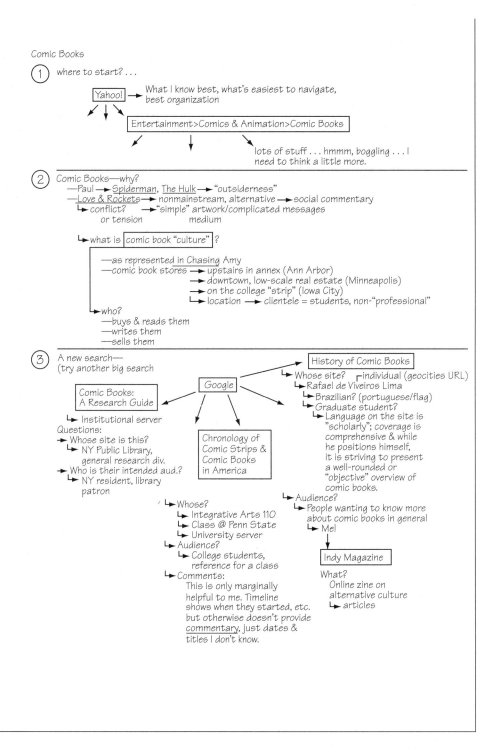

Comic Books

① where to start? . . .

Yahoo! → What I know best, what's easiest to navigate, best organization

Entertainment>Comics & Animation>Comic Books

lots of stuff . . . hmmm, boggling . . . I need to think a little more.

② Comic Books—why?
—Paul → Spiderman, The Hulk → "outsiderness"
—Love & Rockets → nonmainstream, alternative → social commentary
 ↳ conflict?   → "simple" artwork/complicated messages
   or tension   medium

 ↳ what is comic book "culture" ?

 —as represented in Chasing Amy
 —comic book stores → upstairs in annex (Ann Arbor)
               → downtown, low-scale real estate (Minneapolis)
               → on the college "strip" (Iowa City)
               ↳ location → clientele = students, non-"professional"
 ↳ who?
 —buys & reads them
 —writes them
 —sells them

③ A new search—
(try another big search

History of Comic Books
 ↳ Whose site? ┌individual (geocities URL)
 ↳ Rafael de Viveiros Lima
   ↳ Brazilian? (portuguese/flag)
   ↳ Graduate student?
     ↳ Language on the site is "scholarly"; coverage is comprehensive & while he positions himself, it is striving to present a well-rounded or "objective" overview of comic books.

Google

Comic Books: A Research Guide

 ↳ Institutional server
Questions:
► Whose site is this?
 ↳ NY Public Library, general research div.
► Who is their intended aud.?
 ↳ NY resident, library patron

Chronology of Comic Strips & Comic Books in America

 ↳ Audience?
   ↳ People wanting to know more about comic books in general
   ↳ Me!

 ↳ Whose?
   ↳ Integrative Arts 110
   ↳ Class @ Penn State
   ↳ University server
 ↳ Audience?
   ↳ College students, reference for a class
 ↳ Comments:
   This is only marginally helpful to me. Timeline shows when they started, etc. but otherwise doesn't provide commentary, just dates & titles I don't know.

Indy Magazine

What?
 Online zine on alternative culture
 ↳ articles

USING FIELDWORK TO SUGGEST WEBWORK

Using electronic archives, as Sarah Townsend demonstrates on pages 187–95, is a way to supplement and bring to life any kind of topic you choose. Sarah used her Web searches to help her shape her fieldwork project on the culture of comic books before she ventured into the field. Another student, Ivana Nikolic, used her fieldwork project to help her think about the kind of Web search she might conduct to strengthen what she had already done in the field.

When she did this fieldworking project, Ivana had lived in the United States for two and a half years, a refugee from the war in Bosnia. As a student of fieldworking and someone who, in her own words, is "a kid on a mission," she decided to study a homeless shelter in her college town. "I learned that helplessness is probably the most difficult position to be in," she wrote as she positioned herself to do this study. After having both worked and researched in her local shelter, Ivana learned more about homelessness in nonwarring countries and discovered some important things about herself: "I tend to think that my personal experiences have made me more responsive and sensitive to the misfortunes of others; however, they have also lowered my tolerance and understanding for those who seem to have given up trying." Ivana's fieldwork offered her important insights about the shelter she studied—and about her own position in relationship to it.

But Ivana's experiences with one shelter were just a beginning. After writing about her experiences, observations, and interviews she knew that to learn about the picture of homelessness in the United States, she would need to supplement this writing with more reading and online study. Taking the suggestion of her instructor, Lee Torda, Ivana planned to continue her project with more online research. Here is the fieldstudy that she wrote for her class with Lee.

House for the Homeless: A Place to Hang Your Hat
Ivana Nikolic

I was only thirteen years old when my parents, my younger brother, and I left our home in Bosnia in the heat of the war. We have lived as refugees for eight years now. During that time we have started our lives from the very beginning twice, with only three travel bags packed with our pictures and belongings reminding us that we led a normal life before. My parents, once well respected and successful, were either unemployed or struggling to get and keep any job that was offered to them. I was brought up in an environment that highly respected education, and soon I realized that school was my only way out. I realized early on that I can lose everything except for what I can carry with myself, and that was knowledge. Since then, I have been a kid on a mission, determined to succeed, never give up, and make the most of the opportunities that were given to me.

Despite everything that happened to us, or maybe because of it, our family bonds grew stronger. We kept each other sane: we supported each other and never allowed each other to fall into despair. There were many times, though, when just as I thought that we hit the bottom, we would sink a little deeper. I learned that helplessness is probably the most difficult position to be in. After all, ever since the war our lives have been nothing but struggle, and we were in no position to change our situation. We were merely political puppets, suspended on the threads of the bloodthirsty puppet-masters dressed as politicians. I tend to think that my personal experiences have made me more responsive and sensitive to the misfortunes of others; however, they have also lowered my tolerance and understanding for those who seem to have given up trying.

When I moved to the United States two and a half years ago, homeless people were among the first to catch my attention. It broke my heart seeing them on the corners of the main roads, inhaling exhaust and the smell of burned rubber. Dirty and tired, they were holding signs offering to work for food and shelter. I knew how insecure, lost, scared, and lonely some of them must feel, since in a way I have been there too. I couldn't understand. How could the same system that brought me here and gave my family a chance when nobody else would fail so many other people? At first I thought that they were unfortunate people, run down by life or the system, who never found a way to blend in with the rest of the society. As the time went by, my perspective changed.

Most of the refugees that come to the United States don't speak English. While I worked as a Bosnian interpreter and case worker for a refugee resettlement organization, I met many Bosnian, Cuban, Somali, Russian, and Vietnamese refugees. The majority of them spoke little or no English, but they all found jobs within a month or two on their arrival in the United States. Therefore, finding a job was not as difficult as I had thought. That made me think that maybe unemployment was not the major problem of the homeless.

I talked to some of my American friends. "Most of them are drug addicts, alcoholics, or both." "They don't like rules and choose to live that life." "They don't want to be helped." That seemed to be the common American public opinion of the homeless. I could not understand, and what was once sympathy grew into fear that stemmed from not understanding. I grew accustomed to seeing homeless people on the corners without paying much attention. Sometimes, when I would run into them on my way back to my car, I would feel uneasy and often scared. It might be because I thought of them as being desperate. I saw them as people who had lost hope and meaning in life. I allowed myself to base my opinions on what I heard from other people, without ever trying to hear the stories of the homeless themselves. Actually, I never even read one book about them. But I felt ashamed. The more I thought about them, the more interested I was to hear some of the stories firsthand. Where are their families? Do they even have families? What did they do before they stepped into the homeless world? If they could, would they even want to get out of that culture? How many of them had had a misfortune or experienced a tragedy that pushed them so far, and how many chose to live that way? I was ready to listen. Thinking that listening to their stories would help me better understand their culture and that better understanding would diminish fear and stigma, I started to volunteer in a homeless shelter.

A Place to Hang Your Hat

It was 6:45 p.m. Wednesday, and, as always, people were standing in a long line waiting for the doors to the Ramsey House to open. The building is located downtown, next to a health care center. I remember taking refugees to this health care center. There were always people standing and hanging around in front of the building and in the parking lot between the health care center and Ramsey House. There were also always people waiting for the bus at the bus stop across the street. This was rare in other parts of the city, since public transportation was everybody's worst nightmare. As I drove into the parking lot, it seemed that nothing had changed. I heard loud hip-hop and rap music coming from a radio on the shoulder of an old and sick-looking man. His hair was gray and braided. He wore a Jamaican-looking hat. Although he looked tired, his appearance projected an illusion of a young spirit. The others were standing in groups, talking and smoking. It was my third day volunteering, and some people recognized me. They greeted me politely as I walked toward the door.

The lobby of the Ramsey House smelled strongly of lemon-scented disinfectant. A large front desk separated the office space from the lobby. The lobby had 30 chairs arranged around a modern, big-screen TV that was the focal point of the room. In one corner there were a couple of tables where some of the homeless sometimes played chess or cards. On one of the walls there was a display of pictures framed in glass. People of all ages and races were smiling and celebrating. I remembered how before I came, I expected to find a place saturated with religion, and the mere thought made me feel slightly uneasy. However, I was pleasantly surprised when I came. The lobby was saturated with hope and support. There were a lot of references to God, faith, and hope in motivational phrases, such as: "Ain't nothin' gonna come up today that me and the Lord can't handle."

The lobby walls had a display of quilts. One of the quilts had four quadrants, and each quadrant had a message. "Let your life shine. Integrity, love, peace," was embroidered on the upper half, and in the lower half there was a picture of a man playing with a dog bathed by the sunshine. "Saint Francis," read the small letters next to the picture of the man. Above the reception desk there were pictures of Jesus Christ and a cross. On one side there was a sign saying "Our staff does not support violence," and on the other side there was a sticker saying "There is no hope in dope." On the opposite wall there was a large black poster with white letters that read "Believe in the power of work." Next to this poster there was a bulletin board displaying messages in English and Spanish about job openings, TB tests, free job transportation, and other work-related matters. Right above the phone on the front desk there was a sign printed on simple white paper. "A place to hang your hat," was written in small black letters next to a picture of a simple hat on a hook. Just like that poster, this place was simple but carried a warm welcome.

Every night after dinner a volunteer minister held a Bible study. Everybody was welcome to join, but nobody was asked to come. There was also a service during the day, a part of the Chaplaincy Program that was oriented toward spiritual counseling, praying, and worship for guests, clients, and staff. There were neither crosses on every wall nor Bibles on every chair. I felt a strong presence of community and faith, but religion was subtle.

It was 7:00 p.m.—time to check in people for dinner. The air conditioning was broken, and the whole place smelled strongly of lemon-scented disinfectant. The kitchen was large. It could seat about 70 people. A wall surrounded one area of the kitchen. This was where the people stood in a line. Lunch is served every day from 10:30 to 12:30 to anybody who stands in the line. However, dinner is served only to those who check in to spend the night. Ramsey House is a year-round shelter for women and men. Guests, as the staff refers to the homeless, have their own beds assigned, and they have to check in through the kitchen every night. Two security guards with metal detectors check everybody before they approach the check-in table.

It was my first time checking in people. I soon realized that this was probably the most diverse-looking group of people I ever saw classified under the same category—homeless. People from all age groups and racial groups were passing me their cards. Some of them were dressed nicer than I was, and I wondered how many times I passed them on the street never knowing where they went to sleep at night. Some was disabled, tired, and dirty; others looked sick. I was helping George, a full-time staff member. As people were checking in, he was joking with them. Most of them had a very high dose of respect for him, but at the same time they were reserved. He had a slightly militaristic tone of voice; you did not want to make him angry.

I asked George about the people who come here. He told me that most of the people had a drug addiction problem. Some of them were "crackheads." Their families couldn't trust them anymore or couldn't withstand the torture of addiction, so they abandoned them. "People here seldom speak of their families, probably because they've lost touch or realized their mistakes and are ashamed to talk about it. Some of them are infected. You know that, right?" asked George. I assumed that they were, although nobody told me that. A lot of the people in the shelter work and use the shelter as a way to save money until they have enough to move away. Their educational backgrounds vary greatly. There are those who can't read, and those who have master's degrees. However, as much as their individual stories differed and although all of them had their own reasons for being here, they all shared the same dream, and that was to move on.

A significant number of the people in the shelter were trying to get jobs, trying to stay clean of drugs, or trying to get their own apartments. I have a great deal of respect for people who have a goal in their lives, even if they are only short-term goals. When you reach the bottom of the social ladder, a goal or a dream might be your most precious possession. That is what kept me going as a refugee. I realized early on that I can feel sorry for myself, or I can set a goal and instead of passively sitting around and complaining I can work on achieving my goals. I found out that when I was busy thinking about the future and working on getting there, even the worst of troubles seemed less significant. I was too busy to think about them. They were just a thorn on my way to the stars. That is how I learned to respect people that have a goal or a dream. On their way to the fulfillment of their dreams, even if they never get there, they will move on.

A Caravan Stop

New people were checking in, others were leaving. There was a constant flux of people through the shelter. Close friendships were rare, and the occasional conversations between the homeless and me were very friendly but not personal. There was no time to be personal: people had to be fed, laundry had to be done. There was always something to keep me busy. I wondered whether the homeless saw the ritualistic nature of their evenings: check in, eat, listen to George read the rules of the shelter, take new linen, get a shower, chit-chat a bit during the cigarette breaks, then lights out. One night, I was helping in the laundry room, and the endless stream of nameless familiar faces coming in and out of the sweaty, stuffy, and stinky room gave a slightly nomadic feel to the place. The shelter was like a caravan stop for these people on a long tiring journey. It was a temporary place of refuge—a place to hide from their vices as well as from the society that chooses to shun them. The fire alarm went off. Calmly, people started to move toward the entrance. Through the mumbling I heard a couple of them joking, "Somebody tried to smoke one again."

All of us were standing outside on the parking lot. It was very loud. The Jamaican man brought down his radio, and a crackling sound mixed with a beat was pounding on asphalt. A young man in his thirties came and sat down next to me. His name was Alejandro. He was about five feet four and rather skinny. The skin on his hands was rough and broken. It was hard to imagine him doing hard labor, but his hands were his witnesses. I had met him earlier in the laundry room. It was difficult to understand his English, and the noise didn't help either. I asked him where he was from, "Mexico," he said. "I came to America twenty years ago." He lived with his mother in California. "I like California," he said. "Everybody speak Spanish there, but they don't pay good in California. Minimum wage four dollars. Here I get six." His eyes got teary when he mentioned his mother. I found out that his mother and all of his friends were still in California. He did not have anybody here. He carried a rolled-up job-search newspaper. He looked tired. The security guards came out and said that we needed to go back in now. I lost Alejandro in the crowd. I never saw him again. I find myself hoping that he found a job.

Going Back into the World

I met Solomon in the lobby another night. His English was proper and sophisticated, but he had a thick foreign accent. "Where are you from?" I asked.

"Congo. I came to the U.S. two years ago." He was very calm when he talked. His hands barely moved, and even then it was in a slow, preaching manner. He revealed that back home he was a teacher, but here he doesn't know what he will do. I tried to find out why he came here, but he was very reluctant to talk about his past. "Do you have family back home?" I asked. "My mother is still in Congo. She lives in a polygamous marriage. That is not good. There is too much rivalry. I have brothers in Europe, in Germany. I have not spoken to them in a long time," he said. He got very emotional, and as much as I wanted to find out more about his family and how he came here, I couldn't. He was not interested in talking about it. He was not comfortable with my asking questions about him, his family, or his home. He spoke with a certain dose of mystic philosophy. "I like to observe all the people, women and men. All of them. I can see what a person is like by observing them. What makes one a gentleman and one a bum? If you observe people and their reactions carefully, you can find out what sort of an image you project on the world. You can find out who you would like to behave like—find your role models. He said that he doesn't like to talk. "You can find out more by observing," he said.

The whole conversation was somewhat surreal. Here he was, a young, healthy intellectual, sharing his life philosophy with a stranger in the loud and dirty lobby of a homeless shelter. He was stepping over every stereotype I had of homeless people. "A lot of bizarre things have happened since I decided to come to America. I just want to get my life together now. It will take time though," he said calmly. He stared at me with his large tired eyes. I could feel his eyes dragging around my mind like little spies, trying to decipher what I was thinking.

Solomon had applied for a job as a bank teller and as a substitute teacher. Nobody had called him for an interview yet. I saw a glimpse of frustration in his eyes as he talked about how he would like to work as a bank teller just for a little while. I thought it was strange that he insisted on two very hard-to-get positions. I asked if he had considered any other options for employment, but he did not even want to talk about it. A bank teller, a substitute teacher, or nothing. It sounded like he did not consider any other positions because he used to be a teacher and working in hard labor would be demeaning. He made a choice, but I have to admit that the choice seemed odd to me. My father, who had worked in an office all his life, is now working in maintenance, and as strange as it seems, he says that he is happy. He is happy because that job gave him stability, and therefore he doesn't see it as demeaning. In the light of those experiences, I learned that sometimes one has to choose a small compromise for a greater purpose. I assumed that Solomon had either chosen not to compromise, even if that meant staying in the shelter longer, or he had not yet come to terms with reality. And although I wanted Solomon to succeed, I doubted not his ability to do the job well but rather the ability of society to look past its stereotypes.

At one point he said he liked me. I did not know what to say. An uncomfortable "Thank you" came out of my mouth. Our conversation took a cold shower. "Thank you" was not what he was hoping to hear. I took the first chance I had to excuse myself and go help one of the staff members.

Upstairs in the dorms, I met Hope. She was a young, white 18-year-old girl. I first met her a week ago, during my first night of volunteering. It was her first night in the shelter, too. She was scared and devastated to hear that she couldn't have a night-light. She came from a shelter in another city that closed for the summer due to lack of funding and volunteer support. Hope had epilepsy. She told me she had to drop out of school because of her medical problems. She was on medication so she has not had any seizures in a while. Her doctor had told her that her brain was not fully developed at the time of birth and if she had another seizure she would die. Despite all of this, she was unusually talkative and happy. I wanted to find out how she ended up in a homeless shelter, since I remembered that when she came to the shelter, the first thing she tried to do was to call her mother. We sat down and talked.

She was sad because her best friend had left. She met him in the shelter. "I get along with all the guys. I get along better with guys than with girls. 'Cause guys don't steal your boyfriends or talk about you behind your back." I tutor high-school kids, and for a moment there she was just one of those kids. She was worried about her image and wished for colorful and glittery pens. I was not sure whether she even thought about the fact that is she is living in a homeless shelter and that she cannot stay there forever. "My best friend was a guy. Of course. Everybody said I was a 'ho' because I only hang out with guys. But I would still be a virgin if I had not been raped." She told me how one time she had to beat a girl up because she was dating her boyfriend. The girl was pregnant and lost the baby. "I felt really bad. She didn't press charges or anything, 'cause I did not know. If I had known that she was pregnant, I wouldn't have fought her in the first place." She seemed to be too calm talking about all of this. I was more upset just listening to her talk. I couldn't understand how she could be so calm. I found out later that she also had impulse control disorder. This seemed to explain how she could beat up a girl so bad that she lost her baby. Still, she was very calm and relaxed, as if the girl had lost a shoe, not a baby. At that point I started to doubt that she fully understood the consequences of her actions.

Hope told me about her sister, who graduated from college and was living with her boyfriend. Her sister lived close by, and she was her best friend. "My sister is moving out 'cause they started going to church. They are not married, so she is going to move out and get her own place. I am so happy 'cause she's going to church now and all this other stuff. I am really happy for her. I told her maybe I'll move in with her. She said 'O.K.' Yeah, right!" Hope laughed as if this was so far away from possible that one could only laugh at how silly it was. I didn't think that any of that was silly. Wouldn't it be natural for her to live with her sister rather than spend the nights in the homeless shelter? She should have already moved in. I didn't quite understand. I wanted to find out more about her mother. I knew that her mother lived close by and she talked to her over the phone, which I assumed meant that their mother-daughter relationship was not entirely dead.

Her mother lived in a neighboring town. Hope said her mother was a racist because she didn't let her best friend, who was black, spend the night in their house. This made Hope angry, so one day she asked a friend from school, a black friend, to drop her off home. She told her mom that he was her boyfriend. Her mom grounded her, but three weeks later she got a restraining order against Hope and Hope's alleged boyfriend because Hope stood up to her. Hope told her mother that she was setting a bad example for her and she was prejudiced. Well, her mom was not about to listen to her teenage daughter preach to her. Hope still calls her every day, and they talk. She still had great respect for her mother. "I still love my mom. She is the only mom I'll ever have. I respect her thoughts, her wishes, but I told her, I said—I mean I was not trying to be mean or disrespectful, but I told her she couldn't choose my friends or who I date anymore." Her mom got a restraining order against Hope, and it has to be in effect for three years before she can drop it. Unlike Hope, I was shocked, but that was not all. I found out that her father was dying of emphysema and a bleeding ulcer. He did not work. He was on his deathbed according to Hope. He was trying to find a trailer. He lived on his own. She seemed to be closer to her dad than to her mom. She got very emotional talking about her future without him, as if she had already buried him and was even more grateful for the days that she had with him.

I was overwhelmed by Hope's story. My mind was burdened with one question: "How can all this happen to one innocent young human being?" Later, as our conversation continued, I started asking: "Is this really true?" Parts of her story didn't seem to make sense. She told me that her dad bought her a 2000 Eclipse, but she had told me her dad didn't even work and, since she has epilepsy, that she cannot have a driving license until she is 21. I realized that even if she lied about the car, it didn't change anything. She probably needed something to dream about, something to divert her attention from her situation, like the car and going off to college. "I will study journalism," she told me. And as crazy as it seemed to me, she talked about it as if it were nothing. There was not even a slightest doubt in her mind that she might not make it.

I realized early in my study that I came in contact with only a very small number of homeless. The people who were allowed to stay in this shelter had to be clean of alcohol as well as of drugs. Whoever smelled of alcohol or appeared to be high would be kicked out of the shelter. Therefore, I realized that I might have seen only the cream of the crop.

However, I learned that one cannot make generalizations about the homeless. Indeed, the majority of the people in the shelter did have a drug addiction problem and were trying to get rid of the bad habit as well as the bad company. Some of them were more successful than others. They wanted to change and stop the never-ending cycle, or so they said. There, in the shelter, they were offered counseling, support, and programs dealing with drug addiction, and the people who worked there did not judge their character or morality. That is probably why they came there. Some of them, unable or unwilling to escape the vicious circle of addiction, kept coming back. Here, being able to accept your mistakes and face your problems was considered to be a sign of a strong character. Some of the people in the shelter were mentally ill and couldn't help themselves; others were physically disabled, unable to work, living on disability checks or waiting for them to come through. However, all of them—Solomon, Alejandro, Hope, and the others I met—dreamed of and lived for a life outside and after the shelter. For some it will never happen; for some that time will come sooner than they expected. Sitting in the lobby and waiting for their time to come, what keeps them going? What helps them get up in the morning? For most it seemed to be the mere thought that tomorrow they might take their bag, start living, and go home. Maybe the fact that most of the people there appear to be strongly religious explains where this hope that they will make it comes from. Hope was the common thread that I found in this shelter.

As lights were about to go off and I was walking down the stairs, I met one of the older men. He was carrying two large African woven fans and some decorative frames. He was wearing a bright big smile on his face. "Where are you going?" I asked him. "I am moving. I got me a place through Community Village. I am going back into the world. I am going back to living," he said. "Good luck!" I said. "Thank you and good night." That night, in his eyes I saw the biggest flash of hope and happiness ever.

Conclusion

Shortly after the interview, Hope left the shelter. I heard from some of the women that her dad came and took her with him. Unfortunately, George told me that she was kicked out of the shelter. He did not know why, since he was not there that night. I hope that she found a way to live with her dad, mom, or sister. I felt she was too young to be there, anyway. Solomon is still waiting to hear something from the bank or public school system. His frustration seems to grow with every day that passes.

I tried to compare my own experiences to the experiences of the homeless. I shared similar experiences with some of them, and maybe that enabled me to sympathize with them. I learned that "homeless" describes a wide range of people, coming from different cultures, with a wide span of education and a wide variety of reasons for being in the shelter. Like me, most of the people in the shelter had a goal or a dream and hoped that they would succeed and get rid of the need to depend on somebody. I realized that their hope was often rooted in their belief in a higher power. I always believed in myself; however, they have to learn to believe in themselves. But until they do, they put their fate in the hands of their Lord, meanwhile struggling to make it back to the real world.

Reflection is key in ethnographic work, and while all kinds of archives may strengthen a study, in the end, every fieldstudy is also about the self. Here is Ivana's reflection on studying the homeless shelter—what she learned about her self and her own writing and researching process:

Ivana's Reflection

It was interesting to witness how doing this project helped me form a clearer opinion of the homeless culture and how to see how my opinions changed as my research progressed. I was even more surprised to see how much this project helped me look back and reevaluate my experiences as a refugee myself. As much as this research was about the homeless shelter, it was also about me. It helped me see my life in a new light and realize how much I have achieved despite the difficulties I have had. I admit that at times this was disturbing to me, but nonetheless I am grateful because had I not done this project, I may have never had these reflections about my life.

Although ethnographic writing, as with other forms of writing, includes certain kinds of information, it took me some time to realize that fieldwriting is a flexible and fluid form that allows the writer to experiment while trying to find information about the culture. I decided to make my interviews the basis of my project since they provided the best insights into the culture. I must also admit that doing the interviews was the most intimidating part of the whole research project. I was afraid I would ask the wrong questions or open an old wound. I was surprised to find how much people like to talk about themselves. People in a homeless shelter were glad to know that somebody is interested in what they have to say. However, instead of focusing on the interviews so much, I might have written more describing the site, a particular artifact, or something I located from my Web searches. In an ethnographic piece of writing, there is no right or wrong format. The difficult thing is finding the best form for the information. It was painfully difficult for me to come to this revelation, but when I did, it changed my ideas about what fieldwork is really all about—myself in relation to others.

Ivana's description of Ramsey House and especially her portraits of diverse informants—from staff members like George to guests Alejandro, Solomon, Hope, and the Jamaican man—give us a rich portrait of this shelter, and, as readers, we begin to wonder how this shelter compares to others in the United States. To answer this question, the first suggestion we would make to Ivana would be, of course, to do some more research. Her project at this point is the opposite of Sarah Townsend's. Ivana has done lots of "live" fieldwork. She's described the shelter itself based on her fieldnotes, incorporated her own "positioning" as she sees it, and eloquently told the stories of her informants in their words, from her interviews and transcripts—all things Sarah is still planning to do.

Searching the Online Forest to Support Your Journey

Unlike Sarah, who began her research with sources away from her fieldsite, Ivana needs to find ways to incorporate the online information she's already gathered and possibly find more to support what she's already written. Ivana has already performed a search with the words *homeless* and *shelter* with a mainstream search engine, a search that produced results that were overwhelming. She has found 173 websites containing the words *homeless* and *shelter*—with another several hundred links on the sites themselves. Most are homepages for shelters across the United States. So how would these sites help Ivana learn anything specific about Ramsey House?

Let's go back to the three ways to use an electronic archive we described on page 184: (1) as basic secondary-source information, (2) for personal contacts, and (3) as an artifact of the subculture under study. First, Ivana could check the Web for basic written information about the day-to-day issues all homeless shelters face. She could find schedules for when and how meals are served. She could find out how to qualify to stay at shelters. She could determine what different services different shelters offer. Using online data as her secondary resource could help Ivana think about how Ramsey House fits into the larger subculture of homeless shelters more easily than she might at her primary source, the Ramsey House itself. Second, as most of the websites offer contact information, Ivana could easily e-mail a series of questions to any number of homeless shelters, just as Sarah e-mailed Rafael about comic books. She might have e-mail conversations with administrators, volunteers, and perhaps even residents. Unlike online communication using real time, e-mail allows people to choose when to respond during lulls in their own workloads. Imagine how this information would broaden the scope of Ivana's work. And imagine how much more Ivana would need to think about and look for when she returned to the Ramsey House with all this background information.

We've seen how Ivana could use websites for gathering information and personal contact. As we mentioned above, the third way she could use websites is as artifacts in and of themselves—that is, as creations of the members of the subculture. Used this way, a website could give Ivana ways of framing her description and adding depth to her writing, revising a simple narrative into a piece that suggests a broader cultural scope.

Ivana's writing instructor, Lee Torda, offered several suggestions for ways that Ivana could do online research on this topic. Ivana could choose among many options. For example, she could look at websites from different urban regions of the country, perhaps New York City, Chicago, or Los Angeles. She could look at other shelters closer to Ramsey House. Or she could do both. She could read and compare the website of an urban homeless shelter in the San Francisco Bay Area, for example, to the site for a rural shelter in the middle of Maine and then look back to Ramsey House. She might find that the two websites both mention ministry work and are affiliated with a religious organization, which would help explain some of the signs on the Ramsey House walls and some of the religious attitudes, behaviors, and rituals she's already noted and described among both staff and guests. Continuing to take little snapshots from the Web, she might find that the ministry work of the Bay Area shelter is apparent only on its history page, that the Maine shelter has no affiliation on its site, but that a Raleigh, North Carolina, shelter announces its religious affiliation on its splash page. Considering the various websites as artifacts and thinking about how other shelters use their religious affiliations might help Ivana triangulate the data she's collected at her fieldsite.

Another issue Ivana might consider is how websites for homeless shelters discuss their financial considerations. Many list their boards of directors and identify the process by which money is raised and spent. Some display their annual financial reports. Several sites indicate how much of their money comes from government sources and how much comes from donations. Funding is often contrasted with expenditures on administration, drug and alcohol rehab support, employee training, and other programs for shelter residents. How, then, is a shelter a part of its community? And how does Ramsey House compare? Ivana might find this a useful trail of information for another set of interviews. The websites from around the country indicate that the subculture of homeless shelters' relationship to money is complex and important.

Ivana might also notice that several websites have links to webpages that talk about health insurance, mental illness, child abuse and neglect, spousal abuse, the welfare system, and local legislation against squatters' rights. So another important thematic trail she could follow would be to investigate the larger social and cultural problems that stem from and lead to homelessness. She has already seen and described the effects of homelessness on individuals. More knowledge of the larger issues would help broaden her essay. Through electronic archives, Ivana has the opportunity to expand the questions she's already asked, the details she's already found, and, ultimately, the artifacts of the larger subculture she's chosen to study.

Ivana could further enrich her fieldwork essay with Web investigations to give her new ways of understanding the information she has already collected from her fieldsite and new possibilities for interpreting "what goes on there." The real purpose of doing traditional library, archival, or Web research is to strengthen and triangulate data so that it is multilayered and representative of the complexities of the fieldsite. As we stress throughout this book, there is no *one* way to do a fieldstudy. Looking at ways Ivana might redirect and refocus helps show this even more: every fieldworker will write a different study of the fieldsite, even if the site is the same place.

THE RESEARCH PORTFOLIO: REPRESENTING THE UNFLAT STUFF

Whether archives belong to families, local or international institutions, whether they're in big dusty boxes or posted on the World Wide Web, it's hard to know how to use them and what references to include as "stuff" in your research portfolio. What "stuff" can you call yours? How do you represent something that was important to your project when it doesn't fit into a paper portfolio? Why should you include what you decide to include? What does each item mean to your overall research project? We've heard questions from teachers and students puzzling over the value of portfolios as a research tool—as a tool for researchers to document their learning to themselves and to others who might need to assess and evaluate their work.

A high school teacher in a portfolio workshop once asked Bonnie, "What's the difference between a portfolio and a garage sale?" Although at first the question rattled her—she knew the teacher was saying that from his perspective, a portfolio looked like random items of junk sitting in a pile, waiting to be discarded—she eventually thought, "Hmmmm, looking over the array of items at a garage sale and trying to piece together stories of the past is, in fact, *very much* like the reflective work of a portfolio."

Lots of people puzzle over portfolios, wondering how to organize what might appear to someone else as junk. And sometimes the most important "junk" comes in inconvenient sizes and shapes. Perhaps the most provocative question we've every heard about portfolios came from a high school student: "What do we do with the unflat stuff?" A portfolio, because it usually incorporates only two-dimensional materials, most often cannot include "unflat stuff" like performances, audio or videotapes, an informant's treasured, one-of-a-kind artifacts or photos, songs or important sounds, and original documents that are critical parts of your research. Nor can a portfolio house every piece of data you've collected. Not only would it be heavy and unwieldy, but it wouldn't allow you to arrange and rearrange categories as you continue to work with it. In short, to use the terms we use in Chapter 1, a "portfolio of everything" would simply show the "collection" process—and leave no room for the important processes of selection, reflection, and projection.

A well-designed portfolio is all about representation. It is anything but "flat," even if it fits into a three-ring binder with plastic document covers and stick-on notes. Like a well-designed webpage, it displays the items and connections ("links") you've selected to represent the categories of your research, the data you've collected, and the ways your thinking develops as you look it over, plan more research, and then perhaps recategorize further. A high-tech portfolio using web technology can—despite a flat, two-dimensional screen—combine even more data than a paper portfolio, show connections and links even better, incorporate sound and motion, and reorganize itself as you shift your understandings and click your mouse.

A portfolio offers you the chance to sift through the chaos of piles of data and select representations that will enable you to see what you have more easily. Sometimes, with new thinking and lots of data, researchers need something concrete to help them understand abstract ideas. We think portfolios—whether on paper or online—are a deeply important way to bring the process of analysis into a clear and concrete form.

We weren't able to explain our own experience in Muncie, Indiana (see pages 173–76 earlier in this chapter) until we laid out all the representative items and tried to understand the relationships they had with one another. At the time we were visiting, we just grabbed everything we could. It all looked interesting and we weren't sure what was going to be important. But then, later, we studied what we had. We didn't need the whole items themselves (all our notes, all our e-mails, all the books, or the jars, buildings, landscapes, and talk we'd seen and heard). We already knew that data well. Rather, what we needed to understand how to tell our story efficiently to you was a way to represent those items.

Here is a list describing some representative items we would include in a portfolio for our Ball jar project, with some of our thoughts about their significance:

1. An image of a Ball jar. A glass jar is far from flat, but represents the industry and craft that defines the history and culture we discovered in Muncie. We might take a snapshot, photocopy a picture from a book, or use a commercial postcard.

2. A section from the exhibition's background script, with a photo of the building and grounds. Although we'd be tempted to include brochures describing many interesting things from the museum—for instance, the hundred-year-old preserved pears—they are not relevant to the focus we took for our project. We did, though, learn a lot about the life of the Ball family from the script about the rehabilitation of the grounds and the dollhouse, and from looking at the grounds themselves.

3. An excerpt from the transcript of the interview with Almeda Mullin. Curator Beth Campell's interview with Mullin gave us an exciting and detailed window into the life of one glass factory worker in the early part of the twentieth century. It wasn't until we had these two items together (the information about Elisabeth Ball's dollhouse and the interview with Almeda Mullin) that we realized we had evidence of the lives of two very different young women who lived in the culture of this town at just about the same time in history. By putting these items together in our portfolio, we represent connections we might otherwise have overlooked.

4. A photocopy of the cover of the tape from Garrison Keillor's radio program, which we ordered from Minnesota Public Radio over the Internet. We'd accompany it, perhaps, by a section of our transcript. The tape, of course, isn't flat either. But our job for the portfolio is simply to represent the tape, not to play it. It comes from a two-tape audio collection of Keillor's monologues called "Mother, Father, Uncle, Aunt."

5. A photocopy of the cover of one of the Middletown books to illustrate Muncie's history of being a sociological spot known as a "typical" American town, driven by the ingenuity of one family, a rich underground natural gas resource, and a supply of ready workers. Although we didn't read all three books, one was very helpful to us and we found it important to know that there were three written over a 50-year period.

6. A few snippets from our notes, correspondences, and e-mails with professor Joe Trimmer, who originally invited us to Ball State University, and Beth Campbell, who spent an afternoon with us at the Minnetrista Cultural Center. Without the help of these people, who were both our contacts and our references, we wouldn't have been able to conduct this short bit of fieldwork.

When you create a portfolio of representative items, you can organize and reorganize, label each item with a sticky note explaining what you think it means, and reflect on what you have selected. As you go through this process, the themes of your project will become clearer. As you discover more connections, as the themes begin to emerge, as you have more items with which to triangulate, you will learn much about your data, yourself in relationship to it, and what you want to share with your readers. Portfolios are wonderful tools for representation and analysis, whether the "stuff" is flat or not.

FieldWriting: Annotated Bibliographies

One useful way to represent the source materials for your fieldwork is to create an *annotated bibliography,* which provides your reader with more information about the published sources you've used than just the basics of author, title, date, and place of publication. Many researchers, writers, and scholars rely on annotated bibliographies to help them sort through masses of material without having to read each and every source. Each bibliographic citation summarizes a large amount of material into just the key concepts of the book, article, or electronic source. To do that well, the researcher must have a good understanding of the original material and its overall importance. Here are some sample entries of annotated sources from this chapter:

Ball, Edward. *Slaves in the Family.* New York: Ballantine, 1998.
  This research into the writer's white and black plantation ancestors employs both 200-year-old archival documents and oral histories. Ball is a skilled writer who presents a vivid and detailed picture of the history and devastating legacy of the institution of slavery and how it impacted millions of American lives for centuries.

Keillor, Garrison. "On Ball Jars." In *Mother, Father, Uncle, Aunt: Stories from Lake Wobegon.* Original broadcast produced and recorded for Minnesota Public Radio. High Bridge Company HBP 56790. Transcription from Tape 1, side A, 1997.
  In this radio show taped in Muncie, Indiana, Garrison Keillor muses on the importance of Ball jars in both historical and humorous ways. Originally presented before a live audience, Keillor's monologue connects American folk humor about Ball canning jars with other features of living in the

Midwest. This transcription was prepared by Bonnie Stone Sunstein, Elizabeth Chiseri-Strater, and Beth McCabe.

Nikolic, Ivana. "House for the Homeless: A Place to Hang Your Hat." Unpublished fieldstudy, 2000.

First-year college student Ivana Nikolic, a Bosnian refugee now living in the United States, conducted a fieldstudy of Ramsey House, a homeless shelter in a southern U.S. city. Volunteering at the homeless shelter and interviewing both guests and staff, Nikolic discovers a range of reasons for homelessness in the United States that work against the stereotypes she previously held.

FIELDWORDS

Archive A physical or electronic place where collections of public and private records and other historical documents, and sometimes artifacts, are stored.

Browser A computer program that allows the user to view electronic material in a graphical format and to use links to navigate among various websites.

Bulletin board A Web-based resource for public discussion and debate, often threaded by topic. *Bulletin board systems* (*BBSs*) were non-Web-based electronic discussions.

Chatroom A synchronous (that is, real-time) electronic discussion medium or space.

Directory A site that delivers Web content that has been collected and indexed by a human being. Also call *subject guide*.

Electronic archive A set of electronic files stored on a publicly accessible server, available for download by way of a file transfer protocol (FTP) program.

E-mail An asynchronous (that is, not real-time) point-to-point, text-based electronic discussion medium.

File transfer protocol (FTP) A means of downloading and uploading files between a local computer and a publicly accessible server. Examples of FTP utilities include Fetch for the Mac and WS_FTP for Windows.

Internet An international network of computers comprising several subcomponents—the Web, e-mail, and other forms of client-server-based information exchange.

Link A piece of text or an image that has been programmed to allow the user to jump from one website to another by clicking on it with a mouse. Also called *hotlink* and *hyperlink*.

Listserv A subscription-based e-mail discussion community, usually assembled around a particular topic of interest or affiliation.

Multiuser domain (MUD) An electronic space for online role-playing. MOO and MUSH are similar media.

Newsgroup An electronic forum for public discussion, arranged and defined according to topic of interest. Newsgroup exchanges are posted on the Usenet network.

Search engine A site that uses robot programs or "spiders" to search the Web in response to a computer-user's request for content.

Server A computer that communicates with client computers (like the local computer on your desk) by serving them with information via an Internet connection. *Server* also refers to the software that allows a computer to interact with other computers.

Uniform Resource Locator (URL) A webpage address that appears as a text string in your Web browser's location field.

Website A set of files that are stored on a publicly accessible server and that can be retrieved and displayed graphically by a Web browser.

World Wide Web (WWW) A part of the Internet comprising graphical sites interpreted by the browser and connected by links.

FieldReading

Alanen, Arnold R., and Robert Z. Melnick, eds. *Preserving Cultural Landscapes in America.* With a foreword by Dolores Hayden. Baltimore: Johns Hopkins UP, 2000.

Allen, Barbara, and William Lynwood Montell. *From Memory to History: Using Oral Sources in Local Historical Research.* Nashville: American Association for State and Local History, 1981.

Anderson, Jay. *Time Machines: The World of Living History.* Nashville: American Association for State and Local History, 1984.

Bloodworth, Bertha E., and Alton C. Morris. *Places in the Sun: The History and Romance of Florida Place-Names.* Gainesville: U Presses of Florida, 1978.

Brooks, Philip Coolidge. *Research in Archives: The Use of Unpublished Primary Sources.* Chicago: U of Chicago P, 1969.

Brundage, W. Fitzhugh, ed. *Where These Memories Grow: History, Memory, and Southern Identity.* Chapel Hill: U of North Carolina P, 2000.

Bunkers, Suzanne L., and Cynthia A. Huff, eds. *Inscribing the Daily: Critical Essays on Women's Diaries.* Amherst: U of Massachusetts P, 1996.

Clayton, Bruce. *Praying for Base Hits: An American Boyhood.* Columbia: U of Missouri P, 1998.

Early, Gerald, ed. *Ain't but a Place: An Anthology of African American Writings about St. Louis.* Columbia: U of Missouri P, 1998.

Gillespie, Emily Hawley, and Judy Nolte Lensink. *A Secret to Be Buried: The Diary and Life of Emily Hawley Gillespie, 1858–1888.* Iowa City: U of Iowa P, 1989.

Isham, Edward. *The Confessions of Edward Isham: A Poor White Life of the Old South.* Edited by Charles C. Bolton and Scott P. Culclasure. Athens: U of Georgia P, 1998.

Jager, Ronald. *Eighty Acres: Elegy for a Family Farm.* With a foreword by Donald Hall. Boston: Beacon, 1990.

Kammen, Carol. *On Doing Local History: Reflections on What Local Historians Do, Why, and What it Means.* Walnut Creek: Altamira Press, 1995.

Mahoney, James. *Local History: A Guide for Research and Writing.* Washington, DC: National Education Association, 1981.

Shapiro, Ann-Louise, ed. *Producing the Past: Making Histories Inside and Outside the Academy.* Middletown, CT: Wesleyan UP, 1997.

Simpson, Jeffrey. *American Elegy: A Family Memoir.* New York: Dutton, 1996.

Stocking, Kathleen. *Letters from the Leelanau: Essays of People and Place.* Ann Arbor: U of Michigan P, 1990.

Sullivan, Chester. *Sullivan's Hollow.* Jackson: UP of Mississippi, 1978.

Syring, David. *Places in the World a Person Could Walk: Family, Stories, Home, and Place in the Texas Hill Country.* Austin: U of Texas P, 2000.

Weitzman, David. *Underfoot: An Everyday Guide to Exploring the American Past.* New York: Scribners, 1976.

Williams, Terry Tempest. *Refuge: An Unnatural History of Family and Place.* New York: Vintage, 1992.

FIELDPOEM

The Attic and Its Nails
Naomi Shihab Nye

It's hard up there. You dig in a box for whatever the moment requires: sweater, wreath, the other half of the walky-talky, and find twelve things you forgot about which delay the original search, since now that you found them you have to think about them. Do I want to keep this, bring it downstairs? Of course your life feels very different from the life you had when you packed it up there. Maybe your life has another kind of room in it now, maybe it feels more crowded. Maybe you think looking at this old ceramic cup with the pocked white glaze that you made in college would uplift you in the mornings. Your search takes on an urgent ratlike quality as you rip paper out of boxes, shredding and piling it. Probably by now you've stood up too fast and speared your head on one of the nails that holds the roof shingles down. They're lined up all along the rafters, poking through, aimed. Now you have to think about tetanus, rusty nails, the hearty human skull. A little dizzy for awhile, you're too occupied to remember what sent you up into the dark.

Commentary

Alison Barnes

In the poem "The Attic and Its Nails," Naomi Shihab Nye takes us to an attic where we dig through objects that have been packed away. With the use of the second person, Nye allows readers to feel like we are the "you" in the poem, and we quickly lose ourselves in a world where objects remind us of histories and stories of the past. As we tear through boxes trying to uncover more forgotten fragments from our lives, we lose track of the present moment, of the low rafters above us. When we bump our heads, Nye reminds us, "Now you have to think about tetanus, rusty nails, the hearty human skull." It is here, with the human skull, that Nye leaves us to contemplate our urgent need for memory and why objects can seem to contain the knowledge of our lives.

Nye's attic is an example of a family archive, and this chapter shows how objects that have been stored in an attic may be important artifacts in your fieldwork. In addition to family archives, you have read about institutional, museum, and electronic archives. The information and artifacts available to you through these archives can likewise be valuable in your fieldwork. Archives may help you support your fieldwork, or, as you approach, organize, and make sense of these treasure troves of culture and knowledge, give you a starting point for choosing a fieldwork topic.

Alison Barnes is a poet and a photographer. She is currently working on a collection of poems based on the first eighty years of photography.

Researching Place:
The Spatial Gaze

"Gaze" is the act of seeing; it is an act of selective perception. Much of what we see is shaped by our experiences, and our "gaze" has a direct bearing on what we think. And what we see and think, to take the process one step further, has a bearing upon what we say and what and how we write.

—PAUL STOLLER

The word *fieldworking* implies place. When researchers venture "into the field," they enter the surroundings of the "other." Researchers step out of familiar territory and into unfamiliar landscapes. But no matter where they conduct their research, they take their **perspectives** along. When you return to a place where you spent time in your early years, like your grandmother's apartment or a childhood playground, you're probably surprised that the place seems different, maybe smaller or larger than you imagined. And if you visit a kindergarten room, you notice that the scale is designed for small people: you bend down to look at the fish in the fishtank or the gerbils in their cages; you stuff yourself into a tiny plastic chair or fold your legs to your chin during rug time. Your spatial memory and your spatial assumptions depend on your past experiences and your present situation.

As anthropologist Paul Stoller implies in the quotation above, what we see depends on how we filter or select what we see. What we see also depends on *how* we look—how we open ourselves to the acts of seeing. Just as we all read differently at different times in our lives, we also perceive differently. You might not have noticed that the antique stove in your grandmother's kitchen ran on gas until you started to cook yourself. Or as a child, you may not have realized that the reasons for rug time in kindergarten often had more to do with the teacher's desire to establish community than with the fun you had leaving your desk. Stoller's expression "the spatial gaze" represents the fieldworker's stance and worldview. Anthropologists use the term worldview to encompass an informant's entire cultural perspective. Of course, how we understand an informant's worldview is dependent on our own.

This chapter is about researching place: remembering your personal geography, learning how to look at your fieldsite, detailing and mapping space, finding unity and tension within a place, and locating a **focal point**. We are always part of the places we study. Whether they are familiar or unfamiliar, we always stand in relationship to those places. No matter how far outside we may situate ourselves or how close in, there can be no place description without an author. And authoring a place description requires personal involvement. You must always decide on an angle of vision when you take a picture; describing a place is much the same as choosing the perspective from which to shoot.

You may have selected a fieldsite by now and spent some time learning how to "read" it and some of its cultural materials. Researching place takes a long time; this chapter extends many of the skills of reading a cultural site that you may have tried in Chapter 3. Understanding how informants use the space in a fieldsite constitutes the researcher's data. For this reason, fieldworkers train themselves to look through the eyes of both the insider (emic perspective) and the outsider (etic perspective) at once to locate their own perspectives. Studying and writing about how informants interact in their spaces help the fieldworker learn the informants' perspective.

A SENSE OF PLACE: PERSONAL GEOGRAPHY

Each of us has a sense of place, whether we've moved great distances or stayed within the same spaces all our lives. That sense of place evokes a kind of loyalty linked to a familiar landscape that comforts us, even when it is not beautiful or particularly comfortable. Elizabeth grew up near strip-mined land in southern Ohio, which to most people is ecologically irresponsible. And yet that flat blackened landscape recalls strong and familiar sensations for her. Some of us, like Elizabeth, don't recognize our sense of place until we leave it, either by changing schools or homes, going to college, joining the service, traveling, or just growing up.

Even in a new place, something can evoke past sensations, uncovering a geographical memory and bringing with it a sudden surge of images. Ropes slapping against a flagpole in the Midwest may recall the sound of halyards slapping against an aluminum mast on a sailboat in the San Francisco Bay. The smell of a friend's skin cream on a winter day in Idaho can transport us to a searing beach on the New Jersey shore. Our personal geographies influence our spatial gaze; they influence how we look.

Bonnie grew up in Jenkintown, Pennsylvania, a suburb of Philadelphia. She remembers a tall bank clock next to the Snack Shop. With its black Roman numerals and latticed hands, it stood at the intersection where she learned to drive a car. The clock marks a flurry of adolescent images. Every morning, Miss Lobach, the ancient cross-eyed Latin teacher who lived above the drugstore, shuffled past that clock on her daily walk to school. Each afternoon, the Snack Shop sold cherry Cokes for a dime—and charged a penny for each straw to dissuade teenagers from blowing wrappers across the chrome counter at one another. Later, the clock became a gathering site for political rallies, with adults and teenagers chanting and waving handmade protest signs. Thirty years later and 1,200 miles away, in Iowa City, another bank clock reminds Bonnie of those memories, that intersection, and all that happened there.

Barry Lopez, nonfiction and travel writer, calls for Americans to regain their sense of geography in his essay "Losing Our Sense of Place." He writes that Americans "profess a sincere and fierce love for the American landscape, for our rolling prairies, free-flowing rivers, and 'purple mountains' majesty'; but it is hard to imagine, actually, where this particular landscape is" (page 39). Lopez critiques the romanticized versions of scenery that appear on calendars, in television advertising, and in magazines where there are "no distracting people... and few artifacts of human life. The animals are all beautiful, diligent, one might even say well-behaved. Nature's unruliness, the power of rivers and skies to intimidate, and any evidence of disastrous human land management practices are all but invisible" (page 40).

Lopez feels that as a nation we need to become more conscious of our scenery by taking time to become intimate with specific landscapes and by finding local people who hold geographical knowledge: "These local geniuses of American landscape...are people in whom geography thrives. They are the antithesis of geographical ignorance.... Their knowledge is intimate rather than encyclopedic, human but not necessarily scholarly" (page 42). Such geography experts, the "local geniuses of landscape," would make good research informants because they have, in Lopez's words, "the voice of memory over the land." Just as Elizabeth carried a strong sense of southern Ohio's scarred landscape and Bonnie retains images of one street corner in her small Philadelphia suburb, memories of landscapes both small and large influence the way we see other places as well as what we don't allow ourselves to see.

Writer William Least Heat-Moon set out to travel what are considered old, back-road highways, which on early maps were marked in blue in contrast to the red lines that were used for the main highways. In his nonfiction book *Blue Highways*, Heat-Moon, jobless and separated from his wife, records how he headed out to travel these "blue" roads in his truck, which he rigged for sleeping and living. The truck, "Ghost Dancing," was named for the ritual ceremonies of the Plains Indians, who danced for the return of the old ways of life to replace the new ways. Heat-Moon took to the blue highways, he writes, to the "open road in search of places where change did not mean ruin and where time and men and deeds connected" (page 12). His long trip covered the four corners of the United States, beginning as he headed east from Missouri; south to Tennessee, North Carolina, and Georgia; and west through Louisiana to Dime Box, Texas, and New Mexico. From there he moved northwest up through Utah and California to Liberty Bond, Washington; headed east again along the upper portions of the Midwest through Montana, Minnesota, and Michigan into the "downeast" corner of Maine; and finally drove south through New Jersey and back home to Missouri. In the following excerpts, Heat-Moon shows us "Ghost Dancing," then, in his chapter "South by Southwest," stops off Highway 29 in Texas to take a look at the desert and to take stock of how he sees as well as what he sees.

South by Southwest

from *Blue Highways: A Journey into America*
William Least Heat-Moon

Driving through the washed land in my small self-propelled box—a "wheel estate," a mechanic had called it—I felt clean and almost disentangled. I had what I needed for now, much of it stowed under the wooden bunk:

1   sleeping bag and blanket;
1   Coleman cooler (empty but for a can of chopped liver a friend had given me so there would *always* be something to eat);
1   Rubbermaid basin and a plastic gallon jug (the sink);
1   Sears, Roebuck portable toilet;
1   Optimus 8R white gas cook stove (hardly bigger than a can of beans);
1   knapsack of utensils, a pot, a skillet;
1   U.S. Navy seabag of clothes;
1   tool kit;
1   satchel of notebooks, pens, road atlas, and a microcassette recorder;
2   Nikon F2 35mm cameras and five lenses;
2   vade mecums: Whitman's *Leaves of Grass* and Neihardt's *Black Elk Speaks*.

In my billfold were four gasoline credit cards and twenty-six dollars. Hidden under the dash were the remnants of my savings account: $428.

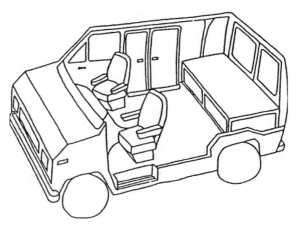

Ghost Dancing.

Straight as a chief's countenance, the road lay ahead, curves so long and gradual as to be imperceptible except on the map. For nearly a hundred miles due west of Eldorado, not a single town. It was the Texas some people see as barren waste when they cross it, the part they later describe at the motel bar as "nothing." They say, "There's nothing out there."

Driving through the miles of nothing, I decided to test the hypothesis and stopped somewhere in western Crockett County on the top of a broad mesa, just off Texas 29. At a distance, the land looked so rocky and dry, a religious man could believe that the First Hand never got around to the creation in here. Still, somebody had decided to string barbed wire around it.

No plant grew higher than my head. For a while, I heard only miles of wind against the Ghost; but after the ringing in my ears stopped, I heard myself breathing, then a bird note, an answering call, another kind of birdsong, and another: mockingbird, mourning dove, an enigma. I heard the high *zizz* of flies the color of gray flannel and the deep buzz of a blue bumblebee. I made a list of nothing in particular:

1. mockingbird
2. mourning dove
3. enigma bird (heard not saw)
4. gray flies
5. blue bumblebee
6. two circling buzzards (not yet, boys)
7. orange ants
8. black ants
9. orange-black ants (what's been going on?)
10. three species of spiders
11. opossum skull
12. jackrabbit (chewed on cactus)
13. deer (left scat)
14. coyote (left tracks)
15. small rodent (den full of seed hulls under rock)
16. snake (skin hooked on cactus spine)
17. prickly pear cactus (yellow blossoms)
18. hedgehog cactus (orange blossoms)
19. barrel cactus (red blossoms)
20. devil's pincushion (no blossoms)
21. catclaw (no better name)
22. two species of grass (neither green, both alive)

23. yellow flowers (blossoms smaller than peppercorns)
24. sage (indicates alkali-free soil)
25. mesquite (three-foot plants with eighty-foot roots to reach water that fell as rain two thousand years ago)
26. greasewood (oh, yes)
27. joint fir (steeped stems make Brigham Young tea)
28. earth
29. sky
30. wind (always)

That was all the nothing I could identify then, but had I waited until dark when the desert really comes to life, I could have done better. To say nothing is out here is incorrect; to say the desert is stingy with everything except space and light, stone and earth is closer to the truth.

I drove on. The low sun turned the mesa rimrock to silhouettes, angular and weird and unearthly; had someone said the far side of Saturn looked just like this, I would have believed him. The road dropped to the Pecos River, now dammed to such docility I couldn't imagine it formerly demarking the western edge of a rudimentary white civilization. Even the old wagonmen felt the unease of isolation when they crossed the Pecos, a small but once serious river that has had many names: Rio de las Vacas (River of Cows—perhaps a reference to bison), Rio Salado (Salty River), Rio Puerco (Dirty River).

West of the Pecos, a strangely truncated cone rose from the valley. In the oblique evening light, its silhouette looked like a Mayan temple, so perfect was it symmetry. I stopped again, started climbing, stirring a panic of lizards on the way up. From the top, the rubbled land below—veined with the highway and arroyos, topographical relief absorbed in the dusk—looked like a roadmap.

The desert, more than any other terrain, shows its age, shows time because so little vegetation covers the ancient erosions of wind and storm. What appears is tawny grit once stone and stone crumbling to grit. Everywhere rock, earth's oldest thing. Even desert creatures come from a time older than the woodland animals, and they, in answer to the arduousness, have retained prehistoric coverings of chitin and lapped scale and primitive defenses of spine and stinger, fang and poison, shell and claw.

The night, taking up the shadows and details, wiped the face of the desert into a simple, uncluttered blackness until there were only three things: land, wind, stars. I was there too, but my presence I felt more than saw. It was as if I had been reduced to mind, to an edge of consciousness. Men, ascetics, in all eras have gone into deserts to lose themselves—Jesus, Saint Anthony, Saint Basil, and numberless medicine men—maybe because such a losing happens almost as a matter of course here if you avail yourself. The Sioux once chanted, "All over the sky a sacred voice is calling."

Back to the highway, on with the headlamps, down Six Shooter Draw. In the distance, deer, just shadows in the lights, began moving toward the desert willows in the wet bottoms. Stephen Vincent Benét:

When Daniel Boone goes by, at night,
The phantom deer arise
And all lost, wild America
Is burning in their eyes.

From the top of another high mesa: twelve miles west in the flat valley floor, the lights of Fort Stockton blinked white, blue, red, and yellow in the heat like a mirage. How is it that desert towns look so fine and big at night? It must be that little is hidden. The glistering ahead could have been a golden city of Cibola. But the reality of Fort Stockton was plywood and concrete block and the plastic signs of Holiday Inn and Mobil Oil.

The desert had given me an appetite that would have made carrion crow stuffed with saltbush taste good. I found a Mexican cafe of adobe, with a white-washed log ceiling, creekstone fireplace, and jukebox pumping out mariachi music. It was like a bunkhouse. I ate burritos, chile rellenos, and pinto beans, all ladled over with a fine, incendiary sauce the color of sludge from an old steel drum. At the next table sat three big, round men: an Indian wearing a silver headband, a Chicano in a droopy Pancho Villa mustache, and a Negro in faded overalls. I thought what a litany of grievances that table could recite. But the more I looked, the more I believed they were someone's vision of the West, maybe someone making ads for Levy's bread, the ads that used to begin "You don't have to be Jewish."

Recalling a Sense of Place

B O X 17

Purpose

We carry our sense of place, our personal geography, into our fieldwork. To research place, it is important to retrieve and record our own internal landscape and make it explicit to ourselves. What images do we remember from particular landscapes? What details do we recall about places we've visited? Why do these sensations return to us at particular moments in time? Why those images, details, and sensations—and not others? Writer Barry Lopez, whom we mention on page 219, suggests in his essay "Losing Our Sense of Place" that the intimate link between landscape and memory comes through the act of writing and "through the power of observation, the gifts of eye and ear, of tongue and nose and finger, that a place first rises up in our mind; afterward, it is memory that carries the place, that allows it to grow in depth and complexity. For as long as our records go back, we have held these two things dear, landscape and memory" (p. 38).

Action

Choose a spot that brings back a rush of sensory details—sights, sounds, smells, textures, and tastes. It doesn't need to be an enormous natural wonder like the Grand Canyon. Try describing a private spot—a certain tree in your backyard, a basketball court, a relative's dining room, the corner of a city lot, the interior of a closet, or a window seat that catches the sunlight. As you think about the specifics of this place—its details and sensations—you'll probably remember a dominant impression, a cluster of images, or a person connected to the place. These are all part of your internal landscape. Write a few short descriptive paragraphs with as many details as you can to share with your writing partner.

Response

Our student Harvey Du Marce wrote about his home, a Sioux reservation in South Dakota. To write his paragraph, in his double-entry journal he first made a list of sensory details and then added a column of personal reflections based on his memories:

Sensory Detail	Reflections
hot, August, 90 degrees	burned out landscape—a symbol?
dry brown prairie grass	familiar landscape
buzzing crickets	comforting sound of home
distant hills	childhood imagination, excitement
mother—white patch in dark hair	quiet affection
soft voice, fixes food	regret, guilt for going away to school
small, cool living room	neatness, comfort, welcoming
clinging vines on windows	brings nature in
star quilts to keep out sun	traditional design—both craft and utility
corn soup, fry bread, chokecherries	nostalgic childhood foods

Harvey's descriptive details evoke a strong sense of place, of both the prairie and the interior of his childhood home. These paragraphs illustrate his spatial gaze as he sweeps across the land around the reservation, moving in closer to his mother's house. In these short paragraphs, he combines both the large and small details of his own internal landscape:

I came home to the reservation that August. The weather was hot and dry. The green grass around my mother's house had burned brown and crisp. A pulsating buzz of crickets caught my ear. The sound came from behind the house; it would rise collectively and then slowly fade in the tree line. My mother intuitively sensed my return as she stood on the porch. She looked the same from a distance; I imagined her gentle open face still had a smooth quality. I thought I saw a small patch of white in her short black hair.

I could not reconcile myself with this landscape, which was once a part of my life, and perhaps it would always be part of me. I momentarily forgot who I was. Could I be the restless young man who left the reservation 10 years ago? Was I really the college-educated person? The crickets and my mother's soft voice merged somewhere in the back of my mind.

When I walked into the house, she greeted me with affection. My long absence did not seem to matter to her, but it mattered to me. Two star quilts hung over the living room windows to keep out the heat of the day. No air conditioner hummed, but inside the house was cool and comfortable. The living room was small. A thick green strand of clinging vines covered the west window, turning the room into a blend of shade and light. I noticed that my mother's cherished and manicured vines had finally reached the roof of the house.

When I sat down on the old sofa, I looked out the south window and saw a range of dark blue hills in the distance. The hills were old and eternal like the earth. As a child, those hills stirred my imagination the way a wind lifts an eagle. Over the years, my imagination had eroded and decayed until only its roof still existed in a far corner of my soul. My dreams were now ordinary.

Homemade corn soup and fry bread smells wafted out of the kitchen. I turned away from the window. Mother put a bowl of the steaming soup and two pieces of fry bread on the table and called to me to come and eat. We would talk later.

A SENSE OF PLACE: SELECTIVE PERCEPTION

Most anthropologists begin their fieldwork in distant places, teaching themselves how to see the local landscape through the eyes of the people in the culture. Folklorist Henry Glassie's *Passing the Time in Ballymenone: Culture and History of an Ulster Community* is a full-length ethnographic study (10 years, 852 pages) of storytelling, conversation, and music making in a small community in Northern Ireland. While he passed the time at evening *ceili* (fireside sessions), Glassie also learned how to look at the northern Irish landscape. Over time, his gaze expanded to include evenings spent inside the neighbors' cottages as he farmed with them during the day and researched their geography, genealogy,

local and national history, politics, economics, and cultural values. He came to
see the influences of his informants' daily living on their verbal art of ceiliing.
Gradually, Ballymenone's landscape took hold of him, drawing him into the
study of his informants' world. In this short excerpt, which introduces a ceili session at the Flanagans', Glassie begins with a verbal snapshot of the landscape, a
wide-angle sweep of the hillside, and ends with a close-up of the neighbors as
they gather around the hearth:

> The house cattle should have been onto the hillsides early in April, but
> summer came lashing wet winds down the brown hedges and through bleak
> fields. Across the bog and over the hills, air lay bone cold. Some of the cows,
> they say, starved in their byres, dying on beds of sodden rushes, and into the
> minds of men waiting for the sun blew years when black frost shriveled the
> spuds on the ridges, years when turf lay on the spread through the summer,
> and winter closed down without food for the belly or fuel for the hearth.
> The bright, warm days expected in May and June never came. In running
> gray skies, in the dank sloughs of the gaps, summer broke, damp, chilled.
>
> Now it is calm. Fat cattle move slowly in the blue harvest evening. Lush
> grasslands swell and fold in the haze. Some of last year's potatoes and turf
> and hay remain, heaped into pits on the moss ground, thatched in lumps on
> the bog, piled in haysheds, built into rotund pecks along the lanes. Old
> defenses against hard times, displays of industry cover the land.
>
> A month ago summer ended in a blaze of sunshine and a frenzy of
> work. Hay was rooked, turf was clamped. Sun and warm winds drove out
> the wet. Once built into rounded conical rooks, and clamps the shape of
> ancient oratories, hay and turf are considered won. That is their word for
> victory in the cyclical war fought with the hand-tools they call weapons: the
> pitchfork and the spade.
>
> Now it is quiet, an interlude in work and worry. The main crop potatoes
> are not yet ready to dig, nor is it time to transplant winter cabbage, shear the
> corn, or drive the cattle onto the sweet aftergrass of the meadows. Work
> slows but does not stop. It is a time for gathering in the spoils of war, draw-
> ing turf and hay home, and it is time to hack back hedges with billhooks and
> cart broken turf to gardens built on barren land. Gently, the next campaign
> begins.
>
> Turf and hay are won. For a month the new potatoes, the Epicures, have
> been boiled for dinner. It is a time, too, for mild extravagance. This year's
> potatoes are boiled in lavish numbers, fires built of this year's turf are unnec-
> essarily hearty. Winter's word is bitter. In its depths, when winds pound at
> the walls of home, potatoes will be sparingly spent and the fire will be
> stretched with gathered sticks, but today victory expands in little luxuries.
>
> Joe Flanagan turns from the sack of turf next to the open front door.
> Damp green and blue melt behind him. He cradles an armload. Peter lifts a
> violin from its case in the corner and settles on a stool by the hearth. Dinner

is done, the hens are fed, empty teacups sit on the floor. Joe tongs live coals from the fire, lines them in front of the hearthstone, and sweeps the ashes off to his side with a besom of heather bound round with twine. (95–96)

In this short passage, Glassie writes from the stance of the Ballymenone residents, capturing the lilting rhythms of their language, seeing what they would see, using words they would use to describe the setting. His first line describes a history of recent weather conditions, noting that the "cattle should have been onto the hillsides in April," that summer "came lashing wet winds," that the "bright, warm days expected in May and June never came," and that when summer finally came it was damp and chilled. He writes with the knowledge of the weather's effect on the current daily lives and livelihoods of the villagers but also its importance in the past when harsher weather affected the potato harvest: "years when black frost shriveled the spuds," "when turf lay on the spread through the summer," and "when winter closed down without food for the belly or fuel for the hearth." His description focuses on the features of the landscape that the villagers themselves would notice: bog, rushes, spuds, turf and hay, cattle. His eye rests on the things their eyes would rest on.

Just as Harvey structured his own personal spatial memories, Glassie's description also begins with a large but detailed sweep of the landscape—fattened cattle moving on lush grasslands in a hazy blue harvest evening—and continues into a small space—here, the Flanagan hearthstone with empty teacups sitting on the floor. His spatial gaze moves from outside to inside, creating a mood and a setting for the ceili (storytelling session). Though Glassie writes using the third-person point of view, this description is not objective. In fact, some scholars believe that Glassie romanticizes the Irish culture in descriptions such as this. Like all of us, Glassie operates with a spatial gaze framed by his own biases, assumptions, and cultural baggage. He might ask himself these questions about his descriptions, as all of us should about our fieldsites:

- Why do I focus on this element of the landscape and not that?
- What is my reason for narrowing my gaze to any specific place?
- What spaces have I rejected as I've narrowed my gaze?
- Why do I use the metaphors and descriptions I do?
- Which metaphors and descriptions did I abandon as inappropriate?
- Where in my fieldnotes do I find evidence for this description?
- What have I rejected, and why?

Spatial details are an important part of the fieldworker's data. All fieldworkers describe their informants in a setting, working from an abundance of evidence: fieldnotes, photos, maps, and background history gathered over time. Researchers cannot lean entirely on visual details; the ethnographic "eye" should also record sounds, textures, tastes, and smells. Important details also come from noticing and documenting, as Glassie does, conditions of color, weather, light, shape, time, season, atmosphere, and ambiance. Choosing details is an act of selective **perception.** As we write, we revise our worldviews. The point of doing fieldwork is to learn to see not just the other but ourselves as well. The spatial gaze demands that we look—and then look back again at ourselves.

B O X 18

Writing a Verbal Snapshot

Purpose

Your fieldnotes are a rich source of data from which you can select key details to begin to create verbal snapshots for your project. Choose a small portion of your fieldsite to describe for this exercise. Whether you have recorded your data as a list, double-entry fieldnotes as Harvey DuMarce did in Box 17 (see page 224), or as a narrative, read and review those fieldnotes, and underline, tag, or highlight five to 10 details that stand out for you at your fieldsite. What detail did your informant call to your attention that you might not have noticed? What is the most typical? The most unusual? One that stood out for you?

Writing a place description involves more than making an inventory or listing details. Your description needs to suggest the overall sense of place you are trying to understand and should mirror your informants' perspective as well. Sometimes one small detail from your data can expand into a rich image that reflects a dominant theme within the culture. For example, Glassie (see page 227) gives us the image of Joe sweeping the hearth with a "besom of heather bound round with twine," which evokes the poetic and domestic sides of Irish culture. It would have been a quite different description had he written, "Joe swept the floor with a homemade broom." Such a sentence would imply more of an outsider's perspective than an insider's, and one of the goals of fieldworking is to include your informant's worldview.

Action

Comb through your data to determine categories of sights, sounds, smells, textures, and tastes; weather, atmospheric conditions, colors, light, shapes. Categorizing will help you write your description, and it will also help you fill in the missing data in your fieldwork. Noticing the gaps helps you determine where, or in what ways, your data might be incomplete. "Do I need different sensory details? More about the setting at different times of day? Do I want to focus on a certain spot in this place where important activity is going on? What details do I need more of? What did I forget to take in?" Asking these questions will help you decide if you want to return to your fieldsite to gather more evidence.

After writing a short description based on your notes about setting details, share a page or two with a colleague to see if you've successfully created a sense of place and to discuss what you might research further. As you respond to your partner, point out your most telling details. Which details evoke larger images? Which details uncover cultural information about the place? Which details seem to represent the informant's perspective? Do any specific words seem like insider language?

Response

Jason Ceynar's fieldwork project, "Life in the Stacks," was a study of the culture of the university library where he worked. Although his focus was the stories his coworkers told, the settings were key places where librarians and aides interacted (or, in this case, didn't interact). This is Jason's description of the periodical sorting room:

> When I walk into the bound periodical sorting room, my feeling of claustrophobia disappears. In the stacks I'm trapped on all sides by towering bookshelves; in here I'm able to move around with relative ease. The shelves in this room are pushed up against the walls. I always look forward to sorting periodicals because of the relative cheerfulness of these surroundings. The lighting in this room is much brighter than it is out in the stacks. This really perks me up after an hour of tedious reshelving. The room's color scheme also puts the atmosphere in the stacks to shame. The rosy-beige colored walls and floor tiles that alternate between burgundy and light brown are far superior to the stacks' dull gray decor. I try to spend as much time as I can sorting periodicals so I don't have to leave this atmosphere.
>
> Today I'm the only one in the sorting room. I wander over to the wooden table in the middle of the room, which is piled high with books. I move some of the books aside to read my coworkers' graffiti, which adorns the table top: "Spam," "For a good time call Mark," "Ivory Soap," "United we stand, Divided we fall." A coworker walks in, and I concern myself with looking busy. I've never talked to this girl; she likes to keep to herself. We exchange a quick glance and a smile and go about our business. The reshelving room is normally a social area. It's one of the few places that we can talk freely while we work. We work alone in the stacks, so it's a welcome change to have some human interaction. I'm disappointed that I won't have somebody to converse with today. I sit down on a stool and begin to put the "A" books in order. I notice scuff marks on the wall behind the backless shelves—red, brown, green, and blue—probably made by colorful bound journals that were carelessly tossed on the shelves. A newspaper crinkles behind me; my introverted friend must be taking a break. To my left is a wall of windows that looks into a hallway that leads to

the English as a foreign language department. Occasionally I make eye contact with people as they walk down this hall. It's uncomfortable; our gaze seems to say "We're not supposed to see each other. This is unnatural."

A few of the ceiling tiles are out of place, I notice when I look above me. I can see wires, vents, and insulation. It reminds me of the disrepair out in the stacks, and I remember how lucky I am to have been assigned to the periodical sorting room today. A small white fan whirs in the corner. Ever since I've worked here, this fan has been on, even when it's freezing in the library. Nobody turns it off because nobody knows who turns it on. The paper crinkles behind me again, and I hear my coworker leave the room. As I resume my sorting, I wonder if that girl thought it was strange that I've been writing madly in my notebook. Aaaah, with this silence, I'll never know.

LEARNING HOW TO LOOK: MAPPING SPACE

As a researcher, like Jason (see Box 18), you'll teach yourself how to look, how to "read" a space. Make lists, for instance, of sensory details at your site, interior and exterior, paying attention to more than just visual impressions. Track who goes in and out of the fieldsite at different times of day and how they use different areas. Draw actual maps or diagrams, which give you information that would be difficult to get merely through observation. Research the space further by talking to informants or by studying documents that describe it. As you take notes, record your assumptions about how the space is used. As you follow up on these initial notes, you will discover surprising information about the place. Through recording, listing, mapping, and researching, you'll learn about how the people you're studying use their space.

Henry Glassie, in his study of the ceili sessions, mapped the visiting patterns among four houses in Ballymenone to determine how the neighbors' and families' relationships interconnected, how his informants' stories influenced each other, and how the evening visits between houses mirrored the informants' work during the day. By mapping the space, Glassie obtained information that would be difficult to understand any other way. Fieldworkers who study cultures for long periods of time make extensive inventories of household goods and cultural artifacts; study kinship patterns, genealogies, and family records; sketch and photograph buildings, implements, and topography; categorize local flora and fauna; and conduct surveys among the locals. Sometimes a culture's archives can assist the fieldworker in developing a sense of place. (For more on archives, see Chapter 4).

Karen Downing, the student whose fieldnotes we showed you in Chapter 2 (see p. 87, studied the Photo Phantasies subculture for a much shorter period of time; nevertheless, she takes advantage of many of these fieldworking skills and displays artifacts from her research in her portfolio. She includes cover pages from glamour magazines and books about the beauty culture, a marketing flyer and promotional package for customers of Photo Phantasies, a company document for employees called "Business Culture" that outlines its beliefs and values, and the manager's favorite poem, which hung in her office. These are the archives of the business, which help Karen understand more fully how the space represents the glamour photography culture. Using these archival records and the lists of details from her fieldnotes as background, Karen sketched a map of the store itself (see Figure 5.1). Her map eventually helped her understand the use of space at Photo Phantasies and its relationship to the business as a whole. She learned that the store organized its layout so efficiently that the customer would be unconscious of either the small size of the store or the underlying hard sell. In her portfolio, Karen reflects on her map: "A map of the PP store (very much not in scale!). What my drawing doesn't show is just how small this store actually is. The layout reflects the theme that efficiency equals greater sales. Everything moves in a progressive way, from one step to the next, like a well-orchestrated dance."

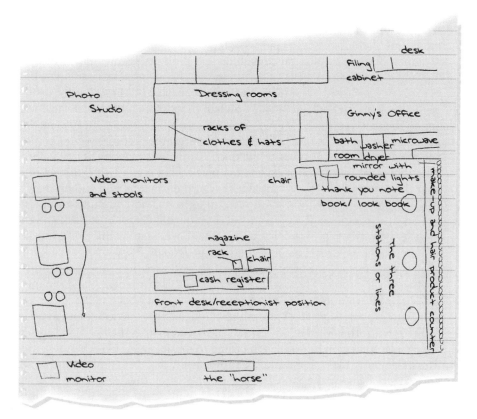

Figure 5.1. Karen Downing's map of the Photo Phantasies store.

The following section from her final essay describing Photo Phantasies draws from all of her background research, her map, and her fieldnotes to create a verbal snapshot of the store. In this excerpt, as Karen waits for her appointment with Ginny James, the manager, she pulls out her research journal and records fieldnotes about what she sees, worried, at the same time, that the receptionist might be watching her. Here's her place description:

The store is perhaps 30 feet by 30 feet, but each inch of space is used. There are three black vinyl chairs facing a mirrored wall and a counter where I assume makeup and hair are done. A sign hanging above this area reads "Professional Makeup Artists." I look around for these people, but no one is working near the three chairs, nor is anyone in the store but the receptionist. Surrounding the four-foot-high mirror on the wall are round light bulbs that remind me of movie stars' dressing rooms. On the counter, an array of curling irons, blow dryers, Q-tips, mousse, static guard, and hair spray joins tray after tray of makeup. Above the mirror is the wall of "Phantasy Phaces": Photo Phantasies photographs, each measuring three feet on a side, arranged to look like film coming off a movie reel. All the photographs are of women, except for two little girls and one couple.

In front of my chair are racks of clothing—denim jackets with gold studs, gold lamé blouses, a coat with red, white, and blue stars and stripes, sequined blazers, beaded bustiers, blue and pink boas, and shelves of hats. Beyond the wardrobe selections, there are three dressing rooms without mirrors or seats inside. Each one has a white mesh hamper for clothes and a white hook on the wall and a black curtain that can be pulled over the opening to the dressing room.

Next to the racks of clothes is the photography sitting room. I cannot see much of that room because the door is only halfway open, but I can see part of a royal blue background and a black vinyl stool. I can only assume that the camera is in there somewhere. On the other side of the photography sitting room are three computer monitors. The computer monitors, placed in a straight row, are off to the right of the receptionist desk and the cash register. My high school students who have been to Photo Phantasies tell me that after they have had their pictures taken, they change back into their street clothes and meet a salesperson who uses the computer monitor to display the proofs. There is no wait time—a customer can see her photographs on the monitor seconds after the pictures have been taken.

After 15 minutes, the receptionist touches me on the shoulder. She looks down at the notes in my journal as I look down at the floor, feeling like I have just been caught doing something inappropriate. "Cool handwriting! It kinda looks like calligraphy! Ginny's ready for you now." She points toward the back of the store, past the racks of clothes to a door near the dressing rooms. The door is open. I stand there, waiting for Ginny to look up. After several moments, I knock and say hello.

Mapping Space: A Meal in the Making

Purpose

This is a version of a mapping exercise we completed in our own training as fieldworkers and have since adapted for our classes. The point of the exercise is to record and gather observations during a half-hour of an everyday routine. We suggest watching people making a meal, but you can choose any daily routine that involves at least two people. It is best to work collaboratively so that you and your partner can collect a range of data. For example, one person can focus on body language and use of space while the other focuses on spoken language. You and your partner can compare the pre-research assumptions you bring to the site and discuss possible conclusions as you work through your data together.

Action

Here are some things to consider:

1. *Obtain access.* Choose a site in which at least two people—children and parent, housemates, spouses, friends—are engaged in the daily mealtime routines. Choose people who will feel comfortable being watched, as this exercise demands such close observation that you will not be able to help make the meal or set the table. Of course, if your informants choose to invite you to eat with them, that's another choice. Be sure, as any good guest would, to offer something in return. You might bring flowers or dessert.

2. *Record your assumptions.* Speculate on what you think you'll see. What do you already know about these people and their relationship? Their kitchen? Their lifestyle?

3. *Take notes on the overall setting.* What details of place seem relevant? How does the eating area fit into the overall plan of the home? Is it casual or formal? Be sure to be specific with relevant details. Note "8 hand-painted Delft plates" rather than "pile of plates."

4. *Map the space.* Draw a diagram of the kitchen or the place where the meal is being prepared. Use it to show where your informants move within the space. Colored markers or pencils can be useful to designate each informant's movements.

5. *Describe the activities.* Develop a system for recording the movements of each informant. What are the meal makers doing? Pay attention to what's going on—phone interruptions, neighbors' and children's visits, other incidents that break the flow of the activity. What utensils and objects do your informants use? How do they use them? Make a time line, noting how long each activity takes.

6. *Tape-record the conversation or take notes by hand.* How much of talk is related to the meal-making interaction itself? How much is everyday talk? What talk is related to the power relationships among the meal makers? Who initiates talk? Who is silent? Who interrupts? Who gives directions and who follows? If males and females are involved, are there gender-related issues or differences?

7. *Talk with your partner.* Expand your fieldnotes together, talk about your findings, and speculate on what your conclusions might be. What do you agree on? What do you see differently?

8. *Write up the data collaboratively (two to three pages).* Attach to this description your fieldnotes, the transcripts, your map, and your notes from discussions with your partner. It is rewarding to see the amount of data two researchers can collect in a half-hour's time.

Response

While she was researching her Photo Phantasies project (see p. 247), Karen Downing did this exercise to learn more about observing and mapping space. The first part of this exercise represents the data Karen and her partner gathered in the field. Her written commentary represents the reflexive analysis they did away from the field.

With a colleague, Liesl, Karen spent a half-hour at the home of Ellen Friar, watching Ellen and her daughter, Paula, prepare dinner. Together, Karen and Liesl gathered over 12 pages of fieldnotes, transcripts, and maps. After their observation, they collaborated on the following set of notes. In looking over their data, they found that their map provided the most important information about the use of the space.

Date: February 13

Time: 5:45 p.m.

Participants: Ellen (E), mother; Paula (P), 20-year-old daughter

Nonparticipating characters Bill (B), Ellen's husband and Paula's father; Frank (F), Paula's boyfriend; Liesl (L) and Karen (K), observers

1. *Obtain access.* We called Ellen and explained the dinner exercise. She was curious and willing to allow us to observe. She explained that her husband, Bill, and Paula's boyfriend, Frank, would not be part of the preparation but would be eating the dinner. She asked us to come on a Wednesday, when Paula was home from work and would be teaching Ellen how to make faji-tas, a meal she had learned from a family in Arizona. "It will be a nice change for me to let Paula cook," she told us, inviting us to eat with them afterward. On Wednesday afternoon, we stopped at Dot's Flower Shop to pick up some red carnations as a small gift of appreciation.

2. *Record your assumptions.* We entered with very different assumptions because Liesl knew the family and Karen didn't. Liesl assumed that Ellen would prepare most of the meal. Liesl also felt that Ellen would be very curious about our observation because she's a teacher herself. Karen felt she would make a good collaborator as she carried no preconceptions about the family, but she had more speculations. Karen wondered, though, how much their researcher presence would affect the preparation. She speculated about how typical this half-hour would be. Would sitting in their kitchen with a tape recorder and two notepads make the family self-conscious? Would the mother and daughter behave normally with two researchers watching their every move?

3. *Take notes on the overall setting.* The house is about three years old, and the Friars are the first family to live there.... We note that the kitchen is an alcove, or C-shaped room, that opens to the dining room. It includes a counter or bar area with stools that look into the kitchen from the dining room side.... The kitchen has green marble-patterned countertops and light pine cupboards. Appliances are all white (refrigerator, stove, microwave, dishwasher, coffeepot) and match the white wall paint and white floor tile. A matching green rug is placed to one side. The electric griddle, chicken, onions, condiments, and utensils ready and waiting on the counter space suggest that they have prepared for us. On the desk near the fridge, a small portable radio is tuned softly to National Public Radio. E wears a red sweatshirt with valentine hearts, matching sweatpants, socks, and slippers. She is small (approx 5'3"/110 lbs), thin face, dark brown hair. P is dressed in a navy blue sweatshirt and stretch pants with socks. She is larger then E (approx 5'6"/160 lbs), full face, blonde hair.

4. *Map the space* (see Map A).

5 and 6. *Describe the activities and record the conversation.*

5:48 p.m.

E asks "What do I do?" She stands idly waiting in the middle of the kitchen for Paula to give her directions.

P points to the chicken and E begins to slice it very thin with an enormous knife.

P begins chopping onions on plastic cutting board, away from E.

E says "We don't usually cook this way—you know, make this food like this. I just didn't cook when you weren't here, not just for Bob and me. Now that you're here, we're cooking more." E explains that it is hard to plan ahead. She stops chopping and waves the knife. She turns to P. "I come home from work, feed the dog, then get dinner—its rush rush. You know, rush in, rush out." E begins chopping again. "I want you to notice that your father scrubbed the burner and got all that

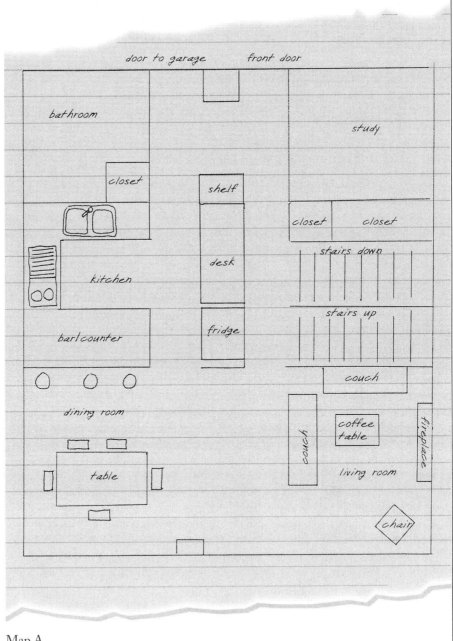

Map A.

gunk off." E points to the burner. P does not respond. "He did a good job. It's pretty clean. Can you see?" P does not respond.

5:55

P puts tortilla chips on table and returns to kitchen, where she throws the chicken onto the griddle.

"It's almost done." E says, "Hmmm, good."

E is cleaning all utensils, cutting boards, and dishes. E rinses everything thoroughly and places it all in the dishwasher.

6:03

E says "OK, I think we're about ready." She takes six brown dishes from the cupboard and sets one at each place at the table.

F enters the kitchen and whispers something in P's ear. P rolls her eyes, and F leaves the kitchen-dining area.

E says "Maybe we should have some salad, or I could cut up some fruit?"

P says "Mom…no, it's fine."

E says "Well, the table looks so sparse! There's hardly a thing on it! Oh! Wait! I do have some fruit bars!" E takes a small plastic container from the cupboard. She removes some lemon squares from it and places them on a plate.

P asks "When did you make those?"

E laughs "That's right! If you had known about them, there would be none for dinner!"

7. *Talk with your partner.* Afterward, since there was such little talk, we wondered how each person knew what duties to perform. We thought P and E negotiated the tiny space fairly well without getting in each other's way or being confused over their duties. E remained mostly stationary or in one immediate area, while P moved about. Were we imagining a tension between P and E? E seemed to be the outgoing director of the action and P the quiet subversive follower. There seemed to be real control issues between them. Even though P was teaching E how to make the dinner, E seemed to control P's actions. As Map B shows, P moved in and out of the kitchen area twice as often as E, who worked mostly in one place. E seems concerned about neatness and cleaning up after a mess is made. The kitchen may be a haven or sanctuary for her. E struck us as a great talker, a facilitator of conversation but not the best listener. What did F whisper to P that caused her eyes to roll? Would he have done that if we weren't there? Or would he have spoken instead of whispered? We wondered what E really thought about P's live-in boyfriend. Did our presence seem to interrupt any of their movements? Our follow-up

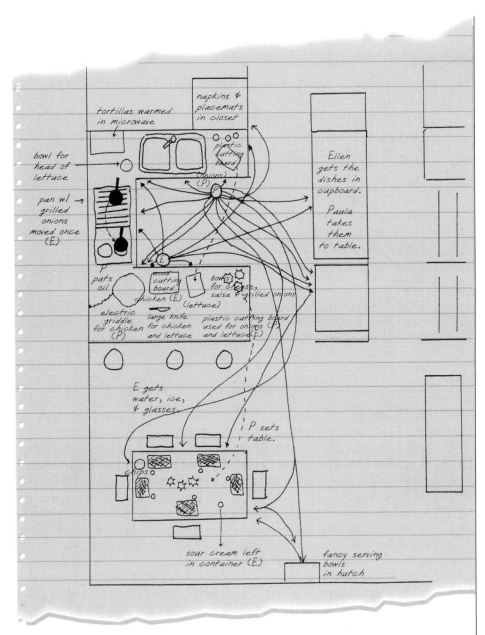

Map B.

questions would consider the themes of power relationship and spatial ownership.

8. *Write up the data collaboratively.*

Dinner Exercise: Final Draft (Excerpts)

Liesl Fowler and Karen Downing

Families are complex systems that operate with many unstated rules and roles for their members. We each know this from our experiences within our own family units. Familiar familial settings often reveal the most about family members because feelings of comfort and safety are inherent in an intimate setting. Perhaps no more comfortable setting exists for this group than the dinner table.

An aspect of family of continual issue is power and control among the various members of the group. Simple dinner conversation can be very telling about the roles each plays in the family unit. Dinner preparations also can distinguish between real and perceived control of the family. This moment of preparation is where we focused our study....

The main dynamic we observed was a dichotomy of power. Overtly, Ellen attempted to dominate the advance preparations for the meal: she had fewer duties during the meal preparation, but those duties were essential; she maintained a constant level of talk during the preparation; and she kept her work in the focal point of the kitchen. Covertly, Paula controlled the conversation through passivity. While she moved from the kitchen to the dining room during the meal preparations, Paula's contributions were extraneous. The wrestling back and forth between mother and daughter over control was central to their relationship. Although this would seem to be a conflict, their interaction was synchronized and familiar. The differences between mother and daughter serve as the foundation for their relationship....

Paula and Ellen navigated the small kitchen despite their size differences and the many preparational tasks. Neither ever stated who was going to undertake each task. Peripheral duties—cutting onions, taking food out of the refrigerator, setting the table, transferring food from container to serving dishes—were Paula's responsibilities. Paula was in constant motion from kitchen counter to sink to refrigerator to dining room. Ellen cut the chicken carefully and deliberately; each piece was nearly identical in size. Her chopping of the lettuce was done in much the same fashion. Ellen remained very much in one section of the kitchen cooking the chicken in the skillet and the onions on the stove. She frequently cleaned Paula's work-stations with a damp cloth as Paula moved on to the other tasks. They seemed to never be in each other's way. If Paula entered Ellen's "space," Ellen silently shifted to another area momentarily, and vice versa.

The conversation between mother and daughter floated from the tasks before them to work and family. The dialogue was dominated by Ellen's questions about Paula's job and friends and boyfriend. Paula's responses were either short or nonexistent. Paula made no verbal response to statements her mother made about Frank but met the remarks with eye-rolling and sighing behind her mother's back. Ellen either seemed oblivious to this behavior or accepted it as a characteristic of the way they communicate. Ellen functioned as the vehicle for conversation keeping the spaces filled with speech. On the rare occasion that Paula would verbally respond, Ellen responded vaguely or in a noncommittal way:

E: So you don't work all week?

P: All week?! I work on Sunday! With the high school chick. I'll have to do everything!

E: Hmmmmm…

Paula generated only one topic for discussion:

P: They [onions] aren't cooking, it isn't hot enough here.

E: *(Exerting her control)* Yes it is now. But I'll move them over to the small burner.

Our final excerpt is the only example of unmasked tension. Ellen's desire to control the meal preparations, her brush-off of Paula's comment, and Ellen's joking assumptions about Paula's potential behavior indicate the struggle between mother and daughter:

E: *(Gesturing toward the table)* Maybe we should have some salad or I could cut up some fruit?

P: *(Rolling her eyes)* Mom, no, it's fine.

E: Well, the table looks so sparse. There's hardly a thing on it…. Oh, wait! I do have some bars! (Ellen takes a small plastic container from cupboard and removes several dessert-like bars and places them on a plate.)

P: *(Whirling around with glasses in her hands)* When did you make those!?

E: *(Laughing)* That's right! If you had known about them, there would be none for dinner.

P: *(Rolling her eyes and quickly turning her back on her mother)* You mean, if ANYONE had known about them!

At that point in the conversation, Paula's boyfriend entered the kitchen and the focus switched to his being in the way when he dropped his backpack in the middle of the meal preparation.

From our observations of the Friars' meal preparation, we feel that the synchronized wrestling of power between this mother and daughter is indicative of their complex relationship.

LEARNING HOW TO LOOK: FINDING A FOCAL POINT

Mapping places is one of the first ways researchers learn how informants in a culture see and use their space. Glassie's map helped him understand the visiting patterns among the Irish neighbors, Karen's map showed her how the Photo Phantasies management used space, and Karen and Liesl's map highlighted dinner making as the playing field for a power struggle between a mother and a daughter.

By looking at how space is used, fieldworkers come to understand the fieldsite—not just what it looks like but also how their informants inhabit it. Mapping helps researchers lay out masses of data that might otherwise be overwhelming. Studying fieldsite maps alongside other information about the culture and its informants can help you find a focal point within data. Mapping helps you see as a researcher, and your narrative description of the space helps the reader see what you've seen.

Sometimes by mapping the fieldsite, you locate a focal point in the space you're studying. A focal point is a spot, an area, or a place where the insiders' activities cluster. In the dinner exercise, all of the important activities take place within the kitchen counter space, with fewer steps taken outside toward the dining room. Researchers often comb their data looking for focal points in their fieldsites.

In anthropologist Barbara Myerhoff's full-length ethnography *Number Our Days,* she describes the researcher's problem of how to select a focal point from masses of data. In this passage, she explains her organizational dilemma as well as her solution:

The amount and variety of information accumulated in a field study is overwhelming. There is no definite or correct solution to the problem of what to include, how to cut up the pie of social reality, when precisely to leave or stop....

Of the three hundred Center members, I met and talked with about a half.... Of these, I knew eighty personally, and interviewed and spent most of my time with thirty-six. I tape recorded extensive interviews with these, ranging from two to sixteen hours, visited nearly all in their homes, took trips with them from time to time outside the neighborhood—to doctors, social workers, shopping, funerals, visiting their friends in old age homes and hospitals, and often following my subjects to convalescent homes and hospitals; I went to many funerals and memorial services. Apart from these excursions and my interviews with outsiders who knew Center people well—teachers, rabbis, local politicians, volunteers—I concentrated on the Center and its external extensions, the benches, boardwalk, and hotel and apartment lobbies where they congregated. (28–29)

Myerhoff's study is of elderly Jews, many of them Holocaust survivors, who spend their days at the Aliyah Senior Citizens' Center in Venice, California, but live independently in apartments. The center elders are immigrants who raised their families into mainstream America; most of them are now forgotten and in poverty. Myerhoff follows them around the community, tracking their daily routines to and from the center and into their homes. From the data that Myerhoff collected, she selected the Senior Center and its external extensions—a set of benches near the beach and the boardwalk—as her focal points.

When Myerhoff takes her readers on a tour around the center, she notes the cacophony of verbal data that characterizes the culture of the place. She chooses advertisements and posters that proclaim "'Hot Kosher Meal—Nutritious—65 cents," signs in both Yiddish and English, "Today at 2:00 Jewish History Class. Teacher, Clara Shapiro. *Very educational.*" "Sunday at 1:00. Special Event: Films on Israel. *Refreshments. Come. Enjoy."*

Myerhoff also describes the walls, decorated by center elders, that slide us through their cultural history: paintings of traditional ceremonies and life in the European shtetl, portraits of Jewish heroes, and artifacts like "a large wooden Star of David illuminated by a string of Christmas lights." A wall-length mural, painted by the elders, portrays "their common journey from the past to the present," a shtetl street scene, a boat full of immigrants arriving at Ellis Island, picketers bearing signs such as "Protest Treatment." Finally, the walls return us to the seniors' everyday life with two pictures of themselves, celebrating the Sabbath inside the center and seated on benches along the boardwalk.

While most of her study's data revolves around the activities inside the Senior Center, Myerhoff pulls her reader toward her other focal point—the benches outside, which face both the ocean and the boardwalk. She uses these benches as her vantage point, as her informants do, to survey the surrounding cultural scene. Myerhoff observes that the benches serve as a village plaza, a public place for social interaction. In the following description, she analyzes the seniors' bench behavior—and what the behavior represents—as an outside extension of the Center:

As the morning wears on, the benches fill. Benches are attached back to back, one side facing the ocean, one side the boardwalk. The people on the ocean side swivel around to face their friends, the boardwalk, and the Center.

Bench behavior is highly stylized. The half-dozen or so benches immediately to the north and south of the Center are the territory of the members, segregated by sex and conversation topic. The men's benches are devoted to abstract, ideological concerns—philosophical debate, politics, religion, and economics. The women's benches are given more to talk about immediate, personal matters—children, food, health, neighbors, love affairs, scandals, and "managing." Men and women talk about Israel and its welfare, and about being a Jew and about Center politics. On the benches, reputations are made and broken, controversies explored, leaders selected, factions formed and dissolved. Here is the outdoor dimension of Center life, like a village plaza, a focus of protracted, intense sociability.

The surrounding scene rarely penetrates the invisible, pulsing membrane of the Center community. The old people are too absorbed in their own talk to attend to the setting. Surfers, sunbathers, children, dogs, bicyclists, winos, hippies, voyeurs, photographers, panhandlers, artists, junkies, roller skaters, peddlers, and police are omnipresent all year round. Every social class, age, race, and sexual preference is represented. Jesus cults, Hare Krishna parades, and sidewalk preachers jostle steel bands and itinerant musicians. As colorful and flamboyant as the scene is by day, it is as dangerous by night. Muggings, theft, rape, harassment, and occasional murders make it a perilous neighborhood for the old people after dark. (4–5)

In these paragraphs, Myerhoff observes her informants enacting their engendered and cultural roles within the setting. She documents months of recorded conversation by noting men's and women's separate topics but also the topics—critical to their cultural history—that they share. Myerhoff sees these cultural roles acted against the backdrop of the benches as part of the boardwalk's staged setting outside the center.

Not only does she gaze outward at the landscape, but she also looks inward with a reflexive gaze at her own internal landscape to examine how she is affected by the place she studies. As a Jewish woman of a younger generation and a former social worker, perched on the benches that define the boundaries between inside and outside, she acknowledges her role as researcher within this social drama. Myerhoff uses the benches to meditate on her own relationship with the seniors; she uses the benches as her informants do:

I sat on the benches outside the Center and thought about how strange it was to be back in the neighborhood where sixteen years before I had lived and for a time had been a social worker with elderly citizens on public relief. Then the area was known as "Oshini Beach." The word *shini* still made me cringe. As a child I had been taunted with it. Like many second-generation Americans, I wasn't sure what being a Jew meant. When I was a child our family had avoided the words *Jew* and *Yid.* (11)

Myerhoff's reflexivity on the place she is researching becomes an integral part of the text, linking her informants' lives with her own internal landscape and personal memory. The reflexive researcher includes herself as part of the data, not just to draw attention to herself, but to draw attention to the fact that she is the one looking at this place, telling this story, and writing these descriptions.

BOX 20 Finding a Focal Point

Purpose

In this box, we'd like you to review the data you've collected about your field-site: fieldnotes, descriptive paragraphs, cultural artifacts, archival documents, and maps. As you read through your material and reflect on what you have gathered, look for the focal points of your site, either from your vantage point or that of your informants. Are there any contradictions?

Action

Write a description of one focal point you find in your setting. Consider whether there are any ways in which your own perspective influences you to see what you do see in this site. Share a draft of your focal point description with a colleague to see if it creates the image you're after.

Response

Karen Downing, as she studies the glamour photography business Photo Phantasies, finds a contradiction when she matches her fieldnotes with the map of the space and the cultural artifacts she gathered. This contradiction is in the image of its "hostesses," who stand outside the door greeting customers with compliments but are trained in hard-sell tactics for roping customers into the store. In her fieldnotes, she describes the "horse," a sitting area and display table that is used to promote the Photo Phantasies business and to solicit customers. In Karen's reflective fieldnotes, she suggests that the horse serves "to take 'em for a ride," admitting her cynicism and her feminist perspective toward the beauty culture. After viewing a training video that outlines the company's customer service policies, she summarizes the purpose of the "horse":

> A Photo Phantasies hostess should man the horse, the brochure stand outside the store, at all times, particularly when the mall is busy. The hostess should greet the people in the mall as they pass and tell them about the professional makeup salon and photo studio. She should show them the "Look Book" with the before and after pictures of previous customers, give them a brochure, take them on a tour of the store, explain the Photo Phantasies process, and work to get an appointment set up on the spot. "Yes or no" questions should be avoided—the focus is on selling the concept.

The "horse" is a place detail that illuminates the values of the beauty culture; the illusion of beauty can be sold to any customer. A salesperson posts herself at the "horse," ready to rope in her customer and tie up the transaction with the biggest package of photos she can sell.

LEARNING HOW TO LOOK: IDENTIFYING UNITY AND TENSION

Karen's description of the "horse" and the "hostesses" who "man" the sales table (see Box 20) serves to confirm other details she's already accumulated about her Photo Phantasies fieldsite and the beauty business it represents. Her interview with Ginny the manager, her description and map of the store's space, and her viewing of training videos unify Karen's growing skepticism.

At the Sunday evening sales meeting, Karen records details that further confirm the contrast between the company's beauty sell and the everyday reality of this mall business. As she sits in the meeting, forgotten in the black chair, she takes fieldnotes about the employees who present themselves in rather ordinary ways. She writes, "While I understand this is after-hours, I have a hard time believing these are the same people who are responsible for creating beauty and self-confidence in others. Their appearance contrasts with the prototypical image of the Photo Phantasies employee I saw in two videos." She also notes three slumped women picking at their nail polish and chewing gum, a photographer who smells of body odor, and a makeup artist eating frozen yogurt who scrapes the bottom of her cup with a plastic spoon as she balances a sleeping child in her lap.

The store manager's pep talk to her staff confirms Karen's growing insights about Photo Phantasies' daily work. The manager points out the uses of the space that Karen has already mapped, that different areas of store space have entirely different purposes. Ginny reminds her staff about one simple rule for using those areas: "We praise each other in front, and we talk about bad things in back. That's what my office is there for." This guideline is such a major part of the business policy that whenever employees begin to say something negative, they are instructed to "touch the red heart on your name tag."

To write about the culture you've researched, you must look, as Karen did, for a unifying perspective. Much of fieldwork involves confirming unity—unity of themes and patterns that hang together in the data. Disparate data sources—maps, interviews, observations, and reflections—accumulate to form a coherent whole. Looking for unity in masses of data is much like Samuel Scudder looking at the fish, as we discuss in Chapter 2. At first, you'll see very little, but over time and with close study, important unifying details will come together, like the symmetry of the fish, which took so long for Scudder to see.

But it is equally important for a researcher to locate disconfirming data, discontinuity, and tensions. Tensions show up in data at moments of contradiction when multiple or opposing perspectives collide. For Karen, the first tension in her study arises when she realizes that not all people share her attitude toward having beauty pictures taken. After Karen spends $62 on a pair of Reeboks at the mall and $10 on a bouquet of irises at the grocery store, she holds a conversation with a checkout clerk over what it means to "treat yourself." Karen is jarred when she realizes that for some people, having their pictures taken at Photo Phantasies might be a treat. Here is part of her short exchange with Darlene, a familiar clerk who's never spoken with her before. In this passage, Karen begins to recognize the discontinuities between her own values and those of others. In a way, this moment serves as a disconfirming source of data. Whenever a researcher senses tension, she needs to recognize and record it:

"God, these are beautiful. How much?" The woman on the other side of the counter smiles as she picks up my flowers and brings them close to her face. I have been checking out movies here for 10 years, and she has never asked me anything other than perfunctory information.

"Uh, ten dollars, I think. Aren't they great? And not really all that expensive. I bought them as a treat." I grin at her with my lips pressed together.

"Are there any left? I just may get some. A treat, like you said. It's either flowers or Photo Phantasies. I've been wanting to do that for so…"

"Photo Phantasies?" I raise my eyebrows at this notion.

"God, yes." As she turns to retrieve my movie, I see her name tag reads "Darlene." "I mean, what could be a better treat? I wanna go in there, have 'em do up my hair and my makeup, put on all those cool clothes, take a whole bunch of pictures, and then go out on the town lookin' so hot! I'd leave my kids with my mother and stay out as late as I wanted. Hopefully, plenty of men would be willin' to buy me drinks."

"Yeah. Hmmm." I don't know how to respond to this because Darlene's version of a treat or an indulgence is not mine. I hate the idea of having my picture taken. Period. And having my picture taken in clothes and hair and makeup that turn me into someone I'm not? Never! I know the feminist rhetoric—a woman's body is hers to do with as she pleases. And I think I believe this feminist rhetoric, or I would like to think I do. But a Photo Phantasies makeover? What a waste of money for something that won't last.

"We'll see. Maybe someday." As Darlene says this, she pushes up the sleeves of her white uniform and sighs. Her two-inch red nails with chipped polish click the price of my movie into the cash register. I am on the verge of suggesting that Darlene get a massage instead of a makeover when I stop short. I see a smudged blue pen mark on her cheek and the trace of dark circles under her eyes.

"No, not someday. Now. Why wait?" Suddenly, I want Darlene to leave the grocery store this instant and drive straight to Forum West [Mall]. I am surprised by my encouragement, but I empathize with her, despite our different ideas of indulgence. "This is weird, but here, look what I just happen to have." I reach into my coat pocket and take out the Photo Phantasies brochure. "I was just at the mall. They gave me this. Here. You can have it. I think they're doing some kind of model search. You should go. Give it a try." It did not escape me that I sounded just like Bettie from the Photo Phantasies store....

"A model search? Wow. No way. That's so cool! I can have this? Really? Cool! Thanks. I just may go. I just may." Darlene tucks the hot pink brochure into the front pocket of her white uniform and hands me the movie.

"Do it!" I say, smiling. "And remember me when you get discovered."

Darlene smiles, showing the white of her teeth. "Maybe when you come back, I'll have pictures to show you." I think about her comment while I wait in the checkout line to pay for my $10 flowers, which I know won't last a week. I buy them anyway.

It is this conversation with Darlene that causes Karen to unpack the personal "baggage" about beauty photography that she brings to her project and to examine her assumptions. Her encounter at the checkout is a moment of insight in which Karen sees Photo Phantasies through the eye of the "other." This tension prompts her to reflect on her own investments of time and money—Reeboks and a bunch of irises—which show her that she's guided her study with her own values, not those of the "other." Karen recognizes what disturbs her. She realizes she must now research Photo Phantasies from the insider's position.

If Karen had continued to look only for unity by just interviewing customers who shared her perspective, she might have discarded her encounter with Darlene as data. After interviewing customers who were, in fact, proud and satisfied with their beauty photographs, she understood the value of beauty photography through their eyes, not just her own. In spite of her own resistances throughout the project, Karen reaches a dramatic and ironic conclusion about the subculture of Photo Phantasies. At the end of her paper, she writes, "Sometimes things are not what they seem."

Here is Karen's study, "Strike a Pose," in its entirety.

Strike a Pose
Karen Downing

It's not easy to create a myth and to emulate it at the same time.... What is ultimately clear is that even the attempted myth must be made a model for imitating, a drama to be tried on for fit.... It is a mold, a prescription of characters, a plot.

—JEROME BUTLER IN *The Beauty Myth*

Smiling Women

As I pull open one of the heavy glass doors at Forum West Mall, a medium-sized suburban shopping mall, I am overwhelmed by sensations. Bells and laughs and sirens from the Fun Factory layer on top of piped-in Muzak. Large, colorful movie posters advertise *Man of the House*, A *Goofy Movie*, and *The Pebble and the Penguin*. People are everywhere—men and women in business suits eating lunch, several teenagers smoking by the reflecting pond, mothers running errands with babies in tow, older people exercise-walking in fitness gear. The smells of freshly baked bread from Subway, sugary caramel corn, greasy pizza, and fried tacos hang in the air. There are yellow benches and tables and leafy trees reaching toward skylights and winding staircases and two automatic teller machines and a lingerie store and a department store and an engraving stand. I experience all of this just 10 feet inside the mall.

As a teenager, I would spend hours at Forum West each weekend, roaming through the stores with various best friends. Now, as a woman in my twenties, when I go to the mall, I go with a purpose. Today I am in the mall to look for tennis shoes. To get to Durham's Discount Sporting Goods, I must pass two food stands and three other shops. I walk quickly, head down, thinking about walking shoes versus cross-trainers, Reeboks versus Nikes. I pass Chopstixs, an Asian fast-food restaurant that provides plastic forks instead of chopsticks with their meals. Up ahead I see the Disney Store, or rather I hear the Disney Store—strains of the *Little Mermaid* soundtrack carry out into the mall. To my right, a group of middle school girls are huddled together, each clutching shopping bags that encourage "Take home a little magic—take home Disney." They giggle as they try on Mickey Mouse ears. I pull closer toward the storefronts. Durham's is only 12 feet away.

"Hi, let me tell you about Photo Phantasies. My name is Bettie. What's yours?" This woman was slumped against a display rack, picking her fingernails, until she saw me. I smile at Bettie and try to pass, but she keeps speaking to me.

"Look! 'Somewhere in America, a new model is waiting to be discovered. It could be you! Just ask how. Today!'" Bettie reads the words in bold print on the display as I notice the photograph under the words. It is of a girl who is possibly in her late teens or early twenties. She is smiling at the camera. Her brown hair cascades around her face and rests on her shoulders. Her brown eyes and lipsticked mouth reflect a glimmer of light.

"The Photo Phantasies process is simple and fun! It's a celebration! And you could be chosen to be a model! With those eyes, I think you'd stand a good chance! We may just have openings right now. At least take a brochure home. Talk to your friends! You should do it! It's fun!" Although Bettie does not have a southern accent, I hear her words and cannot resist adding a slight twang to her speech.

I take the brochure, smile again, and walk away. She calls out these parting words: "You'd look great! Just great! I promise!" I hear these words as I see an image on a television monitor located at the far left side of the store, just an inch or two from the threshold. The woman on the monitor is smiling at me. She's wearing a red hat that fans out from her face. Gold and rhinestone earrings dangle from her ears. She looks like she is posing for a camera, or so I assume, although I can't actually see a camera. She drops her shoulder and tilts her head to the right. She smiles. And then she moves. This time, the photographer steps into the image on the screen. He lowers the woman's chin with his hand. He adjusts the bustier that she is wearing by tugging it down on the right side, his hands close to the woman's waist. He steps out of the picture. She's still. Ready. Looking right at me, this woman on the television monitor smiles. I fold the Photo Phantasies brochure, put it inside my coat pocket, and walk into the sports store.

After I buy my $62.00 Reebok cross-trainers from a man dressed in an umpire's uniform, I drive to my grocery store. I pick up some bananas and 12 long-stem irises before checking out a movie to watch that night with my husband. I take the movie to the pharmacy counter and put the flowers down while I search for my rental card.

"God, these are beautiful. How much?" The woman on the other side of the counter smiles as she picks up my flowers and brings them close to her face. I have been checking out movies here for 10 years, and she has never asked me anything other than perfunctory information.

"Uh, ten dollars, I think. Aren't they great? And not really all that expensive. I bought them as a treat." I grin at her with my lips pressed together.

"Are there any left? I just may get some. A treat, like you said. It's either flowers or Photo Phantasies. I've been wanting to do that for so…"

"Photo Phantasies?" I raise my eyebrows at this notion.

"God, yes." As she turns to retrieve my movie, I see her name tag reads "Darlene." "I mean, what could be a better treat? I wanna go in there, have 'em do up my hair and my makeup, put on all those cool clothes, take a whole bunch of pictures, and then go out on the town lookin' so hot! I'd leave my kids with my mother and stay out as late as I wanted. Hopefully, plenty of men would be willin' to buy me drinks."

"Yeah. Hmmm." I don't know how to respond to this because Darlene's version of a treat or an indulgence is not mine. I hate the idea of having my picture taken. Period. And having my picture taken in clothes and hair and makeup that turn me into someone I'm not? Never! I know the feminist rhetoric—a woman's body is hers to do with as she pleases. And I think I believe this feminist rhetoric, or I would like to think I do. But a Photo Phantasies makeover? What a waste of money for something that won't last.

"We'll see. Maybe someday." As Darlene says this, she pushes up the sleeves of her white uniform and sighs. Her two-inch red nails with chipped polish click the price of my movie into the cash register. I am on the verge of suggesting that Darlene get a massage instead of a makeover when I stop short. I see a smudged blue pen mark on her cheek and the trace of dark circles under her eyes.

"No, not someday. Now. Why wait?" Suddenly, I want Darlene to leave the grocery store this instant and drive straight to Forum West. I am surprised by my encouragement, but I empathize with her, despite our differing ideas of indul-gence. "This is weird, but here, look what I just happen to have." I reach into my coat pocket and take out the Photo Phantasies brochure. "I was just at the mall. They gave me this. Here. You can have it. I think they're doing some kind of model search. You should go. Give it a try." It did not escape me that I sounded just like Bettie from the Photo Phantasies store. I fought off the southern twang.

"A model search? Wow. No way. That's so cool! I can have this? Really? Cool! Thanks. I just may go. I just may." Darlene tucks the hot pink brochure into the front pocket of her white uniform and hands me the movie.

"Do it!" I say, smiling. "And remember me when you get discovered."

Darlene smiles, showing the white of her teeth. "Maybe when you come back, I'll have pictures to show you." I think about her comment while I wait in the checkout line to pay for my $10 flowers, which I know won't last a week. I buy them anyway.

Composing an Image: Before

"Hello, this is Photo Phantasies. My name is Mindy. Today's a great day." I am not calling Photo Phantasies to inquire about specials. I am not calling because I want to know if they have any free time today for a last-minute appointment. I am not calling to see if a $220 package of photographs has arrived. I am calling to speak to Ginny James, the manager. When I make this request and tell Mindy who I am, she says, "Oh. Hang on a sec," in a voice with-out intonation. Her hand covers the receiver, muffling sounds.

When I talk with Ginny, I will not say that I have an aversion to her store and the whole Photo Phantasies concept. I will tell her that I am fascinated by the photographs my high school students, always female, bring to school to show off. I will present myself as curious.

"This is Ginny James. It's a great day! What can I do for you?" Her voice rises at the end of the question.

I tell Ginny my name and ask her if she has received the letter I sent four days ago requesting to visit her store.

"Letter? What letter are your referring to?"

I am caught off guard by her response and feel slightly uneasy. I take a deep breath before explaining my "research project."

Silence. And more silence. Finally, this from Ginny: "I'll need this in writ-ing. Call me back after 11:30. That's when the mail comes. If there's no letter, you'll need to provide adequate documentation. You'll have to deliver it in per-son." Despite the mall noise in the background, I sense immediately that Ginny is guarded with me. Her changed tone results in sentences with periods, no longer exclamation points. I wait until 12:30 and try again.

"Hello, this is Photo Phantasies. My name is Stacey! It's a great day and we're searching for models! How may I help you?"

When I finally talk with Ginny during this second phone call, she leaves out the conversational niceties. Yes, my letter had arrived in the mail after all. "I'll have to clear this request with headquarters, which I can do tomorrow. I'm leaving for a Photo Phantasies meeting in Chicago. What kind of class is this for? Business? Sociology? I'll call you Wednesday night and leave a message about whether or not it's OK."

Wednesday night, no reply.

Friday morning, no reply.

My third call to Photo Phantasies is on Friday afternoon. "Hello, this is Photo Phantasies. My name is Ginny! Ask me about our model search! How may I help you?"

"Ginny, this is Karen Downing. You may help me by telling me that headquarters granted me permission to spend some time in your store." I try to be personable and charming.

"Karen Downing?"

"Yes, the one that sent the letter about doing research for…"

"Oh. Right. Well. Yes. You can come to the store, but I don't want an extra body around when customers are here. You could come to an in-store training session from 5:30 to 6:30 on Sunday night. And I have some material about Photo Phantasies that you could read."

"Huh. Well…huh. Ummm…when could I come out to pick up the material?"

"Saturdays are nuts. Sunday's the meeting day. Monday's my paper day… and I'm still catching up from Chicago…" She trails off into a sigh.

"How about today? This afternoon?"

"Fine." Click. When she hangs up, I realize that in three phone calls, I have never heard the official Photo Phantasies telephone goodbye.

I leave the house to go to the mall at 11:30, even though I know that, technically, it's not yet afternoon. But I have work to do in the afternoon and would rather not face more traffic and a busier mall. Before I leave, I think about what I am wearing. My standard look—black turtleneck and brown jeans, minimal gold jewelry, lipstick, powder, blush and eyeliner, curly and full hair tucked behind my right ear. I decide not to do anything different to my appearance for this particular errand, but I am aware that I am thinking about how I look a lot more than I normally would. I hear the words of my mother, the words I have grown up with: "You need more blush! And remember the lipstick! Without it, you don't look alive!" Today, I follow her advice, advice I usually ignore, and add just a bit more makeup to be sure it's noticeable. I am glad my husband is at work. Although he would not come right out and say I am wearing too much makeup, he would give me the slightest hint of a goodbye kiss and then say, "Lipstick." I know just what he means.

Once inside the mall, I walk through a lunchtime crowd of over 100 people who fill the tables and wait at the food stands. Most of the people are dressed in business clothes; some carry briefcases and cellular phones and Gap bags. I round the bend beyond the food court and am practically inside Photo Phantasies before I know it.

"Hi! May I help you?"

I wonder if this is Mindy or Sharon or Ginny or some employee I have yet to talk with on the phone. There are three other people behind the counter besides the receptionist—two women and one man. I glance at them, noting only that they all wear either black or white clothes. I introduce myself and say I have come to the store to pick up some material from Ginny James. At the sound of her name, three of the people behind the counter stop what they are doing, move over to the right side of the counter, and begin organizing and sorting papers, their bodies still half-turned in my direction.

"I'm Ginny. I thought you said you would be by this afternoon." This from one of the women behind the counter, dressed all in white, probably in her early to mid-forties. She has glasses on, and her brown hair is pulled back into a ponytail tied with a white fabric bow. She glances up at the wall behind me, where I assume she reads a clock.

"Is this too early?"

"Yep." She taps her pen against her chest and continues to stare behind me, eyes lifted, toward the wall.

"When would be better for you?"

"This afternoon. Like I said, 1:30." And with that her eyes leave the wall, pass over me, and return to the papers in front of her.

Composing an Image: After

At exactly 1:30, I return to Photo Phantasies for a second time. I am told by the receptionist that Ginny is busy. I ask if I may take a seat while I wait. She points to a black vinyl chair in the corner. Sitting there, I hear crying children and Disney music and footsteps on tile, even though my back is to the mall. I am almost thankful that Ginny is busy; I have a chance to look around. I pull out my journal, glancing behind to see if the receptionist is watching. Thankfully, she is examining the face of a teenage girl under the bright lights of the makeup station's mirror. I look around the store. Next to my chair is a black magazine rack with *Glamour* and *Elle* and *Mirabella*. I have already read the first two magazines, but I don't mind the chance to page through *Mirabella*. The walls of the store are white and the carpet is gray with muted lines of rose running throughout in a zigzag pattern. Pop music, loud enough to cover some of the mall noise, comes from overhead speakers.

The store is perhaps 30 feet by 30 feet, but each inch of space is used. There are three black vinyl chairs facing a mirrored wall and a counter where I assume makeup and hair are done. A sign hanging above the area reads "Professional Makeup Artists." I look around for these people, but no one is working near the three chairs, nor is anyone in the store but the receptionist. Surrounding the four-foot-high mirror on the wall are round light bulbs that remind me of a movie star's dressing room. On the counter, an array of curling irons, blow dryers, Q-tips, mousse, static guard, and hair spray joins tray after tray of makeup. Above the mirror is the wall of "Phantasy Phaces"—Photo Phantasy photographs, each measuring three feet on a side, arranged to look like film coming off a movie reel. All of the photographs are of women, except for two little girls and one couple.

In front of my chair are racks of clothing—denim jackets with gold studs, gold lamé blouses, a coat with red, white, and blue stars and stripes, sequined blazers, beaded bustiers, blue and pink boas, and shelves of hats. Beyond the wardrobe selections, there are three dressing rooms without mirrors or seats inside. Each one has a white mesh hamper for clothes and a white hook on the wall and a black curtain that can be pulled over the opening to the dressing room.

Next to the racks of clothes is the photography sitting room. I cannot see much of that room because the door is only halfway open, but I can see part of a royal blue background and a black vinyl stool. I can only assume that the camera is in there somewhere. On the other side of the photography sitting room are three computer monitors. The computer monitors, placed in a straight row, stand off to the right of the receptionist desk and the cash register. My high school students who have been to Photo Phantasies tell me that after they have had their pictures taken, they change back into their street clothes and meet a salesperson who uses the computer monitor to display the proofs. There is no wait time—a customer can see her photographs on the monitor seconds after the pictures have been taken.

After 15 minutes, the receptionist touches me on the shoulder. She looks down at the notes in my journal as I look down at the floor, feeling like I have just been caught doing something inappropriate. "Cool handwriting! It kinda looks like calligraphy! Ginny's ready for you now." She points toward the back of the store, past the racks of clothes to a door near the dressing rooms. The door is open. I stand there, waiting for Ginny to look up. After several moments, I knock and say hello.

"Oh, right. Sit here. 'Scuse the mess. I'm still not caught up from Chicago. Let's see, you want to know about Photo Phantasies. Well, here's some information." Ginny continues without waiting for me to look through material.

"There are almost 400 Photo Phantasies studios in the United States. Our corporation's name is Bright Star. Our main goal is retail. We sell an excellent product. We believe in a good work environment and pay our employees well, based on a series of incentives. I'm a manager, coach, cheerleader, and toilet cleaner. Here at Photo Phantasies we have a team philosophy. I'm here to make sure we're victorious." Ginny leans back in her chair, away from me. She holds a pen in her hand that she points in my direction when she wants to stress a point. She looks right at me and does not pause to allow me time to get her words into my notes. I feel like I am listening to a well-rehearsed speech. When she stops to swallow, I ask her how long she has been with Photo Phantasies.

"I've been on board since February 6. I used to be an assistant buyer at another store, and then I single-handedly turned around the gift shop at the museum. But I reached a point where I wanted to do more than sell underwear or stuffed dinosaurs. I wanted to give something back to society. Here I am, managing a Photo Phantasies."

When I ask her about what she thinks Photo Phantasies gives back to society, Ginny does not hesitate, "Self-confidence. An escape. An opportunity to feel good about who you are. It all starts with the initial call to the store. From there on out, this place is about a party atmosphere. And that's no hype. Those of us that work here are artists, waiting to transform."

She stops speaking for a moment and studies my face. "Your eyes. That's what I would concentrate on if I were going to do you. They're your best feature. I'd play those up for sure."

Part of me resents the fact that this woman who has just met me thinks she has the authority to point out my best feature; the other part of me shamelessly succumbs to her comment with a blush.

"We fulfill dreams at Photo Phantasies. Everyone wants to enter a modeling contest. We make it happen. The ol' Miss America dream—it comes alive here. I know, there's all this talk about how that can be damaging, but I put that aside because we're in the business of making people—everyone—beautiful."

I ask her if there has ever been a customer who has presented a challenge. She looks away and smiles. "I probably shouldn't tell you this, but oh well. One day, right after I started, we were short a makeup artist. I had to run the show. So this woman comes in and wants a Photo Phantasies experience. Yeah. Well, let me just say, she was Irish. You know what I mean when I say that? She had that skin that looked like she'd spent too much time out tending sheep. She had wrinkles and a sunburn, and she was broken out, plus she had a cold sore."

I find myself laughing aloud at this, but I wonder if Ginny views my response as laughing at the woman. What I think I am laughing at is the contrast between the woman described and the woman pictured in Photo Phantasies advertisements.

"She was a tough one to build up, but I did it. I looked at her like she was a lump of clay. As an artist, it was my job to shape her. See that angel up there?" She points to an angel figurine, dressed in a white robe with gold glitter on her face and in her hair. "I made that to watch over the place. And just like I made that, I made this Irish woman. I put so much base makeup on her, she looked flawless. And you know what? Those pictures turned out great, and she was thrilled. I think she spent over $100 on a package. And why not? When would she ever look as good?"

The receptionist has been standing in the doorway, waiting for Ginny to finish talking. She walks over to Ginny and whispers something in her ear. Ginny says in my direction, "One moment, I've got to take this call. 'Hello, this is Ginny! It's a great day at Photo Phantasies. How may I help you?"

With the receiver cradled between her head and her shoulder, Ginny shuffles the papers around on her desk and says a few "uh huhs" into the phone.

"No, there's no problem at all! Let me put you on hold for just one moment, and I will consult the scheduling book, just to make sure! Thanks so much for your patience!" As she puts the phone down, she rolls her eyes at me. "Hang on. I've gotta sort this person out."

Alone in her office, I have the chance to look around. She is right. The office is a "mess," and it probably does not help matters that it looks to be no larger than an oversized closet. On one side of the office, there is a stacked washer and dryer. Lint from previous loads gathers on the floor in front of the machines. On the counter, cleaning supplies, Big Gulp cups, and empty cans of diet soda surround a microwave. On the wall are two calendars labeled "Sales Goals" and "Sales Reality." I am too far away to read the numbers that are penciled on each date. Next to this on the wall is a plaque recognizing achievement in regional sales gift certificates. Underneath this, an article from a London newspaper about the "Queen for a Day" concept in England, the Anglo version of Photo Phantasies, I assume.

Underneath Ginny's desk are five purses of varying sizes. I gather that the people who work here use Ginny's office for their belongings, too. On the top of the desk are stacks of paper, notebooks, Post-it notes, and a fax machine. Ginny has her own Photo Phantasies photograph, taken with her wearing a straw hat and a denim jacket with sunflowers embroidered on the collar. Right beside this photograph is a picture of a witch, complete with broom and black cat. Above the witch picture, a Post-it note reads "Before." Above the Photo Phantasies photograph, a Post-it note reads "After." Next to these pictures is the poem "Warning" by Jenny Joseph. "When I am an old woman I shall wear purple...." To the left of my chair is a black storage cabinet about six feet in height. On it is a sign-up sheet for employee meetings with Ginny, as well as some promotional material and sales material. From the latter, I read, "Remember, you need to celebrate the perfect pose. When you look at the pictures with the customer, pick out a specific feature to celebrate. Tell her that her hair is gorgeous in that pose. Celebrate! Celebrate! Celebrate!" The sales tip is stuck to the storage cabinet with a magnet that advertises a local group of surgeons specializing in plastic and reconstructive surgery.

Playing Your Part

Before I leave Photo Phantasies, Ginny gives me two company videos. Not until the day I need to return the tapes do I finally watch them. Somehow, having the videos in my home makes me feel oddly connected to the store, as if I work there and am watching these videos to improve my job performance.

Still in my pajamas at 10:00 Sunday morning, I settle in on the couch to see just how Photo Phantasies presents itself. The first video is titled *Photo Phantasies' 12 Steps of Customer Service*. To illustrate each of the 12 steps, several employees of the Bright Star Corporation act out a skit. Dressed in black T-shirts and khaki pants, the employees first model the wrong way to serve a customer before proceeding to the right way, making constant reference to the "before and after" theme.

After watching the first couple of steps to effective customer service, I realize that "customer service" is actually a Photo Phantasies euphemism for "increasing sales." The 12 steps of customer service are as follows:

1. *The horse.* A Photo Phantasies hostess should man the horse, the brochure stand outside the store, at all times, particularly when the mall is busy. The hostess should greet people as they pass and tell them about the professional makeup salon and photo studio. She should show them the "Look Book" with the before and after pictures of previous customers, give them a brochure, take them on a tour of the store, explain the Photo Phantasies process, and work to get an appointment set up on the spot. "Yes or no" questions should be avoided—the focus is on selling the concept.

2. *The photo inquiry.* When the customer calls to set up an appointment, the receptionist must be sure to use the client's name whenever possible during the phone call. Explain the Photo Phantasies process thoroughly, reminding the customer to arrive for the appointment without makeup and with clean, unstyled hair. Receptionists should tell callers about specials, remind them to bring credit cards for immediate photo purchases, and secure all appointments with credit cards in case the customer cancels a scheduled appointment.

3. *Booking the appointment.* The video recommends that appointments be booked within seven days of a customer's phone call so that there is less time for a change of mind. Appointments should first be scheduled during slow hours, like weekdays and mornings. Suggestion selling is important. The customer should be reassured that her pictures will look great and that she will want to buy enough for everyone she knows.

4. *The confirmation call.* Forty-eight hours in advance of an appointment employees are encouraged to contact the customer just to say how much the staff is looking forward to the appointment. The customer should be encouraged to bring a friend and share the experience. And again, the client should be reminded that she will want to purchase pictures the day of her appointment.

5. *The front counter greeting.* This step urges employees to use customers' names immediately, for they are likely to be embarrassed, particularly if they arrived without makeup and are nervous about the unfamiliar situation. The front counter greeting should involve filling out a bio card so that employees can get to know customers better and make them feel at ease.

6. *In the makeup chair.* This step involves compliments. "You're going to look absolutely beautiful." The employee is encouraged to build up rapport so that the customer shares feelings. Makeup artists should write down two things about each customer and pass that note along to the photographer. That way the photographer will know what to say to increase sales. "What kind of look do you want? Something sexy?" If the customer feels like she has been listened to, she will buy more. The

makeup artists should point out their own photos on their name tags and talk about how much fun the process was for them.

7. *Transition to photo.* Everyone in the store should affirm how attractive the customer looks once she has put on her wardrobe selections. "You look absolutely gorgeous. What a great color for you!" The makeup artist should introduce the customer to the photographer. The photographer should say, "It will be so much fun to be a model!" and play this opportunity up as every woman's fantasy.

8. *The photo session.* During this step, the model theme continues with comments like "You're a natural for this" and "You look like you could be a model. Have you ever been one before?" Suggestions sell with comments like "This shot would be perfect for your husband. You look sexy!"

9. *The video sale.* The salesperson should tell the customer she is pretty. With each picture, the salesperson needs to make a specific suggestion to the customer, for instance, by telling the customer how she might use this photograph for display at work or that photograph for gifts.

10. *Ringing the sale.* The receptionist should tell the customer that her pictures are great and tell her how much fun the experience must have been for her. In addition, the receptionist should encourage customers to upgrade to a higher-priced photo package or to buy the proofs, too.

11. *Exiting the customer.* It is recommended that employees use customers' names when mentioning how much they look forward to seeing the proofs.

12. *Delivering the order.* The final step involves opening up the photo package and looking at the pictures. Employees should be excited because excitement is contagious. Customers should be told that they can order more photographs now that they see how good the results are. Again, employees should use customers' names as much as possible.

The second video, *Preemployment Screening,* lasts only about 15 minutes. This is the video a potential employee would watch before a job interview. I am still in my pajamas on the couch and have now been joined by my husband, who stretches in the living room before his jog. Together, we talk back to the video, offering sarcastic responses to the information provided.

Preemployment Screening is composed of a series of quick images set to fast-paced music. It begins with a testimonial from a Photo Phantasies manager about how employees change lives and attitudes and have a good time doing it. Customers, according to this manager, can go anywhere to have their pictures taken, but they come to Photo Phantasies for the magic. It is this atmosphere that makes them want to order pictures. Images of stores are flashed on the screen with voice-over testimonials from customers.

Next, a narrator talks to the camera. She is probably in her late twenties, southern, and wearing a dress. She is filmed inside stores and inside the company's central photo processing lab. Using the "before and after" theme, the video shows what bad employees do and what good employees do. A gum-chewing, magazine-reading employee turns into a complimentary, smiling hostess. Star performers at Photo Phantasies make $7 to $9 an hour, based on a set rate plus commission. They are expected to look the part, which means wearing makeup, doing their nails, styling their hair, and wearing fashionable black or white clothing. Male employees must have a neat appearance and wear a tie. There are parties and trips for employees, but before any fun can be had, duties must be done. All employees clean, vacuum, wipe, dust, and scrub equipment. Teamwork is the key. If one person succeeds, then everyone in the store is successful. The goal of a Photo Phantasies employee is to bring out a customer's potential. When the customer feels beautiful, she is self-confident. She will want to buy the image that reflects that self-confidence. Before closing with "From all of us at Photo Phantasies, keep smiling!" the narrator asks the viewer if she has what it takes to be part of the magic, to be a part of the Photo Phantasies team. Not everyone, she reminds us, is cut out for the part.

Sunday evening at Photo Phantasies. Thirty minutes after the mall has closed and only a few people pass outside the steel gate that now separates the store from the mall, I have again arrived early, this time for the staff in-service meeting. Just as before, I am pointed to the black vinyl chair in the corner and forgotten. I page through the book of thank-you notes on display next to the "Look Book." The black notebook holds at least a dozen thank-you notes from students in local small-town high schools who appreciate the store's donation to after-prom parties. The donations are always the same—free sittings but never free photographs. There are a few letters from organizations like dieters' clubs and girl scout troops. Each thanks Photo Phantasies for a free sittings donation. I am struck by the method behind Photo Phantasies' generosity. The audience appears, always, to be female, and the donation appears, always, to be made with the potential for profit. Only one letter comes from an individual. It is handwritten on stationery headed "From the desk of someone waiting to be DISCOVERED." Sheila O'Riley's note reads, "My customers asked if I was going to Hollywood. They thought I looked like a model. It was a special experience. I was able to live my childhood dream. Thank you!" I speculate about Sheila O'Riley's occupation and wonder if any of the "Phantasy Phaces" photographs that gaze down on me is of her.

At 5:50, the staff in-service gets under way. Ginny is seated on a stool at the front counter, this time dressed in a blue print outfit. There are seven staff members present, both men and women, some of whom I recognize from my two previous visits to the store. One person is eating a waffle cone, another has a large serving of frozen yogurt, and two people are drinking out of the Big Gulps I saw in Ginny's office. The employee "look" for this meeting is jeans or leggings, tennis shoes, and sweatshirts. While I understand that this meeting is after-hours, I have a hard time believing that these are the same people who are responsible for creating beauty and self-confidence in others. Their appearance contrasts with the prototypical image of the Photo Phantasies I saw in the two videos.

Ginny begins the meeting. "This won't take long if we concentrate. First of all, I want to remind all of you of a very simple rule. We praise each other in front, and we talk about bad things in back. That's what my office is there for. Pass this around to those people who aren't here. Naturally, they're the ones that need to hear it the most."

The employees show no reaction to her words. Three women slump in the chairs their customers sat in just an hour ago. Now the employees pick at their nail polish and chew gum. A photographer seated near me smells of body odor.

The rest of the meeting focuses on how to make the Photo Phantasies team more efficient. Ginny gives the employees an assignment for the next meeting. "Think about ways that other areas can help you. How can the photographer help the sales folks? Let us know. We need to pay attention to each other's needs. Communicate. If we communicate, we're more likely to work on schedule. Maybe we need to get stopwatches at each station. Remember, this is supposed to be a two-hour process for the customer. If we're efficient, we serve more customers. If we serve more customers, our sales average puts money in our paycheck."

"Yeah, well, I have a question," a man with blond hair who looks to be in his early twenties interjects. "Corporate's always talking about role playing. Role playing will make us more efficient, blah, blah, blah. When are we supposed to do this? We just don't have time. 'Oh, excuse me, customer, we're going to role play now.'"

"Sunday nights," Ginny responds immediately. "Sunday nights, like right now, is the time to practice for the real thing. That's what these meetings are for." Her comments meet with no response from the group. A child, under a year old, sleeps on her mother's lap. The mother, a professional makeup artist I saw in the store before, continues eating her frozen yogurt, scraping at the bottom of the cup with a plastic spoon.

After glancing down at a clipboard, Ginny continues. "OK, we have an opportunity to have a whole bunch of fun on Tuesday. It's a power day. I've made up copies of lists of customers who bought pictures in December who were born between 1939 and 1972. We'll call all of these people. It'll be telemarketing all day long. Each of you will have a booking sheet. Our goal is to set up fifty to a hundred appointments. You will all be given scripts for telemarketing. This is a Corporate idea. Seventy percent of our customers said they would return in one to five years. Only five percent have."

Again, no response from the employees, except for the same blond man who spoke earlier. "Cool idea! The people we call will be customers that have been here and liked it." Ginny turns toward this man.

"You know, you're doing a great job! Last week, you were one of the Booksey Twins. And we know who the other one was!"

Everyone looks now at the woman with the baby. She half-smiles while looking down at the carpet. Ginny says, "Keep it up!" She pauses for a moment and then finishes. "That's what I mean. That's the kind of stuff we need to be saying to one another on the floor. The other stuff—back in my office."

She finishes her agenda by telling the employees about the Easter parade theme that kicks off next week. Instead of black and white, the employees will be allowed to wear pastels for the week. They will wear Easter bonnets or bunny ears. Parade music will be played in the store. Children will get Easter candy, and adult customers will be given plastic Easter eggs with slips of paper announcing the current special inside the egg. A few plastic eggs will have coupons for free sittings. A customer appreciation table will be set up in the front of the store with Irish linens and finger sandwiches and fruit and coffee. In the back in Ginny's office, the employees will have their own table with veggies, dip, and pretzels. The employees will get grab bag prizes for the most bookings or the most sales during the Easter parade. But before the fun happens, some work needs to get done. The clothes need to be arranged, the phone stations need to be organized, and makeup and hair stations need to be cleaned.

It is 6:30 p.m., the official end of the meeting, when the first employee leaves the store with his portable phone that never rang. Several clusters of employees are talking among themselves about bunny ears and what to do if the makeup artists take too long and throw off the time schedule. Ginny gives the group one more assignment. "Those of you who are successful, if you have any tips, share them with the rest of us. That's the way our paychecks will increase."

This assignment seems to spark something in the employees. They begin calling out ideas.

"If we confirm appointments correctly, they should be ready to buy."

"Keep it rolling—that will eliminate objections."

"It's not a negative that they pay for their pictures at the time they're taken because the pictures come in a week. Just tell them, 'You'll really like the pictures. They'll be great!'"

"Why should they bring a friend? Because it's more money for us? No, because it's more fun for the customer." This tip meets with laughter by the whole group, even Ginny.

"Remember, attitudes mean everything. When you're about to say something negative, touch the red heart sticker on your name tag. Come out smiling, and you'll feel better."

"It's a party-party atmosphere here. That's with the customer, now with one another."

"Here's my tip. Pretend you're the customer. What would tick you off? What would make you feel great?"

As I get up to leave, I pass by Ginny and whisper a "thank you" in her direction. She asks me what I think. I hesitate before responding and then opt for something as neutral as possible. "It sounds like a lot of hard work."

"As a customer, you'd never guess what goes on behind the scenes, would you?"

Putting on a Face

As I tell people about my research project, I hear this time and time again. "Oh, Photo Phantasies. My mom (sister, aunt, best friend, neighbor) went there. She loved it!"

It seems there is no shortage of possible informants I could talk to about their Photo Phantasies experiences. I end up speaking with two women, both of whom are connected to Lynn, my mother's friend. The first, Robin, will soon be Lynn's daughter-in-law, and the second, Norma, is Lynn's mother-in-law.

I call Robin on the telephone, my list of questions by my side. At last I feel like I have some control over my research process. If Photo Phantasies will not allow me to be in the store when customers are there, I will find my own customers to interview. I manage to catch Robin between her two jobs, full time at the post office and part time at a lumber store. She went to Photo Phantasies a year ago with her mother, her aunt, and her cousin on the occasion of her mother's 48th birthday. Robin was nervous about the appointment before she went because she did not really know what to expect, but she tells me now it was a lot of fun being pampered. She notes that the makeup people asked her a lot of questions, trying hard to make her comfortable with the look they created. They "glitzed her up," but Robin was already comfortable wearing a fair amount of makeup, so this did not bother her. When I asked her if she had concerns about anything during the process, she admitted she did.

"Before I went, I was concerned about the size of the clothes. You see, I'm not exactly petite. I worried that nothing would fit me. But they had thought about that and with zippers hidden in the back of the tops and those loose drapes, they get around the size issue. I worried about my double chin in the pictures but the photographer told me she would take care of that. I also didn't like having to wear a tube top underneath the clothes. When you do the wardrobe changes, that's all you're in. Because the photographer was a woman, I felt OK about it."

Robin liked her pictures when she saw them on the video screen. She bought her proofs, two 8 × 10s, four 5 × 7s, and two or three sets of wallet-size pictures. She also paid for her mother's pictures as her birthday present. Lynn brought Robin's pictures to the house, so I had seen the photographs. I remember Robin's brown eyes and one picture of her in which she wore a gold lamé drape and gold earrings. I ask her if she thinks the pictures look like her. "Yes, I'm comfortable with them. They do look like me, in a different way. I do myself everyday, so I wasn't surprised by a glitzed-up version of what I see all the time. Sometimes people will look at the pictures and tell me that they don't think it looks like me at all. I tell them that it does. What I say to myself when I hear those comments is that they don't know the real me."

I conduct my interview with Norma, Lynn's mother-in-law, in person. I arrive at her house at 2:00 on a Monday afternoon. She has sent her husband away "so we can girl-talk in private." Before I set my bag and tape recorder down, she takes me over to the bookshelf and talks me through the 20 or so photographs of her family that line the shelves. She tells me who everyone is and points out a physical characteristic in each person she thinks stands out. "I know you aren't supposed to have pictures of your family in the living room," she tells me, "but they're all so beautiful. I just have to."

She asks me to sit in the recliner, gives me a cup of coffee, and settles in on the couch. She tells me she is 76 years old, a fact I have a hard time believing. Her skin has only a few wrinkles. She has permed gray hair ("It's thick, feel it!"), and she wears glasses with pink, green, and blue flecks of color on the blue frames. I ask her what prompted her to go to Photo Phantasies, and she tells me it was her husband who encouraged her to go. She saw an advertisement on television about a Photo Phantasies special, so she made an appointment, and her husband drove her to the mall.

"I went without my face to the mall. I was petrified that someone might see me. I looked like a real hag. Yep, I was walking around the mall without my face on. Every morning, my husband tells me to put on my face. That day, I had an excuse why I couldn't."

Norma rises from the couch and goes into the other room to look for her pictures. She returns with one wallet-size photograph. In the picture, her hair and makeup look much the same as they do today. She is wearing the same glasses, and she has a satiny pink drape around her shoulders, plus pearl earrings and a pearl necklace.

"They snap a picture of everything that you have on, everything they put on you. Finally, after they tried a bunch of things on me, I said, "Would you mind if I asked for something to be put on me that is pastel?" They had me in cowgirl clothes and hats and gloves. It wasn't me. I felt like a little girl dressing up. Finally, I asked for something soft and feminine and pastel. I bought eight wallet-size photos so my kids and grandkids could each have one. I didn't buy any of the ones with dangly stuff, just this one. It's me, more me. It's me."

I tell Norma how nice her pictures are. And I mean it. They are beautiful, and they do look just like her. After I leave Norma's house, I have a two-hour drive to the university. For miles, I think about Norma's comment, "putting on my face." Surrealistic, sci-fi images come to mind, images of faceless women waking up in the morning and groping around the nightstand for their faces. I am reminded of an old roommate of mine. The first thing she did when she woke up in the morning was put on her glasses, which she always kept by her alarm clock. Without those glasses, she could not see well enough to get out of bed safely. She wore her glasses for the 10-step walk to the bathroom, where she would immediately put in her contact lenses. Her glasses went into a case for the day, until the 10-step walk to the bedroom at night.

I always felt a surge of tenderness when I saw my roommate in her glasses. I was struck by the vulnerability and honesty of her situation in those moments. In much the same way, I feel this about Robin and Norma when they are without "their faces." I talked to each of them for 45 minutes with perhaps only a quarter of our conversations dealing with Photo Phantasies. In each interview, what began with makeup, hair, and photos quickly moved into more personal territory. Robin told me about working two jobs while trying to plan a wedding. We swapped wedding horror stories about insensitive grooms, difficult mothers, and demanding bridesmaids. Norma told me about her family and about God. She talked about her grandson, who is giving his parents a hard time right now, and about a letter she wrote to him that included passages of Scripture. I told her about some times when I was nasty with my parents and why I may have behaved the way I did. These women allowed me to question them about Photo Phantasies, and in a short time, they revealed much more to me. They revealed to me the part of them that is always there, underneath "the face." In the short time I spoke with them, I moved from researcher to female, quickly putting aside any academic concerns about Photo Phantasies that I may have had at the beginning of the conversation. We moved past surface differences to a common ground our gender shares.

Before Norma left the room to get her Photo Phantasies photo, she gave me a joke to read, one she carries around in her wallet. Cut out from *Redbook* years ago, the joke concerns a school psychologist's visit to a teacher's classroom. The psychologist is convinced that the students are not paying attention to the teacher. When the students leave for recess, the psychologist informs the teacher he plans to conduct an experiment after the students return. When the students come back to the room, the psychologist asks the students to call out a number and tells the students he will write the number on the chalkboard. One student calls out "14," and the psychologist writes "41." None of the students says anything. Another student volunteers "56," and the researcher writes "65" on the chalkboard. Again, no reply. Another, no reply. Another student says "88," and then pauses. The same student says to the psychologist, "See what you can do with that." Norma chuckled over the joke and said, "Guess that little boy showed the smart psychologist just how to look at things." I smiled back, knowing just how the psychologist feels. Sometimes things are not what they seem.

Works Cited

Faludi, Susan. *Backlash: The Undeclared War against American Women*. New York: Crown, 1991.

Joseph, Jenny. "Warning." *When I Am an Old Woman I Shall Wear Purple*. Ed. Sandra Martz. Watsonville, CA: Papier-Mache, 1987.

Wolf, Naomi. *The Beauty Myth: How Images of Beauty Are Used against Women*. New York: Morrow, 1991.

Karen's reflexive conclusion about Photo Phantasies invited layers of insights: that a hard-selling business meant to create illusions could, in fact, build self-esteem in customers and that her own negative attitude about the beauty culture almost blocked her understanding during her research. In her portfolio reflection, she writes about starting the project "very smug and haughty.... I scoffed at the notion and I scoffed at the women who swallowed the absurd 'Model for a Day' rhetoric Photo Phantasies features in their ads. I was out to prove myself right." As the research continued, however, and she began to interview customers, she found herself "championing their desires and validating their experiences" from their perspective. When she stepped back to consider her own values, such as a gym membership and new exercise clothes, she saw "a level of vanity and indulgence inherent" in her own choices. And finally, she accepted Photo Phantasies as "not *my* way, but *a* way," and she admits that the culture of Photo Phantasies could be viewed "as a microcosm for a much larger female culture" to which she also, unavoidably, belongs.

Karen's study shows us that researchers can impose their own values on the places they study unless they are reflective about the process of their own fieldwork. As educated middle-class American women, Karen and her informants exercised personal choices about ways to join or not join the **mainstream** American beauty culture. To indulge herself, Karen chooses Reeboks, exercise clothes, and health clubs over beauty photos, and she admits this in her writing. All researchers need to explain—to themselves and to their readers—the differences between their values and those of others they study, separating their attitudes and assumptions both on and off the page. Her readers can sense Karen's tension as they read her writing. One reader, Andrew Platt, who never met Karen, responded to a draft of her project. Andrew asks two questions, "Is anyone else really being hurt here?" and "So what else is new?" He writes:

> "Humankind cannot bear very much reality," said T. S. Eliot. We all need fantasy. Without it, reality is far too great for us to even remotely handle. Some pull or buy themselves out of it, but aren't they just buying themselves into a new nonreality? What I mean to say is, the customer in this situation buys into a fantasy, the salesperson promises it, the makeup artist creates the illusion, the photographer captures it. The store manager proves to his/her employees that a group effort is necessary to fulfill their obligation to keep America beautiful. The store manager, herself a product of manipulation, lives within a fantasy that all anybody truly wants is to be physically pleasing. The big man at the top has spent a lifetime convincing himself that all he really needs is more money to find happiness, regardless of how many he may deceive in order to do so.
>
> So who's being hurt? We all are continuing that age-old fallacy that love and happiness can be found in exterior beauty. But can we ever imagine that to change? I don't think so. I honestly wish I could say I don't care, say, "Let them throw away their money. Let them buy their temporary luxury," but I cannot do it without feeling a snapping at my heart and a voice snatched up in the back of my throat wanting to scream, "No, please, no."

It's wonderful the distance that Karen places herself at. She too is attracted to the beautiful. She too worries about her appearance, but with a cynical eye, or I should say, a cynical mind still inhabiting a very human body. She is affected—both repulsed and amused.

LEARNING HOW TO LOOK: COLONIZED SPACES

Fieldworkers look for the tension in the way informants inhabit their spaces because sometimes informants inhabit spaces not of their own choosing. Andrew recognizes the tensions Karen writes about: between her own attitude toward the beauty culture and that of her informants, between the management and the customers. Her affect is one of amusement and repulsion at the same time. If Karen had researched even further some of the employees she observed, she might have found that they, too, feel tensions in their everyday jobs of creating glamour. The Photo Phantasies photographer, for example, may prefer to be outside shooting pictures of the natural landscape rather than the artificial images he is paid to create for customers. The woman with the baby on her lap at the employee sales meeting might prefer to stay at home with her child rather than work in a cramped store at the mall. While these people may disagree with the Photo Phantasies dogma, may prefer to be working elsewhere, or may feel oppressed by their economic situation, they do have choices. They have some control over the spaces they inhabit every day.

But lack of control in cultural spaces can present itself on a much larger scale. When people inhabit spaces over which they have no control, they are considered to be *colonized*. In particular, when a **dominant** or powerful culture forces itself on a less powerful group, assuming control over its territories and people, this constitutes **colonization**. Researchers must recognize the vantage point of their own dominant culture and guard against describing others in terms that belong solely to their own culture's values and belief systems. Colonization can involve imposing your own culture's sense of time, place, religion, food, rituals, hygiene, education, morals, and even story structures. Descriptive words about other places and people—like *quaint, picturesque, simple, primitive, native,* or *backward*—imply cultural value judgments. When researchers write about cultures other than their own, they must try to separate their belief systems from those they study. This is a difficult—and sometimes impossible—task.

For example, about a century ago, anthropologists who studied religion in cultures that practiced witchcraft and sorcery needed to acknowledge how their own Judeo-Christian backgrounds influenced what they saw, as well as how they wrote about it. Many did not. One anthropologist whose cultural background guided her study of the spiritual practices of hoodoo was Zora Neale Hurston, whose work you'll read in Chapter 6. Hurston was among the first American fieldworkers to return to her own home culture, study oral storytelling and other folk practices there, and write about herself as she did it. She was a trained anthropologist who focused on the orality of her own people while weaving herself deftly into her fieldwriting account. Contemporary fieldworkers who study **marginalized** groups such as the homeless, gang members, immigrants, or the elderly must be careful not to let their value systems dominate their fieldwork. One way they guard against **ethnocentrism** is to write about their personal reactions and their belief systems throughout the research process, sometimes in their journals, sometimes in double-entry fieldnotes, and sometimes in letters to their colleagues. Writing about it doesn't solve the problem of colonization, but writing can expose it.

In this book, you will read the fieldwork of many researchers who faced the challenge of writing about subcultures with very different value systems. For example, in Chapter 6, you'll read two studies of waitresses' joking, gossip, and stories in which the researchers were careful not to impose any occupational stereotypes on their informants. And in Chapter 7, Paul Russ, who conducted interviews with AIDS survivors, had to recognize his assumptions about the people who contracted the disease as he worked with them. Cindie Marshall admits how her own white-collar background influenced how she saw the biker bar culture that she writes about in Chapter 7.

Colonization can take place both in the field and in the writing process. In the field, it happens when researchers don't adopt the informants' perspective. Karen Downing, for example, had to recognize that her own value system made her prefer Reeboks and irises over a Photo Phantasies package. In the writing process, colonization happens when we use our own language rather than allow our informants' language to describe their spaces. Henry Glassie's description of the broom as a "besom of heather bound round with twine" is the phrasing of his Northern Irish informants, not his own.

In all the studies we've mentioned, informants exercised choice within their fieldsites over whether or not to allow researchers to study there. In a few cases, researchers were denied full entry, as in Jake's study of the skinheads, or the access involved sticky negotiations, as in Karen's at Photo Phantasies. But in all cases, the informants had the power to offer or deny access to the fieldworker. When informants inhabit spaces that are not of their own choosing, as in studies of institutions such as prisons, hospitals, or even schools, researchers may have to leave out some of their best information to protect the privacy and safety of their informants.

Barbara Myerhoff's elderly Jews, for example, found themselves at the end of their lives in sometimes cramped and uncomfortable spaces, not by their own choice but because of economics, family transience, and an inadequate social welfare system. Although Myerhoff realizes that the Senior Center provides the elderly with a safe community, her freedom as a researcher and control of her own cultural space is far greater than that of her informants. In her book, she reflects on her informants' lack of power and her own sense of guilt. She fears that her research and writing will colonize them because she holds so much more power within the culture than they do:

I had become a tasteless ethnic joke, paralyzed by Jewish guilt: about my relative youth and strength, about having a future where they did not, about my ability to come and go as I chose while they had to await my visits and my convenience, when I relished food that I knew they could not digest, when I slept soundly through the night warmed by my husband's body, knowing the old people were sleeping alone in cold rooms. (27)

Myerhoff is very sensitive to the possibility that unconsciously and unwillingly, a researcher can colonize her informants and their space. And unconsciously and unwillingly, too, informants can allow themselves to be colonized. To illustrate from an informant's point of view how it feels to be colonized, how another country's dominant values and belief systems can overtake an entire community's perspective on itself, we share Jamaica Kincaid's nonfiction essay "On Seeing England for the First Time." This reflective memoir is about growing up on the island of Antigua, a British colony in the West Indies. As a child, Kincaid did not realize that England's cultural values overtook her Caribbean island life, but as an adult she writes about its domineering influences on her childhood. As you read her essay, notice how many of the British cultural practices and values she mentions are shaped by the dominant English culture—an ocean away from Antigua.

On Seeing England for the First Time

Jamaica Kincaid

When I saw England for the first time, I was a child in school sitting at a desk. The England I was looking at was laid out on a map gently, beautifully, delicately, a very special jewel; it lay on a bed of sky blue—the background of the map—its yellow form mysterious, because though it looked like a leg of mutton, it could not really look like anything so familiar as a leg of mutton because it was England—with shadings of pink and green, unlike any shadings of pink and green I had seen before, squiggly veins of red running in every direction. England was a special jewel all right, and only special people got to wear it. The people who got to wear England were English people. They wore it well and they wore it everywhere: in jungles, in deserts, on plains, on top of the highest mountains, on all the oceans, on all the seas. When my teacher had pinned this map up on the blackboard, she said, "This is England"—and she said it with authority, seriousness, and adoration, and we all sat up. It was as if she had said, "This is Jerusalem, the place you will go to when you die but only if you have been good." We understood then—we were meant to understand then—that England was to be our source of myth and the source from which we got our sense of reality, our sense of what was meaningful, our sense of what was meaningless—and much about our own lives and much about the very idea of us headed that last list.

At the time I was a child sitting at my desk seeing England for the first time, I was already very familiar with the greatness of it. Each morning before I left for school, I ate a breakfast of half a grapefruit, an egg, bread and butter and a slice of cheese, and a cup of cocoa; or half a grapefruit, a bowl of oat porridge, bread and butter and a slice of cheese, and a cup of cocoa. The can of cocoa was often left on the table in front of me. It had written on it the name of the company, the year the company was established, and the words "Made in England." Those words, "Made in England," were written on the box the oats came in too. They would also have been written on the box the shoes I was wearing came in; the bolt of gray linen cloth lying on the shelf of a store from which my mother had bought three yards to make the uniform that I was wearing had written along its edge those three words. The shoes I wore were made in England, so were my socks and cotton undergarments and the satin ribbons I wore tied at the end of two plaits of my hair. My father, who might have sat next to me at breakfast, was a carpenter and cabinetmaker. The shoes he wore to work would have been made in England, as were his khaki shirt and trousers, his underpants and undershirt, his socks and brown felt hat. Felt was not the proper material from which a hat that was expected to provide shade from the hot sun should have been made, but my father must have seen and admired a picture of an Englishman wearing such a hat in England, and this picture that he saw must have been so compelling that it caused him to wear the wrong hat for a hot climate most of his long life. And this hat—a brown felt hat—became so central to his character that it was the first thing he put on in the morning as he stepped out of bed and the last thing he took off before he stepped back into bed at night. As we sat at breakfast, a car might go by. The car, a Hillman or a Zephyr, was made in England. The very idea of the meal itself, breakfast, and its substantial quality and quantity, was an idea from England; we somehow knew that in England they began the day with this meal called breakfast, and a proper breakfast was a big breakfast. No one I knew liked eating so much food so early in the day; it made us feel sleepy, tired. But this breakfast business was "Made in England" like almost everything else that surrounded us, the exceptions being the sea, the sky, and the air we breathed.

At the time I saw this map—seeing England for the first time—I did not say to myself, "Ah, so that's what it looks like," because there was no longing in me to put a shape to those three words that ran through every part of my life no matter how small; for me to have had such a longing would have meant that I lived in a certain atmosphere, an atmosphere in which those three words were felt as a burden. But I did not live in such an atmosphere. When my teacher showed us the map, she asked us to study it carefully, because no test we would ever take would be complete without this statement: "Draw a map of England." I did not know then that the statement "Draw a map of England" was something far worse than a declaration of war, for a flat-out declaration of war would have put me on alert. In fact, there was no need for war—I had long ago been conquered. I did not know then that this statement was part of a process that would result in my erasure—not my physical erasure, but my erasure all the same. I did not know then that this statement was meant to make me feel awe and small whenever I heard the word "England": awe at the power of its existence, small because I was not from it.

After that there were many times of seeing England for the first time. I saw England in history. I knew the names of all the kings of England. I knew the names of their children, their wives, their disappointments, their triumphs, the names of people who betrayed them. I knew the dates on which they were born and the dates they died. I knew their conquests and was made to feel good if I figured in them; I knew their defeats.

This view—the naming of the kings, their deeds, their disappointments—was the vivid view, the forceful view. There were other views, subtler ones, softer, almost not there—but these softer views were the ones that made the most lasting impression on me, the ones that made me really feel like nothing. "When morning touched the sky" was one phrase, for no morning touched the sky where I lived. The morning where I lived came on abruptly, with a shock of heat and loud noises. "Evening approaches" was another. But the evenings where I lived did not approach; in fact, I had no evening—I had night and I had day, and they came and went in a mechanical way: on, off, on, off. And then there were gentle mountains and low blue skies and moors over which people took walks for nothing but pleasure, when where I lived a walk was an act of labor, a burden, something only death or the automobile could relieve. And the weather there was so remarkable because the rain fell gently always, and the wind blew in gusts that were sometimes deep, and the air was various shades of gray, each an appealing shade for a dress to be worn when a portrait was being painted; and when it rained at twilight, wonderful things happened: People bumped into each other unexpectedly and that would lead to all sorts of turns of events—a plot, the mere weather caused plots.

The reality of my life, the life I led at the time I was being shown these views of England for the first time, for the second time, for the one hundred millionth time, was this: The sun shone with what sometimes seemed to be a deliberate cruelty; we must have done something to deserve that. My dresses did not rustle in the evening air as I strolled to the theater (I had no evening, I had no theater; my dresses were made of a cheap cotton, the weave of which would give way after not too many washings). I got up in the morning, I did my chores (fetched water from the public pipe for my mother, swept the yard), I washed myself, I went to a woman to have my hair combed freshly every day (because before we were allowed into our classroom our teachers would inspect us, and children who had not bathed that day, or had dirt under their fingernails, or whose hair had not been combed anew that day might not be allowed to attend class). I ate that breakfast. I walked to school. At school we gathered in an auditorium and sang a hymn, "All Things Bright and Beautiful," and looking down on us as we sang were portraits of the queen of England and her husband; they wore jewels and medals and they smiled. I was a Brownie. At each meeting we would form a little group around a flagpole, and after raising the Union Jack, we would say, "I promise to do my best, to do my duty to God and the queen, to help other people every day and obey the scouts' law."

But who were these people and why had I never seen them? I mean, really seen them, in the place where they lived? I have never been to England. England! I had seen England's representatives. I had seen the governor-general at the public grounds at a ceremony celebrating the queen's birthday. I had seen an old princess and I had seen a young princess. They had both been extremely not beautiful, but who among us would have told them that? I had never seen England, really seen it. I had only met a representative, seen a picture, read books, memorized its history. I had never set foot, my own foot, in it.

The space between the idea of something and its reality is always wide and deep and dark. The longer they are kept apart—idea of thing, reality of thing—the wider the width, the deeper the depth, the thicker and darker the darkness. This space starts out empty, there is nothing in it, but it rapidly becomes filled up with obsession or desire or hatred or love—sometimes all of these things, sometimes some of these things. That the idea of something and its reality are often two completely different things is something no one ever remembers; and so when they meet and find that they are not compatible, the weaker of the two, idea or reality, dies.

And so finally, when I was a grown-up woman, the mother of two children, the wife of someone, a person who resides in a powerful country that takes up more than its fair share of a continent, the owner of a house with many rooms in it and of two automobiles, with the desire and will (which I very much act upon) to take from the world more than I give back to it, more than I deserve, more than I need, finally then, I saw England, the real England, for the first time. In me, the space between the idea of it and its reality had become filled with hatred, and so when at last I saw it I wanted to take it into my hands and tear it into little pieces and then crumble it up as if it were clay, child's clay. That was impossible, and so I could only indulge in not-favorable opinions.

If I had told an English person what I thought, that I find England ugly, that I hate England; the weather is like a jail sentence; the English are a very ugly people; the food in England is like a jail sentence; the hair of English people is so straight, so dead-looking; the English have an unbearable smell so different from the smell of people I know, real people of course, I would have been told that I was a person full of prejudice. Apart from the fact that it is I—that is, the people who look like me—who would make that English person aware of the unpleasantness of such a thing, the idea of such a thing, prejudice, that person would have been only partly right, sort of right: I may be capable of prejudice, but my prejudices have no weight to them, my prejudices have no force behind them, my prejudices remain opinions, my prejudices remain my personal opinion. And a great feeling of rage and disappointment came over me as I looked at England, my head full of personal opinions that could not have public, my public, approval. The people I come from are powerless to do evil on a grand scale.

The moment I wished every sentence, everything I knew, that began with England would end with "and then it all died, we don't know how, it just all died" was when I saw the white cliffs of Dover. I had sung hymns and recited poems that were about a longing to see the white cliffs of Dover again. At the time I sang the hymns and recited the poems, I could really long to see them again because I had never seen them at all, nor had anyone around me at the time. But there we were, groups of people longing for something we had never seen. And so there they were, the white cliffs, but they were not that pearly, majestic thing I used to sing about, that thing that created such a feeling in these people that when they died in the place where I lived they had themselves buried facing a direction that would allow them to see the white cliffs of Dover when they were resurrected, as surely they would be. The white cliffs of Dover, when finally I saw them, were cliffs, but they were not white; you could only call them that if the word "white" meant something special to you; they were steep; they were so steep, the correct height from which all my views of England, starting with the map before me in my classroom and ending with the trip I had just taken, should jump and die and disappear forever.

Kincaid depicts herself in this essay as a colonized child who, later as an adult, breaks away from the dominant English culture and grows to understand its enormous influence on her worldview. The British controlled not only these Caribbean islanders' government, economics, and political practices, as she shows us, but also their personal geography, their everyday cultural practices, and even their spatial gaze—the way they viewed their surrounding landscape. In this essay, Kincaid takes us into her home, her school, and her island surroundings so that we can see through her eyes what it meant to be overtaken by another culture.

She uses the map of England as a concrete image to show us how the spatial gaze restricts her ability to see and be heard. English cultural values seep through her descriptive language: the map looks like a leg of mutton with squiggly veins of red; the shades of pink and green are unfamiliar. The idea of England itself is a special jewel for only special people, echoing its well-known crown jewels. When Kincaid is asked in school to draw a map of England, she feels conquered and erased. Her spatial gaze is both symbolic and concrete as she describes the tension between a concept, her ideas of England, and its reality, which she eventually encounters. Kincaid suggests the mysterious space between her childhood image of England and its actualization in her adulthood: "The space between the idea of something and its reality is always wide and deep and dark. The longer they are kept apart—idea of thing, reality of thing—the wider the width, the deeper the depth, the thicker and darker the darkness. [...] and so when they meet and find that they are not compatible, the weaker of the two, idea or reality, dies." In Kincaid's case, it was the idea of England that died when she finally chose to go to England on her own and saw its reality: "not a picture, not a painting, not [...] a story in a book, but England, for the first time." To her, the real England was an ugly place—from the white cliffs of Dover to the food and weather to the dead-looking, smelly English who had imposed their values on her people.

The British spatial gaze had been instilled in her as a child. She grew up feeling a tension between what she actually saw and what she was told to see. Her internal landscape was based on her everyday experiences living on Antigua, but the landscape she read about, sang about, and learned about was based on a more powerful island in an entirely different geography. While she sang "When Morning Touched the Sky," she lived a life where "no morning touched the sky." "The morning where I lived," she writes, "came on abruptly, with a shock of heat and loud noises" and "the sun shone with what sometimes seemed to be a deliberate cruelty [...]." Kincaid finds dissonance between the English literary images of gentle mountains and moors "over which people took walks for nothing but pleasure" and her local knowledge that where she lived "a walk was an act of labor"; her people did not take strolls but trudged in hot fields and had no leisure time.

There is not only a mismatch in the spatial gaze and the personal landscape Kincaid describes but also a mismatch between the English cultural practices imposed on Antiguans and what might have been more appropriate ones for their island lives. One focal point she uses is the big English breakfast with grapefruit, eggs, cheese, porridge, oatmeal, and cocoa made in England. This breakfast, along with her hair ribbons, socks, and cotton underwear, her father's khaki shirt, and his brown felt hat, forced on her family the daily practices of the British culture. While these practices were all unconscious, she understood even as a child that they were inappropriate. Islanders, for example, felt sleepy from eating "so much food" early in the hot morning, and she instinctively knew that her father's brown felt hat, which he had selected from a picture of an Englishman wearing one, should have been a hat more suited to the Caribbean climate. All these practices, she suggests, were "'Made in England' like almost everything else that surrounded us."

Kincaid achieves this powerful portrait of a colonized child with expert writing. She evokes a sense of place and brings us into that childhood landscape, making us as readers feel colonized too, and perhaps a little guilty. She selects sensory details of time, place, weather, color, smells, textures, sounds, tastes, and sights, creating verbal snapshots of both Antigua and England, real and imagined. Through her descriptive language, we learn to map the space that she has mapped as a child. She uses as her focal point an actual map of England forced on her at her British-run school and carries this focal point throughout her memoir until she reaches the real England in her adulthood, when she is no longer colonized by British practices.

We don't need to be living in a colonized country to experience colonization. Within our own dominant American culture, many subgroups unconsciously colonize others. In fact, Karen's study of Photo Phantasies gives a clear example. American women—customers, employees, managers, mall shoppers, and even skeptics like Karen—find themselves accepting, and sometimes even internalizing, the values of beauty, costumes, jewelry, and makeup as represented in the glamour photography business. What's important about researching place is to understand how we acquire our spatial gaze, how that gaze informs our look at others, and what's behind the gaze of others who look back at us.

THE RESEARCH PORTFOLIO: LEARNING FROM YOUR DATA

Many people think of portfolios as things meant primarily for display, summaries of accomplishments or designs to present to someone for assessment. Artists submit their portfolios to juries for art shows or to gallery owners and private customers. Financial advisors present portfolios as options for their clients' investment possibilities and potentials. Students often find themselves assembling portfolios of written products to fulfill course requirements or institutional evaluations.

But your research portfolio can serve a very different purpose. It can become a tool for documenting your learning and analyzing your research process. Think of your portfolio as a cultural site—in this case, your personal fieldsite—and the artifacts you choose to place in your portfolio as data that teach you about your own fieldworking process. The readers of your portfolio (which, of course, include you) will need to know why you have collected and selected the cultural artifacts you display. Your portfolio might include, too, a representation of what data you've rejected, what you've left out, or what data you might collect more of in the future. Your own reflections on your portfolio artifacts need to accompany the selections to document your learning process. By writing reflections about each artifact, you'll learn about your unifying themes and be able to find tensions and notice gaps in your data.

As the researcher, then, you are an intimate part of your data, and yet you can learn from it. In Chapter 3's portfolio suggestions, you reflected on how you read and write, how you select and position yourself in the field. In this chapter, we'd like you to think about what you can learn from laying out your data, looking at the range and depth of artifacts and information from the field and from your background research from maps, archives, documents, and books.

Karen Downing's portfolio contained 12 artifacts, her complete study, and a reflective essay based on her analysis of her process. She presented each artifact in a plastic slipcover and wrote an reflection about it on a stick-on note attached to each. On the following pages, we reproduce nine of Karen's artifacts from the list below, along with the reflective essay Karen wrote after her study's completion. She used reflective notes she had written throughout her fieldproject as a basis for the essay.

Karen Downing's Portfolio

Artifacts

1. A typed page, labeled "Assumptions" (p. 275).
2. A map of the store (p. 276).
3. A promotional flyer for Photo Phantasies (not pictured): "This came in the mail in a mailing of coupons and real estate options. On the back of this is an ad for 'Long John Silver's Big Fish Deals, $3.99 for combination platter #4.' Both ads prey on getting a good deal for a small price. The text of the PP ad indicates the model theme prevalent in PP rhetoric."
4. A bright pink promotional checklist for customers to pick up in the store (p. 277).
5. The three-page business statement for employees, printed on fax paper (p. 278).
6. A copy of the poem that Ginny James had posted in her office (p. 279).
7. A list of guiding questions for interviewing informants (p. 280).
8. The transcript of a conversation with Mrs. Conway, a customer (p. 281).
9. A set of notes torn out of her fieldnotes from a stenographer's notebook (p. 282).
10. Collage of fashion words (p. 283).
11. Cover from the bestselling book *Backlash: The Undeclared War against Women* by Susan Faludi (not pictured).
12. A photo of Karen, her friend Amy, and Amy's husband (not pictured).

FieldStudy

"Strike a Pose" (see pp. 247–63 earlier in this chapter)

Portfolio Reflection

"A Pose on 'Strike a Pose'" (pp. 284–85)

Assumptions

I should start first with the whole mall culture. I spent many weekend hours
circling that place with Carolyn. We would poke around the stores, fingering the
clothes, knowing we would rarely make a purchase. We would then go downstairs and
each order a piece of pizza and a Coke at Scottos or whatever it was called. We had
no P.P.—that hadn't made its way to __ yet. I doubt very much that I would have
been going to it even if it were in the mall. I could picture certain girls—Jill Jacobs,
Sundi Geisler, Nikki Hampton—going for the big photo shoot and then bringing the
pictures into school to pass around or making up a cute little gift package for their
boyfriends. Maybe since I never had a serious boyfriend, I had no compelling reason
to go.

Ok, now I'm on to something here. I associate P.P. with a certain kind of woman,
of which I am not one. It's not even necessary that this imaginary woman be
beautiful, but she would be someone who has her bedroom done in matching patterns,
believes in window treatments, has coordinating clothes for workouts, and lives in a
new apartment. I see these women in the making in some of my students, the ones
that bring in their P.P. pictures to school and ask me which one is my favorite. The
other students in the class will flock around and ooh and ahhh and say how wonderful
this girl looks as I stand by and wonder just what the heck all this attention means.

There is something quite overwhelming to me about getting my picture taken. I cried
for five years straight growing up each time my parents assembled us in August to pose
for the annual Christmas card wearing our coordinating wool sweaters with our white dog.
My parents were out of town during my senior pictures, and to this day my mother
still laments how bad the shots are because she didn't get to pick out my outfit
or advise me on hair and make-up. What I remember about sorority pictures is pretty
limited, although I was one of the few girls that only had one half-way decent proof to
choose from. My tongue always poked out between my lips and my smile had a way of
sloping quite unattractively. My hair was always a crap shoot—would or wouldn't the
curls cooperate at that particular moment.

So for me to hear the woman behind the pharmacy counter tell me that she's
thinking of going to treat herself, I don't quite get it. It was my bunch of irises
that spurred her into sharing this with me. "I just want to do it, __
those pictures. I want to find a babysitter, have everything pos__
 then go out for the evening and have a great time. God, what__
myself encouraging this woman to do just that, giving her t__
short line" and all that other Hallmarky stuff. As I wal__
had a feminist dilemma on my hands. Part of me knew it w__
the physical appearance bit. Maybe I should have told he__
white grocery store uniform—that she would look just gre__
she believed it. But the other part of me thought, right__
and treat yourself. And if make-up and hairstyling and p__
gosh darn, you go right ahead. Inspires a muddle of thin__
strong emotions. I'd love to say that looking good doesn__
but it does. I choose to shape my look through exercise __
that's me. Where do I get off being holier than thou? Bu__
That combines two things that I can't stand.

> My assumptions, written
> before I began the research
> process. I "discovered" this
> on my disk late last
> week—interesting that I
> "forgot" about this. My
> dilemma about PP is evident
>   here.

PORTFOLIO

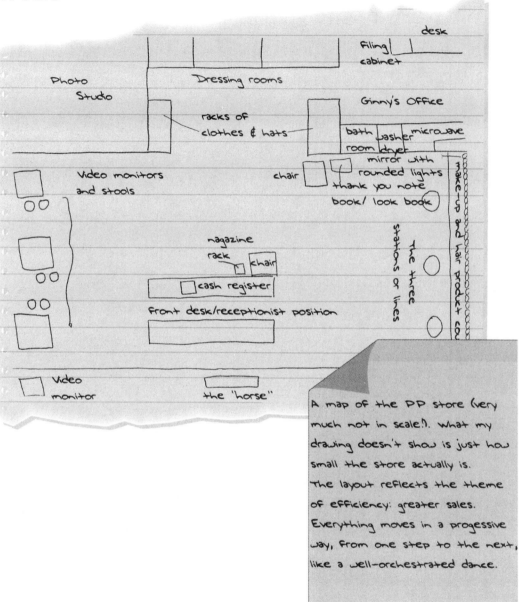

A map of the PP store (very much not in scale!). What my drawing doesn't show is just how small the store actually is.

The layout reflects the theme of efficiency: greater sales. Everything moves in a progressive way, from one step to the next, like a well-orchestrated dance.

CHECKLIST

HIGH FASHION PHOTOGRAPHY

HAVE YOU THOUGHT OF EVERYONE?

- *Husband* ☐
- *Wife* ☐
- *Mom* ☐
- *Dad* ☐
- *Grandparents* ☐
- *Children* ☐
- *Uncle* ☐
- *Aunt* ☐
- *Brother/Sister* ☐
- *Cousin* ☐
- *Friend* ☐
- *Boyfriend/Girlfriend* ☐
- *Wedding Attendants* ☐
- *Classmates* ☐
- *In-laws* ☐
- *You* ☐

REMEMBER THESE PHOTOGRAPH GIVING OCCASI...

Birthdays

Valenti...

Ch...

Anni...

We...

Grad...

Mother's Da...

Secret...

Tha...

Engagem...

...

Su...

Housewarming

A "needs" sheet from PP. The purpose is to have the customer begin thinking about buying photos right when she comes in for her appointment. "Suggestion selling in pretty pink." (A Ginny James quote.)

PORTFOLIO

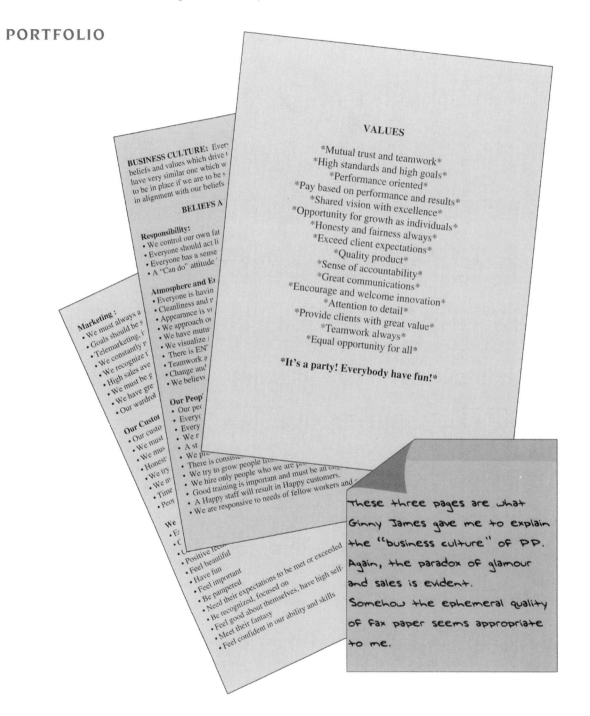

VALUES

Mutual trust and teamwork
High standards and high goals
Performance oriented
Pay based on performance and results
Shared vision with excellence
Opportunity for growth as individuals
Honesty and fairness always
Exceed client expectations
Quality product
Sense of accountability
Great communications
Encourage and welcome innovation
Attention to detail
Provide clients with great value
Teamwork always
Equal opportunity for all

It's a party! Everybody have fun!

BUSINESS CULTURE: Every
beliefs and values which drive
have very similar one which w
to be in place if we are to be s
in alignment with our beliefs

BELIEFS A

Responsibility:
• We control our own fat
• Everyone should act li
• Everyone has a sense
• A "Can do" attitude

Atmosphere and E
• Everyone is havin
• Cleanliness and r
• Appearance is ve
• We approach o
• We have mutu
• We visualize
• There is EN
• Teamwork
• Change and
• We believe

Our Peop
• Our pe
• Every
• Every
• We r
• A st
• We p
• There is consist
• We try to grow people fro
• We hire only people who we are pr
• Good training is important and must be an on
• A Happy staff will result in Happy customers.
• We are responsive to needs of fellow workers and c

Marketing :
• We must always a
• Goals should be s
• Telemarketing. i
• We constantly r
• We recognize t
• High sales ave
• We must be g
• We have gre
• Our wardrol

Our Custo
• Our custo
• We must
• We mus
• Honest
• We try
• We m
• Time
• Peo

We
• E
• C
• Positive reco
• Feel beautiful
• Have fun
• Feel important
• Be pampered
• Need their expectations to be met or exceeded
• Be recognized, focused on
• Feel good about themselves, have high self-
• Meet their fantasy
• Feel confident in our ability and skills

These three pages are what Ginny James gave me to explain the "business culture" of P.P. Again, the paradox of glamour and sales is evident. Somehow the ephemeral quality of fax paper seems appropriate to me.

Warning
Jenny Joseph

When I am an old woman I shall wear purple
With a red hat which doesn't go, and doesn't suit me.
And I shall spend my pension on brandy and summer gloves
And satin sandals, and say we've no money for butter.
I shall sit down on the pavement when I'm tired
And gobble up samples in shops and press alarm bells
And run my stick along the public railings
And make up for the sobriety of my youth.
I shall go out in my slippers in the rain
And pick the flowers in other people's gardens
And learn to spit.

You can wear terrible shirts and grow more fat
And eat three pounds of sausages at a go
Or only bread and pickle for a week
And hoard pens and pencils and beermats and things in boxes.

But now we must have clothes that keep us dry
And pay our rent and not swear in the street
And set a good example for the children.
We must have friends to dinner and read the papers.

But maybe I ought to practise a little now?
So people who knew me are not too shocked and surprised
When suddenly I am old, and start to wear purple.

A copy of a poem Ginny James had in her office. She had it next to her witch picture and her PP photo. The sentiment expressed in the poem seems so contrary to the PP philosophy. This is just one of the many paradoxes I encountered there.

PORTFOLIO

Questions for informants who have been to Photo Phantasies

1. How did you decide to go?

2. Who went with you?

3. How did you feel before the appointment?

4. Tell me about the process in the store—what parts did you like, dislike?

5. What did you talk about with the stylists?

6. What clothes did you pick out?

7. What was it like to have your picture taken?

8. Watching the video images, did you feel any pressure to make a purchase? Did you feel pressure before that?

9. Did you like the pictures?

10. How have you used the photos?

11. Would you go again?

The two interviews I did with informants who had been to PP gave me a feeling of control over the material. While I did ask all of these questions, the conversations with these two women really opened up and quickly became centered on much larger issues, like marriage and family.

transcription of a conversation with Mrs. Conway
place--her house on the east side of town
date and time--April 24, 1995 2:00 on Monday afternoon

I have never met Mrs. Conway before, but I know her daughter-in-law who is my mother's cleaning lady. I spoke with Mrs. Conway on the phone about setting up an interview time and she gave me directions to her house. When I arrived, the first thing she did was show me the photographs of her family members and tell me a little about each of them. In her description, she talked mainly about how each of them looked, what things she thought stood out about them physically. Mrs. Conway is 76 years old and has permed gray hair ("It's thick, feel it!"). She is wearing glasses with pink and green and blue flecks of color on blue frames. She offered me coffee and we began talking about how she decided to go to Photo Phantasies. Her husband had always wanted her to go to PP. Mrs. Conway saw that they were having a special and decided to go. Her husband drove her to the mall and waited for her in the store during the process.

K: So you went out without make-up on...
Mrs. C.:   Uh huh.
K: ...and you just washed your hair...
Mrs. C.:   Yes, I was petrified that someone might see me without my face on at the mall.
            Yep, I was walking around the mall without my face.
K: Ah!!
Mrs. C.:   And you know, they do your hair and your make-up.
K: So you got right in, and what did they do first? Hair?
Mrs. C.:   They do the make-up, I think. Here, do you want to see the pictures?
K: Absolutely!
            Mrs. C. gets up from the couch and walks into the kitchen. From the other room:
Mrs. C.:   Do you know Michael? (Her son.)
K: Yes, I love Mike. In fact Robin (her future daughter-in-law) told me that Mike has offered to give her and Joel $2,000 if they
            would elope to Las Vegas instead of having a wedding. That sounds like Mike...
Mrs. C.:   Oh, yes (still in the other room)
K: That sounds just like him.
            Mrs. C. returns to the living room and hands me two wallet size photos of the same PP. In the photographs, she is wearing a
            satiny pink drape around her shoulders, pearl earrings and a pearl necklace. Her make-up and hair looks much the same as it does
            today in her house.
K: Ah. These are gor-geee-ous!
Mrs. C.:   Thanks. (She giggles.)
K: Oh, my word!
Mrs. C.:   Boy, I'll tell you, they're expensive.
K: That's kind of what I thought, too.
Mrs. C.:   They are. Let me tell you, you don't get them for $14.95 like the ad promises.
K: That's sort of the trick. That price might get you in there, but that doesn't get you anything. Sure, you could walk away
            without ordering anything, but...
Mrs. C.:   Well, they snap a picture of everything that you have on, everything they put on you, and then they show you the pictures
            on one of those screens.
K: One of those video screens?
Mrs. C.:   A video screen. They put all these things on you. Finally after they tried a bunch of
            I asked for something to be put on me that is pastel?"
K: Where they doing you up in glitter?
Mrs. C.:   Everything. Cowgirl, hats...
K: Cowgirl?
Mrs. C.:   ...gloves, but...it wasn't me.
K: So you didn't get to pick your clothes?
Mrs. C.:   No, I only asked for something soft and feminine and pastel.
K: And these are absolutely perfect. How about the jewelry? Did you do
Mrs. C.:   No, they did that.
K: Are these the only ones that you bought?
Mrs. C.:   I bought eight so the kids could each have one.
K: So you didn't but any with the dangly stuff?
Mrs. C.:   No, I just went for that one cause...It's me, more me.
K: Yeh, that's what you want.
Mrs. C.:   It's me.

A copy of my transcript from a conversation with Mrs. Conway. This was the only time I was able to use a tape recorder when gathering information. I like re-reading this. It reminds me of how affirming I am about her pictures. It shows a real genuine connection to her.

PORTFOLIO

Composing An Image: After
-describe store
-contrast with descrip. of office
-Ginny mixed me[...]
        - selling v[...]
        - artists
        - create
        - custom
        - phone

Playing Your Par[...]
-describe sales v[...]
-describe employ[...]
-describe thank [...]
-describe staff m[...]

Putting On Your [...]
        -interview
        -me

map of pp
make-over pic.
Vogue cover

Talking with customers. M/F managers.
Bright star stores.
Ads in paper-rigorous test taking
Process, references, 90 days prob.
All in white.
Extensive training now-prob. in the
past
"On-board" since Feb. 6. Asst. buyer
for Yonkers, worked at MH- more
than selling underwear. Wanted to
give something back to society.
Worked at Science center Shop-
Turned it around.
Christmas w/5 kids-3 step and
marriage.
-How the phone is answered.
-Party atmosphere.
"Not hype."
Artists.
My eye color is my best feature.
Mother-daughter. Look at features.
Ancestral pictures.
"I see my mother"-grateful to
age that way. She's beautiful.

One of my many organizational
attempts done throughout the
"writing up" process. I've
included this as a reminder of
how a researcher shapes her
text.

Not even two months, yet she acts
so confident, knowledgeable

What? making people feel better
about themselves?

This is a treat, special occasion
Oh really? What about the handout
on the closest door which seemed
to suggest that compliments sell.

I blush. Feel embarrassed and
flattered. "I could do such good
things w/those eyes."

emphasis on photos as keepsake

That's a selling pt. in their eyes. How
Ginny felt when she saw her pictures.

A collage of words from the fashion magazines I look at. This shows my lookist side. Ahh!

I know I shouldn't enjoy all this—the ole feminist voice comes out—but I do love the self-indulgent quality of these magazines.

A Pose on "Strike a Pose"

Karen Downing

When I think back over this research process, I'm reminded of something Professor Richard Horwitz said when he spoke to our class. About selecting subjects for ethnography, Horwitz advised, "Think about an experience that is really moving to you, an experience that brings out strong conflicting emotions, possibly within yourself, possibly in relation to yourself and others." That, in a pithy quote, is just what Photo Phantasies is for me.

When I started this project, I was very smug and haughty about PP. I scoffed at the notion, and I scoffed at the women who swallowed the absurd "model for a day" rhetoric PP featured in their ads. I was out to prove myself right. I had a heck of a time gaining access to the kind of information I thought I both wanted and needed. From the beginning, I felt off balance and not in control when dealing with Ginny James, the manager of the PP store at the Forum West Mall. But as the research process went on, I learned that the story I was getting—restricted access and all—was indeed a story, and a very compelling one at that. I was amazed by the conflicting messages embedded in the PP dogma, like saying "customer service" when they actually mean "things we need to do to increase sales." I could laugh at the videos, roll my eyes at some of the things the receptionist said about being an artist, and sit in the corner at the staff in-service meeting furiously scribbling away in my journal. But as soon as I started talking with women, women who either wanted to go to PP or who had experienced PP, I was surprised by my reaction. Not only could I understand their desire to go; I found myself championing their desires and validating their experiences after very brief conversations with them. When I stepped back from my initial stance, I began to see PP as a way for women to treat themselves. Not *my* way, but *a* way. I started thinking about the things I do to treat myself—haircuts and a gym membership and new exercise clothes—and had to admit to the level of vanity and indulgence inherent in my own choices.

The PP topic was so full of metaphors. Early on, it became easy for me to see how the metaphors could shape my text. And not surprisingly, the metaphors I came up with seemed applicable to the paradoxes within myself as well as within PP. So the outsider was an insider, and before I knew it, the lines started intersecting all over the place, just like the metaphors. That's probably because the culture of PP could be viewed as a microcosm for a much larger female culture, something I'm naturally a part of, like it or not.

If I had more time with this project, there are other areas I'd want to explore. I would do more readings and interviews on the subject of beauty. What little reading I did made me all the more curious about other sources and other ideas. I would interview women of diverse backgrounds who had been to PP. That way, I would have a more complete picture than any two interviews provided. Believe it or not, I now feel like I could go for the PP experience. (Easy to say after the project is turned in!) It wasn't until I talked with Robin and Norma that I began to feel I could handle immersing myself that completely in the culture, photo session and all. (Mind you, it would only be for the sake of the project!) Finally, I would want more time to simply "look at my fish." Because my research took a while, I found I had very little time to let all of this soak in. Consequently, my final few pages of my piece, which I view as very important, feel tacked on and not as insightful as I would like. In truth, though, PP touches on some issues I could spend a lifetime sorting out and still never be satisfied with the insight I have.

FieldWriting: The Grammar of Observation

As a fieldwriter, your job is to describe your site as accurately as you can, combining your informants' perspectives with your own. Writers in other genres, like William Least Heat-Moon and Jamaica Kincaid, can create place descriptions based on their own spatial gazes, influenced by their political perspectives and their personal passions. Kincaid writes as a colonized islander, with an antagonistic stance toward the British influence over her culture. Heat-Moon records with a travel writer's gaze, pointing his readers to overlooked markers in the American landscape. For both of these writers of nonfiction, their responsibility was to render their versions of reality—of that place and its people—for their readers.

But the fieldwriter has a double responsibility. You must represent your own perspective at the same time you are representing your informants' perspectives of the fieldsite. And through reflection, you must discuss your role as constructor of this doubled version of reality. Karen, for example, enters Photo Phantasies with a cynical attitude toward the glamour industry. But as she takes fieldnotes, she records her informants' enthusiastic perspectives, and in the end, her fieldwork documents her own changed attitude toward beauty photography. Neither Kincaid nor Heat-Moon conducted fieldwork, and although both writers make us feel intimately connected with the places they write about, neither is trying to write ethnographically. For this reason, Kincaid, for example, doesn't need to interview her father to get his perspective on his brown felt hat or her mother about her big English breakfasts. But Karen Downing, as a fieldwriter, is responsible for representing the Photo Phantasies customers, for including their spatial gazes along with her own.

Fieldwriting places special demands on us as writers. We write on the basis of our collected data—our fieldnotes, expanded versions of them, and reflections about them. When we assemble and draft our final researched account, we revise it many times because fieldwriting, like all writing, is a recursive process. But fieldwriters must return often to their evidence—fieldnotes, transcripts, artifacts, reflections—to verify the account. For example, you may have noticed that many words and phrases Karen jotted into her fieldnotes appear in her final paper. Throughout our drafts, we must be aware of the words we choose. The special demand of fieldwriting is that descriptive material must have corresponding verification in the data. That's why it's called field research.

Over the years, as we and our students have conducted research, we've developed some strategies specific to fieldwriting, what we call the "grammar of observation." Here are a few ways we help our students revise their fieldprojects, based on working with four elementary parts of speech.

Nouns

Fieldwriters write from an abundance of detail, making lists in their fieldnotes of actual people, places, and things that both they and their informants observe. Sometimes these lists appear in a final text, such as Myerhoff's description of Venice, California, from the benches where the seniors sit:

> Surfers, sunbathers, children, dogs, bicyclists, winos, hippies, voyeurs, photographers, panhandlers, artists, junkies, roller skaters, peddlers, and police are omnipresent all year round. Every social class, age, race, and sexual preference is represented. Jesus cults, Hare Krishna parades, sidewalk preachers jostle steel bands and itinerant musicians.

But more often, fieldwriters cull such lists for strong, telling nouns that will organize a description or provide a focal point. Karen Downing focused on the "horse" outside Photo Phantasies, Myerhoff on the benches, Glassie on the hearth. And in Kincaid's nonfiction essay, she used the same technique with her description of the map of England. A focal point is often a noun, a concrete object in the informants' space that represents even more than it actually is. A focal point can serve as a metaphor, a frame to set off more complex cultural themes. The horse outside Photo Phantasies "took the customers for a ride," Myerhoff's benches held the elderly at the boundary between their outside and inside worlds, and Glassie's hearth was a space for storytelling and music-making among neighbors. An effective fieldwriter searches through fieldnotes to identify important nouns that hold cultural meanings in those spaces and uses them to write up the research study. Sometimes these nouns are also metaphors—like the horse, the benches, and the hearth—that can be linked to larger cultural themes.

Verbs

Strong verbs assist all writers because they bring action to the page. A strong verb can capture motion in one word. From the list *walk, saunter, lumber, dart, toddle, slither, sneak, clomp, traipse, schlep, dawdle,* and *pace, walk* is obviously the weakest but the one that would most readily come to mind. Forcing yourself to find the right verb makes you look more closely at the action in your fieldsite so that you can describe it. Finding the right verb makes you a more accurate field-writer. But finding the right verb may not happen until you've drafted and redrafted.

In many passages of this book, we struggled to use lively verbs that would pace our writing and free it of clutter. For instance, in the opening of this chapter, we replaced ordinary verbs with stronger ones like *bend, stuff, filter, select, evoke, recall, slap, transport,* and *retrieve.* Sometimes we even invented verbs, as when we used *junked* to describe Elizabeth's drafting process at the end of Chapter 1.

As we wrote, we alerted ourselves to passive verb forms and reworked those sentences. For example, one sentence included two passive verb constructions: "The spatial gaze *is enhanced* by the fieldworker's ability *to have been taught* to be a good observer." Our polished version was shorter and moved forward: "The spatial gaze demands that we look—and then look back again." Cleaning your sentence of verb clutter is actually a challenging task.

Try what we call a "verb pass." Scan through your text, and highlight or circle the tired, flabby, and overused verbs that flatten prose. Most often, these are forms of the verb *be* or passive voice constructions. Excise these with no remorse. Substitute more precise and more interesting verbs to describe the actions you've observed. Haul the action forward with active, not passive, verbs. Locate focal points, metaphors, and cultural themes in your data to get ideas for new verb choices. For example, when we wrote about Karen's image of the Photo Phantasies "horse" and her idea that it "took customers for a ride," we couldn't resist adding that the horse was ready to "rope in" its customers and "tie up" the transactions.

Adjectives and Adverbs

Cultural assumptions can hide inside the adjectives and adverbs you use. When you write "The dinner table was arranged *beautifully*" or "The *perky* dog greeted me with a *frenzied* lick" or "The *very sultry* atmosphere was *warm and friendly*" or "The *dull, dirty* apartment was crammed with *cheap blue* pottery," the qualifying words convey value judgments that are not verifiable because they belong to you. As a fieldwriter, let your reader make the judgment from the material you present. And let your informants and your other data contribute that material.

Karen Downing is a high school English teacher and a student of writing herself working toward her Master of Fine Arts degree in nonfiction. She found fieldwriting challenging because she wrote—and she taught her students to write—with lots of adjectives and adverbs to add color and "texture." When she realized that fieldwriters must question each qualifier they use, she knew she'd need to pay particular attention to how she wrote about Photo Phantasies. As you can see, her study offers very sharp and close observations, which are expressed with strong nouns and verbs. She reserved her assumptions and value judgments for portions of the paper devoted to discussing them.

With Karen's permission, we have altered a portion of her study, in which she describes Ginny James's office, by stuffing adjectives and adverbs into her clean sentences. We loaded up these paragraphs to show how a writer can bury attitudes under adjectives and adverbs. To see how qualifiers impose a researcher's value judgments and hide cultural assumptions, compare our versions of her description with Karen's on page 255. Each of our versions emphasizes a different set of assumptions.

Version 1

Underneath Ginny's untidy desk, there are five bulging purses of varying sizes, from sleek, expensive leather clutches to cheap plastic bags. I gather from this backstage mess that the disorganized people who mechanically work here also need to use Ginny's sleazy office for their unprofessional belongings. On the top of Ginny's trashy desk, there are sloppy stacks of paper and torn notebooks and curled Post-it notes and a noisy, out-of-date, obsolete fax machine. She has her own ridiculously posed Photo Phantasies photograph, taken hurriedly, with her wearing a yellowed straw hat and a faded denim jacket with garish sunflowers embroidered haphazardly on the collar. Right beside this tacky photograph is a picture of an old haggy witch complete with bent broom and a wicked scraggly black cat.

Version 2

Underneath Ginny's meticulous desk, there are five neatly arranged purses of varying sizes, organized carefully from large to small. I gather that the efficient, tidy people who cheerfully work here need to use Ginny's neat office for their modest personal belongings, too. On the top of Ginny's antique cherry desk, there are straight stacks of brightly colored paper and well-organized matching burgundy notebooks and recently purchased Post-it notes and a quiet, understated fax machine. She has her own sedately posed Photo Phantasies photograph, taken carefully with her wearing a jaunty straw hat and an imported denim jacket with delicate sunflowers hand-embroidered on the dainty collar. Right beside this elegant photograph is a picture of a spiritual witch, complete with hand-crafted broom and a sleek, assured black cat.

The grammar of observation is really just the grammar of good writing: strong specific nouns, accurate active verbs, and adjectives and adverbs that add texture without masquerading cultural bias. All writers face a responsibility to bring their observations—as they see them—to the page. But fieldwriters face a doubled ethical challenge: to translate their informants' voices and perspectives for their readers yet still acknowledge their own presence in the text. This challenge requires careful observation, focused selection and verification of detail, and a deep awareness of the role of the self in writing about the other.

FIELDWORDS

Colonization The takeover of less powerful people by more powerful people who demand conformity to their group's ideas and values, as in a territory ruled or annexed by another country.

Dominate To control, govern, or rule.

Ethnocentrism Assuming one's own perspective is natural and accepting it as the norm rather than challenging one's own values and belief systems.

Focal point A central place in the fieldsite where ideas, artifacts, or people converge. A focal point can sometimes provide a guide for writing fieldstudies.

Mainstream The prevailing or dominant influence within a culture.

Marginalization The process of pushing nonmainstream people toward the edges of society to prevent their access to power.

Perception The taking in of information, observing, or understanding by means of the senses.

Perspective A point of view; an angle of vision (the "spatial gaze," the "ethnographic ear").

FIELDREADING

Baldwin, James. "Stranger in the Village." *Notes of a Native Son.* Boston: Beacon, 1955.

Glassie, Henry. *Passing the Time in Ballymenone: Culture and History of an Ulster Community.* Philadelphia: U Pennsylvania P, 1982.

Goffman, Erving. *Behavior in Public Places.* New York: Free, 1963.

Guterson, David. "Enclosed. Encyclopedia. Endured. One Week at the Mall of America." *Harper's* (Aug. 1993): 49–56.

Heat-Moon, William Least. *Blue Highways.* New York: Little Brown, 1999.

hooks, bell. "Choosing the Margin as a Space for Radical Openness." *Yearning: Race and Gender in the Cultural Marketplace.* Boston: South End, 1990.

Horwitz, Richard P. *The Strip: An American Place.* Lincoln: U Nebraska P, 1985.

Jacobs, Jane. "The Use of Sidewalks: Control." *Death and Life of Great American Cities.* New York: Random, 1961.

Lopez, Barry. "Losing Our Sense of Place." *Teacher Magazine* (Feb. 1990): 38–44.

Marshall, Paule. *The Chosen Place, The Timeless People.* New York: Vintage, 1992.

Moore, Alexander. "Walt Disney World: Bounded Ritual Space and the Playful Pilgrimage Center." *Anthropological Quarterly* 53.4 (1980): 207–18.

Morris, Desmond. "Territorial Behavior." *Manwatching. A Field Guide to Human Behavior.* New York: Abrams, 1977.

Morris, Mary. *Nothing to Declare: Memoirs of a Woman Traveling Alone.* Boston: Houghton, 1988.

Myerhoff, Barbara. *Number Our Days.* New York: Touchstone-Simon, 1978.

Naipul, V. S. *A Turn in the South.* New York: Knopf, 1989.

Rose, Dan. *Black American Street Life: South Philadelphia, 1969–1971.* Philadelphia: U Pennsylvania P, 1987.

Stack, Carol B. *All Our Kin: Strategies for Survival in a Black Community.* New York: Harper, 1974.

Stoller, Paul. *The Taste of Ethnographic Things: The Senses in Anthropology.* Philadelphia: U Pennsylvania P, 1989.

Whyte, William Foote. *Street Corner Society: The Social Structure of an Italian Slum.* 4th ed. Chicago: U Chicago P, 1993.

FIELDPOEM

Scouting

Philip Levine

I'm the man who gets off the bus
at the bare junction of nothing
with nothing, and then heads back
to where we've been as though
the future were stashed somewhere
in that tangle of events we call
"Where I come from." Where I
came from the fences ran right
down to the road, and the lone woman
leaning back on her front porch as she
quietly smoked asked me what did
I want. Confused as always, I
answered, "Water," and she came to me
with a frosted bottle and a cup,
shook my hand, and said, "Good luck."
That was forty years ago, you say,
when anything was possible. No,
it was yesterday, the gray icebox
sat on the front porch, the crop
was tobacco and not yet in, you
could hear it sighing out back.

The rocker gradually slowed as
she came toward me but never
stopped and the two of us went on
living in time. One of her eyes
had a pale cast and looked nowhere
or into the future where without
regrets she would give up the power
to grant life, and I would darken
like wood left in the rain and then
fade into only a hint of the grain.
I went higher up the mountain
until my breath came in gasps,
my sight darkened, and I slept
to the side of the road to waken
chilled in the sudden July cold,
alone and well. What is it like
to come to, nowhere, in darkness,
not knowing who you are, not
caring if the wind calms, the stars
stall in their sudden orbits,
the cities below go on without
you, screaming and singing?
I don't have the answer. I'm
scouting, getting the feel
of the land, the way the fields
step down the mountainsides
hugging their battered, sagging
wire fences to themselves as though
both day and night they needed
to know their limits. Almost still,
the silent dogs wound into sleep,
the gray cabins breathing steadily
in moonlight, tomorrow wakening
slowly in the clumps of mountain oak
and pine where streams once ran
down the little white rock gullies.
You can feel the whole country
wanting to waken into a child's dream,
you can feel the moment reaching
back to contain your life and forward
to whatever the dawn brings you to.
In the dark you can love this place.

From What Work Is

Commentary
by Stacy Clovis

The poet writes of the necessity of limitless sight, for where he comes from has been a place of limits, as fences and roads have been designated as the boundaries of *how* and *what* he sees. There is the tension of unfulfilled sight, especially when the woman in her rocking chair asks him what he wants, to which water is the reply. A connection can be made between the boundless element of water and the pure nature of seeing. Even though the actual landscape is etched in such a way that the land itself is conscious of its own boundaries, the author is able to see beyond such designation. The poet seems to realize that to "see" he must go higher up the mountain to where he awakens in darkness and finds that he no longer knows himself as he once did, nor does he care for all that once maintained his attentions. He places himself in an unspecific nowhere, yet he transforms the darkness into a place that it is possible for him to love, for even his conception of darkness has changed. He has learned that scouting is much more than gathering information about a place; it is a way of erasing one's original limits.

This chapter suggests many of the same ideas, for as fieldworkers we must widen our perspectives when entering a fieldsite. A researcher is required to step outside of familiar territory into an unfamiliar and perhaps unsettling landscape. At the same time, we as ethnographic researchers also have a spatial gaze that is formed by our backgrounds, cultural assumptions, or biases. This spatial gaze involves the outward looking into the landscape or fieldsite but also the inward reflective gaze into oneself and the elements that have shaped our personal understanding of our surroundings, even if they be unfamiliar to us. We take our own personal geographies into our fieldsites, and these should be viewed as a starting place for further discoveries to be made about ourselves and those we have chosen to observe and study. The ethnographic eye absorbs much more than merely visual images; it gathers information about relationships, including the layout of the fieldsite, the informants who inhabit this place, and the ways in which both affect one another. As fieldworkers, we have the dual responsibility of accurately presenting our own perspectives as well as the informants' views. This can be seen as a unified perspective because the limits of one become erased when entering the limits of another.

Stacy Clovis has recently graduated with her MFA in poetry from the University of North Carolina at Greensboro. She has plans to continue teaching, writing, and pursuing the horizon line.

CHAPTER 6

Researching Language: The Cultural Translator

…The simple act of listening is crucial to the concept of language, more crucial even than reading and writing, and language in turn is crucial to human society. There is proof of that, I think, in all the histories and prehistories of human experience.

—N. SCOTT MOMADAY

It is difficult to realize how language both shapes and reflects our culture because it's so intrinsic to our everyday lives. As Scott Momaday reminds us, listening is a crucial skill that both builds and binds cultures. This chapter is about listening to language and translating what it has to say about culture. You'll read, write, and research language and language events—the use of words in everyday talk. You'll also research more formal oral "performances": jokes, stories, sayings, and legends.

Although some **linguists** claim that there is no thought without language, we think much of daily life moves along *without* the language of *words*. The visual and musical arts, dance and athletics, and scientific notation are all examples of nonverbal languages with which we communicate. Fieldworkers notice and record a culture's *nonverbal* languages in an attempt to learn more about the people they study. But they depend on *verbal* language as an intricate tool for at least three purposes. First, as a tool for the mind, verbal language brings nonverbal thoughts to the surface of consciousness. Second, for some fieldworkers, language becomes the topic of their research, illustrating how a culture shares knowledge through words. Finally, because researchers write, language provides them with the means to communicate knowledge about others.

Language, then, shapes the thoughts in your mind, can provide a subject for your research, and communicates your ideas to others. This tool we call language is equipped with a kind of filter. It filters out cultural specifics, keeping outsiders away from understanding. You've probably felt outside the range of some groups' languages: musicians, nurses, computer technicians, and athletes are just a few examples of groups that talk their own insider language.

In the same way, a language can clarify a culture for the insiders, reminding them of their membership. Institutional language, for example, provides insider communication among people who work for the company. Without knowing it, a college uses terms to construct the insider business of being a student, and it filters that role from outsiders. The terms *credit hours, drop-adds, GPA, major,* and *minor* are more than a familiar vocabulary; they form a set of terms displaying insider membership in the subculture of academics. And as students know, these terms are all but incomprehensible to the outsider hearing them for the first time. When taking a general education course, you're introduced to the vocabulary of that field. In a music appreciation course, for example, you learn new meanings for familiar words: *score, signature, beat, measure, repeat.*

As you pay attention to the way language serves as a tool with an insider-outsider filter, you'll learn about your informants' perspectives. Listening to language will help you move further inside a culture and become intimate with it. You'll introduce yourself to a subculture as you describe its settings, daily events, and behaviors and learn more by examining its histories and artifacts. But it's not until you listen to and record its language that you'll become familiar enough to understand the connection of language to a culture's way of being. Even though you are using your own language to capture your informants' language, your job is to listen for theirs. You serve, in a way, as a cultural translator, always placing the insider's perspective in the foreground and your outsider's perspective in the background.

RESEARCHING LANGUAGE: LINKING BODY AND CULTURE

Your earliest attempts at recording and questioning the language of informants will probably involve description of their *body language* and reflection on it. When we think about human expression, we often think first, and perhaps only, of speech. But fieldworkers often learn early in their work that speech, or verbal communication, is only one of several modes that communicate individual and collective meaning about a culture. Early in his study of truckers (see Chapter 1), Rick Zollo felt the significance of body language. Asking questions of Morris, a lease operator of his own rig, Rick sensed he had asked one question too many. In his final project Rick writes, "The question of time raised Morris's suspicions again, and instead of answering, he fixed me with a hard gaze. Sensing I had crossed some invisible boundary, I thanked him for his time. Obviously, my question related to logbook procedures, and I made a mental note to avoid that type of inquiry."

By being attentive to body language, Rick realized his intrusion and backed off, respecting Morris's need for privacy. At the same time, Rick made mental notes that deepened his understanding of his subject. The sooner and the more sensitively you discover, interpret, and use the nonverbal conventions of the culture you're studying, the more successful you'll be.

Since the 1950s, anthropologists, folklorists, linguists, and rhetoricians have contributed much to our understanding of the body as a means of nonverbal expression. With Ray Birdwhistell's 1952 *Introduction to Kinesics,* researchers began to study body communication (kinesics)—how individuals express themselves through body position and motion (facial expression, eye contact, posture, and gesture). Of course, we all engage in the study of **kinesics** informally, particularly in college classrooms, when we notice someone who slumps over her desk, puts her feet on another chair, or refuses to make eye contact with others. Still other researchers extended the study of individual body communication to **proxemics**—how individuals communicate nonverbally when in groups. Members of sports teams are experts at proxemics, communicating meaning constantly with their bodies as they strategize together throughout a game. And so do the fans watching from the stands. If you have ever entered an unfamiliar coffeehouse or bar, you may find yourself startled by how people use that public space to send messages. There is a stance that some men and women adopt that means they are "available." No words are used, but the meaning is communicated as clearly as if they were wearing signs. On airplanes, people signal whether they want to talk to their seat companions or remain silent merely by the way they hold a book or a folder. And there is an unspoken set of rules that govern the use of an automatic cash machine: the person next in line stands at a respectful distance to signal that he cannot see numbers you enter. If you have ever ventured into a culture to find yourself startled by unfamiliar uses of personal or public space, you know the significant role that body language plays in human expression.

Through the physical display of our bodies to others, we signal not only who we are but also who we are in relation to those who "read" us. The body is not just a physical object; it is a social object. For this reason, studying how your informants dress or adorn their bodies and how they use them will tell you much about how they see themselves and their cultures. In Jake's participation with the skinheads (Chapter 3), one of the most obvious features that linked this group together was that every member of the group had a shaved head. This common marking for skinheads, Jake discovered, meant that they did not want their membership to be secret or underground.

Understanding the language of the body can come about in at least two ways. First, you can document body language in fieldnotes (this is better than waltzing up to informants and asking questions that will leave you sorry and them feeling awkward or abused). Second, early in your fieldwork, you might decide to observe and describe how members of the culture adorn their bodies—features of clothing, accessories, and body decoration (like makeup, tattoos, piercings, and hairstyles). Rick Zollo's study of the truck drivers in Chapter 1 considered the "cowboy" dress of truckers and how that shaped their image of themselves.

Of course, one way to build reflexivity into your fieldnotes is to consider your own body in relation to the people you study. What sense do you get of their perceptions of your adornment? What, in terms of body language, is the relationship of self and other? In the study she titled "Strike a Pose" (see Chapter 5), Karen Downing reflected on her own makeup habits as she prepared to meet the manager of Photo Phantasies. Her thoughts were prompted by the prospect of being in the gaze of a differently constructed group of women and led her to hear her mother's voice inside her head.

From an initial focus on adornment, you might next begin to consider a person's body as a kinesic form of expression. Reflect on the patterns of movement you observe and what these patterns communicate, not just to outsiders (in this case, you) but also to other members of the culture—to the insiders. Had Karen Downing spent a bit more time reading the body language of her informants at Photo Phantasies, she would have additional data, information that might help us understand to what degree employees of the store "buy into" the images they sell. And if Karen had posed for Photo Phantasies herself, she might have added another dimension of feeling about herself in that space.

Finally, you might broaden your study of the body to consider how the people you study share and possess space. In other words, what do you notice about the proxemics of the culture? In Chapter 5, we discussed the importance of describing spaces. Now we hope you can discover strategies that will help you document how your informants inhabit space. As you take fieldnotes and reflect on them, you may come to discover underlying reasons why people in the location you've chosen move and communicate as they do. Perhaps these reasons have something to do with informants' "fixed positions" (gender, race, class, or age); perhaps they do not. Elizabeth's longest fieldstudy, a book called *Academic Literacies,* shows one of her informants, Nick, a college student, as he stretches himself over three chairs when he works in a writing group with three women— a kind of defense against them because he was afraid they would assault his text. And it was a "male thing" to take more space than was allotted to him. Had she not noticed this silent body language, Elizabeth might have never discovered this important dimension of Nick's work with his female peers.

As an interpreter of body language, your job as fieldworker is to discover not just what bodies say but why they say what they do. Another way, of course, to elicit information about body language is to ask informants themselves. Keep in mind that questions about body language require a good deal of rapport, particularly if your informant (or the culture) views the body as a taboo subject. But if it strikes you that an informant might ponder your questions without taking offense, think about the observations and ask for an insider's perspective. For instance, Elizabeth, merely by asking Nick, "Why did you need three chairs?" learned a lot about how he felt having three women read drafts of his writing. If your informant is willing to think consciously about his or her adornment, movement, and use of space, you will have a wonderful opportunity to test and revise your thinking.

RESEARCHING LANGUAGE: LINKING WORD AND CULTURE

Listening to the spoken language of your informant is an important way to learn about a culture. One key word, like one key piece of clothing or a gesture, can unlock information about the habits and beliefs, geography and history of a whole group of people. Your job as a fieldworker is to act as a cultural translator, recording and questioning the meanings of key words, phrases, and ideas that might serve as clues to "step in" to your informant's culture.

A fieldworker questioning our colleague Danling Fu, who grew up in the People's Republic of China, might be astonished to discover the array of Chinese words for silk. There are over 20 words that refer to how silk is made: words that denote shininess, smoothness, thickness, weight, and purity. Learning that there are so many silk words would be a signal to a fieldworker to investigate more about the cultural significance of silk. As Danling's friends, we knew only two things: that there were many words for silk in Chinese and that she had kept pet silkworms as a child. We wanted to see how these two facts might show us more about Chinese culture, so we interviewed her as a fieldworker would. We indicate our research strategies in italics.

B&E: Were you unusual, or do all Chinese children keep pet silkworms?
(We wanted to start with what we knew—that she had a pet silkworm when she was a child.)

D: Our relationship with worms is like yours with cats and dogs. I grew up in Jiangsu province, a silk-producing place, and all children kept silkworms. Every family does it. The full name we use is "baby silkworms." We care for them, keep them clean, learn to hold them tenderly, and watch the whole life cycle process.

B&E: How do you care for them?
(Although we were looking for language—words and stories—we wanted to give her time to remember details about keeping silkworms. We also wanted to hear more about the process because we knew that would illustrate more about the whole culture.)

D: In early spring, we put eggs—thousands of little eggs, laid by the silk moth the year before—on little squares of paper in a shoebox. We put them in the sun for warmth. Sometimes we start them in school, like American children grow seeds in paper cups or chick eggs in incubators. Eventually, a worm hatches—so tiny, so black, smaller than an ant. As the leaves come out, we feed them to the little worms. Day by day, we watch them grow bigger, as thick as a little finger, in different shades of white and black.

B&E: Do children compete over how many silkworms they have?
(We wondered if Chinese children keep pet silkworms, whether they have rules for ownership, if they trade or have contests, and if that would suggest anything more about the culture itself. We weren't prepared for her answer, because our thinking was so American, so based on our sense of competition.)

D: Yes, but only because we all want a few to live so we can care for them. They eat a lot of leaves, and we don't have enough of them. In cities, families protect their trees because children steal each other's leaves. Sometimes I would buy extra leaves from farmers to feed my worms. Each year, if I had a ten percent survival rate, I would consider it a victory.

B&E: So where does the silk come in? What do you do with the silk?
(The discussion was beginning to move in a different direction. We wanted to know about silk; she wanted to talk about keeping pets. We tried to redirect it.)

D: Until their last moment of life, they produce silk. These worms are hard workers, a good image for Chinese people. When they are ready to build the cocoon in the summer, they become transparent—they look like the silk itself. And we build little hills for them with straw. The cocoons are red and pink and yellow—so beautiful on the straw hills. My mother used them as decorations in the house.

B&E: But then what? How do you get the silk out of the cocoon?
(It was fun to visualize those little straw mountains with the colorful cocoons. But we hoped that she'd describe a very specific cultural practice there, that it might lead to more interesting insider knowledge. She did, and it did.)

D: We put the cocoon in hot water. And then we pull out a silk thread, very carefully. You wouldn't believe how long it is. One cocoon makes one very long silk thread—yards and yards of silk. We wrap it around a bamboo chopstick, and then we have the thread to play with.

B&E: Do you play games with the silk thread? Weave with it?
(The silk thread and bamboo pole sounded like the beginning of a children's game. Would children's games tell us more about the culture? Again we were biased by our own culture and surprised at her answer.)

D: Not really. It's only just a part of watching the whole process and learning about life and production. Life and productivity are the main parts of our culture. Such a little body, so much hard work. It just gives and gives and gives until the moment it dies. You know, we use every part of the process.

B&E: What do you mean by "every part of the process"?
(Her answer takes an interesting direction. Games with silk aren't as important to her as learning about the life cycle and how production is tied to life.)

D: Well, besides the silk, we watch the males and females produce the eggs together. We even use the waste. We dry it and stuff pillows. We eat the cocoon.

B&E: Yuk! Ugh! Are you kidding? You eat the cocoon?
(We laughed as we teased our friend. We recognized our own assumptions about acceptable food and saw that the message was still tied to productivity—the Chinese don't want to waste anything).

D: Yep. It's good. We deep-fry the inside. Tastes like a peanut.

B&E: So the silkworm is a pet, but you use so much of it to learn about other things.

(We wanted to see what other insider cultural information might come when we asked what they learned from keeping these pets.)

D: The worm is so soft, so tender. That's why we call it "baby silkworm"; we learn to care for it like a baby. These worms live really clean lives. We change the papers and the boxes. We scrape the leaves and the waste when we feed them. We need cheap pets you know, in China. We cannot feed them our food like you do with your pets because we don't even have enough for ourselves.

(Without realizing it, she offers an important insight—that Chinese pets must not threaten human needs but must offer children a chance to learn about life.)

B&E: So children learn about the life cycle with these pets? And you have all those words about how silk is made: texture, shininess, thickness, weight. It's about life and production, as you said?

(We wanted to summarize what we had already heard her say, reemphasize why we interviewed her to begin with, and offer her an opportunity to elaborate, hoping we'd hear more about how silk and silkworms figure into Chinese language. We were hoping for more, but we couldn't force it.)

D: Yes, we have a children's song. It says "Be faithful. Even when you die, you can still contribute without taking anything. Like a silkworm." The silkworm gives us songs, metaphors, and images of our culture.

(Aha, a song! The song holds many of the very values she's been describing: economy, production, collaboration, and the cycle of life. And she recognizes it as she tells us.)

B&E: Wow, all those images of production. Bet that worked well during the Cultural Revolution.

(We knew Danling had been a teenager during the Cultural Revolution.)

D: *(laughs)* Yes, there are a lot of revolutionary songs with silkworms in them.

(If it had a song, would a culture that keeps silkworms and has many words for silk also have other forms of "verbal art"—stories, proverbs, and the like—that revealed its beliefs? She was telling us more about exactly what we wanted to know. This was exciting data.)

B&E: Are there any legends or proverbs about silkworms?

D: Well, not proverbs, exactly, but there are many stories. There's an image-story like "The Tortoise and the Hare." We say that to get something done with patience and consistency, it's like a silkworm, eating a leaf bit by bit, little by little. That little mouth eats so quietly, so fast. Overnight it can consume so many leaves.

(Ah, a relevant saying: to live a productive life takes patience and consistency. A cultural truth with a silkworm as the main character.)

B&E: And are there other sayings about the silk itself?

D: A silk thread, when it's in a cocoon, is so long, so intricate, so soft, and so tangled. It is difficult to figure out where the beginning is and where the end is. When we have a complicated problem, we say we are "tangled by a silk thread."

(And the silk thread even figures into explaining problems—another indicator of its importance in the culture.)

B&E: So there's the silkworm as a pet and so many words about silk. Language and learning and life.

(She was really remembering, and we didn't want to stop or redirect her line of thought. But we wanted her to know we were interested. So we offered another summary. Her own lovely statement summarizes—from her own perspective—better than we ever could from ours.)

D: With silkworms, we see the whole process. We see how silk comes into our lives—not only how we wear it, but how we live with it.

This interview taught us much about Chinese culture—not only how Chinese wear silk, as Danling put it, but also how they "live with it." Two key words that were far more important in her language than in ours, *silk* and *silkworm*, show the extent to which thought determines language—how a culture creates the words it needs. Our focus on these words unleashed information about Chinese history, metaphors, images, sayings, and songs. Danling's digressions on the care and feeding of pet silkworms revealed the cultural values of hard work, sacrifice, and productivity, not to mention the practice of eating cocoons. Because Danling is bilingual and bicultural, she assisted in our cultural translation.

Since Danling is our friend and fellow researcher, we felt comfortable interviewing her, and we were able to explore information more easily than an outsider might. We want our interview with Danling to serve as a model for you, but we realize that she was able to translate as many insiders cannot do. Most of us begin as outsiders who don't know our informants, nor do we have key words in mind when we begin our interviews. Outsider status is the point of entry for all fieldworkers, and practice in listening to insider language is a good way to "step in" toward the inside.

Ethnopoetics

One way to present a transcript and to analyze it for its themes, rhythms, and language patterns is what folklorists and sociolinguists call **ethnopoetic notation.** Folklorist Dennis Tedlock used it to study and record Navajo speech. It also was adapted by sociolinguist Deborah Tannen, author of the bestseller *You Just Don't Understand: Women and Men in Conversation*, to analyze conversations in everyday living and in the workplace. Ethnopoetic notation is a procedure in which a language researcher turns oral speech into poetic form. Transforming oral speech into poetry allows a closer look, not only at an informant's language but also at the informant's perspective. As you take the words, lay them out on a page, and identify repetitions, pauses, and themes, you capture the rhythms of your informant's everyday speech. Here is an excerpt from Danling's transcript, transformed into poetry on the page:

> In early spring we put eggs, thousands of little eggs
>> laid by the silk moth
>> the year before
>> on little squares of paper
>> in a shoebox.
>
> We put them in the sun for warmth; sometimes we start them in school
>> like American children
>> grow seeds
>>> in paper cups
>> or chicken eggs
>>> in incubators.
>
> Eventually, a worm hatches
>> so tiny
>> so black
>> smaller than an ant.
>
> As the leaves come out, we feed them to the little worms.
>> Day by day,
>> we watch them grow bigger
>> as thick as a little finger
>> in different shades
>>> of white
>>> and black.

This layout of Danling's oral language in poetic form is similar to the oral context in which our conversation took place. The poetic notation allows you to see where she pauses and clusters images together: "so tiny / so black / smaller than an ant." In this poem, her figures of speech also stand out ("as thick as a little finger") and her cultural comparison is clear ("like American children / grow seeds / in paper cups / or chicken eggs / in incubators"). Ethnopoetic notation preserves the integrity of the oral conversation more closely than a written transcript. Although a word-for-word transcribed interview may seem more authentic, in fact, by writing it down we remove language from its oral context entirely. The process of ethnopoetic notation allows the researcher to recapture and study informants' language and thought more closely.

B
O
X
21

Listening for "The Word": Creating a Glossary

Purpose

Special languages, jargon, slang and the special use of everyday language are important clues to understanding a culture or subculture. Knowing what terms insiders use will help you step away from your outsider status, and analyzing the words—and their uses—will assist you in seeing what's important to insiders.

Action

Listen for key words in your fieldsite, and create a glossary of insider language. It will be important to get informants' permission to take fieldnotes or tape-record your conversation. As you listen, you may want to repeat what you hear so that your informants can add to, correct, or respond further to the insider language they are sharing with you. Later, you will also need to confirm your list of terms with informants in your fieldsite. Try to collect as much insider language as you can. Do you notice certain everyday words being used in new ways? Are there names for things that are entirely new to you? In this exercise, we want you to sharpen your listening skills to make yourself alert to language at your research site.

Rick Zollo gathered a glossary from two instructors at the trucking school he attended. Rick first heard these words at Iowa 80, but it was not until he sat through some of the formal instruction, read the written material, and interviewed these truckers that he could confirm the meanings of a trucker's vocabulary. Notice that Rick has organized the glossary in alphabetical order and that his definitions are short, concise, and parallel in structure. Here are a few samples:

bear bait   A truck driving faster than the flow of traffic.

bear trap   A radar trap.

chicken coop   A truck weighing station.

chicken lights   Flashy lights surrounding a trailer.

comic book   A trucker's log, required by the U.S. Department of Transportation.

double nickel   55 m.p.h. speed limit for trucks.

parking lot   Trailer hauling motor vehicles.

Response

Sara Voreis studied a traveling theater production by sitting in one spot back-stage and watching as the production grew from planning through rehearsals to two public productions in her university's theater. Here she presents a glossary that she gathered from interviews, field observations, and a theater terminology handout given to all who work backstage and onstage at the theater.

arbor   A metal frame that holds the counterweights used to balance flown scenery. Sometimes referred to as the *carriage* or *arbor cradle.* See also **fly rail.**

biscuit   A stationary speaker hooked into the headset system located in the shop.

bricks   Counterweights. Also referred to as *steels.*

crew head (or crew chief)   A union leader who communicates directly with his workers, the house stage manager, and the road crew chief.

cyclorama (cyc)   The light pink plastic rear projection screen used far upstage.

dimmers   Controls that regulate the amount of light coming out of a lighting unit.

fly rail   The area above stage where the weight system is operated. See also **single purchase system.**

ghosting   After lights have been shut down, they still glow a bit. Said to light the way for a theater ghost.

heavy on the fly   A lot of work to do on the fly rail; busy.

legs   Black velour drapes hung vertically to mask the wings and frame the stage.

loading   Placing bricks onto a cable to balance the weight of equipment lowered from the ceiling.

road crew (or roadies)   Stagehands who travel with a specific show.

shell   Large wall-like pieces set up on either side of the stage and from the ceiling to project sound into the audience. The ceiling pieces are "flown in."

single purchase system   Equal weight system that works from the floor to the operating area to balance equipment from the ceiling.

tripping   The process and equipment used to "fly in" the ceiling pieces.

wing   The space on each side of the stage.

After you've gathered and alphabetized a list, try clustering words into categories. Sara realized that, except for the crew head and roadies (road crew), the words she'd collected were all names of equipment used on the stage or actions that stage crew or equipment perform to create a stage set. The excerpt from Rick's list showed him that truckers use familiar words in unfamiliar ways to develop important insider understandings. The terms *silk* and *baby silkworms,* in our interview with Danling, signaled cultural meanings about life cycles and the value of productivity. Categorization is the beginning of analysis.

RESEARCHING OCCUPATION: RECORDING INSIDER LANGUAGE

Anthropologists, sociologists, and folklorists have always been interested in the language of occupations. They have studied and written about, for example, flight attendants, police, cab drivers, bartenders, nurses, farmers, fishermen, factory workers, and waitresses. To research insider occupational language, you cannot be merely an observer, but you must become a participant-observer, asking questions. As you read these short studies of waitresses, notice that a few phrases of occupational language reveal entire sets of rules, rituals, and ways of thinking. Insider language—a word, a term, or a phrase—can trigger whole stories that illustrate the perspective inside a subculture.

In her full-length ethnography called *Dishing It Out: Power and Resistance among Waitresses in a New Jersey Restaurant,* anthropologist Greta Foff Paules includes a list of waitresses' insider terms, which includes "the floor," "call out," "walk out," and "pulling bus pans" as grassroot expressions coined by the workers themselves to discuss their own work situations. This is not officially sanctioned language that we would find in a manual, guidebook, or even a photocopied set of rules for working in a restaurant. It's interesting, though, that occupational terms are stable. Whether you are a waitress in California, Texas, or New Jersey, you'll know that a "station" is a waitresses' service area and that to be "stiffed" by a customer means that you've been left no tip.

Here are two "stiffing" stories from two different fieldworkers. They both show how waitresses, when stiffed, retaliate. Our colleague Donna Qualley, who was a part-time waitress herself for many years, studied the way waitresses talked among themselves about their work at Norton's Seafood restaurant. Donna recorded this dialogue, shared between an older waitress named Rae, her younger coworker Erin, and herself:

> "I had this young couple."
>
> "How old?" Erin interjects.
>
> "In their twenties, I would guess. They order two fish and chips and two glasses of water."
>
> "Cheap. I'm surprised they didn't ask to split one meal," Erin mumbles.
>
> "When they are done I put the check on the table and tell them I will be right back to collect it for them. I go into the kitchen and when I come back, there is a ten-dollar bill, a dime, a nickel, and a penny on the table."
>
> "How much is the bill?" I ask.
>
> "Ten fifteen."
>
> "That makes me so mad..." Erin begins.
>
> "But," Rae smiles, "the woman had left her coat on the chair. They were in such a hurry to get out she forgot her coat! I grab the coat, check, and money, and then I see her coming back for her coat..."
>
> "I hope you kept it until they left a better tip," I laugh.
>
> "I said to this woman, 'Oh, did you come back for your change?'"

"You really said that? How much was the bill again?" Erin asks.

"Ten fifteen, and they left me ten sixteen. Well, this woman turns all red and apologetic and says, 'We didn't have any money—we thought this was a takeout place.' Yeah, right. They knew what they were doing."

This conversation, taken from long transcripts of recorded waitress talk, is part of Donna's fieldwork study, which shows how talk and gossip bind waitresses as they work. Waitresses, an occupational group that can be oppressed at times, retaliate with gossip against the rude behavior of customers who stiff them.

Greta Paules's study of waitressing, this one conducted at Route, a family-style chain restaurant, illustrates a waitress's outrage at being "stiffed." This waitress, in an attempt to cut her losses, resists waiting on regular customers who previously left without tipping her.

This party of two guys come in and they order thirty to forty dollars' worth of food…and they stiff us. Every time. So Kaddie told them, "If you don't tip us, we're not going to wait on you." They said, "We'll tip you." So Kaddie waited on them, and they tipped her. The next night they came in, I waited on them and they didn't tip me. The third time they came in [the manager] put them in my station and I told [the manager] straight up, "I'm not waiting on them…" So when they came in the next night…[they] said, "Are you going to give us a table?" I said, "You going to tip me? I'm not going to wait on you."(31)

Both of these stories center on the insider term *stiffing*, which means "leaving no tip." In the context of waitressing, the stories that surround the term convey a whole set of behaviors and attitudes toward the occupational term and the event itself. Out of context the occupational term does not convey the waitresses' worldview in the same way that the story, which includes the event, does.

Another insider expression used at Norton's Seafood refers to a waitress who is "in the weeds," which means extremely busy. A waitress who is "in the weeds" might do something extraordinary under such pressure. In Donna's fieldwork, Carrie's story is an example of what happens to a waitress in this context:

I was carrying this huge oval tray, and it was filled with food. And a man stood up right in front of me and said, "I want my beer now." So I handed him the tray and went and got his beer. He stood in the aisle holding the tray. He didn't know what to do. I thought, "If anyone sees this, I'm going to get fired." But it was just "I want my beer now" and me with fifteen dinners on my tray. "OK sir," I said, set the beer on the table, and took the tray. I didn't know what else to do. I didn't want to yell at him—I wanted to throw the tray at him.

Occupations that form subcultures, like waitressing, often convey their insider terms through stories, words, and phrases. Like Carrie's being stuck "in the weeds," too tangled and overwhelmed to get out, insider terms sometimes serve as metaphors. Occupational folklorists have suggested that the relationship between job terms and a group's cultural worldview is so strong that the terminology literally shapes the perspective of the workers. Most waitresses agree that to be busy feels like being caught "in the weeds" and to be insulted by a customer evokes retaliation against those who "stiff" them. Learning occupational terms and swapping stories shape behaviors and values. In the case of these waitresses, the incidents were reminders of caution against customer disrespect and efficiency in the face of customer demands. The occupational language and its accompanying stories help initiate new waitresses into the profession and reaffirm seasoned waitresses' experience. Occupational language reflects an insider's perspective.

In this chapter, we've offered two very different models for listening to language. We set up our interview with Danling with specific questions about language use in her culture. We directed questions toward our goal, but we didn't stop her when she seemed a little off the track. Because informants know more than outsiders do about their own culture, researchers must trust that digressions may lead to important knowledge.

In Donna Qualley's study of waitresses, the best stories came when she just hung out and listened. Although she had worked in the restaurant herself, she had never stopped to listen in quite that way. When Donna set out to identify occupational terms through the stories she heard, she made fieldnotes of waitresses' talk and began to sift out the categories of insider language that she hadn't even noticed as a member of the culture.

Whether you are an insider or an outsider to the subculture you study, whether you conduct a formal interview or collect words, phrases, and stories informally, you can learn much from listening to language. Your goal is to try to describe language from your informant's perspective and analyze what it tells you about the occupation it represents. If you choose to tape-record, you will need the information we provide in this chapter about taping and transcribing oral language.

BOX 22 Describing Insider Language: Occupational Terms

Purpose

Collecting the **verbal art** of a subculture is an important way of understanding it: insiders teach one another how to belong by sharing special terms, proverbs, jokes, sayings, and especially stories. As you spend time in your fieldsite, you may find your informant wanting to explain techniques, rules, rituals, or processes of their occupations—and at those times you'll probably hear much verbal art. Like the researchers who studied waitresses (pp. 304–06), you may hear some good stories. The best way to get a good story, of course, is to hang out long enough to hear one.

Action

In your fieldsite, select an occupation or a person who uses specific occupational language. Spend some time watching the work and listening to the workers and their language. Record fieldnotes or tape insider language, if possible. When you've gathered some terms or phrases and unfamiliar usages, arrange to interview an informant. From your informant, find out as much as you can about the history and uses of these occupational terms or phrases. Ask your informant to tell a story that illustrates the term. You may ask, "What do you mean by X?" or "Tell me how Y works" or "How do you use Z?"

Response

In this reflective response, Donna Qualley writes about how she gathered waitresses' stories. She acted as a kind of cultural translator between the waitresses' lives and her academic life as college student, instructor, and waitress:

> In a sense I think I had earned the right to consider myself bicultural since I had worked in that place for eight years. I had not only witnessed but participated in the kind of cathartic talk I describe, weekend after weekend and summer after summer. What set me apart was my double perspective—my academic take on everything. I could take these conversations and place them in other arenas, adding new layers of meaning. My part-time status at the university was always recognized, so I was not one of them completely. And yet when waitresses told their stories, I recognized them as my own. For in the eyes of the customer, we were all the same. Particularly, when I was a student and literally needed Norton's to survive…being stiffed was a very serious story. We all felt each other's situation keenly. We recognized the type of tale we were telling.
>
> What was different is that when I actively began to do research, to take notes both on the job and at times when I wasn't working, just the act of writing—of actively looking, of fleshing out my notes as fieldnotes at the end of a shift—caused me to see more connections than previously and to articulate them more fully. And I suppose in a way it was different for the waitresses, too, in that I was making their lives matter to someone else. And when I interviewed several waitresses alone, I think this also made them feel their lives were important. People came up to me with their stories. "Put this in your book," they would say. The cooks and the busboys got snippety when they found out they weren't going to be "in it." They had an idea of something like "Norton's: The Untold Story." But my research project was to focus on the gossip and stories of waitresses and what that revealed about the occupation of serving others.

Taping and Transcribing

Interviews provide the bones of any fieldwork project. You need your informants' actual words to support your findings. Without informants' voices, you have no perspective to share except your own. You bring to life the language of the people whose culture you study as you record them.

The process of taping and transcribing interviews has been advanced by sophisticated tape recorders and word processors. It's no coincidence that interviewing and collecting oral histories has become more popular in recent years with these accessible technologies; it's nice that cassette recorders are small, relatively inexpensive, and easily available. With a counting feature to keep track of slices of conversation and a pause button to slow down the transcription process, a simple cassette recorder becomes a valuable tool for the interviewer. Computer software—from simple word processors to the specialized programs that create databases and recombine information—cuts down the tedium of sorting, classifying, and organizing huge piles of written data.

But transcribing is tedious business nonetheless. Most researchers estimate three or more hours of transcribing for each hour of recording. You don't want to tape everything you hear, nor do you want to transcribe it all. That's why it's important to prepare ahead with research and guiding questions but also with adequate equipment and knowledge about using it. We'd like to share some advice to make your taping and transcribing go smoothly.

1. *Obtain your equipment.* Borrow or purchase quality equipment. What's good for taping a concert or copying a friend's CD may not be the best equipment for recording an interview. You'll need a tape recorder that has a counting feature to track and locate sections of the interview and also a microphone that will be sensitive enough to pick up the human voice. Some tape recorders have built-in microphones, but often it is necessary to attach a separate directional mike to maximize the voice and minimize peripheral noise. Check to see if you can borrow interview equipment. Departments of anthropology, sociology, English, theater, and journalism often lend equipment to students.

2. *Prepare your equipment.* Batteries can die when you least want them to, so you'll need to have an AC adapter as an additional power source. It is safer to use electrical outlets as your power source than to depend on batteries. Test your equipment before entering your fieldsite by recording the date, your name, and your informant's name. Then, when you arrive at your interview, play it back. Most fieldworkers have stories about lost interviews due to bad tapes or malfunctioning equipment. Elizabeth, for example, only took one 60-minute tape to a two-hour interview session. After the first hour, her informant kept talking. Pretending she was still recording, she took notes furiously by hand. Check not only the length of each tape you purchase but also its quality. Medium-quality tape is quite adequate (higher-quality tape is made for recording music; low-quality tape can stretch or break). When you arrive on site, be sure to have extra

batteries, extra tape, tape labels, a notepad and pencil, and perhaps a camera to gather contextual information. Remember to wear a wristwatch so that you can quietly keep track of interview time.

3. *Organize your interview time.* Ask the informant to suggest a convenient place and time for the interview. Arrive a few minutes early to set up and test your equipment. Try to minimize interruptions once you are at the fieldsite. Arrange your tapes and notepads close by so that you won't bang or shuffle, distracting your informant or cluttering your tape with extraneous noise.

4. *Organize and listen to your audiotapes.* Nothing is more frustrating to the energetic researcher than a box full of unlabeled tapes. Use the stick-on labels that accompany the tapes to identify the date, day, time, place, and person whom you are interviewing. After recording, listen to the whole tape as soon as possible to get an idea of what may be valuable to transcribe. (We sometimes do this in our spare time, on our car tape players and on our headsets.) You may want to outline the topics covered and take notes to highlight the major themes or to think about what questions you'll want to ask in the next interview. Don't let your tapes gather dust until you have time to transcribe them fully. This initial listening process enhances your memory of the interview and the overall sense of purpose for your project.

5. *Log all your tapes.* Set the counter feature on the tape recorder to identify relevant chunks of data. List the topics and note the corresponding numbers on a piece of paper—for example, "015–138: CV: talks about her late mother's flower shop and her history of gardening" or "249–282: good quote on nature and spirituality." Summarizing your material and noting where it appears on the tape will allow for easy retrieval later. The more time you spend logging and describing what's on the tapes, the less time you'll need for actual transcription. Over time, you will develop your own system.

6. *Transcribe your tapes.* As soon as possible after the interview, transcribe your audiotapes. Use the pause button on the recorder to freeze the tape and the rewind buttons and play to reverse and review any material you need to hear again. If you are fortunate enough to have a foot switch (often used by professional transcribers), you can start and stop the tape with your foot and continue keyboarding as you listen. Transcribe word for word, using parentheses or brackets to indicate pauses, laughing, interruptions, sections you want to leave out, or words that seem unintelligible: "[CV talks about having a cold]" or "[unintelligible: maybe "hunch," "bunch," or "lunch"; check with CV]."

7. *Use your computer.* Word processors have features that enhance transcribing. You can make a separate file for each informant or separate interviews according to themes. The computer allows you to format a pattern of organization as you transcribe (date, person, topic). Be sure to back up important disks once you have a lot of data transcribed.

8. *Bring language to paper.* As a transcriber, you must bring your informant's speech to life as accurately and as appropriately as you can. When you

transcribe oral language, you will find it difficult to capture intonations, speech rhythms, and regional accents on the page. Most researchers agree that a person's grammar should remain as spoken. If an informant says "I done," for example, it's not appropriate to alter it to "I did." If, when you share a transcript later with your informant and she chooses to change it, respect that change. All speakers "code-shift" between what linguists call "speech registers," which depend on topic, audience, and background such as regional or ethnic identity. For example, Bonnie's grandmother code-shifted with Yiddish expressions among her Mah-Jongg partners, but she'd use mainstream accented Philadelphia English in a department store. Many characteristics of oral language have no equivalents in print. It is too difficult for either transcriber or reader to attempt to capture or understand oral **dialect** in written form. "Pahk the cah in Hahvahd Yahd" is a respelling of a Boston accent, meant to show how it sounds. But to a reader who's never heard it—even to an insider, a Bostonian who isn't conscious of her accent—the written version of her oral dialect looks artificial and complicates the reading process. Anthropologists and folklorists have long debated how to record oral language and currently discourage the use of spelling as a way to approximate oral language.

9. *Share your transcript.* Offer the transcripts to your informant to read for accuracy, but realize that you won't get many takers. Most informants would rather not plow through a whole transcript but would rather wait for your finished, edited version of the interview. In any case, the informant needs the opportunity to read what you've written. In some instances, the informant may make corrections or ask for deletions. But most of the time, the written interview becomes a kind of gift in exchange for the time spent interviewing.

RESEARCHING VERBAL PERFORMANCE: THE CURSE AND THE CULTURE

Our waitress stories fit the category of occupational folklore, but they are also what folklorists and anthropologists call "performance events" or examples of "verbal art." Performance events include a wide range of expressive art, from informal to formal: jokes, proverbs and taboos, songs and chants, urban legends, curses and spells, myths and tales, traditional stories, and entire ceremonies complete with storytelling and ritual verbal behaviors (like weddings, initiations, retirements, and seasonal celebrations). These **performances** use spontaneous verbal art; they are unrehearsed, unscripted, and not often staged. This concept of verbal performance comes from folklore and depends on three features: a performer who is an insider to the culture, a recognizable oral performance, and an audience of insiders.

As the waitresses told their stories, away from customers, they engaged in the performance event of occupational storytelling. Their stories were spontaneous and unrehearsed. Audience, storyteller, and researcher understood this performance event. The performers were waitresses who signaled to the insider audience with their shared terms—"I got stiffed last night"—that they were about to offer a story. The researchers who collected those stories were insiders to the occupational culture and understood the key terms, which alerted them to turn on the tape recorder.

In the same way that a folk object, like the basket or quilt we described in Chapter 3, is an expressive art form that blends cultural tradition with individual creativity, so does a verbal performance. A joke, for example, has a traditional core—either of content (the chicken crosses the road) or of form ("Knock, knock!" "Who's there?"). But jokes and stories have **variants;** they change according to the performer's creativity, personal history, and culture ("Oh, I heard a different version of that where I lived").

So the twin laws of folklore—tradition and creativity—are present in our verbal performance events, although we are not consciously aware of them. Telling a joke and gossiping, both verbal performances, are so automatic and integrated into our conversational lives that we don't often stand back to analyze them. But we all know someone who is a good joke teller, and we depend on certain people to give us the latest gossip. We also notice when an outsider "doesn't get" a joke—"You had to be there." Only insiders to a subculture have the cultural knowledge to "get it."

Like a joke or a story, a curse is a kind of verbal performance that exists in many cultures. It is closely connected with other verbal arts in a culture: songs and chants, for example. Looking at the curses of a culture helps us understand its taboos, history and geography, values and beliefs. Zora Neale Hurston, an anthropologist working in the 1930s, was one of the first ethnographers to study the folk tales and magic practices of her own culture, recounted in her book *Mules and Men.* Unlike Reema's boy, the insensitive researcher in Willow Springs (in *Mama Day* by Gloria Nayler—see Chapter 3), Hurston traveled to her native Eatonville, Florida, knowing that there was a rich collection of folk tales to gather there among her people. She used her status as an insider to work her way toward New Orleans to study hoodoo, a uniquely American practice, blended from a mixture of African and Haitian black magic (voodoo) and New Orleans French Catholic religious beliefs.

Hurston learns a curse from hoodoo doctor Luke Turner, who agrees to take her on as a pupil, having himself learned hoodoo from an infamous conjurer named Marie Laveau. From Turner, Hurston also learns the process for putting a curse on someone: sending the names of your enemies to their house sealed with the wax from a porcupine plant and mixing a package of damnation powders for them. Then the conjurer etches the enemy's name with a needle on a black candle dressed in vinegar and sets it on the altar, pays 15 cents to the spirit of death, and invokes this curse-prayer:

> To the Man God: O Great One, I have been sorely tried by my enemies and have been blasphemed and lied against. My good thoughts and my honest actions have been turned to bad actions and dishonest ideas. My home has

been disrespected, my children have been cursed and ill-treated. My dear ones have been backbitten and their virtue questioned. O Man God, I beg that this that I ask for my enemies shall come to pass:

That the South wind shall scorch their bodies and make them wither and shall not be tempered to them. That the North wind shall freeze their blood and numb their muscles and that it shall not be tempered to them. That the west wind shall blow away their life's breath and will not leave their hair grow, and that their finger nails shall fall off and their bones shall crumble. That the East wind shall make their minds grow dark, their sight shall fail and their seed dry up so that they shall not multiply.

I ask that their fathers and mothers from their furthest generation will not intercede for them before the great throne, and the wombs of their women shall not bear fruit except for strangers, and that they shall become extinct. I pray that the children who may come shall be weak of mind and paralyzed of limb and that they themselves shall curse them in their turn for ever turning the breath of life into their bodies. I pray that disease and death shall be forever with them and that their worldly goods shall not prosper and that their crops shall not multiply and that their cows, their sheep, and their hogs and all their living beasts shall die of starvation and thirst. I pray that their house shall be unroofed and that the rain, thunder and lightning shall find the innermost recesses of their home and that the foundation shall crumble and the floods tear it asunder. I pray that the sun shall not shed its rays on them in benevolence, but instead it shall beat down on them and burn them and destroy them. I pray that the moon shall not give them peace, but instead shall deride them and decry them and cause their minds to shrivel. I pray that their friends shall betray them and cause them loss of power, of gold and of silver, and that their enemies shall smite them until they beg for mercy which shall not be given them. I pray that their tongues shall forget how to speak in sweet words, and that it shall be paralyzed and that all about them will be desolation, pestilence and death. O Man God, I ask you for all these things because they have dragged me in the dust and destroyed my good name; broken my heart and caused me to curse the day that I was born. So be it. (197–198)

This curse, collected by Hurston, is a good example of verbal performance art. As a fieldworker, she tries to capture the performer's oral style in her writing. If you read this curse aloud or to a friend, you would understand the full force of its performance features, which link it closely to a wide range of spiritual traditions that invite audience participation. It opens with an evocation "To the Man God: O Great One," and ends with the closing "So be it."

Anthropologists would recognize this curse and its African American, French Creole, and Haitian voodoo roots, as many verbal art forms share traditional and universal features. The hoodoo curses the enemy's most basic cultural elements: disease and death, crops and weather, fertility and birth. The variations on this curse (the "creative spin" or "variant"), specific to these conjurers, includes creative use of language that shows the voice and rhythms of this New Orleans subculture: "their finger nails shall fall off and their bones shall crumble," "their house shall be unroofed and […] the rain, thunder and lightning shall find the innermost recesses of their home."

Curses and spiritual performances, like seances, tarot readings, and fortune telling—even religious sermons—reveal aspects of a culture's belief system. Less formal oral performances like proverbs, jokes, and sayings reveal the everyday rules and rituals that a culture lives by. All cultures and subcultures have sayings, which are often not only entertaining but also didactic—they teach youngsters and newcomers the values and traditions that a culture holds true. Even though there is a traditional core (form or content), each culture's proverbs and sayings are creative and unique. Verbal art is valued in a culture because its shared oral tradition allows each person to bring creativity to each rendering of the performance.

Gathering Verbal Art: Proverbs, Jokes, and Sayings   BOX 23

Purpose

Curses, chants, jokes, proverbs, and sayings are all types of verbal art, as are stories—and insiders "perform" them for other insiders' benefit to instruct as well as affirm the features of having insider status. In this activity, you will gather examples of verbal art and reflect on them. This is a good time to supplement your knowledge—and your field data—with library research. The folklore section in your library holds a treasury of many forms of verbal art—collections of proverbs, jokes, and stories particular to certain cultures and subcultures. You might even want to look in the reference room for two works: Stith Thompson's *Motif-Index of Folk Literature* and Antti Aarne's *The Types of the Folk-Tale: A Classification and Bibliography*. These two valuable reference indices categorize types and themes of folk narratives and other verbal art from around the world and throughout history. Of course, you may be able to collect quite a few pieces of verbal art just by requesting it from the people around you.

Action

If you are working on a major project, you may want to relate this exercise to your fieldwork. If not, try it with any subculture that interests you. Begin data collection by choosing a form and a theme: a certain type of joke told about a certain kind of profession, proverbs, childhood chants, or jump-rope rhymes about a certain theme. After you've collected a few examples, categorize them in a list, and try some analysis. Here are a few questions that might help you: What are the common themes? What words reappear in different ways? What do the variations tell you about the unique features of culture from which these words came? What behaviors do they encourage or discourage? If you were an outsider to this culture, what could you learn from these pieces of verbal art?

Response

Lori Bateman was researching a Swedish American cultural center, and she gathered this cluster of proverbs:

> It is better to stumble with your feet than with your tongue.
>
> The one who wants to lie should have a good memory.
>
> Many know much, but nobody knows everything.
>
> Better to ask for directions twice than get lost once.

Lori writes, "These first four proverbs all deal with verbal actions and stress honesty and caution. Sweden is a northern environment, and rural areas are sparsely populated. Attention to honesty and caution would be important survival skills in such a place." And then she adds:

> Love is like the dew; it falls on weeds as well as on lilies.
>
> One cannot make soup out of beauty.

"To me, these two proverbs tie together and deal with appearance. Beauty is acknowledged in both proverbs, but the emphasis in the first is that everyone finds a partner, and in the second, that beauty alone will not provide a person with what they need. These proverbs really hit home for me because when I was a child my father would use the English proverb 'Pretty is as pretty does' with me, along with the Swedish 'One cannot make soup out of beauty' to make me focus more on my actions and skills rather than my appearance."

Another category Lori found in her collection of verbal art (which contained prayers and song as well) was a group of proverbs that concerned eating or drinking. Here are a few of those, followed by Lori's analysis:

> What fills your heart is revealed by your mouth.
>
> Better without bread than without hope.
>
> Let the food hush your tongue.
>
> When it rains soup, the poor man has no spoon.
>
> What is eaten from the pot never comes to the platter.
>
> Drink and eat, but do not forget God, death, and the judgment.
>
> Where wine goes in, wit goes out.

Lori speculates about this grouping: "I found a few of these proverbs on the back of a cookbook and heard the others at the Swedish cultural center.

I thought it was interesting that so many images of eating could supply double meanings for spiritual nourishment and moral behavior. Maybe there are so many proverbs using food imagery because of the Swedish tradition of smorgasbords and the focus on food-centered celebrations. I'll have to ask my informants what they think about that."

RESEARCHING VERBAL PERFORMANCE: URBAN LEGENDS

So far in this chapter we've suggested that you collect performance events: everyday stories of a subculture and more ritualized language events (jokes, curses, proverbs) that fall into the category of **lore**. We are just as unconscious of our folklore as we are of our everyday language. The lore we pass along in our culture, like curses, stories, tales, and songs, is much more than mere superstition. Our folklore serves to control our anxieties, explain our deepest fears, and teach us how to go about living in our cultures. Like the waitresses' gossip and the conjurers' curses, lore conveys a traditional core as well as variants, depending on the teller.

A culture's myths, one form of lore, are never taken as truth, whereas legends and tales have enough truthful elements to serve as what we might consider folk history. We hear American lore without recognizing it: about dead ancestors (your uncle who almost made a fortune), about famous historical figures (George Washington wouldn't tell a lie), and cultural heroes (John Henry built the railroad and Rip Van Winkle awoke to a changed world after a 20-year sleep). We retell legends without consciously recognizing the cultural belief systems they symbolize: capitalism, honesty, hard work, progress.

One class of folklore narrative is the *urban legend,* set in contemporary times, including elements that are believable to us. Like other verbal art, urban legends encompass belief systems and can also be considered cautionary tales for ways of behaving in our modern life. Urban legends, like ghost stories, are told in places where people come together to eat and sleep temporarily, as in a camp or a dorm. Like all folklore, urban legends travel from one site to another. We have found from our students that a legend told in Des Moines, Iowa, may have a variant in the outer banks of North Carolina. Wherever you grew up, you probably heard about a woman with a ribbon around her neck, a haunted family tombstone, a bloody hook, or rat meat in a fast-food hamburger.

Jan Harald Brunvand, a famous folklorist, has collected examples of urban legends, weird and macabre tales that often feel like truth. Here is an excerpt from his book *The Vanishing Hitchhiker: American Urban Legends and Their Meanings,* which describes many variants of the urban legend that folklorists call "The Roommate's Death."

The Roommate's Death

Jan Harald Brunvand

Another especially popular example of the American adolescent shocker story is the widely-known legend of "The Roommate's Death." It shares several themes with other urban legends. As in "The Killer in the Backseat" and "The Baby-sitter and the Man Upstairs," it is usually a lone woman in the story who is threatened—or thinks she is—by a strange man. As in "The Hook" and "The Boyfriend's Death," the assailant is often said to be an escaped criminal or a maniac. Finally, as in the latter legend, the actual commission of the crime is never described; only the resulting mutilated corpse is. The scratching sounds outside the girl's place of refuge are an additional element of suspense. Here is a version told by a University of Kansas student in 1965 set in Corbin Hall, a freshman women's dormitory there:

> These two girls in Corbin had stayed late over Christmas vacation. One of them had to wait for a later train, and the other wanted to go to a fraternity party given that night of vacation. The dorm assistant was in her room—sacked out. They waited and waited for the intercom, and then they heard this knocking and knocking outside in front of the dorm. So the girl thought it was her date and she went down. But she didn't come back and she didn't come back. So real late that night this other girl heard a scratching and gasping down the hall. She couldn't lock the door, so she locked herself in the closet. In the morning she let herself out and her roommate had had her throat cut and if the other girl had opened the door earlier, she [the dead roommate] would have been saved.

At all the campuses where the story is told the reasons for the girls' remaining alone in the dorm vary, but they are always realistic and plausible. The girls' homes may be too far away for them to visit during vacation, such as in Hawaii or a foreign country. In some cases they wanted to avoid a campus meeting or other obligation. What separates the two roommates may be either that one goes out for food, or to answer the door, or to use the rest room. The girl who is left behind may hear the scratching noise either at her room door or at the closet door, if she hides there. Sometimes her hair turns white or gray overnight from the shock of the experience (an old folk motif). The implication in the story is that some maniac is after her (as is suspected about the pursuer in "The Killer in the Backseat"); but the truth is that her own roommate needs help, and she might have supplied it had she only acted more decisively when the noises were first heard. Usually some special emphasis is put on the victim's fingernails, scratched to bloody stumps by her desperate efforts to signal for help.

A story told by a California teenager, remembered from about 1964, seems to combine motifs of "The Baby-sitter and the Man Upstairs" with "The Roommate's Death." The text is unusually detailed with names and the circumstances of the crime:

> Linda accepted a baby-sitting job for a wealthy family who lived in a two-story home up in the hills for whom she had never baby-sat for before. Linda was rather hesitant as the house was rather isolated and so she asked a girlfriend, Sharon, to go along with her, promising Sharon half of the baby-sitting fee she would earn. Sharon accepted Linda's offer and the two girls went up to the big two-story house.
>
> The night was an especially dark and windy one and rain was threatening. All went well for the girls as they read stories aloud to the three little boys they were sitting for and they had no problem putting the boys to bed in the upstairs part of the house. When this was done, the girls settled down to watching television.
>
> It was not long before the telephone rang. Linda answered the telephone, only to hear the heavy breathing of the caller on the other end. She attempted to elicit a response from the caller but he merely hung up. Thinking little of it and not wanting to panic Sharon, Linda went back to watching her television program, remarking that the caller had dialed a wrong number. Upon receiving the second call at which time the caller first engaged in a bit of heavy breathing and then instructed them to check on the children, the two girls became frightened and decided to call the operator for assistance. The operator instructed the girls to keep the caller on the line as long as possible should he call again so that she might be able to trace the call. The operator would check back with them.
>
> The two girls then decided between themselves that one should stay downstairs to answer the phone. It was Sharon who volunteered to go upstairs. Shortly, the telephone rang again and Linda did as the operator had instructed her. Within a few minutes, the operator called back telling Linda to leave the house immediately with her friend because she had traced the calls to the upstairs phone.
>
> Linda immediately hung up the telephone and proceeded to run to the stairway to call Sharon. She then heard a thumping sound coming from the stairway and when she approached the stairs she saw her friend dragging herself down the stairs by her chin, all of her limbs severed from her body. The three boys also lay dead upstairs in their beds.

Once again, the Indiana University Folklore Archive has provided the best published report on variants of "The Roommate's Death," Linda Dégh's summary of thirty-one texts and several subtypes and related plots collected since 1961. The most significant feature, according to her report, is the frequent appearance of a male rescuer at the end of the story. In one version, for example, two girls are left behind alone in the dorm by their roommate when she goes downstairs for food; they hear noises, and so stay in their room all night without opening the door. Finally the mailman comes around the next morning, and they call him from the window:

> The mailman came in the front door and went up the stairs, and told the girls to stay in their room, that everything was all right but that they were to stay in their rooms [sic]. But the girls didn't listen to him 'cause he had said it was all right, so they came out into the hall. When they opened the door, they saw their girlfriend on the floor with a hatchet in her head.

In other Indiana texts the helpful male is a handyman, a milkman, or the brother of one of the roommates.

According to folklorist Beverly Crane, the male-female characters are only one pair of a series of significant opposites, which also includes home and away, intellectual versus emotional behavior, life and death, and several others. A male is needed to resolve the female's uncertainty—motivated by her emotional fear—about how to act in a new situation. Another male has mutilated and killed her roommate with a blow to her head, "the one part of the body with which women are not supposed to compete." The girls, Crane suggested, are doubly out of place in the beginning, having left the haven of home to engage in intellectual pursuits, and having remained alone in the campus dormitory instead of rejoining the family on a holiday. Ironically, the injured girl must use her fingernails, intended to be long, lovely, feminine adornments, in order to scratch for help. But because her roommate fails to investigate the sound, the victim dies, her once pretty nails now bloody stumps. Crane concluded this ingenious interpretation with these generalizations:

> The points of value implicit in this narrative are then twofold. If women wish to depend on traditional attitudes and responses they had best stay in a place where these attitudes and responses are best able to protect them. If, however, women do choose to venture into the realm of equality with men, they must become less dependent, more self-sufficient, more confident in their own abilities, and, above all, more willing to assume responsibility for themselves and others.

One might not expect to find feminist messages embedded in the spooky stories told by teenagers, but Beverly Crane's case is plausible and well argued. Furthermore, it is not at all unusual to find up-to-date social commentary in other modern folklore—witness the many religious and sexual jokes and legends circulated by people who would not openly criticize a church or the traditional social mores. Folklore does not just purvey the old codes of morality and behavior; it can also absorb newer ideas. What needs to be done to analyze this is to collect what Alan Dundes calls "oral-literary criticism," the informants' own comments about their lore. How clearly would the girls who tell these stories perceive—or even accept—the messages extrapolated by scholars? And a related question: Have any stories with clear liberationist themes replaced older ones cautioning young women to stay home, be good, and—next best—be careful, and call a man if they need help?

After reading Brunvand's article, Courtney Schmidt wrote about her process of collecting an urban tale and its variants in her dorm:

The Roommate's Death

I walked up and down the fifth floor of Harkin Residence Hall searching for a wonderful storyteller. As I soon found out, only one person was willing to step forward, and this was after a lot of coaching. Many people claimed "not to know any stories," and the people who did have stories proved to be very quiet once the recorder play button was hit. Finally, one brave soul out of the bunch put aside her shyness and spoke to share the following:

> This story is one of the first ones I heard here. I had heard it through my hall. It is about a girl who came in late one night from a date and found it odd that her door was unlocked. But being very tired, she decided not to turn on the light and not to wake up her roommate since it was extremely late. She got up the next morning to find a note on the mirror, in red lipstick, saying, "Aren't you glad you didn't turn on the light?" She looked over on the bed to find her roommate had been slaughtered.

Once my friend told this story, the rest of the group surrounding her wanted to tell their own—off the record. One girl told me that the message wasn't written in lipstick but in blood. Another girl told me that the victim had been raped before being slaughtered. Yet another shared that the girl had originally gone to a party that others had warned her about.

After the group told stories, I told them about urban folklore and explained how these stories are most often targeted to females and try to teach them how to act the correct way according to society's standards. I informed them that the basic theme of this legend revolved around the situation when, "as the adolescent moves out from home into the larger world, the world's danger may close in on him or her" (Brunvand 396). The girls and I agreed that the college freshman experience was indeed that of moving into a bigger world and that the story also had a huge warning to all those living in the hall. "If you don't lock your doors, the same thing could happen to you." The tale also contained a sexual theme, which stated that if you go out with a boy and come home late, you are probably up to no good. The roommate's death would be a direct punishment for not being discreet and not insisting that your date take you home right after the movie.

One of the messages of this story is for women to assume traditional roles—or else. I mean, what was the woman doing in college anyway? After I pointed out these ideas about the urban legend, the girls became very angry, and most of them admitted that they had never thought about it that way. Into the night hours, they started taking old horror stories and analyzing them, even adding in the males as the "scairdy-cats" and laughing. I'm glad I could give them a little food for thought.

Like Courtney, our students went out, collected, and analyzed urban legends and shared their findings. Their urban legends, all cautionary tales, fell into three thematic categories: romance, food, and strangers. The first is a story about a high school romance, one you may have heard in a variant form in your own part of the country. This version takes place in North Carolina:

The Spillway

There is a story about this girl in high school. And she wasn't very wild. In fact, she had never been on a date. One night, she snuck out of her house to go on a date with a guy she had just met that day. She thought he was taking her to a movie, but her date convinced her that they needed to get to know each other better. So they drove down by the spillway, a bridge by a lake. Over the course of the evening, he persuaded her to have sex with him in a car. They both thought that since it was her first time, she could not get pregnant. But after about three months, the girl found out she was pregnant. She didn't want to go through the humiliation of telling her family. She stole the boy's keys while he was in gym class, got in his car, and drove it down to the spillway. She ran the car off the bridge, killing herself. It is said that if a guy and a girl go down to the spillway and set their keys on the hood of their car, the girl will come by and start the car.

This urban legend serves to caution young women about having sex on the first date and includes folk beliefs about pregnancy. It feeds on young women's fears of family humiliation and community rejection. The gym class, the keys, and the car are details of our contemporary lives, but they are also symbols of power and freedom in our culture. The legend's main character uses these symbols to destroy herself. This tale has many elements of theme and structure that are traditional in lots of cultures, both modern and ancient. But if you were an outsider listening to this story, you would learn a lot about teenage culture in contemporary middle-class America: the place where kids park, the culture of the car, and a warning not to get into a similar situation.

Our next urban tale, which also includes a car, centers on the very American culture of the shopping mall. This legend elaborates on the traditional dictum "Never talk to strangers":

The Mall, the Car, and the Stranger

One day at the local mall, a young woman returned from shopping to her parked car. She thought that she had just had a normal day of shopping until she looked in and saw a little old woman sitting on the passenger's side. She walked up to the old woman and asked her what she was doing in the car. The old woman told her she was just tired. And then she asked the young woman if she could please give her a ride home. The young woman said no and asked the old lady to please get out of her car. The old woman persisted by saying how tired she was and how she only needed a ride home. Then the young woman decided to not argue anymore and to ask for help from the security officers at the mall. Soon the young woman and the security police returned to the car and found the old woman still sitting there. The security officer asked the old woman to get out of the car, but she would not budge. He had to take her by the arms and drag her out of the car. While they were doing this, the woman hit her head on the car door and her wig fell off. It turned out that the woman was not a woman at all but a man dressed as a woman. The police handcuffed him and praised the young woman for her action, saying that if she had taken the old woman's word for being tired and given her a ride home, she would probably never have made it.

This urban folktale centers around the fear of strangers, warning young women against an "outsider" who appears inside the young woman's car and tries to deceive her. It has traditional elements we might find in tales from many cultures: a stranger in disguise and a young woman who defends herself (with help from cultural authorities) against danger. But the legend uses details from suburban life: a mall with security police, an automobile as a private space that should never invite intruders. And it appears quiet believable to any insider who lives and shops in contemporary America.

Like the mall story, urban legends are so loaded with familiar details that they seem quite believable. When we hear them, we are often fooled into thinking that they actually happened—recently, locally, among people who know people just like the people we know.

We suspect that you've heard urban legends about food, romance, strangers, and certainly many more themes, such as sudden wealth or poverty, mysterious disappearances of people, or superhuman feats. But we wonder if you've ever stopped to analyze which parts link back to traditional tales, which parts suggest cultural warnings or lessons, and which parts make them so believable to the insiders in our own culture.

Collecting Urban Folk Tales

BOX 24

Purpose

If you were gathering legends in an unfamiliar culture, you'd notice elements of cultural tradition in those stories as well as details specific to that culture. As a fieldworker studying any culture or subculture, you'll want to collect important pieces of narrative folklore in order to interpret the teachings, anxieties, and fears of that group. Hearing these stories allows you to focus on the values that shape the subculture. If you have been working in your fieldsite long enough, you might collect urban legends that will relate to your project or to the subculture you are investigating.

Action

Record several urban legends or local ghost stories from willing storytellers as Courtney did (see page 319). Choose one representative story to transcribe and share with a group of fellow fieldworkers. Be prepared to talk about some of the research issues you faced: finding a storyteller, taping and transcribing the story, and analyzing underlying themes, values, and beliefs.

Which of the stories are similar to others you have heard before? What parts seem to be the traditional core, and which parts seem to be the creative variants? How do the details in the variant parts illustrate the values and belief systems in the culture or subculture? What fears, concerns, or anxieties does each story seem to address? What cultural lesson does it teach?

After you do some analysis, you might want to do some library research. Because of all these similarities and differences in folk narratives, folklorists keep carefully organized reference indexes. Most university libraries have Antti Aarne's *The Types of the Folk-Tale* and Stith Thompson's *Motif-Index of Folk Literature,* which we mentioned earlier in this chapter. You may also want to read urban tales published by folklorists like Jan Harald Brunvand. Hundreds of reference works are listed in both general catalogs and social science indexes in the categories of language, mythology, folklore, popular culture, anthropology, and ethnology. Library research will help you see the universal themes in folklore in all cultures and also help you track the details specific to the time and place of your own tale. You may want to write up your research findings, along with the story itself, to include in your research portfolio.

Response

Folklore researchers understand that urban folklore conveys underlying fears and values within the culture. Debbie Smith collected a story about food. Although she was attending college in North Carolina, the story came from her elementary school days in Florida. Other students provided many variants from places where they had lived. When you read it, you may recognize this traditional urban legend from a variant you've heard. While outsiders to this culture of fifth graders might reject this legend as absurd, insider elementary children find it entirely plausible:

The Cafeteria Pizza

At lunch in my fifth grade, my class sat in the cafeteria wishing for any food other than what the cafeteria ladies made. We settled into the entertainment of vying for the story that could gross everyone else out. Over our shepherd's pie and gray peas and chocolate milk, tale after tale was offered depicting all things disgusting to our entranced audience.

And then a nerd, Andre, came through with the story to end all cafeteria stories. He told us about the mad cafeteria worker at another school who was tired of feeding all the nagging kids. He had been fired once but returned to seek his revenge. One night, he entered the school and sliced open all the boxes of processed pizza and carefully put in pieces of broken razor blades into each pizza. The next day, they had served about 50 slices before they found a piece of shiny sausage and went to ask the teacher about it. All the kids were taken to the hospital, but no one suffered from fatal cuts inside their throats. And they never found the maniacal cafeteria worker. We lost our appetites as we pondered this story and its consequences. The next day our school served pizza.

Our anxieties about food run deeper than we realize. In contemporary life, we often eat prepared, frozen, or institutional food. We don't always know the people who make it, we don't always make it ourselves, we don't even see it being made, so many of our urban legends center on food preparation. This tale is a variant of many modern urban legends about mysterious or sinister food preparation: an angry cafeteria worker takes revenge on fifth graders. But it also holds important cultural lessons: watch out for unidentified revenge seekers who lurk around in unexpected places, don't nag cafeteria workers, and be satisfied with boring but safe food. This urban legend is believable because the teller says "it happened at another school" and the worker returned for revenge. We read news stories daily that share very similar details, so it is difficult to find the specifics that would make us doubt the story.

When we first discover forms of verbal art like urban legends, we're often surprised to notice that they have such traditional and universal characteristics. Although we've told them and heard them for much of our lives, it's interesting to see how many cultural values they carry. As with the themes of urban legends, we grow up with the frames of other kinds of narratives, such as fairy tales, which begin early in our childhoods. The fairy tale is another form of verbal art that draws on oral traditions and reflects the values and belief systems of a culture. But unlike urban legends, which attempt to prove that they're true, everyone knows that a fairy tale is fiction and accepts that from the outset.

Fairy tales move through history and across cultures as verbal performance. Folklorists can document versions of Cinderella, Sleeping Beauty, Dracula, and Red Riding Hood, for instance, in hundreds of cultures. One of our students who grew up in Belize decided to write his grandfather's Mayan version of

Hansel and Gretel, a well-known tale for centuries among his people, but one that had not been previously written down. Louis was surprised to learn that it had variants in other cultures. His Mayan version had three children instead of two: Delores, Sebastian, and José. Instead of a forest leading to a little cottage, the three siblings cleared their way through a jungle, "slept the night in one big bunch under a fig tree," and came upon an ominous tropical hut. Instead of an old witch's hot oven, there was a talking dog inside with a pot of boiling water who threatened the children. But the basic traditional elements were unchanged: siblings must collaborate and look out for each other to survive when their parents are absent.

Fairy tales or magic tales (*märchen*) are not just stories for children; they are another way a culture preserves its traditions, values, and belief systems—what scholars call our *unconscious culture* or *unexamined mythology*. We don't often realize that the very nature of fairy tales means that there is no one original, authentic version. Those of us who listened to Grimm's fairy tales learned the nineteenth-century Western European versions written into books by the Grimm brothers and first published in Germany in 1812. But growing up in twentieth-century North America, many of us also took in variants of those traditional fairy tales in Disney movies and more contemporary children's books and theater, TV productions, and audiotapes. Even though we are sometimes unaware of it, a great deal of classical literature originated in traditional folk tales. Because our mainstream American culture is so based on both print and electronic media, much of what we know to be our fairy tales come to us not as oral, shifting stories from a storyteller but in published form. We may have to look to our families and our ethnic or regional backgrounds to find more traditional oral forms of fairy tales.

Whether we've learned them from movies and books or from a relative, our fairy tales exist as unexamined mythology in our minds. Although most of us know better, a woman whistling the song from the Disney version of *Snow White*, "Someday My Prince Will Come," might have an unconscious belief that she will be saved from a jealous controlling person, get married, and live happily ever after. Simultaneously, her boyfriend might expect to charge his way toward a docile, forever smooth-skinned princess who can cook, clean, and transform his home each day while he's gone.

As with other forms of verbal performance, informed audiences of insiders know a fairy tale when they hear one. They know it is a fiction and that there will be recognizable recurring features: a central human character or two, recognizable beginnings and endings ("Once upon a time," "And they lived happily ever after"), talking animals or distorted humans who express certain truths or have magical powers, and a series of trials or tests. Informed audiences know that the story will somehow illustrate an important piece of knowledge in the culture. As with other forms of folklore, the fairy tale has a traditional core (recognizable and recurrent features) and creative variants (details specific to the culture in which the tale takes place, and special details the storyteller adds to make it his or her own version).

RESEARCHING STORIES: DISCOVERING DIFFERENCE

Verbal lore—culturally saturated words (like *silk* for Danling Fu), occupational phrases (like waitresses who are "in the weeds"), audience-directed verbal performance events (such as sharing a joke or proverb or casting a curse or spell), family stories, urban legends, and fairy tales—reveals not only how a group uses language but also much about a culture's rituals, beliefs and fears, and history. All these language events help the fieldworker translate insider ideas about a culture for outsiders to that culture. The most accessible language event for people researching another culture is to listen to storytelling, both for what the story is (the core version and different tellers' variants) and for how and to whom the story is told (the context, the conditions, and the audience).

In the following reading from an ethnographic study of everyday language practices, *Ways with Words: Language, Life, and Work in Communities and Classrooms,* researcher Shirley Brice Heath contrasts the storytelling traditions of two different communities that are only miles apart in the Piedmont Carolinas, an area near Elizabeth's university. Both communities, which Heath calls by the pseudonyms Roadville and Trackton, are made up of working-class residents who convey information, gossip, and stories in culturally specific ways. As you read this selection, which contrasts one section ("A Piece of Truth") about Roadville with another section ("Talkin' Junk") about Trackton, notice the differences in storytelling styles between the two communities. As always in fieldreading, look for things you recognize. You'll probably find some in both of these sections, whether you live near the Piedmont Carolinas or not, and this reading may help you analyze the storytelling practices of people in your own community.

In Roadville and in Trackton

Shirley Brice Heath

In Roadville

A *Piece of Truth*

Roadville residents worry about many things. Yet no Roadville home is a somber place where folks spend all their time worrying about money, their children's futures, and their fate at the hands of the mill. They create numerous occasions for celebration, most often with family members and church friends. On these occasions, they regale each other with "stories." To an outsider, these stories seem as though they should be embarrassing, even insulting to people present. It is difficult for the outsider to learn when to laugh, for Roadville people seem to laugh at the story's central character, usually the story-teller or someone else who is present.

A "story" in Roadville is "something you tell on yourself, or on your buddy, you know, it's all in good fun, and a li'l something to laugh about." Though this definition was given by a male, women define their stories in similar ways, stressing they are "good fun," and "don't mean no harm." Stories recount an actual event either witnessed by others or previously told in the presence of others and declared by them "a good story." Roadville residents recognize the purpose of the stories is to make people laugh by making fun of either the story-teller or a close friend in sharing an event and the particular actions of individuals within that event. However, stories "told on" someone other than the story-teller are never told unless the central character or someone who is clearly designated his representative is present. The Dee children sometimes tell stories on their father who died shortly after the family moved to Roadville, but they do so only in Mrs. Dee's presence with numerous positive adjectives describing their father's gruff nature. Rob Macken, on occasion, is the dominant character in stories which make fun of his ever-present willingness to point out where other folks are wrong. But Rob is always present on these occasions, and he is clearly included in the telling ("Ain't that right, Rob?" "Now you know that's the truth, hain't it?"), as story-tellers cautiously move through their tale about him, gauging how far to go by his response to the story.

Outside close family groups, stories are told only in sex-segregated groups. Women invite stories of other women, men regale each other with tales of their escapades on hunting and fishing trips, or their run-ins (quarrels) with their wives and children. Topics for women's stories are exploits in cooking, shopping, adventures at the beauty shop, bingo games, the local amusement park, their gardens, and sometimes events in their children's lives. Topics for men are big-fishing expeditions, escapades of their hunting dogs, times they have made fools of themselves, and exploits in particular areas of their expertise (gardening and raising a 90-lb pumpkin, a 30-lb cabbage, etc.). If a story is told to an initial audience and declared a good story on that occasion, this audience (or others who hear about the story) can then invite the story-teller to retell the story to yet other audiences. Thus, an invitation to tell a story is usually necessary. Stories are often requested with a question: "Has Betty burned any biscuits lately?" "Brought any possums home lately?" Marked behavior—transgressions from the behavioral norm generally expected of a "good hunter," "good cook," "good handyman," or a "good Christian"—is the usual focus of the story. The foolishness in the tale is a piece of truth about everyone present, and all join in a mutual laugh at not only the story's central character, but at themselves as well. One story triggers another, as person after person reaffirms a familiarity with the kind of experience just recounted. Such stories test publicly the strength of relationships and openly declare bonds of kinship and friendship. When the social bond is currently strong, such stories can be told with no "hard feelings." Only rarely, and then generally under the influence of alcohol or the strain of a test in the relationship from another source (job competition, an unpaid loan), does a story-telling become the occasion for an open expression of hostility.

Common experience in events similar to those of the story becomes an expression of social unity, a commitment to maintenance of the norms of the church and of the roles within the mill community's life. In telling a story, an individual shows that he belongs to the group: he knows about either himself or the subject of the story, and he understands the norms which were broken by the story's central character. Oldtimers, especially those who came to Roadville in the 1930s, frequently assert their long familiarity with certain norms as they tell stories on the young folks and on those members of their own family who moved away. There is always an unspoken understanding that some experiences common to the oldtimers can never be known by the young folks, yet they have benefited from the lessons and values these experiences enabled their parents to pass on to them.

In any social gathering, either the story-teller who himself announces he has a story or the individual who invites another to tell a story is, for the moment, in control of the entire group. He manages the flow of talk, the staging of the story, and dictates the topic to which all will adhere in at least those portions of their discourse which immediately follow the story-telling. At a church circle meeting, many of the neighborhood women had gathered, and Mrs. Macken was responsible for refreshments on this occasion. The business and lesson of the circle had ended, and she was preparing the refreshments, while the women milled about waiting for her to signal she was ready for them. Mrs. Macken looked up from arranging cookies on a plate and announced Sue had a story to tell. This was something she could not normally have done, since as a relative newcomer, a schoolteacher, and a known malcontent in Roadville, her status was not high enough to allow her to announce a story for someone who was as much of an oldtimer as Sue. However, as the hostess of the circle, she had some temporary rank.

Roadville Text IV

MRS. MACKEN:	Sue, you oughta tell about those rolls you made the other day, make folks glad you didn't try to serve fancy rolls today.
MRS. DEE:	Sue, what'd you do, do you have a new recipe?
MRS. MACKEN:	You might call it that
SUE:	|
	I, hh, wanna=
MARTHA:	=Now Millie [Mrs. Macken], you hush and let Sue give us *her* story.
SUE:	Well, as a matter of fact, I did have this new recipe, one I got out of *Better Homes and Gardens*, and I thought I'd try it, uh, you see, it called for scalded milk, and I had just started the milk when the telephone rang, and I went to get it. It was Leona/*casting her eyes at Mrs. Macken*/. I thought I turned the stove off, and when I came back, the burner was off, uh, so I didn't think anything about it, poured the milk in on the yeast, and went to kneading. Felt a little hot. Well, anyway,

put the stuff out to rise, and came back, and it looked almost like Stone Mountain, thought that's a strange recipe, so I kneaded it again, and set it out in rolls. This time I had rocks, uh, sorta like 'em, the kind that roll up all smooth at the beach. Well, I wasn't gonna throw that stuff all out, so I cooked it. Turned out even harder than those rocks, if that's possible, and nobody would eat 'em, couldn't even soften 'em in buttermilk. I was trying to explain how the recipe was so funny, you know, see, how I didn't know what I did wrong, and Sally piped up and said 'Like yeah, when you was on phone, I came in, saw this white stuff a-boiling, and I turned it off.' (pause) Then I knew, you know, that milk was too hot, killed the yeast/*looking around at the women*/. Guess I'll learn to keep my mind on my own business and off other folks'.

The story was punctuated by gestures of kneading, turns of the head in puzzlement, and looks at the audience to see if they acknowledged understanding of the metaphors and similes. Stone Mountain is a campground in the region which everyone at the circle meeting had visited; it rises out of the ground like a giant smooth-backed whale. The beach is a favorite summer vacation spot for Roadville families, and the women often collect the smooth rocks from the beach to put on top of the dirt in their flower pots.

Several conventions of stories and story-telling in Roadville stand out in this incident. The highest status members present, Mrs. Dee and her grand-daughter Martha, renounce Sue's story and subtly convey that Mrs. Macken stepped out of line by asking Sue to tell a story on this occasion. Within her narrative, Sue follows a major requirement of a "good story": it must be factual, and any exaggeration or hyperbole must be so qualified as to let the audience know the story-teller does not accept such descriptions as literally true. Sue qualifies her Stone Mountain description with "almost," her equation of the rolls with rocks by "sorta like 'em," and her final comparison of the rolls to rocks with "if that's possible." She attempts to stick strictly to the truth and exaggerates only with hedges and qualifications.

Perhaps the most obligatory convention Sue follows is that which requires a Roadville story to have a moral or summary message which highlights the weakness admitted in the tale. "Stories" in these settings are similar to testimonials given at revival meetings and prayer sessions. On these occasions, individuals are invited to give a testimonial or to "tell your story." These narratives are characterized by a factual detailing of temporal and spatial descriptions and recounting of conversations by direct quotation ("Then the Lord said to me:"). Such testimonials frequently have to do with "bringing a young man to his senses" and having received answers to specific prayers. The detailing of the actual event is often finished off with Scriptural quotation, making it clear that the story bears out the promise of "the Word." Sue's story is confession-like, and its summing up carries a double meaning, both a literal one ("on my own business" = cooking) and a figurative one ("on my own business" = general affairs). Any woman in the group can quote Scripture describing the sins of which the tongue is capable (for example, James 3:6 which likens the tongue to a fire which spreads evil).

Unspoken here is the sin of Sue and Leona—gossip—the recounting and evaluating of the activities and personalities of others. Gossip is a frequent sermon topic and a behavior looked upon as a characteristic female weakness. Leona, who is not present at the circle meeting, is a known gossip, who occasionally telephones several of the women to fill them in on news in the neighborhood. All of the women know, but none says explicitly, that any phone call with Leona is likely to bring trouble, both to those who are the topics of her phone conversation and to those who are weak enough to listen to her. The story, told at the end of a church circle meeting, appears to be an innocent piece of female chatter, but it carries a message to all present which reminds them of their own weakness in listening to Leona. All the women have gossiped, and all have given in to listening to Leona at one time or another. Yet on this public occasion, all avoid direct negative talk about either Leona or anyone else, since engaging in this censured activity in such a public setting where more than two individuals are present would be foolish. Instead Sue's story is an occasion in which all recognize their common, but unspoken, Christian ideal of disciplined tongue. The major understandings and background knowledge on which a full interpretation of the story depends are unarticulated.

Sue's story carries subtle messages about the values and practices of the culture out of which the story comes. She reaffirms that the most frequent gossip in Roadville takes place between only two people, with an unstated and often unfulfilled agreement that neither will reveal her participation to others; breaches of such trust are frequent causes of female disagreement. Moreover, Sue asserts her maintenance of certain community norms for home-makers: she makes her bread "from scratch" instead of buying store goods; she is unwilling to throw out food; she has obviously trained Sally, her daughter, to be attentive to kitchen matters. Picking up, or recognizing all of this information depends on the familiarity with Roadville's norms and daily customs which the women of the church circle share.

In several ways, stories such as Sue's are similar to Biblical parables, a frequent source for sermons and Bible lessons, and a literary source familiar to all. Parables told by Jesus recount daily experiences common to the people of his day. Often parables end with a summary statement which is both a condemnation of one or more of the story's characters and a warning to those who would hear and understand the parable for its relevance to their own lives. In a parable, two items or events are placed side by side for comparison. The details of the story bring out its principal point or primary meaning, but there is little or no emotional expressiveness within the story evaluating the actions of the characters. The action is named and detailed, but its meaning to the characters is not set forth in exposition or through a report of the emotions of those involved. Biblical parables often open with formulas such as "The Kingdom of heaven is like unto this..." (Matthew 13:24, 13:31, 13:33, 13:44, 13:45, 20:1, 25:1), or admonitions to listen: "Listen then if you have ears" (Matthew 13:9) and "Listen and understand" (Matthew 15:10). Roadville's parable-like stories often open with announcement of the comparison of the events of the story to another situation: "That's like what happened to me..." Both men and women often open their stories with the simple comment "They say..." or a metaphor such as "We've got another bulldog on our hands" (referring to a fighting personality who is the central character in an upcoming story). In ways similar to Biblical parables, Roadville folks share with their listeners experiences which provide a lesson with a meaning for the life of all. The story is told using direct discourse whenever possible: "And he goes 'Now, you look out.'" or "Like yeah when you was on the phone..."

For the best of the parable-like stories, that is, those which are told repeatedly or are handed down in families over generations, the retelling of the entire story is often not necessary. Only its summary point need be repeated to remind listeners of the lesson behind the story. Proverbs or well-known sayings also carry lessons stating the general will of the community and ideals of Roadville families. Understanding of these depends, as do parable-like stories, on comparing one thing to another, for example, seeing similarities across nature.

> A whistlin' girl and a crowin' hen will come to no good end.
>
> A rollin' stone gathers no moss.
>
> A stitch in time saves nine.
>
> Rain before seven, clear by eleven.

For those activities which are traditionally part of the daily routine of mill families' lives—agriculture, weather, male-female relations, pregnancy and childbirth—proverbial guides to behavior abound. Proverbs help determine when certain crops are planted and harvested, predict rain, sunshine, good fishing or bad, link personality traits to physical features, and dictate behaviors of mothers-to-be. The anonymous and collective voices of those who have abided by these lessons in their experiences remind Roadville residents of behavioral norms and reinforce expectations of predictable actions and attitudes among community members.

The Bible's parables and proverbs are sometimes quite consciously used as a written model for Roadville's oral stories and proverbs. However, few written sources, other than the Bible, seem to influence either the content or the structure of oral stories in Roadville. Access to written stories, other than those in the Bible, is relatively rare. Women buy home and garden magazines and read their stories of successful remodeling or sewing projects—testimonials on the merits of budget shopping, thriftiness, and tenacity in do-it-yourself projects. Some women buy "True Story" magazines and publications which feature the personal stories of movie and television personalities, but they do not usually read these publicly. Some women occasionally buy paperback novels, and when asked about their hobbies, they often include reading, but then add comments such as "There's no time for it, for reading, you know, for pleasure or anything like that."

In church-related activities, they not only use stories from the Bible, but they occasionally hear certain other types of content-related stories. The circle meeting at which Sue was asked to tell her story is an example of one such activity. In such meetings, women share study of a designated Bible passage or a book of the Bible. The leader often reads from other short story-like materials to illustrate the need to follow the precepts covered in the Biblical passage. Throughout the discussion, however, there are numerous references to "our own stories [the experiences of those present]" which better relate to the Bible message than do the printed materials supplied for Bible study. Men's and women's Bible study groups prefer that a pastor or an elder lead them. The pastor sometimes suggests to lay leaders that they use a book of exposition of the Scriptures (especially when the Bible study focuses on a particular book of the Bible, such as Revelation). Some members of the Bible study group may be assigned portions of supplementary materials to read and discuss at the next Bible study. However, such efforts usually fail miserably. Roadville men and women do not like to read in public and do not wish to admit their lack of understanding of expository materials. They state strong preferences that, if any written materials are used to expand on Biblical passages, the pastor, and not they, should do it. As Mrs. Turner's mother explained. "I believe what the preacher speaks to be the truth, because I feel he is our leader, and I don't feel, well, I feel like *he* is tellin' us the right thing."

Thus, in interpreting the Bible, church members prefer either their own stories or Biblical accounts to written stories—whether factual expositions or tales of the lives of other modern-day Christians. Their own stories are often modeled on Biblical parables, but they are also personal accounts of what God's Word has meant to them. They reject depersonalized written accounts which come from unfamiliar sources. They use their own stories told on themselves and their friends to entertain and instruct, as they highlight personal and communal weaknesses and their struggles either to overcome them or to live with them....

In Trackton

Talkin' Junk

Trackton folks see the truth and the facts in stories in ways which differ greatly from those of Roadville. Good story-tellers in Trackton may base their stories on an actual event, but they creatively fictionalize the details surrounding the real event, and the outcome of the story may not even resemble what indeed happened. The best stories are "junk," and anyone who can "talk junk" is a good story-teller. Talkin' junk includes laying on highly exaggerated compliments and making wildly exaggerated comparisons as well as telling narratives. Straightforward factual accounts are relatively rare in Trackton and are usually told only on serious occasions: to give a specific piece of information to someone who has requested it, to provide an account of the troubles of a highly respected individual, or to exchange information about daily rounds of activities when neither party wishes to intensify the interaction or draw it out. Trackton's "stories," on the other hand, are intended to intensify social interactions and to give all parties an opportunity to share in not only the unity of the common experience on which the story may be based, but also in the humor of the wide-ranging language play and imagination which embellish the narrative.

From a very early age, Trackton children learn to appreciate the value of a good story for capturing an audience's attention or winning favors. Boys, especially on those occasions when they are teased or challenged in the plaza, hear their antics become the basis of exaggerated tales told by adults and older children to those not present at the time of the challenge. Children hear themselves made into characters in stories told again and again. They hear adults use stories form the Bible or from their youth to scold or warn against misbehavior.... Children's misdeeds provoke the punchline or summing up of a story which they are not told, but are left to imagine: "Dat póliceman'll come 'n git you, like he did Frog." The story behind this summary is never told, but is held out as something to be recreated anew in the imagination of every child who hears this threat.

Trackton children can create and tell stories about themselves, but they must be clever if they are to hold the audience's attention and to maintain any extended conversational space in an on-going discourse. Young children repeatedly try to break into adult discourse with a story, but if they do not succeed in relating the first few lines of their story to the on-going topic or otherwise exciting the listeners' interests, they are ignored. An adult's accusation, on the other hand, gives children an open stage for creating a story, but this one must also be "good," i.e., highly exaggerated, skillful in language play, and full of satisfactory comparisons to redirect the adult's attention from the infraction provoking the accusation.

Adults and older siblings do not make up sustained chronological narratives specially for young children, and adults do not read to young children. The flow of time in Trackton, which admits few scheduled blocks of time for routinized activities, does not lend itself to a bedtime schedule of reading a story. The homes provide barely enough space for the necessary activities of family living, and there is no separate room, book corner, or even outdoor seat where a child and parent can read together out of the constant flow of human interactions. The stage of the plaza almost always offers live action and is tough competition for book-reading. Stories exchanged among adults do not carry moral summaries or admonitions about behavior; instead they focus on detailing of events and personalities, and they stress conflict and resolution or attempts at resolution. Thus adults see no reason to direct these stories to children for teaching purposes. When stories are told among adults, young children are not excluded from the audience, even if the content refers to adult affairs, sexual exploits, crooked politicians, drunk ministers, or wayward choir-leaders. If children respond to such stories with laughter or verbal comments, they are simply warned to "keep it to yo'self." Some adult stories are told only in sex-segregated situations. Men recount to their buddies stories they would not want their wives or the womenfolk to know about; women share with each other stories of quarrels with their menfolk or other women. Many men know about formulaic toasts (long epic-like accounts of either individual exploits or struggles of black people) from visitors from up-North or men returned from the armed services, but these are clearly external to the Trackton man's repertoire, and they do not come up in their social gatherings. Instead, Trackton men and their friends focus on stories which tell of their own current adventures or recount fairly recent adventures of particular personalities known to all present. All of these are highly self-assertive or extol the strength and cleverness of specific individuals.

Women choose similar topics for their stories: events which have happened to them, things they have seen, or events they have heard about. Considerable license is taken with these stories, however, and each individual is expected to tell the story, not as she has heard it, but with her own particular style. Women tell stories of their exploits at the employment office, adventures at work in the mill, or episodes in the lives of friends, husbands, or mutual acquaintances. Laced through with evaluative comments ("Didja ever hear of such a thing?" "You know how he ak [act] when he drunk." "You been like dat."), the stories invite participation from listeners. In fact, such participation is necessary reinforcement for the story-teller. Perhaps the most characteristic feature of story-telling by adults is the dramatic use of dialogue. Dovie Lou told the following story one afternoon to a group of six women sitting on the porch of Lillie Mae's house. The Henning family was transient and had been in Trackton only a few weeks.

Trackton Text V

> DOVIE LOU: Now you know me—I'm Dovie Lou, and you may think I'ma put up wid that stuff off Hennin's ol' lady, right? Who, who, after all, gives a hoot about her—or him, for dat matter? I been here quite a while—gonna be here a time yet too. She holler off her porch "Yo man, he over in Darby Sat'day nite." I say "Shit, what you know 'bout my man? My man." It was a rainy night, you know ain't no use gettin' fussied up to go out on a night like dat. Tessie 'n I go play bingo. But dat ol' woman, she ak like she some Channel Two reporter or sump'n:

"P.B. Evans was seen today on the corner of Center and Main Street. He hadda bottle in each hip pocket, and one under his Lóndon Fóg hat. Sadie Lou [a well-known stripper in a local topless bar] was helpin' him across the street, holin' her white mink in front of him to keep his shíny shoes from gettin' wet. The weather tomorrow promises to be cloudy for some."

What she think she doin', tellin' *me/looks around to audience/*'bout my ol' man? Sayin' "He lookin' mighty fine, yes sireeeeee." (long pause) She betta keep */casting a sharp look in the direction of the Hennings' house/* her big mouf 'n stay shut up in dat house.

Throughout the story, the audience laughed, nodded, and provided "yeah," "you right," "you know it." Dovie Lou's shift to the exaggerated Standard English of the Channel Two reporter brought gales of laughter from the audience.

Numerous cultural assertions are made in the story. The evaluative introduction establishes Dovie Lou as an oldtimer, a fixture in the neighborhood, and Henning and his old lady as relative newcomers. Dovie Lou announces herself a victor before the story begins. Later, she makes it clear that she knew her man, P.B. Evans, was out that night, and that she had had a chance to go out with him, but had decided it was not worth getting "fussied up" to go out in the rain. Instead, she and a girlfriend had gone to play bingo. She uses the TV report to show exaggeration, to report her man out with a famous stripper, and also to brag about the fancy dress of her man who wears name-brand clothes and has a reputation for keeping himself "fine." The final point of the story asserts that her animosity to the Henning woman is not over. Dovie Lou warns that the newcomer should stay inside and not join the neighborhood women on their porches. Once Dovie Lou's anger wears off or she is reunited with her man publicly, she can fend off Henning's wife's stories. Dovie Lou's story is based on fact: Henning's wife had said something to Dovie Lou about her man being out with another woman. But beyond this basis in fact, Dovie Lou's story is highly creative, and she ranges far from the true facts to tell a story which extols her strengths and announces her faith in her ultimate victory over both her wayward man and her "big-mouth" neighbor....

The Traditions of Story-Telling

People in both Trackton and Roadville spend a lot of time telling stories. Yet the form, occasions, content, and functions of their stories differ greatly. They structure their stories differently; they hold different scales of features on which stories are recognized as *stories* and judged as good or bad. The patterns of interaction surrounding the actual telling of a story vary considerably from Roadville to Trackton. One community allows only stories which are factual and have little exaggeration; the other uses reality only as the germ of a highly creative fictionalized account. One uses stories to reaffirm group membership and behavioral norms, the other to assert individual strengths and powers. Children in the two communities hear different kinds of stories; they develop competence in telling stories in highly contrasting ways.

Roadville story-tellers use formulaic openings: a statement of a comparison or a question asked either by the story-teller or by the individual who has invited the telling of the story. Their stories maintain a strict chronicity, with direct discourse reported, and no explicit exposition of meaning or direct expression of evaluation of the behavior of the main character allowed. Stories end with a summary statement of a moral or a proverb, or a Biblical quotation. Trackton story-tellers use few formulaic openings, except the story-teller's own introduction of himself. Frequently, an abstract begins the story, asserting that the point of the story is to parade the strengths and victories of the story-teller. Stories maintain little chronicity; they move from event to event with numerous interspersions of evaluation of the behaviors of story characters and reiterations of the point of the story. Stories have no formulaic closing, but may have a reassertion of the strengths of the main character, which may be only the opening to yet another tale of adventure.

In Roadville, a story must be invited or announced by someone other than the story-teller. Only certain community members are designated good story-tellers. A story is recognized by the group as an assertion of community membership and agreement on behavioral norms. The marked behavior of the story-teller and audience alike is seen as exemplifying the weaknesses of all and the need for persistence in overcoming such weaknesses. Trackton story-tellers, from a young age, must be aggressive in inserting their stories into an on-going stream of discourse. Story-telling is highly competitive. Everyone in a conversation may want to tell a story, so only the most aggressive wins out. The stress is on the strengths of the individual who is the story's main character, and the story is not likely to unify listeners in any sort of agreement, but to provoke challenges and counterchallenges to the character's ways of overcoming an adversary. The "best stories" often call forth highly diverse additional stories, all designed not to unify the group, but to set out the individual merits of each member of the group.

Roadville members reaffirm their commitment to community and church values by giving factual accounts of their own weaknesses and the lessons learned in overcoming these. Trackton members announce boldly their individual strength in having been creative, persistent, and undaunted in the face of conflict. In Roadville, the sources of stories are personal experience and a familiarity with Biblical parables, church-related stories of Christian life, and testimonials given in church and home lesson-circles. Their stories are tales of transgressions which make the point of reiterating the expected norms of behavior of man, woman, hunter, fisherman, worker, and Christian. The stories of Roadville are true to the facts of an event; they qualify exaggeration and hedge if they might seem to be veering from an accurate reporting of events.

The content of Trackton's stories, on the other hand, ranges widely, and there is "truth" only in the universals of human strength and persistence praised and illustrated in the tale. Fact is often hard to find, though it is usually the seed of the story. Playsongs, ritual insults, cheers, and stories are assertions of the strong over the weak, of the power of the person featured in the story. Anyone other than the story-teller/main character may be subjected to mockery, ridicule, and challenges to show he is not weak, poor, or ugly.

In both communities, stories entertain; they provide fun, laughter, and frames for other speech events which provide a lesson or a witty display of verbal skill. In Roadville, a proverb, witty saying, or Scriptural quotation inserted into a story adds to both the entertainment value of the story and to its unifying role. Group knowledge of a proverb or saying, or approval of Scriptural quotation reinforces the communal experience which forms the basis of Roadville's stories. In Trackton, various types of language play, imitations of other community members or TV personalities, dramatic gestures and shifts of voice quality, and rhetorical questions and expressions of emotional evaluations add humor and draw out the interaction of story-teller and audience. Though both communities use their stories to entertain, Roadville adults see their stories as didactic: the purpose of a story is to make a point—a point about the conventions of behavior. Audience and story-teller are drawn together in a common bond through acceptance of the merits of the story's point for all. In Trackton, stories often have no point; they may go on as long as the audience enjoys the story-teller's entertainment. Thus a story-teller may intend on his first entry into a stream of discourse to tell only one story, but he may find the audience reception such that he can move from the first story into another, and yet another. Trackton audiences are unified by the story only in that they recognize the entertainment value of the story, and they approve stories which extol the virtues of an individual. Stories do not teach lessons about proper behavior; they tell of individuals who excel by outwitting the rules of conventional behavior.

Shirley Brice Heath's study of language and life in contrasting communities focuses on communication styles. As a researcher, Heath spent over a decade recording data from fieldnotes, audio- and videotapes, logs, pictures, and artifacts. She provides a textured study of "ways with words" among groups who shared a common geography but not cultural backgrounds or values.

THE RESEARCH PORTFOLIO: SYNTHESIS

As you've worked your way through the exercises in this chapter, you've researched, read, and written a lot. Whether you chose to focus on your main fieldworking project or have done each exercise separately, you've probably piled up a lot of writing—transcripts, lists, short analyses, and written examples of verbal art.

One of the jobs of a research portfolio is to help you synthesize what you have collected and selected. It offers you an opportunity to reflect on what you've learned and on how your research writing fits into the larger picture of your research. It suggests how all this material will help you shape your future goals—both for the project and for yourself as a reader, writer, and researcher.

You've read excerpts from a classic published ethnography (Zora Neale Hurston's hoodoo doctor from *Mules and Men*), a folklorist's article about urban legends (Jan Harald Brunvand's discussion of "The Roommate's Death"), and ethnographer Shirley Brice Heath's study of everyday language practices. You've also read work that we, our colleagues, and our students have done: the interview with Danling Fu, Sara Voreis's and Rick Zollo's glossaries, Donna Qualley's waitress stories and reflection on her position, and Lori Bateman's collections of sayings and proverbs.

And if you've tried one or more of the exercises, you have linked your own research project to extended writing about language in a cultural site. You may have:

- Classified insider language by exploring the word,
- Clustered, categorized, and analyzed language used in occupational groups,
- Gathered and interpreted a range of verbal art (proverbs, jokes, sayings, chants, and curses), and
- Collected, written, and shared urban folktales.

At this point, for your portfolio, we suggest three ways to synthesize your studies of language and language use: focusing on personal history, use of language, and verbal art. You will want to write reflections and share them with your portfolio partner, and you will want to synthesize what all of these exercises, coupled with the readings, have taught you so far.

Personal History

What is your own personal history with verbal art?   In this chapter, we have offered several personal accounts of verbal art, but we have not invited you to think about your own. Here is an opportunity to synthesize with a personal reflection, applying what you've learned about verbal art by looking back at your own history. You may want to focus on one of these questions, or you may instead want to write a traditional story from your own cultural background to put in your portfolio:

- What proverbs or sayings governed your growing-up life?
- What special family language "events" happened in your home? At family celebrations? In the subculture of your workplace, your school, your church, or another subculture to which you belong?
- What kinds of stories were important in your background? Who were the important storytellers? How many different audiences have you been a member of? What has been your own role as a storyteller?

Use of Language

What have you learned about language and language use? The many forms of verbal art that you have studied and collected offer you an array of ways to look at language use and storytelling. Write a reflective analysis of yourself at this point as a language researcher:

- As you survey all the data, what themes do you see about your process as a researcher?
- Which themes do you seem particularly interested in? Which themes do you seem to discard?
- How did your expectations match the data you actually assembled? What kinds of assumptions did you make before you began your research on language? What surprised you?
- What kinds of personal filters interfered with your interpretations?
- What language behavior do you want to know more about? How would you go about obtaining more data?
- What have you learned about language and language use that will be important to you as a reader, a writer, and a researcher?

Verbal Art

What do you now know about verbal art for your research project? If you related all your exercises to your fieldsite, you have done important work toward your final project. As you reread all the data you've collected, which of the exercises will be most useful for describing the language practices of the subculture you are researching? Using these guidelines, write a reflective response about yourself as a language researcher at this cultural site:

- What words, phrases, or insider languages have given you insights into the culture you are studying?
- How do you serve as a "cultural translator" with your informants?
- What has surprised you most about the language use of the people at your site? What verbal behaviors would you like to know more about? How would you go about getting that data?
- What forms of verbal art (proverbs, jokes, curses, chants, stories, urban legends) have you looked for and found at your site?
- How have your informants reacted to your interest in their use of language? What were they eager to share? What made them nervous? What have you learned from them about researching language?
- What have you learned about yourself as a researcher of language? What are you good at? What kinds of skills do you need to practice?

FIELDWRITING: DIALOGUE ON THE PAGE

In the fieldwriting section in Chapter 3, we reviewed how to cite your published and unpublished written data sources accurately for your reader. But we recognize that in doing fieldwork, the researcher has a special responsibility to use informants' words as carefully as any written source material. Fieldwriters choose the most appropriate way to represent oral language on the written page when they record informants' voices—on tape, in fieldnotes, and in transcripts and texts.

As fieldwriters, we need to create texts that embrace our informants' diverse voices and also include our own. Their voices speak of human difference, and it is that difference we need to preserve. When we research verbal art—gather words, assemble terms and sayings, conduct interviews and record stories—our data is language, the language of our informants. Rather than overwriting or erasing our informants' language, we want their voices to tell the fieldwork story along with ours.

When we wrote this chapter, we faced this very dilemma. We wanted to include informants we knew in our personal lives: our friends Danling Fu, whom we interviewed, and Donna Qualley, whose waitress gossip study we quote. We wanted to include our students' research from their informants: glossaries, lists of proverbs and sayings, and urban legends. And we wanted these voices to join those of the published writers, which came from our quirky collection of books—folklore, fiction, journalism, and nonfiction related to oral language. We combined these different sources in our chapter, oral and written, to illustrate the chapter's theme: how language represents culture.

To show this connection between oral language and culture, we made choices about how best to represent language on the page. When you write about your fieldwork, you'll choose among options, too. The fieldworkers whose projects we feature bring their informants' words to life using transcripts, ethnopoetics, and dialogue. They are able to do this only because they documented original conversations in their fieldnotes or in transcripts. Fieldworkers *cannot legitimately make up informants' words,* any more than scholars can legitimately plagiarize someone else's texts. It is critical to represent people's words with accuracy, for their integrity and for our own.

One way to present informants' language on the page is by borrowing dialogue techniques from fiction, as Rick Zollo did in Chapter 1 with Delia Moon. And in this chapter, you've read Donna Qualley's waitress gossip at Norton's Seafood restaurant, which she presents in the form of a fictional conversation. Here, in this conversation between waitresses Rae and Erin, you'll see the standard conventions for writing conversation in dialogue: indenting each time the speaker shifts, framing each sentence with quotation marks, and using strong verbs to indicate response (notice that instead of *says,* Donna uses verbs like *interjects, mumbles, begins,* and *laugh*). Donna doesn't need to identify Erin or Rae each time they speak because the indentations and punctuation do it for her. As the researcher, Donna identifies herself in the conversation only twice, by using *I* outside the quotation.

"I had this young couple."

"How old?" Erin interjects.

"In their twenties I would guess. They order two fish and chips and two glasses of water."

"Cheap. I'm surprised they didn't ask to split one meal," Erin mumbles.

"When they are done I put the check on the table and tell them I will be right back to collect it for them. I go into the kitchen and when I come back, there is a ten-dollar bill, a dime, a nickel, and a penny on the table."

"How much is the bill?" I ask.

"Ten fifteen."

"That makes me so mad…" Erin begins.

"But," Rae smiles, "the woman had left her coat on the chair. They were in such a hurry to get out she forgot her coat! I grab the coat, check, and money, and then I see her coming back for her coat…"

"I hope you kept it until they left a better tip," I laugh.

"I said to this woman, 'Oh, did you come back for your change?'"

"You really said that? How much was the bill again?" Erin asks.

"Ten fifteen, and they left me ten sixteen. Well, this woman turns all red and apologetic and says, 'We didn't have any money—we thought this was a takeout place.' Yeah, right. They knew what they were doing."

The waitress story from Greta Paules's book *Dishing It Out: Power and Resistance among Waitresses in a New Jersey Restaurant* illustrates another way to present an informant's dialogue. In this quotation, a waitress tells a whole stiffing story about herself and her friend Kaddie, and the researcher records it. Note that within this quoted transcript, the waitress quotes her friend, Kaddie, who participated in the stiffing story.

This party of two guys come in and they order thirty to forty dollars' worth of food…and they stiff us. Every time. So Kaddie told them, "If you don't tip us, we're not going to wait on you." They said, "We'll tip you." So Kaddie waited on them, and they tipped her. The next night they came in, I waited on them and they didn't tip me. The third time they came in [the manager] put them in my station and I told [the manager] straight up, "I'm not waiting on them…" So when they came in the next night…[they] said, "Are you going to give us a table?" I said, "You going to tip me? I'm not going to wait on you." (31)

Sometimes, for variety and conciseness, a fieldwriter chooses to summarize rather than use a direct quote when she writes dialogue. Karen Downing combines summary and direct quotation to describe her phone encounter with Ginny James at Photo Phantasies:

When I finally talk with Ginny during this second phone call, she leaves out the conversational niceties. Yes, my letter had arrived in the mail after all.

"I'll have to clear this request with headquarters, which I can do tomorrow. I'm leaving for a Photo Phantasies meeting in Chicago. What kind of class is this for? Business? Sociology? I'll call you Wednesday night and leave a message about whether or not it's OK."

Bringing oral language to the page presents a challenge to the fieldwriter. We've shown you several ways we've done it in this chapter, including transcripts, ethnopoetic notation, and dialogue—directly quoted and summarized. When you work with the spoken words of an informant, your goal is to preserve the integrity of the informant's original verbal art and respect it. As with any art form, how you choose to display your informants' language for the reader must be a conscious and carefully considered choice.

FieldWords

Dialect A regional variation in language, such as English spoken in Tidewater Virginia, Downeast Maine, or South Texas.

Ethnopoetic notation A procedure for analysis of transcripts in which a language researcher turns oral speech into poetic or fictive form.

Kinesics The study of how individuals express themselves through body position and motion (facial expression, eye contact, posture, and gesture).

Linguist A person who studies language and language behaviors.

Lore The implicit rituals, beliefs, language, stories, or traditional behaviors that surround a culture or subculture.

Performance In performance theory, an interaction between a performer and an audience who understands many of the cultural values and behaviors surrounding the act (joke, story, saying, curse).

Proxemics The study of how individuals communicate nonverbally when in groups.

Variant An alteration from the traditional core of a folk art, according to a performer's or artisan's specific history, cultural understanding, and personal creativity.

Verbal art Language behaviors within a culture or subculture, ranging from informal everyday events (grunts, shouts, taunts, jokes, gossip, stories) to more highly ritualized forms (proverbs and taboos, songs and chants, urban legends, curses and spells, myths and tales, traditional stories and ceremonies).

FIELDREADING

Aarne, Antti. *The Types of the Folk-Tale: A Classification and Bibliography.* New York: Franklin, 1971.

Berger, Peter L., and Thomas Luckman. *The Social Construction of Reality.* New York: Anchor-Doubleday, 1967.

Brunvand, Jan Harald. *The Vanishing Hitchhiker: American Urban Legends and Their Meanings.* New York: Norton, 1981.

Chiseri-Strater, Elizabeth. *Academic Literacies: The Public and Private Discourse of University Students.* Portsmouth: Boynton/Cook, 1991.

Gleason, Norma, ed. *Proverbs from around the World.* New York: Citadel, 1992.

Heath, Shirley Brice. *Ways with Words: Language, Life, and Work in Communities and Classrooms.* New York: Cambridge UP, 1983.

Hurston, Zora Neale. *Mules and Men.* 1935. New York: Harper, 1990.

Ives, Edward. *The Tape-Recorded Interview: A Manual for Fieldworkers in Folklore and Oral History.* Knoxville: U Tennessee P, 1980.

Jackson, Bruce. *Fieldwork.* Urbana: U of Illinois P, 1987.

Kochman, Thomas. *Black and White Styles in Conflict.* Chicago: U Chicago P, 1981.

Moffatt, Michael. "The Discourse of the Dorm: Race, Friendship, and Culture among College Youth." *Symbolizing America.* Ed. Herve Varenne. Lincoln: U Nebraska P, 1986.

Momaday, N. Scott. *House Made of Dawn.* New York: Harper, 1966.

Paules, Greta Foff. *Dishing It Out: Power and Resistance among Waitresses in a New Jersey Restaurant.* Philadelphia: Temple UP, 1991.

Spradley, James P. *The Ethnographic Interview.* Fort Worth: Holt, 1979.

Spradley, James P., and Brenda Mann. *The Cocktail Waitress: Women's Work in a Male World.* New York: Wiley, 1975.

Tannen, Deborah. *You Just Don't Understand: Women and Men in Conversation.* New York: Morrow, 1990.

Thompson, Stith. *Motif-Index of Folk Literature.* Bloomington: Indiana UP, 1965.

Turner, Patricia. *I Heard It through the Grapevine: Rumor in African-American Culture.* Berkeley: U California P, 1993.

Zipes, Jack. *Don't Bet on the Prince: Contemporary Feminist Fairy Tales in North America and England.* New York: Routledge, 1987.

See also:

General Reference Works: "Language Dictionaries" for slang, allusions, jargon, and symbols, "Thematic Indexes," and "Folklore Guides."

Social and Behavioral Sciences: Mythology, folklore and popular culture dictionaries, specialized encyclopedias and handbooks.

FieldPoem

Comment on Ethnopoetics and Literacy
Wendy Rose

for Jerome

I gradually came to understand that the words on the pages were trapped words. Anyone could learn to decipher the symbols and turn the trapped words loose again into speech. The ink of the print trapped the thoughts; they could no more get away than a domboo could get out of a pit.

—MODUPE, AFRICAN WRITER

Pick the words
from the evening rain
with throats exposed,
bound and thrown, quickly
thrust the spike in
bladeside down and turn,
now pull it up
from the neck
and drain them all
side by side,
guts on the ground,
paws in a small pile,
everything severed
and stripped down to bone.

Re-make the bodies
in different positions—
another with one forefoot lifted;
strengthen those dead bones with sticks,
puff out that hanging skin with cotton,
make the muscles bunch again with clay.
Where once they scanned the sky
or the ground for hawk shadows,
put tiny glass balls or bits of amber.
Admire what you have done.

Re-arrange the figures
into a natural scene.
Paint the background
into jungle or desert,

scatter sand or leaves
around their claws. Remember
how you danced to their beauty,
how you caught your breath watching them run,
how you moved your head
listening to them call to each other
to mate in the moonlight.

You make them move
with the tip of your finger.

You think that now
they will live forever.

Commentary

by Carol Mimi Harvey

Words can strip the life from lived experience, reducing the sights, sounds, smells, feelings and tastes of fieldwork to mere listings, neat categories.

Words can also share the confounding, the lyrical, the magic of life with all its surprises, shocks, fascinations, and exquisite variety. Words should never plant life rigid and not natural—the "truth" of lives caught for all time—in some museum-exhibit text, caught in the headlights of a "scientist's" gaze.

This poem reminds me to write sensuous tales, fictions, poetry, field memories and all the other ways of sharing those dances in the moonlight, those voices calling to me, those people and places from my fieldwork that will live forever in my memory. This poem demands that I write anything but dry, musty, analytical, lifeless ethnographies. How else to capture the extraordinary of everyday life? How else to share with my readers the stranger-than-fiction, Alice-Down-the-Rabbit-Hole quality of my lived fieldwork experiences? I owe it to myself. I owe it to the extraordinary people with whom I have worked. I owe it to my readers who have not had, and may never have, the wonderful experience of doing fieldwork with the people whose lives I struggle to re-create…with words.

Carol Mimi Harvey received her M.A. in Asian studies and adult education from the University of Victoria, British Columbia, Canada. She is currently pursuing doctoral work in communication studies with a focus on the ethnography of communication.

7

Researching People:
The Collaborative Listener

Ethnography is interaction, collaboration. What it demands is not hypotheses, which may unnaturally close study down, obscuring the integrity of the other, but the ability to converse intimately.

—HENRY GLASSIE

Researching people means "stepping in" to the worldviews of others. When we talk with people in the field or study the stuff of their lives—their stories, artifacts, and surroundings—we enter their perspectives by partly "stepping out" of our own. Insider and outsider stances are symbiotic; they support each other. You already know how to talk and listen to others from meeting new people. You've learned that you don't begin a conversation with a new person by talking only about yourself or failing to allow time or space for the other person to participate and collaborate in the conversation.

In an informal way, you are always gathering data about people's backgrounds and perspectives—their worldviews. "So where are you from?" "How do you like it here?" "How come someone from Texas wants to go to school in Minnesota?" "Did you know anyone when you first came here?" Not only do you ask questions about people's backgrounds, but you also notice their artifacts and adornments—the things with which they represent themselves: T-shirts, jewelry, particular kinds of shoes or hairstyles. The speculations and questions we form about others cause us to make hypotheses about the people we meet. We may ask questions, or we may just listen. But unless we listen closely, we'll never understand others from their perspectives. We need to know what it's like for *that* person in *this* place. Our colleague Mark Shadle writes:

> At its best, this practice is called "cosmology"—the way each of us orders the world around us. Paradoxically, the only way we can find order for ourselves is to negotiate with others doing the same thing. This means that we must learn to respect in both nature and culture..."sensitive chaos."

In the quotation that begins this chapter, folklorist Henry Glassie stresses the interactive nature of field research, suggesting that we shed hypotheses that close down study. You may have formulated a hunch about someone only to find out through new data that your hypothesis is off-base. For example, you may dismiss the middle-aged woman who sits in your political science class and reminds you of your mother. But when you're assigned to a study group with her, you discover that as an army nurse who has traveled all over the world, she knows more about international politics than anyone else in the group. Glassie warns us not to close down study and mask our informants' integrity because this can prevent us from learning from them. The army nurse, as familiar as she may appear, turns into a great informant about international politics. The only way to learn with her is to be a listener. To learn from others, we must converse collaboratively. Fieldworkers and informants construct meaning together.

This chapter will help you strengthen the everyday skills of listening, questioning, and researching people who interest you. You'll gather, analyze, write, and reflect on family stories. You'll experience interactive ways to conduct interviews and **oral histories**. You'll look for and discover meaning in your informants' everyday cultural artifacts. And you'll read some examples of how other fieldworkers have researched and written about people's lives.

GATHERING FAMILY STORIES

We often think of stories as pure entertainment, but as we discuss in Chapter 6, there are many forms of storytelling—gossip, chants, curses, urban legends, and fairy tales, for example. Stories, like material artifacts, serve to tell us about our informants' worldviews and function as data in our fieldwork. Informants have entire repertoires of stories based on their childhoods, their interests, their occupations. When a fieldworker meets an informant, part of the listening process involves gathering the informant's stories. Our job as researchers is to elicit our informants' stories, record them, and carefully analyze what they mean. Researchers who study verbal art think about stories in these ways:

- Stories preserve a culture's values and beliefs.
- Stories help individuals endure, transform, or reject cultural values for themselves.
- Stories exist because of the interrelationship between tellers and audiences.

Waitresses' stories and gossip (see Chapter 6) illustrate that one place where cultures pass on their values and beliefs is the job site. Waitresses build a kind of kinship—with insider language and stories that teach ways of behaving on the job. But the most influential kinship structure is, of course, the family. And stories begin in our families.

Families are not cultures, but they bridge the gap between individuals and their cultures. Because families are small enough units of people, we can, through interaction and collaboration, achieve intimate understandings. To understand someone's culture, we often need to understand the person's family, too. Through the individual we come to understand the culture, and through the culture we come to understand the individual. **Family stories** help us do that, and collecting them from our informants is part of the process of researching people.

Throughout your childhood, you heard and shared stories, but you may never have thought about them as verbal artifacts, to be analyzed for their core themes and variants. Family stories are narratives about family members, both living and deceased. They're the stories we grow up on—like the time your cousin Mattie was jilted the night before her wedding, or your uncle Tyrone, who remarried his high school sweetheart at 85 after his triple bypass, or your aunt Thelma, who took to her bed after raising 12 children, or the time Uncle Fritz won the state lottery and spent it all in a month. Because we first hear them when we're young, these stories influence and shape us.

In many cultures, family storytelling sessions are a deliberate way of passing along values. They are often expected events, almost ritualized performances. Judith Ortiz Cofer, in a memoir of her Puerto Rican childhood, writes about how the younger females in her extended family were encouraged to eavesdrop on the adult storytelling ritual:

> At three or four o'clock in the afternoon, the hour of the *café con leche*, the women of my family gathered in Mama's living room to speak of important things and retell family stories meant to be overheard by us young girls, their daughters.... It was on these rockers that my mother, her sisters, and my grandmother sat these afternoons of my childhood to tell their stories, teaching each other, and my cousin and me, what it was like to be a woman, more specifically, a Puerto Rican woman. They talked about life on the island, and life in Los Nueva Yores, their way of referring to the United States from New York City to California: the other place, not home, all the same. They told real-life stories, though, as I later learned, always embellishing them with a little or a lot of dramatic detail. And they told *cuentos*, the morality and cautionary tales told by the women in our family for generations; stories that became part of my subconscious as I grew up in two worlds. (64–65)

These stories from Cofer's childhood were not merely afternoon entertainment. Her family's stories recorded history and carried instructions about behaviors, rules, and beliefs. Like the legends, folk tales, and proverbs of specific cultures, family stories reflect the ways of acting and even of viewing the world sanctioned or approved by a family. Cofer's relatives conserve cultural traditions of their old country, Puerto Rico, and translate them into the "Los Nueva Yores" culture.

In addition to preserving cultural values, many writers suggest that the act of storytelling is also an act of individual survival. To endure in our families and the culture at large, we must explain our lives to ourselves. First we share our stories, and then we reflect on what they mean. Our own storytelling memories teach us about our personal histories. Why did I remember that story? What is important about that incident my father told me? What other stories does this one remind me of? Is my version the same as my cousin's? When you think of a family story, try to decide why it survived, and which tellers have different versions, what parts of the story remain the same no matter who tells it, and how you've refashioned it for your own purposes.

We'd like to recall one of our own family stories for you. This is a story of family endurance in which five members reshape their own versions for their own purposes, playing out their personal histories in particular ways. A hostile teenager was sent to his room for complaining about the lumpy mashed potatoes during the family supper. He stormed away from the table, throwing his sneaker backward over his shoulder as he walked up the stairs. It landed in the massive bowl of mashed potatoes, splattering his five siblings and his parents and turning his defiance into comedy. On the surface, this is just a funny family anecdote, not a serious "family story." But its themes show why it survived and what it might teach each member.

After this incident, everyone in the family learned that "when you throw something without looking, you never know exactly where it will land" and that even a person who is sent away from the family table holds the power to ruin a meal. In his absence, he can be the most present. The father's version of the story focuses on the shattered bowl. The older brother refashions it as a story about how the younger brother always found a way to get attention. The younger sister remembers wiping hot mashed potatoes off the crying baby's face. And the mother tells the story about making potato pancakes the next morning from the leftovers.

Within the family, the core of this story always includes the humor of the event, the mashed potatoes, and the central character of the angry teenager tossing his shoe backward as he walks up the stairs. Each family member's variant emphasizes an individual's values: power, property, jealousy, protection, economy. For the tellers, the story illustrates their own endurance within this family, emphasizing the values they hold most important. For example, the sister who protects the baby tells the story to her children about how she saved Aunt Alisha from being permanently scarred (by mashed potatoes?). And the hostile teenager tells this story to his own son as a warning against angry defiance. No one in the family may recognize the themes in each version, but a fieldworker would look for them and then try to confirm them with other data about the family's values. She would look at the theme of each member's version to see how it reflects their culture as a whole. In our interview with Danling Fu in Chapter 6, we uncovered cultural themes about the life cycle and the value of productivity when she recalled a Chinese song and a proverb about silkworms. Danling herself was unconscious of the values embedded in her verbal art. But in the process of the interview, as she told us about caring for pets in a crowded country and the importance of working hard, we confirmed the same themes that were in the song and the proverb.

When the values of the family and their culture converge, family stories can convey strong lessons, even warnings, to family members. Families are not cultures. They are extended kinship units, sanctioned by a culture's legal system to acknowledge rights or limitations for groups of related people. Like schools and churches, family units help nourish and conserve features of the larger culture. Individual family members can escape kinship boundaries more easily than they can escape the constraints of the culture as a whole.

In the following reading, a chapter from *The Woman Warrior*, by Maxine Hong Kingston, a mother tells a family story to her daughter to instill in her the cultural values of monogamy and sexual fidelity, values that have followed their Chinese family to San Francisco. Listening to her mother's story does not help the daughter escape her culture's values. But forming the story into a version for herself helps her endure and transcend the values that her mother handed down. As you read this, we hope you'll think about stories from your own family that convey teachings, warnings, or cultural messages.

No Name Woman

Maxine Hong Kingston

"You must not tell anyone," my mother said, "what I am about to tell you. In China your father had a sister who killed herself. She jumped into the family well. We say that your father has all brothers because it is as if she had never been born.

"In 1924 just a few days after our village celebrated seventeen hurry-up weddings—to make sure that every young man who went 'out on the road' would responsibly come home—your father and his brothers and your grandfather and his brothers and your aunt's new husband sailed for America, the Gold Mountain. It was your grandfather's last trip. Those lucky enough to get contracts waved goodbye from the decks. They fed and guarded the stowaways and helped them off in Cuba, New York, Bali, Hawaii. 'We'll meet in California next year,' they said. All of them sent money home.

"I remember looking at your aunt one day when she and I were dressing; I had not noticed before that she had such a protruding melon of a stomach. But I did not think, 'She's pregnant,' until she began to look like other pregnant women, her shirt pulling and the white tops of her black pants showing. She could not have been pregnant, you see, because her husband had been gone for years. No one said anything. We did not discuss it. In early summer she was ready to have the child, long after the time when it could have been possible.

"The village had also been counting. On the night the baby was to be born the villagers raided our house. Some were crying. Like a great saw, teeth strung with lights, files of people walked zigzag across our land, tearing the rice. Their lanterns doubled in the disturbed black water, which drained away through the broken bunds. As the villagers closed in, we could see that some of them, probably men and women we knew well, wore white masks. The people with long hair hung it over their faces. Women with short hair made it stand up on end. Some had tied white bands around their foreheads, arms, and legs.

"At first they threw mud and rocks at the house. Then they threw eggs and began slaughtering our stock. We could hear the animals scream their deaths—the roosters, the pigs, a last great roar from the ox. Familiar wild heads flared in our night windows; the villagers encircled us. Some of the faces stopped to peer at us, their eyes rushing like searchlights. The hands flattened against the panes, framed heads, and left red prints.

"The villagers broke in the front and the back doors at the same time, even though we had not locked the doors against them. Their knives dripped with the blood of our animals. They smeared blood on the doors and walls. One woman swung a chicken whose throat she had slit, splattering blood in red arcs about her. We stood together in the middle of our house, in the family hall with the pictures and tables of the ancestors around us, and looked straight ahead.

"At that time the house had only two wings. When the men came back, we would build two more to enclose our courtyard and a third one to begin a second courtyard. The villagers pushed through both wings, even your grandparents' rooms, to find your aunt's, which was also mine until the men returned. From this room a new wing for one of the younger families would grow. They ripped up her clothes and shoes and broke her combs, grinding them underfoot. They tore her work from the loom. They scattered the cooking fire and rolled the new weaving in it. We could hear them in the kitchen breaking our bowls and banging the pots. They overturned the great waist-high earthenware jugs; duck eggs, pickled fruits, vegetables burst out and mixed in acrid torrents. The old woman from the next field swept a broom through the air and loosed the spirits-of-the-broom over our heads. 'Pig.' 'Ghost.' 'Pig,' they sobbed and scolded while they ruined our house.

"When they left, they took sugar and oranges to bless themselves. They cut pieces from the dead animals. Some of them took bowls that were not broken and clothes that were not torn. Afterward we swept up the rice and sewed it back up into sacks. But the smells from the spilled preserves lasted. Your aunt gave birth in the pigsty that night. The next morning when I went for the water, I found her and the baby plugging up the family well.

"Don't let your father know that I told you. He denies her. Now that you have started to menstruate, what happened to her could happen to you. Don't humiliate us. You wouldn't like to be forgotten as if you had never been born. The villagers are watchful."

Whenever she had to warn us about life, my mother told stories that ran like this one, a story to grow up on. She tested our strength to establish realities. Those in the emigrant generations who could not reassert brute survival died young and far from home. Those of us in the first American generations have had to figure out how the invisible world the emigrants built around our childhoods fits in solid America.

The emigrants confused the gods by diverting their curses, misleading them with crooked streets and false names. They must try to confuse their off-spring as well, who, I suppose, threaten them in similar ways—always trying to get things straight, always trying to name the unspeakable. The Chinese I know hide their names; sojourners take new names when their lives change and guard their real names with silence.

Chinese-Americans, when you try to understand what things in you are Chinese, how do you separate what is peculiar to childhood, to poverty, insan-ities, one family, your mother who marked your growing with stories, from what is Chinese? What is Chinese tradition and what is the movies?

If I want to learn what clothes my aunt wore, whether flashy or ordinary, I would have to begin, "Remember Father's drowned-in-the-well sister?" I can-not ask that. My mother has told me once and for all the useful parts. She will add nothing unless powered by Necessity, a riverbank that guides her life. She plants vegetable gardens rather than lawns; she carries the odd-shaped toma-toes home from the fields and eats food left for the gods.

Whenever we did frivolous things, we used up energy; we flew high kites. We children came up off the ground over the melting cones our parents brought home from work and the American movies on New Year's Day—*Oh, You Beautiful Doll* with Betty Grable one year, and *She Wore a Yellow Ribbon* with John Wayne another year. After the one carnival ride each, we paid in guilt; our tired father counted his change on the dark walk home.

Adultery is extravagance. Could people who hatch their own chicks and eat the embryos and the heads for delicacies and boil the feet in vinegar for party food, leaving only the gravel, eating even the gizzard lining—could such people engender a prodigal aunt? To be a woman, to have a daughter in starva-tion time was a waste enough. My aunt could not have been the lone romantic who gave up everything for sex. Women in the old China did not choose. Some man had commanded her to lie with him and be his secret evil. I wonder whether he masked himself when he joined the raid on her family.

Perhaps she had encountered him in the fields or on the mountain where his daughters-in-law collected fuel. Or perhaps he first noticed her in the mar-ketplace. He was not a stranger because the village housed no strangers. She had to have dealings with him other than sex. Perhaps he worked an adjoining field, or he sold her the cloth for the dress she sewed and wore. His demand must have surprised, then terrified her. She obeyed him; she always did as she was told.

When the family found a young man in the next village to be her husband, she had stood tractably beside the best rooster, his proxy, and promised before they met that she would be his forever. She was lucky that he was her age and she would be the first wife, an advantage secure now. The night she first saw him, he had sex with her. Then he left for America. She had almost for-gotten what he looked like. When she tried to envision him, she only saw the black and white face in the group photograph the men had had taken before leaving.

The other man was not, after all, much different from her husband. They both gave orders: she followed. "If you tell your family, I'll beat you. I'll kill you. Be here again next week." No one talked sex, ever. And she might have separated the rapes from the rest of living if only she did not have to buy her oil from him or gather wood in the same forest. I want her fear to have lasted just as long as rape lasted so that the fear could have been contained. No drawn-out fear. But women at sex hazarded birth and hence lifetimes. The fear did not stop but permeated everywhere. She told the man, "I think I'm pregnant." He organized the raid against her.

On nights when my mother and father talked about their life back home, sometimes they mentioned an "outcast table" whose business they still seemed to be settling, their voices tight. In a commensal tradition, where food is precious, the powerful older people made wrong-doers eat alone. Instead of letting them start separate new lives like the Japanese, who could become samurais and geishas, the Chinese family, faces averted but eyes glowering sideways, hung on to the offenders and fed them leftovers. My aunt must have lived in the same house as my parents and eaten at an outcast table. My mother spoke about the raid as if she had seen it, when she and my aunt, a daughter-in-law to a different household, should not have been living together at all. Daughters-in-law lived with their husbands' parents, not their own; a synonym for marriage in Chinese is "taking a daughter-in-law." Her husband's parents could have sold her, mortgaged her, stoned her. But they had sent her back to her own mother and father, a mysterious act hinting at disgraces not told me. Perhaps they had thrown her out to deflect the avengers.

She was the only daughter; her four brothers went with her father, husband, and uncles "out on the road" and for some years became western men. When the goods were divided among the family, three of the brothers took land, and the youngest, my father, chose an education. After my grandparents gave their daughter away to her husband's family, they had dispensed all the adventure and all the property. They expected her alone to keep the traditional ways, which her brothers, now among the barbarians, could fumble without detection. The heavy, deep-rooted women were to maintain the past against the flood, safe for returning. But the rare urge west had fixed upon our family, and so my aunt crossed boundaries not delineated in space.

The work of preservation demands that the feelings playing about in one's guts not be turned into action. Just watch their passing like cherry blossoms. But perhaps my aunt, my forerunner, caught in a slow life, let dreams grow and fade and after some months or years went toward what persisted. Fear at the enormities of the forbidden kept her desires delicate, wire and bone. She looked at a man because she liked the way the hair was tucked behind his ears, or she liked the question-mark line of a long torso curving at the shoulder and straight at the hip. For warm eyes or a soft voice or a slow walk—that's all—a few hairs, a line, a brightness, a sound, a pace, she gave up family. She offered us up for a charm that vanished with tiredness, a pigtail that didn't toss when the wind died. Why, the wrong lighting could erase the dearest thing about him.

It could very well have been, however, that my aunt did not take subtle enjoyment of her friend, but, a wild woman, kept rollicking company. Imagining her free with sex doesn't fit, though. I don't know any women like that, or men either. Unless I see her life branching into mine, she gives me no ancestral help.

To sustain her being in love, she often worked at herself in the mirror, guessing at the colors and shapes that would interest him, changing them frequently in order to hit on the right combination. She wanted him to look back.

On a farm near the sea, a woman who tended her appearance reaped a reputation for eccentricity. All the married women blunt-cut their hair in flaps about their ears or pulled it back in tight buns. No nonsense. Neither style blew easily into heart-catching tangles. And at their weddings they displayed themselves in their long hair for the last time. "It brushed the backs of my knees," my mother tells me. "It was braided, and even so, it brushed the backs of my knees."

At the mirror my aunt combed individuality into her bob. A bun could have been contrived to escape into black streamers blowing in the wind or in quiet wisps about her face, but only the older women in our picture album wear buns. She brushed her hair back from her forehead, tucking the flaps behind her ears. She looped a piece of thread, knotted into a circle between her index fingers and thumbs, and ran the double strand across her forehead. When she closed her fingers as if she were making a pair of shadow geese bite, the string twisted together catching the little hairs. Then she pulled the thread away from her skin, ripping the hairs out neatly, her eyes watering from the needles of pain. Opening her fingers, she cleaned the thread, then rolled it along her hairline and the tops of her eyebrows. My mother did the same to me and my sisters and herself. I used to believe that the expression "caught by the short hairs" meant a captive held with a depilatory string. It especially hurt at the temples, but my mother said we were lucky we didn't have to have our feet bound when we were seven. Sisters used to sit on their beds and cry together, she said, as their mothers or their slave removed the bandages for a few minutes each night and let the blood gush back into their veins. I hope that the man my aunt loved appreciated a smooth brow, that he wasn't just a tits-and-ass man.

Once my aunt found a freckle on her chin, at a spot that the almanac said predestined her for unhappiness. She dug it out with a hot needle and washed the wound with peroxide.

More attention to her looks than these pullings of hairs and pickings at spots would have caused gossip among the villagers. They owned work clothes and good clothes, and they wore good clothes for feasting the new seasons. But since a woman combing her hair hexes beginnings, my aunt rarely found an occasion to look her best. Women looked like great sea snails—the corded wood, babies, and laundry they carried were the whorls on their backs. The Chinese did not admire a bent back; goddesses and warriors stood straight.

Still there must have been a marvelous freeing of beauty when a worker laid down her burden and stretched and arched.

Such commonplace loveliness, however, was not enough for my aunt. She dreamed of a lover for the fifteen days of New Year's, the time for families to exchange visits, money, and food. She plied her secret comb. And sure enough she cursed the year, the family, the village, and herself.

Even as her hair lured her imminent lover, many other men looked at her. Uncles, cousins, nephews, brothers would have looked, too, had they been home between journeys. Perhaps they had already been restraining their curiosity, and they left, fearful that their glances, like a field of nesting birds, might be startled and caught. Poverty hurt, and that was their first reason for leaving. But another, final reason for leaving the crowded house was the never-said.

She may have been unusually beloved, the precious only daughter, spoiled and mirror gazing because of the affection the family lavished on her. When her husband left, they welcomed the chance to take her back from the in-laws; she could live like the little daughter for just a while longer. There are stories that my grandfather was different from other people, "crazy ever since the little Jap bayoneted him in the head." He used to put his naked penis on the dinner table, laughing. And one day he brought home a baby girl, wrapped up inside his brown western-style greatcoat. He had traded one of his sons, probably my father, the youngest, for her. My grandmother made him trade back. When he finally got a daughter of his own, he doted on her. They must have all loved her, except perhaps my father, the only brother who never went back to China, having once been traded for a girl.

Brothers and sisters, newly men and women, had to efface their sexual color and present plain miens. Disturbing hair and eyes, a smile like no other, threatened the ideal of five generations living under one roof. To focus blurs, people shouted face to face and yelled from room to room. The immigrants I know have loud voices, unmodulated to American tones even after years away from the village where they called their friendships out across the fields. I have not been able to stop my mother's screams in public libraries or over telephones. Walking erect (knees straight, toes pointed forward, not pigeon-toed, which is Chinese-feminine) and speaking in an inaudible voice, I have tried to turn myself American-feminine. Chinese communication was loud, public. Only sick people had to whisper. But at the dinner table, where the family members came nearest one another, no one could talk, not the outcasts nor any eaters. Every word that falls from the mouth is a coin lost. Silently they gave and accepted food with both hands. A preoccupied child who took his bowl with one hand got a sideways glare. A complete moment of total attention is due everyone alike. Children and lovers have no singularity here, but my aunt used a secret voice, a separate attentiveness.

She kept the man's name to herself throughout her labor and dying; she did not accuse him that he be punished with her. To save her inseminator's name she gave silent birth.

He may have been somebody in her own household, but intercourse with a man outside the family would have been no less abhorrent. All the village were kinsmen, and the titles shouted in loud country voices never let kinship be forgotten. Any man within visiting distance would have been neutralized as a lover—"brother," "younger brother," "older brother"—one hundred and fifteen relationship titles. Parents researched birth charts probably not so much to assure good fortune as to circumvent incest in a population that has but one hundred surnames. Everybody has eight million relatives. How useless then sexual mannerisms, how dangerous.

As if it came from an atavism deeper than fear, I used to add "brother" silently to boys' names. It hexed the boys, who would or would not ask me to dance and made them less scary and as familiar and deserving of benevolence as girls.

But, of course, I hexed myself also—no dates. I should have stood up, both arms waving, and shouted out across libraries, "Hey, you! Love me back." I had no idea, though, how to make attraction selective, how to control its direction and magnitude. If I made myself American-pretty so that the five or six Chinese boys in the class fell in love with me, everyone else—the Caucasian, Negro, and Japanese boys—would too. Sisterliness, dignified and honorable, made much more sense.

Attraction eludes control so stubbornly that whole societies designed to organize relationships among people cannot keep order, not even when they bind people to one another from childhood and raise them together. Among the very poor and the wealthy, brothers married their adopted sisters, like doves. Our family allowed some romance, paying adult brides' prices and providing dowries so that their sons and daughters could marry strangers. Marriage promises to turn strangers into friendly relatives—a nation of siblings.

In the village structure, spirits shimmered among the live creatures, balanced and held in equilibrium by time and land. But one human being flaring up into violence could open up a black hole, a maelstrom that pulled in the sky. The frightened villagers, who depended on one another to maintain the real, went to my aunt to show her a personal, physical representation of the break she had made in the "roundness." Misallying couples snapped off the future, which was to be embodied in true offspring. The villagers punished her for acting as if she could have a private life, secret and apart from them.

If my aunt had betrayed the family at a time of large grain yields and peace, when many boys were born, and wings were being built on many houses, perhaps she might have escaped such severe punishment. But the men—hungry, greedy, tired of planting in dry soil—had been forced to leave the village in order to send food-money home. There were ghost plagues, bandit plagues, wars with the Japanese, floods. My Chinese brother and sister had died of an unknown sickness. Adultery, perhaps only a mistake during good times, became a crime when the village needed food.

The round moon cakes and round doorways, the round tables of graduated size that fit one roundness inside another, round windows and rice bowls—

these talismans had lost their power to warn this family of the law: a family must be whole, faithfully keeping the descent line by having sons to feed the old and the dead, who in turn look after the family. The villagers came to show my aunt and her lover-in-hiding a broken house. The villagers were speeding up the circling of events because she was too shortsighted to see that her infidelity had already harmed the village, that waves of consequences would return unpredictably, sometimes in disguise, as now, to hurt her. This roundness had to be made coin-sized so that she would see its circumference: punish her at the birth of her baby. Awaken her to the inexorable. People who refused fatalism because they could invent small resources insisted on culpability. Deny accidents and wrest fault from the stars.

After the villagers left, their lanterns now scattering in various directions toward home, the family broke their silence and cursed her. "Aiaa, we're going to die. Death is coming. Death is coming. Look what you've done. You've killed us. Ghost! Dead ghost! Ghost! You've never been born." She ran out into the fields, far enough from the house so that she could no longer hear their voices, and pressed herself against the earth, her own land no more. When she felt the birth coming, she thought that she had been hurt. Her body seized together. "They've hurt me too much," she thought. "This is gall, and it will kill me." With forehead and knees against the earth, her body convulsed and then relaxed. She turned on her back, lay on the ground. The black well of sky and stars went out and out and out forever; her body and her complexity seemed to disappear. She was one of the stars, a bright dot in blackness, without home, without a companion, in eternal cold and silence. An agoraphobia rose in her, speeding higher and higher, bigger and bigger; she would not be able to contain it; there would be no end to fear.

Flayed, unprotected against space, she felt pain return, focusing her body. This pain chilled her—a cold, steady kind of surface pain. Inside, spasmodically, the other pain, the pain of the child, heated her. For hours she lay on the ground, alternately body and space. Sometimes a vision of normal comfort obliterated reality: she saw the family in the evening gambling at the dinner table, the young people massaging their elders' backs. She saw them congratulating one another, high joy on the mornings the rice shoots came up. When these pictures burst, the stars drew yet further apart. Black space opened.

She got to her feet to fight better and remembered that old-fashioned women gave birth in their pigsties to fool the jealous, pain-dealing gods, who do not snatch piglets. Before the next spasms could stop her, she ran to the pigsty, each step a rushing out into emptiness. She climbed over the fence and knelt in the dirt. It was good to have a fence enclosing her, a tribal person alone.

Laboring, this woman who had carried her child as a foreign growth that sickened her every day, expelled it at last. She reached down to touch the hot, wet, moving mass, surely smaller than anything human, and could feel that it was human after all—fingers, toes, nails, nose. She pulled it up on to her belly, and it lay curled there, butt in the air, feet precisely tucked one under the other. She opened her loose shirt and buttoned the child inside. After resting, it squirmed and thrashed and she pushed it up to her breast. It turned its head this way and that until it found her nipple. There, it made little snuffling noises. She clenched her teeth at its preciousness, lovely as a young calf, a piglet, a little dog.

She may have gone to the pigsty as a last act of responsibility: she would protect this child as she had protected its father. It would look after her soul, leaving supplies on her grave. But how would this tiny child without family find her grave when there would be no marker for her anywhere, neither in the earth nor the family hall? No one would give her a family hall name. She had taken the child with her into the wastes. At its birth the two of them had felt the same raw pain of separation, a wound that only the family pressing tight could close. A child with no descent line would not soften her life but only trail after her, ghost-like, begging her to give it purpose. At dawn the villagers on their way to the fields would stand around the fence and look.

Full of milk, the little ghost slept. When it awoke, she hardened her breasts against the milk that crying loosens. Toward morning she picked up the baby and walked to the well.

Carrying the baby to the well shows loving. Otherwise abandon it. Turn its face into the mud. Mothers who love their children take them along. It was probably a girl; there is some hope of forgiveness for boys.

"Don't tell anyone you had an aunt. Your father does not want to hear her name. She has never been born." I have believed that sex was unspeakable and words so strong and fathers so frail that "aunt" would do my father mysterious harm. I have thought that my family, having settled among immigrants who had also been their neighbors in the ancestral land, needed to clean their name, and a wrong word would incite the kinspeople even here. But there is more to this silence: they want me to participate in her punishment. And I have.

In the twenty years since I heard this story I have not asked for details nor said my aunt's name; I do not know it. People who can comfort the dead can also chase after them to hurt them further—a reverse ancestor worship. The real punishment was not the raid swiftly inflicted by the villagers, but the family's deliberately forgetting her. Her betrayal so maddened them, they saw to it that she would suffer forever, even after death. Always hungry, always needing, she would have to beg food from other ghosts, snatch and steal it from those whose living descendants give them gifts. She would have to fight the ghosts massed at crossroads for the buns a few thoughtful citizens leave to decoy her away from village and home so that the ancestral spirits could feast unharassed. At peace, they could act like gods, not ghosts, their descent lines providing them with paper suits and dresses, spirit money, paper houses, paper automobiles, chicken, meat, and rice into eternity—essences delivered up in smoke and flames, steam and incense rising from each rice bowl. In an attempt to make the Chinese care for people outside the family, Chairman Mao encourages us now to give our paper replicas to the spirits of outstanding soldiers and workers, no matter whose ancestors they may be. My aunt remains forever hungry. Goods are not distributed evenly among the dead.

My aunt haunts me—her ghost drawn to me because now, after fifty years of neglect, I alone devote pages of paper to her, though not origamied into houses and clothes. I do not think she always means me well. I am telling on her, and she was a spite suicide, drowning herself in the drinking water. The Chinese are always very frightened of the drowned one, whose weeping ghost, wet hair hanging and skin bloated, waits silently by the water to pull down a substitute.

Kingston's family tale about the Chinese community's violence and revenge gives the daughter a lesson "to grow up on," warning her against ruining the family name. The story teaches indirect messages such as "adultery is an extravagance" and "women are keepers of secret knowledge." You may have noticed other cultural messages in this story. You may reread it, looking just for those indirect messages carried from one generation to the next. In "No Name Woman," we can see that there is a stable core of details in the story of the aunt. But the Chinese American daughter, listener and recipient, transforms and reinvents the story while her mother tells it, creating a variant. In her refashioning, she uses embellishments that were not part of the core.

Elizabeth's family tells a story about her mother, Alice, and her fiancé, David Perry, who was a respected high school English teacher. One day, when David left town on an errand, Alice went "motoring" with three friends, two of whom were males. They had an accident in the Model T, and Alice broke her arm. Hearing about the accident, David rushed to the hospital and ripped the engagement ring from the finger of Alice's broken arm, sure that she had been unfaithful to him. When he later discovered that this wasn't true, that Alice had just been on a friendly drive, he tried to reconcile, but to no avail. Three months later, on the rebound, Alice instead married Elizabeth's father. They remained married for over 50 years.

So what does this family story reveal? Because Alice broke the same arm twice again later in her life, perhaps the story—and the broken arms—recalled an early love for David Perry. In Alice's version to her daughters, this story conveyed the importance of ignoring gossip and rumors, retaining belief and faith in the one you love in spite of circumstances. Clearly, Alice was a steadfast woman, married for over half a century. As this story has been retold over the years by Alice's sisters, the fate of David Perry has changed in different versions. In Aunt June's version, he remained a bachelor all his life. And in Aunt Louise's, David had a teenage daughter named Allison who was never allowed to drive in boys' cars. Elizabeth tells this story to her two daughters with a lesson that echoes her contemporary feminist leanings. In her version, David Perry was her mother's only true love, and upon his loss, Alice could see no other choice but to marry someone else. This is the reason, she instructs her daughters, that every girl should have a profession and not rely on marriage.

Family stories are often transformed in oral retellings, but they clearly change when they are written down. In "No Name Woman," the aunt's ghost so haunts the narrator that she is driven to write, in part to make sense of what she has been told: "I alone devote pages of paper to her." Although family stories belong to the oral narrative tradition, writing them down helps us analyze their meaning and potential relevance to our own lives. Think about a family story—not necessarily a gloomy one like Kingston's. Stories about lost and found loves, courtship, and marriage are often shared as family tales.

Writing a Family Story

BOX 25

Purpose

We're not always conscious of how our family stories serve us, nor are our informants. But they are worth exploring as a rich source of data when we want to better understand our own lives—and the lives of the people with whom we're working. As scholar Elizabeth Stone, in *Black Sheep and Kissing Cousins: How Our Family Stories Shape Us,* writes,

> What struck me about my own family stories was first, how much under my skin they were; second, once my childhood was over, how little deliberate attention I ever paid to them; and third, how thoroughly invisible they were to anyone else. Going about my daily life, I certainly never told them aloud and never even alluded to them.... Those who say that America is a land of rootless nomads who travel light, uninstructed by memory and family ties, have missed part of the evidence.
>
> The family storytelling that has always gone on in my family goes on in families everywhere. Like me, people grow up and walk around with their stories under their skin, sometimes as weightless pleasures but sometimes painfully tattooed with them. ...one of the family's first jobs is to persuade its members they're special, more wonderful than the neighboring barbarians. The persuasion consists of stories showing family members demonstrating admirable traits, which it claims are family traits. Attention to the stories' actual truth is never the family's most compelling consideration. Encouraging belief is. The family survival depends on the shared sensibility of its members.

Action

Recall a family story you've heard many times. It may fall into one of these categories: fortunes gained and lost, heroes, "black sheep," eccentric or oddball relatives, acts of retribution and revenge, or family feuds. After writing the story, analyze its meaning. When is this story most often told, and why? What kinds of warnings or messages does this story convey? For the family? For an outsider? What kind of lesson does the story teach? How does your story reflect your family's values? How has it changed or altered through various retellings? Which family members would have different versions?

Response

Cheri Krcelic wrote this family story about her parents' courtship.

The Blind Date

I've heard the story of how my parents met all through my life, but I never paid it much mind until now. My mom has used this story time and time again to teach me lessons about forming first impressions. I used to think it was just comical, but now I realize how it has affected my life.

My mother was only 18 years old when she met my father. She was a southern girl, born and raised in a small town in Mississippi. She was brought up by her parents on a farm. She often told stories of how her mother would cut off the heads of chickens in their kitchen and how it terrified her to watch the headless chickens run around the kitchen in a frenzy.

My father was from a small factory town in Pennsylvania. His parents divorced when he was young, and he was living with his mother and two younger brothers. When my father was in the tenth grade, he dropped out of school and got various jobs as a mechanic to support his family. My father eventually got his GED and then entered the Navy and was by the age of 21 stationed at a naval base in Mississippi where my mother lived.

My mother had just graduated from high school and was working full time and still living at home with her parents. Her mother was a hypochondriac, and her father suffered from heart trouble. My mother had not begun to make any real plans for her future.

My mother was set up to go out on a blind date by a friend of hers. The guy she was to have gone out with bailed out at the last minute, and my dad was begged, and finally convinced, to be the last-minute replacement. My mom says that it was love at first sight the moment she laid eyes on him. Little did she know the adventure she was in for that night.

My mom and dad headed for the drive-in movies, accompanied by the couple who had brought them together. Once they reached their destination, the two guys brought out a case of beer. My mom was wearing a long blonde wig that night. She said that every time my dad tried to put his arm around her, the wig would go lopsided. She finally realized that my dad knew she didn't really have blonde hair, so she took it off and stuck it in the rear window of the car. This would help her later.

During the course of the evening, my mom and her best friend ventured from the car to the restrooms. On their way back, they couldn't remember where the car was parked. They began to walk up and down the rows of cars, looking for their dates. Finally, when my dad lit a cigarette, the blonde wig shined through the rear window, and my mom and her friend found their way back.

By the time the movie was over, my mom took it upon herself to drive them all home in order to meet her curfew. On the way out of the drive-in, my mom accidentally wrecked the car. The three others immediately sobered up, and my mom figured this was a good time to inform my dad that she didn't have a driver's license. After finding this out, my dad switched seats and took the blame for the accident.

One month after this disastrous blind date, my dad proposed to my mom. Three months later, they got married. They have been together ever since.

My mother used this story to teach me to be less judgmental and also to give me hope. If I ever came home upset because a date didn't go well, she'd tell me this story to remind me that sometimes the best things come out of bad events. She also wanted to convey that sometimes people alter their appearances in order to make a better impression, just as she had done when she wore the blonde wig and pretended that she could drive. This story has helped me give others a second chance instead of judging them by first impressions.

This story has shaped my own romantic life. I always thought that my mother exaggerated the part of the story about "love at first sight" and didn't think it was possible. When I met my fiancé, I knew the moment I saw him that no matter what, he was the one.

Family stories like Cheri Krcelic's preserve family beliefs through morality lessons with subliminal messages and subconscious instructions. Some family stories, like Kingston's, act as cautionary tales, or what Cofer calls *cuentos,* to pass on warnings about behavior to the next generation. Through storytelling, family tales can be transformed and reshaped to make them fit the teller's needs and life circumstances as the little girl does in Kingston's story, and as each family member does in the story about the mashed potatoes. As Elizabeth Stone also suggests, family stories also allow individuals to break away from the family's values and form their own. Stone writes, "Still, to make one's family stories one's own in the truest sense is to achieve the greatest autonomy—the autonomy of one's point of view—while keeping hold of the best of one's connection to family." (224)

As they transform family stories, tellers can remain loyal to the family unit but be released from it as well. Cheri, for instance, learns about first impressions and quick judgments from her parents' blind date story. In future versions, however, to her own children perhaps, Cheri might reshape the details. She could include the movie title, she might omit the part about the case of beer and the drinking, or she may change the amount of time between the blind date and the marriage. But Cheri also uses her family story to support her own love-at-first-sight narrative. She admits that although she had heard her mother's story, she didn't entirely believe in love at first sight until she met her own fiancé. So such stories can connect us with our families while allowing us our identities as we reshape them to fit our own lives and our own audiences.

When we hear a family story, as Cheri did, and retell it in our own words, it becomes our own story as much as the teller's. The embellishments Cheri would make with each retelling depend on her audience. Sharing it with her friends, her fiancé, her professor, or her own future children will demand different versions. However, if Cheri decides to write this story as told by either of her parents, she will need to record their versions—using their words rather than her own. When the hostile adolescent who threw his shoe into the mashed potatoes tells this story 20 years later to his son, he downplays the family humor and emphasizes the consequences of a teenager's defiance. Elizabeth found herself deliberately reshaping the David Perry story for her daughters to share with them her own contemporary beliefs about marriage.

ONE FAMILY STORY: THE CORE AND ITS VARIANTS

Donna Niday decided to study one of her family's stories, "The Baby on the Roof." She expected to get different perspectives from the five Riggs sisters— her own mother and her four aunts who grew up on a farm in the rural Midwest of the 1920s. She wanted to record her family's history through the stories she had heard over the years. She began by interviewing her cousins to see what they remembered about the story, which would have been passed down to them by their mothers. Just as she suspected, each of Donna's cousins told the story with different details and points of emphasis. She confirmed the aunts' family reputations: "she was the daring one" or "she was always the chicken." Interviewing her cousins made it clear to Donna that she wanted to tape-record each aunt telling the tale of the baby on the roof.

Donna was realistic enough to know that here would be no "true" version of the tale, but the story would have a stable core, a basic frame, shared among the sisters. She also anticipated that there would be many variants, differences in details according to the tellers. She interviewed each elderly sister in her home, allowing time to look through family photo albums together and to visit before tape-recording the stories. As she listened and recorded, Donna gathered both the core story and its variants.

The oldest sister, Eleanor, who claimed responsibility for the secret family event, told the core story this way, emphasizing herself and the baby:

I took Mary to the top of the house when Mom went out to work. You know, all four of us took the ladder—went down to the barn and got the big ladder. Mom just said to take care of Mary, and I did. I took her everywhere I went. Mary was six months old. Well, she was born in January. This would be June, I suppose, when we were doing hay. I knew she'd lay wherever you put her. And so there was a flat place there on the roof. There wasn't any danger—I don't think there was ever any danger of her getting away at all. Yeah, we could see them mowing. If Mom had ever looked toward the house, she would have had a heart attack to see her kids up on the roof. Especially when we were supposed to be looking after the baby. Yeah, well see, I was ten when Mary was born, so I was ten then, a little past ten. I should have known better, but it shows that you can't trust ten-year-olds. I never got punished for that because Mom never did find out.

And so, with Eleanor's version, Donna had the core family story: four sisters spent the day on the roof with their six-month-old baby sister while their mother and father mowed the fields. Each sister provided her own variation. One remembers that the parents were mowing hay; another insists they were cutting oats. Such details would also change the time of the story from June to late summer or early fall. The sisters debate other details. Donna's mother rejects the idea

(Photo: Donna Niday)

The "Baby on the Roof" farmhouse.

that they got a ladder from the barn, saying they climbed on a chair or rain barrel to reach the lower part of the farmhouse roof, which was accessible from their bedrooms. Another of the sisters tells the story as if she remained on the ground while the others climbed to the roof. When they challenge her version, this sister admits that she probably did follow the others. She confesses jealousy of the new baby: until then, she had been the baby of the family. "They weren't worried about me," she recalls. "They were only worried about Mary, the baby."

Mary's version of the story deviates the most. She claims that she fell off the roof and that her sisters climbed down and put her "right back on." Because Mary's variant has no support from the other sisters, she retreats by saying, "Maybe I just dreamed that, but it seems like I fell off when I was up there. Of course, I wasn't really old enough to remember."

After taping and transcribing all five versions of this story, Donna proposes that the "baby on the roof" story displays defiance of authority and rebellion against rules for these otherwise compliant farm girls. She also thinks that the story illustrates "pluck and adventure," as no harm was actually done. Donna admits that her mother and aunts would deny that these stories convey any meaning other than "pure entertainment" and confesses that any analysis of the meaning of these stories is her own. She recognizes that each sister embellished the story based on her family reputation, individual temperament, and storytelling ability. Donna's conclusions are consistent with what we know: that a story has a stable core of details but also many variants according to the tellers. In tape-recording these stories, Donna served as a dual audience for the storytelling that took place: between aunts and their niece and between a mother and her daughter. Had the sisters told their story to another family member, like a grandchild, that audience would have affected the variants of the core story.

Donna repaid her aunts and her mother for their time with a copy of her research essay, "Secrets among Sisters: Stories of the Five Riggs Sisters," and she created a family album complete with photos of the old farmhouse from many angles, with several different views of the roof. Donna used her family photos as cultural artifacts. In a different project, she might also have used written artifacts such as family journals and diaries and letters among the sisters. Such material from a family's archives adds depth to a research project.

Donna followed several important steps in gathering her family stories, steps that any fieldworker considers:

- She conducted preliminary research by interviewing the people involved—in this case, her mother and aunts. Had they all told the same story, the project would not have illustrated the core and variants inherent in family stories.

- She interviewed her informants in their own home settings, making all participants comfortable as she taped and asked questions. To accomplish this, she traveled to four states and made some very long phone calls. She didn't rush her project; she allowed time for scheduling, visiting, interviewing, transcribing, sharing the transcripts, and writing her paper.

- She triangulated her data in two ways. First, by checking the five stories against one another, she could see how one story might verify another or disconfirm it. She shared her work with the sisters as she went along and afterward so that they might confirm, disconfirm, or add to each other's stories. The number of stories she gathered helped her build substantial evidence, which contributed to her analysis of the interview data. She analyzed her data by making a chart that detailed the core elements of the story and the variations in each one.

- She acknowledged the importance of her informants' participation. In this case, as they were her relatives, she presented her essay and the album as a gift in return for the time and energy they spent helping her learn how to listen to family stories. This kind of **reciprocity** is crucial to the ethics of fieldworking.

Stories and Variants

Purpose

Stories that are passed down within a culture help to shape a culture's self-identity. But it's also true that the variants (each teller's version) of a story can explain even more. Knowing how the variants differ helps us find clues about informants, their worldviews, and how a culture has changed over time. If you are working in a fieldsite, you will want to find any important stories that have come out of a shared event, an important moment, or a special person whom everyone knows. For example, at a business you might gather stories about the boss and the boss's son or daughter from several workers as well as from the boss and his children. Retirement and holiday parties, Friday afternoon celebrations (TGIFs), and break-time rituals are all events that yield stories in the workplace. In families, dinners, vacations, and events like holidays, birthdays, weddings, and funerals often prompt storytelling. Malls, cafeterias, game rooms, dorm lounges, and sporting events are sites that invite storytelling as well.

Action

Try to collect one story and its variants. You may want to record one storyteller as he or she tells the same story to three or four different audiences—a grandparent, for example, telling a family story to grandchildren, to adult children, to neighbors, and to a spouse. Or a teacher's signature story—as it was told to different students at different times in different years. In these, you will find that the variants change according to the teller's perception of the audience's needs on particular occasions.

Another way to gather stories and variants is to focus on a moment in time and people's stories about those moments, like John F. Kennedy's assassination in November 1963, the *Challenger* disaster in January 1986, or the millennium celebrations of New Year's Eve 1999. As we wrote this paragraph, in fact, we found ourselves sharing our own stories about where we were during these moments. Elizabeth met her first husband, Michael Chiseri, at a bar in New York City as each waited for a date who didn't arrive from Washington, D.C., because of delays caused by the 1963 assassination of John F. Kennedy. Bonnie was a high school senior sitting in a writing class and writing about her feelings at that moment. When Neil Armstrong and Buzz Aldrin landed on the moon in July 1969, Bonnie watched them through an appliance shop window on a street in Greece, surrounded by emotional Athenians celebrating this U.S. technological triumph. Elizabeth then was living on her father's farm for the summer, thinking about going back to the land while watching this major advance forward.

Choose a way to collect several variants of one story. It is important to record the teller's version on audio- or videotape or by careful word-for-word notetaking. In each of these examples, whether you record several versions of one story or several stories about one event, you will need to look for the unchanging core elements as well as the variants' details. After gathering stories on tape or on paper, analyze your data. Here are some things to look for. First, include the core details of the story: What facts are stable? What's the chronology of the story? What characters are key? What is the central conflict in the story? What is the theme? Does it contain a cultural message or lesson? And then, what are some of the variants as each teller offers her own version: What are the features that change? Look at the list to speculate about why they change. What do the variants suggest about the tellers? About their audiences? You may find some features that don't fit the other versions, and those will provide clues about the tellers' positions and attitudes toward the story and the cultural themes that the story contains.

Response

School administrator Mary McCullough recorded a family story about the complex heritage of land ownership in her family. She and her siblings tell variants of the story, and their children retain different features of it. But here she writes the story as her father tells it:

> "That was some deal," Dad said. He sat on the couch, his arms folded across his chest, head tilted slightly to his right. "Your Mama paid for the land, but there was no will. Her Mama promised it to her, but there was no will. It was something to try to get it all straightened out."
>
> The farm that my mom and her sixteen siblings grew up on is located in Virginia. According to the story as Dad tells it, Mom was the only one who was working and could give her parents the money to expand their farm. There is no detailed information about how much

they had, but with Mom's money, they were able to buy a few additional acres. At the time, they promised her thirty-five acres. However, Mom did not record any information about this deal at the county land office or ask for receipts. When my grandparents died, there were no written records of the transaction and no will. When someone dies without a will, the property is divided up among the living siblings. In the event of their death, their part is divided into smaller pieces for their children. And on it goes.

When Mom became ill, Dad set out to recover her investment. She said she did not want to make a fuss. Dad says he felt that she should be able to leave her children more than a child's part, not enough as far as he was concerned. His journey began with locating everyone dead and living, going up and down the east coast, taking money with him to buy people out—quite a sacrifice as Dad didn't have lots of money. He used his savings, he tells us, for this.

When family members found out what he was doing, they became suspicious and sent messages through the sisters to Mom: "He's trying to get it all for himself."

He countered with, "I am trying to save it. If I don't do it, the white man's gonna get it." Dad kept every piece of paper—receipts, names, addresses, anything and everything. In his story, he tells about how it almost went to court. He retained lawyers, had to fire one and hire another. If the acreage went on the market, Dad knew he could easily lose to the highest bidder. Of course, he said, that wouldn't be a black person or anyone in our family. No one was rich. He fired the lawyer because he wasn't interested in the lawyer's mission—only in his own. This is the story he tells my sister, my brother, and me. He takes out all the documents and shows them to us. He wants us to remember which drawer in his desk holds the papers.

Over time, Dad was able to buy enough parts to accumulate twenty-two of the thirty-five acres originally promised to Mom. After that, he set out to have all the parcels surveyed and to make sure that each owner of a parcel would have a deed and a map. So Mom was able to give her three children their deeded, surveyed acres before she died. We take turns paying taxes and keep all of the receipts. We pay the taxes far in advance of when the money is due so that we don't get reminders from Dad.

Dad wants us to understand the value of land and what it offers. He is a woodsman who has seen changes in the environment, like the extinction of certain animals and birds. He remembers a kind of abundance that no longer exists; he mentions that he doesn't see chinkapins anymore and hasn't heard a whippoorwill's call in a long time. He sees more and more land posted with "No Trespassing" signs. He tells us never to sell.

"You can't make more land," he says. We let him know that we understand what it took for him to recover something given in words but not written, not recorded, not saved. We assure him of that by paying the taxes on time and keeping the papers in order. Pieces of paper, we've learned from him, count for more than some people's word. I learned these lessons from his storytelling:

Just because someone is your blood relative doesn't mean they won't betray you.

Do what you have to do, even when others might not agree or like you for it.

Keep official records, and protect what belongs to you and yours.

It takes time to straighten out mistakes. Do it right the first time.

It is important to make a will.

Nothing worth doing can be done quickly.

Be considerate of those who will be here after you.

I don't think my Dad is conscious of all that he's taught us in this story, now our own story, which we each tell a little differently.

THE INTERVIEW: LEARNING TO ASK

With time and experience, each of us assembles a kind of personal archive, a collection of stories from our family, our workplace, and the people we've encountered. People's story repertoires are verbal artifacts; they become data for the fieldworker. As a fieldworker, you'll dig into these archives, uncover your informants' stories, and look for what they tell you about your informants' perspectives. Fieldworkers listen and record stories from the point of view of the informant—not their own. Letting people speak for themselves by telling about their lives seems an easy enough principle to follow. But in fact, there are some important strategies for both asking questions and listening to responses. Those strategies are part of interviewing—learning to ask and learning to listen.

Interviewing involves an ironic contradiction: you must be both structured and flexible at the same time. While it's critical to prepare for an interview with a list of planned questions to guide your talk, it is equally important to follow your informant's lead. Sometimes the best interviews come from a comment, a story, an artifact, or a phrase you couldn't have anticipated. The energy that drives a good interview—for both you and your informant—comes from expecting the unexpected.

It's happened to both of us as interviewers. As part of a two-year project, Elizabeth conducted in-depth interviews with a college student who was a dancer. Anna identified with the modern dancers at the university and also lived a lifestyle with interests in animal rights, organic foods, and ecological causes. Over time, Elizabeth wondered about a particular necklace that Anna always wore. She speculated that it served as a spiritual talisman or represented a political affiliation. When she asked Anna, she discovered the unexpected. The necklace actually held the key to Anna's apartment—a much less dramatic answer than Elizabeth anticipated. Anna claimed that she didn't trust herself to keep her key anywhere but around her neck, and that information provided a clue to her temperament that Elizabeth wouldn't have known if she hadn't asked and had persisted in her own speculations.

In a shorter project, Bonnie interviewed a school superintendent over a period of eight months. As Ken discussed his beliefs about education, Bonnie connected his ideas with the writings of progressivist philosopher John Dewey. At the time, she was reading educational philosophy herself and was greatly influenced by Dewey's ideas. To her, Ken seemed to be a contemporary incarnation of Dewey. Eventually, toward the end of their interviews, Bonnie asked Ken which of Dewey's works had been the most important to him. "Dewey?" he asked, "John Dewey? Never exactly got around to reading him."

No matter how hard we try to lay aside our assumptions when we interview others, we will always carry them with us. Rather than ignoring our hunches, we need to form questions around them, follow them through, and see where they will lead us. Asking Anna about her necklace, a personal artifact, led Elizabeth to new understandings about Anna's self-concept and habits that later became important in her analysis of Anna's literacy. Bonnie's admiration for Dewey had little to do directly with Ken's educational philosophy. Her follow-up questions centered on the scholars who did shape Ken's theories. It is our job to reveal our informant's perspectives and experiences rather than our own. And so our questions must allow us to learn something new, something that our informant knows and we don't. We must learn how to ask.

Asking involves collaborative listening. When we interview, we are not extracting information like a dentist pulls a tooth, but we make meaning together like two dancers, one leading and one following. Interview questions range between closed and open. Closed questions are like those we fill out in popular magazines or application forms: How many years of schooling have you had? Do you rent your apartment? Do you own a car? Do you have any distinguishing birthmarks? Do you use bar or liquid soap? Do you drink sweetened or unsweetened tea, caffeinated or decaffeinated coffee? Some closed questions are essential for gathering background data: Where did you grow up? How many siblings did you have? What was your favorite subject in school? But these questions often yield single phrases as answers and can shut down further talk. Closed questions can start an awkward volley of single questions and abbreviated answers.

To avoid asking too many closed questions, you'll need to prepare ahead of time by doing informal research about your informants and the topics they represent. For example, if you are interviewing a woman in the air force, you may want to read something about the history of women in aviation. Reading a book about the

WAFs (Women in the Air Force) will prepare you for your interview. You might also consult an expert in the field or telephone government offices to request informational materials so that you avoid asking questions that you could answer for yourself, like "How many years have women been allowed to fly planes in the U.S. Air Force?" When you are able to do background research, your knowledge of the topic and the informant's background will demonstrate your level of interest, put the informant at ease, and create a more comfortable interview situation.

Open questions, by contrast, help elicit your informant's perspective and allow for more conversational exchange. Because there is no single answer to open-ended questions, you will need to listen, respond, and follow the informant's lead. Because there is no single answer, you can allow yourself to engage in a lively, authentic response. In other words, simply being an interested "other" makes a good field interviewer. Here are some very general open questions—sometimes called *experiential* and *descriptive*—that encourage the informant to share experiences or to describe them from his or her own point of view:

- Tell me more about the time when…
- Describe the people who were most important to…
- Describe the first time you…
- Tell me about the person who taught you about…
- What stands out for you when you remember…
- Tell me the story behind that interesting item you have.
- Describe a typical day in your life.

When thinking of questions to ask an informant, make your informant your teacher. You want to learn about his or her expertise, knowledge, beliefs, and worldview. An interview can begin with a focus on almost any topic, as long as it involves the informant's point of view.

B O X 27

Using a Cultural Artifact: An Interview

Purpose

This exercise mirrors the process of conducting interviews over time with an informant. It emphasizes working with the informant's perspective, making extensive and accurate observations, speculating and theorizing, confirming and disconfirming ideas, writing up notes, listening well, sharing ideas collaboratively, and reflecting on your data.

To introduce interviewing in our courses, we use an artifact exchange. This exercise allows people to investigate the meaning of an object from another person's point of view. It follows the model we used when we interviewed our friend Danling in Chapter 6 about silk and silkworms. (see p. 297). This interview focuses on a concrete object, an artifact rather than language connotations.

Action

Choose a partner from among your colleagues. You will act as both interviewer and informant. Select an interesting artifact that your partner is either wearing or carrying: a key chain, a piece of jewelry, an item of clothing. Both partners should be sure the artifact is one the owner feels comfortable talking about. If, for example, the interviewer says, "Tell me about that pin you are wearing," but the informant knows that her watch has more meaning or her bookbag holds a story, the interviewer should follow her lead. Once you've each chosen an artifact, try the following process. Begin by writing observational and personal notes as a form of background research before interviewing:

1. *Take observational notes.* Take quiet time to inspect, describe, and take notes on your informant's artifact. Pay attention to its form and speculate about its function. Where do you think it comes from? What is it used for?

2. *Take personal notes.* What does it remind you of? What do you already know about things similar to it? How does it connect to your own experience? What are your hunches about the artifact? In other words, what assumptions do you have about it? (For example, you may be taking notes on someone's ring and find yourself speculating about how much it costs and whether the owner of the artifact is wealthy). It is important here to identify your assumptions and not mask them.

3. *Interview the informant.* Ask questions and take notes on the story behind the artifact. What people are involved in it? Why is it important to them? How does the owner use it? Value it? What's the cultural background behind it? After recording your informant's responses, read your observational notes to each other to verify or clarify the information.

4. *Theorize.* Think of a metaphor that describes the object. How does the artifact reflect something you know about the informant? Could you find background material about the artifact? Where would you look? How does the artifact relate to history or culture? If, for example, your informant wears earrings made of spoons, you might research spoon making, spoon collecting, or the introduction of the spoon in polite society. Maybe this person had a famous cook in the family, played the spoons as a folk instrument, or used these as baby spoons in childhood.

5. *Write.* In several paragraphs about the observations, the interview, and your theories, create a written account of the artifact and its relationship to your informant. Give a draft to your informant for a response.

6. *Exchange.* The informant writes a response to your written account, detailing what was interesting and surprising. At this point, the informant can point out what you didn't notice, say, or ask that might be important to a further understanding of the artifact. You will want to exchange your responses again, explaining what you learned from the first exchange.

7. *Reflect.* Write about what you learned about yourself as an interviewer. What are your strengths? Your weaknesses? What assumptions or preconceptions did you find that you had that interfered with your interviewing skills? How might you change this?

8. *Change roles and repeat this process.*

Response

Here is an excerpt from the artifact exercise, written by EunJoo Kang about Ming-Chi Own's watch. In the final draft of her essay, EunJoo, the interviewer, interweaves many of her original notes with information added by Ming-Chi from both the oral interview and the written exchange:

> When I tried to locate an artifact on my classmate, Ming-Chi, I was first caught by her necklace. It was golden and very thin. I asked if it had any story behind it, but she said that it did not, she just wore it. So I changed my eyes to a different object. I saw that she was wearing a watch.
>
> Ming-Chi's watch is small and gold-plated and square. It has seven colors: gold, steel, silver, dark gray, light gray, brown, and black on the band. It has a snake leather band with an omega symbol on it. The band does not look new and does not seem cheap either because I could read the omega symbol, which is [used by] one of the most famous Swiss watch companies. The band has seven holes and two loops. The watch itself was made in Japan by Seiko. I recognized Seiko as another good and famous watch company.
>
> How I saw this watch depended on what I was likely to look at, what I was oriented to seeing. I should confess that once I dreamed to be a fine artist. And I find I have a tendency to look at objects by their colors, shapes, design, and usage all at the same time. This was borne out by my noting the seven colors in the watch. Ming-Chi seemed surprised at my finding so many colors in her watch. That told me something. Not everyone sees the same things. To Ming-Chi, the color had little meaning. Instead, her watch focused on keeping schedules and being on time.
>
> Ming-Chi shared that the watch was purchased by her father in Singapore. She got the watch as a graduation gift. She attended college in Australia, far from her family in Singapore. It was not common for families to send their daughters to foreign countries to study, but

Ming-Chi's father trusted her to be able to live by herself in Australia. Her father was happy with his grown daughter and bought her a watch that she could wear for a long time. And she did, as shown by the many scratches on it.

The most obvious thing to associate Ming-Chi's watch with is a concept of time. Even though she is from another culture, she had obviously adjusted to Western ideas of time. She has adjusted to our culture in which time is counted as "length," but time can be considered either monochronic, which comes from Western Europe, or polychronic. In monochronic time, for example, a host expects his guest would visit and leave by set times. In contrast, polychronic time is measured by quality and not length. Polychronic time should be measured by substance and satisfaction and not just by beginnings and endings. This is clearly a more Eastern way of observing time. I wonder whether or not Ming-Chi has experienced this way of being in time.

I am surprised at myself for finding this depth with an ordinary watch my classmate is wearing. This chance to look at a small artifact and describe it makes me understand what the ethnographic fieldworker does.

In interviews, sometimes researchers use cultural artifacts to enter into the informant's perspective. When we invite informants to tell stories about their artifacts, we learn not only about the artifacts themselves (Ming-Chi's watch) but also, indirectly, about other aspects of their world that they might not think to talk about. Artifacts, like stories, can mediate between individuals and their cultures.

In their short, informal conversation that began with a wristwatch, EunJoo uncovered the story of Ming-Chi's multicultural life: from Singapore to Australia to the United States. The watch gave them both, as Eastern students living in the West, an opportunity to theorize about different cultural attitudes toward time. Using Ming-Chi's watch as a focal point gave both the interviewer and the informant intense interaction and talk. Stories surfaced from Ming-Chi about herself as a student, a daughter, a foreigner in two cultures, and an amateur philosopher. Without the watch as mediator, it would have taken much longer to achieve such collaboration. That's why EunJoo was so surprised to find herself learning so much from looking at, speculating on, and thinking about her classmate's "ordinary watch."

Cultural artifacts provide data for a fieldworking project, much as stories do. Fieldworkers try to describe a wide range of artifacts from their individual informants and the culture at large to document their findings. If EunJoo were to write a full oral history of Ming-Chi, she might choose to include descriptions of some of the following cultural artifacts: letters from Ming-Chi's father, a catalog and her school records from Australia, and her passport, family photos, or articles and books describing the complex mix of English and Chinese cultures in Singapore.

THE INTERVIEW: LEARNING HOW TO LISTEN

Although most people think that the key to a good interview is asking a set of good questions, we and our students have found that the real key to interviewing is being a good listener. Think about your favorite television or radio talk show personalities. What do they do to make their informants comfortable and keep conversation flowing? Think about someone you know who you've always considered a good listener. Why does that person make you feel that way?

Good listeners guide the direction of thoughts; they don't interrupt or move conversation back to themselves. Good listeners use their body language to let informants understand that their informants' words are important to them, not allowing their eyes to wander, not fiddling, not checking their watches. They encourage response with verbal acknowledgments and follow-up questions, with embellishments and examples. As Henry Glassie suggests in the quote that opens this chapter, interviewers need to keep the conversation open by keeping the "other" in the foreground.

But to be a good listener as a field interviewer, you must also have structured plans with focused questions. And you must be willing to change them as the conversation moves in different directions. With open questions, background research, and genuine interest in your informant, you'll find yourself holding a collaborative conversation from which you'll both learn. It is the process, not the preplanned information, that makes an interview successful.

Paul Russ conducted interviews with five AIDS survivors for an ethnographic film, *Healing without a Cure: Stories of People Living with AIDS,* sponsored by a local health agency. He developed a list of open and closed questions to prepare for and guide his interviewing process. Paul was a journalist teaching himself to do fieldwork and was very conscious of the difference between open and closed questions. He knew that closed questions would provide him with similar baseline data for all of his informants. For this reason, he formulated some questions that had one specific answer: "How many months have you lived with your diagnosis?" "When did you first request a 'buddy' from the health service?" "Does your family know about your diagnosis?" But the overall goal of his project was to capture how individuals coped with their diagnoses daily, drawing on their own unique resources. He wanted to avoid creating a stereotypical profile of a "day in the life of a person living with AIDS" since he knew that no one AIDS patient's way of coping could possibly illustrate another's.

The field interview draws on both collaboration and interaction. Being a good listener means becoming an active participant in the lives you're studying during the time you're in the field. It means posing questions from your informants' point of view, inviting them to answer from their perspective, from their own worldview. Paul constructed open questions to allow his informants to speak from their lived experiences. Here are a few of his open questions: "What did you already know about AIDS when you were diagnosed?" "How did others respond to you and your diagnosis?" "What has helped you most on a day-to-day basis to live with the virus?" "Have people treated you differently since you were diagnosed?"

In the following excerpt from his hundreds of pages of transcripts, Paul talks with Jessie, a man who had been living with his diagnosis for eight years. For Paul, this interview was a struggle because Jessie hadn't talked much with others about AIDS. And because Paul chose to study people whose lives were very fragile, he paid particular attention to the interactive process between himself and his informants. In the following transcript, Paul uses Jessie's dog Princess just as another interviewer might have used an artifact to get further information:

P: What was your reaction when you were first diagnosed?
(This is one of the questions Paul posed to each of his five informants. Because he was making a training film for public health volunteers, he wanted to record people's initial reactions on discovering that they had a publicly controversial illness.)

J: My first reaction? How am I going to tell my family. And I put it in my mind that I would not tell anyone until it became noticeable. And I wondered who would take care of me.... I knew sometimes AIDS victims go blind. I panicked a little bit, and I started thinking of all the things I have to do to make my life livable.... I started thinking about the things I could do to make it go easier. And I started thinking of things I would miss.

P: Like Princess, your dog?
(Paul knew from previous talks that Jessie's dog was an important part of his daily life.)

J: I've had Princess for three years. I had another red dachshund, but she got away. I got Princess as a Christmas gift.... She comforts me. She knows when I'm not feeling right. She comes and rubs me. She goes places with me. If I'm in the garden, she's right there. She can't let me out of her sight. Sometimes I talk to her, late at night, we just lay there. She seems like she understands.... I don't think she can live without me. If something happens to me, she'll be so confused. I think she'll be so lonely, she'll go off somewhere and just die.... I want to give her to somebody. Maybe an older person, someone I believe will take care of her.
(In this part of the interview, the dog prompted Jessie to open his feelings to Paul. By following up on Jessie's comment about "things he'd miss," Paul deepened their interaction and intensified their talk. It was not the dog

herself that was important in this exchange but what Princess represented from Jessie's perspective. Paul did not intend to make Jessie talk about his fear of dying, but it happened naturally as he talked about Princess. At this point, Paul found a way to ask another one of the prepared questions that he used with each of his informants. And Jessie's answer brought them back to Princess.)

P: What's your typical day like?

J: My typical day is feeding Princess, letting her out, doing my housework. I like to do my work before noon because I'm addicted to soap operas.... I like to work in the yard. I've got a garden. I have some herbs. And I like every now and then to pray. I go to the library. I do a great deal of reading.
(Paul continued to interview Jessie about his spirituality and his reading habits. He brought this interview around to another preplanned question that he asked of all his AIDS informants.)

P: What advice do you have for the newly diagnosed?

J: Don't panic. You do have a tendency to blow it out of proportion. And find a friend, a real friend, to help you filter out the negative. Ask your doctor questions. Let it out and forgive. Forgive yourself, you're only human. And forgive the person you think gave it to you. Then you will learn that the key to spirituality is to abandon yourself.... I don't want a sad funeral. I want music, more music than anything else. I don't want my family to go under because of this disease.

Paul's interviews eventually became a training film for volunteers at the Triad Health Project and area schools that wanted to participate in AIDS support and education. In the film, Paul has the advantage of presenting his data, not just through verbal display but visually as well. As Paul conducts his interviews, we hear his voice and see his informants—their surroundings and artifacts, their gestures and body language, and the tones of voices as they respond to Paul.

BOX 28

Establishing Rapport

Purpose

You can tell from reading the interview with Jessie (see pages 375–76) that Paul Russ worked hard to establish rapport with his informant. He achieves this connection with Jessie by turning his interviews into a collaborative and interactive process in which he makes himself sensitive to Jessie's feelings, position, and worldview.

Action

In this activity, you will reflect on your relationship with an informant and gain greater understanding of yourself as a researcher. Write a short paper about your subjective attitude toward an informant. Think about whether you've felt tentative or hesitant toward your informant, feelings that you may not want to write about in your final paper but that you acknowledge and understand as part of your researcher self. Use the following list to guide you:

1. Describe your first meeting with your informant. What did you notice about yourself as you began the interview process?
2. Describe any gender, class, race, or age differences that may have affected the way you approached your informant.
3. Discuss ways you tried either to acknowledge or to erase these differences and the extent to which you were successful.
4. Discuss how your rapport changed over time in talking with and understanding your informant and her worldview.

Response

Paul Russ faced many race and class differences when he interviewed his informants about how they lived with AIDS. The most obvious was health, since his informants were facing death and he was not. Paul's response describes the many conflicting feelings he had when he interviewed Jessie:

> I picked up Jessie to drive him to the Health Project office for the interview. At first, we didn't conduct the interviews at his house. I'm not sure if he was uncomfortable about me seeing the inside of his house, if he didn't want the neighbors seeing a tall white guy carrying a bunch of camera equipment into this house. Anyway, as Jessie rode in my car, I was incredibly aware of the two different worlds we came from. I had a bad case of white man's guilt. As he sat in my car, I apologized for the dog hair left from taking my two dogs to the vet. He said that it was fine, that he was used to it. Then he mentioned his dog, Princess. It was the first thing we had to talk about. Jessie admitted that he had little family support to cope with AIDS and that Princess was his family. I shared that my dog had had a difficult pregnancy and that I almost lost her. That's when he first opened up to me about his fear of living without Princess or Princess living without him. When it later came up in our interview, it was an obvious opportunity to encourage Jessie to speak personally.
>
> It was essential to establish common ground with him because I felt I had nothing in common with Jessie. Perhaps this was because he did not come from where I came from and, perhaps, because he did not look like me. And while I've never considered myself prejudiced, I realize that we all have prejudices deeply buried inside no matter how

intelligent or informed we are. In order to know him with some degree of intimacy, I had to be vulnerable and share myself. I had to address the baggage of race, class, education. I did this with all the informants in my project, and it scared me because being friends with someone who is facing mortality requires an emotional investment. I knew I had to establish a friendship.

While I was making a personal connection with Jessie, I also had professional distance. With everything that came out of Jessie's mouth, I was thinking about how it could be used in the final project. For me, interviewing is very active. It's not passive at all. You have to listen for meaning and listen for what's not being said. I had trouble getting Jessie to speak from the heart. His responses to early questions were pressed. I knew that if I were writing his story for a reader, I could project a much clearer sense of his identity than he gave me on camera. I knew that. But I wasn't writing his story. My mission was to record him telling his story in his own words. So I looked for opportunities to help him reveal himself to me. Princess was one of these opportunities.

Fieldworkers must turn interview transcripts into writing, making a kind of verbal film. As interesting as interview transcripts are to the researcher, they are only partial representations of the actual interview process. Folklorist Elliott Oring observes, "Lives are not transcriptions of events. They are artful and enduring symbolic constitutions which demand our engagement and identification. They are to be perceived and understood as wholes" (258). To bring an informant's life to the page, you must use a transcript within your own text, sometimes describing the setting, the informant's physical appearances, particular mannerisms, and language patterns and intonations. The transcript by itself has little meaning until you bring it to life.

Cindie Marshall conducted a semester-long field project at Ralph's Sports Bar, frequented by men and women who describe themselves as bikers. Cindie had returned to school while she continued to work at a law firm, and she completed this study in a second-semester freshman writing course. In "Ralph's Sports Bar," she combines her skills as a listener, an interviewer, and most of all a writer. In her study, her informants speak in their own voices, but Cindie contextualizes them, offering readers a look into the biker subculture as it exists at Ralph's. In her data analysis, she identifies three categories of biker patrons as they interact side by side at Ralph's: the "rednecks," the "regular bikers," and the "white-collar weekend professionals." Cindie uses her interviews with two key informants, Alice and Teardrop, to verify her data, along with her own extensive fieldnotes. As you read Cindie's research study, notice all the fieldworking skills she brings together.

Ralph's Sports Bar

Cindie Marshall

The Arrival

Ralph's Sports Bar isn't a sports bar at all really. When someone says "sports bar," I think of a bar that is neatly kept, full of white-collar professionals, a big-screen TV, billiard tables, and more than likely a dartboard or two. Oh, and let's not forget the line of high-dollar sports cars parked outside. Well, that does not come close to describing Ralph's Sports Bar.

As I pulled into the half-paved, half-graveled parking lot, the first thing I saw on the side of the small red-brick building was a large sign that said, "Urinate inside, not out here." I suppose had I been anywhere else I would have been shocked by the sign. However, I had come here to seek out bikers, and this small sign depicted just what I had expected of them. I am not quite sure how I came by such a negative image of bikers. Like anything else in life, I suppose I was conditioned to think this way. My white-collar family raised me to believe that there were different classes in the world and that my class was just better than theirs. The truth is that the sign struck another chord as well. The

"Ralph's" Sports Bar.

(Photo: Minshall Strater)

one thing I had always admired about them was the fact they didn't care what people like me thought of them. It is inspiring to think that there are actually people who simply "do their thing."

After seeing that sign, I was hesitant to continue with my mission. But I had come here to seek out bikers and find out everything I could about them, and that was exactly what I had to do.

Unfamiliar Surroundings

I got out of my car and walked up toward the front of the building. On my approach, I could see three men and a woman sitting at an outdoor table, drinking beer and laughing. The table was brown plastic and was well worn. The four mismatched wooden chairs were unstable and varied in color. The concrete around them was littered with old cigarette butts, bottle caps, and other debris.

Beside the table was a small sidewalk area. This area served as a parking strip for Harley Davidson motorcycles. I had driven by the bar the weekend before and saw the bikes meticulously aligned, handlebar to handlebar, back tire to back tire. I noticed there were none there this evening and wondered if I would find any bikers at all.

As I turned from the table area toward the front entrance, I was greeted by a sign proclaiming my arrival at "Ralph's Sports Bar." The sign was so big, it took up half of the right-hand wall of the building. The entrance doors were glass that had been painted jet black and propped open with wooden straight-back chairs.

I entered the smoke-filled building to the sounds of Ozzie Osborne's "No More Tears" screaming from the jukebox. The smell of stale beer, cigarette ashes, and body odor was overwhelming.

Along the right-hand wall were four small pool tables with an even smaller one on a platform at the rear of the building. The pool tables were well worn, with cigarette burns, beer stains, and rips in the felt. Taking up the bulk of the right-hand wall was a huge 8 by 20 handpainted mural. It was a picture of the red dog from the Red Dog beer commercial. Through the mural ran a banner that said, "Mad Dog Ralphman." The space remaining on the wall was filled with black velvet paintings of dogs playing pool. Most of these pictures were hung on the wall with tape or a punch pin and left unframed.

Immediately on the left was the L-shaped bar. On the wall to the left of the bar was a huge bulletin board covered by pictures of patrons both old and new. Most of the pictures captured smiling men and women while they toasted the camera with their beer. As you walked around the bar, it led to a small room. The room had a wooden table in the center and was surrounded by poker machines. I could only surmise that this room served as the arcade.

From the front door looking down the left wall of the building, there were two booths. They looked like they could have been in McDonald's at one point, with their yellow seats and tabletops. Behind the two booths was the jukebox.

"Ralph's" Sports Bar parking lot.

And beyond the jukebox were two more booths. As you passed the last booth, there was a wooden ramp leading to the bathrooms. (After entering the bathroom, I understood why one would opt to go outside.) The left wall was littered with pictures of Harley Davidson riders playing pool. It was a collection from the "Harley Davidson 25th Anniversary" prints. They were mounted in bent frames with shattered glass covering various snapshots of bikers at play. There were also a variety of neon signs scattered along the wall advertising Budweiser beer.

How Do You Read the Signs?

There were signs everywhere! I read them in hopes of finding out what behavior would be expected of me during my visit as well as what behavior I could expect from the patrons of this bar. The first thing that caught my eye was a sign that stated, "Break a cue, pay $25.00 or be barred." That wasn't the behavioral expectation I had hoped to find. And the bad news was, there were more. On the front door was a sign that stated, "We do not buy stolen merchandise." On the wall over the bar was a handwritten sign that said, "Ale law: no beer sold after 2 p.m." On each poker machine there was a handwritten sign that said, "By N.C. law no gambling allowed." What did all of these signs really mean? By talking to the owner's girlfriend, prior to my visit, I knew that stolen merchandise was sold and bought. I knew that if I played poker, I could cash in my points for money. I also knew that alcohol was served on many occasions as late as the patrons wanted to drink. What's more, I knew that drugs came and went out of this bar as frequently as the patrons. So these signs were really placed on the walls as a sign to the local police that the rules were in place and illegal activity was prohibited at Ralph's.

People Watching

There were thirteen people when I arrived; eight were men and five were women. I did not see the biker group that I had seen while driving by the previous weekend and was disappointed that they would not be the focus of my research. Since my target group was not there, I made my way to the back of the bar, where I thought I would be least conspicuous in my attempt to observe the culture of the bar.

The patrons were scattered around the bar in small groups. One group sat at the bar; they were all men who were mainly clad in black glasses (the doors were open and sun was coming in), blue jeans, T-shirts, and black leather boots of some sort. Each of them had chains attaching their wallets to their belts and had hair that was unkempt and hung at least to their shoulders.

The largest group in the bar surrounded the pool tables. This group was comprised of most of the remaining men and all of the women. They were clad in T-shirts, dirty blue jeans, and brown leather work boots. They were mainly involved in shooting pool and drinking beer, and some of them were dancing to the jukebox between shots.

At the back of the bar, closer to where I was located, were the remaining group of men. They were neatly dressed in blue jeans, button-down shirts, and tennis shoes. This group sat quietly talking while drinking their beers.

As I watched these three groups of people, I concluded that each section of the bar was the territory of distinct groups. The "bikers" were at the bar, the "rednecks" were at the pool tables, and the "white-collar professionals" made their way to the back booths. Each group was made up of individuals who were similarly dressed. They stayed in their own group and did not intermingle with the other groups unless it was a necessity. Anyone who wanted to get a beer had to speak to the bikers at the bar; otherwise you couldn't get to the bartender.

Everyone in the bar eyed me suspiciously during my visit. I appeared to be very different from the other women. I didn't dress like them, walk like them, or talk like them. Because of the illegal activity that goes on in the bar, I also guessed they were probably wondering if I was an undercover cop. After observing these groups for a couple of hours, I realized that given the way they marked their boundaries, they probably wouldn't be very inviting to a stranger asking a lot of questions about their "culture." Especially a female stranger who obviously didn't appear to belong there to begin with.

I decided that I would go to the table out front and perhaps there I could find someone to answer my questions. At the very least, I could get some fresh air and think about my approach.

Talking to Teardrop

When I arrived at the table, there was a woman sitting alone, drinking a beer. She had obviously had a lot to drink. But we talked for a minute, and she was really quite nice. I introduced myself, and she said her name was Teardrop. It was dark outside, so I couldn't see her very well. We talked about the weather for a few minutes, and that led her to tell me that she had moved here from Michigan three years ago and that she came to Ralph's every day.

I knew that this was my opportunity to talk to a patron. I wasn't sure which group she belonged in, but if she came to Ralph's every day, she must be in one of them. On a long shot, I asked her if she would like to shoot a game of pool. She agreed, and I was delighted. This was an opportunity to do two things—ask questions and be seen with a regular patron of the bar. I guessed that if others saw me talking to her, at the least her friends would be more relaxed about talking to me.

Once we were inside, I saw that Teardrop was wearing new Lee jeans, a nice pale yellow sweater, and a heart-shaped brooch. Her hair was brown but was showing signs of graying. She had it neatly pulled back, and her bangs were teased and carefully sprayed in place. It wasn't until she laughed that I noticed she was missing her front teeth, both top and bottom. She had a small tattoo around her wrist that served as a bracelet. It was dark green and was in the shape of a vine. Most of the tattoo was covered by the watch she was wearing.

As we played pool, I noticed something else. She had a very small black spot under her left eye, high on her cheek. At first I thought it was a mole or a birthmark. But after looking at it carefully, I noticed that it was a black tattoo in the shape of a teardrop. I asked her if it was a teardrop and she said yes; that was how she got her name.

When I asked her about her tattoo, she starting really talking to me. She told me that when she was 13, she had been kidnapped by a group of bikers. The biker that kidnapped her had eventually sold her to a fellow biker. This went on for years, being sold from biker to biker. Finally, three years ago, she got away from them. The teardrop was there because she couldn't cry anymore.

After hearing Teardrop's story, my admiration for the bikers' "do your own thing" attitude was lost. I had always been one who appreciated the freedom to express oneself, but this went far beyond freedom. What Teardrop had described was sheer abuse, and she wore that abuse both on her face, in the shape of a teardrop, and in her smile, which was darkened by missing teeth.

After talking with Teardrop, I left the bar to reflect on all that I had seen. I wanted to know why the groups in the bar kept themselves segregated. I also wanted to know why three groups in the bar would come together in a place just to be segregated. The only way I could get the answers to my questions was to talk to a person who had been in all three groups and had spent a lot of time at the bar. The likely candidate would be Alice.

Conversation with Alice

Alice was the receptionist at the law firm that I worked at. Her boyfriend, Ralph, owned the bar. She had worked there prior to coming to the law firm, and she could probably tell me all I wanted to know about these groups.

Alice agreed to my interview, and I prepared a list of the three groups, outlining what I thought their characteristics were. I felt that it was important to understand the groups before trying to understand their connection to this bar or to each other. Alice read my list, and we began our interview.

Characteristics of the "Rednecks"

We both agreed that one of the groups we would call "rednecks" for lack of a better term. My list conveyed the following characteristics for rednecks: they would be lazy; they would value freedom; they would not like or adhere to any rules imposed on them; they would have no self-pride, either in their work or appearance; they would demean women; they would have no materialistic values; they would have no work ethic; and they would have no moral code among themselves—it would be every man for himself.

After reviewing my list, Alice commented that actually, "they are hardworking and take pride in their jobs. Because they like to be able to say 'I do something well.'... Most of them are blue-collar workers—construction workers, electricians, people who do things with their hands. They're good at what they do to a certain extent. A lot of them do change jobs frequently because of the drinking problem that they have, and I think the majority of them do have drinking problems.... They are lazy in the sense that they don't aspire to be anything more than what they are."

We discussed how they treated their women, and Alice was quick to point out "that's the biggest thing that they do.... It makes them feel like they are bigger." We had talked prior to the interview about how uncomfortable I was at this bar. It seemed that all the men treated the women with little or no respect.

On the subject of the rednecks' commitment to their fellow rednecks, I felt that it would be every man for himself. I doubted that the rednecks had lasting bonds or would stand up for a buddy in trouble. Alice said that she had "seen where one night two guys would sit there and be buddy-buddy and would fight together side by side. Two weeks later, they would fight each other."

Overall, the only real corrections Alice made to my list of characteristics was that she strongly disagreed with my idea that rednecks were lazy. She said that they were not lazy and that they all worked. I asked her later outside the interview how they could all be working yet spending their entire day at Ralph's. She told me those individuals worked third shift and would simply go to work drunk.

Characteristics of the Bikers

I had made a similar list of characteristics for the bikers at Ralph's. I had decided that they, too, would value freedom and not like rules imposed on them, much like the rednecks. However, they would have a higher moral code among themselves. I guessed that they didn't care what other people thought of them and therefore would not be materialistic. They would likely believe in making their own way and have a higher work ethic than the rednecks. I would categorize them as more the "weekend warrior" type. I also concluded that unlike the rednecks, they were probably ritualistic in the way they meticulously parked their bikes. As for their treatment of women, after talking with Teardrop, my view on that was clear. To the bikers, women were property, and that was all.

Alice started her revision of my list by first telling me that "there are even two different classes of bikers.... There are some bikers that are construction workers, moochers, low lifes. They live from day to day in how they get their money, how they live. They come from a culture of brotherhood and "my buddy." They are more clannish in that, if a guy drives a bike, they will stand beside him no matter what. But also, there are a lot of bikers that come in there that are white-collar workers; they do this on the weekend and like to be someone different. They change their persona and how people perceive them. They put on their leather pants and leather jackets and ride these motorcycles all weekend long and go back to their jobs. There are four or five of them that nobody knows.... They are businessmen who own companies over in High Point...but you would never guess it by the way they look when they are sitting there on the weekends drinking."

When we talked about the stereotypical biker, I asked her if she felt they "treat women the same way the rednecks do." (I was fairly sure about how the bikers treated women but unclear about the rednecks.) She said no. It was more of a kind of ownership. She said, "'My old lady' and 'my old man,' this is the way they talk. Rednecks are a little more respectful... 'this is my wife' or 'this is my girlfriend.' I think that the 'old lady' and 'old man' can change from week to week. I have seen [bikers] swap women around as if they were pieces of property." Surprisingly enough, she made her point about the way bikers treat women by telling me Teardrop's story.

We talked about the bikers and how they felt about freedom. Alice pointed out, "You will find that most of the bikers will be outside, they will not be inside the bar.... Bikers like the openness and the freedom—that's why they're bikers."

Conclusion

Alice is fascinating because she has been very deeply connected to all three of these groups. Therefore, she is a reliable source of information on all three groups. She works at Ralph's bar at night and at a law firm during the day. Unlike the white-collar biker, who takes on a persona to escape on the weekend, Alice truly does cross the line of the cultural boundaries. I believe that her stereotypes and ideas about each of these groups are based on her living in that culture. As she put it, "I've been there. I've been a drinker and down on my luck and slept in my car. I've been just where they are on many occasions...."

My own stereotypes show in my list of characteristics that I mapped out for Alice to review. I am in the category of the white-collar professional. I have a high work ethic and would probably be tagged by the rednecks or the bikers as materialistic. But it really is more than that. I have pride in myself, and I value the opinions of others. I am uncertain where my stereotypes were born. In all fairness, I would have to say they came from the media, my parents, my friends, and my own attitudes about what is right and wrong.

As for Alice, it is clear that she, too, has stereotyped these groups. Even though she's been involved with each, when asked, "Which culture are you most comfortable with?" she replied, "The rednecks." During the interview, her tone of voice was forceful when she attempted to dispel the stereotype that I presented of rednecks' being lazy.

After talking with Alice and visiting the bar, my question still remained: Why would these distinctly different groups of people, each representing a unique culture, come to one small bar, each mapping their turf and intentionally staying separated? Alice felt that the common bond was Ralph. Ralph moved easily between the cultures and was actually a part of each group. She said that he did it much the same as she did, the difference being that Ralph held the role of "leader" or "policer" of each group. It was because of Ralph that the groups could all drink their beer in harmony while at the bar.

I feel that it goes much deeper than that. The one common bond that all of these groups share is love of freedom. I think that the culture of Ralph's Sports Bar is based on that love of freedom. All these people go to Ralph's to escape, to be free of the watchful eyes of a judgmental society. They like the comfort of not worrying what anyone else will think because they know no one will care or judge their actions.

The white-collar, part-time biker enjoys the freedom of wearing his leather and riding his Harley on the weekend without anyone knowing. The redneck enjoys the freedom to drink his beer and be totally wild if he wishes.

It all comes down to freedom. The group to which you belong simply indicates whether that freedom is experienced for a brief moment or for a lifetime; it states the extent to which the freedom is valued.

Commentary: With More Time...

I would love to have had more time to visit this bar and try to become part of this culture. I am certain that there are errors in my list of characteristics, and I know that these characteristics do not apply to every individual. It would have been interesting to make connections in the bar and test my ideas; to prove or disprove the stereotypes that I have about each group. With that research perhaps it would be more clear where the stereotypes actually come from. I have asked myself that question over and over again while writing this paper. At this point, I cannot clearly say where they come from. I think it is a combination of many sources.

I am still very intrigued with the biker culture. I wish I could have talked with more female bikers to get their ideas on the treatment-of-women issue. Teardrop really changed my attitude.

Three Distinct Cultures

My list of characteristics associated with each culture based on my observations at the bar. (Alice's corrections and additions are in italics.)

REDNECKS
Value freedom; do not like rules imposed on them
Lazy
No work ethic (*Hardworking, but all they do is work and drink*)
No self-pride; either in work or appearance
Demean women, think of them as possessions
Would rather drink than work or do anything else
No moral code among themselves; every man for himself
Minimal to nonexistent educational background
Don't care what other people think of them
Not materialistic or subject to cultural pressure such as fashion

BIKERS
Value freedom
Higher moral code than rednecks; stand up for each other; group is more important
than the individual
Don't care what other people think of them
Believe in making their own way; higher work ethic than rednecks; "weekend warrior"
Not materialistic in terms of possessions but they are in terms of fashion; they all tend
to want and have the same type of clothing
Ritualistic

PROFESSIONAL/WHITE-COLLAR
Materialistic
Care what others think of them; tend to worry a lot about the image they project
High work ethic; must work to obtain more material goods; more important than
drinking; would give up weekend freedom to gain more material things
Attitude of being above the other two cultures

INTERVIEW WITH ALICE
C: Let's go over the category list. You believe the rednecks value their freedom and
are hardworking.

A: I think that they are hardworking and take pride in their jobs. Because they like
to be able to say, "I do something well." But their whole goal in what I have
viewed is that "I work to drink and I drink to work."

C: What kind of work do they do normally?

A: Most of them are blue-collar workers--construction workers, electricians, people
who do things with their hands. They're good at what they do to a certain extent.
A lot of them do change jobs frequently because of the drinking problem that
they have, and I think the majority of them do have drinking problems.

C: We talked about their being lazy, and we concluded that they're lazy in the
sense that they don't aspire to be anything more than what they are.

A: Yes. If their daddy taught them how to do construction or to build houses, they
don't make goals other than that.

C: And no self-pride in terms of their appearance?

A: Yes.

C: And we talked about how they demean women.

A: Yes, very much so. That's the biggest thing that they do. It makes them feel stronger and feel like better people. It makes them feel like they are bigger.

C: We talked about every man for himself, and you were saying that there were no lasting bonds between the members of this particular culture within the bar.

A: This is true. Because I have seen where one night two guys would sit there and be buddy-buddy and would fight together side by side. Two weeks later, they would fight each other. If the situation changes. The alcohol changes people's personalities, and it varies day to day who is buddy-buddy.

C: The other culture that I saw when I was there is--you have your rednecks and you have your bikers. What is the difference between the bikers and the rednecks?

A: I think that there are even two different classes of bikers.

C: In this bar?

A: In this bar. In the sense that there are some bikers that are construction workers, moochers, low lifes. They live from day to day in how they get their money, how they live. They come from a culture of brotherhood and "my buddy." They are more clannish in that, if a guy drives a bike, they will stand beside him no matter what. But also, there are a lot of bikers that come in there that are white-collar workers; they do this on the weekend and like to be someone different. They change their persona and how people perceive them. They put on their leather pants and leather jackets and ride these motorcycles all weekend long and go back to their jobs. There are four or five of them that nobody knows. They are very honest and they tell you what they do, that they are businessmen who own companies over in High Point and one thing and another. But you would never guess it by the way they look when they are sitting there on the weekends drinking. (*Need to ask her how these guys are treated by the full-time bikers. Do they tell the full-time bikers about their other identity?*)

C: So those particular guys really fit both in among the bikers and the white-collar professionals.

A: Yes.

C: So they are just choosing what culture they want to be in on weekends basically. They could go into the biker thing or the professional white-collar worker thing if they wanted to, just whichever way they wanted to go.

A: Yeah.

One of the strengths of Cindie's study is that she acquires different perspectives about Ralph's Sports Bar, which mirror the three categories of patrons she is attempting to understand. One is the perspective of the "white-collar weekend professional." Cindie positions herself honestly at the outset as part of this group, admitting her own stereotypes as she reflects: "I am not quite sure how I came by such a negative image of bikers. Like anything else in life, I suppose I was conditioned to think this way. My white-collar family raised me to believe that there were different classes in the world and that my class was just better than theirs [the bikers]." The second perspective is what Cindie calls the "regular bikers," and her informant Teardrop has belonged to that "regular biker" culture much of her life. Although no longer a biker's girlfriend, Teardrop speaks from insider experience. The third perspective comes from Alice, Cindie's colleague at the law firm and Ralph's girlfriend, who defends the "redneck" position. Since "redneck" is such a negative term, Cindie would have to work hard to find out what Alice implied when she used it. In the South, *redneck* traditionally refers to a manual laborer, someone whose neck is burned from picking crops under the hot sun.

Cindie was fortunate to find Teardrop, who was in many ways an ideal informant. Teardrop frequents Ralph's every day, so she is an insider to the culture. But Teardrop had "stepped out" of the biker culture long enough to be able to reflect on it. As a female, she held a unique view of this predominantly male group. Teardrop was also an ideal informant because Cindie interacted with her informally, gathering data as they shot pool together. During their pool game, Teardrop offered the story about the meaning of her tear-shaped tattoo. Cindie didn't tape-record the story but remembered it and wrote it into her fieldnotes. While shooting pool, she didn't worry about forgetting Teardrop's story because it was indelible; the tattoo was there "because she couldn't cry anymore." Cindie learned this story from Teardrop as they interacted, each gaining trust for the other. Had Cindie pulled out her tape recorder and tried to interview Teardrop by asking, "So tell me how you got your name?" she probably wouldn't have heard Teardrop's story. It was the process of interaction and rapport that allowed Cindie to acquire such good insider data.

Cindie's interview with Alice was entirely different because it was structured and planned. Cindie prepared a list of questions based on her own fieldnote observations of the three categories of patrons at the bar. Because Alice was already a friend from the law firm where Cindie worked, she didn't need to establish rapport. As Ralph's girlfriend, Alice was a different kind of insider at the bar who identified with both the rednecks and the white-collar professionals. In this way, Alice had a position of double access.

Alice confirmed and extended Cindie's understanding of the "white-collar biker" with her own observations and insider status. Alice knew that this group was neither "regular" nor "redneck," that these people transformed themselves for the weekends. "They change their persona and how people perceive them. They put on their leather pants and leather jackets and ride these motorcycles all weekend long and go back to their jobs." While Cindie used Alice both to verify and to disconfirm her own observations, Alice rejected some of Cindie's stereotypes of rednecks: "During the interview, her tone of voice was forceful," Cindie wrote, when Alice "attempted to dispel the stereotype...of rednecks' being lazy." Alice also confirmed Cindie's observations about two groups of patrons at Ralph's Sports Bar.

Both Teardrop's and Alice's perspectives give weight and evidence to Cindie's own field observations, allowing her to confirm and disconfirm her data. As we point out throughout this book, when researchers use multiple data sources (interviews, fieldnotes, artifacts, and library or archival documents), they triangulate their findings. In this semester-long study, Cindie collected and analyzed varied sources (interviews, fieldnotes, and artifacts), but if she were to layer her data further in another revision, she would need to interview different patrons, selecting among informants in her three categories. Cindie's perspective was that of a woman who interviewed other women about a predominantly male subculture. To learn more about the male biking culture, she'd have to conduct research with a few of the male bikers and also probably with Ralph, the owner.

Cindie's final written account illustrates the systematic process of fieldworking. Short fieldwork accounts like this one may display different points of emphasis, depending on the topic, the data, and the researcher's interests. Some may foreground the culture; others may foreground the people. Whereas Rick Zollo's "Friday Night at Iowa 80," which we reproduce in Chapter 1, included many informant interviews, his final account focuses on the culture of trucking using his informants mainly to support his account of the culture. Karen Downing's study of Photo Phantasies (presented in Chapter 5) achieves a balance between looking at the glamour culture and looking at the people who inhabit it: herself, the customers, the management, and the staff. And unlike the fictional researcher Reema's boy in *Mama Day*, who pokes his tape recorder into everyone's face (see Chapter 3), Cindie Marshall learned how to ask, how to listen, and how to collaborate with her informants at Ralph's Sports Bar.

Because Cindie's final account is smoothly written and her research skills are well integrated, it might not be apparent that she has engaged in many aspects of the fieldworking process. A summary of her many fieldworking strategies reveals, however, that Cindie was able to do all of the following:

- *Prepare for the field.*

  She gained access through her colleague Alice, an insider at Ralph's.

  She read other research studies and material about fieldworking.

  She drafted a research proposal that explained her interest in the biker subculture.

  She wrote about her assumptions and uncovered her prejudices about bikers and rednecks.

- *Use the researcher's tools.*

  She established rapport by hanging out at Ralph's and by locating Teardrop, an insider informant.

  She observed, taking detailed fieldnotes about the physical environment.

  She participated in the culture by shooting pool with Teardrop, talking and interacting at the same time.

  She gathered descriptions of many cultural artifacts, taking photos and noting the signs outside and inside and what these implied.

  She interviewed two informants, Alice formally and Teardrop informally, taking fieldnotes on their physical characteristics as well as their stories.

  She transcribed Alice's interview, selecting potential sections to use in her final project.

■ *Interpret the fieldwork.*

She read her data, proposal, fieldnotes, interview notes, and transcripts, looking for themes and patterns.

She categorized her data into findings according to the three groups she observed.

She made meaning collaboratively with her informants:

> With Alice, she verified her categories and disconfirmed her own cultural stereotypes in her interview.

> With Teardrop, she reflected on her data, particularly after her interview, and expanded her findings with insights about the treatment of women within the biking culture.

She reflected on how her data described a subculture.

■ *Present the findings.*

She acknowledged and wrote about her position as an outsider.

She used descriptive details in her writing, selecting particular written artifacts (various signs) that convey the meaning of the culture: "urinate inside, not out here" and "we do not buy stolen merchandise."

She turned her informants into characters by melding her fieldnotes and her transcripts.

She integrated her informants' voices with her narrative by using direct quotations from her transcripts.

She designed sections with subheadings to guide her reader through the project: "The Arrival," "Unfamiliar Surroundings," "How Do You Read the Signs?" "People Watching," "Talking to Teardrop," "Conversation with Alice," "Characteristics of the 'Rednecks'," "Characteristics of the Bikers," "Conclusion," and her commentary called "With More Time…."

She drew conclusions without shutting down further exploration of the topic as she reflected on what other sorts of data she would need to continue her research in her final commentary called "With More Time…."

Analyzing Your Interviewing Skills

BOX 29

Purpose

Reviewing and analyzing an excerpt from your transcripts can help you refine your interviewing skills and see ways to improve them. Pausing to look closely at your interviewing and transcribing techniques may smooth the way for the rest of your project.

Action

Select and transcribe a short section from a key interview, no more than a page, to share. Play the corresponding portion of the audiotape as your colleagues read the transcript and listen. Have your colleagues jot down notes and suggestions about your interview so that you can discuss their observations together afterward:

- Has the interviewer established rapport with the informant?
- Who talks the most, the informant or the interviewer? Does that seem to work?
- What was the best question the interviewer asked? Why?
- What question might have extended to another question? Why?
- How did the interviewer encourage your informant to be specific?
- Were any of the questions closed?

Try using the line-by-line analysis in a small section, like the ones we've presented in the interview with Danling Fu in Chapter 6, Paul Russ's interview with Jessie (pp. 375–76), and the following example from Cindie Marshall.

Response

Here we'll analyze one of Cindie's transcripts, a portion of her interview with Alice. In this excerpt, both interviewer and informant struggle with what they mean by the word *redneck* and its associated cultural stereotypes. Fieldworkers need to be sensitive to words that have different meanings for insiders in a culture. From her outsider perspective, Cindie knew that the word *redneck* is a loaded term and that it's used differently in different areas of the country. She was eager for Alice to help her clarify what it meant to different groups at Ralph's.

> C: You believe the rednecks value their freedom and are hardworking.
> *(Cindie wants confirmation from Alice about one group of people she has observed frequenting Ralph's Sports Bar. She tried to get Alice to untangle her own perspective about this category of patrons in the bar.)*

> A: I think that they are hardworking and take pride in their jobs. Because they like to be able to say, "I do something well." But their whole goal in what I have viewed is that "I work to drink and I drink to work."

> C: What kind of work do they do normally?
> *(Cindie follows Alice's lead, asking for more information, trying to find out more about what they each mean when they use the term* redneck. *When the researcher recognizes that one word has different meanings among different informants, she ought to try to understand it.)*

A: Most of them are blue-collar workers—construction workers, electricians, people who do things with their hands. They're good at what they do to a certain extent. A lot of them do change jobs frequently because of the drinking problems that they have, and I think the majority of them do have drinking problems.

C: We talked about their being lazy, and we concluded that they're lazy in the sense that they don't aspire to be anything more than what they are.
(Rather than trying to get more information from Alice about biker patrons who "do things with their hands," Cindie introduces her own stereotype—that bikers are lazy, an idea that she and Alice had discussed before. Cindie's question represents her indecision about whether her stereotypes of bikers were true or if they came from movies.)

A: Yes. If their daddy taught them how to do construction or to build houses, they don't make goals other than that.
(Alice tried to move the conversation away from yet another stereotype—that bikers are lazy—by offering her own observation: that bikers seem to have limited career goals. Both interviewer and informant struggle to understand each other's stereotypes.)

C: And no self-pride in terms of their appearance?
(This is a leading question and in the end a closed question. Alice has no choice but to answer yes or no. Later in the interview, Cindie asks a descriptive question that prompts Alice to talk about what bikers actually do like to wear.)

A: Yes.

C: And we talked about how they demean women.
(Cindie raises yet another topic based on earlier conversations with Alice and also based on stereotypes of bikers that, in her later interview with Teardrop, prove to be true.)

A: Yes, very much so. That's the biggest thing that they do. It makes them feel stronger and feel like better people. It makes them feel like they are bigger.

GATHERING ORAL HISTORIES

An oral history is a life's story shared collaboratively with a fieldworker, emphasizing the individual's life against the cultural significance of that life. Cindie Marshall uses her interviews to support her research on the biker subculture.

But if she were to do an oral history, she would have interviewed Teardrop in depth to record her whole life's story. Teardrop's role as a biker's companion would be a major part of her oral history, but the emphasis would be on Teardrop. Donna Niday's family story project did not focus on any single sister's whole life. But if Donna were to undertake an oral history, the "baby on the roof" story would become only a minor part of the study of one sister's life as a midwestern farm girl. Paul Russ recorded enough information from five people living with AIDS to write oral histories about each one, but instead his goal was to produce a documentary film.

In an oral history, the fieldworker gathers real-life stories about the past experiences of a particular person, family, region, occupation, craft, skill, or topic. The fieldworker records spoken recollections and personal reflections from living people about their past lives, creating a history. One of the most successful contemporary oral history projects in this country comes from the fieldwork of high school students in rural Georgia. In the 1970s, teenagers in Rabun Gap, Georgia, began to document the stories, folk arts, and crafts of elderly people in their Appalachian community. They wrote about making moonshine, building log cabins, faith healing, dressing hogs, and farming practices in their mountain culture and published their fieldwork in the many *Foxfire* anthologies.

Anthropological fieldworkers who record an entire life's history as well as speculate on the relationship between that life and the culture it represents are called **ethnohistorians**, and their studies span many years. Over 10 years' time, Henry Glassie visited, interviewed, and wrote about one 4-square-mile Irish community in *Passing the Time in Ballymenone* (you can read a brief excerpt on p. 226). Shirley Brice Heath, who researched literacy in the Piedmonts of the southeastern United States in her study *Ways with Words*, spent 14 years gathering data from parents, teachers, and children there (see pp. 325–36 for an excerpt). Ruth Behar wrote a life history of Esperanza, a Mexican street peddler, in her book *Translated Woman*, which we discuss briefly in Chapter 8. Behar traveled back and forth between the United States and Mexico for over five years collecting data and writing about Esperanza.

But not all oral histories need to be full-length ethnographic studies. During the Great Depression in the United States of the 1930s, when writers were among the many unemployed, the government sponsored the Federal Writer's Project, which put writers to work as interviewers. Among them were Claude McKay, Richard Wright, Saul Bellow, Loren Eisley, and Ralph Ellison. This project's goal was to record the life histories of ordinary American people whose stories had never been told: carpenters, cigar makers, dairy people, seamstresses, peddlers, railroad men, textile workers, salesladies, and chicken farmers were among the informants.

One collection of these life histories, *These Are Our Lives* (1939), assembled by R. R. Humphries for the Federal Writer's Project, includes the life story of Lee Lincoln, a man who learns to read and write as an adult. The fieldworker, Jennette Edwards, inserts her own observations and description into the interview while quoting Lee's words directly as she collected them. As you read this piece, remember it was written in 1939, when black Americans were called Negroes, when jobs were difficult to get, and $65 a month was a decent living. As you read this piece, you may want to think about other cultural assumptions, attitudes, and beliefs that have changed in the past six decades.

I Can Read and I Can Write

Jennette Edwards

The Negro houses on Jackson Avenue are strung out like ragged clothes on a wash line. Unpainted. Run down. Lee Lincoln's house—centering the East side of the Seventh block—stands lopsided from added rooms. One room takes care of Lee. Home-made book cases, racks, stands, tables, piled to the limit with books, crowd the room.

"I can read and I can write and I can figure," Lee said. "Every day I am thankful that I had a chance to learn. A man can't get anywheres much these days without schooling."

Lee wore the blue overall uniform of freight packers on the L. & N. railroad. His powerfully built frame tallied with his occupation. Lee pointed out his books with pride. He talked slowly, carefully.

"I'm fifty-three years old, still studying. Still buying books. I have almost five hundred books here on all kinds of subjects. Lots of them I have read from cover to cover."

He took a pair of silver rimmed spectacles from his inside coat pocket and fitted the hooks to his ears.

"My parents didn't have time to fool with schooling for themselves or any of us children. They were sharecroppers. By the time we would get five or six years old, the cotton field got us. I can remember playing about Pappy and Mammy and the older children when they were making the crop and at picking time, wishing I was old enough to help. Before long I was right there slaving too."

Lee pulled a dark oak rocker to a clear space in the center of the matting rug for his visitor. He settled in a straight chair.

"We didn't make much money. Not ever enough to get along easy. But from year to year we'd manage to get by some way. Corn pone, sorghum and sowbelly was the most we had to eat. I didn't mind. I like 'em to this day. Going to the meeting on Sunday or to some neighborhood shindig at night was the way we had our fun."

Lee took off his glasses and polished the lenses with a clean white cotton handkerchief.

"Mammy died when I was sixteen. Then I pulled out for myself. I worked around for different planters for a couple of years. Then I got a job on the L. &

N. Railroad at Memphis trucking outbound freight. It was the best job I had ever had and I was set on not getting fired."

He sighted the glasses for clearness.

"That was the job that learned me a man's got to have schooling to get anywheres. Signboards were posted on the freight cars with the name of the town where the car was to go. You had to know how to read to know what to load up. When the boss would say, 'This truck-load goes to the Nashville car,' I'd ask one of the truckers on the quiet—'Which one's the Nashville car?' One day the Boss heard me. He called me over, picked up a freight bill. 'Read what that says, Lee,' he said pointing to the words, 'The Louisville & Nashville Railroad.' I was scared stiff. I knew it wasn't any use to give a guess. Mammy and Pappy had learned me that a lie always got you in a fiddle. 'I just don't know, Boss,' I said right out. 'I can't read a line.'"

Lee shifted his weight in the chair. A smile of satisfaction spread over his honest face.

"Next day at noon-time the Boss brought a first reader book and a tablet and a pencil. He commenced to teach me to read and spell. I was mighty tickled when I could tell him what some of the words were. At noon-times while I was eating my lunch and every night I studied. Before long I could read most of the signs that said where the freight went. I learned how to write my name. I learned to copy and read back everything in the primer. My, I was one proud Negro! Boss was tickled, too. I never will forget him. Never. He was the best man I ever knew. I've got a little picture of him. I never have framed it. I got a lady artist to fix it on a card for me and I keep it for a bookmarker."

Lee left his chair and went to the iron bed in the far corner of the room. He pulled back the clean quilt—tucked at the head over the pillows—and found the book with last night's reading place marked. He left the book face down on the quilt and brought back the boss' picture.

"There he is. Fine-looking, don't you think? I never will forget him, because he was so good to me and learned me to read and write. I worked at that freight trucking job until the railroad transferred me to Nashville. That was a big promotion. I was made a regular officer. I had a badge with 'L. & N. Railway Police' on it. I worked all up and down the line on excursion trains and in the Nashville yards. I was about thirty years old then. I knew I never would have gotten that promotion if I hadn't picked up what little education I had. I kept right on. I went to night school two or three terms. For more than two years while I was an officer I got a white man to come to my room two nights a week and teach me. I paid him fifty cents a night and there wasn't a night that I didn't learn more than a dollar's worth. He was real educated and had a lot of patience with me. Pretty soon I could read newspapers as good as white people and books too. There were a lot of words I didn't know the sense of, so I got me a dictionary. I paid twenty-two dollars for it."

Lee went to the center table and straightened the scattered newspapers and books. He dusted off the large dictionary for display.

"My teacher told me this was a good one. It is, too. Wish I knew just half the words in it. He was all set on me getting good books. One hour of my lesson he would teach me words and reading and the other hour arithmetic. He would work up all sorts of simple problems he thought I'd have need of in work. He never did just stick to the book. I never will forget the night he told me how to take the carded weight of a carload of coal, figure how many tons and bushels was in the car. Then how much it would bring at so much a ton. Now that was fun. Just as much fun as reading those freight car names. I got so at lunch hour I'd pick out a car of coal in the yard every day, maybe more than one, figure up tons and bushels. He showed me how to figure lumber, too. I planned and figured ever' bit of the lumber for my coal house last fall. Figured it all by myself. I was right proud when my figuring came out just exactly like the lumber man's."

Lee got things on the center table settled to his liking. He rubbed his large hands clean on his pants legs and came back to his chair.

"I know I can read and figure better than I can write. I got to worrying about people not knowing what I meant if I put it down, so I got me a typewriter. They can read my letters now. I am secretary of my union and that typewriter is a big help there. Minutes look nice. Most anything makes a good show when you get it fixed up like print. I use it to make out my rent receipts. This house here I don't use but one room—this one. I pay the whole house rent and sublet all but this room. I've got two families here now. They're good renters, pay on time. The difference in what I pay rent and what I get from them helps me a lot since I lost my good job."

Lee slowly buttoned up the brass buttons of his overall jacket.

"About three years ago I got cut off from the railroad police 'cause I was the only Negro officer left on the system. They put me back to trucking freight, though I mostly packs freight in the cars to go out. I watch for thieving on the platform. I don't get paid for that, just paid for packing freight. They told me I'd have to take this job or nothing as they had to cut expenses. I took it. There were a lot of white men officers that didn't have thirty-two years experience behind 'em like I did. Not easy to pick up a job when you getting along in years—I had to take it. Everything that had been coming in for so long went out sooner than I got it. My wife, now, was one to help a man save. She could have helped. She was a good woman. I spent more'n two thousand dollars on doctor's bills for her. Maybe they eased her some. I don't know. Anyway doctors didn't save her."

Lee rammed his hands deep in his pants pockets.

"Since she died I never have come across a woman I felt like I could trust. We didn't have any children. I never was much on raking up relatives, so I'm going it by myself. I do my own cooking, most of the cleaning too. One of the women that rents does my washing. I had a little saved together from my officer's salary after I got the main of the doctors' bills paid. I had it in a bank. It busted along with the rest of them. The bank got all I had but wages—and those about a fourth of what I got as an officer."

Lee took off his glasses. He unbuttoned the top buttons of his coat and stored them in the inside pocket.

"If I can just keep my job I'll be satisfied. I'd rather work for what I get. There's lots better folks than me out of work now.

"I ain't going to have a preacher telling me I lost my officer's job for some wrong living. I didn't. I don't hold much with churches and less with the preachers. I loaned my preacher twenty-five dollars more'n two years back. I haven't heard a word about it since. If a man lives best he can he'll get along. I'm getting along. You can't do a big lot of things on sixty-five dollars a month but you can live and help a few out besides. A preacher's after my money a sight more than he is my soul."

Lee left his chair and went back to the dictionary. He was silent while he hunted a word.

"I thought so. Not any such word. That Methodist preacher tried to trip me on it last time he came here snooping. I seldom go to church. I do like a good moving picture when I'm not too tired to set. I go to union meeting once a week. I'm secretary."

He closed the dictionary noisily.

"I'd rather get a good case of beer and settle right here with time enough to read on any book I pick up than anything I know of in the world. I remember when I used to have to drink and play poker and shoot craps to make me feel big. I don't now. I don't crave going around a lot like I used to."

This interview is a good example of several techniques for writing up oral histories. The writer begins Lee's story with a simile describing the houses on his street, "strung out like ragged clothes on a wash line." Although the interview begins with Edwards's observations, the story belongs to Lee. The writer strikes an important balance between Lee's voice and her descriptions of his clothing and his mannerisms ("[he] took off his glasses and polished the lenses with a clean white cotton handkerchief"). Edwards includes details about body language as Lee tells his story ("he dusted off the large dictionary for display," "[he] shifted his weight in the chair," "he rubbed his large hands clean on his pants legs and came back to his chair"). The writer retains Lee's language patterns ("That was the job that learned me a man's got to have schooling to get anywheres"), doesn't alter his grammar ("This house here I don't use but one room—this one"), and keeps his colloquial expressions as they were ("A preacher's after my money a sight more than he is my soul.").

Although at first the reader may not understand why the fieldworker chooses the particular details she does, none is extraneous. The details themselves bring Lee's story to life with an emphasis on the artifacts of reading and literacy: glasses, the dictionary, his mentor's picture. Edwards ends with her own observations as Lee closes the dictionary "noisily." In this oral history, the fieldwriter keeps herself in the background, allowing Lee to remain in the foreground telling his own story.

Starting an Oral History

Purpose

Many oral histories today are gathered from ordinary people who have lived through extraordinary times and experiences, as Lee Lincoln did (see "I Can Read and I Can Write," p. 395). Contemporary informants can share their life histories and experiences from, for example, the Cultural Revolution in China; the Vietnam, Korean, and Gulf wars; the women's movement; the civil rights movement in the United States; the Holocaust in Europe; the disassembling of the Berlin Wall; or the end of apartheid in South Africa. Other oral histories can record the everyday life of an occupation that no longer exists, like Jack Santino's study of Pullman porters, "Miles of Smiles"; Theodore Rosengarten's life history of Nat Shaw, a black sharecropper; or A. B. Spellman's study of jazz musicians, *Black Music: Four Lives.* Studs Terkel's journalistic oral histories are probably among the best known. His collections of occupational stories, *Working,* and of Depression stories, *In Hard Times,* offer examples of short histories from real people whose voices are seldom heard or recorded.

Possible projects for an oral history are limited only by your imagination and access to the people you wish to interview. Many people begin an oral history by interviewing their relatives, friends, or teachers about living through a particular era or a time of personal struggle that resulted in dramatic life changes. Perhaps you know someone who's lived through a major catastrophe (such as an earthquake, a hurricane, a tornado, or a flood) or someone who's been caught personally in a political or social entanglement (like war, bankruptcy, or discrimination). Such people make good subjects for oral history.

Many local and compelling oral history projects can emerge in unexpected places and on unexpected topics. Think about someone you know who has a particular skill, such as cooking ethnic food, whittling wooden figures, weaving, or embroidering, or an unusual hobby such as clogging, playing the bagpipes, or raising llamas. Someone's lifelong passion can yield fascinating oral histories—whether the interest is doll or coin collecting, fly fishing, boar or duck hunting, identifying wildflowers, mushroom hunting, or bird watching. Good subjects for oral histories also hide in places where people spend their time alone—for example, in garages tinkering with engines or in antique shops restoring items others have discarded.

Action

If you're interested in pursuing an oral history project, spend some time interviewing someone who fascinates you. Like any other interviewing project, all of the information you record in your fieldnotes may not be what you'll use in a final write-up, but you'll need to record it nonetheless. As Jennette Edwards used Lee Lincoln's surroundings to support his talk, your choices of details in an oral history will help you feature your subject without distracting the reader from the life story as it is told in the informant's own words. An elaborate oral history takes a great deal of time, like many of the other research projects we describe in this book. We hope that what you'll learn by reading and writing oral history is that it's important to foreground the informant and her words and to background the topic, yourself, and her surroundings.

Response

Many wonder but few, like Ivana Nikolic in Chapter 4, dare to ask how some people become homeless. Our colleague Steve VanderStaay's book *Street Lives* is a collection of oral histories of homeless Americans. Steve's project was a large one, and as a professional writer, teacher, and researcher, he could devote many years to completing it. For six years, Steve interviewed people across the country, visiting soup kitchens and homeless shelters, city parks and alleys, tape recorder in hand, gathering stories. He found that many of the homeless wanted to share their stories and welcomed him as a listener. In his introduction, Steve claims that many of the narratives he presents "contradict current and accepted notions of homelessness.... I learned that our present crisis of homelessness, while fueled by social trends and forces, is most essentially a personal one: a crisis in the life of someone with hopes, dreams, and a name. Someone we can know"(x).

In the following oral history, a homeless mother, Tanya, shares her gradual life struggle. We meet her in Philadelphia four years after she had been a college student and soon after she had lost her children to the welfare system. In this example of oral history, Steve as the interviewer remains in the background, foregrounding Tanya's story in her own voice. Unlike Edwards's history of Lee Lincoln, Steve separates—in italics—his words from those of his informant.

Tanya

Steve VanderStaay

PHILADELPHIA, PENNSYLVANIA *Tanya is a quiet, gentle woman with soft features and a languid, pensive expression that rarely changes. She speaks slowly, breaking up her narrative with long, motionless pauses. Tanya spends large portions of her day thinking and staring, and remains puzzled and confused about all that has happened to her.*

Another portion of Tanya's testimony appears in the chapter "The Homeless Mentally Ill." She is an African American and perhaps 30 years old.

This is not really the first time I've been homeless, but this is the first time I've been homeless since I've had a child. Lots of times they tell me, "You should sell your body. Go over there in that hotel, get fifty dollars overnight." I don't do it, but when people get down and out, see, their mind is like…well it's open. Anything somebody got to offer, if you're homeless you're gonna hop on it most of the time.

Jobs is it, I guess, 'cause, the prices these days…a one-bedroom apartment is at least $320, and you have to pay your own utilities, such as your gas and electric. And a lot of people out here that are working are not even getting enough to keep up with those bills. You try anyway, you know. You put a little bit on this and a little bit on that, but that's how people end up being homeless. All of a sudden they'll cut the electric off. You'll say, "Oh, well, I'm not gonna let that bother me." They cut the gas off: "I won't let that bother me, I'm gettin' in enough income to pay my rent so I'm just gonna pay that."

Then the landlord gonna come out: "I don't want you livin' here, I'm gonna find somebody that's gonna take care of the place." Which they can. And you're out there again, trying to find a place to live.

And then you lose your kids. 'Cause you ain't got a place, or they don't think the way you live is fittin'. Most of the girls here in this shelter, their children have been taken away from them that way. And it leaves them homeless. It leaves you homeless if you have been a mother for so many years and you don't have a work history. Just like the situation I had. When they took my children away from me, that's when it all started.

I was like…left alone. I spent the first nights in University City, under an awning. It's part of the University of Pennsylvania, across the street from a big bank. It's a big area; most of the time I was there. Or I would wrap up in a blanket and just, you know, go right off to sleep on a vent. I was hoping someone would see me and tell me how to get back on my feet, but it didn't happen.

Then I found a little shelter where you could go during the day. It was for women. Nights you would have to find some place to go. Just by going to the shelter I'd meet people who had an apartment and they would say, "Well, you can stay the night" or "You can stay a couple of days, but I can't let you stay forever." And it just kept going and going and going.

There were a couple of McDonald's and Burger King's and Roy Rogers that would stay open all night and they noticed me. You know, "Oh I seen that girl around a lot this year." And they'd say, "Hey, do you want something to eat?" And I'd say yes and they'd say, "Well here, you can't eat it in here, and don't hang around, don't let people notice that you're, you know, that you're…outdoors."

I stayed in subways too. Most of the people stay around 30th Street Station. Or sleep on the street. I mean these days you can just lie down on the sidewalk. As long as you don't look like you fell off somethin' or you're sick nobody'll say anything to ya.

THE INFORMANT'S PERSPECTIVE:
"AN ANTHROPOLOGIST ON MARS"

Most field interviews in their final form look smooth and polished, as if nothing had ever gone wrong throughout the process of working with an informant. They make it seem that there have been no fumbling, false starts, missed appointments, or muddled communication and that the equipment always worked. Because fieldworking takes a long time, once interviewers and informants establish rapport, the early messiness and hesitations of the relationship fade into the background. Paul Russ admits to his initial discomfort with Jessie, for example, but even his transcripts show a rather smooth interviewing process. When there are troubles with interviewing, most researchers decide not to highlight them. But they talk and write about them a lot. Our favorite interviewer's story comes from the *Foxfire* collection (edited by Eliot "Wig" Wigginton and others). In this excerpt, a high school student named Paul Gillespie, working alongside his teacher Wigginton, interviews an elderly informant named Aunt Arie at her house in the Appalachian Mountains. Aunt Arie had been interviewed many times; she had been the subject of a *Life* magazine article and much oral history research. But Paul was a novice interviewer, as you will see in this excerpt about students' interviewing experiences. Aunt Arie is 90 years old, and the year is 1963.

> [W]e walked in on her on Thanksgiving morning. She had her back to the door, and we startled her. There she was trying to carve the eyeballs out of a hog's head. I was almost sick to my stomach, so Wig helped operate on this hog's head while I turned my head and held the microphone of the tape recorder in the general vicinity of the action.
>
> They struggled for at least fifteen minutes, maybe more, and then I witnessed one of the most amazing events of my life. Aunt Arie took an eyeball, went to the back door, and flung it out. When she threw it, the eyeball went up on the tin roof of an adjoining outbuilding, rolled off, snagged on the clothesline, and hung there bobbing like a yo-yo. I had Wig's Pentax, so I took a picture of it, and it appeared in a subsequent issue of the magazine. It was very funny, remarkable. (56)

We close this chapter with a selection from one fieldworker whose smooth and polished storytelling intrigues us but whose primary work is in medicine. Oliver Sacks describes himself as a "neuroanthropologist in the field," but he is neither an oral historian nor an anthropologist. He's a doctor who specializes in disorders of the nervous system and uses some fieldworking strategies to understand the perspectives of his patients. Rather than examining them in a hospital setting, Sacks visits his patients in their own contexts to explore their lives "as they live in the real world." In fact, in the preface to his bestselling collection of interviews, *An Anthropologist on Mars: Seven Paradoxical Tales,* he describes his fieldwork as "house calls at the far borders of human experience" (xx).

In one interview, he visits Temple Grandin, a woman with autism who, as a professor of animal science at Colorado State University, studies animal behavior. In this interview, Sacks describes autism's neurological issues as "a triad of impairments: of social interaction, of verbal and non-verbal communication, and of play and imaginative activities" (246). A common stereotype is that autistic people have no concept of feelings for others or even for themselves. Autistic children are often bypassed and misunderstood, both in and out of school, and some autistic people spend their lives institutionalized. Sacks wanted to find out about autism from an insider's perspective. He knew that Grandin was unusual because she had successfully integrated herself into society, had written a book about autism, and was professionally recognized in her field. After researching autism from a medical point of view, he realized that he needed a person to give it voice, to create a portrait of the autistic person. Grandin told him that in her daily life, she feels like an outsider, like a researcher from another planet who is constantly studying the culture in which she lives to understand it. She provided Sacks with a critical understanding of her autistic worldview—as well as the title for his study—with the comment, "Much of the time I feel like an anthropologist on Mars."

Sacks arranged to interview Grandin in her office and in her home. He recounts his first meeting with Grandin at the university, detailing her physical features, clothing, body language, and the deviations of her gait and handshake. Sacks shows us this meeting, rather than tells us about it, through selected detail, creating a portrait of Temple Grandin:

> I made my way to the university campus and located the Animal Science Building, where Temple was waiting to greet me. She is a tall, strongly built woman in her mid-forties; she was wearing jeans, a knit shirt, western boots, her habitual dress. Her clothing, her appearance, her manner, were plain, frank, and forthright; I had the distinct impression of a sturdy, nononsense cattlewoman, with an indifference to social conventions, appearance, or ornament, an absence of frills, an absolute directness of manner and mind. When she raised her arm in greeting, the arm went too high, seemed to get caught for a moment in a sort of spasm or fixed posture—a hint, an echo, of the stereotypies she once had. Then she gave me a strong handshake and led the way down to her office. [Her gait seemed to me slightly clumsy or uncouth, as is often the case with autistic adults. Temple attributes this to a simple ataxia associated with impaired development of the vestibule system and part of the cerebellum. Later I did a brief neurological exam, focusing on her cerebellar function and balance; I did indeed find a little ataxia, but insufficient, I thought, to explain her odd gait.] (256).

In a later section of his article, Sacks visits Grandin at her house. Notice that each of the details he offers is like a puzzle piece, fitting one item at a time into this description. Sacks depicts her range of interests at her home by describing her collection of identification badges and caps from hundreds of conferences, contrasting those, for example, from the American Psychiatric Association and the American Meat Institute. When he looks in her bedroom and finds the "squeeze machine," he doesn't rely only on her description or on her 20-minute demonstration of the machine. Sacks actually enters Grandin's invention, lies in it, and experiences the sensations she designed it to provide.

An Anthropologist on Mars
Oliver Sacks

Early the next morning, a Saturday, Temple picked me up in her four-wheel-drive, a rugged vehicle she drives all over the West to visit farms, ranches, corrals, and meat plants. As we headed for her house, I quizzed her about the work she had done for her Ph.D.; her thesis on the effects of enriched and impoverished environments on the development of pigs' brains. She told me about the great differences that developed between the two groups—how sociable and delightful the "enriched" pigs became, how hyperexcitable and aggressive (and almost "autistic") the "impoverished" ones were by contrast. (She wondered whether impoverishment of experience was not a contributing factor in human autism.) "I got to love my enriched pigs," she said. "I was very attached. I was so attached I couldn't kill them." The animals had to be sacrificed at the end of the experiment so their brains could be examined. She described how the pigs, at the end, trusting her, let her lead them on their last walk, and how she had calmed them, by stroking them and talking to them, while they were killed. She was very distressed at their deaths—"I wept and wept."

She had just finished the story when we arrived at her home—a small two-story town house, some distance from the campus. Downstairs was comfortable, with the usual amenities—a sofa, armchairs, a television, pictures on the wall—but I had the sense that it was rarely used. There was an immense sepia print of her grandfather's farm in Grandin, North Dakota, in 1880; her other grandfather, she told me, had invented the automatic pilot for planes. These two were the progenitors, she feels, of her agricultural and engineering talents. Upstairs was her study, with her typewriter (but no word processor), absolutely bursting with manuscripts and books—books everywhere, spilling out of the study into every room in the house. (My own little house was once described as "a machine for working," and I had a somewhat similar impression of Temple's.) On one wall was a large cowhide with a huge collection of identity badges and caps, from the hundreds of conferences she has lectured at. I was amused to see, side by side, an I.D. from the American Meat Institute and one from the American Psychiatric Association. Temple has published more than a hundred papers, divided between those on animal

behavior and facilities management and those on autism. The intimate blending of the two was epitomized by the medley of badges side by side.

Finally, without diffidence or embarrassment (emotions unknown to her),
Temple showed me her bedroom, an austere room with whitewashed walls and
a single bed and, next to the bed, a very large, strange-looking object. "What is
that?" I asked.

"That's my squeeze machine," Temple replied. "Some people call it my hug
machine."

The device had two heavy, slanting wooden sides, perhaps four by three
feet each, pleasantly upholstered with a thick, soft padding. They were joined
by hinges to a long, narrow bottom board to create a V-shaped, body-sized
trough. There was a complex control box at one end, with heavy-duty tubes
leading off to another device, in a closet. Temple showed me this as well. "It's
an industrial compressor," she said, "the kind they use for filling tires."

"And what does this do?"

"It exerts a firm but comfortable pressure on the body, from the shoulders
to the knees," Temple said. "Either a steady pressure or a variable one or a pulsating one, as you wish," she added. "You crawl into it—I'll show you—and
turn the compressor on, and you have all the controls in your hand, here, right
in front of you."

When I asked her why one should seek to submit oneself to such pressure,
she told me. When she was a little girl, she said, she had longed to be hugged
but had at the same time been terrified of all contact. When she was hugged,
especially by a favorite (but vast) aunt, she felt overwhelmed, overcome by
sensation; she had a sense of peacefulness and pleasure, but also of terror and
engulfment. She started to have daydreams—she was just five at the time—of
a magic machine that could squeeze her powerfully but gently, in a huglike
way, and in a way entirely commanded and controlled by her. Years later, as an
adolescent, she had seen a picture of a squeeze chute designed to hold or
restrain calves and realized that that was it: a little modification to make it
suitable for human use, and it could be her magic machine. She had considered other devices—inflatable suits, which could exert an even pressure
all over the body—but the squeeze chute, in its simplicity, was quite irresistible.

Being of a practical turn of mind, she soon made her fantasy come true.
The early models were crude, with some snags and glitches, but she eventually
evolved a totally comfortable, predictable system, capable of administering a
"hug" with whatever parameters she desired. Her squeeze machine had worked
exactly as she hoped, yielding the very sense of calmness and pleasure she had
dreamed of since childhood. She could not have gone through the stormy days
of college without her squeeze machine, she said. She could not turn to
human beings for solace and comfort, but she could always turn to it. The
machine, which she neither exhibited nor concealed but kept openly in her
room at college, excited derision and suspicion and was seen by psychiatrists
as a "regression" or "fixation"—something that needed to be psychoanalyzed

and resolved. With her characteristic stubbornness, tenacity, single-mindedness, and bravery—along with a complete absence of inhibition or hesitation—Temple ignored all these comments and reactions and determined to find a scientific "validation" of her feelings.

Both before and after writing her doctoral thesis, she made a systematic investigation of the effects of deep pressure in autistic people, college students, and animals, and recently a paper of hers on this was published in the *Journal of Child and Adolescent Psychopharmacology*. Today, her squeeze machine, variously modified, is receiving extensive clinical trials. She has also become the world's foremost designer of squeeze chutes for cattle and has published, in the meat-industry and veterinary literature, many articles on the theory and practice of humane restraint and gentle holding.

While telling me this, Temple knelt down, then eased herself, facedown and at full length, into the "V," turned on the compressor (it took a minute for the master cylinder to fill), and twisted the controls. The sides converged, clasping her firmly, and then, as she made a small adjustment, relaxed their grip slightly. It was the most bizarre thing I had ever seen, and yet, for all its oddness, it was moving and simple. Certainly there was no doubt of its effect. Temple's voice, often loud and hard, became softer and gentler as she lay in her machine. "I concentrate on how gently I can do it," she said, and then spoke of the necessity of "totally giving in to it... I'm getting real relaxed now," she added quietly. "I guess others get this through relation with other people."

It is not just pleasure or relaxation that Temple gets from the machine but, she maintains, a feeling for others. As she lies in her machine, she says, her thoughts often turn to her mother, her favorite aunt, her teachers. She feels their love for her, and hers for them. She feels that the machine opens a door into an otherwise closed emotional world and allows her, almost teaches her, to feel empathy for others.

After twenty minutes or so, she emerged, visibly calmer, emotionally less rigid (she says that a cat can easily sense the difference in her at these times), and asked me if I would care to try the machine.

Indeed, I was curious and scrambled into it, feeling a little foolish and self-conscious—but less so than I might have been, because Temple herself was so wholly lacking in self-consciousness. She turned the compressor on again and filled the master cylinder, and I experimented gingerly with the controls. It was indeed a sweet, calming feeling—one that reminded me of my deep-diving days long ago, when I felt the pressure of the water on my diving suit as a whole-body embrace.

As you can tell from this interview with Temple Grandin, the process of interviewing, of asking and listening collaboratively, allows us to gain the perspective of an "other." Examining our own assumptions and worldviews from the vantage points of others exposes us to our quirks and shortcomings and cultural biases. In the process of understanding others, we come to more fully understand ourselves.

THE RESEARCH PORTFOLIO: REFLECTIVE DOCUMENTATION

Whether you've chosen to learn to research people by continuing your major fieldwork project or by trying separate short studies, we hope you've seen that the researcher-informant relationship is a symbiotic one. It is full of interaction, collaboration, and mutual teaching and learning. In this chapter, we focus on how people are a dominant source of data in the field—through family stories, remembered histories, responses to questions, the personal artifacts they consider important, and your own observation of them. You've exercised the skills of gathering and analyzing family stories and oral histories, and you've conducted some interviews and transcript analyses.

We wanted the readings to illustrate that people, when we research them with their cooperation, teach us much about their cultures. With the professional readings, you met Judith Ortiz Cofer's Puerto Rican New Yorker relatives, Maxine Hong Kingston's No Name Woman, Jennette Edwards's Lee Lincoln in 1939, Steve VanderStaay's Tanya, the homeless mother, and Oliver Sacks's Temple Grandin, the autistic scientist who feels like an anthropologist on Mars. Our own and our students' work offered more readings: Cheri Krcelic's and Elizabeth's family stories of their parents' courtship, Donna Niday's five Riggs girls' "baby on the roof" stories, Paul Russ's Jessie, who was living with AIDS, EunJoo Kang's investigation of Ming-Chi Own's wristwatch, and Cindie Marshall's journey into the culture of Ralph's biker bar.

The research portfolio is an important place to record, keep track of, and make sense of the skills you've learned, the routines and organization you've used, and your responses to readings that illustrate how other fieldworkers have written about their work. Listing and categorizing your research processes illustrates your progress as a fieldworker. We like to call this charting process "reflective documentation." Just as we reviewed Cindie Marshall's research process for the completed version of "Ralph's Sports Bar," you might review and document your fieldworking skills at this point in your project. This chapter's portfolio suggestions focus on documentation of your research skills and not on the actual stories, oral histories, and interviews you've collected, the products of your research process.

For your portfolio, try listing, mapping, outlining, or charting the skills you've learned and the variety and amounts of material you've gathered. You may want to document each of your projects from this chapter separately: family stories, oral histories, and interviews. Or if you are working on a large project, use the questions to document what is relevant to your project. Here is an outline, framed around the same fieldworking strategies as our summary of Cindie's work. You might choose a few questions under each category, try to work with them all, or document your work in a different way.

I. Prepare for the field.
   A. What did you read to prepare for your fieldwork? Where did you find it?
   B. What did you learn from reading the fieldwork of others?
   C. How did you select your informants? How did you prepare before meeting them?
   D. How did you gain access to your informants and your fieldsites? Were there any problems? What might you do next time?
   E. What assumptions did you have going into the field? How did you record them? What did you expect to see, and what did you actually find?

II. Use the researcher's tools.
   A. How did you record your fieldnotes? Did you separate observational notes from personal notes? Did you invent your own method for organizing your fieldnotes?
   B. What equipment did you use? What would you want if you could do this work again?
   C. How did you transcribe your tape recordings?
   D. What interviewing skills did you develop? What skills would you like to work on?
   E. What different types of data did you gather? Print sources? Cultural artifacts? Stories and interviews?

III. Interpret your fieldwork.
   A. Which initial impressions turned out to be part of your final piece? Which ideas did you discard?
   B. What strategies did you develop to categorize your data? Did you use patterns that were linear? Thematic? Chronological? Abstract to concrete? Concrete to abstract?
   C. What strategies did you develop to analyze your data? What didn't fit?
   D. What is your favorite piece of data—or data source—and why?

IV. Present your findings.
   A. What decisions did you make about writing up your fieldwork?
   B. How much of your voice is in the final project? How much of your informants' voices?
   C. What details did you select to illustrate key points to bring your informants to life?
   D. Did you use subheadings to guide your reader in your final paper or some other way to organize your material?

You might decide to use these questions to help you write an essay or commentary about your process as a researcher.

FieldWriting: From Details to Verbal Portraiture

To bring their informants to the page from a pile of data, fieldwriters must pay close attention to informants' personal characteristics and surroundings and write about details that relate to the overall themes they want to highlight. Creating verbal portraits means studying your fieldnotes, selecting your most relevant details, and drafting sentences that portray the informant against a cultural backdrop. In this chapter, the fieldwriters who gave us portraits—Jennette Edwards, Steve VanderStaay, Paul Russ, Oliver Sacks—wrote them on the basis of carefully gathered observations from their fieldnotes and other sources and their own interpretations confirmed by their data.

Details of Character

Choosing the details to describe an interview with an informant is hard work. Fieldwriters must gather and record far more information than they will ever use because during data collection, they won't yet know the themes they'll eventually want to highlight. Written portraits of an informant require noting the same kinds of character details that fiction writers use: physical features, material artifacts, body language, oral language patterns, and personal history. But those details are borne in fieldnotes, interviews, artifacts, and documents. Cindie Marshall's fieldnotes about Teardrop provided the details she needed to create her verbal portrait. Some examples of them follow:

- *Physical features*   vine-shaped tattoo around wrist; brown hair with gray, neatly pulled back, teased and sprayed bangs; top and bottom front teeth missing; small black spot under left eye, high on cheek
- *Material artifacts*   new Lee jeans, pale yellow sweater, heart-shaped brooch, wristwatch
- *Body language*   sitting alone drinking beer, shooting pool
- *Personal history*   goes to Ralph's every day, moved from Michigan three years ago, kidnapped by bikers at 13 and sold from biker to biker for years

From her list of these specific character details, Cindie created a tightly written portrait of Teardrop, and she tried not to interject her own judgments. She presents the descriptions of the most startling details—Teardrop's missing teeth and her tattoos—without judgmental qualifiers. Those details affect the reader because she presents them without value statements. In spite of these attempts, she was probably unaware, as we all are, that she did interpret a few details with qualifiers. Here are three examples of adverbs and adjectives that reflect Cindie's assumptions: a "nice" pale yellow sweater, "carefully sprayed" and "neatly pulled back" hair. To write verbal portraiture, fieldwriters must know their fieldnotes so well that they'll select the ones that most reveal a character—

like Teardrop's tattoo, which Cindie at first mistook for a mole or a birthmark. Here is an excerpt from Cindie's description of Teardrop; the character details that help her create her portrait are in italics.

> When I arrived at the table, there was a woman *sitting alone,* drinking a beer.... I introduced myself, and she said her *name was Teardrop.* It was dark outside, so I couldn't see her very well. We talked about the weather for a few minutes, and that led her to tell me that she had *moved here from Michigan* three years ago and that *she came to Ralph's every day....*
>
> Once we were inside, I saw that Teardrop was wearing *new Lee jeans,* a *nice pale yellow sweater,* and a *heart-shaped brooch.* Her *hair was brown* but was showing *signs of graying.* She had it *neatly pulled back,* and her *bangs were teased and carefully sprayed* in place. It wasn't until she laughed that I noticed she was *missing her front teeth, both top and bottom.* She had a *small tattoo* around her wrist that served as a bracelet. It was *dark green* and was in the *shape of a vine.* Most of the tattoo was covered by the *watch* she was wearing.
>
> As we *played pool,* I noticed something else. She had a very *small black spot* under her left eye, high on her cheek. At first I thought it was a birthmark. But after looking at it carefully, I noticed that it was a *black tattoo in the shape of a teardrop.* I asked her if it was a teardrop and she said yes; that was *how she got her name.*

Details of Setting

When fieldwriters paint verbal portraits, they also create a backdrop for their informants. In Chapter 5, we discuss how writers present landscapes or what we call "verbal snapshots." In addition to her portrait of Teardrop, Cindie creates a cultural backdrop for the other patrons at Ralph's Sports Bar using her fieldnote observations. As we show in Chapter 5 with Myerhoff's details of the Senior Center, Glassie's details of the Irish landscape, and Karen Downing's description of the Photo Phantasies store, setting details must be organized from notes about time, place, weather, color, and other sensory impressions at the fieldsite.

To bring her reader into Ralph's, Cindie moves from exterior to interior. She selects details of texture and space to represent Ralph's Sports Bar outside, focusing first on the half-paved, half-graveled parking lot with Harleys "meticulously aligned, handlebar to handlebar, back tire to back tire." She zooms in on a large exterior sign that announces "Urinate inside, not out here."

As she moves inside, she describes tastes and smells in an atmosphere of smoke, stale beer, cigarette ashes, and body odor. And Cindie also listens to the sounds of Ozzie Osborne's "No More Tears" screaming from the jukebox, a detail with special significance that supports the "teardrop" theme. She chooses among much visual data to represent the biker subculture: four pool tables, McDonald's-type plastic booths, neon Budweiser signs, and black velvet paintings of dogs playing pool. But her major interior visual focus is on the printed signs in the bar that give her clues to insiders' shared values: "Break a cue, pay $25.00 or be barred" is not a gentle sign. "We do not buy stolen merchandise" may imply that they do. The handwritten sign on each poker machine smacks of irony: "No gambling allowed." And Cindie's selection of details to present an image of Ralph's, a so-called sports bar, defies her earlier assumptions about such bars, "full of white-collar professionals [and] a big-screen TV," and with a "line of high-dollar sports cars parked outside."

Details of Theme

As you write your informants into your text, you might draw on an important metaphor or theme buried in your notes about the place or the person. Field-writers must choose details to support the themes they want to highlight, like the houses on Lee's street "strung out like ragged clothes on a wash line," which offer a contrast to the literate man who lives inside, and Temple Grandin's squeeze machine, which she invents to comfort her animals and also herself. One artifact might uncover an important theme, as EunJoo's focus on Ming-Chi's watch began a discussion of cultural differences about time and the dog hairs in Paul Russ's car got Jessie talking about his fears about his dog, Princess. Lee Lincoln's story about learning to read was enhanced by the writer Edwards's decision to describe his glasses, the dictionary he paid for, and his book collection. And Steve VanderStaay, in his portrait of Tanya, highlighted her descriptions of temporary housing: shelters, temporary apartments, sidewalks, and outdoor sleeping spaces.

In fieldworking, themes don't emerge directly from lists in fieldnotes, words in transcripts, or library books and collected artifacts, but such sources suggest them. Themes *do come* from active interpretation of your data, as you study it, triangulate it, organize it, reflect on it, and write about it. Themes are bigger than the actual details you record, but those details, as they cluster into categories of data and images from your observations, generate larger interpretations.

For example, in her study of Ralph's Sports Bar, Cindie's themes work off of the contrasts she observed within the subculture in the biker bar. She arrives at Ralph's with a mental image of what a sports bar is like, and immediately that image contrasts with the reality of this biker sports bar. She is greeted by the sign "Urinate inside, not out here" and realizes that the sports here are limited to playing pool and biking. As she spends more time and takes more notes, Cindie sees other contrasting themes within this subculture.

Another set of contrasting themes is that of bikers as a community of independent people who "do their own thing," but Cindie sees that within this sub-culture, they come together only to be separated: "I also wanted to know why three groups in a bar would come together in a place just to be segregated." Cindie interprets still another contrast when she notices that the biking subculture includes many women. Her fieldnotes report 13 people at the bar, 8 men and 5 women. But this inclusion is deceptive when her informant Teardrop describes her life as a biker woman: "What Teardrop had described was sheer abuse, and she wore that abuse both on her face, in the shape of a teardrop, and in her smile, which was darkened by missing teeth."

Fieldwriting is a skill that requires close observation, careful documentation, and the rendering of data into thick descriptions of informants within their cultural spaces. To be an accurate and sensitive fieldwriter, you'll need to manipulate your multiple data sources, call on your informants' voices, examine your reflective writing, and craft a text so that it will give your reader a sense of participating in the fieldwork you've experienced.

FIELDWORDS

Ethnohistorian A trained ethnographer who conducts oral and life histories.

Family stories Narratives shared in extended families about other family members that convey messages about acceptable behaviors, rules of conduct, or shared values.

Oral history Real-life stories recorded about the past, gathered from living people about their experiences, crafts, skills, or occupations.

Rapport A feeling of connection and trust established between people.

Reciprocity Giving back, a mutual exchange of favors and rights. In fieldwork, it is important to give something to the informant in exchange for time spent.

FIELDREADING

Behar, Ruth. *Translated Woman: Crossing the Border with Esperanza's Story.* Boston: Beacon, 1993.

Bohannan, Paul, and Dirk van der Elst. *Asking and Listening: Ethnography as Personal Adaptation.* Prospect Heights: Waveland, 1998.

Cofer, Judith Ortiz. "A Partial Remembrance of a Puerto Rican Childhood." *Silent Dancing.* Houston: Arte Publico, 1990.

Geertz, Clifford. "Thick Description: Toward an Interpretive Theory of Culture." *The Interpretation of Cultures.* New York: Basic, 1973.

Glassie, Henry. *Passing the Time in Ballymenone: Culture and History of an Ulster Community.* Philadelphia: U Pennsylvania P, 1982.

Heath, Shirley Brice. *Ways with Words: Language, Life, and Work in Communities and Classrooms.* New York: Cambridge UP, 1983.

Humphries, R. R., ed. *These Are Our Lives.* Chapel Hill: U North Carolina P, 1939.

Kingston, Maxine Hong. *The Woman Warrior: Memoirs of a Girlhood among Ghosts.* New York: Vintage, 1977.

Rosengarten, Theodore. *All God's Dangers and the Life of Nat Shaw.* New York: Harper, 1966.

Russ, Paul. *Healing without a Cure: Stories of People Living with AIDS.* Film. 1994.

Sacks, Oliver. *An Anthropologist on Mars: Seven Paradoxical Tales.* New York: Knopf, 1995.

Santino, Jack. "Miles of Smiles, Years of Struggle: The Negotiation of Black Occupational Identity through Personal Experience Narrative." *Journal of American Folklore* 96 (1983): 393–410.

Shostak, Marjorie. *The Life and Works of a !Kung Woman.* New York: Vintage, 1981.

Spellman, A. B. *Black Music: Four Lives.* New York: Shocken, 1970.

Stone, Elizabeth. *Black Sheep and Kissing Cousins: How Our Family Stories Shape Us.* New York: Times, 1988.

Terkel, Studs. *In Hard Times: An Oral History of the Great Depression.* New York: Pantheon, 1970.

Terkel, Studs. *Working: People Talk about What They Do All Day and How They Feel about What They Do.* New York: Pantheon, 1974.

VanderStaay, Steve. *Street Lives: An Oral History of Homeless Americans.* Philadelphia: New Society, 1992.

Wigginton, Eliot, et al., eds. *Foxfire: Twenty-five Years.* New York: Doubleday, 1991.

FIELDPOEM

Why We Tell Stories
Lisel Mueller

For Linda Nemec Foster

1

Because we used to have leaves
and on damp days
our muscles feel a tug,
painful now, from when roots
pulled us into the ground

and because our children believe
they can fly, an instinct retained
from when the bones in our arms

were shaped like zithers and broke
neatly under their feathers

and because before we had lungs
we knew how far it was to the bottom
as we floated open-eyed
like painted scarves through the scenery
of dreams, and because we awakened

and learned to speak

2

We sat by the fire in our caves,
and because we were poor, we made up a tale
about a treasure mountain
that would open only for us

and because we were always defeated,
we invented impossible riddles
only we could solve,
monsters only we could kill,
women who could love no one else

and because we had survived
sisters and brothers, daughters and sons,
we discovered bones that rose
from the dark earth and sang
as white birds in the trees

3

Because the story of our life
becomes our life

Because each of us tells
the same story
but tells it differently

and none of us tells it
the same way twice

Because grandmothers looking like spiders
want to enchant the children
and grandfathers need to convince us
what happened happened because of them

and though we listen only
haphazardly, with one ear,
we will begin our story
with the word *and*

Commentary
by Dan Albergotti

Lisel Mueller's "Why We Tell Stories" makes a bold claim with its title, but
the poem fully delivers on its implicit promise. Divided into three sections,
the poem illustrates that the essential uses of telling stories are to make
sense of reality, to create possibilities beyond reality, and to make ourselves
most fully human. The first section responds to the title's charge with
straightforward, fragmentary answers. The speaker suggests that one
impulse toward storytelling is the revelation of our memory, a rich
storehouse that reaches back deep into time, even to an evolutionary past
when "we used to have leaves" and later "feathers." We tell stories to order
our past and make sense of our present state. In the second section of the
poem, the speaker tells stories of storytelling, particularly the kind of
storytelling that goes beyond the explanation of reality, the kind that
imagines worlds and begins outside that reality. Such stories create "a
treasure mountain / that would open only for us." They give us a world
better than that provided by reality and thus a temporary escape. And
similar stories can even save us from despair. The poem's third section,
composed like the first of "because" clauses, shows that storytelling is
essential to our becoming fully developed as individuals and as members of
the human family. We each tell a "story of our life/ [that] becomes our life";
but we also each tell "the same story," though we tell it differently. We
create a unique identity even through the common stories that we tell, and
we share that identity with others through those stories, especially when
they are told to family members. The poem's final images of grandparents
telling stories to their grandchildren emphasize how the great human story
is carried through time. It is a story that must begin with "and" and that
cannot be governed by end punctuation.

   This poem's revelations about storytelling's functions are illuminating
for the ethnographer who interviews subjects in the field. As fieldworkers,
we must appreciate storytelling's role in constructing the past and present
of our informants. Their stories are not merely narratives but keys to their

*Dan Albergotti holds a Ph.D. in English Literature from the University of South
Carolina and is completing an M.F.A. in poetry at the University of North
Carolina at Greensboro.*

worldviews. We may find that the differences in the ways various insiders tell the same story open a window to their positions and roles within the culture. We must also remember that storytelling is a creative act as well—that its function is not only to preserve objective facts but to find preserving truth through fiction. The stories of our research subjects do not only supply us with data—they give us insight into those subjects' hopes and fears.

We also have to recognize that our subjects' stories always begin with "and" and that they are contributions to larger stories—not only to the stories of their families, cultures, or subcultures but to the grand human story. The informant's story is always deeply connected to the researcher's through our common humanity, and the researcher is always stepping into the culture's story from the moment she enters the field.

CHAPTER 8

FieldWriting: From Down Draft to Up Draft

Finding somewhere to stand in a text that is supposed to be at one and the same time an intimate view and a cool assessment is almost as much of a challenge as gaining the view and making the assessment in the first place.

—CLIFFORD GEERTZ

If, toward the end of your fieldwork project, you want to move into your closet and live with your shoes to make room for piles and piles of data, you might consider writing as an alternative. At this point in your study, you've probably accumulated stacks of fieldwriting—fieldnotes and journal entries, short observations and descriptions, transcribed interviews, artifacts and documents, responses to readings, and reflections—in your organized, reorganized, and even re-reorganized portfolio. Anthropologists describe the deskwork involved in fieldwork—that period of time when you begin to sort through your data to figure out what you have and what you might still need—as a period of confusion which can only be solved by writing, by shaping your data into text. Of course, the good news is that you've been writing all along. Our colleague Wendy Bishop uses the phrase "writing it down in order to write it up" to describe the process of moving data into text. Those piles of data are evidence that you've "written it down." Now your challenge will be to find an appropriate way to "write it up."

You have many choices for writing up your fieldstudy. How you choose to tell your tale, what parts of the data you choose to include, and what you choose as a theme (a thesis, a focus) are critical for shaping your study toward readers. In this sense, your data have the power to guide your choices. But your power as a writer lies in your rhetorical decisions as you analyze, question, manipulate, and present your data. These decisions of voice, purpose, and audience are the same decisions all writers make, as we have discussed throughout this book.

As anthropologist Clifford Geertz observes above, working out your rhetorical stance in your study is as much of a challenge as working your way into a fieldsite. As you discover "somewhere to stand" in your text, you are negotiating between your "intimate view" (stepping in) of the field experience and your "cool assessment" of it (stepping out). These terms, *stepping in* and *stepping out,* we borrow from Hortense Powdermaker and describe in Chapter 2. As we hope you've noticed in all the fieldstudies you've read, the writer constructs an I to accompany the reader through the text. How you construct yourself as part of your study is dependent on the constructed "I" working with all the other voices in your study. This chapter shows you how to shape both your data and your researcher stance as you shape your writing. Writing and analysis take place at the same time. This is not a linear process; in other words, as you reread your data, you'll simultaneously discover theories about what you've seen in the field. Gradually you'll develop an idea or a theme that will explain your theory and help you draft your draft.

Theory may sound like a scary word or a word that belongs only to physics, mathematics, or literature professors. But theory, in reality, is a continuous, unconscious part of everyday living. Our colleague Don Graves is fond of saying, "You can't get out of bed in the morning without a theory." We don't realize how often we depend on our theories. Graves offers the metaphor of a school dance to show us how theories operate in anyone's research process:

> I think doing research is like chaperoning an eighth grade dance. You can't wait to see which ungainly guy is going to dance with which ungainly girl. You have all those ideas and theories bouncing around like so many ungainly adolescents. So, you experiment by pairing them up. That's where the writing comes in. You put two ideas on the page, right next to each other, and see if they dance. It's a bit herky-jerky at first but then they get a bit smoother as you work and rework them, it's exciting. When students do research they aren't going to know anything until they write. They say, "I can't write yet, I don't have anything." Of course, it's the theories that save time. You know a little better who to send out together on the dance floor. A kind of wild image. Poetry and research dance well together. Theories and metaphors dance well together. Einstein got his theory of relativity from a metaphor.

So anyone (and everyone) can and does develop a theory. But we have trouble making our complicated ideas explicit unless we've first recorded them. And often, in the recording, we find a hidden metaphor, a nascent idea, a nugget of data that reminds us of the growing themes of our study. As author E. M. Forster commented, "How do I know what I think until I see what I say?" Writing begets writing. The process of drafting holds a generative power. Language, unarticulated but felt, turns into words and ideas as it moves from mind to page, from notes to drafts.

To us, the word **draft** suggests wind blowing through a piece of writing—with little or big holes left to fill as you craft your writing into something your reader will understand. All writers have their own styles of drafting. Just as fieldworkers establish various habits for organizing information during data collection, so do writers develop successful drafting habits. First drafts need to be exploratory, and sometimes we must force them out of a very strange paradox.

We write to release ourselves from that stuck-tight, closed-up feeling that we can't write because we don't know the answers to—or the meaning of—what we want to say. But to understand the theories behind what we think and feel, we must write. We learn more about what we know as we draft. Writing a first draft is not the same as freewriting, which we discussed in Chapter 2. *Freewriting* uncorks your writing process and helps you become fluid, fast, and fluent. *Drafting* frees all the ideas and research about a topic that you've been holding in your mind. With subsequent drafts, you can fill in the holes—for yourself and for your readers. But the trick in getting that first draft written is to "just do it."

RESISTING WRITING

From our own experiences we know that even when you're prepared to begin writing, it's difficult to "just do it." There are myriad and insidious ways to avoid writing. One writer we know spent most of a year vacuuming when she should have been writing. Other writers hang out, cook, swim, jog, sharpen pencils, iron, spend hours on the Internet—anything but write. While we write this book, in fact, we eat candy, make coffee, take breaks and naps, talk to our friends and families on the phone, take long walks in the afternoons, and give ourselves little rewards when we finally put our thoughts into words.

Even professional writers procrastinate. Our colleague Don Murray has gathered quotes from writers about their writing processes and habits and has described his own writing processes to students and teachers. In his book *Shoptalk: Learning to Write with Writers,* Murray says: "The single quality that distinguishes the unpublished writer from the published is not talent but work habits."

Here are a few of our favorite quotes from his book that describe the stubborn stage when we must begin to turn fieldnotes into fieldwriting or jottings into a coherent paper:

> *Woody Allen:* If you work only three to five hours a day, you become quite productive. It's the steadiness that counts.
>
> *Isaac Asimov:* Rituals? Ridiculous! My only ritual is to sit close enough to the typewriter so that my fingers touch the keys.
>
> *Annie Dillard:* Writing…is like rearing children—willpower has very little to do with it. If you have a little baby crying in the middle of the night, and if you depend only on willpower to get you out of bed to feed the baby, that baby will starve. You do it out of love.
>
> *Madeline L'Engle:* Inspiration usually comes during work, rather than before it.
>
> *John McPhee:* After college, I sat all day in a captain's chair up on 84th Street trying to write plays for live television. Each morning I would thread my bathrobe sash through the spokes of the chair and tie myself in.

You may have felt that the process comes easily, that inspiration is always at hand for the "born writer." But as these quotes from well-known writers attest, writers are not born but dependent on work habits, daily discipline, and reader response, as well as the voices of other writers they've read.

DRAFTING DRAFTS

And so it's time to write a first draft. Spread out your notebooks, your data, stick-on notes, highlighters, scissors, file boxes, and research portfolio. Prepare to let the data speak to you as you sift through what you have. You may decide, for example, in a first sweep through your data that you'll be able to use a memorable quote from a transcript, a key image from your field descriptions, or a reflective piece you've written about your own positioning. It's reassuring then to highlight your notes, attach sticky notes to what you have, spread out your computer printouts or consult your bookmarked websites, and somehow find the data you might use. Check your research journal for notes you have written about your own thoughts as they've come up along with the comments on the artifacts you've assembled in your portfolio. This initial sweep should also help you locate gaps and missing spots that call for further information and perhaps even further research. Evaluating your raw material, of course, is not just a mechanical process. Selecting the best snippets of language, describing and reflecting on your data, requires time and thought.

In your first draft, you will pull many data sources together into sections, so it is important to think carefully about different ways you might organize. Some people lay their data on the floor and move pages around. Some use the categories they've arranged in their portfolios. Others experiment using color-coded hanging file folders to review, organize, and change the patterns of their data. Of course, you can cluster and shift data into files on a computer using keywords as guides. Whichever methods you use, try to be flexible so you can order and reorder your disparate data as the themes emerge in your mind. This is an intellectually challenging process. Fieldworkers always accumulate too much data, far more than they can use, and must learn to let go of the data that doesn't work with the other data, fit the focus, triangulate with other data, or enrich the study. Selecting appropriate data is perhaps the most complicated part of creating a first draft.

Anne Lamott is a professional writer whose book *Bird by Bird: Some Instructions on Writing and Life* considers not only writing but the writer's habits of mind. Her book title comes from a family story. When her brother, at age 10, became overwhelmed while writing a report on birds, her writer father's comforting line was "Bird by bird, Buddy. Just take it bird by bird." In the following section, Lamott writes about the power and the usefulness of first drafts, of getting ideas on paper just for the purpose of later expanding, clarifying, and organizing them. For many writers, just like the case of Lamott's brother, there's reassurance in allowing yourself to write a messy first draft, knowing that each subsequent draft will refine what's already there. We like Lamott's father's advice, and we hope you too will be able to allow yourself to take your writing "bird by bird," one section, one draft, at a time.

Shitty First Drafts
Anne Lamott

Now, practically even better news than that of short assignments is the idea of shitty first drafts. All good writers write them. This is how they end up with good second drafts and terrific third drafts. People tend to look at successful writers, writers who are getting their books published and maybe even doing well financially, and think that they sit down at their desks every morning feeling like a million dollars, feeling great about who they are and how much talent they have and what a great story they have to tell; that they take in a few deep breaths, push back their sleeves, roll their necks a few times to get all the cricks out, and dive in, typing fully formed passages as fast as a court reporter. But this is just the fantasy of the uninitiated. I know some very great writers, writers you love who write beautifully and have made a great deal of money, and not *one* of them sits down routinely feeling wildly enthusiastic and confident. Not one of them writes elegant first drafts. All right, one of them does, but we do not like her very much. We do not think that she has a rich inner life or that God likes her or can even stand her. (Although when I mentioned this to my priest friend Tom, he said you can safely assume you've created God in your own image when it turns out that God hates all the same people you do.)

Very few writers really know what they are doing until they've done it. Nor do they go about their business feeling dewy and thrilled. They do not type a few stiff warm-up sentences and then find themselves bounding along like huskies across the snow. One writer I know tells me that he sits down every morning and says to himself nicely, "It's not like you don't have a choice, because you do—you can either type or kill yourself." We all often feel like we are pulling teeth, even those writers whose prose ends up being the most natural and fluid. The right words and sentences just do not come pouring out like ticker tape most of the time. Now, Muriel Spark is said to have felt that she was taking dictation from God every morning—sitting there, one supposes, plugged into a Dictaphone, typing away, humming. But this is a very hostile and aggressive position. One might hope for bad things to rain down on a person like this.

For me and most of the other writers I know, writing is not rapturous. In fact, the only way I can get anything written at all is to write really, really shitty first drafts.

The first draft is the child's draft, where you let it all pour out and then let it romp all over the place, knowing that no one is going to see it and that you can shape it later. You just let this childlike part of you channel whatever voices and visions come through and onto the page. If one of the characters wants to say, "Well, so what, Mr. Poopy Pants?," you let her. No one is going to see it. If the kid wants to get into really sentimental, weepy, emotional territory, you let him. Just get it all down on paper, because there may be something great in those six crazy pages that you would never have gotten to by more rational, grown-up means. There may be something in the very last line of the very last paragraph on page six that you just love, that is so beautiful or wild that you now know what you're supposed to be writing about, more or less, or in what direction you might go—but there was no way to get to this without first getting through the first five and a half pages.

I used to write food reviews for *California* magazine before it folded. (My writing food reviews had nothing to do with the magazine folding, although every single review did cause a couple of canceled subscriptions. Some readers took umbrage at my comparing mounds of vegetable puree with various ex-presidents' brains.) These reviews always took two days to write. First I'd go to a restaurant several times with a few opinionated, articulate friends in tow. I'd sit there writing down everything anyone said that was at all interesting or funny. Then on the following Monday I'd sit down at my desk with my notes, and try to write the review. Even after I'd been doing this for years, panic would set in. I'd try to write a lead, but instead I'd write a couple of dreadful sentences, xx them out, try again, xx everything out, and then feel despair and worry settle on my chest like an x-ray apron. It's over, I'd think, calmly. I'm not going to be able to get the magic to work this time. I'm ruined. I'm through. I'm toast. Maybe, I'd think, I can get my old job back as a clerk-typist. But probably not. I'd get up and study my teeth in the mirror for a while. Then I'd stop, remember to breathe, make a few phone calls, hit the kitchen and chow down. Eventually I'd go back and sit down at my desk, and sigh for the next ten minutes. Finally I would pick up my one-inch picture frame, stare into it as if for the answer, and every time the answer would come: all I had to do was to write a really shitty first draft of, say, the opening paragraph. And no one was going to see it.

So I'd start writing without reining myself in. It was almost just typing, just making my fingers move. And the writing would be *terrible*. I'd write a lead paragraph that was a whole page, even though the entire review could only be three pages long, and then I'd start writing up descriptions of the food, one dish at a time, bird by bird, and the critics would be sitting on my shoulders, commenting like cartoon characters. They'd be pretending to snore, or rolling their eyes at my overwrought descriptions, no matter how hard I tried to tone those descriptions down, no matter how conscious I was of what a friend said to me gently in my early days of restaurant reviewing. "Annie," she said, "it is just a piece of *chicken*. It is just a bit of *cake*."

But because by then I had been writing for so long, I would eventually let myself trust the process—sort of, more or less. I'd write a first draft that was maybe twice as long as it should be, with a self-indulgent and boring beginning, stupefying descriptions of the meal, lots of quotes from my black-humored friends that made them sound more like the Manson girls than food lovers, and no ending to speak of. The whole thing would be so long and incoherent and hideous that for the rest of the day I'd obsess about getting creamed by a car before I could write a decent second draft. I'd worry that people would read what I'd written and believe that the accident had really been a suicide, that I had panicked because my talent was waning and my mind was shot.

The next day, though, I'd sit down, go through it all with a colored pen, take out everything I possibly could, find a new lead somewhere on the second page, figure out a kicky place to end it, and then write a second draft. It always turned out fine, sometimes even funny and weird and helpful. I'd go over it one more time and mail it in.

Then, a month later, when it was time for another review, the whole process would start again, complete with the fears that people would find my first draft before I could rewrite it.

Almost all good writing begins with terrible first efforts. You need to start somewhere. Start by getting something—anything—down on paper. A friend of mine says that the first draft is the down draft—you just get it down. The second draft is the up draft—you fix it up. You try to say what you have to say more accurately. And the third draft is the dental draft, where you check every tooth, to see if it's loose or cramped or decayed, or even, God help us, healthy.

What I've learned to do when I sit down to work on a shitty first draft is to quiet the voices in my head. First there's the vinegar-lipped Reader Lady, who says primly, "Well, *that's* not very interesting, is it?" And there's the emaciated German male who writes these Orwellian memos detailing your thought crimes. And there are your parents, agonizing over your lack of loyalty and discretion; and there's William Burroughs, dozing off or shooting up because he finds you as bold and articulate as a houseplant; and so on. And there are also the dogs: let's not forget the dogs, the dogs in their pen who will surely hurtle and snarl their way out if you ever *stop* writing, because writing is, for some of us, the latch that keeps the door of the pen closed, keeps those crazy ravenous dogs contained.

Quieting these voices is at least half the battle I fight daily. But this is better than it used to be. It used to be 87 percent. Left to its own devices, my mind spends much of its time having conversations with people who aren't there. I walk along defending myself to people, or exchanging repartee with them, or rationalizing my behavior, or seducing them with gossip, or pretending I'm on their TV talk show or whatever. I speed or run an aging yellow light or don't come to a full stop, and one nanosecond later am explaining to imaginary cops exactly why I had to do what I did, or insisting that I did not in fact do it.

I happened to mention this to a hypnotist I saw many years ago, and he looked at me very nicely. At first I thought he was feeling around on the floor for the silent alarm button, but then he gave me the following exercise, which I still use to this day.

Close your eyes and get quiet for a minute, until the chatter starts up. Then isolate one of the voices and imagine the person speaking as a mouse. Pick it up by the tail and drop it into a mason jar. Then isolate another voice, pick it up by the tail, drop it in the jar. And so on. Drop in any high-maintenance parental units, drop in any contractors, lawyers, colleagues, children, anyone who is whining in your head. Then put the lid on, and watch all these mouse people clawing at the glass, jabbering away, trying to make you feel like shit because you won't do what they want—won't give them more money, won't be more successful, won't see them more often. Then imagine that there is a volume-control button on the bottle. Turn it all the way up for a minute, and listen to the stream of angry, neglected, guilt-mongering voices. Then turn it all the way down and watch the frantic mice lunge at the glass, trying to get to you. Leave it down, and get back to your shitty first draft.

A writer friend of mine suggests opening the jar and shooting them all in the head. But I think he's a little angry, and I'm sure nothing like this would ever occur to you.

We like Lamott's description of the drafting process. First comes the "down draft," which is the most difficult task for the writer to achieve. In the case of fieldwork, your job in a down draft is to organize and manipulate your many layers of data. Then come your subsequent "up drafts"—as you slowly fix up your text for a reader.

As you work through your up drafts, we hope you'll review all our chapter sections called "FieldWriting," which we've connected to each chapter's theme. For example, you'll find "Establishing a Voice" in our first chapter (Stepping In and Stepping Out), "The Grammar of Observation" in Chapter 5 (Researching Place), and "From Details to Verbal Portraiture" in Chapter 7 as we write about writing about people. The placement of these sections is in fact an example of how we've rearranged how we wrote about writing, just as you might want to rearrange your data several different times. In the first edition of this book, published in 1997, we had only one chapter specifically about writing, and it was at the end. Our readers asked for more, and they wanted to read about writing earlier in the book. So for this edition, we eventually settled on the organizational pattern of linking a fieldwriting section to each chapter, a beginning (Chapter 2) and ending (Chapter 8) about writing. We considered hauling all of the "Field-Writing" sections into this last chapter. We decided that would be overwhelming, and it wouldn't help you at the beginning of your fieldwriting, so as we revised, we moved around our discussions of writing. Since we think writing is critical to every stage of fieldwork, we decided to signal that to you by including discussions of writing in little sections throughout the book as well as in the chapters we've devoted to fieldwriting. And so, although we've known from the beginning of this project that this book is as much about writing as it is about fieldwork, we had to shift our patterns of organization and revise over and over again.

Revising is *not* editing. The term **revision** implies a reseeing and reimagining of the original material. Both editing and revising can take place during the drafting process, but revision always involves making substantial changes, not just fine-tuning a sentence or two. As you draft and redraft, adding and subtracting pieces of data and discovering new connections, you should not bother to make your writing look perfect. Save the editing for later. Revision is the first job after the first draft. To revise means to rewrite with an eye toward emerging ideas, themes, and voice. And then it means to draft again.

Eventually, of course, comes what Anne Lamott calls in the preceding piece the "dental draft," in which the writer must polish and edit carefully to meet the expectations and conventions appropriate for the intended audience. This dental draft is the last stage of manuscript preparation before the publishing, however it's done—and this is an important distinction. The process of working a dental draft is quite separate from the process of revision. Your instructor probably has a policy (what Lamott might call a dental policy) that describes the conventions a piece of writing must follow in its final form. As long as you focus on the acceptable editing format for the kinds of readers you're addressing, you may find useful suggestions for the final polishing stage in the many good handbooks and online resources that are available.

QUESTIONING YOUR DRAFT

And so we go back to revision. Once you've written a first draft, whether it's "shitty" or not, you have something to work with that's not just piles of paper and sticky notes. You can fold further data into the draft, deciding what you'll put in the foreground of your study and what you'll use for the background. This phase is a little like interviewing your draft using guiding questions about your fieldwork material and your relationship to it. Just as interviewing requires both preparation and openness, questioning your draft also requires that you give it both structure and room for discovery. In this section we look back at questions you've been asking all along—of your fieldnotes and your fieldworking process—and we present some new questions that focus more tightly on the fieldwriting process. Although we dislike presenting our suggestions in a linear order, we hope you'll understand that we mean these questions to support you in all the active and recursive processes of questioning, drafting, requestioning, and redrafting.

In Chapter 2, we presented three key questions for you to use regularly as you take fieldnotes and gather data. We hope you've found them useful as you've collected and written material for your fieldproject:

What surprised me? (to track your assumptions)
What intrigued me? (to track your positions)
What disturbed me? (to track your tensions)

These three questions help you understand your shifting assumptions, and tracking your changing research positions helps you construct your researcher's voice as it will guide your reader through your study. Analyzing your tensions as they appear and sometimes disappear allows you to develop a relationship with your reader by being honest about what disturbs you—and how you come to understand this through the course of your study. To explain more specifically how asking these questions has assisted researchers, we'd like to return briefly to some of the studies you may have already read in this book:

What Surprised Me?

Rick Zollo's surprise was in the truckers' logbook. (See Chapter 1 for Rick's study.) As Rick talked to Dan and other truckers about their jobs, they pointed him to the logbook and its restrictions on their lives. He began to see that his assumption that truckers lived an unfettered life was not entirely true. The logbook showed that they were subject to government restrictions, fines, and scrutiny from the police and the U.S. Department of Transportation. Karen Downing's study (see Chapter 5) uncovered many assumptions for her as she encountered other peoples' perspectives on the beauty culture: Ginny, the manager of Photo Phantasies, sees her work as important ("giving back to society"). Darlene, the checker at the supermarket, sees glamour photos as both "an indulgence and a treat." Karen's mother's friends, who are as old as seventy-six, loved having their pictures taken. Ivana Nikolic, who studied the homeless (see Chapter 4), was shocked that this group of people even existed in the United States and found them "tired, scared, and lonely." And Cindie Marshall (see Chapter 7) was surprised to find that she felt more comfortable talking with Teardrop than the bikers she set out to study, who turned out to be less stereotypical and more varied than she'd initially assumed.

What Intrigued Me?

For Rick, the comparison between cowboys and truckers was something that attracted him at the beginning and helped him develop a metaphor to guide him through his study. Since he'd always been intrigued by "the open road," his position as a closet cowboy helped him connect with the trucker culture. Karen was intrigued by the glossy photos on the wall, the wardrobe selections (metal-studded denim jackets and gold lamé blouses), the horse (which provided her with a focus for her study), the business side of Photo Phantasies and how programmed it was, and the idea that "putting on a face" could be empowering. As a middle-class woman and teacher, her position emerged as she found herself fascinated by the details of this culture's business and fashion underlife. Ivana's position as a U.S. resident and former refugee moved her to volunteer at the homeless shelter and then to do a research project so that she could better understand that unemployment was not the major problem of the homeless. An artifact, a sign ("Urinate inside, not out here"), intrigued Cindie and reminded her that she was both attracted to and afraid of bikers and their culture.

What Disturbed Me?

Over time, Rick was disturbed to find out how political the trucking industry is and how truckers face many of the same kinds of constraints in their work as office workers do. Karen felt tension mount throughout her study as she began to track her own feminist stance—that a woman should have control over her own body—when she started to realize that the beauty culture, too, allowed that same control. As a former outsider to American culture, Ivana felt ashamed that she had allowed other peoples' opinions to shape her understanding of the homeless. But she also felt a tension between her family's story and the stories she heard at the shelter. Cindie was disturbed that the artifacts she observed implied illegal activities at Ralph's Sports Bar: drugs, stolen goods, and gambling. She was further disturbed by Teardrop's story, which exposed the brutality of some bikers and their abuse of women.

We'd like to introduce you to Sam Samuels and his study in the following reading. Sam relied on these three key questions throughout his study of a telemarketing firm. He entered this fieldsite with curiosity, with anger about the telemarketers who often interrupted his busy life, and with the knowledge that some of his own college students worked part time at this local company. Sam wrote this essay while playing multiple roles: he is a teacher, a journalist, and a student. You'll see evidence of these positions as you read his essay. He allows himself to offer personal judgments as he describes the telemarketing site and its employees. The more visits he made to the site, the more he was struck by the parallels between these workers and the factory workers of several generations ago. He studied books and articles about working, assembly lines, and telemarketing.

Sam's "On the Line" reads as a seamless nonfiction essay, much like Studs Terkel's classic studies in *Working*, but in both cases in-depth ethnographic interviews and field observations form the backbone of the writing. Sam writes, "I'd say 75 percent of the material I gathered didn't make it into the final piece.... There will be other drafts of this piece.... The material that did not make it into this one may resurface. I had a lot of choices. This could have centered solely on the efforts of the workers to unionize.... It might have been about the divided workforce, interviewing an equal number of college kids and 'grown-ups' with family responsibilities. But I started with a special interest in the older workers, and that was as far as I got this semester." As you read this essay, you may be as engaged, entertained, and instructed as we were when we found ourselves, with Sam as our guide, stepping in to the subculture of the telemarketing world.

On the Line
Sam Samuels

The black desktop phone in Eugenia Easton's cubicle is a relic. She's a TSR, a telephone sales representative. She's on the line seven and a half hours a day. But the phone itself is little more than a quaint paperweight. The essential wiring passes right through it into a lightweight headset that frees her hands to scroll through her computerized script and punch in new data on the customers—those who don't hang up on her. An efficient and comfortable setup, outside of the occasional outbreak of head lice.

Visiting EPIC Teleservices where Eugenia does her calling, I became acutely aware that she is in every sense of the word an assembly-line worker in the service economy. Ben Hamper wrote in *Rivethead: Tales from the Assembly Line* about what it's like to be a General Motors shop rat. He was a third-generation GM worker; in his book he describes being shuffled from one location on the line to another, getting laid off and rehired, battling the clock for every grudging tick it grants him, and inventing strategies to remain sane as one identical Chevy Suburban chassis after another rolls by to accept its requisite number of rivets from his rivet gun. Eugenia too mans an assembly line—a virtual assembly line on which the products that roll by aren't Suburbans or Oldsmobiles but us.

That's her problem. We, the object of her labors, have yet to be successfully standardized. Hamper's work is a traditional assembly-line job, where the work is so purely physical that it allows his mind the freedom to wander, to divert itself from its task and create fantasy worlds and schemes on company time. For Eugenia, though, the task is an odd hybrid of routinized brain work. Just enough of her intellect is required to keep her customers engaged that there's little opportunity for on-the-job creativity. We, her product, have been targeted, listed, and lumped into demographic groups according to our values, lifestyles, credit histories, and past purchasing behavior, but still we persist in being people—hanging up, being out, saying no, mouthing off, blowing up, and faking coronary arrests on the line.

I'm one of the angry ones, or at least I used to be. Before getting to know some telemarketers, I used to engage in lengthy arguments with them when they interrupted my dinner, eventually realizing that until I actually hung up the phone they weren't going to budge. The arguments were like this one, partially reconstructed from memory:

Me: "I don't like being called at home. I have a policy never to buy anything over the phone. Please take me off your list."

TSR: "I'll just put you down as irate."

Me: "Excuse me?"

TSR: "I'm putting you down as irate."

Me: "You don't have to put me down as irate. I'm not irate. I'm being pretty calm and reasonable. I just don't want to be called any more at home."

TSR: "That's just what we have to do to get somebody off the list. Put them down as irate."

My defensiveness that day served only to waste two people's time, and by the time I got through arguing why I was not irate, I was irate. It would have been kinder just to hang up on this poor person, whom I now believe was probably a novice TSR. Eugenia would never waste her valuable time on an obvious no-sale like me. She's not one of the legion of college or high-school students doing this ho-hum job to pay their way through school. I've taught some of them. The first time it occurred to me that telemarketers might have faces was in my own classroom. I'd just been tirading against telemarketers as my prime example of the accelerating collapse of American society. After class one of my better students approached me, confessed that she'd phone-sold her way through high school, and asked if I could please not be so rude to telemarketers or hang up on them any more. I began to question my views of perhaps not the whole industry but at least the individuals at the other end of the line. After all, when I was a teenager, I earned my stereo set dishing ice cream at a swim club.

In Iowa, however, there aren't nearly as many swim clubs as there are telemarketing centers. Most of these kids look forward to something different. But not Eugenia: she's a lifer, and over the eight years of calling she's gotten to be very, very good.

When I first meet her, she's just a voice. Vince Feldstein, the center manager, has cheerfully agreed to let me listen in on some telemarketing calls. I just walk in and introduce myself. I am surprised at how willing Vince is to let me hang out at the center. I've been reading Barbara Garson's *All the Livelong Day: The Meaning and Demeaning of Routine Work*, in which she interviews all kinds of workers to gain a feeling for the nature of repetitive jobs. Garson talks about how impossible it is to get past the security officers and receptionists that guard the portals of most American workplaces; she eventually has to resort to taking a job herself to get inside an office. I'm feeling incredibly lucky. All I did was call and drop by, and now Vince is giving me a guided tour, an interview, and even offering me a headset to eavesdrop with. Heck, if I'm not careful, he might offer me a job.

Just looking around the room, I find that my preconception is correct: the workers are roughly divided into college students and older workers, with college students as the large majority. It's the older workers I'm after, the ones who make their livelihood at this. I ask Vince to pick somebody really skilled. He walks me over to an empty cubicle, offers me a headset, and then fiddles with the computer for a while. Text begins flashing by, and my headset comes alive with conversation. The caller can't hear me, but I can hear her and the customers. Managers and supervisors listen in like this all the time, Vince tells me with a conspiratorial grin. Sometimes the corporate clients even listen in from their office out of town.

"Do they listen at random? Or do you give them the best callers to listen to?" I ask.

With a wink, Vince answers, "We usually know who they get."

"Can I switch around and change who I'm listening to?"

"I can switch it for you, but it takes a while. Why don't you listen to Eugenia for a bit first. She's one of the best," Vince offers. I can see why he got into sales. He's young, perhaps not yet thirty, with close-cropped blond hair and a vibrantly perky face. Like most people in this invisible profession, he wears no tie or any other special clothing to mark his position within the office. He's risen through the ranks, from TSR himself to supervisor to receptionist to center manager. He's even overseen the opening of several new centers, including this one about four years ago. Vince is also a student, a married one taking the long route through college by working full-time. Weekends, he DJs at parties. He's very helpful to me—almost supernaturally helpful, as long as the conversation goes his way. I'm getting a taste of the kind of friendly force that gets people ahead in the telemarketing world.

I settle in to my cubicle. It's 1:00 in the afternoon, and break time is at 2:00, so I have an hour to listen to Eugenia. Vince has placed me in an empty row. The office is a long basement divided lengthwise down the middle. Along the north side is a large break room with some circular tables, Vince's enclosed office, and a training room with lots of flip charts and dry-erase boards. A center staircase leads down from the shopping mall upstairs and ends in the reception area, bisecting the space. The south wall is lined with tiny cubicles separated by shoulder-high partitions covered in sound-absorbing grey burlap. There's a main aisle that runs the length of the center, and off that are eight smaller aisles, each of which has a dozen cubicles at which the TSRs sit with their backs to the aisle. At the far end of each aisle, mounted on the wall, is a white tote board for each team, as well as a set of four clocks, one for each time zone. You never know from one call to the next what part of the country you'll be talking to. I do a little mental calculation. Ninety-six Americans might be getting calls from this center at any one time.

Right now the center is only about one-third full because it's the middle of the day. The really busy time, Vince tells me, is evenings. Along the main aisle, at the end of each set of cubicles, are the eight supervisors' work stations. These are desks equipped with computers and phone setups but raised because the supervisors never sit down. From this location they can survey their whole team from above, listen in on calls, and watch their workers' screens scroll by. Mostly they sort of stalk around whipping their teams up with whatever form of encouragement they can think of. Some sound like cheerleaders, some like auctioneers, some like taskmasters.

Eugenia's supervisor, Franco, is of this third variety. He paces up and down behind his team's backs. He's tall with jet black hair and also looks to be around thirty. I'm surprised at the youth of even the highest-level people here. There are a couple of hundred employees of this center, but nobody looks like a corporate authority figure—no grey-haired suits, even in management. It seems when you get old at EPIC, you have two choices: get promoted out of the center, or stay a TSR for life. The real leadership takes place from a remote location. Clients are wooed, scripts written, and phone lists compiled somewhere else. Then the work is shipped to this center in computerized form for lower-down managers to oversee. Franco has Mediterranean-olive skin, a slight Italian accent, and a very hard face. As I speak to more workers later, I'll hear rumors about him. Eugenia calls him dominating. Rick, who's no longer working here, suspects that Franco is a management spy: Franco got promoted from TSR to supervisor quite suddenly and at the exact time that the workers' efforts to unionize were quelled by an information leak to management. Right now he's adjusting the figures on the tote board: "Have: 66. Need: 72." His team has an hour to make six more sales. All around me, I hear the mingled voices of TSRs at various points in their calls. This center deals almost entirely in credit cards.

"If you do have any questions, please call 1-800…"

"If he's married, is his spouse available?"

"You've been chosen to receive the new…"

"No, no message."

"Do you open your parents' mail?"

On goes my headset, and even though it leaves my left ear uncovered, the quiet din is filtered out surprisingly effectively. Eugenia is working fast. I'm hard pressed to try to write down most of what is said. The computer in front of me is matching her computer, so I get to read on the screen exactly what she's reading, notice her little deviations from the script, and watch her record the course of each call. The computer thinks of everything for her, prompting her at every turn. If the customer is not home but somebody else is, there's a space for her to note that. The computer absorbs it all: "Spoke to lead. Spoke to spouse. AM tape machine. PM tape machine. Reschedule. Unavailable. Divorced."

Customer: "I already have six cards."

Eugenia: "Do those cards have a low APR rate of…"

Customer: "Look, I already have a consolidation loan, and I'm paying it off. I don't want more cards."

Eugenia: "I certainly understand that, Mr. Maile. (Click.) Mr. Maile? Mr. Maile?" Pause. He's definitely gone. "Thank you for your time, Mr. Maile, and if you do have any questions please call 1-800…"

Who is she talking to? This guy has hung up. There's a brief pause while Eugenia regroups but not too long. She doesn't do the dialing herself. She's a phone worker who never hears a dial tone all day. All she does is push a

button, and the computer routes the next available call for her. Even Lily Tom-
lin's operator got to count: "One ringy dingy! Two ringy dingies!" Not Eugenia.
The computer doesn't give her the call until the customer or his spouse,
answering machine, or toddler picks up. It also times her, keeping track of how
long she waits between calls. Nearly everything about this sales process has
been automated, even supervising the TSRs. Only the essential moment of
interaction is left to a person, and that's kept to a minimum.

The next customer is out. A woman offers to take a message.

"There's no real message. If he's married," Eugenia says to the man's obvious wife, "is his spouse available?"

Now I'm catching on. The computer script doesn't say, "There's no real
message" anywhere. I overhear other TSRs use the phrase, "There no message."
The insertion of the word *real* appears to be Eugenia's own innovation. It's
subtle. It implies a lot. It means that there is a message, just not a "real" one,
so perhaps you could talk to me instead, and if not, I'll be calling back. This
call, too ends in a hangup. Again, Eugenia ends with her set speech:

"Mrs. Tunstill? Mrs. Tunstill?" Pause. "I certainly understand how you feel,
Mrs. Tunstill. Thank you for your time, and if you do have any questions, please
call 1-800…"

Again, to nobody. This is one thing that makes her such a good TSR. She's
like a batter who follows through on her swing even after the ball has been
whiffed and nestles safely in the catcher's mitt. Keeping the mood alive, keeping the flow going. After listening to a lot of these calls, though, I begin to
notice that Eugenia does allow herself a little comment here and there. The
words are always the same in this windup, but the tone varies. While a customer is there, her speaking voice is monotonous, unemotional, the boiled-
down essence of every bored telephone operator I've ever spoken to. It seems
to reassure people. Once they've hung up on her, tiny hints of sarcasm, even
bitterness, creep into her voice as she delivers her concluding courtesies into
the empty ether.

I listen to more. Some are successful calls, and I get to hear what the later
parts of the script say.

"For security purposes, may I have your date of birth or mother's maiden
name?"

This line comes after the person has confirmed all the information that
Eugenia already knows, their name, address, and other vital information. Now
she needs some really personal data, and this is the point where, with amazing
regularity, the customer balks:

"What is this call about?"

Up to this point, the customers have been yessing and uh-huh-ing along,
as if perfectly comfortable and conditioned to the fact that some total stranger
knows everything about them. But now, when they have to cough up some intimate details like their birth date, they need a recap. Which Eugenia is only too
happy to provide.

No money changes hands during these calls. Technically, this is not a purchase. The customers have been preapproved for a line of credit, and they are required to give their consent before the card can be issued to them. In a successful call, the customer says yes, and then they receive the card "inactive" in the mail. Then they have to activate it by calling another number. Eugenia gives them the option of reading them the fine-print terms of the credit card, but most are fairly punch-drunk by that point in the script and ask to have it just sent to them. Like Mrs. Baker, who said, "I might as well wait and read it because I can't understand what you're talking about."

Or this woman:

"May I ask what your annual household income is?"

"I'm just on a fixed income."

"Would you say that's $15,000?"

"It's about the lowest income you can get."

"Would that be about $15,000?"

"It's the lowest you can get."

"We'll put in $15,000. That'll help you." Help her what? Get access to more credit than she can possibly pay off in her remaining golden years?

I stand up. I'm getting crampy, and I've only been here forty-five minutes. This is giving me powerful memories of my forty-hour-a-week job as a legal word-processor, how confining and tense it was to maintain a rapid rate of highly concentrated, adrenalated work while 95 percent of my body had to remain still.

Up to now, I've been listening completely unnoticed. Apparently there is enough job turnover here and enough surprise visits from clients that the sight of a stranger in a headset is nothing special. I take advantage of my anonymity to scan the row of workers facing me and see if I can guess which is Eugenia. Finally, I spot someone whose mouth is in synch with the voice on my set.

She's wearing a sweatshirt with the EPIC logo embroidered on it. It's baggy, and the way she's settled into her seat suggests a sack of onions that's settled into its bin for the long haul, each one rolled as close to the bottom of the bag as it can get. She's in her fifties. Her hair is medium length, light brown, with what looks like a permanent case of static electricity. Roseanne Arnold with all the air let out.

Now a customer is complaining. Once somebody acquiesces to the credit card, Eugenia has to repeat the whole transaction with a tape recorder running. These completed calls, or "completes," are taped and sent on to a quality-control department at another location. I can tell this is happening because my and Eugenia's computers flash "Currently Recording." That way, if the customer claims they were duped, there's a permanent record that the conversation went along lines that are approved by the company's legal experts. There is no backing out. But this customer misunderstands. When Eugenia tells her she's about to turn on the tape machine, she bursts:

"You mean you've been taping me this whole time?"

In fact, she hasn't. She's only about to start taping, but Eugenia can't afford to anger this person. "I'm turning it off, I'm turning it off." Perhaps there's some way this call can be salvaged?

Nope. Click.

Some people don't like to be rude. They want to console Eugenia for not making a sale or take the blame for it themselves. "No," explains one man as he refuses the easy credit he's being offered, "I wouldn't be entrusted. Thank you." Click.

Or this one: "You can send it, but I have a purseful, and I don't use them." Click.

To which Eugenia responds into the ether, "I can't send it if you don't give me information."

The hour is almost over. The tote board now reads "Have: 72. Need: 72." The next few minutes are gravy. Anybody who exceeds their goal by two calls per hour gets an extra ten minutes in their break. Eugenia is recording, which means a sale.

"Now that's two!"

Which initiates a last-minute flurry of enthusiasm from the rest of Franco's team.

"Franco! I got two this hour!"

"I had two sales this hour!"

"I got two this hour!" This is Eugenia, but I almost don't recognize her voice. She's alive and sassy now that she's not talking into the headset.

A male voice with a pronounced Indian accent announces, "I had fifteen this hour." I'll hear later about how accents can actually help you rather than hinder you as the management claims. Especially English accents, but Indian accents seem to evoke some of that erudition and trust as well. Would you turn down a credit card from Gandhi?

"You had fifteen?" says Eugenia brimming with good-natured sarcasm. "Oh, yeah!"

"Just five more minutes, guys," announces Franco. "Five minutes until break."

Eugenia goes into high gear, but nobody's biting. One no after another.

"We have more credit than we need."

"Once I have it, I use it. That's the problem."

Somebody asks a tricky question about her "fine-print" recitation:

"And what is the interest rate *after* November?"

"Then it reverts to a variable rate of 17.4 percent."

"Not interested!" Click.

"Break!" barks Franco. "Make sure you are back in ten minutes. You are responsible. Enjoy your break."

"I think if my head hurt any worse, it would pop," says Eugenia to nobody in particular.

At break time, most of the college age workers scramble out of the building to smoke, leaving the few lifers to rattle around in the nearly empty break room with the vending machines and the inspirational posters. "If we don't take care of the customers, someone else will" is the corporate homily on one poster, which depicts a candle being lit by the flame of another candle. "There is nobody who totally lacks the courage to change—Rollo May," declares another. "EPIC: Every Person Is a Consumer," says a third.

Eugenia sits down nearby. I introduce myself and tell her about my project.

"You're not from 20/20 or something like that are you?"

No, I reassure her. I'm not doing an exposé of how she's some illegal scam artist. She smiles, reassured.

"That's good. They had one on last week." Everybody's always trying to show how terrible telemarketers are. Yes, she'll talk to me. But we have only ten minutes. I don't tell her that I've just been listening to her for an hour. For the first time, I notice that her teeth are small, pointy, brown, and far apart from each other.

"I've been here four and a half years. Before that, I had the same job at MCI. I got fired for low productivity."

Bob, who had joined us, chimes in, "Oh, yeah, they'll do that over there." He's another lifer, and like Eugenia he's all decked out in corporate logos. His T-shirt has a giant credit card on it, the card they're currently selling. I ask if they've won these clothes for being good callers.

"Yeah," brags Eugenia, "I won lots of stuff. T-shirts. Back at my station I got a jacket I won. It's real warm, but my husband wore it mostly for the past few years." She leads me over to a bulletin board next to the microwave oven and shows me a brochure of the various trinkets the workers can win—in lieu of a comprehensive benefits package, I remark inwardly. There are clothes, watches, and pens with EPIC's pyramid-shaped logo. What were the designers thinking of when they made this logo? Hadn't they ever heard of pyramid schemes? "When they get these new recruits in, they have this EPIC cup they give them after two weeks, to congratulate them."

Two weeks seems to be a real milestone in this occupation. Kathy, the third worker who joins us in the break room, started two weeks ago. Of the four people in her training group, she's the only one left. "Couldn't take the rejection," she explains. She herself has little choice. A hip displacement recently put an end to her twelve-year career as a nurse, and she has to do work that's sedentary.

Eugenia chimes in. "I've been calling for eight years now. It's all I can do because I've got rheumatoid arthritis. I had this arthroscopic surgery, and I can't be on my feet for eight hours. Sometimes I'd like to be doing something else." On the wall of EPIC's break room, next to the employee of the month and the board listing "11 Keys to Success," is a plaque from the Iowa Commission of Persons with Disabilities giving EPIC its Large Employer Award. It seems like an ideal place to work if you can't stand up or walk around all day. Since the supervisors all walk around, though, I ask myself whether this limits a disabled person's chances of advancement.

"Lately, I haven't been winning much," continues Eugenia. "I got this supervisor, Franco. He's sort of dominating, and I had a dominating father, so I can't talk to him either. But I don't do it for the prizes or anything. I do it to do a good job."

Bob seems more cynical, less accepting than Eugenia or Kathy. I ask him if he would mind being interviewed some time.

"You have a set of questions you want to ask us? You want to pick our brains, find out what makes us tick? Find out why anybody would do this?" This last question is not to me but proclaimed to the heavens with his hands upward, as if really seeking an answer from some higher power.

"How'd you guess?" I ask, hoping to humor him into an interview.

"I got eight years of higher education here." Bob agrees to talk to me after work some time. So does Eugenia. I ask for their numbers. They refuse, but they all write down mine and promise to call me.

One thing about telemarketers. They're stingy about giving out their phone numbers.

References

Alger, Alexandra. "Whose Phone Is It, Anyway?" *Forbes* (July 29, 1996), 104.

Garson, Barbara. *All the Livelong Day: The Meaning and Demeaning of Routine Work.* New York: Doubleday, 1975.

Hamper, Ben. *Rivethead: Tales from the Assembly Line.* New York: Warner, 1986.

Rudnitsky, Howard. "Ring, Ring, Jingle, Jingle." *Forbes* (May 20, 1996), 65.

Singer, Barry. "It's Seven P.M. and Five Percent of Omaha is Calling. Want Twenty-eight Steaks and a Radio?" *New York Times Magazine* (Dec. 3, 1995), 68.

Sam's essay blurs the boundaries between ethnographic and journalistic writing in interesting ways: his research method represents careful and thorough fieldwork, yet his stylistic approach allows his value judgments to seep through in phrases like this description of Eugenia, his main informant, who is a "lifer" at EPIC ("the way she's settled into her seat suggests a sack of onions that's settled into its bin for the long haul, each one rolled as close to the bottom of the bag as it can get.... Roseanne Arnold with all the air let out").

But although Sam allowed himself to use such metaphors to show his own values as he watched his site, he closely monitored his changing assumptions, positions, and tensions throughout his research process the way all fieldworkers should. What surprised him? Having had his own annoying conversations with telemarketers, Sam had assumed much about the telemarketer/customer relationship. He'd not thought much about their working from scripted conversations. As he listened to Eugenia's conversations, he was shocked that she often finished talking to the customer even when the customer had hung up the phone. He was surprised that sometimes accents evoked trust in customers, that the employees were decked out in corporate logo clothing, and that some people at EPIC really liked their jobs. The more he observed, the more he questioned his assumptions.

What intrigued him? As he watched the telemarketers, he recalled his own position as a young worker dishing ice cream at a swim club. But here, in these times, as he noted, "there aren't nearly as many swim clubs as there are telemarketing centers." He noticed that Vince, the center manager, was friendly, had a "vibrantly perky face," and was "almost supernaturally helpful," which erased the sense of otherness Sam had carried with him to this site. Both Vince and Eugenia became completely embodied people rather than mere telephone voices in what Sam refers to as "this invisible profession."

What disturbed him? The tension Sam felt, more and more often as he continued his study, had to do with the working conditions at the place. Specifically, he noted the small, confined workspace in which Eugenia sat most of the time, her supervisors' practice of listening in on her conversations and monitoring her sales, the competition to earn more than the 10-minute breaktime, as well as the rewards of T-shirts, watches, and pens that substituted for health care benefits. Sam also shares with his reader an awareness that although many physically disabled people can work for this company, they may not ever have the opportunity to become supervisors. After you've reviewed your questions about your own assumptions, positions, and tensions, as Sam did, you'll be better able to question your draft to further guide you in the writing process.

THICKENING YOUR DRAFT

Anthropologist Clifford Geertz, whose quote introduces this chapter, borrowed the term "thick description" from philosopher Gilbert Ryle to explain the process of compiling layers of data to reveal evidence of your having "been there" in the field as you re-create and re-present your experience for a reader. He explains this data-texturing process in a well-known essay called "Thick Description: Toward an Interpretive Theory of Culture." In that essay, he offers an example to distinguish between "thick" and "thin" description by discussing the difference between two physically indistinguishable facial movements that in our culture carry markedly different interpretations. Geertz summarizes Ryle's idea as he explains his notion of the ethnographer's need to write description "thick" with cultural interpretation:

> Consider, he says, two boys rapidly contracting the eyelids of their right eyes. In one, this is an involuntary twitch; in the other, a conspiratorial signal to a friend. The two movements are, as movements, identical; from an I-am-a-camera, "phenomenalistic" observation of them alone, one could not tell which was twitch and which was wink, or indeed whether or both or either was twitch or wink. Yet the difference, however unphotographable, between a twitch and a wink is vast; as anyone unfortunate enough to have the first taken for the second knows.... [A]s Ryle points out, the winker has done two things, contracted his eyelids and winked, while the twitcher has

done only one, contracted his eyelids. Contracting your eyelids on purpose when there exists a public code in which doing so counts as a conspiratorial signal is winking. That's all there is to it: a speck of behavior, a fleck of culture, and—*voilà!*—a gesture. (7)

Thickening your draft helps you write with a fieldworker's lens. "Right down at the factual base, the hard rock, insofar as there is any," writes Geertz in another part of his essay on thick description, "we are already explicating: and worse, explicating explications. Winks upon winks upon winks" (9). The process of creating thick description reflects the process of triangulation, which we've discussed at various points in this book. Triangulating data is the heart of the fieldworking process, distinguishing it from library research or observational reportage. You must consider all the data in this process, even data that do not fit neatly into your plan. And this triangulation process is intimately connected to writing your text; as our colleague Thomas Newkirk says, "the scholarship is in the *rendering*." Turning a draft (your choices from "the scholarship") into a thick multilayered text ("the rendering"), you may want to use another triad of questions:

1. **What's going on here?**
2. **Where's the culture?**
3. **What's the story?**

First, "What's going on here?" asks descriptive questions of your data—about informants' rituals and routines, about how people and places interact. "Where's the culture?" refers to descriptions of language practices, place observations, background research, and artifacts you've gathered in the field to understand the group and its history. The final question, "What's the story?" includes a description of what we like to call *twin tales*—your informants' perspectives and also your own perspective on the research process.

To explore how these questions work to enhance a first draft, we'd like to introduce you to some excerpts from three students' studies. Although Yolanda, Heather, and Pappi drafted many versions of their fieldstudies, we highlight different strategies each writer used to answer each question—at a different point in the drafting process. As you read through these drafts, notice how each researcher has compiled and layered specific data for the writing.

What's Going on Here?

Yolanda Majors studied the culture of a hair salon, and as we write, she is in the process of publishing her study in a forthcoming collection of essays. As a middle-class African American student, she entered her fieldsite with many assumptions, positions, and tensions. She collected data over several months and tried out several different approaches in her drafts.

Yolanda's challenge as a writer was to present a complex fieldsite—a hair salon that describes itself as "multicultural" and that caters to both black and white customers in a small, predominately white city. Yolanda enters the culture carrying with her warm memories from having spent long days in a predominately black hair salon in a large city. She writes, "everyone knows that gettin' your hair done is, at least, a full-day affair and that the first half is reserved for waiting…. But that's OK, because when you finally emerge from the salon, and your butter is churned, whipped, and hopefully laid, no one can convince you that it was a waste of time."

Yolanda felt ambivalent about this salon from the outset; she hadn't wanted to have a different hair experience from the one she'd had since childhood. As a writer, she realized she needed to show this tension in her descriptions of the places and people at her fieldsite. In this section, "Multiple Mirrors," from one draft she called "Black Hair Don't Lie Flat," she shows how the white and black beauty cultures sit side by side as she contrasts names of beauty products, magazines, lighting, and furniture.

Notice that she quotes from her fieldnotes, letting the reader see her shock at finding a white hairdresser for herself. She does this to show her initial attitude, which showed up in her early fieldnotes when she refers to the stylist as "WG" ("white girl"), until she was comfortable enough with the situation to call her by her name, Darlene. In this draft, Yolanda tries to expose that tension by using both "Darlene" and "WG":

Before I could enter the salon, three framed posters of white models with some serious attitude wearing bright business suits greet me. I pause for a moment to take in these advertisements of female ideal before rolling my eyes at the posters and givin' the doorknob a strong yank. Inside the waiting area I am greeted by the motion bells of the door and two floor shelves stocked with plastic bottles of this, that, and the other.

"Hello?" Moving beneath a tracked spotlight, I make my way toward the L-shaped showcase in black lacquer, functioning as the receptionist desk minus the receptionist and doubling as a display case for a field of beauty products. Aveda, Tressa, Ecoly, brand names with top-dollar advertising in *Mademoiselle* and *Glamour* magazines. I couldn't say that this place was representing the repertoire of products in my bathroom cabinet—Dark and Lovely, African Royale, Cream of Nature—or of the black beauty shops and Korean-owned and -operated beauty-supply stores in the heart of my downtown.

"May I help you?" The "black-white girl" appeared from the back of the store, entering my experience like she owned part of it.

"Yes, I have an appointment with Darlene. My name is Yolanda." In an attempt to locate the best fly-girl-diva voice I had, I ended up sounding defensive.

"Ah right, have a seat, I'll tell her you're here." She looked at me with a raised eyebrow as if I were crazy, yet managed to give me a smirk of a smile.

> *"The WG (white girl) greeted me. Her hair was laid in golden black-girl spirals, and I think that she's wearing the same jeans and sweat shirt she had on the other day. Maybe it's a uniform. If it is, someone should tell her that it's not representing the wannabe chic decor in here"* (from my fieldnotes).
>
> As I scribbled these first thoughts down in my field journal, I realized that my hand was trembling with embarrassment.

In a different draft, Yolanda shifts her stance to focus on a more reflective theme. Here is an excerpt called "Room with a View," in which she describes the same place and the same event and yet focuses on different details. She moves in for a close-up using the salon's mirrors as a metaphor to illustrate the black and white tension. You'll see more subtle nuances as she writes herself into the scene through the metaphor of the mirrors. Rather than taking an observer stance here, she has become part, in her words, of the "cultural cloth":

> As I followed Darlene through a wide, doorless entryway, separating the front reception area of the salon from an adjacent room, I looked around hoping to find something familiar.....Taking a seat I was literally face to face with a reflection of myself, as I sat in Darlene's chair facing the large, black-framed glass. At first I thought it was unusual to have a mirror facing me directly. In all of my encounters with hair salons, mirrors have always been placed on either the side or in the back of the client's view. It made me uncomfortable at first, yet as I gazed into the picture in the glass, a picture of Darlene, her hands, my "nappy" head, our "talk" being pulled together in that mirror, I felt completely connected to the world around me, as if I too were a thread in this cultural cloth.

While Yolanda's two drafts are quite different, neither of them represents "better" or "worse" writing. Both drafts illustrate how one writer experiments with choices—of descriptive details, of how people and places interact, and of how the researcher fits into the scene. As you write and consider the question "What's going on here?" you will select details to recapture your experience—what you've seen, heard, and thought—and design a shape for conveying it to readers.

Where's the Culture?

When you ask the question "Where's the culture?" you are inquiring about the language and artifacts as well as the rituals and behaviors that help the group define its own culture to itself as well as to you. While this question overlaps with "What's going on here?" it focuses on more intricate details of the subculture that become apparent only after repeated visits to the fieldsite, deeper investigations, and accumulations of data. Only the actual informants in the culture can provide answers to this question.

Heather Kiger studied the subculture of bull riding and came to see over a period of time that the performance nature of this sport was much like her own experience with dance. "We are performers who love what we do and have our own fans and supporters who enjoy watching us," she writes. Initially, Heather did not feel this connection to the culture she studied; it took many drafts for her to understand bull riding enough to relate it to dancing. In the first of six drafts, Heather places herself on center stage, where she makes an ethnographic inventory of the artifacts and the rituals of bull riding. This early draft of her piece titled "Let's Go Let's Go Let's Rodeo" is rich in its observation of language, artifacts, and rituals. As you read the following excerpt, you can almost imagine what her fieldnotes contained:

> Stepping onto the grass and rocks from the van, I immediately smell something unpleasant. I turn to the left and figure it is coming from the bulls that are in a pen. I walk over to the gate and see that there are different sections of the pen. To the left of the pen is an area that has a white sign with red letters that says "Contestants Only." I see several contestants in the area, and most of them have women with them, probably wives or girlfriends, so I walk inside the gate. They all have bags with them, so I peek inside one and see that it contains gloves, a rope, a pair of jeans, a thick vest, a pair of cowboy boots, spurs, and a bottle of Tylenol. The contestants all have on jeans, tennis shoes or cowboy boots, a T-shirt, and a cowboy hat. They all have short hair, clean-shaven faces, and look to range in age from nineteen to twenty-six.
>
> I walk over to a section of bleachers next to the announcer's station, which is a low wooden platform with an overhead covering. Behind me is a very small white building with windows, and I can see trophies inside. On the platform are large speakers on each side, and the announcer is on a stool in the center holding a microphone. He is trying to get people to sign up for a game called bull ringo and an event called steer wrestling.

In this early draft, Heather catalogs the signs, the contestants, their clothing, their companions, the contents of their bags, and their physical surroundings. With this rich record of detail, Heather is able to move herself away from simply recording from her own point of view toward describing insiders in the culture. Heather has accomplished a difficult challenge in writing up fieldwork; she's written the first layer of details for herself, with herself as the main character looking at the culture. But in a later draft, a section of her study with the subheading "Man against Beast," Heather becomes able to shift her perspective away from herself to a multilayered description of one insider in the culture, along with the artifacts and rituals that **represent** the whole culture of bull riders:

> It is a Wednesday night, and he is riding down the road singing as loud as he can along with Skinnard on the radio, and his cowboy hat is lying

undisturbed on the dashboard. He has left all his troubles back at home, and riding is the only goal on his mind. His bag is packed and is in the back of the truck. When he gets to Creek Junction, his mind turns away from Skinnard and on to the main event of the night. He gets his bag and heads for the designated area. The audience is just starting to arrive, and Little Texas is blasting from the speakers, "You've got to kick a little." The concession stand is open and already packed with hungry fans.

Before he unpacks his bag, he roams the bullpens and hopes he draws a good one. He goes back to his bag and begins unpacking it by putting his chaps, vest, and rope around the fence. He takes his jeans out and goes to the bathroom to change. When he comes back, he is ready to rosin up his rope, the most important piece of equipment. He slips on his glove and brushes off the remaining dust and grit from the last bull ride, crumbles rosin in this gloved hand, and applies it to the bull rope. This helps him continue to have a good grip on the rope during the extremely bumpy ride. Boots and spurs are the next items to come out of the bag, and then he puts on his long-sleeved buttoned-up shirt. A few of his buddies have arrived, and they start up a bull-riding conversation while moving over to the guy who has the bulls' names to see which one he will ride tonight. His bull is Unforgiven. After they have gone, he returns to his bag, kneels, and begins praying that the ride will be a safe one and that he will walk away uninjured. The last items he puts on before the ride are his chaps and protective vest. The vest serves as the only real protection from the bull. He continues preparing for his ride by stretching out and warming up his legs and arms as a precaution against injury.

In this later draft, Heather works with the same details she used to form the earlier draft but has thickened her description to be more than a list. This time, she places her reader inside the bull-rider's culture, bringing it to life through one bull-rider's actions as he prepares for a ride. Instead of tentatively "peeking" inside a few riders' bags, for example, this time she describes a representative rider as he unpacks and changes into his bull-riding outfit—chaps, vest, and gloves. She gives us the bull's name (Unforgiven), and she shows the bull rider in a ritualistic prayer as he readies himself for his ride.

In an early draft, Heather mentions an intriguing activity in one phrase, "bull bingo." This turns out to be a common practice at bull-riding events, which assists her (and her informants) in defining the bull-riding culture. Later Heather expands it for her readers' understanding: "'Bull bingo,' I find out, is where people sign up to be put in a circle in the arena, and a bull is put in there with them. The bull comes charging at these people, and the last person to move wins a cash prize." Heather's choice of detail uncovers an important shared behavior for audiences in the bull-riding culture—people who gamble their personal safety, putting themselves at risk. But "bull bingo" was an unfamiliar term when she first heard it. For Heather, it needed explanation, and so it will for her readers. While it's an intriguing phrase, "bull bingo" alone would have no meaning for readers had Heather not explained it in her later draft. And because she did, we have the opportunity to see the culture as it plays out beyond the bull-riding ring and into its circle of fans. In answering the question "Where's the Culture?" Heather collected descriptions of language practices, observations of her site, and artifacts she gathered about the subculture of bull riders.

What's the Story?

Every field study has two stories, twin tales, to tell. One story is about the culture itself and what it means through the perspective of informants. The other is the story about you as the researcher and how you did the research. The story about your research process is what compositionist Ken Macrorie has long called the "I-Search Paper." While the story about the culture you're investigating is the critical one, the subplot of how you negotiated your entry, conducted your interviews, and collected other data is also part of your study.

Documentaries about "the making of the movie" offer an insider's look at how a finished film came about, and your story of your fieldwork offers your readers the same perspective. There is no formula for the balance between these twin tales; they form and inform a dialogue between self and other. Whatever way you choose to balance the twin tales, the power of narrative carries your essay to your reader. An important but difficult job of fieldwriting is to allow informants to tell a tale about their lives—and find a way to include yourself as the fieldworker telling the tale.

Pappi Tomas did a fieldstudy of an Irish tailor, Chipper, who owns a small shop. After Pappi gathered data on Chipper, he found himself overwhelmed with the piles of information he'd accumulated—a detailed map of the shop, his "jottings notebook," fieldnotes, a drafting notebook, a newspaper article about Chipper, Web research about the history of tailoring in Ireland, and Chipper's favorite novel about Irish life. Pappi also kept a set of what he called "underground scribblings" in which he explored his positions and identity in terms of "how he would mesh with Chipper and his shop." This writing shows Pappi's anxiety about being respectful to Chipper's words as his own data "balloons." He's understanding the delicate balance between his own researcher's tale and Chipper the tailor's story:

> Oh, but I had so much to work from. My jottings ballooned. My cassette tapes—which I began using after the first interview—suggested to me that there was too much gold pouring from Chipper's mouth to hold in my measly brainpan. They ballooned, too. And soon my "underground scribblings" contained several different drafts of the same material, plus recordings transcribed long after the fact, so that I was incorporating them into the drafting as I made my way through the essay—like laying a brick road and driving over it at the same time....
>
> When it came to drafting, I had good days and bad days as always. I began with "To find out what sort of tailor Chipper is, you might begin with

the walls," which from the start felt like the beginning of the essay. Yet somewhere midway, after I'd shared a draft in process, I was seriously unsure of how to enter this subject. Should it flow narratively? Was this impressionistic beginning forceful enough?

Even now I'm not sure if the voice I settled on is right for the material, or if I settled on a voice at all.... You see, I didn't want a journalistic piece.... I wanted to build a little poetry if I could into the story of Chipper, which of course did not need the likes of me to give it poetry. Chipper himself speaks a poetry all his own, and the extent to which I use his words in the essay shows how fond I am of them. But the interstices (which is how I like to think of my words in relation to his)—I wanted them to sing, too, if not in the same way. It was hard at times....

In his final essay, you'll notice how carefully Pappi integrates his data sources with his own voice and Chipper's. He transcribes and quotes carefully from his tape-recorded interviews, including his rendering of Chipper's speech to show that "Chipper himself speaks a poetry all his own." One of the ways Pappi achieves a seamlessness in his writing is to use "you" (the second-person pronoun), to invite his readers into his text and into Chipper's shop. He decided to use this rhetorical device, the use of "you," after many drafts. In this excerpt from the middle of his study, subtitled "The Cutter around the Corner," notice how Pappi crafts his voice by using twin tales:

"In the old days," Chipper begins, "there were no electrical machines. They were all just treadle." He talks to me now. "I have to turn me back on you now," he says, from the old green sewing machine, which sits in its table under a window against the wall. A "flat machine," he calls it, though it is anything but flat, with a long arching arm to accommodate bulky folds of fabric. A century-old Singer machine, its kind, in the trade, is used as much now as ever. "Of course whenever I went to England, you know, when I was a greenhorn, you know—never saw a power machine. Scared the bloody hell out a' me. I thought it was goin' to run up me arm, you know. And I didn't want to let meself down, you know, that I didn't know anything about a power machine."

A long time ago, that was and hard to imagine, when you watch him thread that machine—around and through and down, up, down. As smooth as wrapping thread around a spool; watch him slide the garment under the needle, lean forward in short, heavy bursts of drumming stitch, and watch him hold a conversation with you, greet a customer just come in, nudging, slanting, easing, spreading the folds through all the while. When you see all this, it is indeed a stretch of fancy to see him sitting there, decades ago, a greenhorn in Ireland, poised with belly aflutter.

Likewise a stretch it is when you watch him mark trousers with shaved chalk and ruler or watch him, number two thimble (thirteen on the American scale) in place, poke the needle through, yank to the side, then, like a firefly, dart up and out, pulling the thread taut, ready for the next stitch. These are the moments of consummate skill that I admire, that I yearn (as we all do, those of us who admire the practiced artist) to experience myself in some craft, be it shaping the curve of a sentence or molding the slope of a collar.

In the last sentence of this excerpt, Pappi connects the artistry and craftsmanship of writing to that of Chipper's tailoring. The idea of practice belongs to all craftspeople, artists, and sportspeople, who share an understanding of the long rehearsals that precede a final performance or product. The rehearsal process of writing is in the revision and the drafts. As we noted earlier in this chapter, many writers admit to the difficulty of disciplining themselves as they write, revise, write again, revise, write again, revise, and more. As Pappi was writing about Chipper's tailor shop, he needed to check his notes many times. Over the course of his visits to the tailor shop, Pappi went through the process of layering his data into his drafts. He changed his mind a lot, learned much about tailoring, and deepened his understanding about Chipper.

In all these excerpts from students' fieldwork, the three questions ("What's going on here?" "Where's the culture?" and "What's the story?") guided the writers' assembly of data. You also may have noticed their struggles to find a place to stand in the text, to construct a voice that would do justice to their data and to themselves as researchers. Their multiple drafts show you that there is no one way to present data, that all writers need to play around to discover a voice that works for them every time they do a writing project.

By now you know that you, as the researcher, are *not* the only character in your fieldwork story. Fieldwriting is multivocal, and you are responsible for other voices as well as your own. Like Yolanda, Heather, and Pappi, you'll want to pay attention to the issue of voice as you draft and redraft. Good fieldwriting allows informants to speak for themselves alongside the writer's cultural interpretations. So how the people talk in your final paper can reveal various relations of power among different people in the group you've studied, your relation to the group as a researcher, and the voices of outside authorities in secondary sources.

Listening to the Voices in Your Draft

BOX 31

by David Seitz, Wayne State University, Michigan

Purpose

Ethnographic writers strive to maintain the individual variations of voices from the fieldsite, allowing for differences of opinion and experience within the common values of the group. As **participant-observers**, their own voices in writing often shift between a cultural insider's and academic researcher's voice as necessary for the purposes of the writing. When ethnographic writers use the outside authority of secondary research, they do not want the voices of these sources to overpower either their informants' views or their own. Your final writing should both show and interpret the power relations between these various voices and allow them equal opportunity to interpret their **worldviews**. This difficult balance of power relations between voices is much easier to develop when you first visibly highlight the voices in your complete first draft.

Highlighting voices helps you hear them more clearly, making sure each remains distinct in terms of language use, what each communicates about the culture of the group, and the contexts for their statements. This activity may also help you better understand the way you represent your relationship with the informants in your fieldsite.

Activity

Highlight in different colors each of the following kinds of voices you can find in your present draft. After highlighting, use the questions about each kind of voice to reflect on your writing choices and strategies. Write a two- or three-paragraph response based on these reflections, and share your insights with a partner.

1. *Each voice from the fieldsite.* How do the similarities and differences in their voices show unity and tensions in the group or social structures?
2. *Your voice as cultural interpreter.* How does your voice compare to those you are researching? Do you speak in more than one voice in your draft? When are you speaking as insider? As outsider?
3. *Voices of secondary print and electronic sources.* Do they overpower the voices from the fieldsite or your own interpretations?

In your response, try to write about how you would want to revise based on your listening closely to these multiple voices: each voice from the fieldsite, your voice as cultural interpreter, and the voices of your sources.

Response

Angela Shaffer studied three young women who worked at a midsize natural history museum. The women operated the front desk and gift shop area, daily greeting customers of all ages, answering questions, selling gifts, and dealing with problem guests. Angela came to understand how the three employees worked together to create a group personality while calling on their individual strengths. Through their humor, informal games, and mutual support, they displayed their beliefs about work, friendship, and even their coworkers and supervisors. Angela wrote a reflective response to this exercise:

I found that I showed well the group dynamics of Laura, Allie, and Leigh when I described their talk and actions. It appeared they were just goofing off at work, but they were actually creating the open work atmosphere they wanted for their future careers—relaxed when possible, efficient when necessary. I opened my draft with their zip code game (where they try to guess the zip codes of incoming customers as an indication of their social class) to demonstrate their creativity and need to break the monotony using their intelligence.

Nevertheless, I could have developed more their individual voices, styles of talk, and humor along with my descriptions. I did, however, draw a scene with dialogue of Allie and Laura showing how they talk with each other compared with their talk with customers. In this moment, Allie and Laura teased each other about their intelligence as they worked over their daily crosswords but shifted to a more distant tone with customers in between their own conversation, never missing a beat between the two.

I now can see several places where I could have let my informants' voices help interpret their actions that I only described for them. In one area I describe Allie and Laura teasing Leigh, the youngest of the three, about her enthusiasm for waiting on customers. I need to show through Leigh's voice how wild she can get about that. Also, I contrast Allie's voice as she's dealing with irate customers with and without her coworkers to back her up. Although I show the difference in Allie's tone in each situation, I could also include Allie's voice interpreting her different approaches. Similarly, when I examined how they present a unified front when faced with their bosses' expectations and their coworkers' slacking off, I could have let them give their views about it.

Doing this exercise showed me the importance of separating my voice from those of my informants and all the institutional voices that surround the museum gift shop.

CULTURE ON THE PAGE: THE EXPERIENCE, RHETORIC, AND AESTHETICS OF REPRESENTATION

Taking a stand on the page involves making lots of narrative choices. How do you decide to combine your data? How will you integrate your informants' voices and perspectives with your own? How will you portray yourself, the others, their culture and yours, and the twin tales you're telling? And, above all, how will you keep your reader interested in reading your words about where you've been, what you've seen, and what you've thought about it all? The answers to these questions will rely on your own artistic choices as well as your experiments with words. In short, knowing the art and craft of writing will allow you to make writerly choices as you draft and revise.

We've developed three lists that encompass some of the most effective writing strategies available to fieldworkers, strategies that will bring life to your work—and bring your work to life. Table 8.1 identifies these experiential, rhetorical, and aesthetic strategies.

Table 8.1.   *Selected Strategies for Cultural Representation*

Experiential	Rhetorical	Aesthetic
Fieldnotes	Positionality	Metaphor and simile
Double-entry notes	Voice of the researcher	Sensory image
Research journals	Voice of the "other"	Concrete image
Interview transcripts	Point of view	Ethnopoetic notation
Photos and artifacts	Analytic section heads (subheads)	Spatial gaze
Notes on readings and other background sources	Analytic titles	

Experiential Strategies

You have many layers of data: fieldnotes, double-entry notes, notes from your background reading, and other fieldwork records like tapes and transcripts, photos and artifacts. We like to call this mass of field material **experiential**—firsthand accounts of your experience at specific times and in specific places. In your fieldwriting, you'll use this material to convince readers that *you were there*—that you saw the places, heard the people, and tried to interpret what they were doing.

Rhetorical Strategies

Another way to represent yourself and your informants originates with the **rhetorical choices** you make as a writer—choices of voice, purpose, and audience. As we mention in Chapter 2, our Western rhetorical tradition owes much to Aristotle's advice about effective communication—ethos, logos, and pathos. Composition scholars refer to similar basic principles when they teach effective written communication—voice, purpose, and audience.

As a fieldworker crafts a final written text using informants' words, background information, field experiences, and observations, she asks questions that help shape a rhetorical stance. These questions can help the fieldwriter determine her purpose and voice and think about the needs of her audience:

1. Whose views of this culture am I representing—mine, my informants', or background information? What is the balance among these sources?

2. How do I organize data? How can I include my informants' perspective or worldview? Through my own? Or through some theme from my data?

3. How am I representing my informants? What data do I use to re-create an informant on the page? Have I given my reader enough details to visualize or "hear" my informant?

4. What sense of place am I offering? What details of setting do I use to organize and locate what I saw? What data do I use to re-create this place? Will my readers feel as if they've been there with me?

5. What assumptions, positions, and tensions do I bring to my interpretations? Where did they come from? Will my reader know enough about me to understand them?

6. Would I offer my reader the same information if I presented it a different way? Could I shift point of view and tell a similar story?

A fieldwriter's answers to these questions can help guide the writing process. Creative options give us much rhetorical power as writers. Table 8.1 (p.448) offers a sample of rhetorical choices, many of which we've already discussed in this book. Not every strategy is useful for every study. Each setting, each culture, and each person suggest different rhetorical decisions about the chronology or the shape of the narrative. What fieldworkers actually experience governs the shape of the written text.

Aesthetic Strategies

Finally, the third column in Table 8.1 suggests that we must employ knowledge of the writer's craft as we choose artistic ways to represent what we've studied. Like good fiction or poetry, a well-written field study needs artful design to allow the reader in. Throughout this book, we've pointed out writers' conscious uses of **aesthetic** features. For example, Harvey DuMarce uses sensory description of his childhood home in Chapter 5—the buzz of crickets and the sound of his mother's soft voice, the contrast between the bright hot light outside her house and the cool shade inside the living room, the smell of the fry bread and steaming corn soup. In Chapter 6, Danling Fu uses simile when she describes silkworms as pets: "Our relationship with worms is like yours with cats and dogs." Her description of the worms themselves draws on imagery and simile: "thick as a little finger," "smaller than an ant," and "tastes like a peanut." She makes a comparison between the silkworm and Chinese workers when she says "Such a little body, so much hard work." She employs the metaphor of the silkworm to describe the whole life cycle: "We see how silk comes into our lives, not only how we wear it but how we live with it." And when we see how easily Danling's prose becomes poetry, we understand the effect her figurative language has in bringing her culture to the page.

CRAFTING A TEXT

In this section, we'd like to show how all these strategies come together for a writer using layer on layer of data to draft a text. The writer happens to be one of us—and her idea for this piece came initially because she had a conversation with the other one. Our example comes from Bonnie's research on a group of deaf teachers in a summer writing program. She hadn't intended to study these particular teachers, but after a midnight conversation with Elizabeth about deafness, she saw the opportunity to include this group of people in her study. (We explore this initial conversation in box 32 on p. 459) Bonnie's study of the deaf writing teachers turned into a seven-page "intertext" (a smallish chapter between larger ones) in her ethnographic book, *Composing a Culture: Inside a Summer Writing Program with High School Teachers*. In "Getting the Words Second Hand: Deaf People Can Do Everything—Except Hear," Bonnie uses many of the formal experiential, rhetorical, and aesthetic writing strategies we've introduced. As you read through this excerpt from her book, notice how she employs them. After the excerpt, we'll discuss how she made her choices.

Getting the Words Second Hand
Deaf People Can Do Everything—Except Hear
Bonnie S. Sunstein

"Everything you hear directly is what we hear second hand." As we sit in the lobby of Sackett Hall, Lee explains to a few of us how it is to be deaf in a hearing world. She and her colleagues, Ruth and Linda, live down the hall and I see them daily in Terry Moher's class with Therese and Dorothy. As temporary neighbors, we've shared food, drink, dorm woes, and writing. They are here with two other colleagues this summer from an English department at a high school for the deaf. As a hearing teacher who has spent a long professional lifetime in public schools, I learn much that I never knew about the languages, culture and politics of deafness.

The university has hired several free-lance sign interpreters for each day of the writing program. They are not always the same people. Every week there is a new crew of interpreters, probably because it is summer and many of them teach or go to school. Few of the rest of us know how to sign, but we can see there are differences in the interpreters' interpretations. Lee explains to me that there is American Sign Language (ASL), considered a language, and Signed English, a coding system. Each interpreter appears different as we watch, but, like translators, their job is to interpret spoken text as closely as possible. To an outsider, the interpreters are performers. As hearing observers, we enjoy watching the texts of our spoken words dance in their hands and on their faces. It adds a poetic dimension to the summer and some dramatic physical action to all our talk about writing. The language of Sign is an artful mix of letters, facial expressions, and gestures.

But the complexities are more than poetic for those who must rely on the interpreters' work for language. As in all languages, we discover, translation is not exact. It is a special verbal literacy that requires quick and careful thinking on the part of the hearing interpreter as well as the deaf recipient. I ask Lee if it's difficult to get oriented to so many different interpreters, and mention that I've noticed major differences in them. "Of course," she signs while her mouth forms the words, her oral English a bit blurry. "You are very observant." In this encounter, we talk about language and writing with a twist I hadn't considered.

On the lawn in front of the dorm, we lie in the bright sun together, pick at the grass, and talk about how crucial it is for all students to maintain the connection between reading and writing, especially those who are "at risk" with physical disabilities like deafness that block mainstream language acquisition. Lee and I watch each other's mouths carefully and we secure our notebooks under our legs. We do not need an interpreter. Occasionally, we need to write out a word that one of us doesn't understand.

Deaf Students Are Bilingual Interpreters

Lee shows me a record she keeps of her students' "malapropisms." Until now, I have not thought of her students as interpreters. To me, their approximations in using English written language are both amusing and poignant. They remind me of all teenagers as they pursue making their own sense of the adult world. But Lee's students' written words illustrate the extra job a deaf adolescent has as she interprets Sign into writing:

"Oh, thank gosh."
"A shovel slaps the snow."
"Going camping, I wear my pack-back."
"There was a terrible plane crush."
"It is time to clam down."
"When I went to my girlfriend's house, I rang the door bellring," and then we had an "argumen."
I put the words in "alphabetable order."
There is a "broadwalk at Ocean City."
I found a "secret passway."
"After the argument, my mouth was wild open."
"I had to go to the hospital to get an x-tray."
"The police arrived in a helicopper."
"The weather is short of warm."
"The dance was wowderful, fan-static."
"I ran the lawnmotor."
"I saw a hummerbird."

In each of these little miscues, there is inherent logic and figurative language. The words illustrate creative understanding of meaning, as well as contextual interpretation. "Wild-open" mouths and beachside "broadwalks," weather that is "short of warm," and crushed planes and police in helicoppers conjure up lucid poetic imagery. We must understand that deaf students are bilingual, and, Lee believes, given an environment rich with reading and writing, they thrive.

We Read with Our Eyes, of Course

Lee is deeply aware of the unnecessary disenfranchisement her students suffer. She and her colleagues tell many stories to support this position. Because her school is a demonstration school in a large city, her students are often "on display" to administrators, politicians, foreign diplomats, and other interested people. The visitors are not always enlightened. She incorporates one of those stories into her own writing about disability and power. In her paper, Lee writes:

> …This spring, one of my classes was visited by a South American dignitary from a country where educating deaf people is not the norm. My students had just finished reading *Sounds of Silence*, a young adult novel by Marilyn Levy that includes a mainstreamed deaf teen as a major character. The dignitary watched with visible awe as the class worked individually and in teams writing an additional chapter to the novel, drafting invitations for the character to come to our school and experience the Deaf culture the students themselves enjoyed.
>
> Our visitor could suppress her confusion no longer. "You mean these deaf students have all READ this book? But how?"
>
> Julie, a junior, confidently stated what was to her the obvious. "With our eyes, of course." And Julie was perfectly correct….

Lee's story illustrates a moment that is at once embarrassing and triumphant. As I see it, this is a story of all marginalized populations in school: the foreign language speaker, the ghetto dialect speaker, the person who is "educable mentally retarded" or physically handicapped. Like Julie and her classmates, our marginalized students deserve *more* fully connected language opportunities in school, *not fewer*. A rich mix of reading, writing, speaking, and listening in the company of other English language users is critical for their literacy. This means reading and writing literature, not executing grammar worksheets. (Sunstein in Stires, ed., 1991)

Deafness as Deficit: A Self-Fulfilling Prophecy

Lee and I discuss the "deficit model" thinking that we see in curricula for students who carry the label "disabled." As long as schools see human difference as deficit, difference will always be sorted out. On the other hand, schools *could* view difference as opportunity, we agree. The mere act of living in the mainstream demands that "disabled" students develop extra abilities: interpreting and signing, jumping comfortably between two national or ethnic cultures, or understanding the biology of a physical or mental handicap. Students with difference have extra information to contribute.

"If our deaf students cannot read and write literature on a level with their hearing peers," Lee writes, "it may very well be that they've never been exposed to real literature at all.... Too long, we have been making deficit assumptions and spoon feeding (sometimes force-feeding) our students with a conceptual mash unable to create or sustain intellectual or linguistic growth. By thinking deaf students incapable of reading and writing real literature, we've created a self-fulfilling prophecy.... Reading and writing are power, and empowered students are hooked for life on their own learning."

It is not any lack of intelligence that prevents a student from fuller literacy; it is often the self-fulfilling prophecy of the "disability testing and remediation" she must endure. If these students are given little pieces of language to exercise their broken parts, they will never have a chance to use English whole, or to see how others use it. As these teachers experience reading and writing for themselves here this summer, they rethink their own teaching practices and reflect on their teacher-training histories. Lee's colleague Ruth writes:

> Teacher training programs set the pace for the field of education of the deaf. When I began teaching deaf children over twenty years ago, I took classes towards a certificate that showed I understood deafness and how it made deaf children different...in Language Development I learned ASL was to be ignored...in Speech and Speechreading the hearing professor was embarrassed about having deaf students in his class...in Audiology we learned about how language development is affected by degree of hearing loss...in Psychology of Deafness, we learned certain personal traits deaf children have, and that the teachers were martyrs...there was rarely a course in American Sign Language, the language that most deaf people used...but there were newly developed systems of signs to help children learn English...

Ruth explains that many educators of deaf students still have a clinical, pathological point of view. As a deaf person herself, she writes "We prefer to be seen as a culture, with a rich heritage passed on by children of deaf parents.... It will be a long time before my rage is completely gone. Like Toni Morrison said of black people, 'historically, we were seldom invited to participate in the discourse even when we were its topic'" (Morrison in Zinsser, 91).

Language Forbidden

Although Lee grew up struggling as a deaf child in a hearing home, her colleagues Ruth and Linda are among the 5 percent of the deaf population who come from deaf families. The deaf child born into a deaf family has a distinct advantage in literacy, Linda tells me, a home environment rich in language.

Their "home language" is American Sign, and English is a learned second language. Linda's parents and grandfather signed stories to her when she was a child, creating a context for learning much the same as in any privileged home. But for deaf children like Lee born into hearing homes, there is minimal communication.

Linda observes that Don Murray's term "inner voice" was a new idea to her (1990). She tests herself. "I noticed that I *do* have a 'deaf voice' based on the dreams I dream. The characters in my dreams have conversations in ASL. With the interpreters, the ones who signed in ASL, I received the messages very comfortably and directly whereas those who signed in Signed English, I had to translate into ASL—especially the phrases, idiomatic expressions, sounds, and puns, and then into English." Linda writes:

> For most of us whose first language is ASL, writing is a laborious chore. We have to translate our native language into English and then put it down on paper. In order to write well, we must read a lot, so we can switch our language into English comfortably when we write.

One of Linda's pieces during the three weeks is a poem called "The Forbidden Language." It details her "seven solid years of battle" during the nineteen-fifties, in a residential school in which ASL was prohibited. At night in the dorms, one student would stand in the doorway, watching for the housemother: "A circle of kids would watch another kid, the storyteller, signing, secretly" and then they would scatter when the housemother came. Although they were punished severely, they "dared to continue the risks." The scars on her sister's thigh clued Linda's parents to the hairbrush beatings they received for signing stories together. A formal, legally filed grievance and a subsequent victory placed Linda and her sister in a different school where signing was respected. Had her parents not been deaf, Linda and her sister and their classmates might have stayed there for more years, deprived of their native language.

A Bond of Stars: The Plastic Spots of Difference

On one night during the first week, Lee, Ruth, and Linda sit in a circle on Lee's bed in their pajamas, eating candy, drinking Diet Coke, joking, and reading one another's writing. Linda is wearing her favorite tee shirt. It is black with white letters across the chest: "Deaf People Can Do Everything—Except Hear." Lee's computer is printing out her latest piece of writing, her cloth-bound journal sits inside her folded legs, and the floor is messy with wads of discarded drafts. They are signing wildly to each other when I walk by.

Ruth invites me to take a walk down the hall with her. She has just discovered a planetarium in her room. She points upward and then turns off the light. The ceiling is covered with plastic stars, affixed in configurations that reproduce a few constellations. They don't twinkle; they glow plastic yellow-green over our heads. We can't talk in the dark, but we jab each other and laugh together at the hidden legacy from a recent college student.

When she turns the light on, the stars disappear. It is a fitting metaphor for the shared literacies we are all experiencing this summer. When the lights go on, the eerie spots of plastic difference disappear. But they become a bond between us, the knowledge that each of us has a secret in the dark worth exploring together. Whether we get the words "straight" or "second hand," it is in talking, reading, and writing about those differences that we can celebrate our human abilities to communicate.

Works Cited

Sunstein, Bonnie S. "Notes from the Kitchen Table: Disabilities and Disconnections." *With Promise: Redefining Reading and Writing for Special Students.* Ed. Susan Stires. Portsmouth: Heinemann, 1989.

Zinsser, William, ed. *Inventing the Truth: The Art and Craft of Memoir.* 2nd ed. New York: Houghton, 1995.

Bonnie's dilemma as a researcher was that over time, she had collected mounds of different kinds of data about the deaf subculture:

- Journal entries from conversations with Elizabeth (who has been hard-of-hearing since childhood), Terry Moher (the deaf teachers' hearing instructor), and the interpreters who were in their daily writing class,

- Observations and fieldnotes about the interpreters in the classroom and public readings,

- Observations and fieldnotes about the three informants in the dorm and in the classroom,

- Taped interviews with each informant, including histories about deafness in their own schooling and family lives and accounts of their teaching,

- Written artifacts from each informant—letters, poetry, informal narratives, and formal essays,

- Photos of the three informants in their dorm rooms, in their classroom, and at summer program activities, such as picnics, readings, and receptions,

- Background source material on the difference between American Sign Language and Signed English, as well as the politics of deafness, and

- Background source material about many kinds of marginalized students in schools.

As she surveyed her mass of data, Bonnie at first had no idea how she would present the three separate and very different stories from her deaf informants, Lee, Ruth, and Linda. They were not the main informants of her study, so they couldn't take "center stage." Nevertheless, she thought of many possibilities: Offering three separate case studies, one about each informant? Writing a chronological account of her significant encounters with every informant throughout the three weeks of the summer writing program? Choosing to show how they entered into the life of the dorm, the tenor of the classroom, and the program's shared events? Bonnie saw that she had enough data to organize her text in any of these ways, but at this point in her project, she wanted to think some more about her audience—which would consist of other teachers of writing.

To begin writing, she asked herself, "What do I want my readers to learn about these teachers and this subculture?" Her decision, interestingly enough, came from two insider clues. One was Linda's T-shirt, which announced "Deaf People Can Do Everything—Except Hear" and turned into the title for the intertext. The other was a quote from Lee in a transcript, "Everything you hear directly is what we hear secondhand," which became Bonnie's lead sentence. Bonnie's decision about how to begin to offer her data to her reader came from what she had learned about the subculture itself—in the very language of her informants.

Experiential Writing Strategies in "Getting the Words Second Hand"

To tell her own researcher's story with the deaf teachers (her part of the twin tales), Bonnie chose data from her fieldnotes that would show the reader how she worked with the deaf teachers, meeting them in their dorms, classes, and outside. She didn't bother with the midnight conversation she'd had in Elizabeth's car (see Box 32). It had been an important catalyst for Bonnie, but it was not relevant for the purposes of the three informants' stories. To help readers believe in the research, it's important that fieldworkers disclose the kinds of relationships they form with their informants. Bonnie does this in the scene on the lawn in which she and Lee communicate without an interpreter. And Bonnie's fieldworking methods come in again in the final scene where, turning out the lights and looking at the plastic ceiling constellations in Ruth's room, she illustrates how she's been invited into the lives of those she's researched. Depicting the actual fieldworking "in process" develops the narrative voice that allows a reader to participate in the story a researcher has to tell.

Rhetorical Strategies in "Getting the Words Second Hand"

Bonnie organized her writing around five main themes or ideas about the deaf that she used as subheadings. Both the title, "Getting the Words Second Hand: Deaf People Can Do Everything—Except Hear," and the five section headings guide her readers through the text without interrupting the narrative flow:

- Deaf Students Are Bilingual Interpreters
- We Read with Our Eyes, of Course

- Deafness as Deficit: A Self-Fulfilling Prophecy
- Language Forbidden
- A Bond of Stars: The Plastic Spots of Difference

Subheadings serve a rhetorical purpose for a fieldwriter; they stand as a kind of outline for the whole. And for readers, these headings quietly signal the important themes that the text will develop. In that sense, the headings themselves help the reader understand your analysis. We'll share more about subheadings in the FieldWriting section at the end of this chapter.

Bonnie made other rhetorical choices for her intertext. Since the book in which it appeared, *Composing a Culture,* is about a summer writing program for teachers, she chose to include the teacher's stories, written, signed, and spoken—as they wrote and told them. She was careful to include as much of the teachers' writing as possible, to achieve a balance between her voice and the voices of the teachers she studied.

She employed still another rhetorical strategy in this piece of writing: background source material about American Sign Language and Signed English. Bonnie hadn't previously known much about sign languages, but after working with these teachers and reading books and articles about the deaf, she wove basic informative material into her text. In the same way, she included information about inclusion and exclusion of marginalized populations in school to give force—theoretical power—to her unstated argument that the deaf are treated unfairly both in and out of schools.

Aesthetic Strategies in "Getting the Words Second Hand"

Writers cannot tell feelings to their readers; they must show the feelings instead. Well-chosen imagery and careful use of aesthetic or poetic devices are not extraneous details. Rather, they can sensitize a reader toward a point of view, an argument, or an idea. For the purposes of fieldwriting, researchers draw on the same aesthetic strategies that all writers use to elicit strong emotional responses from their readers.

The major but subtle metaphor Bonnie evokes in this short piece is that of dance—an idea that came from her earliest talk with Elizabeth, when Bonnie had said the interpreters seemed to be "dancing" words with their hands. So she calls on this metaphor to show how she begins to see sign language as not just physical motion but "an artful mix of letters, facial expressions, and gestures." And just as dance does not translate directly into words, sign language is not an exact translation either. Bonnie learns, with the help of Lee, Ruth, Linda, and the interpreters, that there are both gains and losses in the translation process.

Another metaphor she employs is the plastic stars in Ruth's room. These symbolize how Bonnie began her relationship with the teachers—separated from them by "eerie spots of plastic difference." In fact the differences between the deaf and hearing are important and ever-present, but when Ruth shares the secret of the stars by turning off the lights, chuckling with Bonnie as a friend and fellow teacher, the differences disappear. The metaphor, while somewhat schmaltzy, really did represent Bonnie's emotional response to working with deaf teachers.

THINKING ABOUT LINKING

When you make choices about writing your fieldwork essay, much of your drafting process involves imagining what a reader needs to know. As Bonnie's drafting process and her finished piece have shown, your experiential, rhetorical, and aesthetic choices relate to a sense of your audience. Imagining your readers as you revise is often a difficult task. We've both had many students who suggest that in most of their writing experiences, the reader is really the teacher, and when confronted with a real reader—or an assignment with a purpose other than obtaining a grade—writing is almost an exercise in fantasy. We agree that such is often the case. But fieldwork studies will be interesting to readers both inside and outside the cultures you study. And these days, with the kinds of publications available to all of us, we're changing our notions of what publishing means. The term *publishing* really means "making writing public," and in the twenty-first century we have many more options for writing publicly than we've had before. Novelist Stephen King recently demonstrated how large his audience really is when he wrote his first online novel. The popularity of "zines" comes from how easily and inexpensively they are published and distributed both on the Web and on the street. Underground publishing, in all historical eras, has always been a way that writers can get their work out to a selected audience—and often effect political and cultural change as a result.

So imagining a reader—whether you do it as part of your revision process to find out what ideas and details need more explanation or as part of your design—is critical. Lifetime professional writers often consider the nature and amount of their readership. Christopher ("Chip") Scanlan is a seasoned journalist who has given up writing for a newspaper to teach other journalists. Now that he writes online, Chip recognizes the much larger possibilities he has for readership. "For twenty-two years," he writes, "I had access to an audience at the user end of a printing press. On a good day, my first stories might find their way to readers of the *Milford Citizen* in Connecticut (circulation 6,000 daily, 7,000 Sunday). By 1994, the last pieces I wrote as a national correspondent in the Washington Bureau of Knight-Ridder Newspapers went out to more than twenty million subscribers to the company's twenty-eight dailies and more than 250 other news outlets. Giving up that access had been one of the few downsides of leaving daily journalism until I began writing online."

In his online article "Writing Online Rocks," Chip recognizes the potential power of a much larger world readership online. He mentions in the article that an Internet survey would tag his potential online audience ("world reach") at 275 million or more. But the number of potential readers is not nearly as important to him as the potential diversity of readers' interests. Chip remembers a motto from the 1970s that was emblazoned on stickers all over the news bureau where he worked, and even in its restrooms. The motto was simply "Think Pictures." Now, he writes, "The byword for writing journalism online should be 'Think Links.'" He discusses the relationship between computer links and potential audience:

> Good writing requires great reporting, an overabundance of information. But like the iceberg that doomed the *Titanic*, the power of solid reporting resides below the surface with only the tip revealing the most compelling quotes, examples, and observations. Too often, writers sink their stories with information they can't bear to part with even if it's not relevant ("But I spent three hours interviewing that Deputy Assistant Commissioner of Public Information!").
>
> Links allow you to add content without interfering with the flow of your story. For instance, in "My Cancer Time Bomb," an essay I wrote for Salon.com about the hazards of childhood smoking, I was able to link directly to an abstract of the study that prompted the piece. Readers didn't have to rely solely on my interpretation. In my "Turning Fifty" piece, I referred to a cool life expectancy calculator online so that readers, with a single click, could figure their own lifespan....
>
> Feedback from readers is the best part of online writing. Perhaps because the stories I've written so far have been personal essays, I think of these readers as kindred spirits. They share their lives, their thoughts, their support and advice.

All writers need response, even online writers like Chip Scanlan.

Sharing Data: Partners in Revision

B
O
X
32

Purpose

We believe that all researchers should find collaborative partners, people with whom to share their research plans and talk through the next stage of their projects. All fieldworkers need to invite an interested "other" to help question and talk through their thinking. At different places in this book, especially in the boxes and Research Portfolio sections, we've indicated different ways to use talk to clarify, expand, and reflect on fieldwork projects:

- Portfolio partners to talk over fieldnotes, transcripts, and other data,
- Small groups to share drafts in progress and portfolios as they illustrate your processes,

- Artifact exchanges to understand the cultural objects gathered from the research site,
- Paired reading responses to exchange ideas about readings and background research, and
- Collaborative exercises to learn with another fieldworker about the research process.

Conversation, even casual talk, has power. In this activity, you will see how talk generates both further thinking and further text.

Action

Meet with your research partner, and share some data together. Try choosing something you're feeling unclear or uncertain about. Read your partner's freewriting, look at her fieldnotes or artifacts, and have a conversation. After talking, write again, this time about your own data.

Response

One of our own projects began with just hanging out, sitting in Elizabeth's stuffy gray Dodge Caravan. It was a casual conversation, late on a humid summer night. Bonnie was collecting data about teachers in a summer writing program in which Elizabeth was teaching. Worried about her research, Bonnie blurted out a long monologue. "I'm not seeing anything interesting," she whined. "I just don't know what to focus on, and I'm taking notes on everything. It feels like nothing. I'm not getting any sleep, and it's taking up all my time."

"Oh, I'll bet you are finding interesting things," Elizabeth reassured her. "You just don't know it yet. You're taking fieldnotes, right? All data is something. Tell me what you're seeing." Giving Bonnie no chance to answer, Elizabeth changed the subject. "Hey, how are those deaf teachers doing in Terry's class? Did the interpreters show up today?" Our colleague Terry Moher was teaching a class of high school teachers, three of whom were deaf and taught at an urban high school for the deaf.

"Oh yeah, they're there. And it's really neat to watch the interpreters. Their movements are so expressive—sort of like dancers. Wish I understood what they're doing. Terry was rattled at first by too many extra people in the class—me as researcher and two interpreters at all times. She's got twenty-seven high school teachers in that group now, and she's really enjoying them. But I'm not studying the deaf teachers anyway. Or their interpreters. It just wasn't in my plan."

Ignoring Bonnie's plan, Elizabeth suggested, "So if you want to understand them, why don't you interview them? That's interesting! Why don't you pay more attention to what's happening with the deaf teachers? How are they fitting in? Do they have a chance to talk about their deaf students? These teachers probably have something important to teach us about literacy. You should know that. You're interested in marginalized groups."

Bonnie listened, still wanting to follow her "plan." But she was eager to talk through her anxiety with her friend. Elizabeth continued: "You know, I've always stayed away from deaf people. They kind of scare me because I've been 'hard of hearing' all my life and I'm afraid as I get older, I'll become even more deaf than I already am. Wearing a hearing aid hasn't made me any more sympathetic. But I've really become interested after watching the interpreters at the poetry reading yesterday. How is sign language a language? What kind of translation processes do the interpreters go through? Would I be an entirely different thinker if I had signed all my life instead of talked?"

Elizabeth was really talking to herself, but it made Bonnie think about those three teachers who had not been in her original plans for interviewing. Aloud she replied, "Well, maybe I should take some more notes. We're staying in the same dorm, and last night they bought a dozen donuts and we ate them in the lounge. They all read lips, just like you do sometimes." This brief talk was the beginning of a theme that emerged in Bonnie's research and eventually became part of her full-length study of the writing program that summer. The conversation about the deaf continued throughout the summer in both planned and unplanned ways. Talking to Elizabeth helped Bonnie clarify what she was learning about the culture of the deaf.

At the beginning of her project, Bonnie's collaborative conversation with Elizabeth took her off-course into surprising but important new directions. When we discuss our plans with an "other," we can hear the "self" aloud— which is a different process than thinking alone. Informal conversation often encourages us to stretch, shift, or refashion our plans. Even if we make no changes at all, talk clarifies our thoughts as we shape them into words for another person.

For her project, Bonnie kept a researcher's journal as she studied the summer writing program for teachers. Because the program lasted only three weeks, she disciplined herself to keep detailed fieldnotes, and nightly she reflected on them in her researcher's journal, which she kept as a separate file on her computer. Here are some excerpts from her researcher's journal that very summer night as she was beginning to change her plan:

Memo 7/21/90
    1:25 am
    I feel guilty because I took off two hours from collecting data. Anyway, at midnight, I talked with Eliz in her car, in the driveway. She was so encouraging—said "Bonnie, you can't fail at this. There's no way to fail. You

have great stuff. It's all in how you organize it." Last nite they brought donuts and we sat in the lounge and talked about deaf teachers teaching English to deaf kids. I love watching the interpreters, seeing L, R, and L make strong statements to their class of "hearing" others. Bet they've got a lot to say, and "reading" how they see this experience might tell me a lot about others' experiences too. But I didn't plan to do it. I have enough to do. Maybe I need another year to do more research. These deaf women are really teaching me a lot. Rats! I just don't know enough about it.

But Bonnie knew more than she realized. And she added to her knowledge with more research. Bonnie's journal writing allowed her to trace back her thinking and offered important details—talk and observations—that she used later in her finished text.

REVISING FOR A READER

As we've mentioned so many times in *FieldWorking*, whether a researcher can successfully bring the lives of different cultures onto a page depends very much on how well that fieldworker writes. We agree with writer E. M. Forster's comment, "How do I know what I think until I see what I say?" Research leads to writing, writing leads to reflection and revision of thought—which leads you then into more sharpened research, new reflections, and then more writing. As we've shown in this chapter, detailing your experience with your site, layering and blending your personal tale with the tales of the members of your chosen subculture, and offering your writing to an audience requires revision. You reach your goal through many thoughtful drafts.

We want to share with you a voice whose work has guided our work as long as we've been writing teachers, as well as guided us throughout this chapter. Don Murray is a composition scholar who writes about both risk-taking and rewards involved in the revision process. His attention to revision has helped student and professional writers and writing teachers for the past four decades. Here's a short piece he calls "Some Notes on Revision," which he first presented in a writing class.

Some Notes on Revision
Donald M. Murray

February 15, 1995

- Revision is not failure but opportunity. It is an essential part of the process of thinking that produces a series of drafts that clarify and communicate significant meaning to a reader. Writing is not thought reported but the act of thinking itself.

> The artist Philip Baxter: "I don't paint what I see, I see what I paint."
>
> Murray: "I don't write what I know, I know what I write."
>
> John Kenneth Galbraith: "There are days when the result is so bad that no fewer than five revisions are required. However, when I'm greatly inspired, only four revisions are needed before, as I've often said, I put in that note of spontaneity which even my meanest critics concede."
>
> Neil Simon: "Rewriting is when playwriting really gets to be fun. In baseball you only get three swings and you're out. In rewriting, you get almost as many swings as you want and you know, sooner or later, you'll hit the ball."
>
> Bernard Malamud: "I love the flowers of afterthought."

■ Revision begins before the first draft when writers talk to themselves, make notes, begin to draft in their head and on the screen.

> Wallace Stevens: "The tongue is an eye."

■ Find the edge. Revision is first of all a search for the central tension, the knot, the conflict, the intersection, the questions, the news, the contradiction, the surprise that will involve the reader in the draft.

■ Do not look first for error. Look for what works, develop the strengths. Ironically, the strengths of the draft are often found in the failures, in the places where the writing is new, awkward, not yet clear because the writer has not written it before.

■ Start as near the end as possible. No background information before the draft really begins. Weave in background material when the reader needs it. Often we write our way toward the subject. It is scaffolding similar to the staging we construct to put up a building. It should be taken down before the text is shown to a reader.

■ Revision is fun because of the surprise. The draft teaches us and we are surprised by what we didn't know we knew.

> Saul Bellow: "I'm happy when the revisions are big. I'm not speaking of stylistic revisions, but of revisions in my own understanding."

■ There is a logical sequence to revision:

Message: What do I have to say?
Order: How can I say it?
Develop: What does the reader need to know?
Voice: What is the voice of the draft?

- Write for yourself, *then* your reader.
- Write and edit out loud. Listen to your voice and tune it to the meaning, purpose, and audience of the draft.
- Enter the work. Work within the evolving draft, taking instruction from the evolving work. Enjoy the gift of concentration.

    Bernard Malamud: "If it is winter in the book, spring surprises me when I look up."

- Cut what can be cut. Everything must advance the evolving meaning.

    Kurt Vonnegut, Jr.: "Don't put anything in a story that does not reveal character or advance the action."

- Develop. Answer the reader's questions in the order they will be asked with specific, accurate information.

    John Kenneth Galbraith: "I would want to tell my students of a point strongly pressed, if my memory serves, by Shaw. He once said that as he grew older, be became less and less interested in theory, more and more interested in information. The temptation in writing is just reversed. Nothing is so hard to come by as a new and interesting fact. Nothing so easy on the feet as a generalization."

- When do you stop revising? On deadline or when there are no more surprises as you read and edit the draft.
- The effect on the writer of revision—re-seeing, re-feeling, re-thinking—is powerful.

    E. L. Doctorow: "Everytime you compose a book your composition of yourself is at risk. You put yourself further away from whatever is comfortable to you or you feel at home with. Writing is a lifetime act of self-displacement."
    Don DeLillo: "I think after a while a writer can begin to know himself through his language. He sees someone or something reflected back at him from these constructions. Over the years it's possible for a writer to shape himself as a human being through the language he uses. I think written language, fiction, goes that deep. He not only sees himself but begins to make himself or remake himself."

As we've suggested, there is no formula for revision. How to revise depends on the demands of each draft you've written. So Murray's notes are just that, musings about the process from his perspective and that of other writers. Murray has been collecting writers' quotes for decades and likes to include perspectives from creators in other media. In this short piece, Murray represents revision as play and surprise. His advice about revising includes locating tensions, conflicts, and contradictions in a draft. He tells writers to develop material and to cut it. He suggests reading your work aloud and talking to others about your writing.

Murray never sees revision as a failure or punishment, although many students' early experience is a confusion of editing and revising or simply the fear of having words judged just as they hit the paper for the first time. One of Elizabeth's students, a reluctant reviser, described his negative attitude toward rewriting this way: "If you bang a nail in once, why would you want to take it out and bang it back in again?" Murray is eager to remove that nail and examine it before he pounds it back in. Revision, he's taught us, is a way to gain energy and insight about your topic—far before you commit it to a final polished piece of writing. And it's also a way to gain insights about your self and your writing, since as we revise, we reflect on the meaning of our work—and the way we figured it out. Under the most generous of circumstances, revision can become a way of remaking the self in the process of remaking a text.

THE RESEARCH PORTFOLIO: ONE-PAGE ANALYSIS AND ANNOTATED TABLE OF CONTENTS

You may think at this point that your portfolio resembles a souvenir of your research project. Of course, it's helped you sort through important data and see the array of materials you've used. We hope it's assisted you, too, with your analysis. By capturing your process as you go, we hope your portfolio has offered you insights as you've put more things in, taken things out, and sorted through what's there.

Students sometimes wonder (cynically, as opposed to naïvely, at this point, we hope) about the difference between a scrapbook and a portfolio. A scrapbook, as some of us like to say, is a "pasted down" moment in time. But a portfolio is its opposite: it is a shifting document of your multiple processes of learning, constantly changing as you continue to learn about your research site.

You and your teacher may appreciate what the portfolio's done for your project but perhaps observe some deeper dilemmas: "Okay, okay, we love portfolios but can't afford a utility vehicle to haul them around." "Yeah, I tried it for a while. The more attached I get to my portfolio, the less I want to turn it in. And I might not get it back." "If I ever want to make a webpage about my research site, I'd use most of what's in my portfolio, and now I won't have it because I turned it in." "I don't want a grade on this portfolio. It shows the process of my work, not the product."

Your research portfolio has been a critical part of your fieldwork project— your research assistant, in a way. Although you've shared it with groups and classroom colleagues and even with the people at your research site, you'd hope your teacher could look at every page of your research portfolio, each time it's changed. And the same for every other student researcher. But you also know that's an unrealistic expectation for yourself and for your teacher.

Since our students have had these problems, we've tried to develop a few shortcuts. Although they cannot offer the full impact of a real portfolio (or a research webpage), these shortcuts make it possible for you to include your portfolio as part of your finished work. Your teacher may choose to grade it as part of your research project or allow you to choose pieces from your portfolio to submit for a grade. Everyone's strategy—for portfolio-keeping, for fieldworking, for teaching, for learning, and for grading within an institution's curriculum—is different.

The most important strategy we've developed for portfolios is a simple double strategy. It requires two pieces of paper (well, two parts—and sometimes more than two sheets of paper). Several times each semester, our students submit these two items:

- *An annotated table of contents* made from a list of the artifacts in the portfolio at that time, along with annotations or explanations in short sentences or phrases (taken from the stick-on notes, "reflective windows," "captions," or "thought balloons") to accompany each item. Organizing and reorganizing your portfolio, you've probably begun to see how the items cluster into units. You might organize them chronologically at first or according to type of data. But as you begin to analyze your data, you'll most likely decide that you want to reorganize your portfolio according to the themes that will eventually be the subheadings of your written study (for more on subheadings, see pp. 468–70).

- *A one-page analysis* of the portfolio's current contents (a "portfolio letter," "one-pager," "reflective commentary"). This one-page analysis offers you an opportunity to explore your current ideas about the overall themes in your research: connections between items, between sites and informants, between past and present, between yourself and the people you've met, between your current materials and the writing or organizational goals you still want to meet.

With these two documents summarizing what's in your portfolio, you can get a clearer picture of your research and its progress. Of course, like much in our lives, there's no substitute for the real thing; the strategy is merely to take a snapshot of the rich and textured living research you've experienced. Nevertheless, during regular class data-sharing and writing sessions, offering this "snapshot" of your portfolio gives your teacher and your research partners a chance to view and record one another's emerging body of work several times during a research semester.

And so in this section, we offer you a two-part sample—an annotated table of contents and a reflective analysis of those contents—from Pappi Tomas's fieldwork project (see p. 443). No, these are not the real thing. They're missing the colors, the textures, and the "unflat" surprises of a real portfolio or research website. But samples like these offer a good way to see the essence of portfolios, peruse researchers' works, and learn a lot about fieldworkers.

Portfolio Table of Contents for "The Cutter around the Corner"

Pappi Tomas

1. Map of the shop
2. Photo of the walls
3. Explorations of my subjective positions exercise: age, my vision of the tailor, my identity as a university student and how it would mesh with him in the shop
4. Jottings notebook/fieldnotes: photocopied samples
5. Sample fieldnotes written up
6. Underground scribblings notebook: whole
7. Article from local magazine
8. A book, *Michael Joe: A Novel of Irish Life,* by William C. Murray, one of Chipper's favorite writers, which I decided to read for the local color, the feel of an Irish village
9. Drafting notebook: in which I drafted when I wasn't using a computer when I had an idea for a passage wherever I was

Portfolio Commentary: "Like Laying a Brick Road and Driving over It at the Same Time"

Pappi Tomas

I am glad I approached the research for this project using a portfolio as an organizing tool. I have to say, though, that the portfolio, physical object that it was, did not help me so much as the various notebooks I designated for this or that purpose. But the portfolio helped me organize big ideas and investigate hunches, getting themes to come out. And I guess that was a bigger help than I realized while I was keeping the notebooks straight. The hardest thing was trying to focus myself thematically. I didn't want a this, then this, then this kind of patchwork fieldwork, though that is exactly what I started with.

First the walls of the tailor shop, then the tables, then Chipper's face, Chipper's walk, Chipper's talk. I did have some ideas from the start (that is, from the start of the drafting process)—ideas of what themes I saw and what would make for an interesting essay. I wanted to present Chipper and his shop in a way that would appeal to a range of readers. I'm not sure I succeeded. Still, I think I stuck to my plan, which included a section on the shop itself and an outline of Chipper's history; one on Ireland, one on tailoring history, one on the disappearance of custom tailoring, and finally, one on the community surrounding Chipper's shop. I ended with that because I felt in the end it was the theme that impressed itself on me most intensely. Hence the title, "The Cutter around the Corner."

But maybe I should go back and begin with the process itself because out of the process came most of the problems that frustrated me later in drafting. Right away I settled on the double-entry notebook method. In one, I kept my fieldnotes, dated and punctuated here and there with questions I planned to ask during my next interview. In the other, I reflected on my fieldnotes, recorded unexpected thoughts that occurred to me when I was not intending to think about this project, tried my hand at drafts, test phrases, images, and so on. I called this second notebook my Underground Scribblings, and it was most valuable to me along the way. In it, I think I was feeling my way into the voice, the style, the syntax, and so forth that I would use later.

One of the earliest artifacts that came into my hands was the two-page profile of Chipper from a magazine, a local archive. It was an affectionate piece about a local character and tradition. For me, it served as a kind of yardstick, an internal compass for the sort of piece I wanted to write. I wanted to build a little poetry if I could into Chipper's story, which didn't really need me to give it poetry. Chipper himself speaks a poetry all his own, and the extent to which I use his words shows how fond I am of them. I did try to pay attention to meter, to rhythm, so that a kind of mood would establish itself and carry through.

Okay, but my portfolio shows that I had so much to work from. My scribblings ballooned. My cassette tapes—which I began using after the first interview—ballooned too. There was too much gold pouring out of Chipper's mouth to hold in my brainpan. And soon my Underground Scribblings contained drafts of the same material, transcripts of recording, and I was incorporating them into my writing—like laying a brick road and driving over it at the same time. I couldn't find the time to visit, jot, scribble, record, transcribe, write up fieldnotes, and reflect for every session I had with Chipper. Not with my other studies.... But I can see what I'd do differently in the future....

When it came to drafting the final essay, I had good days and bad days. I began with "To find out what sort of tailor Chipper is, you might begin with the walls," which from the start felt like the right beginning...I had that written right away...had to make moment-by-moment decisions of what to leave out, what pieces served to best illustrate the themes I had chosen, and what information felt simply too valuable to leave out. That's where the portfolio and all its representative items came in.... I wanted to represent as much of Chipper as I could in a limited frame. "Of course, as I told him," Chipper says, "I says, well, you had a good subject." I would agree with this.

FIELDWRITING: ANALYTIC SECTION HEADINGS

One of the best things about writing fieldstudies is that they can and should be completed in sections. As you organize your data, certain parts of the study will stand out as potential sections: topics such as "Entering the Field," "Interviewing Informants," "Understanding Culture," and "Looking at Artifacts" can become your way of organizing information. But once you start writing, you'll see that you can refine your text into sections with even more specific and interesting headings. These headers can do more than just describe what is in each section; they can provide the reader with a type of thematic analysis as well. There is an art to organizing field studies, that of engaging your mind with the features and themes that stand out most, and this is what you want to convey to your audience when writing your section headers. These headers might be key words of the culture, the actual words of your informants, themes from the fieldsite, or descriptive words about the artifacts you find there. In this chapter we listed some of the headers Bonnie used in her study about deaf culture (see pp. 456–57).

When you organize your study with carefully selected subheadings, you are actually making an outline and providing the reader with an analysis of your data at the same time. These headers convey the themes of your study, and you construct them from recurring patterns in the data, from key moments in the interviews, and from a distillation of the observations you have made. We ask our students to keep a working list of their section headings as they write and to revise the headings as they revise their texts. List your headings, and scan them to see if they represent the themes and key ideas of the study you are presenting. When a section stands out as not matching the flow of the others, it will provide you with a clue about what is working best and what sections might need more work.

In one of our favorite full-length ethnographic studies, *Translated Woman*, researcher Ruth Behar makes use of analytic section headings in a most wonderful way. The subtitle of her book, *Crossing the Border with Esperanza's Story*, helps describe the book's main title while providing the reader with further analysis of how the book will be about border crossing. In this ethnographic oral history, Behar crosses the border from the United States to Mexico to interview Esperanza, a street peddler whom she studied for many years. The book also explores Behar's own border crossing as an academic and Cuban immigrant in relation to Esperanza's life story and their cross-cultural encounter. Behar uses headers to provide a thematic outline of her study of Esperanza, a complex and multifaceted woman who experienced many hardships.

The first part of Behar's study is called "Coraje/Rage," evoking the double voice of Spanish and English that the book employs and making the reader aware that all of the subsequent headings will be connected to this theme of rage. One of the things Esperanza recognized as she shared her oral history with Behar was the reflexive understanding that her own mother suffered the abuse and sadness that Esperanza would herself experience throughout life. The subheads of this section of the book are

1. The Mother in the Daughter
2. The Cross of the White Wedding Dress

3. The Rage of a Woman

4. The Daughter in the Mother

5. *Con el perdon suyo, comadre, no vaya a ser que el diablo tenga cernos:* "With Your Pardon, Comarade, Doesn't the Devil Have Horns?"

6. *Mi hija, amarrate las faldas:* "My Daughter, Tie Up Your Skirts"

Working with analytic headings as Behar does provides an interesting way to understand your material and to preview the content of each section for your reader in an artistic way. You may want to review some of the headings in the ethnographic studies we have included in this book to see which ones you feel do more than just summarize what the section will be about. Here, for example, are Rick Zollo's headers from "Friday Night at Iowa 80": A Modern Trucking Village, Truck Stop Restaurant, The Arcade, Iowa 80 Employees, Talking to Truckers, A Trucker's Lament, Town Meeting around the Cash Register, Truck Yard at Night, Old-Timer at the Fuel Center, Conclusion. Note how vivid most of his headers are, with the exception of the final one, Conclusion. Try to make your headers do more analysis than Introduction or Conclusion. Play around with possibilities in shaping an artistic and analytic set of headers for your study.

FIELDWORDS

Aesthetics The perceived artistic beauty, style, and good taste of an object, as in the visual arts, literature, or performance arts such as music or dance. *Aesthetics* also can refer more broadly to pleasing or artistically beautiful appearances of things from hair styles and poetry to athletics.

Draft A text that is not yet in its final form. Writers may make many drafts of any piece of their writing. The final draft usually signals the end of a writing project, but some writers continue to revise their work even after publication.

Experiential writing strategies The forms of exploratory writing—keeping a journal, freewriting, and making notes in a notebook—that reflect the researcher's own feelings and observations in the field. These often are feelings and observations about the researcher's self and her lived experience as a researcher.

Revision The process of reseeing or reimagining a text by changing many different aspects of it. For most writers, the real craft of composing takes place in the process of revising.

Representation In writing, using words to symbolize ideas. In ethnography, how a researcher goes about using language to describe another person, place, or artifact is a highly charged area of discussion because any description is always subjective.

Rhetorical choices The writer's consideration, while drafting, of voice, purpose, and audience.

FieldReading

Behar, Ruth. *The Vulnerable Observer: Anthropology That Breaks Your Heart.* Boston: Beacon, 1996.

Chiseri-Strater, Elizabeth. *Academic Literacies: The Public and Private Discourse of University Students.* Portsmouth: Boynton, 1989.

Fletcher, Ralph. *What a Writer Needs.* Portsmouth: Heinemann, 1993.

Geertz, Clifford. "Thick Description: Toward an Interpretive Theory of Culture." *The Interpretation of Cultures.* New York: Basic, 1973.

Geertz, Clifford. *Works and Lives: The Anthropologist as Author.* Palo Alto: Stanford UP, 1988.

Goffman, Erving. *The Presentation of Self in Everyday Life.* Garden City, NY: Anchor, 1959.

Graves, Donald. *A Reseacher Learns to Write.* Portsmouth: Heinemann, 1983.

King, Stephen. *On Writing: A Memoir of the Craft.* New York: Scribner, 2000.

Lamott, Anne. *Bird by Bird: Some Instructions on Writing and Life.* New York: Pantheon, 1994.

Moore, Lorrie. "How to Become a Writer." *Self-Help: Stories.* New York: Knopf, 1985.

Mortensen, Peter, and G. Kirsch. *Ethics and Representation in Qualitative Studies of Literacy.* Urbana: NCTE, 1996.

Murray, Donald M. *The Craft of Revision.* 2nd ed. New York: Harcourt, 1995.

Murray, Donald M. *Shoptalk: Learning to Write with Writers.* Portsmouth: Boynton, 1990.

Newkirk, Thomas. *The Presentation of Self in Student Writing.* Portsmouth: Boynton, 1997.

Oakley, J., and H. Callaway. *Anthropology and Autobiography.* London: Routledge, 1992.

Qualley, Donna. *Turns of Thought.* Portsmouth: Boynton, 1997.

Rose, D. *Living the Ethnographic Life.* Thousand Oaks: Sage, 1990.

Scanlan, Christopher. *Reporting and Writing: Basics for the Twenty-first Century.* Fort Worth: Harcourt, 2000.

Sunstein, Bonnie S. *Composing a Culture: Inside a Summer Writing Program with High School Teachers.* Portsmouth: Boynton, 1994.

Sunstein, Bonnie, and Jonathan H. Lovell. *The Portfolio Standard: How Students Can Show Us What They Know and Are Able to Do.* Portsmouth: Heinemann, 2000.

Terkel, Studs. *Working: People Talk about What They Do All Day and How They Feel about What They Do.* New York: Pantheon, 1974.

Van Maanen, John. *Representation in Ethnography.* Thousand Oaks: Sage, 1995.

FIELDPOEM

Perhaps the World Ends Here
Joy Harjo

The world begins at a kitchen table. No matter what, we must eat to live.

The gifts of earth are brought and prepared, set on the table. So it has been since creation, and it will go on.

We chase chickens or dogs away from it. Babies teethe at the corners. They scrape their knees under it.

It is here that children are given instructions on what it means to be human. We make men at it, we make women.

At this table we gossip, recall enemies and the ghosts of lovers.

Our dreams drink coffee with us as they put their arms around our children. They laugh with us at our poor falling-down selves and as we put ourselves back together once again at the table.

This table has been a house in the rain, an umbrella in the sun.

Wars have begun and ended at this table. It is a place to hide in the shadow of terror. A place to celebrate the terrible victory.

We have given birth on this table, and have prepared our parents for burial here.

At this table we sing with joy, with sorrow. We pray of suffering and remorse. We give thanks.

Perhaps the world will end at the kitchen table, while we are laughing and crying, eating of the last sweet bite.

Commentary
by Dale Allender

Part of the value of this poem as a model of writing is its rootedness in a particular object as a place from which to explore human relationships and the world. I remember late nights of adolescent identity exploration at the kitchen table with my mother. The conversation nourished my teenage mind and heart. When my wife and I wish to talk to my own teenage son,

Dale Allender is associate executive director of the National Council of Teachers of English (NCTE).

for praise or confrontation, we often sit at the table, plan our discussion, then call him to a chair to share the space and each other. My father always reached for our hands to begin a prayer before a meal when we were children. I do the same after my son has lit candles, my daughter laid out napkins, my wife serves food, and I pour wine and milk.

How often can we look at an inanimate object and see the cycles of life implicitly and explicitly buried within and hovering around? Harjo looks at this cultural artifact—the kitchen table—and explores the symbolic and literal. She works that invisible line between the universal and the particular: the relationship between the table—round or square, or long and narrow; made of wood, marble, or earth—and our lives, a particular life, and life itself.

A FINAL COMMENT

As you move your way through your fieldwork, you will shuttle often between research and writing, and each process will enable the other. Research always involves searching for and finding answers to questions, and fieldwork is no different in that respect. As philosopher Roland Barthes writes, "Research is the name we give to the activity of writing…whatever it searches for, it must not forget its nature as language" (198). Attention to language is critical when we write about the lives of others and bring their culture(s) to the page. As you work with the words of your informants and with your own, as you haul them from your notes and layer them into text for your reader, you will engage in the rigors and joys of writing and researching. We think it's a stimulating kind of process.

Now it's time for us to step out of this chapter—and our book—so that you can step back in to your own fieldwriting project. We hope our advice and experience has been interesting to you and that we've introduced you to students, colleagues, teachers, and writers whose fieldwork and writing will inform and invigorate your own. For us, writing *FieldWriting* has been a rich journey, one we've discussed with you throughout this text as we break through and speak to you about ourselves and our fieldwork. For you, depending on the topic and the courses you're taking, you may want to journey back through the book as you continue your fieldworking and fieldwriting. The best of luck to you from both of us.

APPENDIX A

MLA Documentation Guidelines

In-Text Citations

1. Author named in a signal phrase

Myerhoff claims that "Cultures are, after all, collective, untidy assemblages, authenticated by belief and agreement" (10).

2. Author named in parentheses

Racial identity is not shaped by skin color alone; rather, "everything from skin color to family attitudes to national politics helps shape how we interpret who we are" (Chideya 55).

3. Two or three authors

Eldred and Mortensen argue that American women in the early 1800s developed a political language to assuage tensions over slavery and regionalism (184).

4. Four or more authors

As Hunt, Martin, Rosenwein, Hsia, and Smith show, private philanthropy served as a major institutional structure in ancient Greek society, underwriting everything from the welfare of the Greek poor to international relations (141).

5. Organization as author

Physical activity has been shown to protect against certain forms of cancer "either by balancing caloric intake with energy expenditure or by other mechanisms" (American Cancer Society 43).

6. Unknown author

Railroad maps in the 1850s often "took liberties with locations of stations and other features" to increase property values ("Mapping Tracks" 1).

7. Author of two or more works

Lassiter describes the simplistic images that most children have of Native Americans and shows readers that "the dominant images seem to change little from those most Americans acquire as children" (*Power* 22).

475

8. Two or more authors with the same last name

Rebecca Mead points to an important conflict of interests when she writes, "Nevada has long been the place where Americans go to do things they can't do at home" (74).

9. Multivolume work

Jefferson Davis, a hero of the Mexican War, had "considered his primary talent—or, as he termed it, his 'capacity'—to be military" (2: 3).

10. Literary work

After awakening from his drugged sleep, Demetrius immediately asks the disbelieving Helena, "To what, my love, shall I compare thine eyne?" (3.2.137).

11. Work in an anthology

Contemporary legal definitions of victimhood, Martha Nussbaum argues, can be traced back to Greek tragic plays and "the portrayal of human beings as victims" (361).

12. Bible

When Moses asks God "But who am I...that I should bring the Israelites out of Egypt," we see for the first time one of God's chosen people question what is asked of them (*The Oxford Study Bible*, Ex. 3.11).

13. Indirect source

E. M. Forster points to the necessary relationship between language and knowledge when he asks, "How do I know what I think until I see what I say?" (qtd. in Murray 101).

14. Two or more sources in the same citation

Educators have suggested that portfolios are the best means we have of assessing students' long-term development and should take the place of standardized tests in public schools as they have in alternative schools (Johnson 24; Sedey 165).

15. Entire work or one-page article

In "The Lady or the Tiger" Patricia Williams argues that we are all imitating each other all the time.

16. Work without page numbers

Imitation and emulation, Patricia Williams notes, are natural human processes that introduce ethical concerns in journalism and other professions where "the representation of another is premised on a kind of public trust" (par. 7).

17. Electronic or nonprint source

After living in New York City's East Harlem for five years, anthropologist Philippe Bourgois "constructs a densely textured documentary that affords unparalleled insight into the culture of the street" (Kamiya, par. 3).

Explanatory and Bibliographic Notes

1. SUPERSCRIPT NUMBER IN TEXT

Tompkins argues that the incorporation of personal experience in school life leads to a stronger sense of commitment and connection among students.[1]

2. NOTE

[1]Tompkins, an English professor, may not be aware that several people in the field of education have already made this argument, including Mike Rose, Jerome Bruner, and a number of feminist scholars such as Nel Noddings and JoAnne Pagano.

MLA STYLE FOR A LIST OF WORKS CITED*

Books

1. ONE AUTHOR

Murdock, George. *Social Structure.* New York: Macmillan, 1949.

2. TWO OR THREE AUTHORS

Brown, Lyn Mikel, and Carol Gilligan. *Meeting at the Crossroads: Women's Psychology and Girls' Development.* Cambridge: Harvard UP, 1992.

3. FOUR OR MORE AUTHORS

Belenky, Mary Field, Blythe Clinchy, Nancy Goldberger, and Jill Tarule. *Women's Ways of Knowing: The Development of Self, Voice, and Mind.* New York: Basic, 1986.
or
Belenky, Mary Field, et al. *Women's Ways of Knowing: The Development of Self, Voice, and Mind.* New York: Basic, 1986.

4. ORGANIZATION AS AUTHOR

American Heart Association. *Living Well, Staying Well: Big Health Rewards from Small Lifestyle Changes.* New York: Times, 1995.

5. UNKNOWN AUTHOR

Everyman. Manchester: Manchester UP, 1961.

6. TWO OR MORE BOOKS BY THE SAME AUTHOR(S)

Kozol, Jonathan. *Rachel and Her Children: Homeless Families in America.* New York: Crown, 1988.
---. *Savage Inequalities: Children in America's Schools.* New York: Crown, 1991.

---

*In standard MLA style, using a typewriter, turnovers indent five characters.

7. EDITOR(S)

Franklin, H. Bruce, ed. *The Vietnam War in American Stories, Songs, and Poems.* Boston: Bedford, 1996.

8. AUTHOR AND EDITOR

Cather, Willa. *Later Novels.* Ed. Sharon O'Brien. New York: Library of America, 1990.

9. WORK IN AN ANTHOLOGY OR CHAPTER IN A BOOK WITH AN EDITOR

Murray, Donald M. "Where Do You Find Your Stories?" *Presence of Mind: Writing and the Domain beyond the Cognitive.* Ed. Alice G. Brand and Richard L. Graves. Portsmouth: Boynton, 1994. 291-96.

10. TWO OR MORE ITEMS FROM AN ANTHOLOGY

Reed, Ishmael, ed. *Multi-America: Essays on Cultural Wars and Cultural Peace.* New York: Penguin, 1997.
    Portales, Marco. "Hispanics and the Media." Reed 348-58.
    Silko, Leslie Marmon. "The Border State Patrol." Reed 434-40.

11. TRANSLATION

Kafka, Franz. *The Metamorphosis.* Trans. Stanley Corngold. New York: Bantam, 1972.

12. EDITION OTHER THAN THE FIRST

Whyte, William Foote. *Street Corner Society.* 4th ed. Chicago: U of Chicago P, 1993.

13. ONE VOLUME OF A MULTIVOLUME WORK

Foote, Shelby. *The Civil War.* Vol. 2. New York: Random, 1986. 3 vols.

14. PREFACE, FOREWORD, INTRODUCTION, OR AFTERWORD

Bok, Sissela. Foreword. *An Autobiography: The Story of My Experiments with Truth.* By Mohandas K. Ghandi. Boston: Beacon, 1993. xi-xvii.

15. ARTICLE IN A REFERENCE WORK

Daphony, James. "Louis Armstrong." *The New Grove Dictionary of Music.* London: Macmillan, 1980.

16. BOOK THAT IS PART OF A SERIES

Ancelet, Barry Jean. *Cajun Country.* Folklife in the South Series. Jackson: UP of Mississippi, 1991.

17. REPUBLICATION

Melville, Herman. *Moby-Dick; or The Whale.* 1851. New York: Norton, 1976.

18. GOVERNMENT DOCUMENT

United States. Cong. House. *Memorial Address in the Congress of the United States and Tributes and Eulogy of John Fitzgerald Kennedy: A Late President of the United States.* 88th Cong., 2nd sess. Washington: GPO, 1964.

19. Pamphlet

Smith, Debra. *Answers to Children's Questions about Adoption.* National Adoption Information Clearinghouse Factsheet. Rockville: Cygnus, 1989.

20. Published proceedings of a conference

Jones-Lloyd, Richard, and Andrea A. Lunsford, eds. *The English Coalition Conference: Democracy through Language.* Urbana: NCTE, 1989.

21. Title within a title

Bloom, Harold, ed. *Alice Walker's* The Color Purple: *Modern Critical Interpretations.* New York: Chelsea, 2000.

22. Sacred book

The Oxford Study Bible: Revised English Bible with the Apocrypha. New York: Oxford UP, 1992.

Periodicals

1. Article in a journal paginated by volume

Santino, Jack. "Miles of Smiles, Years of Struggle: The Negotiation of Black Occupational Identity through Personal Experience Narrative." *Journal of American Folklore* 96 (1983): 393-410.

2. Article in a journal paginated by issue

Biondello, Sal. "Self and Other." *Anthropology and Humanism Quarterly* 4.1 (1989): xii.

3. Article in a monthly magazine

Keillor, Garrison. "In Search of Lake Wobegon." *National Geographic* Dec. 2000: 86-109.

4. Article in a weekly magazine

Alger, Alexandra. "Whose Phone Line Is It, Anyway?" *Forbes* 29 July 1996: 104.

5. Article in a newspaper

Brown, Byron. "Church Opens Doors to Vietnamese." *Nashua Telegraph* 10 Aug. 1994: A3.

6. Editorial or letter to the editor

Hallowell, Christopher. "Letting the River Run." Editorial. *New York Times* 4 May 2001: A25.

7. Unsigned article

"Black Astronaut Carries Navajo Flag." *Cedar Rapids Gazette* 10 Feb. 1995: A7.

8. REVIEW

Hacker, Andrew. "The Big College Try." Rev. of *Beer and Circus: How Big-Time College Sports Is Crippling Undergraduate Education,* by Murray Sperber. *New York Review of Books* 12 Apr. 2001: 50-52.

9. ARTICLE WITH A TITLE WITHIN THE TITLE

Barron, James. "Public Lives: 'Titanic,' 'Titanic' Everywhere." *New York Times* 21 July 1998: D4.

Electronic Sources

1. CD-ROM, PERIODICALLY REVISED

National Center for Chronic Disease and Prevention. "Youth Behavior Risk Survey." *Youth 99* Vers. 2 (1999). CD-ROM. Youth Risk Behavior Surveillance System. 2000.

2. SINGLE-ISSUE CD-ROM, DISKETTE, OR MAGNETIC TAPE

Freedman's Bank Records. CD-ROM. Salt Lake City: Church of Latter Day Saints, 2001.

3. MULTIDISC CD-ROM

The Encyclopedia Britannica 2001 Edition. CD-ROM. 2 discs. Chicago: Encylopedia Britannica, 2001.

4. ONLINE SCHOLARLY PROJECT OR REFERENCE DATABASE

"Colonial Missouri." *The Missouri Site of USGenWeb.* Ed. Larry Flesher. 2000. 18 Sept. 2000. <http://www.rootsweb.com/~mogenweb/hints.htm>.

The Vietnam Veterans Oral History and Folklore Project. Ed. Lydia Fish. 2000. Buffalo State College. 23 Oct. 2000. <http://www.buffalostate.edu/~fishlm/folksongs/>.

5. PROFESSIONAL OR PERSONAL WORLD WIDE WEB SITE

Dederick, Emma I. *Music in Usenet Newsgroups.* 5 Mar. 2000. Indiana University School of Music. 17 Oct. 2000. <http://www.music.indiana.edu/music_resources/usenet/html>.

6. ONLINE BOOK

James, Henry. *Daisy Miller.* New York Edition, 1909. *The Henry James Scholar's Guide to Web Sites.* Ed. Richard Hathaway. 21 Feb. 2001. <http://www.newpaltz.edu/~hathaway/daisynye.html>.

7. ARTICLE IN AN ONLINE PERIODICAL

Greenberg, David. "Riot Act." *Slate.* 20 Apr. 2001. <http://slate.msn.com/HistoryLesson/01-04-20/HistoryLesson.asp>.

8. WORK FROM AN ONLINE SUBSCRIPTION SERVICE

Miller, Marjory. "Five Pigs Cloned; Transplants to Humans Touted." *Los Angeles Times*
15 Mar. 2000. America Online. 29 May 2001. Keyword: Human cloning.

9. POSTING TO A DISCUSSION GROUP

Smyth, Gina. "Did They Tie Jim Up?" Online posting. 2 Feb. 1998. Twain, Huckle-
berry Finn. 15 Apr. 1998 <http://denn14.cohums.ohio-state.edu/huck/_
huck/00000027.htm>.

10. E-MAIL MESSAGE

Pradl, Gordon. "Fieldwork Guidelines." E-mail to Emily Dull. 25 Nov. 2000.

11. WORK IN AN INDETERMINATE ELECTRONIC MEDIUM

"Communion." *The Oxford English Dictionary.* 2nd ed. Oxford: Oxford UP, 1992.
Electronic. OhioLink, Ohio State U Lib. 15 Apr. 1998.

Other Sources

1. UNPUBLISHED DISSERTATION

Friedman, Teri. "The Experience of Being a Female Police Officer." Diss. New York
U, 1989.

2. PUBLISHED DISSERTATION

Lehner, Luis. *Gravitational Radiation from Black Hole Spacetimes (General Relativ-
ity).* Diss. U of Pittsburgh, 1998. Ann Arbor: UMI, 1998. AAT9837499.

3. ARTICLE FROM A MICROFORM

Scalon, Leslie. "Black Churches Offered Refuge and Dignity during Slave Era."
Louisville Courier-Journal 20 Nov. 1996. *NewsBank: Social Relations* (1996):
fiche 76, grids A12-13.

4. INTERVIEW

Sampras, Pete. Interview. *Charlie Rose.* PBS. WNET, New York. 19 Dec. 1996.

Thompson, Jenna. Personal interview. 7 Jan. 1999.

5. LETTER

Paul, Sherman. Letter to the author. 21 Feb. 2001.

6. FILM OR VIDEOCASSETTE

Reviving Ophelia: Saving the Selves of Girls. Videocassette. Media Education Foundation, 1998.

7. TELEVISION OR RADIO PROGRAM

Keillor, Garrison. "On Ball Jars." *Mother, Father, Uncle, Aunt: Stories from Lake Wobegon.* Minnesota Public Radio, High Bridge, 1997.

"Meadowlands." *The Sopranos.* Dir. David Chase. Prod. David Chase. HBO. 31 Jan. 1999.

8. Sound recording

Mahler, Gustav. *Symphony Nos. 1 and 5.* Cond. Leonard Bernstein. Vienna Philharmonic Orchestra. Deutsche Grammophone, 2001.

Springsteen, Bruce. "Hungry Heart." *Bruce Springsteen's Greatest Hits.* Sony/Columbia, 1995.

9. Work of art

Guyther, Anthony. *Fish Scales.* Private collection, Vineyard Haven.

10. Lecture or speech

Stone, Oliver. "Searching for the Spiritual." Commencement Address. University of California, Berkeley. 10 May 1994.

11. Performance

Inherit the Wind. By Jerome Lawrence and Robert E. Lee. Dir. Edward Stern. Repertory Theatre, St. Louis. 11 Oct. 2000.

12. Map or chart

New York City. Map. Skokie: Rand, 1997.

13. Cartoon

Chast, Roz. "The Back Page." Cartoon. *New Yorker* 23 & 30 Apr. 2001: 201.

14. Advertisement

State Farm Insurance. Advertisement. *Newsweek* 7 Jan. 2001: 15.

APPENDIX B

APA Documentation Guidelines

IN-TEXT CITATIONS

1. AUTHOR NAMED IN A SIGNAL PHRASE

Ackerman (1991) has argued that physical beauty plays a significant role in our life experiences.

Because 70% of our sensory receptors are located in the eyes, Ackerman (1991) argues, "it is mainly through seeing the world that we appraise and understand it" (p. 230).

2. AUTHOR NAMED IN PARENTHESES

Fieldwork has been described as "house calls at the far borders of human experience" and work that reaches to understand all spectrums of social life and existence (Sacks, 1995, p. xx).

3. TWO AUTHORS

Cole and Cole (1993) claim that we know relatively little about human genotypes because of the ethical dilemmas involved in conducting scientific studies of human genetic expression.

Studies of human genetic expression require scientists to expose organisms of the same genotype to a range of environments, some of which may be unfavorable and unsafe (Cole & Cole, 1993).

4. THREE TO FIVE AUTHORS

Battin, Fisher, Moore, and Silvers (1989) point to the discrepancy between beauty and economic value when they argue that art thieves steal the most valuable works of art they can, not necessarily their favorites.

5. SIX OR MORE AUTHORS

As Gorenstein et al. (1975) show, the Plateau Indians and those of the Northwest Coast were closely connected until ecological conditions altered their natural resources and, in turn, their cultural practices.

6. ORGANIZATION AS AUTHOR

For most of the year this region of Australia is dry, but during the annual monsoon season—between January and March—thunderstorms sweep the land (National Geographic Society, 1998).

7. UNKNOWN AUTHOR

In a North Carolina subdivision that had previously been an apple orchard, soil showed traces of DDT, lead, and arsenic from the pesticides the orchard used ("Apple Orchard Yields Bitter Fruit," 2000).

8. TWO OR MORE AUTHORS WITH THE SAME LAST NAME

J. Page (2001) shows how forensic anthropologists can determine much about fossils and skeletal remains just through their sense of touch.

9. TWO OR MORE SOURCES WITHIN THE SAME PARENTHESES

List sources by different authors in alphabetical order by author's last name, and separate with semicolons: (Baumeister, 2001; Kline, 2001). List works by the same author in chronological order, separated by commas: (Kline, 1998, 2001).

10. SPECIFIC PARTS OF A SOURCE

Nielson et al. (1983, chap. 25) argue that religious movements developed in periods of cultural and social disintegration have most often occurred in nonliterate societies colonized by European nations and the United States.

11. E-MAIL AND OTHER PERSONAL COMMUNICATION

E. Cleary (personal communication, November 4, 1999) supported her previous claims that the spots on the leaves indicated a high level of pollutants in the area.

12. WORLD WIDE WEB SITE

To cite an entire website, include its address in parentheses in your text. If you do this, you do not need to include it in your list of references. To cite part of a text found on the Web, include the chapter or figure, as appropriate. To document a quotation, include the page or paragraph numbers if they are available.

In her online letter, Mary Foley (2001, para. 4) argues that nurses are leaving acute-care settings and opting for jobs that "don't require them to work up to 12 hours a day...and don't impose unsafe working conditions."

Content Notes

1. SUPERSCRIPT NUMERAL IN TEXT

The number of family members who had attended college was an important factor in considering them for the HESOP program.[1]

2. FOOTNOTE

[1]Program organizers Michael Fulton and Regina Kardos developed the standards for entry into the program.

APA STYLE FOR A LIST OF REFERENCES

Books

1. ONE AUTHOR

Kramer, J. (1975). *Trucker: Portrait of the last American cowboy.* New York: McGraw-Hill.

2. TWO OR MORE AUTHORS

Emerson, R., Fretz, R., & Shaw, L. (1995). *Writing ethnographic fieldnotes.* Chicago: University of Chicago Press.

3. ORGANIZATION AS AUTHOR

National Geographic Society. (2001) *Guide to the national parks of the United States.* Washington, DC: Author.

4. UNKNOWN AUTHOR

Mixing oil and (clean) water. (2001, 7 May). *Newsweek,* 6.

5. EDITOR

Atwan, R., & Lightman, A. (Eds.) (2000). *The best American essays of 2000.* New York: Houghton Mifflin.

6. SELECTION IN A BOOK WITH AN EDITOR

Aronson, D. D. (1999). Reproductive technologies are a valid medical treatment. In J. P. Torr (Ed.), *Medical ethics* (pp. 97–101). San Diego: Greenhaven press.

7. TRANSLATION

Barthes, R. (1977). *Image-music-text* (S. Heath, Trans.). New York: Hill and Wang.

8. EDITION OTHER THAN THE FIRST

Mead, M. (1969). *Social organization of Manua* (2nd ed.). Honolulu: Bishop Museum Press.

9. ONE VOLUME OF A MULTIVOLUME WORK

Werner, O., & Schoepfle, G. (1987). *Systematic fieldwork:* Vol. 1. *Foundations of ethnography and interviewing.* Beverly Hills: Sage.

10. ARTICLE IN A REFERENCE WORK

Watkins, C. (1993). Indo-European and the Indo-Europeans. In *The American Heritage college dictionary* (3rd ed., pp. 1573-1579). New York: Houghton Mifflin.

11. REPUBLICATION

Bell, A. G. (1974). *The Bell Telephone.* New York: Arno Press. (Original work published 1908)

12. GOVERNMENT DOCUMENT

U.S. Federal Trade Commission. (1934). *Chain stores. Miscellaneous financial results of chain stores.* Washington, DC: U.S. Government Printing Office.

13. TWO OR MORE WORKS BY THE SAME AUTHOR(S)

Geertz, C. (1973). *The interpretation of cultures.* New York: Basic Books.

Geertz, C. (1983). *Local knowledge: Further essays in interpretive anthropology.* New York: Basic Books.

Periodicals

1. ARTICLE IN A JOURNAL PAGINATED BY VOLUME

Oring, E. (1987). Generating lives: The construction of an autobiography. *Journal of Folklore Research, 24,* 241-262.

2. ARTICLE IN A JOURNAL PAGINATED BY ISSUE

Miner, H. (1956). Body ritual among the Nacirema. *American Anthropologist, 58*(3), 9-12.

3. ARTICLE IN A MAGAZINE

Rudnitsky, H. (1996, May 20). Ring, ring, jingle, jingle. *Forbes, 157,* 65.

4. ARTICLE IN A NEWSPAPER

Wolf, M. (2001, May 31). London ghosts try to haunt New York. *The New York Times,* p. E2.

5. EDITORIAL OR LETTER TO THE EDITOR

Borowitz, A. (2001, May 31). I am set for life [Op-Ed]. *The New York Times,* p. A27.

6. UNSIGNED ARTICLE

Harper's index. (2001, March). *Harper's Magazine, 302,* 15.

7. REVIEW

Paulos, J. A. (2001, Winter). [Review of the book *98.6: Where mathematics comes from*]. *The American Scholar, 70,* 151-152.

8. PUBLISHED INTERVIEW

Clinton, W. (2000, December 28). [Interview with J. Wenner]. *Rolling Stone,* 84-128.

9. TWO OR MORE WORKS BY THE SAME AUTHOR IN THE SAME YEAR

Hoy, P. C. (1992a). *Instinct for survival: Essays.* Athens: University of Georgia Press.

Hoy, P. C. (1992b). *Reading and writing essays: The imaginative tasks.* New York: McGraw Hill.

Electronic Sources

1. INFORMATION RETRIEVED FROM A WORLD WIDE WEB SITE OR A DATABASE ACCESSED VIA THE WEB

Phillips, S., & Richardson, J. (1990). Meeting the learning needs of isolated rural women. *Rural Society.* Retrieved May 19, 2001, from http://csu.edu.au/research/crsr/ruralsoc/v2n4p11.htm

Vanclay, F. (2000). Centre for Rural Social Research. Retrieved May 20, 2001, from http://www.csu.edu.au/research/crsr/centre.htm

2. LISTSERV MESSAGE

Lackey, N. (1995, January 20). From Clare to here. Message posted to Nanci Griffith electronic mailing list, archived at http://www.rahul.net/frankf/Nancy/archives/95130.html

3. NEWSGROUP MESSAGE

Sand, P. (1996, April 20). Java disabled by default in Linux Netscape. Message posted to news://keokuk.unh.edu

4. E-MAIL MESSAGE

The APA's publication manual discourages including e-mail in a list of references and suggests citing e-mail only in text as personal communication.

5. SYNCHRONOUS COMMUNICATION (MUDs, MOOs)

Davis, M. (1995, November 12). Online collaboration [Group discussion]. Retrieved December 8, 1996, from http://www.ipl.org/moo

6. MATERIAL FROM AN INFORMATION SERVICE OR ONLINE DATABASE

Foote, E. (1997). Collaborative learning in community colleges. *ERIC Digest.* Retrieved August 7, 1999, from ERIC online database (No. ED 411 023)

7. SOFTWARE OR COMPUTER PROGRAM

Chem Office 2001 [Computer software]. (2000). Cambridge, MA: CambridgeSoft.

Other Sources

1. TECHNICAL OR RESEARCH REPORTS AND WORKING PAPERS

National Council Panel to Evaluate Alternative Census Methods. (1993). *A census that mirrors America: Interim report.* Washington, DC: National Academy Press.

2. PAPER PRESENTED AT A MEETING OR SYMPOSIUM, UNPUBLISHED

Tesch, R. (1987, April). *Comparing the most widely used methods of qualitative analysis: What do they have in common?* Paper presented at the American Educational Research Association Annual Convention, San Francisco, CA.

3. DISSERTATION, UNPUBLISHED

Steinmetz, A. (1988). *The role of the microcomputer in the social and psychological world of an adolescent male.* Unpublished doctoral dissertation, New York University, New York.

4. POSTER SESSION

Harris, L. M. (1995, June). Race, ethnicity and poverty status of populations living near cement plants and commercial incinerators. Poster session presented at the International Congress of Hazardous Waste: Impact on Human and Ecological Waste, Atlanta.

5. FILM OR VIDEOTAPE

Soderbergh, S. (Director). (2000). *Erin Brockovitch* [Motion picture]. Los Angeles: Dreamworks

6. TELEVISION PROGRAM, SINGLE EPISODE

Lennon, T. (Executive Director), & Steele, S. (Writer). (2000, May 2). Jefferson's blood [Television series episode]. In T. Lennon (Executive Producer), *Frontline.* New York: Public Broadcasting Service.

7. RECORDING

Coltrane, J. (1995). Resolution [Recorded by J. Coltrane]. On *A love supreme* [CD]. Los Angeles: Uni/Impulse. (1964)

Works Cited

Aarne, Antti A. *The Types of the Folktale: A Classification and Bibliography.* Trans. Stith Thompson. New York: Franklin, 1971.

Ackerman, Diane. *A Natural History of the Senses.* New York: Vintage, 1991.

Antin, David. *Tuning.* New York: New Directions, 1984.

Aristotle. *Ars Rhetorica.* W. D. Ross, ed. Oxford, 1959.

Baldwin, James. "Stranger in the Village." *Notes of a Native Son.* Boston: Beacon, 1955.

Barthes, Roland. "Writers, Intellectuals, Teachers." *Image-Music-Text.* Trans. Stephen Heath. New York: Hill, 1977.

Behar, Ruth. *Translated Woman: Crossing the Border with Esperanza's Story.* Boston: Beacon, 1993.

Benedict, Ruth. *Patterns of Culture.* 2nd ed. New York: New American Library, 1953.

Berger, John. *Ways of Seeing.* New York: Penguin, 1972.

Berthoff, Ann. *Forming, Thinking, Writing.* 2nd ed. Portsmouth: Boynton/Cook, 1988.

Birdwhistell, Ray. *Introduction to Kinesics.* Louisville: U of Kentucky P, 1952.

"Black Astronaut Carries Navajo Flag." *Cedar Rapids Gazette* 10 Feb. 1995: A7.

Bowen, Elenore Smith. *Return to Laughter.* New York: Doubleday, 1954.

Brown, Byron. "Church Opens Doors to Vietnamese." *Nashua Telegraph* 10 Aug. 1994: A3.

Brunvand, Jan Harald. *The Vanishing Hitchhiker: American Urban Legends and Their Meanings.* New York: Norton, 1981.

Cantwell, Robert. *Ethnomimesis: Folklore and the Representation of Culture.* Chapel Hill: U of North Carolina P, 1993.

Chiseri-Strater, Elizabeth. *Academic Literacies: The Public and Private Discourse of University Students.* Portsmouth: Boynton/Cook, 1991.

Cofer, Judith Ortiz. "A Partial Remembrance of a Puerto Rican Childhood." *Silent Dancing.* Houston: Arte Publico, 1990.

Didion, Joan. "On Keeping a Notebook." *Slouching toward Bethlehem.* New York: Farrar, 1968.

Edwards, Jeanette, ed. *These Are Our Lives.* New York: Norton, 1939.

Elbow, Peter. *Writing with Power: Techniques for Mastering the Writing Process.* New York: Oxford UP, 1981.

———. *Writing without Teachers.* New York: Oxford UP, 1998.

Gannett, Cinthia. *Gender and the Journal: Diaries and Academic Discourse.* Albany: State U New York P, 1992.

Geertz, Clifford. *The Interpretation of Cultures.* New York: Basic, 1973.

———. *Local Knowledge: Further Essays in Interpretive Anthropology.* New York: Basic, 1983.

Glassie, Henry. *Passing the Time in Ballymenone: Culture and History of an Ulster Community.* Philadelphia: U Pennsylvania P, 1982.

Goodenough, Ward. *Culture, Language, and Society.* Menlo Park, CA: Benjamin/Cummings, 1981.

Graves, Donald. E-mail to the authors. Mar. 1996.

Hall, Edward. *The Silent Language.* Garden City, NY: Doubleday, 1959.

Healing without a Cure: Stories of People Living with AIDS. Dir. Paul Russ. TRIAD Health Project, 1994.

Heath, Shirley Brice. *Ways with Words: Language, Life, and Work in Communities and Classrooms.* New York: Cambridge UP, 1983.

Hurston, Zora Neale. *Mules and Men.* 1935. New York: Harper, 1990.

Jackson, Jean. "I Am a Fieldnote: Fieldnotes as a Symbol of Professional Identity." *Fieldnotes: The Making of Anthropology.* Ed. Roger Sanjek. Ithaca: Cornell UP, 1990.

Kincaid, Jamaica. "On Seeing England for the First Time." *Harper's* Aug. 1991: 13–16.

Kingston, Maxine Hong. *The Woman Warrior: Memories of a Girlhood among Ghosts.* New York: Vintage, 1977.

Lado, Robert. "How to Compare Two Cultures." *Encountering Cultures: Reading and Writing in a Changing World.* Englewood Cliffs, NJ: Blair, 1992.

Lamott, Anne. *Bird by Bird: Some Instructions on Writing and Life.* New York: Pantheon, 1994.

Lopez, Barry. "Losing Our Sense of Place." *Teacher Magazine.* Feb. 1990: 38–44.

Macrorie, Ken. *The Research Paper: Revised Edition of Searching Writing.* Portsmouth: Boynton/Cook, 1988.

Mead, Margaret. *Letters from the Field: 1925–1975.* New York: Harper, 1977.

Metzger, Deena and Barbara Myerhoff. "The Journal as Activity and Genre: On Listening to the Silent Laughter of Mozart," *Semiotica* 30 (1980): 97–114.

Miner, Horace. "Body Ritual among the Nacirema." *American Anthropologist* 58 (1956): 503–507.

Moffatt, Michael. *Coming of Age in New Jersey: College and American Culture.* New Brunswick, NJ: Rutgers UP, 1989.

Momaday, N. Scott. *The Way to Rainy Mountain.* Albuquerque: U of New Mexico P, 1969.

Murray, Donald M. "Notes on Revision." Letter to the authors. 15 Feb. 1995.

———. *Shoptalk: Learning to Write with Writers.* Portsmouth: Boynton/Cook, 1990.

———. "Where Do You Find Your Stories?" *Presence of Mind: Writing and the Domain beyond the Cognitive.* Ed. Alice Brand and Richard Graves. Portsmouth: Boynton/Cook, 1994.

Myerhoff, Barbara. *Number Our Days.* New York: Touchstone, 1978.

Naylor, Gloria. *Mama Day.* New York: Vintage, 1988.

Oring, Elliott. "Generating Lives: The Construction of an Autobiography." *Journal of Folklore Research* 24 (1987): 241–262.

Paules, Greta Foff. *Dishing It Out: Power and Resistance among Waitresses in a New Jersey Restaurant.* Philadelphia: Temple UP, 1991.

Peacock, James L. *The Anthropological Lens: Harsh Light, Soft Focus.* Cambridge: Cambridge UP, 1986.

Powdermaker, Hortense. *Stranger and Friend: The Way of an Anthropologist.* New York: Norton, 1966.

Rosaldo, Renato. *Culture and Truth: The Remaking of Social Analysis.* Boston: Beacon, 1989.

Rosenblatt, Louise. *Literature as Exploration.* New York: Barnes, 1976.

Rule, Rebecca. "Yankee Curse." Hanover, NH: UPNE, 1996.

Sacks, Oliver. *An Anthropologist on Mars: Seven Paradoxical Tales.* New York: Knopf, 1995.

Sanjek, Roger. *Fieldnotes: The Making of Anthropology.* Ithaca: Cornell UP, 1990.

Santino, Jack. "Miles of Smiles, Years of Struggle: The Negotiation of Black Occupational Identity through Personal Experience Narrative." *Journal of American Folklore* 96 (1983): 393–410.

Scudder, Samuel. "In the Library with Agassiz." *Every Saturday* 4 Apr. 1874.

Shadle, Mark. Letter to the authors. Sept. 1995.

Spellman, A.B. *Black Music: Four Lives.* New York: Shocken, 1976.

Stires, Susan, ed. *With Promise: Redefining Reading and Writing for Special Students.* Portsmouth: Heinemann, 1989.

Stoller, Paul. *The Taste of Ethnographic Things: The Senses in Anthropology.* Philadelphia: U of Pennsylvania P, 1989.

Stone, Elizabeth. *Black Sheep and Kissing Cousins: How Our Family Stories Shape Us.* New York: Times, 1988.

Sunstein, Bonnie S. *Composing a Culture: Inside a Summer Writing Program with High School Teachers.* Portsmouth: Boynton/Cook, 1994.

Tannen, Deborah. *You Just Don't Understand: Women and Men in Conversation.* New York: Morrow, 1990.

Tedlock, Dennis. *The Spoken Word and the Work of Interpretation.* Philadelphia: U of Pennsylvania P, 1983.

Terkel, Studs. *Hard Times: An Oral History of the Great Depression.* New York: Pantheon, 1970.

———. *Working: People Talk about What They Do All Day and How They Feel about What They Do.* New York: Pantheon, 1974.

Thompson, Stith. *Motif-Index of Folk Literature.* Bloomington: Indiana UP, 1955.

Toth, Jennifer. *The Mole People: Life in the Tunnels of New York City.* Chicago: Chicago Review, 1993.

VanderStaay, Steve. *Street Lives: An Oral History of Homeless Americans.* Philadelphia: New Society, 1992.

Walker, Alice. "Everyday Use." *In Love and Trouble: Stories of Black Women.* New York: Harcourt, 1967.

Wigginton, Eliot, et al., eds. *Foxfire: Twenty-five Years.* New York: Doubleday, 1991.

Williams, Raymond. *The Sociology of Culture.* New York: Schocken, 1982.

Wolf, Margery. *A Thrice-Told Tale: Feminism, Postmodernism, and Ethnographic Responsibility.* Stanford: Stanford UP, 1992.

Zinsser, William. *Inventing the Truth: The Art and Craft of Memoir.* 2nd ed. New York: Houghton, 1995.

Zipes, Jack. *Don't Bet on the Prince: Contemporary Feminist Fairy Tales in North America and England.* New York: Routledge, 1987.

CREDITS

INDEX

497